D1032284

THOMAS FISCHER

ARMY
— OF THE —
ROMAN
EMPERORS

With contributions by
Ronald Bockius, Dietrich Boschung,
and Thomas Schmidts

Translated by
M. C. Bishop

CASEMATE

Published in the United States in 2019 by
CASEMATE PUBLISHERS
1950 Lawrence Road, Havertown, PA 19083

and in the United Kingdom by
OXBOW BOOKS
The Old Music Hall, 106–108 Cowley Road, Oxford, OX4 1JE

Hardcover Edition: ISBN 978-1-61200-810-3
Digital Edition: ISBN 978-1-61200-811-0 (epub)

First published as *Die Armee der Caesaren: Archäologie und Geschichte* in 2012 (revised 2014)
by Verlag Friedrich Pustet, Regensburg, Germany

Text © 2012, 2014 Thomas Fischer, Ronald Bockius, Dietrich Boschung and Thomas Schmidts

Translation © 2017 M. C. Bishop

English Language Edition © Oxbow Books 2019

All rights reserved. No part of this book may be reproduced or transmitted in any form or by any means,
electronic or mechanical including photocopying, recording or by any information storage and retrieval
system, without permission from the publisher in writing.

Printed in India by Replika Press

Typeset in India by Versatile PreMedia Services. www.versatilepremedia.com

For a complete list of Casemate titles, please contact:

CASEMATE PUBLISHERS (US)
Telephone (610) 853-9131
Fax (610) 853-9146
Email: casemate@casematepublishers.com
www.casematepublishers.com

CASEMATE PUBLISHERS (UK)
Telephone (01865) 241249
Email: casemate-uk@casematepublishers.co.uk
www.casematepublishers.co.uk

Front cover: (Background) Rome, Trajan's Column. (Foreground) Reconstructed Hebron type helmet (iron and copper alloy).
Photo: J. Pogorzelski

CONTENTS

Part IV The buildings of the Roman army   **223**

Part V   The development periods of Roman military history   297

End matter   **374**

TRANSLATOR'S PREFACE

I still remember my excitement when, as a teenager, I was given a copy of the first edition of Graham Webster's *Roman Imperial Army*. It served as my introduction to the serious study of the Roman army and was a much-loved companion through my undergraduate and postgraduate years even if, as was inevitable, it became increasingly more dated as ideas and discoveries moved on and, in a few details, completely and utterly wrong: such is the fate of any textbook. That does not diminish from its intrinsic value, but it does mean that I have spent many years casually looking at the many books produced on the Roman army for one I could recommend to my younger self (or, for that matter, anybody else) and say with confidence 'this is the one for you now'.

It took many years, but when in 2012 my friend Prof. Tom Fischer sent me a copy of his new book, *Die Armee der Caesaren*, I knew this was it. The only problem was that it was in German, which meant somebody would have to translate it into English for a non-German-reading public. Paradoxically, it is well nigh impossible to study the Roman army in any depth without reading German, simply because so many excellent scholars of that institution have come from German-speaking countries. Indeed, the interplay of British (and latterly American) and German, Austrian, and Swiss scholarship on the Roman army has been pivotal since the 19th century.

The challenges for a translator of such a work are many, although the technical vocabulary is strangely not one of them. The first thing an English-speaking exercitologist needs to know is how to distinguish a *Schuppenpanzer* (scale armour) from a *Schienenpanzer* (articulated plate armour), or a *Rasenodermauer* (turf rampart) from a *Holz-Erde-Mauer* (earth-and-timber rampart – although most anglophone scholars tend to just use *Holz-Erde-Mauer*!).

Coping with the German avoidance of the passive voice, or leaving verbs to come panting apologetically home at the end of a sentence after some clausal gymnastics, albeit imperfectly, comes later. A literal translation is not necessarily a readable one, however, and here the translator must walk a tightrope between faithfully rendering the German text into English, while maintaining sense and flow.

This is one reason why the translator (certainly this one) needs help. All the dictionaries in the world (paper or online) cannot match having the assistance of a competent native German speaker on hand to check every word. If they also happen to be exceedingly good at English (at times better than the translator!) and also a specialist on the Roman army, then so much the better. I am fortunate in having been able to turn to Dr Stefanie Hoss, who has relentlessly sorted out some of my messier passages, bad (or wrong) translations, and general infelicities with aplomb and finesse, before I ran the resulting text past Tom for his approval. My gratitude to both of them is boundless.

Having recognized that this book needed to be translated into English, I was indeed fortunate in being able to persuade Clare Litt at Oxbow Books (now part of Casemate Publishers) of the merits of the project. I must thank her for her patience as I ploughed on through several deadlines, barely aware of the famed whooshing sound that Douglas Adams noted define their passing.

This then, born *Die Armee der Caesaren*, is now *Army of the Roman Emperors*. I have learned much by translating it; I hope you do by reading it. If it inspires you to study the Roman army in greater depth, then so much the better.

M. C. Bishop
Pewsey, March 2017

ACKNOWLEDGEMENTS

Many have cooperated on a book like this, which has been in development for decades. There remains the particular necessity, and pleasant task, of expressing gratitude to employees, colleagues, experimental archaeologists and various collectors for technical assistance, information, and constructive criticism, without which the book could not have come about in this form. In particular the following should be mentioned here:

Michael Berger (Munich), Dr Marion Brüggler (Xanten), Dr Alexandra W. Busch (Rome), Prof. Dr Karlheinz Dietz (Würzburg), Michael Drechsler (Cologne), Manfred Eberlein (Munich), Prof. Dr Werner Eck (Cologne), Veronika Fischer MA (Munich), Holger von Grawert (London), Prof. Dr Nicolae Gudea (Cluj-Napoca), Dr Norbert Hanel (Cologne), Jens Horstkotte (Munich), Dr Stefanie Hoss (Nijmegen), Dr Marcus Junkelmann (Oberempfendorf), Christian Levett (Mougins, Museum of Classical Art), Prof. Dr Michael Mackensen (Munich), Ingo Martell MA (Xanten), Susana Matesic MA (Schleswig), Dr Semra Mägele (Cologne), Dr Mark Merrony (Mougins, Museum of Classical Art), Dr Christian Miks (Mainz), Prof. Dr Günter Moosbauer (Osnabrück), Dr Martin Müller (Xanten), Dr Ansgar Nabbefeld (Cologne), PD Dr Salvatore Ortisi (Cologne), Dr Anette Paetz née Schieck (Mannheim), Dr Andreas Pangerl (Munich), Dr Richard Petrovszky (Speyer), Dr Matthias Pfaffenbichler (Vienna), Dr Barbara Pferdehirt (Mainz), Jörg Pogorzelski (Cologne), Dr Johannes Prammer (Straubing), Dr Hans Hojer von Prittwitz und Gaffron (Bonn), Prof. Dr Michel Reddé (Paris), Dr Alexander Reis (Bonn), Dr Marcus Reuter (Xanten), Dr Erika Riedmeier-Fischer (Weilerswist), Dr Wolfgang Risse (Langquaid), Dr Hajo Schalles (Xanten), Prof. Dr Egon Schallmayer (Wiesbaden), Dr Bernd Steidl (Munich), Benjamin Streubl MA (Mayen), Alois Wenninger (Munich), and Martin Wieland MA (Cologne).

Particularly noteworthy in the design and production of the manuscript is the ever-dedicated help of Boris Burandt, Philip Groß MA, Jennifer Schamper MA and, last but not least, Amira Smadi MA (all Archaeological Institute of the University of Cologne).

I owe particular thanks to the dedicated staff of the publishing house Friedrich Pustet for their not always easy work, especially the editor Heidi Krinner-Jancsik, as well as Christiane Abspacher and Sabine Karlstetter.

Cologne, February 2011
Thomas Fischer

INTRODUCTION

The possibility of reaching a clear understanding of Roman warfare, based on its consistent organic development, has unfortunately been prevented by the extensive fragmentation of the relevant monograph literature (…), so that one can say, like Kahrstedt, that one would have to live to be a hundred in order to have read everything; it seems all the more impossible to deal only with the majority of it in a regionally limited summary presentation. For better or worse, the writer must run the risk that the accusation is later made of them by another author that they had not taken into account or refuted in detail their or any other work.

(Georg Veith, 1928)

From the outset, the army was the most important prop for the government and provincial administration of the Caesars during the Roman Principate. With the help of his armies, Augustus was successful in the civil war against Marc Antony and other opponents. After the victory, the new autocrat reduced, reformed, and reorganized the civil war armies as an imperial army, the most important pillars of his power.

By modern standards, the uniformly drilled and armed professional army of the Roman Empire was – in terms of their various duties and the number of their external enemies – amazingly small in size. It is only possible to cite approximate estimates for the total strength of the Roman army during the 1st to 3rd centuries AD. With legions, auxiliaries, marines, and guard units, it should have amounted to between 400,000 and 500,000 men.[1] Local militias could even be used in times of crisis, but there is still no clarity about their structure and scope from research. Against the background of the considerable extent of the Roman Empire around the Mediterranean in the imperial period, peace and security of the Empire were guaranteed by only a relatively small number of professional soldiers. The reasons why so few soldiers were sufficient for the protection and control of the Empire are manifold. In addition to the good training and leadership of the Roman troops, armament and equipment superior to that of their opponents certainly played a particularly large role. Infrastructure – such as strong camps and forts, border inspection facilities, and roads, which facilitated adequate supplies and rapid troop movements – also secured the military superiority of Rome over a long period.

In relation to the enormous extent of the empire, the modest strength of the Roman army of the Imperial era seems even more surprising, if one bears in mind that its tasks in many areas went far beyond what is nowadays associated with the duties and activities of a modern army. First of all, the Roman army fulfilled the classic function, acting as an armed power of the state, as represented by the emperor, in external and internal conflicts. In other words, they guarded the borders, responded to external aggression, led wars of conquest, and also protected the emperor and the political system he represented from internal enemies, in the worst case in costly civil wars.

In addition, however, the troops also undertook functions that are nowadays the job of the police, economic police, customs, and tax authorities. Even that was not enough: as part of their service, Roman soldiers were just as active as road builders, architects, contractors, manufacturers of building materials in quarries and brickyards, and as lumberjacks. The Roman military not only constructed its wooden and stone field and base camps and various other military buildings themselves – from legionary fortress to frontier watchtower – but the experienced military engineers could also build fort baths, roads, canals, bridges, and ships, with the help of trained military craftsmen and ordinary soldiers as labourers and workmen, without any help from civilian forces.

At the same time, the legions frequently made their specialists available to auxiliary troops for more complicated work, as evidenced by many building inscriptions.

Legionary soldiers, mostly centurions, led and monitored the construction of the baths, walls, towers, gates, and internal buildings of auxiliary forts. The troops themselves supplied the building materials for all of these installations: from the mid-1st century AD onwards, legions and auxiliary troops often ran their own brickworks, if suitable clay deposits with convenient connections to water for bulk transport were available. Their products were labelled with the monogram of the unit producing them (brick stamps). Quarries were also operated by the army, with the military fleets able to arrange the transport of building materials.[2] And finally, there is evidence that legionaries were employed for extracting ore using mining technology.[3] Several reasons underlie all of these (from today's perspective) non-military activities. Thus infrastructure certainly played an important role in support of the border provinces, which then also benefited the civilian sector. However, steady employment in times of peace was also a means to prevent soldiers getting out of shape or – even worse – harbouring dangerous notions, if they were unhappy about the political situation.

One result of these non-military activities of Roman soldiers are those buildings – or rather building complexes – which, as a speciality of the Roman army, distinguished them from all other armies in antiquity: regularly laid out camps and forts. Only a few such installations from the time of the Republic compare with large numbers of well-known and researched camps of the early and middle Imperial period. Fortresses are known of all sizes from the period of late antiquity. Incomparably larger and better fortified than the older camps and forts, they illustrate the significant changes in fortification which came with the completion of the reforms of Diocletian (AD 284–305) and Constantine I (306–37). In addition to camps and forts, border fortification systems of all kinds (*limites* and *ripae*), infrastructure such as roads and canals, as well as specialised buildings like military baths, were among the constructional legacy of the Roman military.

With its regular and good pay, the professional Roman army gained an importance in peacetime for those border provinces where it lay in garrison that should not be underestimated: within their immediate surroundings, soldiers as consumers formed a stable basis for agriculture, industry and trade of every kind.[4]

In the Republic, the economic power of the Roman army had already led to the fact that a regular entourage of businessmen, soldiers' hangers-on, and fortune seekers of all kinds escorted the troops on campaign to take advantage of the soldiers' regular pay and booty: the slaves and freedmen of soldiers and officers, farmers and traders, slavers, prostitutes, priests and soothsayers – in addition to the legitimate and illegitimate wives and children of soldiers – were the constant companions of Roman armies. Even the risk of dying with the troops, as happened in AD 9 in the Teutoburg Forest, did not stop them.[5]

After the establishment of permanent camps in the early Imperial period, permanent and even town-like civil settlements were set up around legionary camps (*canabae legionis*) and auxiliary forts (*vici*), where the camp-followers settled down for good. Stable communities, some of them of considerable size, often developed from the early temporary 'booths' (*canabae*). Many of these Roman military sites in the border provinces formed the basis of settlements that still survive (Fischer 1999a).

However, the Roman army was not only implanting and safeguarding Roman civilization at the borders of the Empire through its economic power and infrastructure: in the conquered frontier provinces, members of the subdued nations learned to know and appreciate Roman culture, together with the Latin language and writing, as auxiliary soldiers. Quite early after the conquest of the region in question, most legionary and auxiliary soldiers elected to settle down to live in the border regions following their release from military service as veterans. They cultivated the Roman way of life and thus contributed to the progress of Romanization in even the most remote areas of the empire.

The state of research

From the beginnings of the study of Roman history, research into the Roman military system was at the forefront in the work of historians. Initially, they could rely primarily on the wealth of richly detailed, written literary sources from antiquity, which increasingly were supplemented with published inscriptions. From the 19th century onwards, the rapidly flourishing archaeological research disciplines also started to contribute significant research results to the study of the Roman army.

In the absence of a more recent general work of historical research, the relevant volume of the *Handbuch der Altertumswissenschaft* (*Handbook of Classical Studies*: Krohmayer and Veith 1928) must still be named as the foremost summary in German-speaking countries. A more recent attempt at a synthesis has come from the anglophone countries (Erdkamp 2007). Otherwise, there is an almost endless, and steadily growing, specialised literature on the subject of the Roman army. Meanwhile, the tradition, in the form of literary and written sources, has remained largely unchanged. Yet new epigraphic sources (inscriptions, papyri, ostraca, and graffiti), obtained as archaeological finds, bring ever more new discoveries. One only has to think of the sudden increase in military diplomas in recent years, largely resulting from the use of metal detectors.[6]

Even more dynamic was the increase in knowledge through the work of archaeologists: by means of excavations, the 'science of the spade' provides new discoveries and small finds at installations which are closely related to the activities of the Roman military in ever less manageable amounts. Even if not everything brought to light by excavation in recent decades has as yet been published satisfactorily, the ever-increasing volume of a constant flood of monographs and articles makes it ever more difficult for the expert to maintain even a very general overview. This creates a growing need for summary works, at least for research topics on the Roman military, to keep professionals, members of neighbouring disciplines, and other interested parties up to date. This book attempts such a summary of the contributions that archaeology can make towards the study of the army of the Roman Empire, but it cannot and will not be an all-encompassing guide to Roman warfare in general.

In countries with a territorial share of the former Roman frontier provinces, military archaeology is mainly the subject of provincial Roman archaeology.[7] Therefore, the main focus of the book will comprise the contributions of provincial Roman archaeology to the study of the Roman military.

Iconographic sources for the Roman army are primarily the subject of Classical Archaeology, which has developed the methodological tools to put them in proper context and interpret them; admittedly, not always with sufficient consideration for antiquarian aspects. The increasing specialization of research has meant that, in recent years, the archaeological exploration of Roman maritime and river navigation has become its own special discipline, which includes the study of the Roman navy (Pferdehirt 1995).

In recent years, the rapid increase of the material and the consequent rapid development of relevant studies have inevitably led to growing specialization. The days of the lone, brilliant scientific warrior, with a confident overview of all relevant historical and archaeological aspects of a subject, are numbered. If one nevertheless tries to go it alone, the rapid progress in specialised disciplines carries the implicit danger of spreading outdated or even incorrect views. So in order to gain a broader view beyond the narrow limits of their own discipline, one must work on such a book together with colleagues from related disciplines. This has been attempted in this book. I would like to thank Ronald Bockius, Dietrich Boschung and Thomas Schmidt for readily agreeing to engage in this cooperation.

The work presented here is not intended as another popular, non-fiction book on the history and archaeology of the Roman military like those currently in great demand. Rather, it has been attempted as a technically correct, but nevertheless accessibly written, overall view of Roman military archaeology, including selected aspects of ancient historical and epigraphic research. It is intended for professional researchers, staff and students of related disciplines, and for other readers similarly interested in the Roman military.

Beyond these purely scholarly considerations, there is another reason to produce such a summary of Roman weaponry and military equipment: in recent years, popular representations and reconstructions of the Roman army have enjoyed an unexpected and ultimately barely explicable popularity. Alongside the familiar 'sword-and-sandal' films (Junkelmann 2008), there have been numerous television productions, mostly British or American in origin. In addition, there are ever more relevant computer games in which the Roman military, with its characteristic weaponry, participates. Similarly, the demand for richly illustrated popular books and magazine publications continues unabated. This development of a distinctive subculture, outside professional scholarly literature, raises mixed feelings: some of these publications are of considerable originality and quality, but others repeat outdated or even incorrect information. The creation and widespread public appearance of 'Roman' re-enactment groups (Gilbert 2004; Schrader 2010; Koepfer *et al.* 2012) have greatly assisted popularization of the subject and as yet there seems to be no end to developments in this field. 'Roman groups', *i.e.* enthusiastic amateurs who dress as Roman soldiers in their characteristic armament with a considerable commitment in time and costs, can nowadays frequently be met at 'Roman festivals'. Increasingly, they also appear on television to bring documentaries about Roman history to life. Accordingly, 'Roman' soldiers in this guise are ubiquitous in the daily flood of media images and they dominate the public consciousness.

But are this equipment and armament, which are encountered so often that they have has become a stereotype, always truly authentic? In the current public perception in films, books, computer games, and re-enactment, identical images and ideas of the Roman army and Roman soldiers, their clothing and weapons, which are not based on current research, occur again and again. Mostly they

Figure 1 *Parade by legionary re-enactors from around AD 100, with red- and blue-painted rectangular shields, segmental and mail armour, helmets of the Weisenau type, red tunic, red cloak, Pompeii-type sword, and pilum. Photo: J. Pogorzelski*

show features limited to only a tiny time segment in the centuries-long history of the Roman army: to a time around AD 100. These include a red-painted rectangular shield, plate armour, Weisenau-type helmets, a red tunic, a red cloak, a Pompeii-type sword, and the *pilum* (Figure 1). Translating these colourful images into black and white inevitably reveals their roots: the representations of the Roman army on Trajan's Column, with its supposedly uniform standardization. More than any other, it was the characteristic representations on this monument that allowed the Roman army to appear 'uniform' and thus 'modern'.[8] But is this really true? Or do we get tricked into believing representations frequently transmitted by all sorts of media that have nothing to do with ancient reality?

The constant repetition of images of the Roman army ultimately derived from Trajan's Column has led to their

gaining a considerable and dangerous momentum; in the worst case they will convey factually inaccurate stereotypes to the modern audience, rather than sound, modern scholarly knowledge of Roman armament from a time around AD 100. Quite apart from that, this development has pushed aside the dynamic and steady evolution of weaponry and equipment in the Roman army and with it the conditions in other periods of the Roman Empire. All this is now superseded or even completely ignored by the persistent presence of images of supposedly 'classic' Roman soldiers in pictures of Trajan's Column. Only a few 'Roman re-enactor groups' have been able to disconnect themselves from the predominant imagery of Trajan's Column and are really striving for authenticity and diversity in the selection of models for their armament and equipment. The consequence of this is that they have to produce their equipment and armament themselves, modelling it upon original finds. In contrast to this, most 'weekend Romans' get their equipment from the Internet – manufactured in India and, in many cases, mass-produced items which are no longer authentic.[9] And the defining images of Trajan's Column in many cases served and serve as direct patterns for the weaponry finished in India.

So this book was also written with the declared intention of putting to the test the popular notions and images that are increasingly coming to the fore in the public eye. Where necessary, these images will be critically scrutinized, because the imaginative enthusiasm of amateurs and the dry findings of scholars are not always in harmony!

Actually, this is a shame, because the amount of time and money the many members of 'Roman groups' devote to assembling their equipment is considerable. The errors observed in the composition and details of such reconstructed equipment are easily avoidable and could be readily corrected. This is especially relevant, since many re-enactment groups repeatedly emphasize the claim that they are not conducting a game or mere recreational activity, but that they should be seen as engaging in serious, rigorously scholarly experimental archaeology!

The iconographic sources

The contribution of classical archaeology relates to the iconographic sources, in other words the representations of Roman soldiers and their weapons and equipment. These occur on historical reliefs (Koeppel 1983 to 1992), sarcophagi, and gravestones[10] but rarely on wall paintings. Decorative weapon friezes often show more-or-less-naturalistic depictions of individual weapons. Among the main iconographic sources for the imperial army are reliefs, such as those from the Cancelleria, Trajan's Column, and the Marcus Column, or on the victory monument at Adamclisi. However, one cannot just unquestioningly take the images of these historic monuments or sarcophagus representations as evidence of historical reality. On closer inspection, and through comparison of these representations with original items, it frequently turns out that the depictions are not 'photorealistic' in the modern sense, claiming to offer accurate and realistic representations of weapons, equipment, and episodes from campaigns and battles. Rather, these representations are often either highly simplified and stylized or even show obsolete types of weapons, in a 'classical' Hellenistic Greek form. Therefore, it is definitely necessary to first subject such representations to a critical analysis of the source before viewing them simply as illustrations of historical reality. Dietrich Boschung will deal with these aspects.

On armament, equipment, and the buildings

Most of what is known today about weapons and military equipment in the Roman period is owed to excavations and discoveries on land or at the bottom of the sea or inland bodies of water. But these only form a small and random selection of what once existed. Thus weapons and parts of weapons made from metal tend to be found fairly often. Components of weapons and equipment made from organic materials (*i.e.* wood, leather, or textiles) are only preserved in a few exceptional cases. Likewise, there are often quite diverse reasons and mechanisms for the deposition of weapons and military equipment in the ground; it thus seems useful to also consider selected examples of finds assemblages with relevant material in this book. Finally, a newer area that contributes to the knowledge of Roman weaponry must not be excluded: experimental archaeology.

In a separate chapter, this book will also deal with the buildings of the Roman army; a subject that has been dealt with intensively by provincial Roman archaeology since its establishment. The reason for this is that this branch of research first developed in the UK, Germany, Switzerland, and Austria, countries whose Roman past had in many ways been determined by the Roman military in what had then been the frontier regions of the Roman Empire. This is also true of the Danube areas of Hungary, Slovakia, Croatia, Slovenia, Serbia, Bulgaria, and Romania. In all of these regions, military structures of all kinds were discovered in excavations, from legionary camps to forts, and from frontiers to warships. In these installations, weapons and equipment were found in large quantities, supplemented by water and hoard deposits or finds from civilian settlements.

Generally, civil settlements in the border provinces belong with military infrastructure. Cities and *vici* very often owed not only their establishment to a military garrison, but were also inhabited by former soldiers. On the one hand, the inhabitants of these places directly played a part in the supply of the troops on the border through the production of and trade in weapons, equipment, and all manner of other goods like glassware, pottery, and imported food products; on the other hand, they were of course equally dependent on the members of the military as consumers. The rural settlement system was also directly geared to the supply of the military. Farm units (*villae rusticae*) were concentrated around larger bases or near frontier forts, where military equipment, possibly from veterans, has occasionally been found. In this manner, archaeology is frequently confronted with traces of the Roman army and corresponding archaeological material in the investigation of non-military settlements. Thomas Fischer will deal with all of these areas.

Basic information on the history and structure of the Roman army

Although the totality of Roman warfare, and in particular the Republic, is not the subject of this book, it should nevertheless be briefly summarized here. Large parts of this book, dealing primarily with archaeological research, are incomprehensible without a basic knowledge of the research results in ancient history on the structure, organization, and history of the Roman army.[11]

The Republic

The army of the early Republic was purely a militia, in which conscript citizens had to provide their own weapons and equipment. It is therefore understandable that the cavalry were only recruited from the wealthy classes, later resulting in the *equites*, or equestrian order, the second tier of imperial aristocracy below the senatorial order. This militia army was only called up in time of war and then usually from spring to late summer; a year-round standing army did not yet exist. The expansion of Roman territory in Italy soon brought the inclusion into the Roman army of troops from allies, who formed their own legions, following the Roman model. Just as later, the bulk of the

Figure 2 *Bronze tablet with inscription dedicated to the genius of legio III Gallica: GENIO LEGIONIS III GALL (icae) ANTONINIANAE from the time of Caracalla (AD 198–217). The Legion was in Syria at that time (unprovenanced, private collection). Photo: A. Pangerl*

cavalry came from the allies and not from the Romans. After the Social Wars of 91–89 BC, all free Italians south of the River Po received Roman citizenship. With that special status also allotted to their troops, these now served in the Roman legions. Finally, with the expansion of the empire outside Italy, the incorporation of the *auxilia* took place, with troops who were free provincials without Roman citizenship. Initially, these *auxilia* were not independently operating units, but were each assigned to specific legions. From the Republic to the early Imperial period they were in fact based in the marching camps of these legions and did not yet have their own forts; this only changed in the Claudian period.

The long Punic Wars and the rise of the Roman Empire to a superpower in particular brought with it a crisis for the old militia army. On the one hand, the Roman peasantry was ruined by protracted war service, but on the other increased involvement outside Italy necessitated a year-round standing army.

So it was only logical for Marius to create a professional Roman army during the Jugurthine War (111–105 BC), where landless Roman citizens (proletarians), who before had only provided the light infantry at best, could now voluntarily enlist in the legions and get paid for it. Thus the so-called military reforms by Marius led to the first professional Roman army, which formed the basis of the Roman army of the Empire. The definitive standing professional army, in whose legions only volunteering Roman citizens were included, was formed under Augustus after protracted civil warfare in the years after 27 BC (Actium). Theoretically, compulsory service for all Roman citizens still existed, but this was only ever used in times of need (as in the Marcomannic Wars of the 2nd century under Marcus Aurelius (AD 161–80). But even then it was possible to evade military service by nominating a substitute.

The army of the early Republic (from the 5th century BC) is supposed to have been organized as a Greek-style phalanx (Fig. 3), in which the heavily armoured

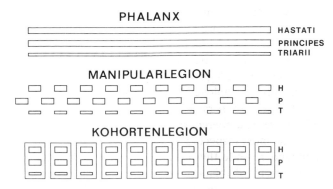

Figure 3 *Diagram showing the phalanx, manipular and cohort legion (after Filtzinger 1983)*

infantry soldiers were placed close together in three lines. However, the lines or ranks of the Early Roman order of battle were broken down by armament and age groups, with the *hastati* in front, the *principes* in the centre, and the *triarii* in the back row. The ratio was 1:1:1/2. Since the *triarii* were older and more experienced soldiers, the Latin proverb *res venit ad triarios* meant, in effect, 'things are now really serious.'

Combat was opened by the *velites*, lightly armed skirmishers. The long line of battle of a legion was soon subdivided into smaller tactical units for better control and was thus made more flexible. Two companies (centuries) were combined in the new tactical unit of the maniple (*manipulus*). Within the legion, the maniples of *hastati*, *principes*, and *triarii* were each numbered from 1 to 10, with the size of the centuries varying. At the beginning of the 3rd century, as the war against Pyrrhus (280–275 BC) finished, the manipular legion according to Polybius looked like this:

1200 *hastati*	= 10 maniples of 120 men	
	= 20 centuries of 60 men	
1200 *principes*	= 10 maniples of 120 men	
	= 20 centuries of 60 men	
600 *triarii*	= 10 maniples of 60 men	
	= 20 centuries of 30 men	

There were a further 1,200 lightly armed *velites*, with an unknown structure. This legion therefore had a total theoretical strength of 4,200 soldiers.

The cohort legion

With Marius' reform of the army around 100 BC, a restructuring of the legions is supposed to have occurred, although this is not explicitly stated anywhere, but it seems feasible that the change occurred around this time. It is only recorded that Marius introduced the *aquila*, the legionary eagle, as the standard of a legion, implemented some technical improvements to the *pilum* (not readily comprehensible from the sources), and reformed the marching pack of the soldiers. The latter earned the soldiers the nickname *muli Mariani* or Marius' mules. After these reforms, the maniple was no longer the basic tactical unit of the legion, but rather the cohort. In battle, the ten cohorts deployed side by side, each divided into the established three ranks of *hastati*, *principes*, and *triarii*. Cohorts were numbered from 1 to 10, with the first cohort being the most respected as a sort of bodyguard for the commander, while the hierarchy of the centurions in a legion respected this scheme: the centurion of the first cohort served as *primus pilus*, the senior centurion in a legion.

Fighting force of 60 centuries of 80 man	4800
Legionary horsemen	120
Craftsmen and store workers, working in the camp	*300
Artisans employed permanently outside the camp	*100
Hospital personnel and veterinary staff	*50
9 (10) legionary staff	*260
Operating with the provincial governor/procurator	*210
Working or travelling with governors/procurators of other provinces	*210
Manning military road, customs, and tax stations	*200
Other privates (*immunes*) and outposted	(150)
Total	6400

Figure 4 *Theoretical strength of an imperial legion. The figures marked with * are estimates (according to v. Petrikovits 1975 and Dietz and Fischer 1996)*

Legions in the Imperial period

The legion of the Imperial period, which had developed from the legion of the Marian reforms was, tactically and administratively, a self-contained military organization. Internally, the legion was divided in many ways. Duty rosters and administrative procedures were subject to strict regulations, as well as the complicated principles of promotion within a sometimes inscrutable hierarchy (v. Domaszewski 1967). After the military reforms of Marius around 100 BC, professional soldiers who already had Roman citizenship upon entry into the force served in the legion. From then onwards, the tactical basis was the cohort, a subunit of about 500 men, which was further divided into six centuries of 80 combat troops. Each legion consisted of ten cohorts, around 5500–6400 men, with (probably only from the Flavian period) the first cohort, as the leading subunit about twice the size of the others, with *c.*800 men. But the actual strength of a legion would rarely have matched the nominal strength. Following H. von Petrikovits (1975), the latter can be simplified as follows (* = pure estimates).

Infantrymen

One should not assume that all soldiers of a legion always stayed in camp in peacetime, for several hundred soldiers were assigned to special duties and were often based far outside their garrison sites.

Among the soldiers of a legion, there were some 5,000 men serving as combat troops. Most were employed as 'common' infantrymen, as *milites gregarii*. They were enrolled in the legion between 17 and 20 years of age, most having previously learned a craft. They now had every chance to advance in the complicated promotion system of the Roman army. The normal period of service for legionary soldiers was 20 years; an honourably discharged veteran then remained with his unit for a further five years (*veteranus sub vexillo*). After 25 years of service, he was able to return to civilian life with a pension (*praemia militiae*), which consisted of cash and/or a land grant. At least in theory: in the early Imperial period there were repeated problems of mutiny, because soldiers were not released on time, but were forced to serve for longer. But it was also possible to continue to serve as a volunteer (*voluntarius*). The veteran with regular service proudly stressed that he was a *missus honesta missione*, 'dismissed with an honourable discharge'. There were also premature retirements as a result of disease (*missio causaria*) or even dishonourable dismissal from the army (*missio ignominiosa*).

The common soldiers performed their daily duties within one of the ten cohorts. With the exception of the first, each cohort in turn consisted of six centuries ('hundreds') each commanded by a centurion. Eighty common soldiers served in every century; the remaining 20 were composed of specialists such as craftsmen, doctors, soldiers with administrative tasks, legionary riders, and so on. Two centuries formed a maniple in the 2nd and 3rd centuries, by then only important administratively and for the cohesion of the soldiers. Thus, each cohort had three maniples, the legion 30 of them; as the types of armament were named in the same way as in the early days of the Republic – *triarii*, *principes* and *hastati* – the maniples carried the same names. Each maniple had its own standard (*signum*).

Each legion possessed 120 horsemen (*equites legionis*). They probably served primarily as dispatch riders and messengers. In battle, they fought together with the legion's auxiliary cavalry, separate from the legion itself.

Legionary commanders and military tribunes

The commander of a legion, the *legatus Augusti pro praetore legionis*, was appointed by the emperor. If only one legion was based in a province, he always also fulfilled the office of governor. He thus administered both the military and the civil administration of a province. The next highest-ranking officer after the legionary legate was a senatorial military tribune, the *tribunus militum laticlavius*. Since this officer, by birth or by the favour of the emperor, was a contender for the post of *quaestor* (minimum age requirement 25 years) and thus of senatorial rank, he was allowed to wear a broad purple border (*latus clavus*) on his tunic. He was very young, usually only 18 to 20 years old. Nevertheless, he was the highest ranking officer after the legionary commander. Lacking a fixed command role, he was a deputy in the event of war. Such a senatorial military tribune often had a brilliant career in the military and the administration before him.

From the second tier of Roman nobility came the equestrian military tribunes who, because of the narrow purple stripe on their tunics, were called *tribuni militum angusticlavii*. There were five of them in a legion. They too were often at the beginning of great careers in the procuratorial service, for which service as an equestrian officer was a precursor. These equestrian tribunes spent most of their time in administrative tasks. Sometimes they also led a cohort, commanded some special detachments, or helped the commander in other important tasks.

Legionary prefects

The military tribunes were serving in the army for only a relatively short term, quickly continuing their career path of mixed military and civilian postings. Accordingly, they cannot really be called professional soldiers. Their practical military experience was probably not very wide-ranging in most cases. However, there was at least one officer in the command structure of each legion who had worked his way up from recruit as a professional soldier in the army: the *praefectus castrorum* (*legionis*). In terms of rank, he was below the senatorial tribune, but above the equestrian tribunes. He belonged to the equestrian order. The area of responsibility of legionary prefects could be described as base commander and logistics officer. He was responsible for the camp and the associated legionary territory, also controlling the entire roster including guard duties. In the period from around the Emperor Domitian (AD 81–96) to Emperor Septimius Severus (AD 193–211), they were called *praefectus castrorum* with the occasional addition of *legionis*, but afterwards just *praefectus legionis*. This title they retained even when, after Gallienus (AD 253–68), they commanded the entire legion, because there were now no longer any senatorial officers in the legion, although they had already done so earlier in the absence of the *legatus legionis* and *tribunus militum laticlavius*. All the above-mentioned officers had their own administrations.

Centurions

Centurions can be described as the military backbone of a legion. These officers – equivalent to the modern rank of captain – were professional soldiers through and through. They usually commanded the centuries, administratively and tactically the smallest subunits of a legion. Ultimately, they were responsible for ensuring that, in the event of war, military operations were performed successfully. Therefore, they had to pay particular attention to the maintenance of discipline in troops in time of peace. As part of this duty they enforced the commands of the legion's high command with the ordinary soldiers. They also monitored the daily routine of the combat troops, drill as well as manoeuvres, preparation of parades, and inspections, and likewise the introduction of new recruits or the cleaning of accommodation. In battle, they were at the forefront. In more peaceful times, centurions also commanded work details of legionaries in mines, quarries, or brick kilns, generally on imperial and state possessions. Sometimes they were temporarily employed as commanders of building detachments, such as for the erection of forts or fort baths for auxiliary units.

As a sign of his disciplinary authority, the centurion carried a vine staff and wore greaves, a transverse crest, and a gold ring although, after Septimius Severus, non-commissioned officers (*principales*) also had these.

Most centurions had been promoted from the lower ranks and only achieved their position after 13 to 20 years of service. The *evocati*, veterans who voluntarily returned to the colours, also had good career opportunities, most of them being promoted directly to centurions.

According to the number of centuries, there were 60 centurions in a legion. They were allotted to the cohorts and again to the maniples. Since each of the three maniples in a cohort comprised two centuries, each had two centurions. Like military tribunes, these were divided between a *prior* (more experienced) and a *posterior* (less experienced). In pithy military language, therefore, the six centurions in each cohort were named according to the old manipular terms *pilus prior* and *pilus posterior*, *princeps prior* and *princeps posterior*, and *hastatus prior* and *hastatus posterior*. The commander of the entire cohort was the *pilus prior*. The cohorts in turn were numbered from the first (*prima*) to the tenth (*decima*), so that each centurion could be precisely identified. Of course, the difference in rank between the centurions of the second to the tenth cohort was not particularly serious. Only the centurions of the first cohort (*primi ordines*) occupied a special position.

This was because the entire first cohort significantly differed from the other nine in many ways. It was almost twice as strong, although it had only six centuries; but it had another 400 soldiers: mainly the ordinary soldiers and NCOs under the legionary prefect, as well as soldiers on long-term duty outside the garrison base. The most senior centurion, the *primus pilus*, also led two centuries (Dobson 1978). This position, apparently only held for one year, could even lead to elevation to equestrian rank. The *primus pilus* was first and foremost the centurions' spokesman with the commander.

After his year in office, this officer (with a minimum age of 50 years) either retired and played a prominent role in his home region or was next promoted to *praefectus castrorum legionis*. With that, his military career was finally over. However, if – after the primipilate – he went to the capital city of Rome and served as a tribune in the fire service (*cohortes vigilum*), city cohorts (*cohortes urbanae*) or in the imperial bodyguard (*cohortes*

praetoriae) as tribune, he could return to the legion as *primipilus iterum* ('*primus pilus* returning for a second time'); then he occupied a special place on the staff of the legion commander and ranked immediately below the senatorial military tribune. Such men had a good chance of being entrusted with a post as an equestrian in command of a legion in Egypt or even with an imperial procuratorship, *i.e.* a high and well-paid administrative office. The majority of the men certainly never got so far and were discharged as centurions. However, during his active career, a centurion did not have to remain with the same legion. The reasons for transfers differed; they might be found on a personal level or could be a result of patronage. Technical specialists also often changed postings.

Principales and immunes

One group of soldiers, entrusted with special tasks, ranked above ordinary soldiers but below centurions. They were called *immunes* (exempt from fatigues, corresponding roughly to modern privates) and *principales* on a slightly higher level (ranking similar to modern NCOs). Since the two terms (the latter first appeared at the beginning of the 2nd century) were not always used unambiguously, it is often not possible to specify the exact rank of individual posts (it is even more difficult to determine possible career structures). In addition, it is to be expected that one or other was subjected to fluctuations in status over time, *i.e.* it would increase or decrease in status. These included the weapons orderlies (*armorum custodes*) assigned to each century. Although they were still among the *immunes* around AD 180, a few decades later they were definitely *principales*. The same was probably true for scribes and copyists, the *librarii* and *exacti*, who, if they worked in the office of the governor, belonged to the *sesquiplicarii*, especially in the 3rd century AD. The main difference between the *immunes* and the *principales* lay in their pay and that the *principales* were exempt from the duties of ordinary soldiers by virtue of rank, while it was granted to the *immunes* specifically to exercise their special duties. In turn, *principales* were further graded according to whether they received one-and-a-half times or twice the basic pay: whether one was a *sesquiplicarius* or *dupl(ic)arius*.

Whoever had achieved this 'non-commissioned officer rank', enjoyed further, additional privileges, such as more spacious accommodation and communal areas in camp. Nevertheless, there were differences even within this rank. For daily routine, it was important whether a *principalis* belonged to the combat troops, and thus served in a century (such as, for example, the *optio*, *tubicen*, and *signifer*) or on the staff. Among staff positions, another two groups are distinguishable: office posts (*officiales*),

a

Rank	Augustus	Domitian	Septimius Severus	Caracalla	Maximinus Thrax
legions					
miles legionis	900	1,200	2,400	3,600	7,200
eques legionis	1050	1,400	2,800	4,200	8,400
centurio legionis	13,500	18,000	36,000	54,000	108,000
primus ordo	27,000	36,000	72,000	108,000	216,000
primuspilus	54,000	72,000	144,000	216,000	432,000
auxiliaries					
miles cohortis	750	1,000	2,000	3,000	6,000
eques cohortis	900	1,200	2,400	3,600	7,200
eques alae	1,050	1,400	2,800	4,200	8,400
centurio cohortis	3,750	5,000	10,000	15,000	30,000
decurio cohortis	4,500	6,000	12,000	18,000	36,000
decurio alae	525	7,000	14,000	21,000	42,000
horse guards					
eques singularis Aug.	(2,800)	5,600	8,400	16,800	
decurio eq. sing. Aug.	(14,000)	28,000	42,000	84,000	

b

Rank	Augustus	Domitian	Septimius Severus	Caracalla	Maximinus Thrax	Total
Prefect	13,500	18,000	36,000	54,000	108,000	1
imaginifer	1,500	2,000	4,000	6,000	12,000	1
6 centuriae						
centurion	3,750	5,000	10,000	15,000	30,000	6
signifer	1,500	2,000	4,000	6,000	12,000	6
optio	1,500	2,000	4,000	6,000	12,000	6
tesserarius	1,125	1,500	3,000	4,500	9,000	6
miles	750	1,000	2,000	3,000	6,000	456
4 turmae						
decurio	4,500	6,000	12,000	18,000	36,000	4
signifer	1,800	2,400	4,800	7,200	14,400	4
duplicarius	1,800	2,400	4,800	7,200	14,400	4
sesquip-licarius	1,350	1,800	3,600	5,400	10,800	4
eques	900	1,200	2,400	3,600	7,200	112

Figure 5a–b Pay in the Roman army in the early and middle Imperial period: a) annual pay in sesterces (HS); b) unit pay in sesterces (HS) using the example of a cohors quingenaria equitata (after Gorecki 1997)

designated according to the rank of their officers, and tactical posts which – seconded from the centuries – served on the staff of the governor, like the eagle-bearer (*aquilifer*). He carried the standard of the whole legion, topped with a golden eagle. Apparently always a member of the first cohort, he was the highest-ranking NCO not in an office. This post was not always achieved after a long period of service. It seems that sometimes eagle-bearers (there were possibly two per legion) had previously been standard-bearers (*signiferi*) and were later even promoted to *centurio*.

The head of the administrative staff was called the *cornicularius*, both in military offices as well as in the civil administration of the relevant *officium* of the governor. He oversaw the lower-ranking clerical staff (*e.g.* the *exacti* and *librarii*), and even undertook clerical work himself, especially in the offices of the lower staff officers. If he worked for the legionary commander and governor, he could hope for promotion to centurion. The *beneficiarii consularis* reported directly to the governor. They were used for special tasks, for instance the financial and economic control along roads (Schallmayer 1990 and 1992). The *signifer* carried the *signum*, a standard with discs attached (Alexandrescu 2010). Apparently, two such standard-bearers belonged to each maniple. In addition, this rank was responsible for monitoring the cohort funds and the savings of the soldiers; he was also responsible for the burial fund. Until the 1st century AD, the *frumentarii* provided their units with grain; accordingly, they derived their name from it (*frumentum* = grain). Later, however, they were used for various tasks: as messengers and as a supervisory officers.

The *optio* commanded the century if the centurion was ill or otherwise incapacitated, also helping him with management tasks. As a kind of 'sergeant', he was waiting to join the centurionate. Each maniple had a *tubicen*, a *tuba* player (or other brass musician), as well as a *cornicen* (horn player) (Alexandrescu 2010).

Roman soldiers were given regular pay, which was differentiated according to the rank and service grade of the troops, in return for their by no means easy duties (Fig. 5). However, there were deductions from pay for weapons and equipment. In addition, a part of the pay was withheld, to be paid out as a bonus upon honourable discharge from the army – here, something approximating one of the principles of modern national insurance was anticipated. A share of booty during war and one-off donatives upon the accession of a new emperor could on occasion supplement pay.

The total number of legions during the Imperial period repeatedly fluctuated due to losses and new formations, but there were never more than 28 units at the same time (Fig. 6).

Legion	Caesar	Augustus	Tiberius	Claudius	Nero	Vespasian	Domitian	Trajan	Hadrian	M. Aurel	Sep Sev	AD 300
I Adiutrix					Misenum 68 Galba (Otho) Bodriacum	Mogontiacum 69/70	Mogontiacum 85; Sirmium 89? until 97	Brigetio 97; Dacia Camp; Parthia; Camp 114–16	Brigetio	Brigetio	Brigetio	Brigetio
I Augusta Germanica		Hispania Gallia 19 BC; Col Agrippina AD 9–	Col Agrippi –16 (Germanicus); Bonna 16–	Bonna	Bonna	69/70						
I Italica					66 Gallia; Cisalp 68; Lugdunum (Vitellius)	Novae 69	Novae	Novae Dacia Camp	Novae	Novae	Novae	Novae
I Minerva							Bonna 82	Moesia; Dacia Camp; Bonna 105	Bonna	Bonna –161; Orient 161–166; Bonna 167–	Bonna	Bonna
I Parthica											Singara (Mesopotam)	
II Adiutrix						69 Ravenna; Noviomagus; 70 Lindum (Brit) 70/71–8	Deva –86/88; Singidunum; 87–9 Aquincum 89	Dacia 101–106 Aquincum 106	Aquincum	Aquincum Orient 161–166	Aquincum	Aquincum
II Augusta		43 BC G Vibius Pansa; 30 BC Hispania T; AD 9 Rhine	17 Argentorate (Germanicus)	Britannia 43 (Vespasianus)	Glevum (Gloucester) 67–	Glevum –75	Isca (Caerleon) 75–	Isca (Caerleon)	Isca (Caerleon)	Isca (Caerleon)	Isca (Caerleon)	Isca
II Italica										Aquilea 165; Locica 170–2; Albing 170–2; Lauriacum 205	Lauriacum	Lauriacum
II Parthica											197; 202 Alba (Rom) Parthia (Caracalla)	Alba
II Traiana								105 Laodicea; 114–16 Parthia; 117 Judea (Egypt)	25 Nicopolis (Egypt)	Nicopolis	Nicopolis	Nicopolis
III Augusta		43 BC G Vibius Pansa; 30 BC Africa	Ammaedra (Africa)	Ammaedra	Ammaedra	Ammaedra 74 Tebessa 75	Tebessa	Tebessa 98 Lambaesis	Lambaesis	Lambaesis	Lambaesis	Lambaesis
III Cyrenaica	(Caesar); (Lepidus)	Egypt 30 BC	Egypt	Egypt	Egypt (Alexandria)	Egypt	Egypt	Egypt; Bostra 106; Parthia 114–16	Bostra (Arabia); Judea 132–5	Bostra	Bostra	Bostra

Figure 6 The legions of the Roman Empire from Augustus to AD 300. Design: A. Pangerl

Legion	Caesar	Augustus	Tiberius	Claudius	Nero	Vespasian	Domitian	Trajan	Hadrian	M. Aurel	Sep Sev	AD 300
III Gallica	(Caesar) 48 BC (Antonius)	Emesa/Apamea (Syria)	Emesa/ Apamea	Emesa/ Apamea	Moesia 67/8; Vespasian vs Vitellius	Raphanea (southern Syria)	Raphanea	Raphanea	Raphanea; Judea 132–5	Raphanea	Syria Phoenicia	Danaba
III Italica										Aquileia 165; Eining 172; Castra Regina 179/80	Castra Regina	Castra Regina
III Parthica											197 Rhesana (Mesopotamia)	
IV Macedonica	(Caesar) 48 BC; 47–44 Macedonia (Antonius) Philippi	Hispania T Juliobriga	Hispania T Juliobriga 39	Mongotiacum 43	Mongotiacum (Vitellius)	Mongotiacum 69/70						
IV Flavia						70 Burnum (Dalmatia)	85 Singidunum Moesia Sup	Singidunum Dacia Camp	Singidunum	Singidunum	Singidunum	Singidunum
IV Scythica	before 30 BC Antonius	30 BC Macedonia; AD 9 Moesia	Macedonia Moesia	Macedonia Moesia	Laodicae (Syria) 66 Zeugma	Zeugma	Zeugma	Zeugma (Euphrates, Balkis, Syria)	Zeugma	Zeugma	Zeugma	
V Alaudae	(Caesar) 52 BC Transalpine Gallia; 47/46 Africa Philippi	Hispania T 30–19 BC Germania; 17 BC Lollius (Eagles in Gallia)	Vetera I 14 (Germanicus)	Vetera I	Vetera I 69 (Vitellius) 61 Armenia	Pannonia? Moesia? 70	? Sarmatia 92 +?					
V Macedonica		Philippi 30 BC–AD 6 Macedonia	Oescus (Moesia)	Oescus	Iudea, Pontus, Egypt 62–71	Oescus 71	Oescus 86; Moesia Inferior	Dacia Camp Troesmis 106	Troesmis	Troesmis –161; Orient 161–166; Potaissa (Dacia) 167	Potaissa	Potaissa; Dacia Ripensis
VI Ferrata	(Caesar) 52 BC Gallia Cisalp; (Lepidus); (Antonius)	Laodicea 30 BC Raphanea	Raphanea	Raphanea	Raphanea	Raphanea	Raphanea	Raphanea	Arabia 119; Judea 132–5 Legio (Caparcotna)	Legio	Legio	Legio
VI Victrix	(Caesar?) 40 BC (Augustus)	40 BC Hispania T	Hispania T	Hispania T	Hispania T Galba 68/9	Novaesium 70	Novaesium	Novaesium 103 Vetera II	Vetera II 122 Eburacum 122	Eburacum (York)	Eburacum	Eburacum
VII Claudia	(Caesar) 59 BC (Augustus); Hispania Gallia; Britannia 54/55	Galatia Dalmatia (Tilurium) 9 AD	Tilurium	Tilurium	56/7 Moesia; 69 Vespasian	Moesia (Viminacium?)	Viminacium	Viminacium Dacia Camp	Viminacium	Viminacium	Viminacium	Viminacium

Figure 6 (Continued)

Legion	Caesar	Augustus	Tiberius	Claudius	Nero	Vespasian	Domitian	Trajan	Hadrian	M. Aurel	Sep Sev	AD 300
VII Gemina					68 Hispania (Galba)	Hispania (Galba) Carnuntum; 69–74; 74 Legio (Hispania)	Legio	Legio	Legio	Legio		
VIII Augusta	(Caesar) 59 BC Hispania (Augustus); 44 BC Illyrica, Gallia Pharsallus	9 AD Pannonia (Poetovia)	Pannonia	Pannonia 45; Novae 45 (Moesia)	Novae Vespas.an (Cerialis)	Novae 70; Argentorate 70	Argentorate	Argentorate	Argentorate	Argentorate	Argentorate	Argentorate
IX Hispania	(Caesar); (Augustus); Gallia Hispania; Illyria-Pannonia	30–19 BC Hispania? Illyricum (Siscia); 9AD Pannonia	Pannonia	Britannia 43	Lindum (Lincoln) 50–71	Lindum –71	Britannia	Britannia	Britannia +120			
X Fretensis	(Caesar?) (Augustus) 40/41	Macedonia	14 AD Syria; 17/8 AD Cyrrhus (Syria)	Cyrrhus	Judea 66–74	Judea; Masada; Jerusalem	Jerusalem	Jerusalem	Jerusalem; Judea 132–5	Jerusalem	Jerusalem	Aela (Red Sea)
X Gemina	(Caesar) 59 BC Equitata; 44 BC (Lepidus); (Antonius); Hispania; Gallia; Britannia; 54/55 'citizens'	30 BC Hispania T; Petavonium	Hispania T; Petavonium	Hispania T; Petavonium	Hispania 62/ Carnuntum Hispania 69; Cerialis (Vespasian) Batavia	Noviomagus 71	Noviomagus 101	Aquincum 101–118; Dacia camp	Vindobona 118	Vindobona	Vindobona	Vindobona
XI Claudia	(Caesar) 58 BC Gallia Transalpina; (Augustus); 40/41 BC Gallia	Illyria; Dalmatia; Burnum	Illyria; Dalmatia; Burnum	Illyria; Dalmatia; Burnum	Illyria; Dalmatia; Burnum (Vespasian Batavians)	Burnum 69; Vindonissa 70	Vindonissa	Vindonissa 100; Brigetio 101; Oescus 106; Durosturum 106; Dacia Camp	Durosturum	Durosturum	Durosturum	Durosturum
XII Fulminata	(Caesar) 58 Alps Lake Geneva; (Antonius); Gallia 44–43 BC	Egypt	AD 14 Syria	Raphanea	Laodicea Judea 66–74 (Titus)	Judea; Jerusalem Melitene (south Cappadocia)	Melitene	Melitene	Melitene	Melitene	Melitene	Melitene

Figure 6 (Continued)

Legion	Caesar	Augustus	Tiberius	Claudius	Nero	Vespasian	Domitian	Trajan	Hadrian	M. Aurel	Sep Sev	AD 300
XIII Gemina	(Caesar) –57 Alps Gallia Rubicon (Antonius)	? Illyricum (Drusus) 15 BC Raetia; AD 9 Rhine	Vindonissa 14 (Germanicus)	Vindonissa 45–6 Poetovio (Pannonia)	Poetovio (Pannonia) opposing Civilis	Poetovio	Poetovio	Vindobona 97–101; Dacia Camp *Sarmizegetusa* 102–5; Apulum 106	Apulum	Apulum	Apulum	274/5 Ratiara Dacia Ripensis
XIV Gemina	(Caesar) 53 BC Gallia Transalp	Illyricum AD 9 Mogontiacum	Mogontiacum	Mogontiacum; Britannia 43 Viroconium	(Britannia) Viroconium 56–67; Lugdunum 67–; (Britannia 69?)	Lugdunum –70; Mogontiacum 70–	Mogontiacum 92/98; Pannonia (Mursia)	97–100?; 100–114 Vindobona Dacian Camp	Carnuntum 117	Carnuntum	Carnuntum	Carnuntum
XV Apollinaris	(41/40 BC) Actium Illyricum; AD 9 Pannonia (Emonia)	Carnuntum 14	Carnuntum	Carnuntum 62; Syria; Iudea, Orient 62–71	Carnuntum 71	Carnuntum	Dacia Camp Carnuntum Parthian Camp 117/8 Satala	Satala (Cappadocia)	Satala	Satala	Satala	Satala
XV Primigenia			..	Mongotiacum 39 (Calig); Vetera I 45/46	Vetera I	Vetera I 69 (Vitellius)						
XVI Gallica		40/41 BC? Actium; Rhine 15/16 BC (Drusus); AD 9 Mogontiacum (Germanicus)	Mogontiacum	Mogontiacum 43 Novaesium	Novaesium (Vitellius)	Novaesium 70/71						
XVI Flavia						70–5 Satala (Northern Cappadocia)	Satala	Satala; Parthian Camp	Samosata	Samosata	Samosata	
XVII		Aquitania (Tiberius); 15 BC Raetia? Novaesium (Varus 9)										

Figure 6 (Continued)

Legion	Caesar	Augustus	Tiberius	Claudius	Nero	Vespasian	Domitian	Trajan	Hadrian	M. Aurel	Sep Sev	AD 300
XVIII		Aquitania (Tiberius); 15 BC Raetia? Vetera I (Varus 9)										
XIX		Gallia (Tiberius) 15 BC Raetia Col Agrippin (Varus 9)										
XX Valeria Victrix		40/41 BC Hispania T; 30 BC Illyria (Burnum); AD 9 Col Agripp (Germanicus)	Col Agripp Novaesium?	Novaesium; Britannia 43; Camulodunum 45–48	(Britannia) Glevum 45–67; Viroconium 67–	(Britannia) Viroconium –88	(Britannia)` Deva 88–	Deva	Deva	Deva	Deva	Deva
XXI Rapax		40/41 BC Gallia Transalp; Biesheim; Raetia Vetera I 9/10–14	Vetera I (Germanicus)	Vetera I 41/44; Vindonissa 47	Vindonissa (Vitellius)	Vindonissa 70; Bonna 70–82	Mogontiacum 82–89; 89–92 Danube					
XXII Deiotariana		Egypt 25 BC	Egypt	Alexandria	Alexandria	Egypt	Egypt	Egypt	Egypt 119			
XXII Primigenia				Mogontiacum 39	Mogontiacum (Vitellius); Carnurtum 70	Mogontioacum 71; Vetera II 71	Vetera II 92/3; Mogontiacum	Mogontiacum	Mogontiacum	Mogontiacum	Mogontiacum	Mogontiacum
XXX Ulpia								Brigetio 103 Dacia Camp	Noviomagus 118–120; Vetera II 120	Vetera II	Vetera II	Vetera II

Figure 6 (Continued)

Auxiliaries (auxilia)

About the same strength as the legions, there was a second part of the Roman army, the so-called *auxilia* or auxiliary troops (Kraft 1951; Spaul 1994 and 2000). In terms of strength, pay, and legal status, these were 'second-rate' units. From the mid-1st century BC, auxiliary troops were mainly used for frontier protection, but when in combat, they operated alongside legionary troops. In the Imperial period, auxiliaries provided all of the cavalry (the few mounted legionaries were insignificant in impact). Those free imperial residents from the provinces who did not initially possess Roman citizenship, the so-called *peregrini* (= strangers) could enrol in the *auxilia*. If they had completed 25 years of service and if they had done nothing wrong, then they could get the coveted Roman citizenship.

In the Republic, auxiliary troops were tightly bound to the legions in organization, garrison, and use. They were also housed with them – albeit spatially separated – in the same camps. After the Augustan period, their position changed: they became increasingly independent units and had, from the Claudian period onwards, their own camps – the auxiliary forts.

Structure

The *auxilia* were divided between cavalry and infantry units into *alae* and *cohortes*, 500 (*quingenaria*) or 1,000 (*milliaria*) men strong. Frequently, there were also mixed units, so-called *cohortes equitatae*.

A *cohors quingenaria peditata* consisted of six centuries, each of 80 infantrymen under the command of a centurion; including the staff, it was about 500 men strong. Their commander, the *praefectus* or *praepositus cohortis*, usually came from the equestrian order.

A *cohors milliaria peditata* consisted of ten centuries, each of 80 infantrymen under the command of a centurion; with staff, it was perhaps about 1,000 men strong. Their commander, the *tribunus cohortis*, usually came from the equestrian order.

The *cohors quingenaria equitata* was a mixture of infantry and cavalry. It consisted of six centuries of 80 men under the command of a centurion. To these were added six *turmae* of cavalry; it was probably about 500 men strong. Their commander, the *praefectus cohortis*, came from the equestrian order.

A *cohors milliaria equitata* was also a mixed unit of infantry and cavalry. It consisted of ten centuries of 80 men commanded by a centurion. In addition, there were ten *turmae* of 24 cavalrymen, so together with staff the unit was over 1,000 men strong. Their commander, the *tribunus cohortis*, came from the equestrian order.

An *ala quingenaria* consisted of 480 horsemen, who were divided into 16 *turmae* of 30, the leader of the *turma* being the *decurio* (not to be confused with that post on a city council). The *ala milliaria* consisted of 1,008 horsemen, who were divided into 24 *turmae* of 42 men. The commander of an *ala quingenaria*, like the *ala milliaria*, was always a *praefectus alae*, drawn from the equestrian order.

Commanders of auxiliary cohorts were appointed by the governor of the province in which they were stationed. In contrast, the commanders of *alae*, the *praefecti alae*, were always appointed directly by the emperor in Rome. They completed their military service after the time of Emperor Claudius (AD 41–54) in three tiers, namely in the career of the *tres militiae* which corresponded to three grades:

1. Prefect of a *cohors quingenaria*;
2. Military tribune in a legion (*tribunus militum legionis angusticlavius*) or as a *tribunus cohortis milliariae*;
3. *praefectus alae quingenariae*.

Then, around the middle of the 2nd century AD, a fourth tier was added for the command of an *ala milliaria* with the *militia quarta*, only rarely achieved, in the *quarta militia equestris*, namely the rank of *praefectus ala milliariae*. This was the highest military rank that an equestrian could attain, very often paving the way for a procuratorship, managing the financial administration of a province.

Nomenclature

While the Romans initially drafted auxiliary troops from the able-bodied young men of newly conquered territories and based them away from the recruitment area, over time the majority of units increasingly came from the hinterland of their base, with only a few exceptions. Often, auxiliary units were named after the tribe from which they had been originally recruited, for example the *cohors Raetorum*. However, if such a Raetian cohort was posted in Britain for a long time, for example, the name became merely traditional, because over time the unit came to be formed mainly from provincials, in other words from Britons. In contrast, there were special forces with indigenous weapons or special abilities that were extremely important to the Roman army. These included, for example, the Batavians from the Lower Rhine. They were not only first-class fighters on foot and on horseback, but they could also do what others apparently could not, crossing water in full armour with their horses. They evidently trained in these skills from early youth. So, along with oriental archers (mainly from Syria), they belonged to those auxiliaries who were not just placed in an area and then raised recruits from around their garrison town, but also kept recruiting from their original recruitment region. Moreover, the officers of these units were aristocrats from the same tribes. There were some auxiliary units (*cohortes civium Romanorum*) in which Roman citizens served too, while *cohortes classicae* were a relic of the Civil War, as they were infantry units formed after 27 BC from marines left over after the battle of Actium.

Auxiliary units were also named after the emperor, or an officer under whom they were founded, for example the *ala Flavia* or *ala Indiana* (after the Treveran noble Julius Indus). There were also numerous honorary names if the whole unit had performed well, for example *pia fidelis* (reliable, loyal) or *victrix* (victorious). Special armament was also occasionally added to the title of the unit, *e.g. sagittariorum* (archers) or *scutata*, meaning the troops fought like a legion, with the *scutum*, the rectangular shield.

Up to the mid-1st century, the *auxilia* were still closely tied to the legions, tactically as well as spatially and in their accommodation. Only with the formation of stable frontiers on the *limites* and *ripae* did the *auxilia* win more independence and were posted further away from the legions to man the frontiers. (However, an interesting exception is the legionary fortress at Bonn where an additional *ala* and a cohort were based alongside *legio I Minervia* until the 3rd century AD.)

Citizenship

With his honourable discharge (*honesta missio*) after 25 or more years of service, better times began for the auxiliary soldier. The savings that had been withheld for him in the unit coffers and that had built up over the years were paid out to him in cash; in addition he now finally received Roman citizenship, extending to his wife and his descendants. Through the 'law of legal marriage' (*ius conubii*), also awarded to him at that time, an existing or proposed matrimonial alliance with a 'foreign' woman was now fully recognized before Roman law. So now he could live in a family recognized by Roman law for the first time! The citizenship acquired via service in the auxiliary troops helped millions of provincials to become the legal and social equals of Roman citizen who had moved to the provinces after the conquest. These privileges, of which the most important were citizenship and legal marriage, were so important that it is no wonder that many soldiers wanted them confirmed in duplicate. These documents had the form of bronze plaques, so-called 'military diplomas' (Fig. 7a–d). They contained the text of the imperial decree of the honourable discharge of this soldier from military service, as well as the date, the names and seals of a number of witnesses, the personal data of each recipient and his wife and children, his direct and indirect superiors, as well

as a list of all troops affected in the relevant province, an extremely important source for Roman military history (Eck and Wolff 1986; Eck 1997 and 2010a; Pferdehirt 2004). The original of this document was posted publicly at the Temple of Minerva in Rome, so the recipient only received a copy.

Numeri

From the late 1st century, the so-called *numeri* appeared, ranking below the *auxilia* (Reuter 1999a). These consisted of 100- to 200-strong guard and reconnaissance units, stationed along fixed lengths of frontier. If such units were mounted, they were called *exploratio*. They were under the command of a *praepositus numeri*, often a centurion seconded from a legion. *Numeri* were used in addition to the *alae* and cohorts for frontiers or to explore and secure areas beyond the frontiers, particularly in more remote forest regions, like the Taunus and Odenwald in Germany or on the Dacian *limes*. In contrast to other *auxilia*, they always seem to have been used in the same province, and always in the same frontier sector; they were not, for example, sent on campaign. This proves that, as local scouts, they were familiar with a particular section of frontier. The names of the *numeri* were often formed from the nations from which they had been raised, as with, for example, the diverse *numeri Brittonum* or *numeri Palmyrenum*. In order to identify a specific unit among the various *numeri Brittonum* in Upper Germany, the name of a river or a source in their territory was added to the name of the unit. An example is the *numerus Brittonum Elantiensium*, named after the River Elz, a tributary of the Neckar.

Guards

The emperor and the provincial governors were protected by guard units (Fig. 8), whose soldiers were detached from the regular army (Busch 2010). These *cohortes praetoriae*, introduced by Augustus, guarded the emperor and his family and went to war with the emperor. They originally numbered nine cohorts of 1,000 men, each made up of 900 infantry and 100 cavalry. From the time of Tiberius (AD 14–37), they were based in the Praetorian Camp in Rome and were for a long time the strongest military power in and around Rome.

Augustus also introduced a mounted guard of Germans, the *Germani corporis custodes*, although their strength and organization are not known. This unit was disbanded under Galba. Only under Trajan was there a mounted guard again, the *equites singulares Augusti*. Furthermore, there were other special units recruited from troops in

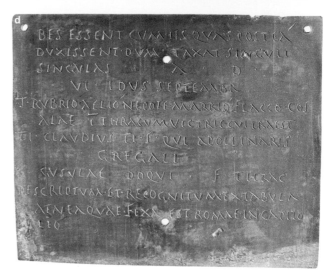

Figure 7a–d *Military diploma for troops in the province of Noricum from the time of Titus (AD 79–81) dated 8 September AD 79. issued for the Thracian Gusula(s), son of Doquus. (a outside, b inside), c outside d inside; after White 2004; Eck and Pangerl 2006; unprovenanced, private property). Photo: A. Pangerl*

Rome, such as the *speculatores Augusti*, *evocati*, *statores*, *frumentarii*, and *speculatores legionis*. In addition, soldiers of the Imperial fleets from Misenum and Ravenna were reassigned to operate the awnings in the circus and in the theatres.

To these regular military units were added the *cohortes urbanae*, the city soldiers, and the *cohortes vigilum*, a kind of military fire service and night watch.

Not until Septimius Severus (AD 193–211) did the military presence of the Praetorians in and around

Rome become much stronger. First, the Praetorians were temporarily disbanded and a legion, *legio II Parthica*, was stationed in Albano, near Rome; then the theoretical strength of the Guard was increased considerably (Fig. 9).

In the praetorian frontier provinces without legionary garrisons, there was a 'guard' for the governor consisting of around 250 cavalrymen and infantrymen, the *equites* and *pedites singulares*, which consisted of selected men from the provincial army. In the provinces with legionary garrisons, the governor's guard consisted of selected legionaries.

Unit	Known to be in Rome	Camp	Organisation	Strength	Ancestry	Status
cohortes praetoriae	27/26 BC–AD 312	*castra praetoria*	cohorts	9–10 cohorts of 500/1,000 men	1st/2nd century: Italian 3rd century: legionaries from the Danube provinces	Roman citizens
speculatores Augusti	27/26 BC–AD 312 (?)	*castra praetoria*	unknown	300	from the *cohortes praetoriae*	Roman citizens
evocati	27/26 BC–AD 312 (?)	*castra praetoria*	numerous, *centuria*	unknown	veterans of the *cohortes praetoriae* and *urbanae*	Roman citizens
statores	27/26 BC–AD 312 (?)	*castra praetoria*	numerous	unknown	from the *cohortes vigilum*	Roman citizens
Germani corporis custodes	Augustus–AD 69	near the *horti Dolabellae*	cohort Decurian	500	low Germany, Batavia area	*peregrini*
equites singulares Augusti	Trajan–AD 312	*castra priora/nova equitum singularium*	*ala equitates*	2nd century: 500/1,000 3rd century: 1,000/2,000	low Germany, Pannonia, Noricum and other provinces	*peregrini*
cohortes urbanae	27 BC–mid-4th century AD	*castra praetoria, stationes, castra (urbana)*	*cohortes quingenariae peditatae*	3 (+2) cohorts of 500–1,500	*cohortes vigilum*	Roman citizens
cohortes vigilum	AD 6– (?)	7 *stationes* 14 *excubitoria*	*cohortes quingenariae peditatae*	7 cohorts of 500–1,000		*liberti*
frumentarii	Trajan–Diocletian	*castra peregrina/ stationes (?)*	numerous	90–100	from the legions	Roman citizens
speculatores legionis	(?)	*castra perigrina*	(?)	(?)	from the legions	Roman citizens
classarii	1st century–(?)	*castra Misenatium/ castra Ravennatium*	*classis*	(?)		*liberti, peregrini*
legio II Parthica	end 2nd century AD	*castra Albana*	legion	10 cohorts of 500/1,000	from the Danube provinces	

Figure 8 *Troops and paramilitary units in Rome during the Imperial period (after Busch 2010)*

Unit	1st century	2nd century	3rd century	early 4th century
cohortes praetoriae	4,500	5,000	10,000	10,000
speculatores Augusti	300 (?)	300 (?)	300 (?)	300 (?)
evocati	(?)	(?)	(?)	(?)
statores	500 (?)	500 (?)	500 (?)	500 (?)
Germani corporis custodes	500	–	–	–
equites singulares Augusti	–	(500) 1,000	(1,000) 2,000	2,000
cohortes urbanae	1,500	2,000	6,000	6,000
cohortes vigilum	3,500	3,500	7,000	7,000
classarii	(?)	(?)	(?)	(?)
frumentarii	–	90–100	90–100	–
speculatores legionis	(?)	(?)	(?)	(?)
legio II Parthica	–	–	5,000–10,000	5,000–10,000
other	(?)	(?)	(?)	(?)
total	10,800 + X	12,900 + X	35,900 + X	35,900 + X

Figure 9 *Theoretical strength of troops in Rome during the Imperial period (after Busch 2010)*

Militias

From the early Imperial period, there were also local militia units in the provinces: *iuniores* or *iuventus* associations are testified, without details of their number, structure and military armament being known. They gained greater importance, especially in the turbulent times of the 3rd century, and were then more frequently attested epigraphically. Thus the inscription on the Augsburg victory altar names *populares,* unspecified militiamen, as jointly responsible for the Roman victory of 24th/25th April 260 over the *Semnones/Iuthungi* (Bakker 1993).

The so-called 'military reform' of the 4th century AD

With few exceptions, the Roman army – legionary and auxiliary troops – was based along the frontiers in permanent legionary camps, as well as *ala*, cohort, and *numerus* forts, from the time of Augustus (Fig. 10). Apart from the Praetorians and bodyguards of the emperor, Italy had no military presence; only from the time of Septimius Severus (193–211) was there a legion south of Rome, in Albano. This meant that the military high command had no significant mobile reserves present in the interior of the empire to deploy alongside the frontier army.

In this system, concentrations of military force, such as were necessary for field campaigns or in the defence of larger attacks, were difficult and time-consuming to accomplish, as ad hoc army groups (*vexillationes*) had to be assembled from the various provincial armies to undertake specific combat missions (Saxer 1967). If the task was completed, the individual components of these *vexillationes* returned to their regular units. While this approach generally worked until the 3rd century, or the practical-minded Romans would not have kept it, during the 4th century the weaknesses of it became increasingly obvious. At a time when there were often multiple simultaneous external attacks on the Rhine and Danube frontiers by Germans, Sarmatians, and other opponents, and in the East by the Parthians and then by the Persians, this system simply collapsed. The withdrawal of troops from a momentarily seemingly less-endangered western frontier for field campaigns in the East now meant that Germanic opponents recognized the weakness and regularly took the opportunity to attack the frontier provinces. In addition, the wars between rival claimants to the throne often meant that the best troops of the Empire fought each other, often to the point of almost total annihilation, from the time of Septimius Severus onwards.

The first large-scale measures to reform the Roman frontier defensive system and get this problem under control can be detected under Gallienus (AD 253–68).

Since the effectiveness of the Persians and Germans was probably that they were mostly mounted, a cavalry formation – which was mobile and stationed in Milan – was set up by the emperor from new units to protect Italy and Rome from threat. They could even catch an opponent if they had already broken through the frontier defences and had penetrated far into the hinterland. In late antiquity, this system was perfected with a functional division of the army (border guard troops in garrisons on the frontier, mobile task forces in the hinterland) and introduced throughout the empire. The older view of this dual system as a new introduction in the context of military reform under Diocletian and Constantine is being increasingly called into question by research. Thus, for example, K. Strobel (2007) and Y. Le Bohec (2010) emphasize the continuous development of the comitatensian or mobile army from the mid-Imperial period onwards. However, fundamental changes in the Roman army arrived in the 4th and 5th centuries AD, but are difficult to reconstruct in detail. In general, the Late Roman military system is much less transparent than those of the Republic and the early to mid-Imperial period. Due to their scarcity, written sources generally play a much smaller role for the military history of late antiquity than for the preceding period; the number of inscriptions generally decreased radically, in other words epigraphic evidence with military implications – which previously constituted the most important source for the organization and distribution of Roman troops – disappeared almost completely. Here, even the text originating in the early 5th century AD, the 'directory of all offices, both civilian and military in the western parts of the empire' (*Notitia dignitatum omnium, tam civilium quam militarium, in partibus Occidentis*), known for short as the *Notitia Dignitatum,* is hardly a substitute. But at least the units of the frontier army and weapon factories are listed in it.

From at least the reign of Constantine I (AD 306–24), the Roman army was divided in two: there were now a frontier army permanently based in frontier forts, the *limitanei* or *riparienses,* and a mobile army operating in the hinterland, the *comitatenses.* The frontier units were largely maintained along earlier lines, in terms of formation and tactical designation (legions, *alae*, and cohorts), but their theoretical strength was significantly lower than that of the same units of the early and mid-Imperial period. This can be seen from fort sizes, compared to the early and middle Imperial period.

According to the *Notitia Dignitatum,* the military command of the frontier troops of the Western Empire lay in the hands of the highest-ranking soldier in this part of the Empire, who held various titles and had diverse areas of competence over the course of time. He was called *magister militum* [*utriusque militiae*] ('master of the army'

Figure 10 *Early modern illustration from the Notitia Dignitatum showing the forts Augustanis (Augsburg), Phoebianis (Bürgle), Submuntorio (Burghöfe), Vallato (Manching?), Ripa Prima (copyist's error), Cambidano (Kempten), Guntia (Günzburg), Foetibus (Füssen) Teriolis (Zirl) and Qunianis (Künzing) in Raetia Secunda. The illustrated manuscript was created in 1551 for the Count Palatine Otto Henry (after Garbsch 1994)*

or 'master of all military branches'), or at the Imperial court *magister peditum praesentalis* ('master of infantry present [at court]'); after *c.* AD 370 he was addressed as Illustrious One (*vir illustris*); the *dux limitis* (frontier sector commander) reported to him. Occasionally, this post was filled by one person for several provinces, like the military commander of the two Raetian provinces. He bore the title of *dux provinciae Raetiae primae et secundae* (General of the First and Second Raetian Provinces) with the rank of Admirable One (*vir spectabilis*).

The Roman navy

The Roman fleet of the Imperial period,[12] like the auxiliary troops of the Roman army, took as recruits free, but legally and socially underprivileged, peregrine residents of the Empire who did not possess Roman citizenship. However, they could gain the coveted Roman citizenship for themselves and their families through military service. However, since naval service was considered more difficult than that of the forces on land and since, with a total of 26–28 years, it was also longer than the 25 years of service for the legions and auxiliary troops, those entering the fleet gained the special privilege of Latin citizenship for themselves from the start – but not for their wives and children. Although this did not offer all the privileges of full Roman citizenship, it was a huge leap forward in legal status for a peregrine provincial. A fleet soldier received full Roman citizenship for himself and his family only upon honourable discharge, after having completed the whole term of service.

Of course, this rule did not apply to the officers who, from the outset, had to possess Roman citizenship. The supreme commander of a fleet, the *praefectus classis*, came from the equestrian order.

In organization and jurisdiction, the Roman fleet was divided into two parts (Fig. 11), with a clear distinction apparent between the sailors and the marines. This went so far that every ship had two commanders, one nautical and one military. The nautical commander bore the title *nauarchus* on larger vessels, on smaller ships *trierarchus;* these designations were quite obviously adopted from the eastern Hellenistic area, albeit with a certain change of meaning.

Military crews were equivalent to the centuries of the land army. These consisted of about 80-strong combat units under the command of a centurion. Therefore, there was a marine captain with the rank of *centurio classicus*. Above all, the sailors were often specialized, there being helmsmen, navigators, a man who was on the lookout in the bow, warning of shoals, a coxswain for the rowers, loadmaster, doctors, and others.

A particular theme in Roman military archaeology – the iconographic and textual sources, and especially the

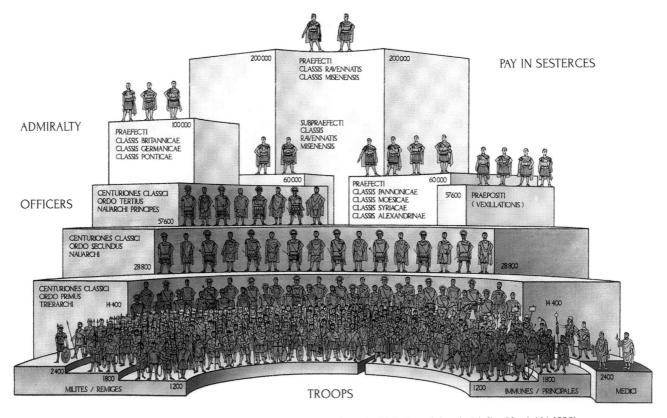

Figure 11 *Diagram showing the hierarchy of the Roman fleets of the early and middle Imperial period (after Pferdehirt 1995)*

original remains of Roman warships – has recently led to the development of a separate direction in research: the study of ancient navigation. The discovery of numerous shipwrecks in the Mediterranean, but also of warships used on the Rhine and Danube, like the ships from Mainz and Oberstimm, has brought further advances here. In particular, the Museum for Ancient Navigation (*Museum für antike Schifffahrt*) in Mainz (affiliated to the nearby *Römisch-Germanisches Zentralmuseum*) has had a major impact in this as an international research institute. The current state of research into the installations of the Roman fleet, the naval bases, and their warships is dealt with in Part VI by Ronald Bockius and Thomas Schmidts.

Notes to Introduction

1. Eck 2010a, 90.
2. For example, the *Classis Germanica*, which – according to inscription *CIL* XIII 8036 from the time of Antoninus Pius – transported trachyte from Drachenfels near Bonn to Xanten for the construction of the forum. See Precht 2008, 351f.
3. However, it is reported that soldiers of *legio II Augusta* did not see this as a task appropriate to their rank and sent a letter of protest to the Emperor Claudius complaining of their posting to the silver mines in the Taunus, on the right bank of the Rhine (Tac, *Ann.* 11.20.3; Eich 2010, 26ff.).
4. Wierschowski 1984; Fischer 2000a; Bender 2010.
5. The possible size of the baggage train can be guesstimated from vague accounts in the context of the civil wars after Nero's death in the years AD 68/69: thus the convoy of Vitellius in his march on Rome was said to be greater than the force of 60,000 men. Likewise, the 40,000 soldiers of the Flavian army at the second Battle of Cremona were allegedly outnumbered by their retinue. See. Tac., *Hist.* 2.87; 3.33; Herod. 7.8.10f.; Speidel 2010, 133.
6. Compare just the enormous increase of newly published military diplomas. For example, in Pferdehirt 2004 or Eck and Pangerl 2008 and 2009 respectively.
7. Fischer 2001; 2010.
8. Strobel 2010, 236.
9. Schrader 2010, 364f.
10. W. Eck in: Beyer 2010a, 174.
11. For this very general overview I have used the following summary literature: Tricholoma 1924–25; Grohmayer and Veith 1963; Webster 1969; v Domaszewski 1967; Dobson 1978; Alföldy, Dobson and Eck 2000; Le Bohec and Wolff 2000; Speidel 2002; Demandt 2007; Le Bohec and Wolff 2004; Strobel 2007; Le Bohec 2010. I would particularly like to thank K. Dietz (Würzburg) for discussion and numerous references.
12. Just see Kienast 1966; Redde 1986; Pferdehirt 1995; Konen 2000.

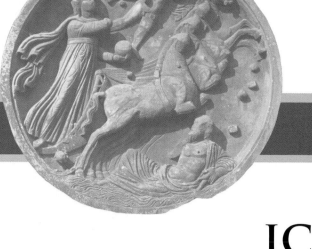

Dietrich Boschung

ICONOGRAPHIC SOURCES FOR THE ROMAN MILITARY

I

1. Introduction

The numerous representations of the Roman military mainly fall into two categories: Roman funerary art, where soldiers are depicted on their gravestones, and state reliefs. They were not produced as an end in themselves, nor were they created with the intention of faithfully illustrating the structure or equipment of the Roman army, but for other reasons: with gravestones, a representative moment was always chosen, showing the depicted with his equipment to the best advantage.[1] With state reliefs, the main purpose of the representations was to display the model behaviour of the exemplary commander in charge, *i.e.* the emperor. Among his main tasks was the provision of appropriate equipment for the soldiers, and especially the leadership of the army. Even if the emperor was not personally involved, he was ultimately responsible as holder of the auspices. The abundance of iconographic sources does not allow a comprehensive treatment of the subject here. Instead, I have restricted myself to a few, particularly informative, monuments. From these, it will become clear that there is no homogeneous convention for the representation of military themes in Roman art.

2. Republican representations

The frieze on the monument of L. Aemilius Paullus at Delphi

By the end of the 19th century, Théophile Homolle had already recognized the association of a four-sided frieze from the sanctuary of Apollo at Delphi with the pillar monument of L. Aemilius Paullus, mentioned in several literary sources, and, as the subject of the representation, the battle between Macedonians and Romans at Pydna (168 BC).[2] Further research has followed him in this,[3] although some points are still very unclear. It seems the monument was initially started for the Macedonian king Perseus, the Roman *imperator* then appropriating the monument as booty after his victory.[4]

The subject of the frieze has been repeatedly associated with individual episodes of the Battle of Pydna,[5] which is described in Livy and Plutarch. Homolle interpreted the striking representation of a fleeing horse without a bridle, occupying the middle of the long side (Fig. 12), with the help of literary information about the onset of battle.[6] However, ownerless horses in flight are also common

Figure 12

Figure 13

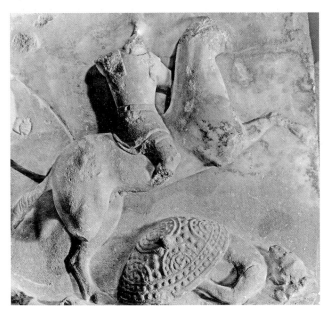

Figure 14

Figure 15

Figures 12–15 *Delphi, frieze from the pillar monument of Aemilius Paulus. Figures 12–13: eastern frieze; Figure 14: southern frieze (detail); Figure 15: western frieze (detail). Images: Cologne Digital Archaeology Laboratory*

in mythological battle scenes, such as Amazonomachy representations from the 5th century BC through to the Roman Imperial period.[7] At the same time, in contrast to the frieze in Delphi, the animal is usually associated with a fallen rider figure in these depictions and provided with a bridle. The motif of the riderless horse is thus presented in a different manner on the Paullus frieze and must be of particular importance, as has often been emphasized.[8]

Other attempts to restore historically attested episodes of the combat in the frieze have been abandoned, however.[9] Like the ownerless fleeing horse, some of the other figures also comply with the iconographic repertoire of mythological representations. These include horses with saddle blankets made from the fur of a predator (panther, lion), collapsed horses, and fallen mounts holding themselves upright with their front legs.[10] The pose of a dying youth, with his head hanging back, crossed legs, and arm falling across his face, also corresponds closely with a traditional representational scheme in Greek art and is similar to the late classical theme of the dying children of Niobe.[11]

Given the traditional character types used, it is all the more striking that the warrior figures have contemporary armament. The frieze is supposed to represent an actual event, but uses preset iconographic elements for this, which are reassembled according to its intent. Topical references, especially the characteristic shields, identify the two sides here. Three round shields are depicted as Macedonian by their decoration of concentric circles and semicircles (Liampi 1998). They are consistently assigned to the losing side: the first shield is carried by a foot soldier standing behind a fallen rider and attacked by two Roman riders; a second soldier with a Macedonian shield is already forced onto his knee under the onslaught of the Romans (Fig. 13); and the third Macedonian shield covers a dead man (Fig. 14). The Macedonian troops are therefore hopelessly inferior in all phases of the fight. The shield of a fallen warrior is recognizable by its shape and distinct curvature as Macedonian. Only one Macedonian foot soldier is seen fighting, but showing his shield from the inside, so the decor is not visible. However, all the soldiers shown with the Roman *scutum* (oval shield) are attacking or fighting (Fig. 15). In four places on the frieze, they are to be found in the immediate vicinity of a falling or dead opponent.

Neither the *scutum* nor the 'Macedonian shield' have been exclusively carried by a single nation. In many cases, the Etruscans and Celts used the *scutum*, but the precise form used here is repeatedly found as the shield of Roman legionaries.[12] Since they are also shown on Roman coins of the 3rd century BC and can be seen on the depiction of a trophy on the coins of Pyrrhus, these defensive weapons seem to have been regarded by both the Romans themselves and by their Hellenistic opponents as typical for the soldiers of Rome.[13] On the Aemilius Paullus monument, the consistent distribution of the two shield forms, taken together with the inscription, suffice to characterize the triumphant side as Romans and the defeated as Macedonians.

The dramatic scenes of the Battle of Pydna reported by Plutarch and Livy are not recognizable in the representation on the frieze. Even the active role of the Macedonian cavalry there is in contrast to the historical accounts, whereby Perseus almost withdrew with the cavalry without engaging. The frieze avoids any hint of the menacing Macedonian phalanx, which had temporarily placed the Romans in serious difficulties. The elephants, whose attack initiated the Macedonian defeat,[14] are also not included in the frieze. Only the fleeing horse, whose depiction is striking in its isolation and not motivated by later events, can be understood as a reference to the initiation of the battle. This can hardly be accidental because, according to the oracles, the manner in which the battle came about meant that the victory of the Romans was preordained by the gods.[15] The frieze shows only a hint of units in close combat on this long side; the two adjacent sides indicate a melee with a more vigorous mixing of the parties. This can be reconciled with the historical accounts, whereby the breakup of the Macedonian phalanx was crucial to the outcome of the battle.

Above the inscription, the front of the frieze depicted the defeat of Perseus, heavily abbreviated:[16] a Roman horseman and a Roman legionary storm over a dead man, clearly indicated as a Macedonian by his shield, in pursuit of fleeing enemies (Fig. 14). If the viewer followed the frieze to the adjacent sides and to the back, they could see how the defeat had occurred and that the Romans had started the fight in accordance with the omens. At no point in the battle are the Macedonian soldiers the equals of the Romans.

The Census Relief in the Louvre

In an entirely different context and in a different way, Roman soldiers appear on the Census Relief from Rome in Paris, dating back to the first half of the 1st century BC.[17] It is divided into three sections, accentuated by the composition, the middle one of which occupies the most space (Fig. 16). It shows a figure-rich sacrificial scene, in which a rectangular altar is the centre of the action. Next to it, on the left and facing the front, a beardless warrior with helmet and armour holds a spear with his raised right hand and rests his left forearm on a round shield, while his hand grasps the hilt of a sword. His head is turned to the altar, with his right foot resting on its base. Neither the shield nor the armour correspond to contemporary forms of weaponry, so it must be a mythological figure who is accepting the sacrifice.

On the other side, a man is wearing a *toga capite velato*, i.e. pulled up over the back of his head, as was appropriate for the Roman ritual of sacrifice. His right hand holds a *patera* above the sacrificial face of the altar, over which an assistant is pouring wine. This is in preparation for a libation, which belongs to the bloodless part of the sacrificial ritual. Two musicians are also playing as part of the sacrificial ritual, a *kithara* player and an *aula* piper, who stand behind the armed deity and two smaller assistants, who assist the sacrificing togate figure and one of whom holds an incense box on his left shoulder. From the left, the sacrificial animals – a bull, a sheep, and a pig – are led to the altar after the preparatory offerings.

In this main scene, two brief depictions are connected to the left and right. That on the left shows two groups of two, each comprising a standing and a sitting togate figure (Fig. 17). The man sitting on the left end of the frieze rests a large unfolded writing tablet on his knees, upon which he makes an entry with his pen. The standing figure looks on and gestures towards the tablet, while he holds a smaller, closed writing tablet to his chest. In the second group, the seated figure turns to the standing man and touches him on the shoulder while he places his right hand in front of his chest in a gesture of oath-taking. Between this group and the sacrifice scene, two soldiers with helmet, mail, sword, and oval shield are standing, one of whom looks towards the oath scene, the other at the sacrifice.

On the right-hand side of the frieze, three more soldiers with helmet, mail, and sword can be seen (Fig. 18). Two of them, who also carry a large oval shield, turn towards each other and are deep in conversation;

Figure 16

Figure 17

Figure 18

Figures 16–18 *Paris, Louvre. Census Monument. Images: Cologne Digital Archaeology Laboratory*

the third takes care of his horse. Even in 1841, the French archaeologist Clarac had realized that the frieze depicts scenes from a Roman census (Clarac 1841); this interpretation is not disputed. The census happened on the Campus Martius – a site outside the city of Rome – and was initially held every five years by two censors (Kubitschek 1899). Every mature Roman citizen had to appear before the censors and, under oath, account for his family and financial circumstances. He was then assigned to one of five tax brackets, according to his assets, and to a voting constituency. This was accompanied by a military muster, whereby citizens had to present themselves and their weapons. In addition, this was combined with a review of the Senate and the equestrians. A violation of the existing moral codes by these gentlemen could be punished with different penalties: admonitions or reprimands, but also reductions in status by transfer to a lower class or by exclusion from senatorial or equestrian

rank. The censors were also responsible for the control of the management of public assets and tax revenue. As assistants to the censor, *iuratores* (oath swearers) are found recording assets. The conclusion of the census was the sacrifice of purification (*lustrum*) for Mars, in which the entire army took part, and which ensured that the census was valid. Lots were drawn for which of the two censors would perform the *lustrum*. Finally the censors led the people back to the city.

The scene on the left side of the frieze therefore represents the actual census (Fig. 17): the seated scribe is in the process of entering the details of the citizen in front of him in the master list of citizens; the citizen in turn has brought a diptych in order to prove his status. The next group of two shows a standing citizen swearing his details to a *iurator*. The soldiers, who are represented at two points on the reliefs, are illustrating the military aspects of the census. They take no special part in the action; they talk to each other and take care of their weapons and their horses (Fig. 17, 18). They are not lined up in formation, but stand there at ease and thereby show their equipment to advantage. They have not been summoned to fight, but to muster.

In the centre is the lustration (Saladino 2004). It is offered to Mars by the censor chosen by lot and it is a *suovetaurilia*, or the sacrifice of a pig, sheep, and bull. Here, the censor vowed a new victim for Mars if he would protect the people until the next lustration. The representation thus emphasizes the sacred side of the census and various aspects of the ritual. The censor at the altar has pulled the *toga* over the back of his head and thus complies with the requirements for a sacrifice according to Roman ritual. Other rules are also strictly adhered to: a *camillus* pours wine into the sacrificial bowl; another is holding incense ready; musicians accompany the sacrifice with their playing; the *hostiae* (sacrificial animals) for the *suovetaurilia* are all male and fully grown; they are – as was required for a favourable sacrifice – willingly led to the sacrificial location. The dramatic moment of the killing, in which the censor would have played only a minor role, is not shown; instead, the bloodless preliminary sacrifice is chosen, in which he is central. While the sacrificial personnel are shown in detail, the celebrants, however, are completely absent. The soldiers, casually turned away, are certainly not intended as participants. They illustrate the military aspect of the census, whereby the Roman army was formed by the muster and classification, and at the same time purified by means of the final lustration ritual.

In antiquity, the census frieze was associated with a three-panel mythological relief depicting the wedding of Poseidon and Amphitrite.[18] This relief differs not only thematically but also stylistically from the census relief and was probably only connected to it in a secondary use in Rome. Together, the friezes decorated the base of a large monument, perhaps a statue group. Here, the mythological part can be understood as a symbol for the mastery of the seas and thus also as a euphemism for a naval victory. If the antiquarian and iconographic studies of the census frieze suggest an origin in the first half of the 1st century BC, the exact dating of the monument and its attribution to a historical personality are as yet still controversial. The most likely connection is with the censors of the year 70 BC – L. Gellius Poplicola and C. Cornelius Lentulus Clodianus – who performed the first census after an interruption under Sulla. At that time, 64 senators were excluded from the Senate (Livy *per.* 98), illustrating how the census could be exploited in the context of domestic political conflicts. However, the relief does not depict exceptional moments, which could appear as politically motivated and therefore problematic; rather, it offers an idealized image of a census, by emphasizing the religious aspects.

The Sant'Omobono base (Bocchus Monument)

Different military aspects are addressed on the so-called Bocchus Monument from the Sullan period, in other words from the first decades of the 1st century BC.[19] Fragments of a large frieze of grey limestone survive which served as panels covering four sides around a large base. The find spot in Rome suggests that it was originally set up at the Temple of Fides on the Capitol.

The centre of the front is occupied by a large round shield, to which archaically stylized personifications of Victory are attaching a laurel garland; the scene is flanked by large candelabra (Fig. 19). The relief decoration of the shield shows two flying cupids, bearing an empty inscription panel, and under them an eagle sitting on a thunderbolt. It has outspread wings and holds a palm branch, which has two wreaths and a *taenia* wound round it. To the right of this depiction is a block presenting an array of different weapons (Fig. 20): first a greave with a frontally viewed head of Hercules on the knee and an extremely animated Victoria below; then an undecorated muscle cuirass; a round shield with a representation of one of the Dioscuri riding a horse; and finally a chamfron. The left third of the front face can be reconstructed as a mirror image to this, as demonstrated by a surviving fragment.

The right side (Fig. 21) is also structured symmetrically and here a relief-decorated round shield is likewise central, in this case with the helmeted head of a goddess, who can be seen as Roma, Minerva, or Virtus. The shield is flanked by two *tropaia*, each hung with a helmet and a cuirass. The neighbouring side is balanced to the left and right with the depiction of a cuirass, which is adorned with a gorgon on the breast, with a hovering Victoria on each of the epaulettes. Another fragment, from the rear face, represents a rectangular shield with curved sides, its relief decoration depicting a winged serpent.

What is striking is the stylized nature of the representation: the weapons and items are not shown in their functional context, but are lined up, without taking into account any change in proportions: candelabra, trophy, round shield, greaves, and breastplate are all adapted to the height of the frieze and are thus approximately equal in height. The stylized arrangement of the objects is in turn matched by the decoration, with mirror symmetry as the dominant principle controlling the overall presentation. This distinguishes the 'Bocchus monument' from the Pergamum weapons friezes, where the irregularity of the arrangement symbolizes the random accumulation of enemy booty captured.[20] There are Hellenistic precursors for a symmetrical arrangement of weaponry as well. The paintings in the Macedonian tomb of Lysias and Callicles

Figure 19

Figure 20

Figure 21

Figures 19–21 *Rome, Capitoline Museums. Base of San Omobono ('Bocchus monument')*

with symbolic references and combined with additional elements. Overlaps and moving figures result in a visual accumulation that could be understood as action only in the middle of the front face (Fig. 19). However, the 'acting' victories stand like statues on their own pedestals and they are shown in archaic, hieratic formal language. The cupids 'acting' similarly and the moving eagle are already part of the shield adornment.

The individual symbols are not difficult to understand in themselves: weapons, trophies, and palm branches point to military successes, while the candelabra are sacrificial equipment within the sacred realm. In figural representations, Victoria is most strongly emphasized as a goddess of victory, reinforcing the already obvious military references in the frieze. She is shown in three different forms: on the epaulettes of the cuirass to one side, she floats down to bestow (or report) a victory. On the front of a greave, she runs up, armed, appearing as a comrade-in-arms, actively bringing about the victory that she personifies. On the centre front, the goddess of victory occurs twice, symmetrically. The archaic formulas of the symmetrical, artistically drawn folds of drapery and stiff, upstanding curls are to be understood as denoting age and respectability. These figures of Victoria contrast conspicuously with other representations of the goddess of victory, appearing as venerable divinities who, although shown like statues, are also endorsing the shield of the victor.

The Dioscuri, Roma (or Minerva?), and Hercules are only indirectly evoked in the decoration of weaponry. They were the tried and trusted tutelary deities of the Romans and helpers in time of war. The eagle on the thunderbolt refers symbolically to Jupiter, the supreme god of Rome, the cupids to Venus, which in this strongly militarily influenced context is not at first readily understandable. The decoration of the weaponry makes it clear that it is not looted weapons that are being shown here, but rather the carefully maintained and preserved ceremonial weapons of the Roman victors.

The frieze has been dated to the time of Sulla with good arguments, some of them stylistic. T. Hölscher has proposed its identification with an historically attested monument which King Bocchus of Mauritania erected in honour of Sulla in 91 BC and whose sculptural group represented the surrender of Jugurtha.[22] Although the identification of the monument is not without problems,[23] the connection with Sulla would explain the allusion to Venus in such a prominent place: she was the patron goddess of Sulla, whose Roman epithet Felix was translated in Greek as Epaphroditus. The reliefs do not provide a specific narrative: rather, they depict a series of symbolic groups and individual emblematic designs that are presented alongside each other and partly have no discernible direct relationship. These individual motifs add up to an overall statement: they recall the tutelary gods of Rome and especially the

in Lefkadia (created *c.*200 BC) show weapons hanging on the wall, including 'Macedonian' shields.[21] However, the symmetrical composition adopted is simpler and more uniform: for instance the lack of a similar combination of victories, candelabra, and trophies. In the Sullan frieze, however, the weapon representations are highly charged

patroness of Sulla, even if only indirectly through the shield design; and they evoke military successes through figures and attributes and elevate them to a sacred level by simultaneously combining them with the two candelabra. The historical events to which the reliefs allude, and which were perhaps explained in a corresponding inscription, are not even shown; the victorious quality of the commander is not limited to a particular situation, but is independent of specific operations. The person being honoured is indeed absent, but at the same time all the elements in it indicate him as the true focus. Perhaps he appeared prominently in the sculptural group on top of the base. The statement being made by the relief must have been evident to the ancient viewer through the overall context (*i.e.* in relation to site, inscription, and sculpture).

These three examples – the Aemilius Paullus monument, the census relief, and the 'Bocchus Monument' – do not allow any fixed representational conventions for military issues to be identified for the period of the Roman Republic. Rather, they vary according to the occasion and original context. It is always about the glory of a single person; neither the Roman people, the Senate, nor the army are guarantors of success or the agents of historical developments; instead this is always an outstanding individual. His performance could be equally well illustrated by a narrative representation as by a stereotypical scene or a symbolic description. These different modes of representation existed simultaneously and side by side. They all exploit the Hellenistic Greek repertoire, but in different ways. Thus the frieze on the Aemilius Paullus monument employed single figure types from Hellenistic mythological friezes and updated them with contemporary armament. The 'Bocchus Monument' extended Hellenistic stereotypes and charged them with a wealth of symbolism.

3 The Early Empire: Augustus to Domitian

The frieze from the Porticus Octaviae

A frieze from the Porticus Octaviae in Rome is formally connected to the representation of the 'Bocchus Monument',[24] reproducing equipment in a symmetrical arrangement and without regard to the actual proportions. At the same time, the compositional scheme is further developed in a way that is characteristic of the Augustan period. The frieze was divided into equal panels by *bucrania*, some of which show the components of ships (Fig. 22). The objects are repeated: *cheniskos* (bow fitting) and *prora* with *rostrum* (prow with battering ram) occur in the frieze (only partially preserved) five times; anchor, rudder and *aplustre* (stern adornments) occur four times. So those decorative and symbolic parts of warships are shown on the frieze that had long been seen as a sign of victorious sea battles. However, the ship parts are not simply piled up, but instead they are rather artfully composed, with the symmetrical arrangement emphasizing the aesthetic standards of presentation. The central axis of this relief of ship trophies, strangely enough, is taken up with a sacrificial accessory, namely a *turibulum* (incense stand).

In fact, the sections with ship components alternate regularly with a second theme, namely that of images of sacred devices.[25] They show instruments that would complement each other functionally in the course of a sacrificial ritual: the *aspergillum* (holy water sprinkler) and *mappa* (towel) were used in ritual purifications; the *acerra* (incense box) and *turibulum* (incense stand) with incense; the *simpulum* (ladle), *urceus* (wine jug) and *patera* (offering dish) with the libation; and the axe and dagger with animal blood sacrifices. The *galerus*

Figure 22 *Rome, Capitoline Museums. Frieze block with ship components and sacrificial equipment*

(leather cap) was a significant part of the costume of the high priest. Some of these sacrificial devices are to be understood as badges of priesthood:[26] the *simpulum* can stand for the priesthood of *pontifices*; the *lituus* for *augures*; the *galerus* and *apex* for the *salii* and *flamines*; and the laurel on the *acerra* and *urceus* can be seen as indicative of the *quindecemviri sacris faciundis* ('fifteen men for the procurement of victims'), one of the four highest colleges of priests. The frieze sections with sacred devices were also symmetrical in respect to the central axis of the ship reliefs to which they are connected. Military success and piety are inextricably interlinked in this frieze; they change constantly over the course of the frieze, but the different portions are always of the same size and thus equivalent.

So the frieze alludes to and interprets historical events without really representing them. The ship components displayed give no indication of the defeated enemy, the occasion of the battle, or the identity of the victor. Depicting the sea battles of Naulochos and Actium would also have been problematic because it would need to show Romans fighting against Romans. In addition, the role of Octavian in the two battles had not exactly been heroic: in the Battle of Naulochos, he is supposed to have lain petrified, flat on his back, and only got up again when Agrippa had won the battle for him (Suetonius, *Augustus* 16.1–2). These difficulties have been solved by omitting the actual event: the reliefs do not depict a particular event, but formulate a general statement – the connection between *pietas* (piety) and victory. The multiple changes and the compositional logic of the representations show that piety and political success are forever linked. It is therefore a particularly striking reference when a sacrificial device appears in the centre of the section with ship trophies and points to the common axis of symmetry. And since traditional *pietas* was restored by Augustus (the attributes of the priesthood, which Augustus had reformed, demonstrate this), political and military successes inevitably appear. The victory of Augustus was not the result of blind chance, which might lead to a very different result next time; rather it was the logical, compelling result of the religious policy of the *princeps*. The victorious general himself does not appear in all this.

While the Porticus Octaviae was named after the sister of Augustus, it was actually financed by Octavian from the spoils of the Dalmatian War (Cassius Dio 49.43.8; Suetonius, *Augustus* 29.4). The frieze thus provides an authentic vision of Octavian, or was at least authorized by him. This view is reflected in the speech that Octavian is supposed to have addressed to his troops before the battle of Actium (Cassius Dio 50.24): in effect, righteousness and piety lead to victory. The Augustan view, that *pietas* and military success were necessarily related, differed fundamentally from the point of view of some late republican generals: Lutatius Catulus credited *Fortuna huiusce diei*, the goddess of fortune of the present day, for his victory over the Cimbri in 101 BC (Plutarch: *Marius* 26.2). In this view, warfare appeared to be a kind of game of chance, success depending upon the ever-changing constellations. The frieze in the Porticus Octaviae proclaimed that this risky state of affairs had been overcome by Augustus.

The silver cup from Boscoreale

While the monuments of the later Augustan period concentrated upon military successes, military events were almost completely suppressed. A significant example of this is demonstrated by two silver *skyphoi* from Boscoreale,[27] one of which shows Augustus as the main character of the two relief representations, the other Tiberius. T. Hölscher has pointed out that they show the Roman campaign of the year 8/7 BC in Germania. Tiberius had at that point defeated the Germans between the Rhine and the Elbe and celebrated a triumph in Rome in 7 BC. In 8 BC, Augustus himself was near the combat zone, but remained on the left bank of the Rhine, while Tiberius crossed it (Cassius Dio 55.6; Velleius Paterculus 2.97.1).

The Tiberius cup shows the *vota nuncupata*, the sacrifice upon Tiberius' departure at the beginning of the campaign on one side (Fig. 23).[28] The process of the bull sacrifice is shown in detail, with the victim held in the correct manner by well-trained staff. By including the temple facade, with its gable ornaments, the location of the event is suggested: the eagle on the pediment shows that the sacrifice takes place in front of a Temple of Jupiter, which stands on a high podium. The front of the temple is divided by four columns into three sections. It is tempting to see in this sacred building the Temple of Jupiter Optimus Maximus, which contained the three *cellae* of the Capitoline Triad.[29] The image on the opposite side (Fig. 24) represents the triumph of Tiberius. Despite their small size, the attributes of the *triumphator* are depicted very accurately: the eagle sceptre; the laurel branch in his right hand; the crown which is held over his head by a slave; his *toga*; and the *quadriga* with its ornate coachwork. In front is a bull that, from its decoration, is shown to be a sacrificial animal, anticipating the sacrifice that will take place at the conclusion of the triumphant procession to the Capitol.

On the Augustus cup, one scene shows the submission of a barbarian tribe before Augustus (Fig. 25). The emperor sits on a *sella castrensis*, but is otherwise pictured in a pointedly civilian manner. He has a large crowd of escorts closely surrounding him, indicating his importance: the lictors with *fasces* mark him as a high curule magistrate; the standing staff officers make clear

Figure 23

Figure 24

Figures 23–24 *Paris, Louvre. Tiberius cup from Boscoreale*

Figure 25 *Paris, Louvre. Augustus cup from Boscoreale*

the role of the emperor as supreme commander, but they are held at a distance by Augustus' lictors. The other side shows Augustus as a civilian official: sitting on the *sella curulis*, in tunic and *toga*, with a scroll in his left hand. But here he appears frontally, like a cult image, and isolated within an empty space. In his outstretched right hand he holds the globe, a symbol of world domination. Around him stand, at a reverent distance, goddesses

and gods. Mars, the ancestor of the Romans, leads in a group of personified provinces from the right. From the left, Venus, the ancestress of the Julii, appears before the seated emperor, to place a Victoria statuette on his globe. Behind her are Honos and Virtus, the personifications of honour and martial prowess.

The four reliefs of the cups just described provide, as is usual with early imperial *skyphos* pairs, a complete sequence of images. They depict Augustus, upon whom the gods have bestowed victory, as ruler of the world. He receives the submission of the barbarians. His son Tiberius departs from Rome as a commander in the war and returns victorious, in triumph, to Rome. The actual military events are not shown. The campaign, which is the reason for the events depicted, remains obscure and is limited to the elaborate presentation of two religious rituals. As in the frieze of the Porticus Octaviae, piety and victory are also permanently and inextricably linked in this event.

Representations from the Julio-Claudian period

Other monuments of the Augustan and Tiberian period show the same distribution of roles between the emperor and the imperial princes as on the Boscoreale cup. The Gemma Augustea,[30] referring to the military successes in the years AD 6–12, also portrays the victory and triumph of Tiberius, but in a different, panegyrical, formal manner (Fig. 26).

In the lower frieze, Roman soldiers erect a *tropaion*; captives squat on the ground or are dragged in. Above, Tiberius, in *tunica* and *toga*, crowned with laurel, dismounts from a four-horse chariot. The *quadriga*, the costumes, and the wreaths match the characteristics of a *triumphator*, recalling the success of Tiberius in AD 12. But here the triumph is not depicted realistically, but exaggerated panegyrically: Tiberius holds the long sceptre of the gods and Victoria, the goddess of victory, serves as his charioteer. Moreover, Germanicus – whom Tiberius had adopted in AD 4 as a young officer – stands next to the chariot. Roma and Augustus are sitting on a bench, the feet of the latter resting on captured weapons. Between their heads is a disc bearing two star signs, the Julian Star (*sidus Iulium*) that marked the deification of Caesar, and the capricorn, the zodiacal sign of the emperor.

The cameo shows the deification of Caesar the father as inevitably predetermining the reign of Augustus, guaranteed by the stars. The emperor is the main character of the cameo scene: all eyes are on him. Just like Jupiter, he sits topless, wearing only a cloak over his hips; like Jupiter, he holds the long sceptre of the gods. The eagle, the familiar of Jupiter, sits at his feet and looks up at him. Next to him, a group of gods are resting: Tellus, Oceanus,

Figure 26 *Vienna, Kunsthistorisches Museum. Gemma Augustea. Photo: Cologne Digital Archaeology Laboratory*

and Oikumene (the personification of the inhabited earth), holding the oak wreath over his head. The striking attribute in the right hand of Augustus is a *lituus*, the attribute of the augurs. It here appears as a sign that it is Augustus holding the auspices for the campaign. For, as commander in chief, the leader of the empire took the auspices, predicting the course of a planned war. Again, the image gives no hint of the campaign, but illustrates the fortunate achievement of an ideal state of affairs. Again, the imperial family appears as the guarantor of Roman victory. Augustus, the pre-determined ruler of the world, supported by the gods, takes the auspices; Tiberius returns victorious in triumph;

the young Germanicus is ready to provide active support as an officer. Three generations of the *domus Augusta* ensure the continuity and durability of the Roman Empire.

These roles survived the Augustan period and are also found on Tiberian monuments. The relief on the sword sheath of the so-called 'Sword of Tiberius'[31] shows the encounter between the Emperor Tiberius and the commander Germanicus (Fig. 27); Tiberius is enthroned between Mars and Victoria Augusta; Germanicus stands before him in armour and hands him a statuette of Victoria, the embodiment of his victories. Again, the roles are clear. No matter how proficient the commander might be, the

Figure 27 *London, British Museum. Decorated plate from a sword scabbard ('Sword of Tiberius')*

Figure 28 *Privately owned. Sesterce of Caligula (RIC)*

guarantor of victory was the Emperor himself. After the death of the younger Drusus (AD 23), Augustus' succession policy was finally in tatters; however, its representation initially continued. This makes the images of the Grand Camée – created in the years AD 23–9 – significant.[32] Again, the Emperor Tiberius is enthroned like Jupiter in the centre with the *aegis* and also holding the *lituus* here. The three sons of Germanicus stand around him in armour; they are sent out by the Emperor, doubtless to great deeds and victories. Of course, any specific reference is lacking here: there were no military undertakings by the princes to celebrate; at best one could hope that they would emulate the shining example of their father in the near future.

The monuments emphasize the responsibility of the emperor for the military and demonstrate that his person guaranteed victories. But at the same time they demonstrate the distance that separates the Jupiter-like emperor from the martial craft of the soldiers. While there are definitely representations of combat in the Augustan and Tiberian period (*e.g.* the Arch of Orange: Amy 1962), the emperor is never directly connected with them. This is important for two reasons. One was that the role of Augustus as a caudillo figurehead in the civil wars had not been forgotten. In addition, the personal bravery of Octavian was not without controversy. His opponents accused him of fleeing from the Battle of Mutina and only surfacing again after two days (Suetonius, *Augustus* 10.4); during the first Battle of Philippi he hid for three days in the marshes (Pliny, *Naturalis Historia* 7.148); at Naulochos, he lay paralysed on his back and only got up once Agrippa had won the battle for him (Suetonius, *Augustus* 16.2). His portrayal as a great warrior might therefore have provoked opposition or at least undesirable associations. In contrast, the solution he chose made any comparison with living or dead war heroes impossible.

This made clear that his position was incomparable and unique.

The representations of the following decades differ in some aspects from Augustan conventions for representation. From the time of Caligula, the attachment of the emperor to his soldiers is emphasized more strongly in official self-representation.[33] A coin of Caligula with the inscription *adlocutio cohortum* shows an address by the emperor to his soldiers (Fig. 28): the emperor is in a *toga* in front of a *sella castrensis*. In his left hand he holds a scroll, while the right he raises to the soldiers in full armour (with helmet, shield, and sword) in front of his podium. They are standing in close formation and hold four standards, on each of which an eagle is perched. The round discs on the standards will have contained the imperial busts which they carried as an expression of loyalty to their emperor.[34] The emperor himself appears unarmed and in civilian garb: he is not inclined to fight with his troops, but he leads them; and in return earns the loyalty of the soldiers. Two coins from the earliest part of the reign of Claudius refer to the strange circumstances of the beginnings of his government, when the Praetorians played a decisive role as king makers. The first bears the inscription *praetor(ianis in fidem) recept(us)*: the togate emperor stands opposite a Praetorian *signifer*, offering his hand. This gesture expresses solidarity, but also implies equality. The other coin, with the inscription *Imper(ator) recept(us)*, shows the Praetorian camp, where the emperor had found refuge.

Figure 29

Figure 30

The Cancelleria reliefs

Despite these changes, a key element of the Augustan concept is still found at the end of the 1st century AD, namely in the Domitianic reliefs from the Cancelleria. They had already been placed into storage in antiquity, but they are likely to have been found close to their original location and to have belonged to a building on the Campus Martius in Rome. One of the two friezes, which certainly belong together,[35] originally showed the departure of the Emperor Domitian to war (Fig. 29); after his assassination, his portrait was altered into a likeness of his successor Nerva. The emperor is placed as the principal figure in the centre of the work (Fig. 30). He wears the *tunica* and *paludamentum*, faces left and is raising his hand towards the front, indicating the direction

of the march. An armed woman in Amazon costume, representing Virtus (personified bravery), supports the emperor by grasping his left forearm. In front of him, Minerva and Mars are moving in the direction the emperor indicates, while simultaneously looking back at him. Minerva, the patron goddess of Domitian, is equipped for war with *aegis*, helmet, round shield, and spear. The bearded god of war, Mars, also has a helmet, shield, and spear, but with a muscled cuirass. His round shield, with a head of Ammon, is like the *clipei* adorning the Forum of Augustus, and therefore it may be that the avenging Mars Ultor was intended here. In front of Mars and behind the emperor walk the lictors, designating the rank of senior officials.

Behind Virtus, the *genius* of the Senate and the *genius* of the Roman people are standing. The *genius Senatus* appears as a worthy bearded man with long hair and, like the senators, whose assembly he embodies, he wears *tunica*, *toga*, and the *calcei patricii*. He holds a sceptre with the bust of the emperor and thus provides an expression of the close connection between ruler and Senate.[36] The *genius populi Romani* appears as an idealized young man with long curly hair, wearing a cloak around his hips which leaves his upper body free, and with a cornucopia. Both have raised their right hands to the emperor. In contrast to the companions of the emperor, they remain in Rome, while the following soldiers set off to follow their emperor. On the extreme right of the frieze are three soldiers in the *paenula* and travel clothing, but equipped with oval shield and *pilum*. The fourth figure preceding them has different equipment, carrying a *hasta*, like the *principales* (NCOs),[37] and a round shield he has not put on, but carries under his arm. This figure is the *armiger*, the armour-bearer of the Emperor. The left end of the frieze is lost, but surviving traces show that a flying Victoria led the procession.

Figure 31

Figures 29–31 *Vatican, Museo Gregoriano Profano. The Cancelleria reliefs. Images: Cologne Digital Archaeology Laboratory*

Thus, the relief shows the *profectio* of the ruler: he is leaving Rome with his soldiers on a military expedition, the victorious outcome of which is announced by the Victoria flying in front (alternatively, Hölscher 2009 sees an *adventus* here). The closest companions to the emperor are the gods Mars, Minerva, and Victoria. The Senate and people of Rome see him off in an appropriate manner. The emperor, as a high civil magistrate, is still travelling with his lictors, but he carries his weapons with him and, if necessary, would fight with his soldiers.

The main figure in the second frieze (Frieze B: Fig. 31) was originally Domitian, but the portrait head was also subsequently changed, in this case to Vespasian. The emperor wears the *toga* and is turning to a second, youthful *togatus*. Behind these are the *genius* of the Roman people and the *genius* of the Senate, who look towards the emperor. A flying Victoria (of which only one leg and a toe survive, because of the fragmentary state of the reliefs), hovering above, brings an oak wreath to set upon the ruler – the highest military decoration, only given for the rescue of a Roman citizen. Again, lictors surround the emperor. At the left-hand end of the frieze, perched on a pedestal, is the goddess Roma; like the Vestal Virgins standing in front of her, she looks toward the emperor.

This frieze, complementing the first, shows the return of the emperor to Rome. Victorious, he is crowned by Victoria, welcomed into Rome by the Senate and people, and awaited by the Vestal Virgins and the city goddess. As with the Tiberius cup from Boscoreale, the victorious war is depicted by two rituals. However, here these are not religious acts indicating the relationship between *pietas* and victory and at the same time acting as a framework for military success. Rather, it is the solemn ceremonies of departure and return, expressing the close but at the same time hierarchical ties between the ruler on one hand and the priesthood, the Senate, and the people on the other. The Cancelleria reliefs combine representational conventions that occur simultaneously but separately in the Augustan period. They show – like the Gemma Augustea – personifications of gods as companions of the emperor, which elevate his person into the mythological realm. Like the Tiberius cup from Boscoreale, they strive for detail in recording reality, such as in the equipment and garb of the lictors or soldiers. These details make the representation plausible and thus validate the panegyric exaggeration. Again, however, the events of war are avoided, description being limited to the events in Rome itself. Thus it is not specified which of the wars of Domitian is intended. Possible confrontations are the wars against the Chatti (AD 83), the Dacians (AD 86–8), and the Sarmatians (AD 92), in all of which Domitian was personally present.

4 Representations from the middle imperial period

Trajan's Column

The Trajanic period reveals a fundamentally different view of the military tasks of the emperor. It found its most impressive expression in the reliefs of Trajan's Column.[38] With a height of 100 ft, an internal spiral staircase illuminated by windows, and a helical frieze nearly 200 m long, it belongs to the grand architectural achievements of antiquity and, due to its near-complete state of preservation – only the crowning statue of the emperor has been lost – is one of the most important monuments of imperial Rome (Fig. 32). The column was financed *ex manubiis* – in other words, from the spoils of the Dacian Wars – and consecrated in AD 113. After the death of the Emperor Trajan, his ashes were buried in its base.

In 155 scenes, the frieze depicts events from the two Dacian wars of Trajan in the years AD 101–2 and 105. These are partly standard combat scenes, but specific events are also shown, with the emperor being repeatedly present. The sequence begins at the bottom and then ascends in an anticlockwise spiral. The first scenes show the Roman frontier, with its military buildings and guards (I–II), then the departure of the Roman army from a well-fortified city and its crossing of the Danube on a pontoon bridge (III–IV; Fig. 33). Other scenes depict the advance into enemy territory (V); the emperor with his advisers (VI); a fortified Roman camp; sacrifice scenes (VIII); speeches (X), and construction (XI). These illustrate the routine of the war, but in addition, exceptional events are shown that may have been of particular importance for the campaign. Among these is the fall of a rider from his mule in the presence of Trajan (IX). Actual combat scenes are also given a lot of space. An example of this is Scene XXIV, probably intended to represent the Battle of Tapae (Cassius Dio 68.8) (Fig. 34). If the general direction of reading is followed, the viewer first sees the result of the battle: two auxiliary soldiers present severed enemy heads to the emperor as a sign of their bravery and prowess. This is followed by the actual battle scene, with the Roman cavalry, legionary, and auxiliary troops. Their Dacian opponents are marked as barbarians by trousers, long beards, long tangled hair, and in part by their headgear; they operate out of the forest. The relentlessness of the struggle is illustrated by the well-known representation of a legionary who fights with the severed head of an enemy between his teeth,[39] but

Figure 32

Figure 33

Figure 34

also by the fact that there are no fleeing Dacians. Jupiter himself intervenes and fights on the side of the Romans. Among the gruesome aspects of war described in detail are the torching of Dacian houses, the deportation of women and children, the slaughter of domestic animals, and the execution of the men (XXIX/XXX). At the end of the first war, there is the submission of the Dacians in the presence of the emperor (LXXV) and a final speech by Trajan (LXXVII; Fig. 35). At the mid-point of the frieze, Victoria, the goddess of victory, appears between two *trophaia*, writing the victories of Trajan on a shield, and thus passing them on for posterity (LXXVIII). Then, with just as many scenes (77) and equally detailed, the second Dacian war is described, ending with the defeat and destruction of the Dacians and the suicide of their king, Decebalus (CXLV).

Although the legibility of the reliefs may have been enhanced for the ancient viewer with paint and metal fittings, the continuous narrative of the reliefs on the column itself could not be followed.[40] Only separate sections could be seen from the adjacent buildings, depicting the Roman army on the march, at sacrifices, or building fortifications and fighting. These details, even if they were only occasionally visible to the ancient viewer, suggest a high level of authenticity, validating the representations as accurate and realistic. It is fitting that mythological and allegorical characters are almost completely absent on the column and where they do occur, are set in their own context. Jupiter appears above the Battle of Tapae, clearly separated from the fighting soldiers (XXIV; see

Fig. 34). Likewise, the writing Victoria is clearly separate from the narrative scenes (LXXVIII). River gods (III) and personifications of places (CL) are isolated from events by composition and size.

The illustrations are in part non-specific, such as sacrifices, *adlocutiones*, and building scenes. Others, however, obviously signify important or spectacular events in the campaigns, such as the march across the pontoon bridge or the suicide of Decebalus. The strong stylization of the entire frieze is apparent by both wars being represented with the same number of scenes and of the same length. The emperor is represented 58 times and in different situations: as a *togatus*, wearing a cuirass, or in civil service costume.[41] He is always elevated in the composition and identifiable from his portrait. Again and again he gets involved, managing the army, speaking to the soldiers, or supervising construction and battles. The success of the army is down to him. Mostly he is found accompanied by advisers and experts, but it is him giving the instructions. Only a small number of scenes have stylistic precursors in the reliefs of the early Imperial period. The *adlocutio* of the emperor has already been seen on the sesterces of Caligula (Fig. 28); the image is extended and varied on Trajan's Column. Similarly, the submission scene, shown at the end of the first Dacian war, was anticipated on the Augustus cup from Boscoreale (Fig. 25) and sacrifices were common in Roman art from the Republican period onwards, and even more so in the early Imperial period. On Trajan's Column, these images are integrated into a continuous sequence of events and thus convey a specific message.

The reliefs of Trajan's Column depict precisely those elements of military events that the Augustan Boscoreale cup and Domitianic Cancelleria reliefs omitted. Conversely, events that are represented there are missing, namely the sacrifice upon departure and the *profectio*, the *adventus* and the triumphal parade of the emperor, which were rituals and ceremonies that took place in Rome itself. However, other monuments of Trajan's time, such as the Arch of Beneventum,[42] definitely depict them, so they were still present as visual themes. What is new was that military campaigns were represented in Rome as a continuous narrative and in such detail that they seem to seamlessly document the emperor's deeds in the field. The frieze thus appears to be a 'visual paraphrase' of literary accounts of the campaigns of Trajan.[43]

The Great Trajanic Frieze

The new interest in the martial deeds of the emperor also informs another frieze, which probably comes from the Forum of Trajan, and thus must have been visible in the immediate vicinity of Trajan's Column. Eight panels, which had been reused and installed in pairs in four different

Figure 35

Figures 32–35 *Rome, Trajan's Column*

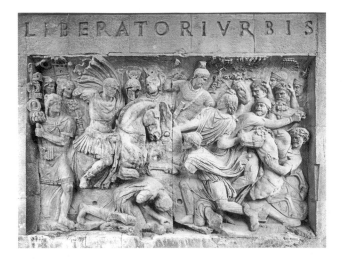

Figure 36

Figure 37

Figures 36–37 *Rome, Arch of Constantine. Reused Trajanic frieze*

places on the Arch of Constantine, as well as a series of fragments, can be used for a partial reconstruction.[44] The main part shows the battle between the Romans and Dacians. The emperor plays a crucial role: at the head of his troops, he rides down the enemy and forces his opponents into flight (Fig. 36). From the other side, the Roman cavalry have encircled and defeated the Dacians. Another scene from the battle is set on the left-hand side (Fig. 37). It shows the return of the victorious emperor to Rome. The military context is illustrated by the fact that Trajan is wearing armour and the *paludamentum*, and that soldiers are accompanying him in the background. Victoria floats behind the emperor, crowning him, and thus distinguishing him as victor. Virtus leads him to an arch which symbolizes one of the gates of Rome. Some fragments belonging to the same frieze show soldiers standing quietly with standards; they may have

belonged to a submission scene.[45] The frieze thus originally contained three scenes relating to military events: the fight against the barbarians, decided by the emperor's personal intervention; the return of the victorious general to Rome; and perhaps the *submissio* of the Dacians. The *adventus* scene continued the conventions of the Domitianic Cancelleria relief by letting the emperor be seen with gods and personifications, thus enhancing a ceremony that actually took place in Rome. In contrast to them, the Great Trajanic Frieze connects these scenes with scenes of the actual war. However, the emperor appears here not as an organizer and leader of the campaign – as on Trajan's Column – but as an heroic fighter.

The Column of Marcus Aurelius

About three generations after the erection of Trajan's Column, another Roman monument borrowed its shape, theme, and narrative form: the Column of Marcus Aurelius (Fig. 38). On both columns, the campaign begins with the crossing of a river bridge over the Danube (Fig. 39). The derivative nature of the column of Marcus Aurelius is also revealed in the structure of the reliefs, in the design of important scenes, and sometimes even in the reproduction of details. The first and most important message of Marcus Aurelius' column is that he was as efficient, energetic, and successful a general as Trajan had been three generations earlier. His wars were as important for the Roman Empire as the Dacian wars and he mastered these challenges with the same energy and alertness as Trajan had done.[46]

The exact dating of the column is controversial because the inscription associated with it has not come down to us. However, the representations refer to the campaigns of Marcus Aurelius against the Germans and Sarmatians in the years 172–5 and 178–80; the completion and dedication of the monument took place after his death.[47] In the 116 scenes, Marcus Aurelius himself appears 59 times. Scene III,[48] for instance, shows the emperor leading the Roman army over the Danube. In the following scenes, he is always talking to the soldiers, as at the end of the first campaign, where he reads out a proclamation.[49] In other scenes he is negotiating with barbarians; sacrificing; monitoring the advance of the Roman troops; directing the fighting; judging prisoners (Fig. 40); watching the removal of booty and prisoners; accepting the submission of the barbarians; and negotiating contracts. All of these depictions make it clear that the emperor personally directs all phases of the campaigns and thereby tirelessly and diligently takes care of all the crucial questions.

Compared to Trajan's Column, the changes are mainly on a formal level initially: the visibility of the individual figures and the legibility of the scenes has been improved on the Marcus Column by reducing the number of turns;

Figure 38

Figures 38–40 *Rome, Marcus Column*

Figure 39

Figure 40

the figures therefore are larger and also presented more clearly. Stylistically, the reliefs are less classical, *i.e.* the figures move in a livelier manner, and they are pictured more dramatically and expressively; the whole relief is more influenced by effects of light and shadow.[50] However, there are also differences in detail: the construction scenes that are presented so impressively on Trajan's Column are largely missing on the Marcus Column; on the other hand, scenes of combat as well as of killing and destruction are more common: the brutality of war against the defeated barbarians is also clearer, just because of the legibility of the images.[51]

A series of reliefs of Marcus Aurelius

The military campaigns of Marcus Aurelius were also the subject of the reliefs on an honorific arch, eight of which were later installed in pairs on the Arch of Constantine; three more were brought to the Capitol in the 16th century, from the church of S. Martina. These eleven reliefs belong to a series and probably decorated a monumental arch to Marcus Aurelius.[52] The sequence of events begins with the emperor embarking upon a campaign and departing from Rome (Fig. 41). The *genius* of the Senate and the *genius* of the Roman people, who stand behind him and remain within the urban area, are bidding the emperor farewell. This is followed by several events from the campaign, an example being a speech of the emperor to his soldiers. Another relief

Figure 41 *Rome, Arch of Constantine. Reused relief from an arch of Marcus Aurelius*

shows an incense offering, which the emperor takes in his *toga* at a portable metal altar. We also know this scene from Trajan's Column, where it is clear that a procession of soldiers is walking around a fortified camp. The sacrifice is therefore a *lustratio*, the ritual purification of the army, carried out by the commander in accordance with his obligations. The success of the commander is manifested in the subjugation of the barbarians. One such relief shows two men who fall to their knees before the mounted emperor and plead with outstretched hands, asking for mercy (Fig. 42). Other enemies are captured by Roman soldiers and led, bound, to the general. The campaign depicts scenes including the establishment of a client king.

The sequence of the six scenes of war is unclear. The *adlocutio* and *lustratio* are standard narrative scenes in war and can therefore be inserted at any point. The establishment of the vassal king is more likely to belong to the end. But what happens next is then clear: after the successful completion of the campaign, the emperor returns to Rome in travelling clothes, accompanied by Mars and Virtus (Fig. 43). In the background, a monumental arch is visible next to the Temple of Fortuna Redux. The goddess Fortuna herself is in the background next to her temple. Beside her appears Felicitas, holding a cornucopia and a *caduceus*, and thereby referring to the prosperity that the return of the emperor brings. Above the emperor hovers the victory goddess, Victoria, making it clear that he returns victorious. Then the depiction of a triumph follows (Fig. 44). The triumphant emperor drives through the city in the richly decorated triumphal *quadriga*. Above the emperor, the goddess Victoria is still hovering. A *tuba* player and a single lictor lead the way. The strangely cramped pose of Marcus Aurelius is explained by the fact that, originally, a second figure was riding in the emperor's chariot: Commodus, who was later, after his fall and *damnatio memoriae*, removed. The destination of the triumphal procession was the Capitol, where the victor was offering a sacrifice to Jupiter Optimus Maximus. Beside the emperor is the *flamen dialis*, the priest responsible for the cult of Jupiter. Behind the emperor appears the *genius* of the Senate. This sacrifice can be located precisely because it takes place in front of the temple of Jupiter Optimus Maximus, the three doors visible on the relief referring to the three *cellae* of the Capitoline Triad. Jupiter, Juno, and Minerva are also seen in multiple figures on the pediment of the temple. The final relief shows the distribution of largesse by the emperor. On a high pedestal, Marcus Aurelius is seated on a *sella curulis* in a *toga*. He is surrounded by togate men and on the instructions of the emperor, an assistant distributes the money to the men, women, and children who have lined up in front of the podium. Again, a figure seated on a *sella curulis* next to the emperor (and therefore his equal) has subsequently been removed: it can only have been Commodus.

Figure 42

Figure 44

Figures 42–44 *Reliefs from an arch of Marcus Aurelius; Fig. 43 reused in the Arch of Constantine; Figs 42 and 44 Rome, Capitoline Museums*

Figure 43

A comparison of this series of reliefs with the Marcus Column shows that both represent the same topic, but with a different focus. While the column is limited entirely to the events of war far from Rome and attempts to describe them in detail, the reliefs emphasize the connection with the city: the emperor leaves Rome and returns there after the end of the war; he celebrates a triumph there and brings Jupiter a victory sacrifice; and finally he endows the city population with a *congiarium*. The events in Rome are precisely located, and thus based on very specific and verifiable occasions. Unlike the column, the close relationship between the emperor and the Senate is important: in the *profectio*, as in the victory sacrifice, the *genius senatus* is close to the emperor. However, the emperor's relationship with the traditional priesthoods, the population, and even the gods of Rome themselves is also depicted as close and harmonious. Finally the dynastic aspect was emphasized by the fact that his son Commodus appears at the side of Marcus Aurelius in two reliefs. In this manner, the reliefs blend the specific events of war into a few standardized situations. As with the column, so in the portrayal on the relief – whatever the emperor does is perfect, both *domi et militiae*, in Rome and on campaign.

The Arch of Severus

The monumental arch of Septimius Severus and his sons in the Roman Forum[53] was established by resolution of the Senate and consecrated between 10th December 202 and 9th December 203 (Fig. 45). According to the inscription, the reason was the restoration of the state, *i.e.* the end of the civil wars, as well as the expansion of the empire. The campaigns of the years AD 197–9 against the Parthians are depicted in four relief panels, which are mounted on both faces over the side passages and together comprise 74 m². Of the twelve scenes, three show sieges and another three the *adlocutio* of the emperor. On each panel, two city views occur. If one begins by examining the left field of the relief panel facing the Forum, then three superimposed set scenes can be distinguished: below is the departure of the Roman army from a city, probably Nisibis; above, a battle, and at the top, an *adlocutio* and a city view. The second panel, right next to it, in fact shows five scenes, which in turn are arranged into three strips, one above the other: below, the storming of a city with a large battering ram; to the right, the subjugation of the barbarians in front of the emperor and, to the left, an address by the emperor; and in the top right, the arrival of the emperor in a city (probably Edessa) and, top left, the *profectio*, the departure of the army. On the side of the arch facing the Capitol, the relief shows (bottom left) the siege of a city by a river, probably

Seleucia,[54] and the surrender of the city (Fig. 46). The fourth panel (below) is the siege of Ctesiphon on the Tigris, and (above) another *adlocutio* (Fig. 47). Among the total of 484 figures in the campaign scenes, the emperor appears eight times. While the figures are usually presented in dense groups, the occurrence of the emperor is significant: he is always shown from the front, placed in front of the crowded group of companions, and is the one person shown with no overlap. Similar observations can be made on the Marcus Column, where the importance of the emperor is consistently emphasized in the same manner.

The representations are partly stereotypical, for instance the *adlocutio* scenes, so that they can be read not only as an event in the course of the campaign, but also as a general expression of the *fides militum erga imperatorem*. Like the reliefs on Trajan's Column, the scenes include landscape elements and thereby appear scenic. According to Herodian (III.9.12), Severus had paintings erected in public in Rome with the struggles and victories of his Parthian War. The reliefs of the arch could hark back to these historical paintings. However, the similarity with the representations on the columns and especially with the Column of Marcus Aurelius is striking, manifested in the use of the same types of scenes (*e.g.* the *adlocutio* scenes), the division into registers, and the progression of the story from the bottom up. The relief areas of the arch look like cut-out and framed parts of the column reliefs.

Figure 45

Figure 46

Figure 47

Figures 45–47 *Rome, Roman Forum. Arch of Septimius Severus*

They were obviously inspired by the detail- and figure-rich representation on the columns. However, the Arch of Severus fixes the viewpoint and selects the images, while with the columns, the viewer makes that selection.

The reliefs described, which should reflect key events of a historical campaign, are integrated into the overall programme of the sculptural decoration of the arch. Immediately above the side passages, and therefore below the great campaign reliefs, a booty frieze is shown repeated four times (Fig. 46): Roman soldiers lead a train of wagons laden with booty, also carrying captive Easterners. In the middle of the display sits a grieving woman with an oriental cap personifying the conquered Eastern territories (Parthia). This train leads to the city goddess Roma, enthroned upon arms; before her, Easterners drop to their knees. Earlier monumental arches (the Arch of Titus in Rome, the Arch of Trajan in Beneventum) have small friezes with detailed representations of a triumphal procession. Although the frieze on the Arch of Severus contains triumphal elements, it does not represent the triumph itself. In particular, it lacks the victor as the main character of the procession. The reason for this choice of representation is that Septimius Severus had rejected a triumph (*Historia Augusta*, *Severus* 16.6). The small frieze mixed two different areas: the booty train can be understood as a depiction of actual operations, but is combined with two personifications, the grieving Parthia and the victorious Roma. The fourfold repetition shows that it is not a one-off event; rather, imperial victory also repeatedly produces material gains. The reliefs of the column base tackle the military issue by presenting captive Parthians and Roman soldiers. The victories above the main passage carry *trophaia* from the Parthian campaign.

The large relief panels depict the foreign policy successes of Severus in great detail and as a continuous narrative. At the same time they ignore the struggles of the civil wars, alluded to in the inscription. The issue of military successes is taken up again in other forms in other areas: in the small frieze with its emphasis on booty given to Roma; in the reliefs of the column base with their depictions of defeated Easterners and victorious Romans; and in the attic reliefs over the main passage with their depictions of the goddess of victory.

5 Representations from the Tetrarchic period

The Arch of Galerius in Thessaloniki

Of the tetrapylon, which was built around AD 300 in Thessaloniki, then the residence of Emperor Galerius, two of the four pylons (with a total of 28 reliefs) remain.[55] The

Figure 48

Figure 50

Figure 49

Figure 51

Figures 48–51 *Thessaloniki, Arch of Galerius*

subject of the reliefs is Gallienus' war against the Sassanids in AD 297/8. The war concluded in 298 with a peace treaty, which ceded northern Mesopotamia and the five provinces beyond the Tigris to the Romans.

Most images promote Galerius as a successful commander. Some of the subjects are quite conventional: travel (Fig. 48), speeches (Fig. 49), battles (Fig. 50), prisoners, and the allegorical exaltation of the emperor. The images presented could also have been used for any previous emperor: Trajan and Septimius Severus had themselves depicted in Parthian campaigns in almost the same scenes. By contrast, some representations are located by inscriptions and thus identified as certain events in the campaign. Thus, the river god adjacent to a fight scene is labelled Tigris (AI Scene 3; similar to A II 5). Others show spectacular successes of the campaign of 297/8, for example the capture of the royal

harem (AI 2). One of the battle scenes (B II 20) illustrates the courage and vigour of the emperor, which decide the fight (Fig. 50). The emperor appears on horseback in the centre of the depiction; he is striking down both an enemy horseman and an infantryman, regardless of personal risk. The eagle of Jupiter holds a wreath over Galerius' head and marks him as victor. Three colossal Roman soldiers represent the power of the Roman army, contrasting conspicuously with the small Persians. A similarly drastically unequal distribution of power is demonstrated in the subjugation scene (A III 9) and in the envoy scene (BI 16) (Fig. 51).

The Arch of Galerius differs from earlier representations of war in the scenes relating to the Tetrarchy, the form of government then newly created by Diocletian. This includes the victory sacrifice, which is offered jointly by Diocletian and Galerius (BI 17; Fig. 51 below). The historic campaign of Galerius, which most reliefs on the arch strive to depict accurately, is integrated into the 'success story' of the Tetrarchy in a further relief (II 19 B), but in a stylized manner. In the centre of this relief, the two Augusti, Diocletian and Maximianus Herculius, sit on a globe, both being crowned by Victoria. Next to them are the Caesars, Galerius and Constantius Chlorus, both of whom raise up a kneeling province. The duplication of events is noteworthy: it occurs simultaneously and in the same manner to the left and right of the enthroned Augusti; Mesopotamia is shown in the east of the empire and Britannia in the west. The Augusti themselves do not need to intervene here, as their watchful presence is enough to guarantee Roman success. The imperial group is flanked by gods and personifications.

The series of reliefs on the arch in Thessaloniki is intended to convey to the viewer that they live in an ideal world: with the help of the gods, the tetrarchy brings stability and victories, which in turn delivers material well-being. This happy state of affairs will last forever, because the system of the Tetrarchy will renew itself periodically. The realism of the depictions is validated by specific references – the labels locating the battle sites and the representation of unique events, such as the capture of the Sassanid harem. Because these events are verifiable and authenticated by the details pictured, this suggests to the viewer that, if the representation is exact in these details, it must also be correct elsewhere.

6   Representations from Late Antiquity

The Arch of Constantine

In the struggle against his rival Maxentius in AD 312, Constantine, son of the Tetrarchic Emperor Constantius Chlorus, had brought cities in Gaul and northern Italy over to his side, partly by conquest, partly won peacefully. After advancing on Rome, the decisive battle, in which Maxentius was killed, took place at the Milvian Bridge on 28 October 312. The very next day, Rome was taken by Constantine. These events were commemorated in the reliefs and the inscription on the arch, which the Senate had erected for Constantine next to the Colosseum.[56] This also used older reliefs as spolia, including parts of the battle from the Great Trajanic Frieze and reliefs from an arch of Marcus Aurelius.

The small frieze attached to the front, above the side passages and (at the same height) on the shorter sides of the arch is of Constantinian date and relates events of the campaign against Maxentius. The illustrations are arranged chronologically, beginning on the smaller western side. First, the *profectio* is shown, the departure of the army from Milan (Fig. 52). The *cornicines* (horn players) and standard bearers lead the way. Some of the following soldiers are shown as *cornuti* with horned helmets, members of an elite Gallic force. Behind the combat troops follows the train with a camel and a horse; at the rear is a cart with two officers. The relief shows a well-ordered, disciplined army, equipped with all the necessities and arrayed in marching order. On the south side of the arch, facing away from the town, the conquest of Verona (Fig. 53) is presented. In the right part, the city with its towers is shown, one of the defenders collapsing, mortally wounded, from the wall. The troops of Constantine are placed to the left of this scene. Behind them stands Constantine, emphasized by his size, in muscle cuirass and wearing a cloak. Following him are the *protectores* (bodyguard) and, on the extreme left, his caparisoned horse. Victoria flies in to crown Constantine.

The right-hand relief on the south side shows the Battle of the Milvian Bridge (Fig. 54). In the centre, the dramatic and decisive moments of the conflict can be seen: the Praetorians of Maxentius sink into the water and are fought from the shore by the troops of Constantine. To the right are a *cornicen* and a trumpeter; to the left, on the approach of the bridge destroyed by Maxentius, Constantine is shown, accompanied by Victoria and Virtus. The two reliefs show the army in action; fighting under the guidance of the emperor himself, his soldiers are orderly, disciplined, and effective.

On the eastern, narrow side, the entry into Rome follows, which took place on 29 October 312 (Fig. 55). The victorious emperor's team of four is driven by Victoria. First are the infantry, followed by cavalrymen with *draco* standards, then more foot soldiers. The entire army is again well equipped and disciplined. The front and back of the column are marked by an arch, so the army is already marching within the city.

On the north side, facing the city, the reliefs show the appearance of Constantine in Rome. The first depicts the *oratio*, his address to the people of Rome. Events are accurately located by the buildings in the background: we can still identify the exact spot where Constantine was standing. The emperor is meeting with the senators in the Roman Forum, in the old traditional capital in the heart of the empire, and he speaks to the people of Rome. This relief shows their close ties with Constantine. This appears as a contrast to the tyrant Maxentius, who allegedly murdered senators and massacred the people. The topographic accuracy guarantees the exact reproduction of the activities and confirms the entire process. The last relief in this cycle shows the distribution of gifts of money and records the *largitas Augusti*, the liberality of the emperor. Again, the emperor is seated in the centre, flanked by two

Figure 52

Figure 53

Figure 54

Figure 55

Figures 52–55 Rome, Arch of Constantine

strictly symmetrically arranged groups. These illustrate the distribution of money in four accounting offices. It takes place in an organized, controlled way: two senators each keep the books and vouch for the orderly course of events.

The six reliefs described form a coherent, self-contained story: the army departs from Milan; it besieges Verona under the guidance of its victorious Emperor Constantine; it defeats the troops of the tyrant on the Tiber with his guidance and moves into Rome; Constantine speaks to the Roman Senate and people of Rome in the Forum; and he enters the consulship in Rome, distributing generous donations on this occasion. The military successes of Constantine thus lead to a happy, harmonious agreement between the emperor, the Senate, and the people. The two military depictions can be found next to each other on the southern side, or in other words on the side facing away from the city centre. Both images show how the emperor

commands his soldiers and in both he is accompanied by Victoria. On the north side, facing the centre of the city and placed side by side, are the two reliefs showing the emperor in Rome itself. In those, the military is almost completely absent; they demonstrate the harmonious relationship between the emperor and the Senate.

The remaining reliefs of the arch, including the reused reliefs, confirm this statement. Within the main passage of the arch, two battle panels from the Great Trajanic Frieze decorate the western wall on the left; they are related by their inscription '*Liberatori urbis*' to the victory over Maxentius (Fig. 36). The head of the main figure was reworked into a portrait of Constantine. The observer sees Constantine, who single-handedly rides down barbaric foes, while the context of the inscription makes it clear that these must be the soldiers of Maxentius. The relief does not show Praetorians and Romans as the opponents, but barbarians: the liberation of the city from Maxentius does not appear as a success in the civil war, but as a victory over external enemies. Two more panels from the Great Trajanic Frieze are mounted on the eastern wall and provided with the explanatory inscription 'Fundatori Quietis' (Fig. 37). The observer sees two scenes: to the left, the emperor, who is led by soldiers, but also by Virtus and Honos, to a gate and simultaneously crowned by Victoria; and to the right a combat scene is again included. The reliefs originally celebrated the victory of Trajan over the Dacians; after the replacement of the head of the emperor, they became depictions of the victories of Constantine. The front sides of the arch's attic are decorated with reliefs, which were also re-used and taken from an arch of Marcus Aurelius.

In addition to the reliefs showing the emperor himself, the arch also has decorative imagery that is more generic. The reliefs of the column bases, for example, mix four themes: victories, soldiers with standards, prisoners next to a *trophaion*, and captive barbarians, who are being led away by Roman soldiers. These themes are not new, nor is their representations on the column bases: they are already found, for example, on the Arch of Severus. What is surprising about the representations is seeing them in context with the inscription, because it does not mention victories over barbarous peoples. So these are generic images that do not refer to a single specific campaign, but celebrate the universal victory of the Roman army, as do the reliefs with victories above the main passage. Looking at the Arch of Constantine as a whole, the large-scale reliefs are dominated by representations of the emperor. Again and again, the emperor appears in a beneficial capacity, which is in part military, and in part civil. On the Arch of Constantine, these depictions are not meant to represent one-off events; rather, they illustrate the virtues of the emperor in typical situations. They are supplemented by more general scenes on the base and spandrel reliefs. Representations of the emperor are missing here, but the depictions point to his universal and permanent victory. The attentive Roman observer knew these symbolic depictions from older monuments and understood that the emperor here asserted virtues that had already been claimed by previous emperors such as Trajan and Severus. That these were not empty promises or even pretence, was vouched for by the series of historical reliefs: they show the efficient and disciplined army of Constantine, his work as a successful general, and his close and trusting relationship with the old capital, Rome. As with the Arch of Galerius, the promise of universal happiness in the relief decoration is validated by referring to concrete actions and successes.

The small historical friezes show the emperor as one figure among many, albeit emphasized by size and composition. However, the reused attic reliefs focus more on the figure of the emperor and his immediate companions. The same theme appears several times in different parts of the decorative reliefs. The military activities of the emperor are shown in the context of historical events, as head of his army, but then as a courageous fighter against the enemies of Rome in the recycled Trajanic reliefs in the passage, with the explanation *Liberatori Urbis*. The emperor appears repeatedly in the company of Victoria and Virtus; bravery and victory are closely associated with him.

A second theme that is used in various forms in the relief decoration of the Arch of Constantine is the close relation of the emperor with Rome. It is shown in three series of reliefs, and, like the emperor's victory, in several different manners. The small friezes clearly show events in Rome, and the appearances of Constantine in Rome are also located precisely in the attic reliefs and in the passage reliefs. But there he is not shown in front of the citizens and senators of Rome, but in the company of gods and personifications. Particularly important is the arrival of the emperor (*adventus*) in Rome, which is shown three times. The distribution of money to the Roman city population is illustrated twice, namely in the Attic reliefs and as a conclusion to the small historical friezes.

This idealized emperor is to be seen against the background of the defeated predecessor, whom the sources paint in the darkest colours. Constantine appears in all respects as the exact opposite of the tyrant: he is brave and victorious, generous, and in harmony with the Senate and people. His dominion is fully legitimized by his virtues, as well as through his lineage and his visual referrals to the good emperors of the 2nd century AD. As with the Arch of Galerius, these depictions reflect an idealized image, a relationship that did not last, and a hope of the Senate, which was not realized. In January 313, Constantine left Rome and then only returned for anniversaries of his accession.

Notes to Part I

1. Cf. Bauchhenß 1978; Tufi 1988; Pflug 1989, 96f;. Boppert 1992; von Moock 1998, 59f.
2. Homolle 1897, 620ff.; 1903, 297–302.
3. Cf. Jacquemin 1999, No. 424; Kotsidu 2000, 443 ff. Cat. No. *318; Boschung 2001, 59–72; E. Schraudolph in Bol 2007, 231–4. 401 Abb. 194a–h.
4. Plutarch, *Aemilius Paullus* 28.2; Kotsidou 2000, 445.
5. Hammond 1984, 31–47.
6. Homolle 1897, 621; Kähler 1965, 12f.; von Vacano 1988, 375.
7. Boschung 2001, 65.
8. von Vacano 1988, 375; Kähler 1965, 13.
9. Boschung 2001, 67.
10. Ibid.
11. Vierneisel-Schlörb 1979, 472ff. No. 43; Geominy 1982, esp. 147ff.
12. Eichberg 1987, 157ff.
13. Ibid., 188f., 284f. Nos 238–42.
14. Hammond 1984, 46.

15. Ibid., 44.
16. On the arrangement, cf. Jacquemin-Laroche 1982, 212.
17. Kähler 1966; Hölscher 1979, 337ff.; Torelli 1982, 5ff. Taf. I,1–4.; Hölscher 1984a, 16ff.; Zanker 1987, 22ff.; Meyer 1993, 45ff.; Fless 1995, 31ff. 103 Cat. No. 2; Lohmann 2009.
18. Wünsche 2005, 120f.; M. Flashar, in Bol 2007, 371f., 420 Abb. 370a–f.
19. Hölscher 1980b, 351ff., 1984a, 17ff., 1988, 384ff. No. 214; Schäfer 1979, 243ff., 1989, 74ff.; Meyer 1991/92, 17ff.; Reusser 1993, 121ff.
20. Polito 1998, 91–95.
21. Miller 1993, 48–59 Taf. 2–3; Polito 1998, esp. 74ff. with further examples.
22. Hölscher 1980b; 1988, 384ff.
23. Reusser 1993, 135ff.
24. Hölscher 1984b, 204ff.; Leoncini 1987, 13ff., 58ff.; Zanker 1987, 130ff.; Hölscher 1988, 364ff. No. 200; Boschung 1999, 202f. Abb. 1.
25. Siebert 1999, 161–289 F1.
26. Zanker 1987, 130f.
27. Hölscher 1980a, 281ff.; Baratte 1986; Kuttner 1995; Boschung 1999, 203f. Abb. 2–5; Alföldi 2001; de Caprariis 2002.
28. Cf. Orlin 2002, 38–45.
29. In my opinion incorrectly disputed by de Caprariis 2002.
30. Kähler 1968; Megow 1987, 155f. A 10 Taf. 3–6; Prückner 1997, 119ff.; Zwierlein-Diehl 2008, 98ff. Nr. 6.
31. Künzl 1988, 558f. No. 383; Zanker 1987, 234f. Abb. 183.
32. Megow 1987, 202 A 85; Boschung 1989, 64f.; Vollenweider-Avisseau 2003, 219ff. No. 275 Taf. 27–31; Giulani 2010.
33. Kent-Overbeck-Stylow 1973, 99 Taf. 46. 47 No. 172. 176; von Kaenel 1986, 7. 10ff. 46ff. 67ff. 162f. Taf. 1. 6ff. Nos 2–44, 430–46, 458–531, 577–90; Boschung 1987, 224.
34. Stäcker 2003, 169ff.
35. Frieze A: Magi 1945; Bergmann 1981, 19ff.; Simon 1985, 543ff.; Hölscher 1992; Meyer 2000, 124–139; Hölscher 2009, 54–8.
36. Boschung 2004, 103f.
37. Eibl 1994, 273–97.
38. Cichorius 1896–1900; Lehmann-Hartleben 1926; Zanker 1970, 529ff.; Gauer 1977; Hölscher 1980a, 290ff.; Settis et al. 1988; Baumer-Hölscher-Winkler, 1991, 261ff.; Krierer 1995, 123ff.; Galinier 2007.
39. Krierer 1995, 128.
40. Galinier 2007, 158–61.
41. Ibid., 59 Abb. 15, 63ff.
42. Fittschen 1972, 742ff.; Simon 1981, 3ff.
43. Zanker 1970, 727.
44. Leander Touati 1987; Galinier 2007, 185ff.
45. Leander Touati 1987, 98ff., esp. 103.
46. Hölscher 2000, 89.
47. Coarelli 2008, 32–7; Löhr 2009.
48. Petersen et al. 1896 Taf. 9–11; Coarelli 2008, 114–18.
49. Petersen et al. 1896 Taf. 63; Coarelli 2008, 222ff.
50. Pirson 1996, bes. 168–71.
51. Ibid., 139–79.
52. Ryberg 1967; Koeppel 1986; Angelicoussis 1984; De Maria 1988, 303ff.; Torelli 1993, 98f.
53. Koeppel 1990, 1ff. 9ff.; Brilliant 1967; De Maria 1988, 305ff.; Krierer 1995, 165f., 218.
54. Brilliant 1967, 195ff.
55. Laubscher 1975; Kolb 2001, 158–62; Mayer 2002, 47–65; Boschung 2006, 360–7.
56. L'Orange-Gerkan 1955; De Maria 1988, 316–19; Pensabene-Panella 1999; Mayer 2002, 185ff.

II

GENERAL REMARKS ON THE ROMAN ARMY

1. Introduction

Within provincial Roman archaeology, research into the armament and equipment of the Roman military has been steadily increasing in recent years – to the point where it is difficult to keep track of the mass of studies on find sites and types of finds published. Our knowledge of the subject has profited in particular from the publication of studies on finds from camps, forts, hoards, and underwater discoveries. These finds mainly consist of the metal components of weapons and equipment, or in other words iron and various non-ferrous metal alloys (bronze and brass). Silver or even gold occur less often and mostly as decoration. In addition, there are slingshot made of lead and sword hilts, bow stiffeners, or other militaria of bone or ivory. Organic material, such as wood, textiles, and leather, only survives in the ground very rarely and, if so, then it is under special conditions of preservation (anaerobic wet conditions, bog finds, and items from extremely dry regions). There are a lot of recent publications covering particular aspects of Roman military archaeology,[1] but synthetic works that cover all aspects are still lacking.

One recent development arouses quite mixed feelings: for some time now, a large amount of Roman weaponry has been circulating in the art market and in private collections in addition to other antiquities that have been traded and collected traditionally. One of the reasons for this is the political upheaval in those countries of the middle and lower Danube regions that once belonged to Yugoslavia, or were behind the Iron Curtain. This has often led to a temporary ineffectiveness in the state protection of monuments, so that large-scale archaeological sites have been looted and destroyed. The finds – unprovenanced, of course – then circulated in the international art trade right down to flea markets (Peterson 1990). However, it would appear that this development has by now ceased, or is at least diminished. Similar cases, albeit on a smaller scale, are known with regard to finds from Britain, Germany, and other European countries, a particularly spectacular example being the 'Crosby Garrett Helmet' (Breeze and Bishop 2013; Figs 334–5). While private collections of Roman militaria are not a new phenomenon – one need only recall the Lipperheide and Guttmann collections and their very different fates.[2] The former was acquired by the Staatliche Antikensammlungen in Berlin and thus remained accessible to the public and the research community. The latter has unfortunately been dispersed throughout the art market by the unexpected death of the collector and consequently is now more or less inaccessible for research. I seriously doubt whether the relevant state institutions, in a rather short-sighted spirit of fundamentalism and political correctness, really acted in the best interests of research here by passing up the chance to transfer this important collection into public ownership.

Among these finds in private ownership are extraordinarily well-preserved pieces and even representatives of previously unknown types, which cannot be ignored by responsible researchers. Technical innovations such as digital photography and the Internet mean that this material has become known to a much greater extent than in previous years. In selecting the pictures for this book, these finds from collections have therefore been preferred to published material wherever possible. In this manner, these unprovenanced and 'homeless' finds can at least be made accessible to international research and given their due importance.

Selection of the material dealt with here

The following chapter 'Arms and military equipment' deals with classes of objects used by or specifically produced for the Roman army.[3] That among these objects there is an overlap with the civil sector, and that researchers do not agree in all individual cases on the military use of these objects, is inevitable. This can be illustrated with a couple of examples: knives, which Roman soldiers carried with them as general purposes tools (kitchen knives/cutlery), will not be considered in this book, although they certainly could constitute effective weapons in the case of an emergency. However, they have been never used purely as regular weapons.

The bronze vessels, which the soldier took with him into the field, will likewise not be considered in all typological and other details, since they are basically no different from pieces found in civilian contexts. This is also the case with vessels made of glass and ceramics used in military bases, although the composition and selection of types and shapes may well differ from those in civilian contexts here. Likewise, in many areas there is no difference between the military and the civilian sectors in the tools and implements of craftsmen in wood, leather- and metalworking, or construction. Although tools and implements are sometimes found in considerable quantities in camps and forts, they are largely ignored in this book. This also applies to medical instruments used by both Roman military and civilian doctors (Krause 2009).

However, there are a number of pioneer tools that have been used primarily by the military and were even used when needed in combat as weapons. There is a passage in Tacitus (*Ann* III, 43; 44–6) where, forced to a standstill by heavily armoured 'iron men' of the Aedui, Roman legionaries, whose *pila* and *gladii* were ineffective, without further ado waded in and hacked at them with hatchets (*secures*) and pioneer axes (*dolabrae*). Turf cutters, entrenching tools, and pruning hooks may be considered military pioneer equipment. Attention will also be given to palisade stakes, leather tents, musical instruments and standards, as well as military decorations.

Single- and twin-axled carts, which in some finds – and also in representations, such as Trajan's and Marcus' Columns – were used as military vehicles, are not dealt with in detail in this book, as they do not differ from civilian vehicles in any detail recognizable to us today.

2.   A history of research

From the Middle Ages to the beginning of critical historical research

During the Middle Ages, the material remains of antiquity were only used as evidence for the past in a very limited manner. They were not used as sources for the history of antiquity in any systematic research. At best, ancient objects were appreciated as giving evidence of the martyrdom of pious Christians. In addition, they often played a role in propping up the prestige of a city, confirming its greater age in comparison to its rivals.[4] At the time, there was no interest in the Roman army as such and even less for its pictorial representations or material remains.

The first piece of genuine weaponry taken for a Roman original find and gaining great public attention in post-antique times is an iron spearhead. However, during the medieval period, this object was not the subject of scholarly reflections on Roman armament, but rather a highly symbolic relic revered by devout believers: the so-called 'Holy Lance' (Fig. 56), counted among the crown jewels of the Holy Roman Empire of the German nation. Preserved for a long time in the Kaiserburg in Nuremberg, it is now part of the collections of the Kunsthistorisches Museum in

Figure 56 *Vienna, Kunsthistorisches Museum. So-called Holy Lance; iron with gold*

Vienna.[5] It was believed to be the tip of the weapon with which a Roman soldier pierced Jesus' side on the cross in order to determine whether he was dead (John 19, 34).

In recent times, serious scholarship could demystify this ancient piece and expose it as a work of post-Roman blacksmithing. Thus the 'Holy Lance' is not an ancient Roman weapon, but rather – as many parallel finds with the very characteristic wings on the socket show – the tip of a winged lance of the 8th to 10th century AD (Paulsen 1967).

Initial approaches to the rediscovery of ancient armour came with the rediscovery of antiquity in the Renaissance. Now art found a new field of activity in illustrating historical events that were not taken from the biblical narrative. In Italy, illustrations from Roman history meant as allegorical representations were now produced for the first time. Historical figures now appeared in Roman-style armament, although at first this was dominated by contemporary weaponry rather than the 'correct' ancient weaponry. That changed, however, as contemporary scholars started to look closely at the ancient world in all its detail.

The rediscovery of ancient weaponry during the Renaissance has not been fully addressed by research yet, but there is an exemplary study on Florentine art in the early Renaissance by M. Pfaffenbichler (1996). He could show that the muscle cuirass (after the Greek *linothorax*) was used in art to identify ancient, biblical, or mythical heroes. It was also used for contemporary ruling figures, when it was wanted to portray them as embodying the time-honoured virtues of antiquity. Pfaffenbichler noted that, in addition to ancient cuirassed statues, Byzantine representations mainly served as inspiration. Sometimes, a detail occurs that originated in a completely different culture, but was then mixed with the ancient muscle cuirass by artists: pauldrons in the form of lion heads. M. Pfaffenbichler stated that this form had crept in during the 14th century from Chinese art in representations of 'antique-ish' armour.

Of course, the artists of this time did not take care to produce accurate representations of Roman armour. As Pfaffenbichler explains in his description of an archaized cuirass of Joshua on the eastern bronze door of the Baptistery of Florence by Lorenzo Ghiberti (1403–1424):

> The head is protected by a hemispherical helmet, which is given a fantastic appearance through its ornamentation, not based on any ancient model. This is the beginning of a development which intensified during the 15th century, and reached its pinnacle in the Alexander Relief of Verocchio, where Alexander's *all'antica* harness is used only as an excuse for a largely anachronistic, but fantastic and decorative form of weaponry.[6]

However, ancient-style armour was not only used for pictures in the visual arts in the Renaissance period. Roman-looking elements were also worked into ceremonial and tournament armour. In its body armour gallery, the Kunsthistorisches Museum in Vienna keeps a half-harness

Figure 57 *Vienna, Kunsthistorisches Museum. Ceremonial armour of the Duke of Urbino, Francesco Maria della Rovere, 1490–1538 with archaising helmet (after Gamber and Beaufort 1990)*

(inv. No. A 498) which was once made for the Duke of Urbino, Francesco Maria della Rovere (1490–1538), by the Milanese armourer Filippo Negroli (Fig. 57). Its helmet deserves special attention, as it is completely different in comparison to contemporary as well as medieval models. With tight curls on the bowl and side panels that integrate cheek pieces together with embossed representations of the ear, this helmet shares amazingly naturalistic similarities with Roman sports helmets (tight curls!) and with early imperial cavalry helmets of the Weyler/Koblenz-Bubenheim type (cheek pieces with naturalistic representation of the ear). Only the forehead diadem is replaced by a loosely arranged band with no ancient prototype, which represents a twisted cloth.[7]

Since such mask helmets and cavalry helmets were not used on the ancient sculpture and reliefs known at the time, one must conclude that they must have derived from original finds serving as templates for this helmet. This only leaves the conclusion that there must have been a collection of antiquities in northern Italy containing original finds of such mask and cavalry helmets, which had been properly classified as Roman. These were then used as a template for the duke's helmet. These pieces have now been lost and can only be attested from the replica.

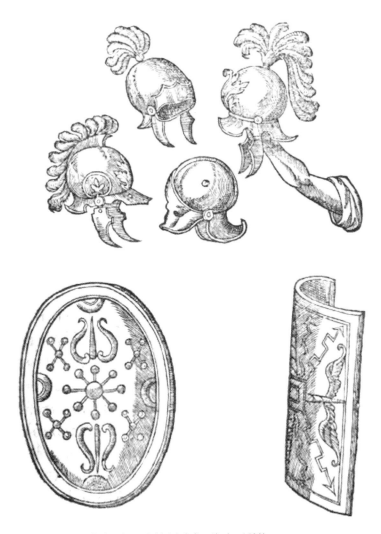

Figure 58 *Roman helmets and shields (after Lipsius 1598)*

Figure 59 *The statue of St George from 1723 by Cosmas Damian Asam (Klosterkirche Rohr/Lower Bavaria). Photo: T. Fischer*

In the 16th and 17th centuries, archaeology began to intensify significantly. Numerous researchers wrote a remarkable wealth of treatises of all kinds. As a consequence, they soon tried to create review papers on the state of archaeology in the form of so-called thesauruses. The researchers who then dealt with the ancient world were not yet known as archaeologists, but were called antiquarians.[8] These antiquarians soon began to deal with Roman warfare and weaponry, although not on the basis of archaeological finds, but only on the basis of ancient textual and representational sources. Trajan's Column was a particular focus for their interest. The first work of synthesis that dealt with Roman warfare and with armament was that of Justus Lipsius, entitled the *De militia Romana Libri Quinque. Commentarius Ad Polybium* (Antwerp 1598) (Fig. 58).

Since the Baroque period, the visual arts in Italy and elsewhere produced an abundance of representations of the 'Roman' warrior. The churches were full of pictures and statues representing archangels and saints in 'ancient'

armour. Clad in ancient-style muscle cuirasses, greaves, and fantastically caparisoned helmets, they interpreted quite freely what had been learned about ancient Roman armament from ancient reliefs and cuirassed statues.

An example of this is a statue of St George from the period around 1723, created for a side altar of the monastery church in Rohr, in the district of Kelheim/Lower Bavaria (Germany) by Cosmas Damian Asam. St George wears a coat of mail in the basic shape of a muscled cuirass and a fantastically caparisoned Attic helmet (Fig. 59). The Stations of the Cross paintings (around 1755) of the Straubing artist Matthias Obermayer, in the monastery church of St Mary in Windberg (district Straubing-Bogen/Lower Bavaria, Germany), provide another example: the soldiers wear an idiosyncratic mix of muscled and segmental cuirasses and a type of pseudo-Attic helmet that could have been borrowed from Trajan's Column (Fig. 60). Numerous allegorical pictures of secular rulers of the Baroque period are shown with this 'antique-ish'

Figure 60 *Roman soldiers. Paintings around 1755 by Matthias Obermayer on a station of the cross in the cloister church of Windberg/Lower Bavaria. Photo: T. Fischer*

armour, surrounded by looted weapons, *tropaia*, and other references to the Roman military then known. These interactions between contemporary art and Roman finds have not yet been the subject of synthetic research by art historians.

All these representations of ancient weaponry were drawn from representational sources alone, mainly from the columns of Trajan and Marcus. The excavations of the cities around Vesuvius were the start of a new era of research into the Roman military: for the first time, scholars were now confronted with original finds of Roman weapons. Thus, during excavations of the 18th century in Stabiae (I), Roman arms (a *gladius* and a dagger) were discovered. None other than J. J. Winckelmann reported on these finds in 1763 and the question of whether they belonged to gladiatorial equipment or military weaponry was subsequently discussed.[9] Nearly identical copies of ancient *gladii* were in daily military use even before it was possible to research Roman arms and especially swords based on original archaeological finds on a larger scale from the mid-19th century onwards: during the early 19th century, in the context of the general enthusiasm for Roman antiquity during the *Empire*, the French army

Figure 61 *French fascine knife (first third of the 19th century) and Roman Pompeii-type gladius blade (privately owned). Photo: A. Pangerl*

under Napoleon and later carried fascine knives in the form of Roman *gladii* (Fig. 61). Their curved blades and solid brass handles in the antique style had visibly been inspired by pictorial representations from the Roman period. These weapons were later adopted by other armies. The American army took them up, but via the Napoleonic

Figure 62 *Ludwig Lindenschmit the Elder (1809–93). Self-portrait of 1879 (detail; from Frey 2009)*

time, from which provincial Roman archaeology emerged in the early 20th century.[11]

However, at first it was mainly representatives of the nascent prehistoric archaeology who also turned to the study of Roman weaponry. The novel aspect was that in addition to ancient representational sources, comparable original finds were also taken into consideration. The latter were brought to light everywhere in the burgeoning excavation activities of enthusiasts for the ancient world. Now an entirely new factor also provided well-preserved Roman weapons: the continuing industrialization of the 19th century saw the importance of major rivers as waterways increasing, while steam power supplied the technical capability to dredge rivers to previously unknown degrees, to straighten them, and also to control the constant risk of flooding. This dredging brought a large number of prehistoric and early historical finds to light. This also happened during the construction of harbours, locks, and hydropower plants. Among these finds, a large number of Roman weapons were found, mainly from the Rhine near Mainz, especially helmets and swords in an unprecedented, excellent state of preservation.[12] Similar concentrations of archaeological water finds were made in other European rivers, like the Danube, Rhône, or Thames.[13]

Using such water discoveries, among other things, Ludwig Lindenschmit the Elder (1809–1893) had an extremely prominent role in the study of Roman weaponry and military equipment in Mainz (Frey 2009). An artist and art teacher by training, he was a co-founder and first director of the Roman-Germanic Central Museum (Römisch-Germanisches Zentralmuseum or RGZM). Lindenschmit (Fig. 62) is now considered one of the principal founders of serious prehistoric and early historic archaeology in the German-speaking world. He was the first to systematically deal with the presentation and classification of original finds of Roman armament and equipment (Figs 63 and 64), including the depictions, such as the soldiers' tombstones from the Rhineland. His little book from 1882 is the first modern summary treatment on the subject of Roman weapons and military equipment. In his series of books *The Antiquities of our Pagan Past* (*die Alterthümer unserer heidnischen Vorzeit*), he presented other important material.[14] Lindenschmit conducted a Europe-wide correspondence about his work with the most important researchers of his time. However, he did not just spread his ideas about Roman military equipment in academic journals. Through his numerous illustrations and museum replicas, in addition to accurate reconstructions of weapons and figures of soldiers from painted plaster, which were made to his specifications and sold at the RGZM (Fig. 65), he shaped the picture of the Roman soldier for the general public, even today.[15]

campaigns they also appeared in large numbers in Russia, where they continued to be carried by military units as a sidearm.

Through the capriciousness of fate, many of these lookalike 'Roman' swords later came to Germany or Austria – for instance as 'souvenirs' during the First and Second World Wars – and were subsequently buried by accident or on purpose, for example at the end of the war in 1945. They then became rusty and patinated, as happens with ancient items if buried for a long period, and are therefore now identified by some collectors and professionals as real Roman swords.[10]

From the 19th century to the First World War

The 19th century saw critical research methodologies introduced permanently into the study of the past which are still applied to historical and archaeological subjects today. The modern research disciplines of ancient history, classical archaeology, and prehistory also developed at that

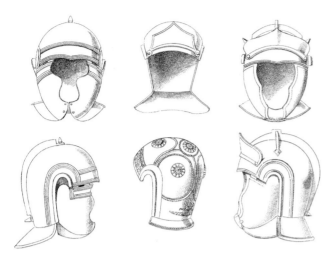

Figure 63 *Roman infantry helmets of the Niederbieber type (after Lindenschmit the Elder, 1882)*

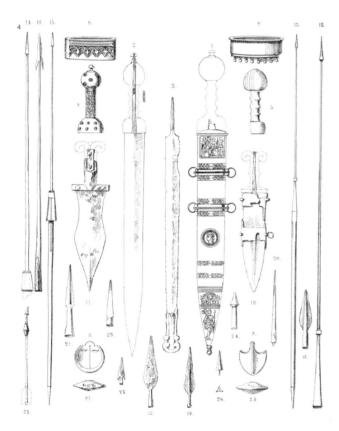

Figure 64 *Roman weapons (after Lindenschmit the Elder, 1882)*

Figure 65 *Figurine of a Roman legionary in RGZM (after Lindenschmit the Elder). Photo: RGZM*

The excavator of the fort of Saalburg in the Taunus (Germany), Louis Jacobi, who had worked there since 1871, continuing the excavations of his predecessors, published numerous Roman weapons and pieces of equipment and also depicted reconstructed Roman soldiers, strongly influenced by Lindenschmit (Fig. 66).[16]

The excavations and publications of the Imperial Frontier Commission (Reichslimeskommission, see ORL;

Brown 1992), founded in 1892, meant a big boom for archaeology in Germany. During the excavation of forts on the Upper German and Raetian Limes, numerous Roman weapons and pieces of equipment came to light, especially in the burning and destruction layers of the 3rd century AD and often in a very good condition. Example are the forts of Niederbieber, Zugmantel, Saalburg, Osterburken, Weißenburg, Pfünz (Fig. 502), and Eining.

Following the example of the German Reichslimeskommission, a Limeskommission was constituted in Austria in 1897 at the then Imperial Academy of Sciences. The practical work was mainly directed by the Imperial and Royal Colonel Maximilian Groller von Mildensee (1838–1920), who was responsible for the large-scale excavations in Lauriacum and Carnuntum. Von Groller published the finds, including many Roman weapons and pieces of equipment, in his own drawings in the 1900 series *The Roman Limes in Austria* (*Der römische Limes in Österreich*). The internationally recognized expert, von Groller also excavated and published features and finds for the

Figure 66 *Roman legionary. Reconstruction (after Lindenschmit the Elder) after finds from the Saalburg (Jacobi 1897)*

publication of the ancient historian Emil Ritterling (1861–1923) at the early imperial fort of Hofheim im Taunus (Ritterling 1912) also brought a major advance: for the first time, a closely dated early imperial auxiliary fort was completely excavated and published. The finds, including Roman weapons and pieces of equipment, were particularly abundant because the camp had been violently destroyed and burned down in the turmoil after Nero's death in AD 68.

The rapid growth of knowledge and material which archaeology achieved in the study of Roman weapons and equipment soon led to the introduction of experimental archaeology. No lesser person was involved in its inception than the French emperor Napoleon III (1808–1873), who worked intensively on the Roman army and initiated the first large-scale excavation in Alesia (Büchsenschütz 2008). He conducted an intensive learned correspondence, for example on the *pilum*, with L. Lindenschmit and invited him to a scientific exchange in Paris (Schoenfelder 2009). In the years 1860/61, Napoleon had a Roman galley rebuilt, but it proved to be a faulty design (Morrisson and Coates 1990). Similarly, he had ancient artillery reconstructed, although it was not very authentic (Junkelmann 2002, 75).

The German artillery officer Major General Erwin Schramm (1856–1935) was both extremely painstaking and successful in this field. After careful study of the literary, pictorial, and archaeological sources, translated for him by renowned classical scholars of his time, he reconstructed numerous functional ancient artillery pieces between 1903 and 1920. He successfully tested these – some in the presence of Kaiser Wilhelm II – in Metz and on the Saalburg (Schramm 1918). He founded modern research into Roman artillery, which was continued – often associated with experimentation – by, among others, E. W. Marsden, D. Baatz, and C. Miks.[17]

In Britain, the excavations conducted within the forts of Hadrian's Wall and the Antonine Wall since the mid-19th century had greatly promoted research into Roman armament and military equipment. In southern England, the excavations at Richborough and the Claudian fort of Hod Hill were of particular importance.[18] Especially important for the research into militaria was James Curle's (1862–1944) 1911 standard work on the Scottish fort of Newstead.

From the end of the First to the end of the Second World War

During the First World War, archaeological research of all kinds came to a virtual standstill. After the war, archaeological work on the Roman period in Germany and Austria lagged far behind the intensity of the pre-war period. During the period of Nazi rule in Germany and

German geographer and archaeologist Adolf Schulten (1870–1960) in Spain, for instance, at Numantia.

In 1901, the Viennese art historian Alois Riegl (1858–1905) published his important study on the 'late Roman art industry'. In it, he presented a whole series of military bronzes, but mainly verified the Roman character of crossbow brooches and Late Roman belt fittings, which he attributed to the Roman army. His work appeared in a second edition in 1923 and was reprinted in 1973 (Riegl 1923). Victor Hoffiller produced an important presentation of material, publishing the militaria from Croatia (Hoffiller 1910–11 and 1912).

The large excavations in the early Roman camps of Haltern, Oberaden, Xanten Vetera I, and Neuss increasingly trained researchers in the art of recognizing and adequately excavating and documenting timber features. In addition, they provided large amounts of mostly well-dated Roman weapons and pieces of equipment. The excavations and

Austria, Roman research and therefore research on the Roman military were further reduced due to ideological resistance. In other European countries and also in the United States, however, research continued unabated.

The Frenchman P. Couissin (1885–1932) undertook important basic research with his work *Les Armes Romaines* in 1926. He tried to summarize the development of Roman armament from the beginning of Rome to late antiquity. Based *inter alia* on Lindenschmit, he studied the archaeological material that was available to him at the time. His division of Roman helmets into the Montefortino, Hagenau, Weisenau, and Niederbieber types is still applicable today. But he was not very critical of the representational sources – whether they were realistic or archaizing – believing them all to provide a realistic impression of antiquity and accordingly including them all in his considerations. This is the reason why, today, Couissin's reconstruction drawings seem rather fanciful and have little to do with current thinking on the armament of Roman soldiers.

However, his ideas have had a lasting impact – right up to the relevant equipment of the classic 'sword and sandal' films from Hollywood or Cinecittà in Rome (see Junkelmann 2009). For a long time, there was no rival or successor to Couissin's work: the relevant chapter in the manual of Krohmayer and Veith that indeed claimed to cover the whole of ancient military history, was extremely modest in terms of weapons and military equipment.[19] The manual occasionally cites Couissin, but almost entirely ignores the demonstrably sound results in the field of weapons research which German-speaking archaeological research had gained. Accordingly, the leading archaeologists of the time were not consulted, only E. Schramm being asked to comment on his work on ancient artillery. There is also a similar lacuna on Roman arms and military equipment in the newer *Companion to the Roman Army* (Erdkamp 2007).

Until then, Roman Britain and the Roman territories on the Rhine and Danube had an almost complete monopoly on the archaeological exploration of Roman armament and equipment, but now the East also became the focus of research. Numerous Roman weapons were discovered during the excavations undertaken in the years 1928–1937 by Yale University and the French Academy of Sciences in the former Roman frontier city of Dura-Europos on the Euphrates, now located in Syria. This town had recently received large numbers of Roman troops, when they were besieged, stormed, and destroyed in 255/56 by the Persians. In the dry desert climate, not only military papyri had been well preserved, but also wooden shields, including leather covers, complete sets of horse armour, and other organic materials, which nowhere else had come to light in such abundance. Important pieces – such as some military bronze fittings, cloak brooches, painted shields,

horse armour, or the wooden shafts of catapult bolts – had already been presented in the preliminary reports, but it would take until 2004 and *The Militaria of Dura-Europos* of S. James before they were fully published.

After the Second World War

In Germany, archaeological research into the Roman military, which was largely dormant during the period of Nazi rule, quickly gained importance and achieved international standing after the war with the introduction of the subject of 'Roman Provincial Archaeology'.[20] In particular, the International Limes Congresses, held since 1949, and which came about with a significant British stimulus, have considerably intensified and internationally networked research into Roman armament and military equipment (Birley 1986). At German universities the relevant investigations started with the work of G. Ulbert, continued by his students.[21] Ulbert's brief summary of Roman arms in the 1st century AD had a wide impact, for there was nothing else like it in German (Ulbert 1968). The other important centres involved in research into Roman armament and military equipment were museums, such as, for example, the Rhineland Regional Museum (Rheinisches Landesmuseum) in Bonn (H. von Petrikovits), the Westphalian Regional Museum (Westfälisches Landesmuseum) in Münster (S. von Schnurbein, J.-S. Kühlborn), the Württemberg State Museum (Württembergisches Landesmuseum) in Stuttgart with its branch museum, the Limes Museum in Aalen (Ph. Filtzinger), and the State Prehistoric Collection (Prähistorische Staatssammlung) in Munich (H.-J. Kellner, J. Garbsch).

Three institutions which are responsible for a substantial part of the research into Roman armament and military equipment are the Roman-Germanic Commission of the German Archaeological Institute (Römisch-Germanische Kommission des Deutschen Archäologischen Instituts) in Frankfurt (H. Schönberger, S. von Schnurbein), the Roman-Germanic Central Museum (Römisch-Germanisches Zentralmuseum) in Mainz (H. Klumbach, G. Waurick, E. Künzl), and the Saalburg-Museum in Bad Homburg vor der Höhe (H. Schönberger, D. Baatz, E. Schallmayer). In Switzerland, at Windisch-Vindonissa, the Vindonissa-Museum (R. Fellmann, M. Hartmann, Ch. Unz) is a traditional centre of Roman military research. Likewise there are related activities in the colony town of Augusta Raurica-Augst (E. Deschler-Erb). The universities in Basel (L. Berger, E. Deschler-Erb) and Bern (R. Fellmann, S. Martin-Kilcher) have promoted research into Roman armament and military equipment.

In Austria, it is the Austrian Archaeological Institute (Österreichische Archäologische Institut); the Vienna Academy of Sciences (Wiener Akademie der Wissenschaften) with its Limeskommission; the University of Vienna; the Federal Monuments Office (Bundesdenkmalamt); and the National Museum (Landesmuseum) in Klagenfurt, which have distinguished themselves with research into the Roman military. A strange fate befell a standard work from Austria, the Vienna dissertation of Hansjörg Ubl, *Weapons and Uniforms of the Roman Army of the Principate from the Grave Reliefs of Noricum and Pannonia* (Ubl 2013). Although the work was not published for a long time (in Austria there are no publication requirements for theses), 'pirated' copies of it have been repeatedly reproduced and it was used and cited in relevant scholarly circles around the world. Now it has finally appeared.

In Britain, Graham Webster's book about the Roman army of the 1st and 2nd centuries AD included brief descriptions of Roman armament and military equipment (Webster 1969). A significant advance in the study of the many pieces of 2nd- and 3rd-century equipment of copper alloy, iron, and bone from the forts of the Upper German-Raetian Limes and beyond, came with Jürgen Oldenstein's thesis published in 1976.

The 'Robinson effect'

Powerful stimuli for research into the Roman military which have come from Britain since 1970s have an unexpected momentum even now. These impulses no longer came just from 'established' archaeological specialists, but also from enthusiastic outsiders. Researching Roman militaria no longer remained the preserve of closed, academic circles, but to an increasing extent integrated interested amateurs and supporters of re-enactment, often through personal relationships. Bishop and Coulston have accurately referred to this phenomenon as the 'Robinson Effect'.[22]

But one could also speak of the 'Corbridge' effect: H. R. Robinson, who as an expert on oriental armour worked as assistant to the Master of Armouries in Her Majesty's Tower of London, was friends with Graham Webster, then one of the leading scholars in the UK working with the Roman military. Through this contact, Robinson was asked to interpret a new discovery from 1964 at the beginning of the 1970s. It was a hoard of scrap metal buried in the northern English fort of Corbridge in the early 2nd century AD.[23] For the first time, this contained large portions of several segmented cuirasses, which – along with items already known from other sites – at last allowed a well-supported reconstruction of this type of armour.

Robinson now turned to the problem of interpretation of the find and the construction and operation of segmental armour from a practical point of view: he built full-size Corbridge cuirasses from the same materials and so, for the first time, a functional reconstruction of this armour was made. Theoretical studies into the representations of Trajan's Column and the finds from the weapons store at Carnuntum, from Newstead, and Rißtissen, had not led to any sustainable result. Inspired by this breakthrough, Robinson further engaged with Roman head and body armour. As a result of this research, which in turn included a wealth of home-made reconstructions, in 1975 he released his definitive work on Roman armour. This book, quickly out of print, meant not only an important step forward for research, but also caused a major boost to the further development of the re-enactment scene.

Soon after, inspired and trained by H. R. Robinson, blacksmith M. Simkins from Nottingham began with the production of replicas of Roman weapons, which he introduced in his own publications.[24] The cooperation of the illustrator P. Connolly on Robinson's standard work proved to be momentous.[25] Connolly not only provided accurate, technical illustration of individual pieces of weaponry, but also brilliant reconstruction drawings of Roman soldiers in a suggestive photo-realistic reconstruction. He was able to draw on a tradition for making naturalistic reconstruction images for Roman Britain, like the rather gloomy graphics of A. Sorrell or the reconstructions by R. Embleton published in numerous magazines.[26] The illustrators A. McBride and G. Sumner, should be mentioned here as successors of Connolly.[27]

This collaboration as an illustrator for Robinson established P. Connolly in his career as an internationally recognized researcher in Roman armament and equipment, incorporating intensive experimental archaeology in his work (Connolly 2002). He became known worldwide, beyond professional circles, for his brilliantly illustrated and meticulously researched factual works on the Greek and Roman military,[28] which he always wrote in close cooperation with relevant subject specialists.

Connolly's factual works, which appeared internationally in large numbers, along with the writings of Robinson, considerably stimulated the serious re-enactment scene in the UK.[29] This movement then quickly spread to the continent, as typified by Marcus Junkelmann and the march of his group across the Alps in 1985 (Fig. 67).[30] The 'Ermine Street Guard', founded in Exeter in 1972 by its leader, C. Haines, is one of the most active and largest Roman groups operating in experimental archaeology.[31] In 1978, based on Robinson's work, triggered by the discovery of the Theilenhofen helmets and encouraged by H.-J. Kellner, J. Garbsch presented all the then-known sports armour together in a monograph. This was done at the Prehistoric State Collection in Munich as part of an exhibition, which was also shown in Nuremberg. The collaboration of professional archaeologists with practitioners and dedicated amateurs – which started in the UK, but soon expanded internationally – was a significant advance in research. A local seminar on 21 March 1983 was held at the University of Sheffield under the leadership of M. C. Bishop, which set a momentous development in motion: for

Figure 67 *The Junkelmann force on 12 May 1985 on the Roman road north of Bressanone. Photo: M. Junkelmann*

this and other internal university research seminars soon became an international conference, which has enjoyed steady popularity with professional researchers, amateur enthusiasts, and practitioners over the years: the Roman Military Equipment Conference (ROMEC). In addition to several meetings in the UK, meetings were held in Germany, France, Croatia, the Netherlands, Austria, Switzerland, and Hungary. The publications of these meetings have now become an important international forum of research on Roman arms and military equipment. Most of the researchers currently working in Belgium, Bulgaria, Denmark, Germany, France, Great Britain, Israel, Italy, the Netherlands, Austria, Poland, Romania, Switzerland, Serbia, Slovakia, Slovenia, Spain, Czech Republic, Hungary, and the USA are represented in it.

Similarly, the Proceedings of the International Limes Congresses are frequently relevant to the subject. In addition, a number of monographs with militaria from individual sites have appeared in recent years, such as those for Augst, Vindonissa, and Xanten.[32] There have also been works on individual types of weapons: Roman helmets (Waurick 1988a; Feugère 1994), Early Imperial daggers and decorated scabbards (Obmann 1999), Roman swords (Miks 2007), and in the same year a study on later imperial swords based on the material from Illerup Ådal (Biborski 2007),

as well as a dissertation on Roman shields (Nabbefeld 2009). An antiquarian archaeological commentary on the representations on Trajan's Column, to which weaponry and equipment are key, was published by D. Richter in 2004, with a second edition in 2010.

For the first time since Couissins' synthetic work of 1926, a French work on the subject was again published in 1993 (2nd ed. 2002) by M. Feugère. M. C. Bishop and J. C. N. Coulston were then influential with their summary synthesis of Roman armament and military equipment from the Republic to late antiquity. Their book *Roman Military Equipment* was soon sold out and reappeared in 2006 in a second, heavily revised edition.[33]

Meanwhile, research had made great progress. Increasingly, scholars were able to include ever larger collections of Roman arms and military equipment from the East and North Africa in their considerations. In 2004, the long-awaited monograph by Simon James on *The Arms and Armour and Other Military Equipment* from Dura-Europos was published, mainly containing material from the period around the middle of the 3rd century AD. Militaria from Sagalassos in Pisidia (van Daele 2005), Dülük Baba Tepesi (Fischer 2011), Zeugma[34] and Qraije on the Euphrates (Gschwind 2009) have been published or are expected to be in the near future. From Israel, closely datable finds from Herodium and Masada have been brought to print (Stiebel 2003; Stiebel and Magness 2007).

Ch. Boube-Piccot had already published her monograph on *Les bronzes antiques du Maroc IV. L'équipement militaire et l'Armement* in 1994.

Until now, German-speaking countries has been lacking an overview of the current state of research on Roman arms and military equipment, apart from brief summaries in the *Lexicon of Germanic Archaeology* (RGA), or other minor contributions.[35] The German edition of this book tried to remedy this situation.

3. Armament and equipment

Change

As might be expected, the Roman military did not retain the same types of equipment and armament throughout the approximately twelve centuries from the Republican period until the end of the Western Roman Empire. Rather, they repeatedly adapted to changing requirements, making developments which can be clearly understood and dated from both representational sources and original finds. One of the problems that arises is that there are different speeds in the development of Roman weapons or rather in their service life: for example, more substantial items, like helmets or swords, were obviously used for longer than more fragile or vulnerable pieces of equipment, such as body armour or the belt. Other weapons and pieces of equipment, like arrows, spears, or entrenching tools, eventually reached their ideal form and changed little after that.

With continuing progress in research, the production date of a weapon can almost always be defined quite closely, but this may be several years or even decades from the point in time when a weapon was finally deposited. The typological development of equipment is not uniformly well understood for all periods of the Roman Empire. Understanding them is highly dependent on well-known representative groups of finds and their more-or-less-precisely dated find contexts. But well-dated find contexts are by no means evenly distributed across all periods from the late Republic to late antiquity. Thus the research situation for the 1st and 3rd century AD is significantly better than for the 2nd century AD, thanks to larger amounts of material (destruction layers and hoards) and numerous well-dated sites. It is also always worth bearing in mind that the actual finds we know are only a tiny fraction of those weapons that once were in use. E. Künzl calculated that, for example, in the nearly 130 years from Augustus (27 BC to AD 14) to Domitian (AD 81 to 96), about a million Roman swords must have existed.[36] J. Obmann, who in 2000 knew of 142 daggers of the 1st century AD with ornate metal sheaths, estimated their former numbers over the same period to between 750,000 and a million.[37] The same would have to apply to helmets and armour. Shields, which as 'consumables' were exposed to a greater rate of attrition, must have been stocked in even higher numbers, even if shield bosses and other metal fittings were likely to have had a high rate of reuse.

Nevertheless, the current state of research on Roman armament allows us to define periods of change in the equipment, whose transitions are of course more or less fluid. It has been repeatedly proven that in some periods not only individual parts of the equipment or weapons fell out of use and were replaced by new types, but that the whole package of the soldier's weapons and equipment changed significantly within a short period.

Occasionally, research has explained this as intentional 'reforms' of equipment, which, commanded from the top, had led to a quick re-arming of all the troops throughout the empire with a different set of weapons or armours. However, this model of a centralized 'reform' of weapons and equipment turns out to be more than questionable on closer inspection, especially since there are hardly any written sources, apart from the change to the *pilum* allegedly decreed by Marius in 100 BC.

So another explanation must be sought for this repeatedly and unequivocally observed phenomenon: a continuous development of individual components of Roman Imperial period weaponry can be discerned as a rule, occasionally accelerated by new inventions,[38] the acquisition of enemy weapons seen as superior,[39] or the spontaneous improvement of their own material in response to superior enemy weapons.[40] Even pure fads have to be allowed for: short-lived phenomena such as the niello decoration on copper-alloy fittings of the Tiberian to Neronian period, ring- and frame-buckle belts of the 3rd century, Late Roman chip carving sets, or on ornate dagger sheaths of the 1st century AD can hardly be explained in exclusively technical or functional terms.

Now, in the Imperial period, there were always larger military conflicts with internal and external enemies, which were accompanied by above-average loss of men (and also material). These had to be replaced by levying and training – in comparison to 'normal' times – more than the average number of new recruits who were then also accordingly equipped and armed. With the help of military diplomas, these mechanisms can now be partly observed in auxiliary units: in peaceful times, the need for new recruits caused by the 'normal' retirement of soldiers upon reaching the appropriate age or death, should have been covered by those provinces where the units were stationed. The only traditional exceptions were Batavian units and oriental archers who were usually levied from their original homelands.

After major conflicts, this was completely different, however. Based on examples from the *c.*1,000 military diplomas known at the moment, W. Eck could demonstrate that the replenishment of units of a certain province depleted in combat could also lead to unusually high recruitment in other provinces (Eck 2010). The replacement of losses was obviously not carried out during hostilities, but afterwards (*ibid.* 103), for in ancient times there was no reserve army, as in modern armies. To equip all the new recruits, large amounts of weapons had to be manufactured, which of course were made after the latest types.[41] Since these types frequently occur in very large archaeological deposits, this misleadingly suggests intentional, 'top-down', deliberate reforms.

However, it should be stressed that currently no direct links have yet been made between the increased recruitment phase indicated by military diplomas, as proposed by Werner Eck, and the archaeological material periods of change or change in armament. In the current state of affairs,[42] the following, to some extent clearly distinguishable, phases in the armament and equipment of the Roman army can be defined:

- the Republic from the 2nd century BC (since the end of the 2nd Punic War);
- from Augustus to Nero;
- from Vespasian to Trajan;
- from Hadrian to Septimius Severus;
- from Caracalla until the reforms of Diocletian;
- Late Antiquity.

Adoption of enemy armament

The Romans always understood how to adopt the weaponry and fighting techniques of defeated enemies and then quite naturally make them their own. They were fully aware of this themselves, as the so-called equestrian treatise of AD 136 by Arrian shows:[43]

> One must therefore also particularly praise the Romans, as in other respects, because they did not let their love for their own traditional institutions stop them adopting useful things from everywhere and naturalizing them. Thus it can be seen that they both acquired certain types of weapons from others – and these were already called 'Roman' because the Romans used them most effectively – as well as military exercises.

These adopted weapons were often immediately adapted to their own fighting style by the Romans and optimized through improvements: examples are the helmets of the Montefortino and Weisenau types that were derived from Celtic models, as well as mail armour,[44] the dagger and short sword (*pugio* and *gladius*) from the Celtiberians, and the long sword (*spatha*) of the Celts. In the 2nd century AD, eastern elements influenced Roman swords leading, for example, to the emergence of the so-called ring-pommel swords or to the adoption of a new technique of attaching the scabbard to the baldric. Whether the Roman 'national' weapon – the *pilum* – was of Iberian or Italic origin,[45] it was not, in any case, a Roman invention. Scale armour, the reflex bow, and various shield shapes were also borrowed from other peoples. Artillery and siege engines were adopted from Hellenistic armies. Finally, in late antiquity, the Romans adopted eastern Parthian-Sassanid helmet shapes. In fact, according to the current state of research, of all the arms only segmental armour was a purely in-house Roman development of the Augustan period.[46] Similarly, in siege warfare (which will not be further considered here), among the war machines, dominated by Greco-Hellenistic machines, only the drawbridge can be shown to be a typical invention of the Romans from the time of the first Punic War.[47] With their help, elements of land warfare, such as the storming of a fortress, could be transferred to naval actions by dropping down the folded-up bridge onto the enemy ship and securing it with a spike.

Uniformity and regional differences

The widespread uniformity of Roman equipment – which barely existed – has been repeatedly emphasized and used to postulate the 'modernity' of the Roman army. Some have even gone so far as to see central production workshops as responsible for this alleged uniformity.[48] These ideas of an almost modern-sounding uniformity of Roman weapons and equipment are certainly influenced by the images of Trajan's Column in Rome (Pogorzelski 2012). The unity represented there, which we perceive as standardization, definitely did not exist in the Roman Empire: however, there were some periods with broader, trans-regional ('national') similarities in armament and equipment and others, where regional elements dominated.

The weapons and equipment of the Augustan period, for instance, seem quite uniform in the Rhine and Danube regions. This probably has something to do with the fact that the bulk of the material was first produced in northern Italy, where the Augustan legions were mainly raised. Production moved to the various garrisons, which then constantly changed.

With troops stationed in the same province for longer periods during the 2nd and 3rd centuries AD on the other hand, distinct local differences in the details can be perceived between the equipment of the Rhine or Danube armies or the troops in Britain. In particular, prolonged stationing of troops in a region favoured the emergence of local workshop and form traditions. Of course we have to take into account that, with the current state of research, eastern armies cannot be properly included in our deliberations, which would certainly result in a more nuanced picture.

With the high mobility of Roman troops, successful weapon and equipment types, but also fashion trends, could rapidly be disseminated over most of the empire. Of course, there were minimum standards for the arming and equipping of all Roman units based on the usual requirements of combat, but similarities in the equipment of Roman soldiers probably occurred less through uniform guidelines than from various local interpretations of the 'regulation armament'. On the other hand, there were also controls by the army, which decided whether a privately-made weapon was suitable for use in the Roman army.[49]

Local differences, which derived from local workshop traditions, are noticeable for certain periods. However, they also depend on a comparable state of research everywhere, which is not always the case. For Upper Germany and Raetia in the 1st century AD, a certain stylistic dominance of workshop traditions in the area of the legionary camp of Vindonissa is observable.[50] Even a cursory comparison of military bronzes from Morocco (Boube-Piccot 1994) with those of the north-west provinces shows both similarities and significant differences; there is some scope for further detailed research here.

Comparing the Danube region with the Rhine provinces and Britain, a wide range of 2nd and 3rd century AD militaria displays major differences: many types are concentrated in Raetia and the nearby Danube regions, which cannot be explained by the state of research in these regions, since it is on a comparable level. Examples are the 'VTERE FELIX' belts, the round perforated plates with suspension as part of a military belt,[51] or bronze projectile points.[52] On the other hand there was a long tradition of 'Celtic' weapons in Britain, such as those with enamel decoration. Such swords or sword scabbard fittings have been collected by C. Miks.[53] The so-called 'Celticizing' style of military bronzes of the second half of the 2nd and the 3rd centuries AD, which then spread into the whole Empire, may derive from there.

Dura-Europos has provided an amazing amount of material of the 3rd century AD which, at first sight, looks as if it could also have come from Upper Germany or the Danube area. Simon James explains this as contemporary, Empire-wide uniform equipment, with which all local units were equipped (James 2004). However, allowance should perhaps also be made for the highly mobile Rhenish-Danubian troops in the Parthian and Persian campaigns of the 3rd century as an explanation for this observation.

Supply of weapons

Upon entering the army, Roman soldiers received an enlistment bonus (*viaticum*) to get to their units.[54] Once there, they apparently had the choice to acquire new weapons from private or military sources or to buy used pieces from the unit, usually from the *custos armorum*,[55] departing soldiers having sold theirs to him. During their period of service, the soldiers were given occasional state subsidies for their clothing, equipment, and weapons, sometimes even gifts of arms.[56] Soldiers themselves had to bear the high cost of over- and undergarments, coats, shoes, armour, helmet, shield, belt, sword, dagger and other weapons, and entrenching tools, cookware, and tarpaulins. The maintenance of armament, equipment, and clothing caused additional regular expenses.

As for the manufacture of weapons, there has been much discussion among researchers about whether this was done in a military or civilian context.[57] From the early Imperial period, there is ample evidence in the camps – at Haltern, for example – in the form of castings, semi-finished products, and so on, which attest to the production and repair of weapons and military equipment by craftsmen. Also *fabricae*, or the troops' own workshops, can be found in every camp and fort, where metal processing and thus probably weapons production and repair took place (Bishop 1985a). Specialized craftsmen were working there, as they are also testified epigraphically, such as a swordsmith (*gladiarius*) in Vindonissa (*CIL* XIII 11504). An Egyptian papyrus of the 2nd or 3rd century AD lists the products of a weapons workshop, which was operated by a legion, including *spathae* and shields.[58] However, in the course of time these workshops seem to have played a more important role during campaigns away from garrison locations. For, ever since larger civilian settlements developed around the permanent bases – *canabae legionis* around legionary camps, *vici* around auxiliary forts – private workshops for weapons and equipment can generally be demonstrated to have existed though finds. As the research of, among others, J. Oldenstein and J. Nicolay[59] has shown for specific examples, there were apparently larger and smaller private companies that produced weapons and equipment and sold it to the soldiers at virtually any *vicus* and each *canaba legionis*.

In a recent written contribution by P. Herz, the share of private enterprises in the supply of the Roman army has been considerably underestimated, as he completely relies on the sparse written sources. He obviously did not know the relevant research of provincial Roman archaeology on this subject, such as the works of Oldenstein, Bishop and Coulston, and Gschwind (Herz 2010). However, as Bishop and Coulston rightly point out, we have far too little information to be able to say for sure where and at what time the private sector was less important, equally significant, or only of peripheral importance (Bishop and Coulston 2006, 234).

A private arms dealer from the time of Commodus is attested on an inscription from Mainz.[60] An altar for the well-being of the emperor was dedicated there by a veteran of *legio XXII Primigenia*, G. Gentilius Victor, who worked as a sword dealer (*negotiator gladiarius*). The amount of 8,000 sesterces for the monument shows that he was doing good business; after all, as a *negotiator* he was more of a wholesaler.[61]

The form in which swords came into the trade is suggested by some original discoveries: from Mainz and the hinterland of Krefeld-Fischeln there are hoard and individual finds of *spathae* with longer than normal tangs. These may be weapons that had yet to be finished for use after sale: they were fitted with handles in the individual hand size of the buyer, and only then would the tangs be reduced accordingly. This blade with an extra long tang may therefore have been the 'standard form', in which new swords arrived for trading. For the most important part of a sword, whose particular qualities mattered, was indeed the blade. The addition of handles and sheaths was done by special craftsmen and left to the individual tastes (and purchasing power) of the buyer.[62] This would also explain why stamps, which were a guarantee of the quality of the blade were often set into the tang and covered by the handle. This is particularly evident in the swords from Germanic sacrificial bogs.[63] The bulk of edged weapons found there are indeed Roman swords, but with Germanic handles and scabbard fittings. This, too, suggests that only the blades were traded and the weapons subsequently furnished to the individual taste of the owner.[64]

References to the production of weapons and equipment, and especially of bronze components, by private enterprises have only so far been comprehensively published for Raetia: such workshops are known here, *e.g.* from the fort settlements of Pfünz, Regensburg-Kumpfmühl, Regensburg-Grossprüfening, and Straubing. During the middle Empire, these workshops seem to have covered all the local requirements in all areas of copper-alloy processing: from horse harness to belts to fibulae (Gschwind 1997). That the troops still had artisans in the 2nd century AD, especially when on military operations away from garrison locations, is not only shown by literary and epigraphic sources: a half-finished cheekpiece for a cavalry helmet was found in a base used briefly during the Marcomannic wars of AD 172–5 at Eining-Unterfeld.[65]

Private weapons manufacturers seem to have also existed away from the main garrison areas, at least during the early Imperial period: back then, northern Italy was the most important centre for raising Roman legions. It was not only necessary to drill and train the recruits before sending them to the hotspots of military confrontations in Spain, Germania, or the Danube, but it was also necessary to have a veritable 'arms industry' in order to equip them with weapons and other accessories. Weapons

workshops excavated with the appropriate methods and then published are rare; an example of such is the workshop at Magdalensberg in Carinthia from the mid-Augustan period. Here, such a centre of arms production – probably of more than just local significance – was discovered and published (Dolenz *et al.* 1995). In this trading and commercial settlement '*ferrum Noricum*', wildly praised in antiquity because of its quality and acquired either in the immediate vicinity or further afield, was probably used for the production of tools and weapons. But non-ferrous metals were also processed: the production of sword and dagger sheaths, military belts, helmets of the Weisenau type and plate armour is proven by failed castings, unfinished items, production waste, and other production traces (ibid.).

In the civilian settlement on the Auerberg near Bernbeuren in the Allgäu, where craftsmen and traders had been settled since the time of Tiberius, clay moulds for the production of massive bronze washers for torsion artillery are known from the early Imperial period. These were obviously intended for legionary troops because, in the early Imperial period, such artillery pieces were only used by them (see Baatz 1994). Whether civilian craftsmen acted as artillery manufacturers on the Auerberg, or whether legionary specialists built or repaired guns, is currently not clear. The question of where this legion's troops were stationed (Augsburg?) is still completely open. For Britain, a weapons workshop from the time of Nero has been identified through relevant archaeological material – including belt fittings and helmets of the Weisenau type – at Colchester-Sheepen (Niblett 1985). Some arms have manufacturer's inscriptions that can hardly have belonged to military *fabricae* but rather to private workshops (Bishop and Coulston 2006, 43–6). The Augustan dagger from Oberammergau has the damascened inscription C ANTONIVS FECIT (Caius Antonius has made it; Ulbert 1971a) on the handle. A *gladius* of the Claudian period with a sheath of relief-decorated bronze sheet is known from a river find in the Rhine at Strasbourg. This contains the stamped factory inscription on the sheet metal of the sheath: Q NONIENVS PVDES AD ARA F ('Quintus Nonienus Pudes made this in Ad Aram'). This piece has always been associated with Cologne (Colonia Claudia Ara Agrippinensium) as a possible production site for the scabbard (and thus probably the sword). However, there are now similar inscriptions on scabbard plates from the area of Vindonissa which relate to Colonia Lugdunum, which also had an altar to the imperial cult. Thus, on a scabbard plate from Vindonissa, there is the inscription C COELIVS VENVST LVGD ('Caius Coelius Venustus made this in Lugdunum'). Therefore, it is also possible that the Strasbourg example came from Lyon and not from Cologne.[66]

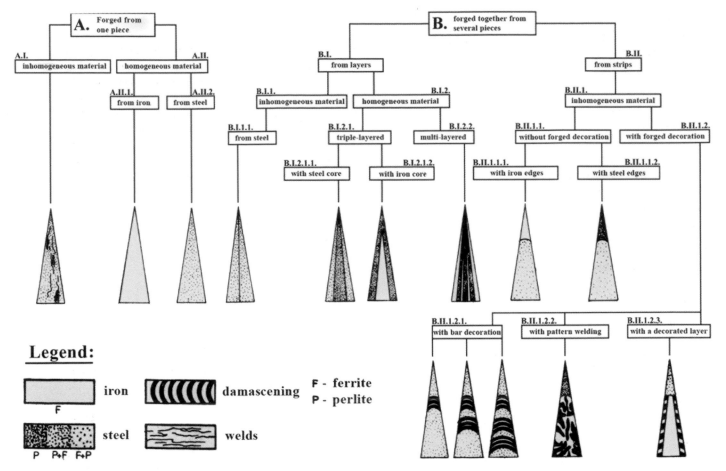

Figure 68 *Scheme of the technological structure of Roman swords, among which there are also damascened pieces (by Miks 2007)*

The technology of weapons production and procurement of raw materials

Iron

Since mines were basically government owned,[67] it is unlikely that the procurement of metal for military use represented a major problem. Not only larger centres were exploited for iron, since they are known for the Iberian Peninsula, Britain, Dacia, Raetia (eastern Swabian Jura) and Noricum, the production site of the famous '*ferrum Noricum*'. In addition, the metal could also be acquired from countless smaller production sites. Iron mining in the Roman Empire has moreover only been studied preliminarily; Eisenberg in the Palatinate, for instance, was only recently revealed as a Roman-period production site of national significance in the German provinces. Cast iron or cast steel was not yet known in ancient times. Iron was smelted in a bloomery furnace and thus produced relatively small, highly contaminated blooms. These had to have undesirable constituents removed through intensive forging afterwards.[68] Smithing slags often occur en masse on archaeological sites, and if they occur together with smelting slag, are characteristic of iron extraction.[69] If they occur alone, they indicate workshops for iron tools and weapons.

The size of pieces of iron being worked in antiquity was limited, because they could not be cast, but could only be made from forged out blooms, which were joined by forge-welding (Baatz *et al.* 1995). Depending on the nature of the desired end product, the iron now had to be processed further. Wrought iron produced by forging blooms was elastic, as a rule, but soft. For the cutting edges of tools and equipment, but especially in weapons (swords, daggers, spearheads), a hard material was needed. But this was also brittle and therefore prone to breakage. Today, the union of these originally opposing properties of iron can be had through using an alloy of cast steel. In ancient times (and up into modern times), much more complicated techniques were necessary: a soft, but elastic, blade core was combined through forge-welding with separate hard, but brittle, cutting edges and thus achieved the desired combination of hard-elastic (Löhberg 1969; Pleiner 1970; Graßler 2012). The technique of damascening yielded even better results, but meant much more work, with thin rods of hard/brittle and soft/elastic iron forged into ingots, which served as the starting material for a high-quality blade (Fig. 68).

Since these bars were also twisted and folded during forging and the various iron rods relied upon as a starting material also differed in colour, the finished product could develop ornamental qualities which were quite popular.[70]

One other decorative technique, used mainly on dagger scabbards, on the grips of ring-pommel swords, and chapes, was inlay with various metals, such as gold, silver, brass, and copper. The desired ornamental patterns were cut into the iron using a graver so that the incisions were undercut. Wire from the above-mentioned materials was then hammered into the cut and the whole thing polished.[71] The silver inlay relatively common on dagger sheaths is hard to imagine as contrasting with a shiny silver iron background, and consequently it indirectly attests bluing. With this technique, the workpiece is heated and then quenched with oil, which results in a blue-black colour. Other decorative techniques occurring on weapons are enamelling, niello decoration and fire gilding.[72]

From the time of Caesar's Gallic Wars, the Romans took vigorous advantage of the Celtic supremacy in forge technology. This is especially visible in helmets: even the oldest Roman helmet types (the Montefortino type and its variants) were in fact derived from Celtic iron helmets, which had been encountered through the Celtic tribes that had penetrated northern and central Italy. But only the form was taken as a model and not the technology, with the iron helmets adapted in copper alloy, which was technically easier to work (casting and raising). When during the Gallic wars, around the middle of the 1st century BC, there again were close military contacts with the Celts, their current iron helmet types were adopted and quickly evolved into the Roman Weisenau type. Now, however, both the form and the complicated manufacturing techniques, namely the forging and finishing of the iron helmet bowl in one piece, were adopted into Roman weapons production. Although there were Weisenau helmets and their successors in copper alloy, their numbers were much smaller than those of iron helmets.

Copper alloy

For copper alloys, the origin of the metals used is easier to narrow down: it was mainly the well-known centres in the eastern provinces and in Spain which provided the copper, although all small local deposits were exploited, as in Gaul and the German provinces. Tin required for the alloy of bronze came mainly from Britain (Cornwall). Around the middle of the 1st century, brass began to be used.[73] It had been discovered in the 1st century AD in Asia Minor and then used as a metal for coinage. This use spread to the Romans, since the golden, shiny brass (*orichalcum*) was easily distinguishable from bronze and copper. From the outset, the deposits exploited for this were natural deposits of mixed copper and zinc (calamine) suitable for the production of brass.[74] The ability to acquire natural, pure zinc in order to use it as alloy with copper from elsewhere to produce brass had been developed early as well (see Fellmann *et al.* 1999). In addition to the mining of copper, tin, and zinc, the reuse of copper alloys played a very important role; scrap metal of all kinds is excavated in private and military workshops for copper-alloy processing everywhere.

By the time of Augustus, brass was used in large amounts for the production of coins and for all kinds of militaria. In addition to its shiny, golden colour, the fact that it was more flexible than bronze certainly played a role. However, distinguishing between brass, bronze, and copper among corroded archaeological finds is a big problem, because they all have a uniform green patina. Only metal analysis can ascertain which metal is used.

During antiquity, the casting of copper alloy was only possible in small batches, as controlled melting in larger crucibles and furnaces was still unknown. When simultaneously pouring molten metal from several small crucibles, there is a risk of premature solidification of the melt and thus casting defects. Therefore, larger workpieces often have attachments and repairs (patches). For non-ferrous metal,[75] hardening by hammering was possible. Items could be decorated with different inlays, and niello decoration was especially very common (Deschler-Erb 2000).

Other materials

Other, mostly organic materials that were needed in large quantities for the production of arms and military equipment – such as leather, textiles, or wood – were purchased from the private sector[76] or procured directly. The latter is the case for timber[77] and the manufacture of canvas is known in the naval base at Cologne-Alteburg.[78] The Romans also procured leather in the form of tributes from dependent tribes, as is testified for the Frisians.[79]

State arms factories in Late Antiquity

In late antiquity, this changes. The *Notitia Dignitatum* now records state arms factories for the central production of weapons.[80] These armouries are recorded in the literary sources for Northern Italy, Northern and Central Gaul, and along the Rhine and Danube, as well as in the eastern provinces. For Britain, North Africa, Spain and Egypt, however, there are no such documents.

So far, we know of the following workshops from the *Notitia*:

- *arcuaria* (bow factories) in Ticinum
- *armorum* or *armorum omnium* (factories for unspecified weapons) in Salona and Argentorate
- *ballistaria* (artillery factory) in Treberi
- *clibanaria* (cuirass factories) in Antioch, Caesarea, and Nicomedia

- *hastaria* (spear factories) in Irenopolis
- *loricaria* (cuirass factory) in Mantua
- *loricaria, ballistaria et clibanaria* (factory for cuirasses, artillery, and heavy armour) in Augustodunum
- *sagittaria* (arrow factory) in Concordia
- *scutaria* (shield factories) in Horreum Margi, Aquincum, Carnuntum, Lauriacum, Cremona, Augustodunum, and Treberi
- *scutaria et armorum* (factories for shields and unspecified weapons) in Damascus, Edessa, Nicomedia, Sardis, Hadrianopolis, Marcianopolis, and Verona
- *scutorum, scordiscorum et armorum* (factories for shields, saddles, and unspecified weapons) in Sirmium
- *spatharia* (factory for swords) in Lucca and Remi

In addition, there were weapons factories for unknown products in Thessaloniki, Naissus, Ratiaria, and Suessiones. It is clear that this list of weapons factories must be incomplete because the helmet factories, for example, or the workshops manufacturing the characteristic metal-studded belt of Late Antiquity are missing in the *Notitia Dignitatum*. The number of sword forges is much too small in comparison to workshops manufacturing shields. However, there is no archaeological evidence for any of these state-owned weapons workshops so far, with the possible exception of Carnuntum. There C. Gugl recently hypothesized that late-period wooden vats in the *via sagularis* on the east side of the legionary camp could be associated with tanneries. This would correspond well with the *scutaria*, the shield factories mentioned in the *Notitia Dignitatum*, where leather was indeed required in large quantities.[81]

In addition to these state-owned large enterprises, decentralized workshops that manufactured metal military equipment still existed. These are attested for forts and civilian settlements through archaeological finds. Examples are lead models, which were used to produce moulds for the manufacture of belt buckles, from Haus Bürgel (near Düsseldorf) or from Mamer (Luxembourg).[82] There are also failed castings or half-finished products, such as the unfinished amphora-shaped strap ends from the hillfort of Entersburg near Hontheim.[83]

Ownership

In the Roman Empire, defensive weapons, swords and daggers, tents, entrenching tools and cooking and tables wares were all effectively privately owned.[84] But this was certainly not so for 'consumables', such as javelins, arrows, slingshot, and other projectiles. The outdated theory that the weapons of Roman soldiers were state-owned can still be found in print, although a number of sources clearly contradict it. Likewise, the view expressed by H. U. Nuber in his thesis,[85] that weapons were only handed over to soldiers in exchange for a deposit, can hardly be credited when confronted with the counterarguments listed below.

First, there are documents on papyri which record the fact that weapons and military equipment were privately obtainable in the Roman Empire: J. F. Gilliam has discussed a papyrus from Egypt, which records how the weapons and equipment of a deceased auxiliary soldier (among them a tent), were acquired by his unit, the money then being given to the mother. He also cites further evidence for the private ownership of weapons and military equipment from information on Egyptian papyri (Gilliam 1967). Papyrus *P. Columbia* Inv. 325 shows that Roman soldiers were apparently accustomed to selling their weapons and equipment to the unit (represented by the *custos armorum*; cf. Speidel 1992) upon leaving active service, the weapons then being sold to the new recruits. The fact that the sum paid out was the property of the soldier, and did not represent the repayment of a deposit sum, which had been put aside for state-owned weapons and equipment,[86] is clear from other sources (see below). Taking all surviving information together, the private ownership of weapons and military equipment was the rule. It seems frequently to have been a payment by instalment: when entering the service, one got a complete set of equipment, which was paid off by deducting amounts from the regular payments until everything was paid.

In fact, every Roman soldier was free to buy new weapons immediately upon entering service or buy better and more beautiful equipment – whether new or used – later, to use perhaps as a 'secondary weapon'. There is just such a case in another Egyptian papyrus from Alexandria: here we learn of a cavalryman in Egypt in AD 27 who has, among other things, deposited a silver dagger sheath with ivory inlay and a silver-plated helmet as collateral for a loan.[87] This would have been impossible if the dagger and helmet were state owned. In addition, the dagger was not standard armament for cavalry. From this we can infer that, in this case, the weapons were privately owned by the soldier and that he had additional equipment for use during his service. It is unimaginable in any army in the world that a soldier could respond with impunity to an enquiry about a missing weapon by innocently stating that he had unfortunately temporarily given it away as security.

It is clear from two letters that the marine Claudius Terentianus wrote to his father in the early 2nd century AD that, in addition to weapons, entrenching tools like the *dolabra* were also available commercially and the private property of soldiers.[88] Claudius had enlisted as a recruit in the fleet and expected to serve in the legion. In the first letter he asks his father Tiberianus, who is apparently a member of a legion himself, to send a sword (*gladius pugnatorius*), a mattock (*dolabra*), an iron hook, two spears, a cloak, and a tunic with belt and trousers. In a second letter he asks for shoes made of soft leather, socks, and a replacement for his *dolabra*, which was taken away by his *optio*.

Ownership inscriptions on the weapons themselves are relevant in the context of private ownership of these pieces as well; they were marked by scoring or punching inscriptions on helmets or parade armour. There are also many ownership tags in bronze that were originally attached to shields, cuirasses, and other military equipment. These have the form of round or rectangular plaques with a rivet on the backside, or small *tabulae ansatae*, often with holes, which were sewn on (Nuber 1972). All these ownership tags bore the name of the owner along with details of the unit (century, *turma*) in which the soldier in question served, and the names of his superior *centurio* or *decurio*.

Archaeological contexts provide additional arguments: weapons occur repeatedly as grave goods in military burials of men, who probably were not Roman, but of barbarian origin. This custom can be observed increasingly from the second half of the 2nd century AD. It is interpreted as a result of the increasing recruitment of Germans into the Roman army, since the addition of weapons to the grave was often obligatory for warriors in German society. Another explanation might be the increase in social prestige of the soldiers' social standing since the time of Severus, resulting in veterans wearing soldierly garb in public and in death (Fischer 1990). Be that as it may, it is inconceivable that state-owned weapons and military equipment would have been placed in soldiers' graves as grave goods.

With the increasing threat to the border provinces through barbarian invasions from the second half of the 2nd century AD, and particularly in the 3rd century AD, there was an increase of military equipment – and not just potential hunting weapons – in private contexts, especially in *villae rusticae* (Fischer, 1990; Pfahl and Reuter 1996). This could have meant that veterans who settled as farmers after their *honesta missio* preferred to keep their weapons for reasons of self-protection, rather than selling them back to their unit as was common earlier.

Similar finds occur in the Batavian region, but are interpreted differently (Nicolay 2007). Here, Roman militaria and components from horse harness are found in considerable quantities in individual indigenous Germanic farms and village settlements from the early and middle Imperial period. J. Nicolay interprets this as the result of the particular Batavian custom of keeping and not selling their weapons and equipment back to the unit after their honourable discharge from the army (*honesta missio*). This is only possible if the weapons were their private property.

In the Late Roman period, the majority of weapons came not from private companies, but from state factories. There is no real tangible evidence, however, that the weapons of the Roman military were now in state ownership. On the contrary: while it is true that the number of ownership marks on weapons decreases sharply, that also applies to all written records of daily life in late antiquity. The few inscriptions on late Roman weapons – as on the cavalry helmet from Deurne in the Netherlands – name both units and individuals, presumably the owners.[89] Otherwise, stamps are only found on shield bosses and name units.[90]

By contrast, there is a large amount of archaeological evidence from Late Antiquity for private control over weapons and military equipment, which in the early and middle Imperial period was rather rare and regionally restricted:[91] the deposition of weapons in graves. This custom, originally Celtic and particularly barbaric German, appears in burials of Roman soldiers with the widespread incorporation of Germans into the Roman army during Late Antiquity. Of the numerous relevant grave goods, especially the military belt, *spathae*, spear- and arrowheads, axes, and shield fittings, I will just cite the examples from northern Gaul and Raetia.[92] Here too, it can safely be assumed that the Roman military administration would hardly have tolerated large quantities of state weapons being abused as grave goods.

Secondary use of weapons

In the ancient world, metal was precious. Therefore, one can presuppose intensive reuse of disused metal objects. Again and again, hoards of scrap or copper-alloy waste are found in camps, forts, or civil settlements. This should be seen as evidence of workshops where disused metal objects were collected for reforging or remelting, among them parts of weapons and military equipment. In addition, there are numerous examples where weapons or their components have been reworked for a secondary use in other purposes.

Military

J. Obmann has published a decorated front panel from a dagger sheath of the early Imperial period from Xanten (Obmann 1999c), which only revealed its secrets during an X-ray examination: The piece had been made from brass and was originally decorated with enamel inlay, which had been turned around and decorated with silver inlay in a secondary use. S. Fortner (Fortner 1995) was able to show that a piece had been re-fashioned for secondary use, based on a late 2nd to early 3rd century AD fitting with incised decoration from the fort of Gelduba/Krefeld-Gellep. Probably originating from the edge of a shield boss fitting with a rectangular base plate, the plate from Krefeld-Gellep was then used either as the ornamental fitting of a scabbard or a breast closure of a cuirass.

L. Borhy has published a 'sports breastplate', probably from Pannonia, which was purchased by the Hungarian National Museum in Budapest from art dealers.[93] It is a closure of sheet metal from regular body armour (scale armour or mail), which is now no longer attributed to 'sports armour'. Borhy rightly notes that the piece was re-fashioned for secondary use from a 'visor' of a cavalry helmet of Heddernheim/Worthing/Bodegraven type. It can therefore be dated to the second half of the 3rd century AD.

A bronze helmet of the Niederbieber type from the second half of the 2nd and the 3rd century AD in the Museo Archeologico in Florence[94] was updated in the Late Roman period and adapted to the crested helmet type common at this time.

Secondary civilian use

As in every period, elements of Roman weaponry and military equipment were also re-used for peaceful purposes in the civilian environment. M. Feugère has pointed to an iron Celtic helmet from St.-Jean-de-Castex-à-Vic-Fecensac (Gers) which, fitted with a handle, served as a bailer.[95] From Pompeii come bronze helmets of the Montefortino type from the 1st century BC, found used as a household funnel or scoop. One had had an iron spout riveted on to it. In this manner the helmet, mounted on a long wooden pole, was used to to empty a cesspit or the like in a second life.[96] Similarly, M. Feugère has published swords from France which were subsequently turned into wood saws.[97] The reworked handle with the upper blade portion of a broken *spatha* was used as a kitchen knife in a cellar deposit from around the middle of the 3rd century AD, in the *vicus* of the small fort of Regensburg-Grossprüfening.[98]

Indications of the private re-use of decorated components of armour are very common in the archaeological record, in particular, those of cavalry helmets or of sports armour serving in a secondary use as fittings and decoration. The fragment from the forehead tiara of a Theilenhofen-type cavalry helmet from the Guttmann Collection[99] was cut into a rectangle and provided with four mounting holes. It was probably used as a fitting for a casket or furniture. Relief-decorated fragments of a greave worked from bronze sheet from the area of the great cemetery of Regensburg (Fig. 69) probably served as a box fitting,[100] like the fragment of a sports armour component, probably a chamfron (Fig. 70), from Heddernheim.[101] This also applies to a Dioscurus which was cut out of the side of a chamfron and provided with rivet or nail holes (Fig. 71).

A small eagle of bronze plate, which had also been cut from a piece of sports armour, bore traces of lead-tin solder on the back. It probably served as the decorated plate of a disc brooch. The piece comes from a woman's grave of the period around AD 200 from the Niedertraubling district of Regensburg.[102]

However, there is also an example from the side of a chamfron simply scrapped in a military or private workshop without regard to the representation of an embossed eagle (Fig. 72). The emblematic bird was just cut

Figure 69 *Box fittings from recycled copper-alloy sheet of a greave from Regensburg (Fischer 2001b)*

into pieces with tin snips – whether to be used as patches or rolled up to be placed in a crucible for melting.

A locket plate from a Pompeii-type *gladius* sheath has been narrowed in secondary use and used as a ferrule, probably from a knife sheath (Fig. 73).

The durability of weapons

Finds that can be closely dated – either intrinsically or through their contexts or other evidence – raise the question how long the period of use of individual pieces of Roman weaponry actually was. It seems logical that

Figure 72 *Cut-up copper-alloy sheet metal of sports armour with representation of an eagle (provenance unknown, privately owned). Photo: A. Pangerl*

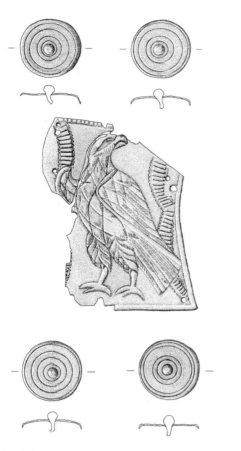

Figure 70 *Box fitting from recycled copper-alloy sheet from the sports armour from Frankfurt-Heddenheim (after Reis 2010)*

Figure 71 *Box fittings from recycled copper-alloy sheet of sports armour (provenance unknown, privately owned). Photo: A. Pangerl*

Figure 73 *Scabbard plate of copper-alloy from a Pompeii-type gladius in a secondary use as a knife sheath (?) (provenance unknown, privately owned). Photo: A. Pangerl*

Figure 74 *Dagger of the Künzing type with an iron scabbard and older emobossed, decorated copper-alloy sheets slid in, partly from a sword scabbard, partly probably from a box (provenance unknown). Recording: Musée Mougins*

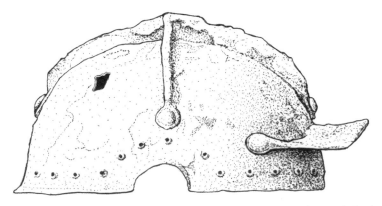

Figure 75 *Florence, Museo Archeologico. High Imperial Roman bronze helmet of the Niederbieber type fashioned into a late Roman helmet (Robinson 1975)*

durable and hefty pieces of weaponry, such as helmets, would – with 'normal use' without the application of external force – have had a long lifespan. In the case of the eponymous bronze helmet of the Montefortino type (Buggenum variant), a 'lifespan' of up to 120 years can be inferred. M. Junkelmann published a Flavian brass helmet of the Weisenau type from the Guttmann Collection, which possibly comes from the Balkans. Its four, or possibly five, successive ownership inscriptions attest to a long service life for this defensive weapon.[103] However, whether it was really used for a century, as Junkelmann states, seems rather doubtful, because this assumes that most of the owners of this helmet survived their 25 years of service.

Finds from gravel extraction in Xanten, which can in my opinion plausibly be associated with the Batavian uprising of the year AD 69, are dominated by helmets of the Hagenau type that should by then have been replaced by helmets of the Weisenau type according to established opinion.[104]

With a Künzing type dagger (provenance unknown, privately owned), the sheet iron scabbard was decorated in an unusual way: it was provided with embossed plates previously cut from non-ferrous metals, originally from the scabbard mouth locket plate of a *spatha* of the Pettau type (Fig. 74) or from a box.

An extreme example of the longevity of a piece of Roman weaponry is provided by a bronze helmet of the Weisenau type from the 2nd century AD of unknown provenance which is preserved in the Museo Archeologico in Florence. It was obviously 'updated' and worn in the Late Roman period after adapting it to the then-standard crested helmet type.[105] This was mainly done by cutting off the projecting neck guard from the bowl and providing it with holes for attaching the movable neck protection and wide cheek guards typical of the time (Fig. 75). The crosspiece on top of the bowl and the brow guard were retained. J. Oldenstein describes a perforated belt fitting from Kreuzweingarten in the Eifel, manufactured in the first half of the 3rd century AD, and then modified in the Late Roman period as a belt buckle (Oldenstein 1979).

The *gladius* displayed on the Claudian tombstone of Annaius from Bingerbrück (Ortisi 2009a) has a realistic representation of web-shaped metal ornaments within the frame scabbard fittings (with Claudian *catellae*). This proves that the sheath of this weapon was manufactured in the early to middle Augustan period and had been in use for at least 50 years.

And finally, the famous sword of Caesar should be noted in this context: this had been stored at the temple of Mars in Cologne and subsequently played a role during the proclamation of the usurper Vitellius in the year AD 68.[106] If it was truly authentic, this weapon would then have been over 120 years old!

4. Find contexts of Roman weapons and equipment parts

All currently known Roman arms and military equipment components have come to us as archaeological finds or finds from water. Not one ancient piece has survived to this day above ground. In common with all archaeological finds from known contexts, Roman militaria have to undergo intense source criticism. This boils down to the simple question: why did this piece survive at all, and why was it found? For the 'normal' fate of Roman arms and military equipment would indeed have been to disappear without a trace.

Metal components disappeared through recycling: bronze, brass, and silver were melted down, iron reforged. The military or civilian secondary use already described usually only formed an interlude on the way. Wooden parts were burned or rotted away, just like leather and textiles. Only the bone components of weapons would have survived the times under normal circumstances, if they were not cut up or otherwise used.

Source criticism in Roman arms and military equipment therefore revolves around the following issues: when, how, and why was a weapon lost at all so that it could pass into the archaeological record? Only when these issues have been diligently resolved can one also try to identify the original context of pieces whose provenance is unknown, for example, from their condition, patina, or other evidence. There are basically two main, differing reasons for preserving Roman arms and military equipment: accidental loss and deliberate deposition.

Accidental loss occurs when metal components of arrows, catapult bolts, javelins or other projectiles such as slingshots are found on a battlefield or around a defended location. These were shot, but then normally collected for reuse. They are only accessible to present-day archaeologists, if they were concealed in the ground because, for example, their wooden shafts had broken off. In battles in captured forts or in street fighting within civilian settlements, larger pieces of weaponry, such as helmets or swords, could be lost, especially when buildings were already burning. This also applies in a clash on a body of water or in a sea battle or shipwreck for instance, when weapons of all kinds sank in a river, a lake, or the sea.

Militaria made of metal or fragments of them only arrived in landfill if they were overlooked. Recent studies of the 'waste behaviour' of the Roman military have shown that rubbish dumps at Roman camps and forts typically contain almost exclusively ceramics, bone, wood, leather, and a few glass fragments.[107] So small-sized metal objects, such as coins, brooches, or militaria in camps, forts, and other settlements usually ended up in the ground unintentionally. Intentionally buried hoards also belong in this category, as the original plan had of course been their recovery, after the danger leading to the deposition had passed.

Grave goods or votive deposits on the other hand represent the intentional 'loss' of Roman arms and military equipment, in which one yielded ownership of the items 'for eternity', entrusting them to the gods.

Finds from camps, forts and other military sites

Many military items, usually small-sized fragments of metal or bone, are found during excavations in abandoned or destroyed Roman legionary bases or auxiliary forts. There are two types of deposits, in which the proportion of larger finds, which would have been reusable in principle, is particularly high compared to other periods. On the one hand, there are the finds in the camps of the early Augustan period from the military occupation of the Rhineland and the area between the Rhine and Elbe up to the end of the first decade AD. Examples are Nijmegen, Oberaden, or Dangstetten, where a surprising number of metal objects were found without any traces of violent destruction of the camps. This seems to result from the fact that, in a time of uncertainty shortly after the occupation, camps often had to be abandoned quickly, leaving material that under normal circumstances would have been kept for recycling.

On the other hand, large numbers of military objects come from the burnt remains of destroyed camps and forts, where metal finds occur in much larger quantities than in camps that were cleared in a planned manner. An example is the camp of Cáceres el Viejo in the Estremadura region of central Spain, which was violently destroyed during the war against Sertorius in 80 BC (Ulbert 1984). The Augustan camp of Haltern (Aliso?) also met a violent end in the year AD 9, resulting in a correspondingly high amount of metal finds of all kinds, including many military items (Harnecker 1997; Müller 2002). In Britain, burnt layers from the Boudican uprising in the year AD 61 produced corresponding material. In a number of camps and forts that ended in fire and destruction during the civil wars and rebellions after Nero's death in the years AD 68/70, unusually high numbers of well-preserved Roman arms and pieces of military equipment were found. One need only think of Vetera I, Hofheim, Rheingönnheim, or Aislingen and Burghöfe. Among later finds, the Marcomannic Wars, which left corresponding amounts of militaria in destroyed camps and forts (e.g. Regensburg Kumpfmühl, Iža, and Musov), stand out.

Most of the relevant material entered the ground through the crises of the 3rd century AD. Locations such as Niederbieber, the Saalburg, Osterburken, Weißenburg, Pfünz, Regensburg, Straubing, and Künzing are just some examples. For the numerous camps that met a violent end in the East during the Persian Wars of the 3rd century, Dura-Europos with its military garrison can be named as an example, captured in AD 255/56 (James 2004 and 2005).

The example of an excavation in the western area of the fleet base at Köln-Alteburg, where two massive Trajanic burnt layers were found, containing numerous finds, including weapons, however, cautions against hasty historical interpretation of such traces of destruction (Fischer 2005): these discoveries are neither repeated at any other site of the camp, nor is there any indication of warlike episodes at this time and in this region. The burnt layers were simply caused by a local accidental fire.

Finds from civilian settlements

There are also always militaria from the excavation of civilian settlements – especially in the border provinces (Bishop 1991). The reasons are manifold: a small number of pieces may be connected to travelling soldiers or veterans living in these settlements. We also have to reckon with the possibility of workshops in these settlements, where military artefacts were manufactured or repaired (Deschler-Erb 1999). Especially during the early phases of the occupation, soldiers or *veterani sub vexillo* may have lived in and protected civilian settlements, as is thought for the early Roman Iron Age hillfort on the Auerberg in Schongau and early Imperial Kempten/Cambodunum (both in Raetia).[108] From Auerberg, several daggers, belt components and other militaria are known. But of particular interest are the remains of clay *cire perdue* moulds for the production of massive bronze clamping rings for catapults that have either been manufactured or repaired on the mountain. Since at this time, artillery was only part of the armament of legions, the discovery raises some questions, which remain enigmatic at present.[109] There are early military items from Kempten, including legionary weaponry, such as the iron spindle-shaped shield boss of a *scutum*.[110]

As in military settlements, militaria also occur in civilian settlements when these have been taken by force, often including fierce street fighting. Such finds and find concentrations have been reported from the Republican period onwards, for example in Spain: here, weapons were found as relics of battles in Gracurris/Alfaro (Iriarte *et al.* 1997) or Osuna (Sievers 1997). A wealth of militaria that entered the archaeological record under these dramatic circumstances occurs in settlements in the German provinces wherever battles raged in the 3rd century AD, be it through civil wars or barbarian invasions: in colony towns like Xanten/Colonia Ulpia Traiana[111] and Augst/Augusta Raurica[112] or in *vici* such as Heddernheim/Nida.[113]

Even rural settlements sometimes provide military objects in regional concentrations: it is clear that an increase of militaria in *villae rusticae* from the Limes hinterland in Upper Germany and Raetia during the High Empire is not only due to potential hunting weapons (Fischer, 1990; Stake and Reuter 1996). This could mean that veterans who settled as farmers after their *honesta missio* preferred to keep their weapons for reasons of self-protection, rather than selling them back to the unit as usual. The increasing vulnerability of the border provinces to barbarian invasions from the second half of the 2nd century AD and particularly in the 3rd century AD may serve as a plausible reason for this development.

Another, very special situation exists for the Batavian region (Nicolay 2007). Here, Roman militaria and components from harness are found in considerable quantities on individual farms and in village settlements of indigenous German type from the Early and High Imperial period. J. Nicolay, as others had done before him, explains this as a particular custom of the Batavians, who did not sell their weapons and equipment back to a unit after the *honesta missio*, but took them home to the village from which once, as young recruits, they had left to serve with the Batavian troops of the Roman army. As mentioned earlier, this discovery strengthens the position of those who advocate privately owned Roman armament and military equipment.

Finds from water

There are basically two explanations for the finds of Roman arms and military equipment from water: through accidental loss in battle, a shipwreck, or simply in a personal accident. Losses in combat include those in the Po in Cremona (Fischer 2004) or in the Rhine at Xanten (Schalles and Schreiter 1993). Unintentional losses are, for example, more likely for river finds from the Rhine near Mainz: there, Early Imperial military equipment apparently came from an old ferry landing, because the finds cease when the first permanent bridge across the Rhine was built in the Flavian period.[114] On the other hand, as is common for finds from prehistoric periods, they might be attributable to ritual reasons, *i.e.* votive offerings in water (Torbrügge 1972; Pauli 1987). For the Roman period, this is still a matter for discussion.[115]

Grave finds

In the early Imperial period and up to the 3rd century AD, cremation prevailed among the Romans, at least in Britain and in the provinces of the Rhine and Danube. Offerings of weapons were not common. Only Celts and Germans were given weapons and military equipment, such as swords, belt fittings, shield fittings, and spearheads, as grave goods in both burials and cremations (van Doorselaer 1963/64). Again and again, the custom of ritually destroying weapons, such as swords and spearheads, by bending and breaking them before they reached the grave can be observed. In the light of these burial customs, the exceptional finds of weapon graves are more noticeable when they occur in the Roman provinces and require an explanation. They most frequently occur among the Treveri (see below) or in Thrace, often represented by cavalry or face-mask helmets only.[116] The survival of older regional burial customs can probably explain this: customs adhered to by the local mounted nobility even when they served in the Roman cavalry. However, human remains found with weapons in Roman archaeological contexts should not always be regarded as regular burials. A human skeleton with a *gladius* and all the fittings of a belt set that came to light near the fort of Rheingönheim (Fig. 110; 239.3), was probably a victim of the Batavian revolt, who came to be buried with his weapons by accident during the uprising. This is also likely for a human skeleton with a ring-pommel sword buried in the collapse of a burning house in the late 2nd century AD in Geneva.[117] Even the skeleton of the legendary standard bearer of Niederbieber, found along with the eponymous helmet (Fig. 183) and the metal components of a *signum*, was not deposited as a regular burial in a grave (Fig. 354). Rather, the man died in the destruction of the fort in AD 259/60 and was accidentally covered by debris. And of course this is also true for the numerous Persian and Roman victims of the collapse of the mine at Tower 19 in Dura-Europos, who were buried together with weapons during the siege of the year AD 255/56.[118]

Regular cremations with weapons from the early Imperial period are mainly known from the Gallic, and especially the Treveran, area (see above). Although the tombs of Treveran nobles at Göblingen-Nospelt in Luxembourg belong to the Augustan period, their armament is still purely in the Celtic-Treveran tradition.[119] This also appears to apply for the weapons grave at Thür near Mayen (von Berg 2006). The rich weaponry of mail, *gladius*, and face-mask helmet, together with early imperial coin dies, in the cremation from Chassenard in Gaul (Beck and Chew 1991) is difficult to explain for the lack of a parallel.

In contrast, the weapons burials found in the cemetery of a rich villa at Wehringen (south of Augsburg in Raetia), which can be dated to the first half of the 2nd century AD, point towards Germanic men, but so far they are isolated finds both in this period and for this region.[120] A weapons grave at Lyon/Lugdunum can be compared to contemporary burials in the Danubian region, which are usually explained with the increased amount of Germanic men in the Roman army (Wuilleumier 1952). One of the oldest Late Roman weapons graves, dating to the period around AD 300, comes from Cologne (Martin-Kilcher 1993; Fig. 76). In contrast, weapon graves from Thrace[121] or Syria[122] should probably be attributed to local traditions instead.

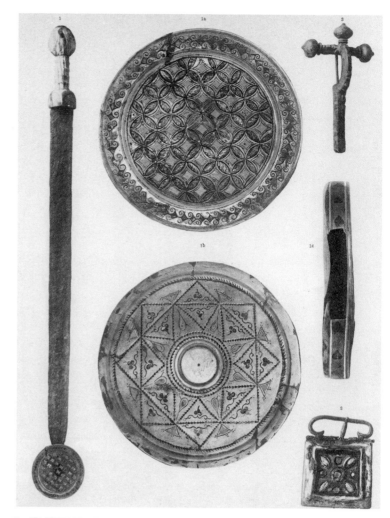

Figure 76 *Grave find from Cologne with belt buckle, spatha with box chape, and crossbow brooch (after Lindenschmit)*

Hoards

Hoards consist of closed finds, which are often in outstanding condition and preserve specific groups of material – mostly made of metal – that are found much less frequently in settlements and burials and then encountered only in fragments. In addition to silver and bronze vessels, kitchen utensils, tools and equipment, religious statuettes, jewelry and other valuable goods, these often include weapons and military equipment, especially in the vicinity of forts and camps. Hoards are collections of mostly still usable objects, deliberately hidden, mainly by burial in the ground, to protect them from robbers or enemies in case of war. Those who had hidden such a hoard intended to retrieve it when the danger was past. If this was not the case and the hoard remained in the ground, it means that the owner had been killed or was prevented for other reasons from recovering their property. Thus hoards always mark uncertain times.

Hoards can be roughly divided into three groups and are mostly distinguished by their reasons for concealment:[123]

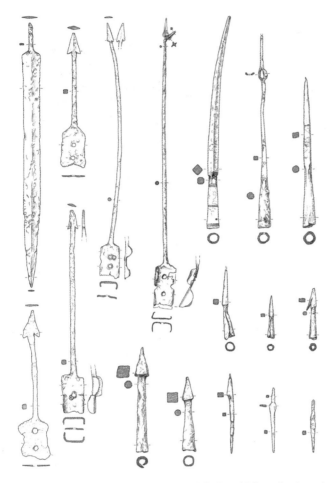

Figure 77 *Selected finds (sword, pila, missile heads) from the hoard from Grad Šmihel/Slovenia (after Horvat 1997)*

Hoards may consist of objects that were hidden by the owner himself, in plenty of time, before an imminent danger. Ernst Künzl, following A. Kaufmann-Heiniman, has called these 'anxiety or panic hoards' (Künzl 2009). They are marked through the collection of items that belong together (temple treasures, household or kitchen inventories, jewelry ensembles, tools and equipment hoards) and are largely undamaged. In those rare cases, in which the find circumstances are known, it could be proven that they were carefully packed, for example in a bronze cauldron or a wooden box before being buried.

In addition, ancient finds complexes occur which have been gathered and hidden after a disaster by looters and metal collectors. In the rare cases where the find circumstances are clear, they were only hastily buried in shallow pits or in ruins. These finds are sometimes very mixed. Alongside undamaged objects they may contain scrap metal, which has often previously been subjected to fire. On the German frontier, marauding tribesmen have been blamed for this, collecting coveted scrap metal after the successful conquest of a fort or a settlement, but not wanting to be burdened with it when venturing further

into the interior of the Empire. Rather, they planned on salvaging these items upon returning, but then often did not come back.

In addition to these hoards with recognizable reasons for concealment, there is a whole range of hoards that cannot be put into any category because of incomplete knowledge about their exact find circumstances. In some cases, assemblages, which were accidentally buried during a disaster (an earthquake or a fire) are often barely distinguishable from an intentionally hidden hoard. The earliest known hoard with Roman arms comes from Slovenia. It is a collection of projectile points, *pila*, swords, caltrops, tools and (now lost) a helmet (probably a variant of the Montefortino type), which was discovered in the hillfort of Grad at Šmihel (Fig. 77). The find dates from the end of the 3rd century to the first half of the 2nd century BC. It is unclear who buried it and for what reason, but it is evidently the remains of a battle that was probably to do with the security of the newly established Roman colony of Aquileia.[124]

Historical references can frequently be used in discussing the causes for the concealment of such hoards. With the right interpretation, hoard events are often used like a historical source in research: in the Roman period, where the historical environment is known in broad terms at least, hoards that can be interpreted as anxiety hoards often allow important conclusions on military events that affected one place or a larger region. This is especially the case when clustered hoards occur in a definable spatial and temporal unit, *i.e.* there is a hoard horizon. For example, in the Upper German-Raetian Limes area and its hinterland, a large number of hoards were found, many of which had Roman weapons. These are obviously connected to the Germanic invasions of the 3rd century AD. Well-known examples of such hoards are the hoards from Straubing (Fig. 78, 79) and Künzing (Fig. 80).

When analysing this hoard horizon, it turned out that a Germanic invasion of Raetia around AD 254 played an important role here. It had completely surprised the Roman garrisons along the Limes, which had been weakened by Valerian I through the removal of a significant portion of the Roman frontier troops in AD 253 for his usurpation and then for his Persian campaign. As a result of this incident in the year AD 254, the Raetian Limes possibly collapsed completely and permanently.[125]

However, there are hoards from other provinces and other periods. A few examples may be cited: silver belt fittings from the late Flavian period come from the Tekije treasure trove in Serbia (Mano Zisi 1957). From Britain we know of a number of highly important hoards, such as the discovery of the Corbridge Hoard with its components of segmental cuirasses (Allason-Jones and Bishop 1988). This collection of finds was interpreted as a box of scrap metal,

Figure 78 *Mask helmets and greaves from the Straubing hoard. Photo: Gäubodenmuseum Straubing*

Figure 80 *Daggers from the large iron hoard in the principia of the fort at Künzing. Photo: M. Eberlein*

Figure 79 *Chamfrons from the Straubing hoard. Photo: Gäubodenmuseum Straubing*

which was carefully packed and probably buried during the sudden departure of the fort garrison. Perhaps the numerous well-preserved military items from the Scottish fort of Newstead should be seen in a similar light: again, this was scrap or excess material from a *fabrica* buried before a sudden withdrawal, which was not recovered for reasons that will probably never be known.[126] A collection of finds of Roman weapons, consisting of an iron infantry helmet, an iron and bronze face mask of a sports helmet, fragments of bronze greaves, including knee plates, remains of bronze scale armour and iron mail, is said to come from a cave near Hebron in Israel. It is associated with the Jewish War of Hadrian (AD 132–5). Unfortunately, we only know the circumstances of the find from unverifiable information from the antiquities trade and not from reputable documentation.[127]

Battlefield and siege finds

In recent years, the number of battlefields and sites of local skirmishes identified archaeologically has increased significantly, which is largely due to the use of the metal detector.[128] There is now so much evidence from all periods that 'battlefield archaeology' has begun to be a discipline in its own right (Meller 2009). Its importance lies in the fact that when traces of battles and minor skirmishes are brought together with historically attested events in safe conjunction – with certain restrictions – historical 'snapshots' remain in the ground which can sometimes be dated to within just a few months.

Apart from all the other aspects, this precise dating is very important for fixing the chronology of militaria and other archaeological material. However, it is important to get away from the notion that finds on battlefields always provide the correct conclusions about the course of the fighting on them. Rather, research has shown that, subsequent to the battle, many changes took place on the battlefield which greatly influence the impression given by the finds. Thus, as an example, looting by victorious opponents significantly alters the density and distribution of weapons finds in the area. The archaeological picture of a battlefield is therefore heavily dependent on whether the Roman army were claiming victory there or had suffered a defeat.

At Ephyra in Epirus, a Macedonian fortress was stormed by Roman troops in the context of the Battle of Pydna (168 BC) and set on fire. In this action, both the catapults of the defenders and the *pila* of the attackers remained in the burnt debris. In the locality of Andagerta in the northern Spanish region of Cantabria, which was discovered and explored by metal detector, it appears to be still unclear whether the remains are of a battle in open terrain or of a besieged strong point.[129]

At the site where the famous Augustan dagger was found on Döttenbichel in Oberammergau (Fig. 277), turned up by the foot of an ox in the 19th century, W. Zanier and others have now unearthed traces of a battle apparently involving the Romans and indigenous Raetians by prospecting with metal detectors and by excavation. It has been convincingly argued to be associated with the Alpine campaign of 15 BC. The finds include, among other things, another dagger and catapult bolts, including those with the stamp of the 19th Legion (Fig. 81), through to numerous trilobate arrowheads that had been shot by oriental archers, and large numbers of iron hobnails (Zanier 1994 and 1995).

The excavator is of the opinion that the weapons found at the Döttenbichel should not be seen as direct evidence of a battle at the site, but were retrieved from a remote battlefield and deposited as offerings on the striking mountain ridge of the Döttenbichel where, apparently next to a settlement, there may have been a sacrificial site of the pre-Roman Raetian Fritzens-Sanzeno culture. However, this interpretation is now no longer plausible, bearing in mind the finds known from the undoubted battlefield site at Harzhorn (see below). While this battlefield dated to the 3rd century AD, almost the same range of military material was found there as at the approximately 250 years older Döttenbichel:

Figure 81 *Munich, Archäologische Staatsslg. Catapult bolt with the stamp of the 19th Legion from Döttenbichel at Oberammergau. Photo: M. Eberlein*

catapult bolts, numerous trilobate arrowheads shot by oriental archers, and large amounts of iron hobnails. Those elements of military equipment that were either very small, or – in the case of projectile points – had been buried and hidden in the ground were missed at both sites, evading retrieval by the victorious Romans, who would otherwise certainly have carefully recovered the tools and equipment of the dead and wounded.

Finds from the gorge of Crap-Ses in the Swiss canton of Graubünden (Figs 82, 83) also belong to the Alpine campaign of 15 BC (Rageth 2010; Rageth and Zanier 2010). Late Republican coins and Roman (projectile points, slingshot, shoe nails, tent pegs, and engineering equipment) and Celtic (sword components, a Raetian Hellebard axe) militaria were found with the help of metal detectors. It seems that here Roman troops fought for the passage through the canyon which was being blocked by locals.

However, a fundamentally different spectrum of finds comes from the battlefield of the year AD 9 at Kalkriese. This is certainly connected to the fact that this place marked a crushing defeat for the Romans, whereas the Döttenbichel and Harzhorn were victorious battles for Rome. In Kalkriese, with only a few projectile points and lead slingshot, completely different finds groups dominate which are also distributed spatially very differently around the battlefield: at one point, a little away from where the concentrations of finds show the fight to have been happening, valuables were found (a purse, a scabbard with silver mounts) obviously hidden in desperation by the owners. At the focal point of the battle, beneath the collapsed German turf ramapart, large metal objects (helmet mask, *dolabra* etc) have survived that would otherwise have been taken by the victors. Again and again concentrations of small-sized shield fittings or smaller parts of personal equipment (armour,

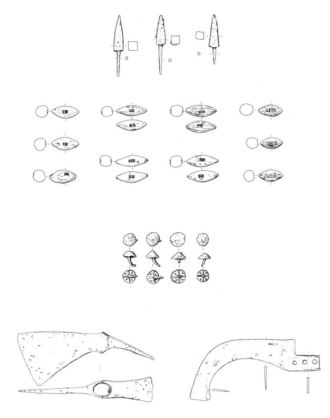

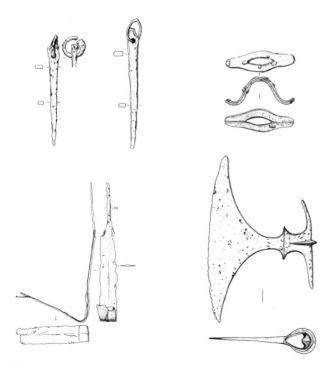

Figure 82 *Crap-Ses-Schlucht/Graubünden. Augustan finds (1 pilum head; 2 slingshot; 3 hobnail; 4–5 engineering tools) from the battlefield of the Alpine campaign 15 BC (after Rageth 2010)*

Figure 83 *Crap-Ses-Schlucht/Graubünden. Roman (6 tent pegs) and Raetian (7–8 sword parts; 9 halberd). Finds from the battlefield of the Alpine campaign 15 BC (according Rageth 2010)*

belt) have been found, which had been overlooked in the ruthless plundering to obtain reusable metal. Because the victorious Germans did not know how to use Roman shields or segmental cuirasses, they were cut up and scrapped on the battlefield (see Varusschlacht 2009; Rost and Wilbers-Rost 2012).

At the southern English hillfort of Maiden Castle, caught up in the Claudian invasion of AD 43, the excavators found the remains of the victims of the Romans: skeletons with traces of the impact of Roman weapons, including head injuries from sword blows and an artillery bolt in a spine.[130]

The fort of Gelduba/Krefeld-Gellep in Lower Germany provides the remains of not one, but two distinct battles: the first from the civil war of the year AD 68, the other from the Frankish invasions of the 3rd century AD. Here, ever better understood evidence of the battle of the year 68 during the Batavian revolt has now been revealed, which can be compared with a fairly detailed description by Tacitus.[131]

At Kalefeld (district Northeim), near the Harzhorn in Lower Saxony, large numbers of catapult bolts, trilobate arrowheads shot by oriental archers, as well as large amounts of iron hobnails have been found. There were also other Roman finds, such as the iron components of carts and coins. These provided a numismatic *terminus post quem* for the reign of Alexander Severus (AD 222–35). The other discoveries do not contradict this dating (Geschwinde *et al.* 2009; Fischer 2013B; Fischer 2013D; Fischer and Moosbauer 2013; Pöppelmann *et al.* 2013). Here, a raid has obviously taken place during a Roman military campaign, which led to an ambush in a defile and a counterattack by the Romans using archers and artillery. The battle ended in victory for the Romans. Researchers agree that the fighting can be placed into the historical context of the German campaign of Maximinus Thrax in AD 235. Recently, the battlefield of Abritus in Bulgaria, where the Goths under their king Kniva destroyed a Roman army in the year AD 251, has been discovered through finds. Both Emperor Trajan Decius (AD 249–51) and his son and heir Herennius Etruscus were killed in this battle (Rodoslava *et al.* 2011; Bursche 2013).

Battles and skirmishes which took place during sieges have to be valued differently. Here, the traces of often very long-term occupation by Roman troops at a site are mixed with short-term find deposition during the conquest of the besieged place. Only specific, clearly definable and datable contexts, like the siege tunnel under Tower 19 at Dura-Europos, datable to the years AD 255/56, or the traces of the short-term siege of Alesia, can really provide precisely datable archaeological material.[132] The situation is different in Numantia, where a prolonged siege took place, leaving a range of differently dated material at the various camps (Luik 2002 and 2009).

Dedications

Again and again, there is literary, epigraphic, and archaeological evidence for the dedication of weapons in sanctuaries.[133] We know from Tacitus, for example, that a sword of Caesar was kept in the temple of Mars at Cologne.[134]

Less common are situations where votive offerings of weapons testified in literature are also archaeologically documented. One example is that of Telamon in northern Italy: this archaeological site simultaneously combines a historically attested battlefield with a historically attested sanctuary. In pits near the sanctuary, numerous *pilum* heads were found that may date back to the Battle of Telamon of the year 225 BC when the Romans successfully repelled a Celtic invasion (Luik 2000). Polybius explicitly mentions the crucial role of *pila* in the victory of the Romans in the battle (*Hist.* 2.30.1).

On the other hand, archaeologically proven weapons dedications often occur where written reports provide no information, such as in Mainz (Klein 1999). From a small shrine of the 3rd century AD, on the vineyard at Eining in Bavaria, come the fittings of an oval shield, in addition to larger parts of a segmental cuirass that were most likely deposited here as a votive offering.[135] Dedications of weapons were also apparently normal in certain sanctuaries on the Lower Rhine: examples are the temple of Empel in the Netherlands, which is supposed to have been dedicated to Hercules Magusanus,[136] and the sanctuary of the Germanic goddess of war Vagdavercustis at Kalkar on the Lower Rhine.[137] Unique among weapons dedications is the occurrence of a bronze washer from torsion artillery in the sacred spring of Aquae Sulis (Bath) in southern England.[138]

Finds from Germanic sacrificial bogs

The Roman militaria from the Germanic sacrificial bogs can only be touched upon briefly here. These very different sacrificial sites are indeed far beyond the Roman Empire and its cultural influence in North German and southern Scandinavian Barbaricum, but are nonetheless of the utmost importance for the study of Roman arms because they contain large quantities of Roman military artefacts, including more Roman sword blades than have ever been found in the whole of the Roman Empire. According to recent research, these finds were not the result of individual finds deposited continuously over long periods, but rather the equipment of defeated Germanic armies, which were submerged in the bog by the victors in a short-term sacrifice ritual. Among these weapons are numerous swords which are more likely to have been the result of trade, but also captured Roman militaria – summarized in the Copenhagen exhibition catalogue *Sieg und Triumpf* in 2003. The sacrificial moors of Ejsbøl,[139] Illerup Ådal,[140] Nydam,[141] Thorberg,[142] and Vimose can be named here as examples for this category.[143]

5.   Legionary or auxiliary equipment?

It has long been discussed among researchers, whether and how it is possible to determine a difference in the arming and equipping of legionary and auxiliary troops. In theory there should be a difference, as the ancient sources repeatedly mention the different manners of fighting of the two types of troops, which should in some way be reflected in armament and equipment. The reality is different: the archaeological differentiation of legionary and auxiliary infantry through their traditional equipment inevitably brings with it fairly substantial and seemingly unsolvable problems. Auxiliary troops certainly wore their traditional weapons in the late Republic and early Empire and that fact distinguished them from the Roman legionary troops (Waurick 1994) – such as Caesar's Gallic and Germanic auxiliaries in the Gallic Wars (Czarnecka 1997). L. Pernet has recently tried to summarize and describe the armament and equipment of Gallo-Celtic auxiliaries of the late Republic (Pernet 2010). However, by the early Imperial period, they are already barely distinguishable, since the auxiliary infantry had equipped itself with Roman weaponry.

Representations of irregular auxiliaries, such as Germanic tribes allied with the Romans on Trajan's Column, for example, should be treated with the greatest suspicion. These are shown with bare torsos and fighting mainly with wooden clubs, a barbarian topos that indeed probably exists to meet urban Roman preconceptions and prejudices, but hardly represents reality.[144] The stereotypical depictions of lightly armed Moorish cavalry with a kind of dreadlock hairstyle (Fig. 84) shown there are also hardly the height of realism: apparently, it was more important for the artists to show these riders without a helmet and armour, in order to characterize them clearly as Moors on the basis of their exotic hairstyle, than to represent them realistically with their protective armament.

As for the distinction between the weapons and equipment of the cavalry and infantry in legions or auxiliary units, on the other hand, things are relatively simple: first, cavalry are marked out in principle from infantry by their differing weapons. Secondly, most of the Roman cavalry in the Early and High Imperial period were auxiliary troops, so that the few legionary cavalry are statistically negligible.

As for the differences between legionary and auxiliary infantrymen, one must first indicate the rather significant discrepancy between the pictorial tradition and historical reality. On Trajan's Column, there is a clear distinction between the legionary and the regular auxiliary infantry in two ways: in body armour and shields. Throughout, legionaries wear the segmental cuirass (Fig. 85), but auxiliary infantrymen a short mail shirt, the bottom hem of which has triangular teeth or semicircular flaps (Fig. 86). The legionaries carry the rectangular shield, which is almost

Figure 84 *Trajan's Column, Numidian cavalry (after Bartoli and Dzur 1941)*

Figure 85 *Trajan's Column, legionaries with segmental cuirasses and rectangular shields (after Bartoli and Dzur 1941)*

always decorated with the obligatory thunderbolts. The auxiliary soldiers, however, both infantry and cavalry, have oval shields with various different decorations: there are vine motifs, wreaths, eagles, rosettes, stars, crescents, and so on. The other German, African, or Sarmatian allies of the Romans on Trajan's Column are also recognizable through their characteristic hairstyles, clothing, and armament. For legionary troops and auxiliary infantry, the mandatory dagger is missing.

The reality, as it appears from the material found in contemporary contexts from legionary bases and auxiliary forts, does not permit such a clear distinction yet: all types of cuirasses come from all types of camps and forts, both those with legionary garrisons and auxiliary forts. Short mail shirts with the lower edges finished with triangular teeth or semicircular lobes have not yet been found. The poor state of preservation and the small-sized fragmentation with which the remains of mail armour are usually found say little about whether it ever has been used. However, in the metopes on the contemporary victory monument at Adamclisi things already look quite different: legionary soldiers never wear segmental cuirasses here, but only scale and mail armour (Fig. 87).

The clear distinction in the images on Trajan's Column, where the curved, rectangular shield is typical of legions, while other shield forms are associated with the auxiliaries,

Figure 86 *Trajan's Column, auxiliary soldiers (after Bartoli and Dzur 1941)*

hardly reflects historical reality either. Rather, this is more likely to be seen as a trick used by the designing sculptor to clearly differentiate between citizen troops and auxiliaries. Recent studies by A. Nabbefeld and A. Busch show that the apparently safe hypothesis of legionary soldiers exclusively carrying the rectangular shield is on decidedly shaky ground in reality (Nabbefeld 2009; Busch 2009).

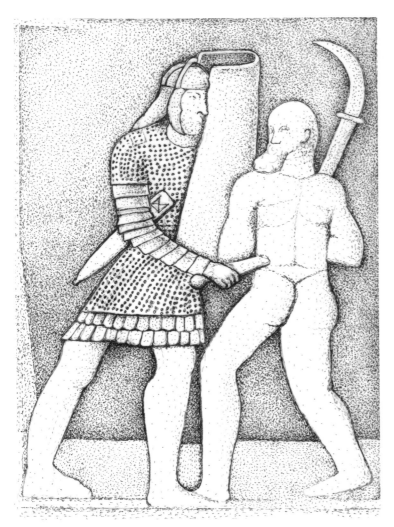

Figure 87 *Metope from the victory monument of Adamclisi. Fight between a legionary (left) and a Dacian armed with a falx (right). Drawing: A. Smadi, Archaeological Institute of the University of Cologne*

Figure 88 *Reconstructed legionary from the time around AD 100 with a Weisenau-type helmet, segmental cuirass, rectangular shield, Pompeii-type gladius, and pilum. Photo: C. Miks*

The *pilum* and the rectangular *scutum* appear to have been largely reserved for the legions in the early and middle imperial period even from the archaeological evidence (Fig. 88). However, the *cohortes scutati* and *cohortes voluntariorum*[145] were also fighting with a *scutum*! No other infantry weapons can be clearly attributed by us today, unless they have ownership inscriptions on them. It is instead becoming more and more apparent from the known material, that helmets, cuirasses, daggers, and swords of the same types were worn by both legionary and auxiliary infantry.

Another possibility, not currently provable from the archaeological evidence, would be that units were distinguishable from each other through the colour and decoration on clothing, such as the tunic and cloak. A lot is certainly to be expected in the near future from the archaeological textile research studies currently in progress, which is advancing the research on the dress of the Roman soldier.[146]

For now, all we know is that the individual legions were clearly distinguished by their shields, probably by colour, unit-specific inscriptions, or symbols. Thus Tacitus reported, in the context of the civil war after Nero's death and the Second Battle of Cremona of 24/25th October of the year AD 69, how a large and dangerous artillery piece on the side of the troops of Vitellius was incapacitated by a daring commando raid by Flavian legionary soldiers (Tac. *Hist.* 3.22.2). The soldiers of this assault force disguised themselves by taking the shields of fallen foes and thus deceiving the enemy. From this we can deduce two things: shields clearly indicated the membership of a particular force by colour, decor, or inscriptions. However, in their other equipment, the soldiers must not have been recognizable – at least at first glance – as members of a particular unit.

The role the shields played in the identification of military units, even for the individual soldier, is confirmed by Vegetius. He writes (in 2.18) that identity tags (*digmata*) of the units and the names of the soldiers were written on the front of their shields. Unfortunately, it is unknown if Early and High Imperial shields are meant, or the traditional shield blazons of Late Antiquity as depicted in the *Notitia Dignitatum*. However, Cassius Dio reports for the year AD 89 that the commander Julianus in the Dacian War introduced the custom of recording the name of the shield carrier and his centurion on the shields.[147]

A possible, but hardly provable, hypothesis is that, among legionary troops, the three battle lines – *hastati* at the front, *principes* in the middle, and the *triarii* in the rear line – each carried different types of shield for protection. An admittedly not very viable indication would be the explanations of Vegetius that *hastati* and *triarii* had a special type of armament.[148] It is true that the period for which that information was provided is virtually impossible to ascertain; the reference to the *semispatha* would perhaps indicate the 3rd and 4th centuries AD.[149]

This begs the question of the extent to which complete units or individual armies were ever fitted out in an identical manner or whether they wore any kind of homogeneous uniform. On Trajan's Column, this is clearly the case, but its problems as an accurate source have already been mentioned several times. Otherwise, as far as original finds are concerned, the archaeological evidence is largely unhelpful. Thus, for example, the question of whether complete units had the same helmet is unclear. Here there is only the multiple find of five identical helmets, apparently derived from the same manufacturer, from the Po at Cremona, probably all belonging to the equipment of marines from Misenum established under Nero in AD 68 as the *legio Classica*. Renamed under Galba to *legio I Adiutrix*, they participated in the First Battle of Cremona, where, as a result of their defeat, some of their equipment entered the river (Fischer 2004). From this we can also conclude that it was necessary to re-equip the marines 'promoted' to legionary soldiers in the emergency conditions of the year AD 68. It seems that they received new helmets, for example, of types characteristic for the legions of that time and were not allowed to continue wearing their old fleet pseudo-Attic helmets.[150]

Praetorians

There are hardly any original discoveries of weapons for the equipment of the Praetorians. An exception is

Figure 89 *Copper-alloy fitting from a belt with inlaid silver inscription of the Praetorian C. Iulius Gratus, soldier of the 5th Praetorian cohort (provenance unknown, privately owned). Photo: A. Pangerl*

the fitting of an Early Imperial belt, privately owned (Fig. 89). The piece, a simple, rectangular, bronze fitting with a silver-inlaid ownership (or votive?) inscription mentions a Praetorian, C. Iulius Gratus, soldier of the 5th Praetorian cohort as owner (or donor). The representational evidence for the Praetorians shows them, when represented in battle equipment, as mainly using the same weapons as those of contemporary legionary soldiers, for example, the Pompeii-type *gladius* and *pugio* including belts (Fig. 90) on the tombstone of Caius Ottiedius Attianus from Assisi[151] or the *pila* on the Cancelleria reliefs.[152] Exceptions are the ancient oval shields (Fig. 91). But there are also representations that show Praetorians in a kind of parade gear with muscle cuirasses, oval shields, and Attic helmets with plumes: for example, on the Great Trajanic Frieze battle scene or the Praetorian relief in the Louvre, which most likely comes from the former.[153] However, we do not have any finds of these Praetorian parade weapons.

In pictorial representations of shields, helmets, and insignia of the Praetorians, scorpions are repeatedly shown, so it can probably be assumed that this was the official emblem of the Praetorian units. In this context, it is worth noting the fact that Scorpio was the star sign of Tiberius Caesar, responsible for building the Praetorian Camp in Rome.[154] Scorpions can be found on weapons on several occasions on the Great Trajanic Frieze, which is partly reused in the Arch of Constantine. They identify their carrier as a Praetorian (the numbering of figures is that of Koeppel 1985, 173–95). Cavalrymen Nos 17, 36, and 47 carry scorpion representations on the cheek pieces of their helmets, as do infantrymen Nos 56, 60, and 61. On a shield (cavalryman No. 68), there are four scorpions (of which the lower is concealed).

On a Domitianic-period relief from Puteoli, now located in Baltimore Museum in Pennsylvania, Praetorians are

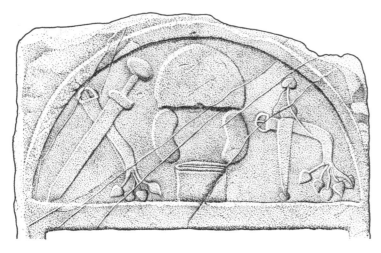

Figure 90 *Praetorian tombstone from Assisi with representation of a gladius, pugio (on belts) and helmet (Museum Assisi). Drawing: A. Smadi, Archaeological Institute of the University of Cologne*

Figure 91 *Reconstructed oval scutum of a Praetorian after a relief from Puteoli in Baltimore. Reconstruction and recording: J. Porgozelski*

Figure 92 *Auxiliary soldiers of the Flavian period. Cavalryman (left) and infantryman (right). Drawing: P. Connolly*

depicted with oval shields with scorpions on them. These served as a model for the reconstruction in Figure 91.[155]

An inscription from the tomb of M. Pompey Asper, who also served in the 3rd Praetorian cohort, according to his *cursus honorum*, shows two standards to the left and right. Both have a rectangular plate with the representation of a scorpion. The tomb comes from Tusculum near Rome and is now kept in the Palazzo Albani in Rome; it dates from the second half of the 1st/early 2nd century AD.[156]

Auxiliary cavalry

The auxiliary cavalry had weapons, such as helmets or hexagonal shields, which are characteristic for these units. The mail and scale armour of the cavalry seemingly do not differ from those of the infantry. In the early Imperial period, breeches, the *spatha*, and the belt are typical of cavalry equipment. The latter does not have any decorative fittings, just a metal buckle (Fig. 92). Additionally, cavalrymen do not wear daggers or segmental armour. From the middle of the 2nd century AD, these differences begin to blur: now infantrymen also carry the *spatha*, and as the 3rd century AD progressed, cavalrymen also wore the ring- or frame-buckle belt. Typical cavalry weapons like light javelins cannot be distinguished from similar infantry weapons in the archaeological material. According to the iconographic sources, these weapons were no different from those of the Guard cavalry (*equites singulares Augusti*) in Rome (Busch 2011).

Auxiliary soldiers with specialized or local armament

Armoured cavalry (cataphractarii, clibanarii)

An exceptional type of cavalry inherited from the East was represented by the armoured cavalrymen (*cataphractarii* or *clibanarii*). The term already appears on a Hellenistic papyrus of the 3rd century BC. In the 1st century AD, the Romans first became acquainted with the armoured cavalrymen fighting for their Sarmatian opponents. Here the protection of man and horse is emphasized, making a shield unnecessary. Sarmatians are shown on Trajan's Column whose representations, with tight-fitting scale armour for horse and rider, can hardly be viewed as realistic (Fig. 93). The occurrence of iron and often quite large armour scales in the Danube region from the period around AD 100 onwards is likely to derive from Sarmatian models. This is not to say that such cuirasses were only worn by armoured horsemen. Also, one generally cannot distinguish whether scale cuirasses, made of iron or non-ferrous metals and mostly only fragmentarily preserved, belonged to the equipment of men or horses.

The first mention of armoured horsemen in the Roman army is late and isolated: under Hadrian, an *ala Gallorum et Pannoniorum cataphractata* may have been established. There is more epigraphic and literary evidence again for these armoured cavalrymen in the 3rd century AD, when they were in use even on the Upper German-Raetian Limes. For the time of Severus Alexander, the *Historia Augusta* reported the Romans had succeeded in killing 10,000 Persian (probably Parthian) armoured cavalry (*cataphractarii, quos illi clibanarios vocant*) and, with the help of captured weaponry, had been able to set up Roman armoured cavalry units. The truth of this statement, however, is highly controversial.

This exceptional force has always interested historians, because they wanted to see in them the forerunners of medieval knight armies. This is scarcely conceivable because the stirrup was not known in ancient times, an important prerequisite for heavy cuirassed horsemen along the lines of medieval knights.

Both man and horse in the armoured cavalry were covered with scale or lamellar cuirasses, the chief weapon being the heavy thrusting spear (*contus*). This was held shieldless with both hands. An incised drawing on a wall at Dura-Europos shows such an armoured cavalryman, and from there also come three sets of horse armour from the well-known undermined Tower 19, although it is unclear whether these are pieces of Roman armoured cavalry equipment from around the middle of the 3rd century AD, or captured Persian armour (Figs 94, 95). Otherwise, special pieces of equipment that could have belonged to *cataphractarii* are unknown. With the exception of tombstones of the 3rd century AD, no indications of these special forces have yet been found in the northwestern provinces. We know of the armoured cavalrymen Valerius Fuscianus from Claudiopolis (Turkey), Valerius Maxantius from Worms (Germany), or Valerius Drusus from Amiens (France) from their tombstones, for example. In the museum of Aswan in Egypt is the funerary statue of an armoured horseman carrying a *spatha* with a box chape on a baldric. It therefore dates to the middle third of the 3rd century AD (Fig. 96).

The efficacy of armoured cavalrymen is probably overestimated. Literary sources tell us repeatedly that the horses collapsed under the weight of their riders who then, hampered by their own armour, were no longer able to get up, because cataphracts, according to the ancient sources, could not get on the horse by themselves, and had to be lifted up by several men. In battle, they could scarcely perform complicated maneouvres: they were usually only able to mount a single frontal shock attack in close formation. If their opponents succeeded in closing up the battle line again after a breakthrough of cataphracts, or even intentionally let them pass through, then the attack dissipated, as happened with Hellenistic war elephants, and they could easily be

Figure 93 *Trajan's Column, Sarmatian horsemen (after Bartoli and Dzur 1941)*

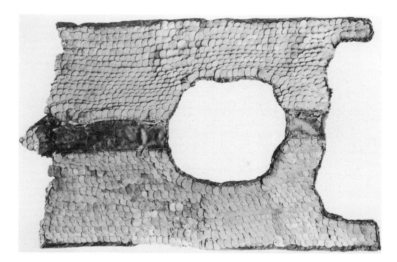

Figure 94

Figure 95

Figure 94–5 *Horse armour from Dura-Europos (after James 2004)*

Figure 96 *Tombstone of an armoured rider from Aswan, Egypt. The spatha on a broad baldric has a box chape (mid-3rd century AD). Photo: V. Fischer*

Figure 97 *Tombstone of an oriental archer with conical helmet, single-edged machete, and reflex bow from Housesteads. Drawing: A. Smadi, Archaeological Institute of the University of Cologne*

dealt with in the rear, isolating them in small groups, and then incapacitating the immobile armoured cavalryman.

Oriental archers

A tombstone from Housesteads on Hadrian's Wall (Fig. 97), as well as representations on Trajan's Column (Fig. 98), show oriental archers from units that had been recruited in Syria. The man from Housesteads is wearing a tunic and a cloak and has a conical helmet made from a single piece; he is armed with a single-edged slashing sword, and the reflex or composite bow, including a protective cover and quiver.[157] The archers on Trajan's Column are similarly depicted (Fig. 99), except that they wear long kaftans.

Conical helmets, like that on the tombstone from [Housesteads] in England, have only been found in the Danube region so far, such as the pieces from Dakovo,[158] Bosnia, or from the area of Intercisa.[159] These helmets with their single-piece bowls should not be confused with the similarly conical, multipart Spangenhelm helmets, which were introduced towards the end of Late Antiquity and the migration period (Miks 2008).

Trilobate arrowheads and bone stiffeners from reflex bows by contrast are frequently found in all frontier provinces. The single-edged slashing sword, as shown on the tombstone from Housesteads, is rarely found in Roman archaeological contexts. We know of such a weapon from Vindonissa, for example. This weapon is in any case certainly not Germanic, as indicated in Unz and Deschler-Erb.[160]

Figure 98 *Trajan's Column, archers of Eastern origin with conical helmet, long kaftan, and reflex bow (after Bartoli and Dzur 1941)*

Figure 99 *Reconstructed archer of Eastern origin with conical helmet, long kaftan, and reflex bow. Drawing: P. Connolly*

However, equipment consisting of long robes, conical helmets, and single-edged slashing swords might not have been worn by all oriental archer units (Fig. 100). From the fort and the environs of the *cohors I Canathenorum sagittariorum milliaria equitata* in Sorviodurum/Straubing on the Raetian Danube frontier, for instance, numerous trilobate arrowheads and bow stiffening laths are known. Otherwise, however, nothing different to the usual equipment of auxiliary troops in Raetia was found – for example, there were no conical helmets or slashing swords. Rather, the numerous weapons finds from Straubing fort match the usual infantry and cavalry weapons (Walke 1965; Prammer 2010, 13–17).

Dacians with the scimitar (sica)

Inscription *RIB* 1914 of *cohors I Aelia Dacorum* from Birdoswald on Hadrian's Wall (Fig. 101), datable to the early 3rd century AD, provides an interesting sidenote. To one side of this is the representation of a typical Dacian scimitar, the *sica*. The question now is whether the weapon depicted on the inscription, exotic by Roman, let alone British, standards,

is only symbolic for the unit or were Dacian troops in Britain really still fighting with the scimitar. To answer this question, only original archaeological material can help. K. Strobel, without further evidence, assumes that the depiction on the inscription is that of the actual weapons of the troops.[161]

Numerus soldiers

The few weapons and equipment finds from *numerus* forts along the Upper German Limes are no different from the armament of contemporary auxiliary troops. The Palmyran *numerus* from Porolissum (Dacia Porolissensis) can probably be associated with the find there of trilobate arrowheads of iron.[162]

Marines

While it is assumed for the period of the Republic that land forces were occasionally used as marines, units fighting as marines are known under the Empire. Their equipment can only be deduced on the quite limited basis of the discoveries from the cities around Vesuvius and the fleet

Figure 100 *Tombstone of mounted archer Flavius Proculus, a native of Philadelphia/ Amman, from Mainz. Drawing: A. Smadi, Archaeological Institute of the University of Cologne*

Figure 101 *Birdoswald (Hadrian's Wall). Inscription of Coh. I Aelia Dacorum with Dacian curved sword on the right-hand side. Drawing: A. Smadi, Archaeological Institute of the University of Cologne*

bases of Köln-Alteburg (Fischer 2005) and Dover (Philp 1981). In addition, there is the problematic literary source, Vegetius (Baatz and Bockius 1997). Overall, it turns out that the known remains of swords, daggers, belts, cuirasses, shields, and spearheads are no different from the finds from contemporary legionary or auxiliary infantry bases. Only the helmets seem to be different: in addition to the discoveries from the two fleet bases, two pseudo-Attic bronze helmets from Pompeii[163] have been assigned by S. Ortisi with good reasons to members of the fleet of Misenum.[164]

Other paramilitary units

Currently there are hardly any safe original finds that can be assigned to arming those public or private special forces such as the fire brigade or bodyguards. However, S. Ortisi was able to identify a particular, single-edged slashing blade in Pompeii with a degree of probability as belonging to the city guards. As for regular military *gladii* in Pompeii, he assumes that some veterans carried them who worked as private bodyguards.[165]

Arming of civilians

In the Roman Empire, civilians were only allowed to carry weapons in public in exceptional cases. Those exceptions were travelling (due to the ubiquitous risk of brigandage) and hunting.[166] Weapons in civilian settlement contexts always lead to the almost unanswerable question of whether the weapons present here were in civilian ownership, or whether they were buried there as a result of combat, such as in civil war situations or in hostile raids. The cases of weapons in ship finds, however, such as the swords from Comacchio[167] or Porto Novo should be fairly clear.[168] These probably belonged to a passenger or crew member, for example the captain.

6.   Rank insignia

Emperor, tribunes, and legates

On cuirassed statues, the emperor and senior officers always wear muscled cuirasses, often combined with an eagle-headed sword. To these can be added the *paludamentum* (general's cloak). Lower ranks like centurions were apparently denied this special equipment, according to the iconographic evidence (see below).

Centurions

The most characteristic features of military rank in the Roman army in the Early and High Imperial period are known for centurions. These present themselves in military garments which – at least in the 2nd and early 3rd century AD – are seen as typical for centurions: dazzlingly white tunics decorated with blue or purple stripes (*clavi*) made from genuine purple.[169] These largely correspond to the garb of the *equites*. They also wear a red sword belt (*balteus*) with gold or gold-coloured decorative buttons and a white disk-shaped or spherical pommel made of bone or ivory.[170] In addition, a blue shoulder cloak is fastened with a silver brooch. We are informed on these commonly depicted details of dress through the study of Egyptian mummy portraits from the Fayum (Fig. 102).[171] Similarly, the painted shroud of a Roman officer from Luxor in Egypt also shows a narrow red belt, decorated with silver buttons.[172]

On tombstones of the 1st century AD, centurions occasionally wear a special form of body armour: it is mail or scale armour, but with the lower edge of the belly semicircular, sometimes with *pteryges*, and with fringed flaps on the lower edge of the cuirass, having the appearance of muscle cuirasses (Fig. 103).[173] Apparently this form of body armour was reserved for the higher echelons (tribunes, legates, and the Emperor), so that the centurions had to be satisfied with a muscle cuirass-'like' protective armament. They thus avoided the rigid form of the muscle cuirass armour and contented themselves with more flexible, more combat-grade body armour which merely imitated the appearance of the cuirasses of higher ranks, because centurions were – unlike tribunes, legates and so on – usually fighting in the front line.

Another clear sign of identification for centurions in the army of the Early and High Imperial period was the upright transverse helmet crest, the *crista transversa*.[174] This was depicted on tombstones from Carnuntum and Ptuj/Poetovio[175] and described by Vegetius (*Epitoma Rei Militaris* 2.16). A helmet of the Weisenau type from the river Kupa in Sisak in Croatia[176] was correctly identified by D'Amato and Sumner as the helmet of a centurion with a *crista transversa* (Figs 104, 105): on top of the helmet bowl, there is one of the common box-like devices for the attachment of a crest. The riveted plates with hinged movable rings commonly

Figure 102 *Mummy portrait from the Fayum in Egypt. Centurion with baldric, 2nd century AD (after Parlasca and Seemann 1999)*

Figure 103 *Tombstone of the centurion M. Favonius Facilis from Colchester. Drawing: A. Smadi, Archaeological Institute of the University of Cologne*

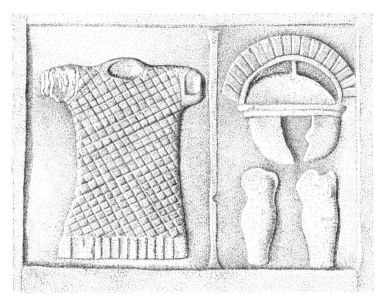

Figure 104 *Weapons from the tombstone of the centurion T. Calidius Severus from Carnuntum. Drawing: A. Smadi, Archaeological Institute of the University of Cologne*

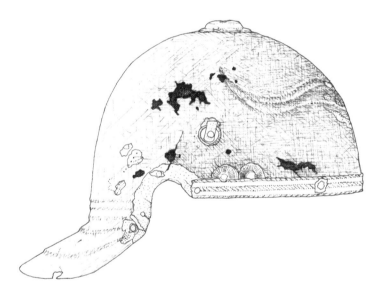

Figure 105 *Iron helmet of the Weisenau type of a centurion with crista transversa (recognisable from the side-mounted attachment rings to fix the helmet crest holder) from the river Kupa in Croatia (after Radman-Livaja 2004). Drawing: A. Smadi, Archaeological Institute of the University of Cologne*

Figure 106 *M. Junkelmann as an early Imperial centurion with a Weisenau-type helmet with crista transversa, vitis, and greaves. Note the suspension method of the Mainz-type gladius on the left. Photo: M. Junkelmann*

associated are present but not, as usual, mounted to the front and rear, but on the right (surviving) and left (only the mounting hole survives) sides of the helmet. Thus, it is clear that the plume was fastened crosswise as a *crista transversa*, and accordingly the helmet belonged to a centurion.

Centurions had the right to wear gold rings. They were also normally equipped with greaves – often decorated – and a *vitis*.[177] This *vitis*, cut from a vine stock, marked the right of the centurion to exercise corporal punishment (Fig. 106). The fact that it was carried not only as a mark of rank, but in fact was often used for flogging, is dramatically attested.[178] In addition, centurions in the 1st century AD wore their *gladius* on the left, not on the right, like other soldiers.[179]

Optiones

In addition to the centurions with their *vitis*, there is a second military office for which a rank insignia is known – the *optio legionis*. He acted as deputy centurion and could also be promoted to that rank. H. Ubl recognized that, on three tombstones on which soldiers are named with the rank of *optio*, there are rod-shaped rank insignia with differently shaped knobs.[180] These are described by Ubl as follows:

The staff of office is decorated the same in all cases. It is as high as a man, consists of a straight, round, and smooth shaft of the thickness of a spear shaft and apparently had no ferrule; at least the reliefs do not represent one. Differences between the three staffs concern the shape of its pommel, with which they are topped. The staff of the *optio* of *legio I Minervia* has a simple, narrow annular ring; that of the *optio* of *legio I Adiutrix* has an elongated, round, and moulded pommel; and that of the *optio* of *legio XX Valeria Victrix* has a small ball.[181]

All of these pieces of evidence date to the first half of the 2nd century AD. It is currently not known whether such a symbol of rank was also common before or after and whether they were part of the permanent equipment of *optiones*.

Pieces of equipment made of precious metals as a sign of military rank?

For the early Imperial period, S. Ortisi has pointed out that silver in the form of belt and scabbard fittings in Roman military was a familiar phenomenon and was hardly suitable for the identification of military ranks (Ortisi 2009a). However, the *gladius* sheath with silver belt set from Kalkriese adorned with silver and gems was, according to an incised inscription, actually owned by a centurion.[182] Around AD 200, *i.e.* in the Severan period, this tendency changed. When publishing silver belt fittings of the 3rd century AD, I have tentatively allocated such pieces of equipment of silver, along with brooches, to higher military ranks. According to representational sources from Egypt, this appears to be true for centurions. Even the belt studded with silver of a member of the bodyguard of Caracalla, which consisted of centurions according to Cassius Dio, confirms this (Fischer 2012). For the Late Roman period, research into belt fittings and crossbow brooches reveals a clear rank hierarchy, which is expressed through the use of the metals bronze, silver, and gold. That this rank hierarchy still existed in the time of Justinian is shown by an incident in Procopius, *Anekdota* VII: a mugger assaulted some nobles in Constantinople, and robbed them of, among other things, their golden brooches and belts. To disguise themselves, they thereafter only used belts and brooches of bronze, although these were actually below their station.

7. On the reconstruction of Roman fighting methods

On the particular combat and fencing techniques of the Roman army there is little in the written sources and it is treated unsystematically. An attempt to gather and edit these scattered sources has not yet taken place; meanwhile, there is for now the study by J C N Coulston (Coulston 2007).

What repeatedly appears in the tradition is the constant drill and the high level of discipline of the standing Roman army. This of course meant intensive training in the use of weapons, especially in the use of the edged weapons of the

sword and dagger. It seems likely that there were particular cuts, stabs, and feints, practised repeatedly in training in antiquity, just like those we know about from medieval, especially late medieval, combat manuals.[183]

Whether such combat manuals were actually written in ancient times is not known, but it seems at least worth considering. However, the ancient sources point to only a single related case: Publius Rutilius Rufus, legate under Quintus Caecilius Metellus in the Jugurthine War from 109–107 BC, first introduced fencing lessons along the lines of the gladiatorial schools for his troops (Val. Max. 2.3.2) in 105 BC. The results were obviously quite impressive, because Marius, who took over Rufus' army a little later, preferred them over his own troops because of their effectiveness (Frontinus, *Stratagemata* 4.2.2). One would assume that these gladiatorial fencing moves were also written down, thus enabling their rapid adoption by the military in the first place. It is also conceivable that his positive experience with good and uniformly trained troops may have persuaded Marius in his decision to establish a Roman professional army.

This would actually be the conclusion of this topic within the limits of this book, which must be based on tangible written sources, were it not for a remarkable attempt by Peter Connolly to define a particular, specifically Roman, close combat technique from the typological transformation of helmets and swords in the early Imperial period (Connolly 1991). He began from the correct observation that the Roman infantry helmet of the Montefortino type and its variants did not change over the centuries. Only in the Augustean period was a completely different design principle introduced with the Weisenau type, allowing the conclusion that there were changes in combat techniques. The enlargement and lowering of the neck guard in other words served the purpose of protecting a warrior who had to fight in a crouching position with the head turned upwards. This is the tactic of a small man who, with a stabbing sword, attempts to get under the guard of a larger opponent by attacking them in the abdominal area.

Connolly proposed this peculiar method for fighting with tall Celts as adversaries who also carried long slashing swords. He also attributed the introduction of brow guards on helmets to this weapon, an idea that he acquired from Russell Robinson.[184] Among other arguments, this change, about a generation after the Romans concluded the Gallic Wars of Caesar victoriously without the helmet brow guard, would be rather remarkable.

Junkelmann has rightly criticized these chronological inconsistencies of this – for him – 'creepy crawly tactic' of Connolly's reconstructed battle stance:

> He [Connolly] anticipates that the Celts were the main opponents
> of the Romans in the western part of the empire and therefore the
> helmet was specifically designed as protection against the Celtic
> slashing sword. But the introduction of helmets with wide hori-

zontal neck guards and brow guards in the years around the birth of Christ falls in the middle of the period between the end of the Gallic War in the middle of the 1st century BC and the invasion of Britain 100 years later, in which the Celts became less significant as opponents of the Romans and the Germans – who were spear fighters and not swordsmen – assumed this role. The Romans would therefore react with a delay of more than 50 years to a situation which no longer existed.[185]

Moreover, Junkelmann argued, he had tested Connolly's 'creepy crawly tactic' experimentally. His usual accomplices, well-trained in the handling and use of ancient weapons – within certain limits set by the criminal law, naturally – could endure this crouched stance in full armour for only a short time without completely cramping up.[186] However, it must be said in Connolly's defence here that he never claimed Roman soldiers were crouched for hours on end in this way 'crawling' across the terrain. In an emergency, only a brief moment would have been enough in that position to undermine the defences of the enemy and to effect the deadly blow.

Anyway, this example may suffice to show how problematic it can be to reconstruct specific battle tactics from the particular characteristics of armament. Unfortunately, the interpretation of archaeological finds has reached limits which cannot, for the time being, be passed.

8.   Comments on the re-enactment scene

A momentous development can be traced back to the initiative of the American experimental archaeologist D. Peterson, which has not necessarily had a positive impact on the standards that all 're-enactment Romans' purport to follow enthusiastically and seriously: namely, to operate strictly scientific experimental archaeology. I am referring to the standardized 'Roman' armament from India, now readily available in huge quantities and at competitive and low prices, for example, over the Internet.[187] While reputable groups like the Ermine Street Guard (among others Haines 2000), the groups of Marcus Junkelmann, the Roman cohort Opladen, the Legio IIX Augusta of Alexander Zimmermann, and others strive to make their equipment as authentic as possible or produce it themselves from original finds, one can now acquire complete sets of 'Roman' equipment 'off the shelf'.[188] These things often bear only a superficial resemblance to faithful replica weapons made from original ancient models, especially if their owners mix the equipment of different periods without hesitation.

These developments have also occurred because the dialogue between 're-enactment Romans' and specialists in the subject has often broken down or never took place at all. This contact, from which both sides can benefit, is essential if the claim of many Roman groups to operate experimental archaeology on a strictly scientific basis, is to be faithfully followed (Griffiths 2000). If this book could help in providing templates for authentic equipment as a first step to really sound experimental archaeology, then one of the motives for its publication would be met!

9.   Forgeries

Fully preserved pieces of Roman weaponry have always been sought after by collectors and museums and were therefore of interest to the art trade, especially since their owners charged handsome prices for these things. The Lipperheide Collection of ancient helmets was already formed in the 19th century in this manner (Bottini et al. 1988). In the late 20th century, Berlin developer Guttmann had collected an amazing assemblage of ancient weapons that was unfortunately squandered and dissipated through the art trade after his sudden death (Junkelmann 1996, 1997 and 2000). Clever counterfeiters and distributors have always tried to use such events to produce counterfeits and pass them as genuine in the trade. This is very often successful. There are amazing forgeries, for example, in the Lipperheide Collection (Bottini et al. 1988), the Toledo Museum of Art (Vermeule 1960), or in the Hamburg Museum of Arts and Crafts.[189]

A recent trend is to take weapons, such as helmets, manufactured in India for re-enactment groups and to then artificially 'age' them by patination and pass them as genuine in the trade. There have been multiple attempts to sell modern replicas of Roman helmets, which had been artificially aged, as 'originals'. This tendency, it is to be feared, is likely to increase. Scholarship will have to be more vigilant and critical in the future if unusual (but also 'normal') pieces appear at dealers or collectors. However, one should not misuse the suspicion of fraud as a killer argument to discredit from the outset all the privately owned finds which are not from 'official' excavations on ideological grounds!

Notes to Part II

1. Johnson 1987; Bishop and Coulston 2006; Miks 2007; Künzl 2008; Nabbefield 2009 and Schallmayer 1997; Wamser 2000; Humer 2007.
2. Bottini et al. 1988; Junkelmann 1996; 1997; 2000, along with various online auction catalogues.
3. Here, I deliberately refer to the brief remarks of Bishop and Coulston 2006, vii.
4. Fischer 2005b, 194f; Snap 2009 92–134.
5. Schramm 1955; Wolf 1997; Worm 2000; Wolf and Kirchweger 2005.

6. Pfaffenbichler 1996, 369 note 13.
7. Gamber and Beaufort 1990, 37–40. For the photo and numerous references I thank M. Pfaffenbichler, KHM Vienna.
8. See Boschung 2005. For the development from antiquarianism to archaeology as a science see in great detail Schnapp 2009, 136–340.
9. Ortisi 2006, 376f.
10. This happened in the 1980s, when just such an archaeological find was submitted to the Prehistoric State Collection in Munich for evaluation by a private citizen. For a long time, J. Garbsch and I struggled in vain over this puzzling piece, then H. Ubl was up by chance from Vienna and unravelled the secret of the mysterious 'gladius'. As a recognized expert for the modern military too, he knew about the origin of the weapon and could help us accordingly with the information.
11. See Fischer 2001; Fischer 2010.
12. Wegner 1976, 12f.
13. See Torbrügge 1972; Pauli, 1987; Künzl 1996, 438–49, Fischer 2004, 61 note 2.
14. Lindenschmit 1858; 1870; 1881; 1882; 1892 1911. Of course he was able to heavily rely on the rich collection of finds from his native city of Mainz.
15. Künzl 2008, 2f; esp. Fig. 1; Miks 2009.
16. Jacobi 1897, 481–92; Taf. 12; 28–41; 45, 46; 52–69. On Louis Jacobi: Schallmayer 1997, 28–32l.
17. Marsden 1969; 1971; Baatz 1994; Miks 2001.
18. On Richborough: Bushe-Fox 1927ff; on Hod Hill: Brailsford 1961.
19. Krohmayer and Veith 1928, 409ff; 521–5.
20. J. Obmann in Fischer 2001, 19f; Fischer 2002; 2010.
21. Festschrift G. Ulbert, 1995 XI–XXIII.
22. Bishop and Coulston, 2006 274f; Künzl 2008 2f.
23. Allason-Jones and Bishop, 1988; Schrader 2009, 359.
24. See only the German version of Simkins and Embleton 2005.
25. See Junkelmann 2002, 83. Künzl 2008, 3; Schrader 2009, 359f; Koepfer et al. 2012.; Himmler 2012.
26. Sorell 1981; Embleton 2003; Simkins and Embleton 2005.
27. Schrader 2009, 360; Sumner and D'Amato 2009.
28. See German editions of Connolly 1976, 1990 and 1990a.
29. Junkelmann 2002, 83.
30. Junkelmann 1986; Gilbert 2004; Schrader 2009, 361.
31. Haines et al. 2000; the group benefits from the fact that they had early contact with professional researchers. H. R. Robinson, P. Connolly, M. C. Bishop, J. C. N. Coulston, C. van Driel-Murray and others have advised the group and benefitted in return for the practical implementation and testing of their theoretical research results (see Schrader 2009, 360).
32. See Deschler-Erb 1999; Unz and Deschler-Erb 1997; Lenz 2006.
33. A smaller preliminary study of this work consisted of only 76 pages: M. C. Bishop and J. C. Coulston, *Roman Military Equipment* (Princes Risborough 1989).
34. Militaria from Zeugma on the Euphrates (Eastern Turkey) are published (Kennedy and Bishop 1998) or their publication is promised: Speidel 2010, 139 mentions (not yet submitted) Roman militaria: '… that in all sondages Roman weapons came to light (mail shirts, armour scales, helmet fragments, arrow- and spearheads, fittings, and washers from catapults, carapult bolts, caltrop, mattocks etc.'.
35. Ulbert et al. 1976; Fischer 1997; Oldenstein 1997; Fahr and Miks 2001.
36. Künzl 2008, 8
37. Obmann 2000, 4.
38. A fundamentally new concept in Roman artillery construction around AD 100 could indicate the invention of an individual. See Baatz 1994, 296f.
39. For instance through taking over eastern armoured cavalry (cataphracts). See Harl 1996.
40. Like the cross-bar reinforce on Roman helmets of the Weisenau type in the Dacian Wars.
41. There is proof in inscription *CIL* XIII 6763 from Mainz, for instance, where a certain Annianus is sent to Transpadana at the end of the reign of Maximinus Thrax (AD 235–8) to raise recruits against 'Hostes publici' and equip them in Mediolanum/Milan with newly manufactured weapons. See Oldenstein 1976, 80, esp. note 135.
42. Bishop and Coulston 2006 also proposed a similar periodization: The Republican Period, From Augustus to Hadrian, The Antonine Revolution, The Army in Crisis, The Dominate.
43. Arrian, *Tactics*, 33, in a translation by F. Kiechle, in Garbsch 1978, 38.
44. On the Celtic origins of mail also Varro, *Ling.* 5.116.
45. Bishop and Coulston 2006, 52.
46. Künzl 2008, 38–41.
47. Krohmayer and Veith 1928, 610.
48. Bishop and Coulston 2006, 233.
49. On state control of arms from private companies see Herz 2010, 124f.
50. A. Böhme, in Schönberger 1978, 217.
51. Fischer 1995, 340ff; Gschwind 2004, 159–63.
52. Deschler-Erb and Schwarz 1993.
53. Miks 2007, 161–4, 322ff.
54. Eich 2009, 56ff.
55. Nicolay 2007, 166–71; Stauner 2004, 48–51; Nicolay 2009, 260; Rau 2010, 468, esp. note 278.
56. Nuber 1972, 502f.
57. In summary, Bishop and Coulston 2006, 233–40.
58. P. Berlin 6765 inv. A. Bruckner and R. Marichal (eds), *Chartae Latinae Antiquiores, Part X, Germany I* (Zurich 1979), No. 409; Bishop and Coulston, 2006, 236.
59. Oldenstein 1976 68–75; Oldenstein 1985; Bishop and Coulston 2006; Nicolay 2007, 131–6.
60. Herz 2010, 127; *CIL* XIII 6677 = *ILS* 2472.
61. As a *negotiator*, he produced no swords, but only traded the products of specialized craftsmen. See Schlippshuh 1974, 11; 68.
62. Decker 1993; Bridger 1994, 83. The considerations employed by Herz 2010, 127 are less likely to be applicable here: 'And I suspect that the sword and dagger were probably delivered with only a simple wood or even leather sheath, in which just the chape and the opening (sic!) were made of metal. More complex models, where the scabbard had for instance plates with decorations of pressed (precious) metal, probably had to be procured by the soldier or officer interested in such things at his own expense.'

63. Miks 2007, 135–9.
64. Ibid., 135. Matešić 2009.
65. Fischer 1985. It is worth noting that the adhering tin shows that this semi-finished product, manufactured in a crisis situation, was made from a recycled bronze vessel.
66. Ettlinger and Hartmann 1984; Miks 2007, 254, esp. note 940.
67. It is likely to be irrelevant whether these had been state-managed or leased to private individuals. See Herz 2010, 112–15.
68. Pleiner 2000, 68f.
69. Ibid., 251–67.
70. Roth 1986, 118ff; Miks 2007, 52–6; for the production of segmental cuirasses, see now Sim and Kaminski 2012.
71. Roth 1986, 53f.
72. Ibid., 54 f; Obmann 2000, 7.
73. For introduction of the brass, especially for militaria, see Istenic 2009.
74. Thus, for example, in the region of Gressenich at Aachen. See Horn 1987, 155; 602f.
75. Gschwandler 1986, 17–46; Armbruster 2001.
76. Stauner 2009, 54ff.
77. See the woodfelling detachment of the 22nd Legion in the Main area mentioned in inscriptions: Speidel 1983 and 2008.
78. Fischer 2000b, 562.
79. Tac. *Ann.* 4.72.1.
80. James 1988; Bishop and Coulston 2006, 238f.
81. Gugl and Kastner 2007, 509f; Gugl 2009.
82. Fischer 2000, 114f.
83. Gilles 1985, 132; Pl. 34, 3.
84. Cf. MacMullen 1960. Bishop and Coulston 2006, 262f., Stauner 2004, 47–51; Herz 2010, 111.
85. Nuber 1972, 495–501.
86. A possibility considered by Herz 2009, 112; Stauner 2004, 49f keeps both options open.
87. Gilliam 1967; Harrauer and Seider 1979; Obmann 2000, 15; Bishop and Coulston 2006, 85.
88. Youtie and Winter 1951, Nos 467/468. Bishop and Coulston 2006, 41.
89. Klumbach 1973, 60 where there is a cursive inscription scratched on the neck guard, which is to be read as M. TITVS LVNAMIS or (less likely) M. TITV HLVNAMIS.
90. Böhme 1974, 113f.
91. For instance in the Treveri region or in Thrace. See Krier and Reinert 1993, 55–70, esp. map Fig. 41.
92. Böhme 1974, 53–114; Keller 1971, 56–78 and 1979, 40ff; 44.
93. Borhy 1990, 301f.
94. Robinson 1975, 84f; Fig. 104–7.
95. Feugère 1994, 689.
96. Ortisi 2009 40. The author was able to observe this timeless secondary use as well during his childhood in a village in the Swabian Alb: on many farms there were two German Wehrmacht helmets – one served for plastering, the other, provided with a welded-on nozzle, as a scoop for emptying out manure and septic tanks.
97. Feugère 1993, 123b.
98. Fischer 1990, 81.
99. Junkelmann 2000, 162 AG 462.
100. Fischer 2001a, 15f.
101. Reis 2001/2002 and 2010, 126; 226f.; Pl. 90, no. 171.

102. Fischer 2000, 287 No. 26. 2. 3. 1. Pl. 184 B. 1.
103. Junkelmann 2000, 178f.
104. See Schalles and Schreiter 1993. For older dating and the theory of the development of helmets of the Hagenau type into those of the Weisenau type around the middle of the 1st century AD see Klumbach 1961, 100f.
105. Robinson 1975, 84f; Figs 104–7.
106. Suetonius, *Vita Vitellii* 8, 2f; Eck 2004, 191.
107. Pers. comm. A. Schubert (Cologne), preparing a dissertation on waste disposal in Roman military camps.
108. Mackensen 1987, 158.
109. On Auerberg cf. G. Ulbert, in Czysz *et al.* 1995, 417 ff; Wamser 2000, 318f.
110. Weber 2000, 32f.
111. See Lenz 2006, 103–6. Components of 3rd century swords and scabbards in particular point towards fighting here.
112. Martin-Kilcher 1985; Deschler-Erb and Schwarz 1993. Due to new ideas on dating, it should be considered whether or not the Augst crested helmet belongs to contexts of the late 3rd century. See Miks 2008, 6f.
113. Reis 2010, 210–45.
114. Künzl 1996, 438–49.
115. Fischer 2004a, 71f.
116. Krier and Reinert 1993, 55–70, esp. Map Fig. 41.
117. Miks 2007, A 220.
118. James 2005, 192–205.
119. Metzler *et al.* 1991, 112–16.
120. Nuber 1985, 52f.
121. See here the grave at Vize (Garbsch 1978, 62). Most of the unprovenanced Roman cavalry weapons, which have reached the art market in recent years probably came from looted tombs of the Moesian-Thracian region.
122. Homs, Tell Oum Hauran, Chisfin; see Garbsch 1978, O4, N1, N2. Gogräfe and Chehadé 1999, 73–80; Miks 2007, A 169ff.
123. Fischer, 1991, 169–73; 1999, 24f and 1995, 346.
124. Horvat 1997, 2002 and 2009, 136f.
125. So a few years earlier than the Upper German Limes, the end of which is taken to be after AD 259/60. Fischer 1999, 27f.; Reuter 2007.
126. Curle 1911; Manning 2006, 15–32.
127. Garbsch 1978, 59.
128. The discovery and study of places like Kalkriese, Döttenbichel, Crap-Ses-Schlucht or Harzhorn would not have been possible without the use of the metal detector.
129. Morillo Cerdán 2000, 7–11.
130. Wheeler 1943; Fischer 2009b, 5.
131. Fahr 2005. The proposition by T. Bechert for the location of this battlefield is less likely now: T. Bechert, in Jilek 2005.
132. On Dura-Europos: James 2005; Bishop and Coulston 2006, 26; on Alesia: Reddé and von Schnurbein 2001.
133. Fischer 2001, 17f; Fischer 2012b.
134. Suetonius, *Vita Vitellii* 8.1; Eck 2004, 191.
135. Fischer 2001, 18.
136. Roymans and Derks 1994; Fischer 2001, 18.
137. Opladen-Kauder and Boedecker 2005; Boedecker 2010.
138. Cunliffe 1988, 8f; Taf. 5.
139. Sieg und Triumpf (sic!) 2003, 240–56.
140. Abegg Wigg and Rau 2008, 19–24.
141. *Sieg und Triumpf* 2003, 258–84; 296–309.

142. Ibid., 412–14, Abegg Wigg and Rau 2008, 55–123.
143. *Sieg und Triumpf* 2003, 224–38; Abegg Wigg and Rau 2008, 137–49.
144. Richter in 2010, 397–417.
145. See van Driel-Murray 1999. Busch 2009, 325f.
146. See Böhme-Schönberger 2009 and the relevant articles in a meeting of 27 and 28.2.2009 in Sheffield, which has been held in the framework of the EU project DressID. These are published in the *Manheimer Geschichtsblätter* 19, 2010, 4–151.
147. Cass. Dio 67.10.1. However, in Vindonissa, for example, such information has already been provided earlier by original finds of shield covers.
148. Vegetius, *Epitoma Rei Militaris* 2.15/16: The critical remarks of A. Busch (Busch 2009) on shields may support these considerations.
149. Miks 2007, 22f.
150. Ortisi 2005, 147.
151. Annibali 1995, 14f.
152. Koeppel 1984, 28–33.
153. Robinson 1975, 142, Fig. 154; 147, pl. 423. Koeppel 1985, 173–95; on Praetorians in general, see now Pogorzelski 2014.
154. Alexandrescu 2010, 225, esp. note 1797; Busch 2011. For discussion and numerous references I thank J. Pogorzelski (Cohors I Praetoria, Cologne).
155. Flower 2001 esp. Figs 1 and 10.
156. Alexandrescu 2010, 329, No. P 11. Taf. 25.
157. Coulston 1985, 341, Figs 26, 27.
158. Robinson 1975, 85 Fig. 237.
159. Bishop and Coulston 2006, 143, no. 4.
160. Unz and Deschler-Erb 1997, 14; Taf. 1.4.
161. Strobel 2010, 296.
162. Gudea 1989, 990, Pl. 81, 9–11.
163. See Robinson 1975, Fig. 150, 151 ('Imperial Gallic A'). The location given in Robinson for these helmets kept in the National Museum of Naples ('probably Herculaneum') can now be corrected with the help of the studies of S. Ortisi (Ortisi 2005, 147). Both helmets come from Pompeii and, along with other weapons, they are from the gladiators' barracks there.
164. Robinson did not want to interpret them as regular military helmets, assigning them instead to the City Guard, but Ortisi considers them to be the helmets of marines of the fleet at Misenum (Ortisi 2005, 47).
165. Ortisi 2006, 382.
166. Brunt 1975; Rice 2010, 241ff.
167. Miks 2007, A 115.
168. Ortisi 2006, 372.
169. For the *clavi* on tunics see Pausch 2003, 104–27. Paetz gen. Schieck 2010, 92f.
170. D'Amato and Sumner 2009, 101, 101 Fig. Paetz gen. Schieck 2010 92f; on sword handles made of bone or ivory, see Miks 2007. 168–77.
171. Speidel 1999; Parlasca and Seemann 1999, 150f; Paetz gen. Schieck 2010, 92f.
172. Parlasca and Seemann 1999, 39 Fig. 31; Paetz gen. Schieck 2010, 92f.
173. Thus, for example, the scale armour of centurion Q. Sertorius Festus of the *Legio XI Claudia Pia Fidelis* from Verona (Robinson 1975 156f., Fig. 442, 444); the mail shirt of the centurion M. Favonius Facilis of the 20th Legion from Colchester (Robinson 1975, 166, Fig. 465).
174. See on this (slightly sceptical) Obmann 1999, 192f. This scepticism is now clearly refuted by the helmet found in the Kupa in Croatia.
175. Illustrated in Junkelmann 1986, Taf. 36; Robinson 1975, 142, Fig. 150.
176. Robinson 1975, 56, pl.121. Radman-Livaja 2004, Plate 26, No. 127, Plate 14, 15; D'Amato and Sumner 2009, 116f., Fig. 136.
177. Testified by numerous representations on gravestones of the 1st century AD. See the centurions Q. Sertorius Festus of the *Legio XI Claudia Pia Fidelis* from Verona (Robinson 1975, 156f., Figs 442, 444) and M. Favonius Facilis of the 20th Legion from Colchester (Robinson 1975, 166, Fig. 465).
178. Tacitus, *Ann.* 1.23.3, reported, in connection with the mutiny of the Rhine legions in AD 14, the centurion Lucilius nicknamed '*cedo alteram*'. During his beatings of soldiers, he frequently used to break his *vitis* on their backs, calling to be given a new one, which earned him his nickname. No wonder he was lynched in the mutiny.
179. Bishop and Coulston 2006, 82.
180. Ubl 2013, 434–7; Bishop and Coulston 2006, 120; 185.
181. Ubl 2013, 436.
182. R. Wiegels in Franzius 1999, 600ff.
183. See the annotated editions of Meister Thalhoffer combat manual of 1467: A. Schulz, *Mittelalterliche Kampfesweisen. Teil I: Das lange Schwert* (Mainz 2006); idem, *Mittelalterliche Kampfesweisen. Teil II: Der Kriegshammer, Schild und Kolben* (Mainz 2007); idem, *Mittelalterliche Kampfesweisen. Teil III: Scheibendolch und Stechschild* (Mainz 2007); J. Graf zu Koenigsegg-Aulendorf and A. Schulze (eds), *Der Königsegger Codex. Die Fechthandschrift des Hauses Königsegg* (Mainz 2010); see also Coulston 2007.
184. Robinson 1975, 26.
185. Junkelmann 2000, 27.
186. Ibid., 26f.
187. Schrader 2009, 364f.
188. However, for many of these Indian Roman weapons, there is still the opportunity to retrofit them as accurate replicas.
189. Manifestly counterfeit Roman helmets can be found, among other things, from this Hamburg Museum, presented as genuine in D'Amato and Sumner 2009, 37, Figs 24, 51, Figs 37, 114, Figs 130, 116, Fig. 135 (with the possibility of forgery mentioned).

COSTUMES, WEAPONS, AND EQUIPMENT OF THE ARMY FROM ORIGINAL ARCHAEOLOGICAL FINDS

III

1. Infantry

Clothing or uniform? There is still a controversial debate about whether or not the clothing and equipment of Roman soldiers should be described as uniform.[1] This was often triggered by the conspicuously homogeneous appearance of the Roman military on Trajan's Column (Richter 2010), but it is important to see their uniformity and the clear differentiation between legionary and auxiliary infantry. Moreover, the debate often centres around ideas that are too modern: does the concept of uniformity refer to completely homogeneous clothing or even to a modern image of a completely identically dressed and equipped army with machine-made industrial products? Thus it is certainly too simplistic.

However, for this reason, in antiquity and the pre-industrial era through to the early modern era, the very concept of uniformity must be understood a little more loosely, because one has to take into account the handmade nature of clothing and equipment in the Roman army. The result was that each piece of clothing and equipment could have unique characteristics, within certain limits, naturally. On top of that, as in modern armies, every soldier in the Roman army apparently had the opportunity to acquire his clothing and equipment according to his financial means and the personal preference of the individual.

One particularly curious example of this is unfortunately unprovenanced: a segmental cuirass was decorated with riveted *denarii* during or after the time of Maximinus (AD 235–8) (Fig. 107). One can only speculate over what ultimately lay behind such a peculiar display of solvency. Yet a Roman military unit, if clothing, equipment, and weapons are taken together, certainly did not present too varied an impression to have made it impossible a priori to speak of uniforms – on the contrary! One only knows that nowadays, in cut, colour, and decoration the clothing of a Roman military unit can no longer be described as uniform. It is not even known whether and to what extent there was such a thing. Esprit de corps and the need for troops to differ markedly in appearance from civilians[2] and opponents alone inevitably made for a certain standardization and uniformity. The suitability of clothing for military purposes, such as a belted tunic that provided legroom, or cloaks and trousers for weather protection, clearly served to distinguish military equipment from everyday civilian clothes, hence the uniformity of the troops. In addition, there may also have been opportunities – important in civil wars – to distinguish individual units from one another by clothing (colour or cut), not just by painting shields.

We can also recognize that, repeatedly, there are certain differences in the clothing on contemporary depictions of soldiers. However, it is impossible with the little material

Figure 107 *Fragment of an iron segmental cuirass of the Newstead type with riveted denarii of Domitian (AD 81–96) and Maximinus Thrax (AD 235–8; unprovenanced, privately owned). Photo: A. Pangerl*

known until now to determine systematic differences in terms of rank insignia within a unit or even between legionary and auxiliary troops, not to mention variations in the clothing between one contemporary unit and another. To what extent the colour of clothing or insignia offered clear opportunities for differentiation to be recognized by outsiders must remain unresolved (Obmann 1999; Böhme-Schönberger 2009). As an exception, we know about arrow-shaped ornaments (*clavi*) on the tunics of officers in the 3rd century AD, as they have survived in Egypt.[3]

Clothing

The clothing of legionary and auxiliary soldiers is known almost exclusively from written and pictorial sources. Here those from the Imperial period predominate. In this period, realistic representations can mainly be found on gravestones and historical reliefs. However, these are not available to the same extent for all of the Imperial period.

Occasional original textile finds from military camps are only preserved in small fragments and give only a little information from the current state of research on the general appearance of the garment.[4] Original finds of better-preserved military clothing which can safely be identified as such are barely known from the Roman Empire, as can be seen for shoes. Otherwise, overarching detailed synthetic studies of the representational sources and original finds are still lacking for military clothing. Here, previously published works only offer a stopgap (Sumner 2002, 2003, and 2009).

Tunics

On his body, the soldier wore a broad, full-length shirt made of wool or linen: the tunic. This consisted of two

parts, a front and a rear part, which were sewn together at the sides. Originally it was sleeveless. It was generously cut, so that it could be worn comfortably, and the military tunic was probably slightly narrower than the civilian, since it was worn under armour.[5] The tunic was calf-length, but was always belted on duty with the military belt, so that its hem reached just above the knee.[6]

Representations on gravestones show that the tunic was subject to considerable change in the Imperial period. This was certainly not only dictated by the phenomenon of fashion, but also depended on the nature of the climate in the region where a unit served in the longer term.

From the Republic until the early Imperial period, soldiers predominantly wore the sleeveless tunic, but even into the 3rd century AD, it was still occasionally found.[7] In the early Imperial period, tunics with short sleeves predominated.[8] These were either cut like a present-day teeshirt, or they did not have any sleeves. Since the tunics were cut generously, in this case, the shoulders formed 'baggy sleeves'. Because of their voluminous nature, tunics could be artfully draped in folds. Thus representations are known on early Imperial gravestones up to the Flavian period variants, whereby tunics have semicircular folds across them on the front. This is the case for legionaries as well as auxiliary soldiers.[9] This fashion then seems to have fallen into disuse and the tunic is from then on worn with a straight hem, which is known from the Augustan period.[10]

The long-sleeved tunic (*tunica manicata*) increasingly occurs from the 3rd century AD as a military garment, as the *tunica militaris*. In late antiquity, they were predominant.[11] From the later 3rd century, such tunics were decorated with *clavi* and other decorative elements, which are not currently thought to show any systematic indication of ranks or units, especially as these ornaments can also be observed on civilian tunics. However, this phenomenon is almost entirely seen on wall paintings and grave finds from the East, especially in Syria and Egypt (Sumner 2003; Paetz gen Schieck 2003). In colder regions and climates it was normal for soldiers, except for the lower tunic, to wear several tunics on top of each other, as Suetonius wrote of Augustus.[12] In winter, this was underwear plus four tunics (Suetonius, *Vita Augusti* 82). Occasionally, in representational sources, the tunics of legionaries engaged in pioneering activities – or any other heavy physical labour – are knotted at one shoulder in a bunch.[13] This is intended to prevent the loose-fitting garment getting in the way while working. As for the colours of military tunics, there is little substantive evidence. The only certainty is that the consistently red tunics that today comprise stereotypical Roman soldiers for a wide audience, do not match the ancient state of affairs. They are so dominant in today's perception because they occur as the ubiquitous garment in the widespread reconstruction drawings of P. Connolly and were adopted by most re-enactment groups simply because of that.

Although there is only a small amount of information about ancient colour, it all points towards white or reddish-white. In Egyptian mummy portaits of the 2nd and 3rd century, for example, there are officers, probably centurions, shown with dazzling white tunics.[14] Otherwise, white to brownish tones are most common in the few remaining coloured pictorial representations.[15] Thus white or natural-coloured through to brown woollen tunics seem to have been the standard clothing for the Roman military, not red.

In a modern experiment by students of the University of Regensburg, it has allegedly proved better to use muted colours because of the high degree of staining of a white tunic by metal debris from armour.[16] However, in this case (if I interpret the picture right), tunics made of linen were used, which could then no longer be washed clean. With woollen tunics, this would not have been the case. Nevertheless, it is not impossible that on special occasions dazzling white or different coloured tunics were worn by soldiers, in any case, as an alternative.

Trousers

For a long time, the trousers of the Celts, Germans, and eastern barbarians, were thought of as an un-Roman, barbaric garment. Even Tacitus found it worth noting that in AD 69, during the civil war after Nero's death, the commander of the Lower German army, A. Caecina Severus, passed through northern Italy 'in trousers, a barbaric garment' (Tacitus, *Hist.* 2.20). Knee-length trousers (*feminalia*) are known only from image sources. They were initially only used by auxiliary cavalrymen (as Lederhosen?) until, later in the 1st century AD, they were then adopted by the infantry – at least in the northern provinces. Knee-length trousers were already included on the reliefs of Trajan's Column as a distinctive garment for Roman legionary and auxiliary infantry.[17] In the letter by Claudius Terentianus, trousers are assigned for marines.[18] From the second half of the 3rd century, and in the Late Roman period, long trousers are by then standard clothing for Roman soldiers. Two areas of origin bear consideration: the earliest evidence can be observed on the so-called sacrifice fresco from Dura-Europos.[19] They are also represented on the triumphal relief of Shapur I from Naqsh-i-Rustam.[20] This could indicate adoption of long trousers from the East. On the other hand, long trousers (*braccae*) are also the characteristic garment of Germanic warriors.[21] Since, in general, Germans served increasingly in the Roman army from the late 2nd century AD, in particular in the Late Roman period, the introduction of long trousers could also be due to influences from the north.

Undergarments

Since the Roman army also had to do their job all year in colder regions, there was a need for warm undergarments.

Beneath the undertunic, there was also the *subligaria* (underpants or loincloths?), mentioned in the Vindolanda tablets.[22]

Belts

The metal-studded leather military belt, which is now commonly referred to in the research jargon as the *cingulum*, served as a sidearm belt in the early Imperial period. The dagger and *gladius* could be worn together on a belt, but there were also often separate belts for the two edged weapons that were then worn crossed over each other ('cowboy fashion') (Fig. 108). A third possibility was that the dagger was attached to the belt, but the *gladius* to a slim shoulder strap, the *balteus*. For the early Imperial period, H. Ubl assumes that a kind of sash or cummerbund was worn under the *cingulum* (Ubl 1989). The sidearm belt probably underwent a name change in the ancient world. Originally it was probably called *balteus*. When this designation passed to the sword baldric, the name *cingulum* or *cingulum militiare* became customary.[23]

The *cingulum*, which secured the full-length tunic in a wide bunch above knee height, was the distinctive mark of the soldier. On duty he had to wear at least a belt and dagger. This also explains the disgrace of the military punishment which involved standing unbelted, pilloried 'as a civilian'.[24] From the Severan period at the latest, the different metals of the belt fittings (non-ferrous metal, silver, gold) seem to mirror the differences in military rank. From that time onwards, as the soldiers' status underwent a social enhancement, veterans probably also wore the *cingulum*, as grave finds from civilian settlements prove.[25] By the time of Justinian, the *cingulum* was still the identifying element designating the soldier's status. There is an illuminating episode in Procopius' *Anekdota* 24: apparently, people had obtained pensions without ever having been soldiers by falsely entering their names into the muster rolls of the military. To identify their (fake) status as soldiers and obtain the illegitimate privileges, they wore the *cingulum*. Justinian had the muster rolls checked and those caught in the act had the *cingulum* taken away, so that they, deprived of the outward signs of the military, no longer received any state benefits and had to go begging.

Figure 108 *Reconstruction drawing of an early imperial legionary without armour, with gladius and pugio on two cingula worn 'cowboy fashion'. Drawing: B. Burandt*

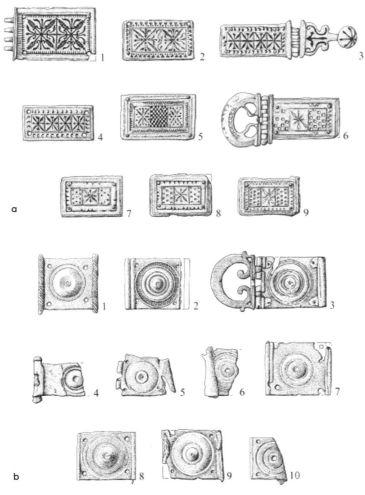

Figure 109a/b *Claudian to Flavian belt fittings of copper alloy from various locations in England (after Grew and Griffiths 1991)*

The metal-plated belt also continued into the Byzantine era, retaining its role as a status symbol, however, but now also imbued with religious symbolism (Albrecht 2010).

CINGULA OF THE 1ST TO THE MID-2ND CENTURY AD

Until the time of the late Republic, the weapon belts of the Roman army were not fastened with buckles, but rather with belt hooks, like those of the Celts and Germans. When the buckle – a strap fastener of metal with a loop, axle, and

tongue – was introduced is still unclear. The first military find site with a few buckles in addition to belt hooks, was the camp of Cáceres el Viejo dated to 80 BC.[26] There are no Caesarian finds, but a buckle can clearly be seen on the *cingulum* of the centurion Minucius on a military gravestone from Padua, which is dated to the period around 42 BC.[27] L. Pernet has now compiled possible late Republican buckles from Spain and Gaul.[28] In the earliest Augustan camps that have produced sufficiently representative amounts of material (Dangstetten, Oberaden, Augsburg-Oberhausen, and Haltern), buckles predominate and there are only a few belt hooks. The last bronze belt hooks with toggle clasps as *cingulum* fasteners are known from Haltern, Vetera I, and Augsburg-Oberhausen (five examples).[29] These pieces comprise the last remnants of the Republican military belt, and accordingly the invention of the buckle can be dated to the time around the middle of the 1st century BC. It then relatively quickly prevailed as a technically superior solution compared to other strap fastenings. From the early Imperial period until the middle of the 2nd century AD, there are hardly any complete sets of *cingula* mounts known. Only individual metal fittings are known, but these in large numbers, mostly found in military camps (Fig. 109). The exceptions are some burials, like that from Rheingönheim (Fig. 110) and a few settlement finds, for example the *cingulum* from the Auerberg.[30] From the incomplete sets of silver fittings from two early Roman Imperial *cingula* in the hoard from Tekije in Serbia, a complete set including the 'apron' can be reconstructed (Fig. 111a/b). In addition, complete or at least near-complete *cingula* were found with the remains of soldiers who are not buried normally, but rather entered the archaeological record in unusual circumstances. One of them is the soldier from Velsen I, lynched and thrown down a well, probably during the Friesian Rebellion of AD 28 (Morel and Bosman 1989). The marine buried alive on the beach at Herculaneum by the eruption of Vesuvius in AD 79 (Ortisi 2009) was also carrying a complete *cingulum*, like the soldier from Rheingönheim,[31] who most likely was killed and buried irregularly in the wake of the unrest after Nero's death in AD 68.

Otherwise, the form and number of fittings of earlier weapon belts can be reconstructed from representational sources, especially military gravestones. It should be noted,

Figure 110 *Early Imperial belt fittings made of tinned copper alloy with red enamel from Rheingönheim (Museum Speyer). Photo: M. Eberlein, Arch Staatsslg. Munich*

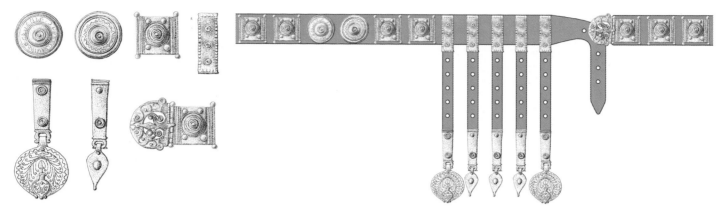

Figure 111a *Flavian belt components of silver (with false hinges) from the hoard from Tekije (after Mano Zisi 1957). Drawing: A. Smadi, Arch Institute University of Cologne*

Figure 111b *Flavian belt made of silver (with false hinges), reconstructed after the finds from the hoard from Tekije (after Mano Zisi 1957). Drawing: A. Smadi, Arch Institute University of Cologne*

Figure 112 *Silver belt components with frogs for sword suspension and false hinges from Pompeii (after Künzl 1977). Drawing: A. Smadi, Arch Institute University of Cologne*

however, that here the correspondence does not extend to the fine details. Thus the rectangular decorative fittings with rosette decoration frequently depicted on gravestones are not reflected in the original finds.

No organic residues of fabric or leather survive on these *cingula*, only the fittings of non-ferrous metals and – very rarely – of silver.[32] The surface is often tinned, but may also have a silver coating.[33] These sets of metal fittings (in the case of the buckle, bone is also known) consist of a buckle, decorative fittings, frog or button-and-loop fasteners for suspending the dagger and the *gladius* (Fig. 111), and an 'apron'. Metal strap ends were not yet common with early *cingula*. However, it is open to question whether each *cingulum* really had all of these components and if there were just simple versions with a buckle and fasteners (see below).

Buckles – *Cingula* buckles turn up from the Augustan period onwards in the archaeological material. E. Deschler-Erb has divided the finds from the 1st to early 2nd century AD into three forms (A, B and C).[34] Form A

Figure 113 *Copper-alloy buckle with openwork fitting (unprovenanced, privately owned). Photo: A. Pangerl*

(Augustan-Claudian) has a semi-circular to oval buckle loop resting on the inside edge of the loop of the fitting towards a bar with moulded decoration (Fig. 113), which is either plain or has voluted decorative terminals projecting

Figure 114 *Buckle with concave-sided frame from the 2nd century AD with the inscription C (enturia) SABINI LVCANI (unprovenced, privately owned). Photo: A. Pangerl*

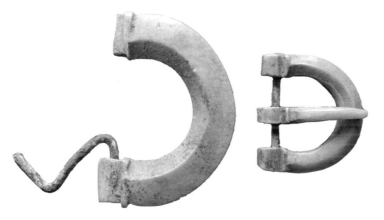

Figure 115 *Belt buckles made of bone, with spindles made of copper alloy (unprovenanced, privately owned). Photo: A. Pangerl*

beyond the loop. Form B (Flavian) is characterized by the terminals of the strap buckles being rolled up and the moulded bar does not extend beyond the width of the loop ends in length. Form C (1st half of the 2nd century AD) is defined by the enamel decoration on the flat buckle loop (see below). The buckle tongues are primarily designed three-pronged, but can also be simple.[35] As E. Deschler-Erb has already correctly stressed, this division could be clarified and refined.[36] Bone buckles with metal spindles are somewhat more rare among the finds (Fig. 115). A special type of belt buckle that occurred parallel to the

other forms from the Flavian period to the second half of the 2nd century AD, consisted of rectangular buckles with inward-curving sides and moulded terminal knobs (Fig. 114). The latest dated piece comes from the vexillation fortress at Eining-Unterfeld, which was occupied during the Marcomannic Wars between AD 172 and 179 by parts of the 3rd Italic Legion and an unknown cavalry unit.[37]

Decorative fittings – For belt mounts, undecorated, rectangular, and square bronze plates with incised circular grooves decorating the front (often with imitation hinges) occur. Moulded decorative circles were a subsequent development. M. Müller was able to disprove the opinion of Deschler-Erb and Peter that belt plates with circular ornamental grooves were an innovation of the Tiberian period.[38] Belt mounts of this type are usually tinned. Belts with simple rectangular mounts or square bronze plates with incised circular grooves dominate Augustan belt finds. The material from Augsburg-Oberhausen offers a similar picture, but it lacks the belt plates with incised circular groove decoration (Hübener 1973). The niello-decorated military equipment, including belt mounts, only occur from the Tiberian period onwards, but quickly became very popular (Fig. 109a).[39] Deschler-Erb sees the niello-inlaid militaria of all kinds as the definitive 'index fossils' (or indicators) of military sites of the Tiberio-Neronian period.[40]

Rectangular belt plates with embossed metal decoration appear in the Tiberian period, then fall into disuse by the Neronian period.[41] Up to the Trajanic period, belt fittings were designed without openwork decoration, but from the Flavian period, they could also be enamelled (see below). In each case, two of these decorative fittings were sometimes provided with separately made protruding knobs (called frogs) which could be up to 2 cm in diameter, and which served to fix the dagger to the belt. However, these were not strictly necessary, because they could be replaced by separate button-and-loop fasteners on a belt (see below). Larger button-and-loop fasteners (more than 2 cm in diameter) served in pairs for the suspension of the sword.

Apron – The apron usually shown in the representational sources (Fig. 116) consists of leather straps, which are densely covered with mostly round decorative mounts; at the end hangs a pendant that can be leaf- or heart-shaped, or lunate (Bishop 1992). If they have been found individually, all of these fittings cannot definitely be assigned to the apron: they were used as multi-functional components elsewhere, for example on harness.[42] This is also true for the embossed studs of the Flavian-Trajan period that can occur on aprons (Ulbert 1971; Feugère 1985) (Fig. 117). S. Ortisi was recently able to prove that they could also belong to the so-called *catellae*, an additional decoration of the sword scabbard (Ortisi 2009b).

Despite the frequent representations there are surprisingly few components that can be indisputably

Figure 116 *Graffito from an early Imperial tuff quarry in Kruft. It shows a soldier with loincloth, cingulum, and clearly emphasized apron with oversized double pickaxe. Photo: B. Streubl*

Figure 117 *Embossed studs made of copper alloy, probably from the apron (unprovenanced, privately owned). Photo: A. Pangerl*

assigned to the apron through their find contexts: there is one leather strap with metal fittings from Mainz already published by Lindenschmit (Fig. 118). Metal components found together and probably belonging to a single apron come from Vindonissa[43] and Oberstimm, for example. The latter set of copper-alloy apron fittings was found in rubbish deposits on top of the Trajanic-Hadrianic boats, which filled the harbour basin.[44]

Button-and-loop fasteners – Dagger sheaths have four rings, like those of the early Imperial *gladii*, on which the weapon could be attached to the belt (see below). For suspension, frogs or button-and-loop fasteners, often found in Roman military camps of the 1st and 2nd century AD, were made of copper alloy, but none can definitely be dated to the 3rd century.[45] These were sewn through the loop to a textile or leather belt or otherwise attached (Fig. 119).

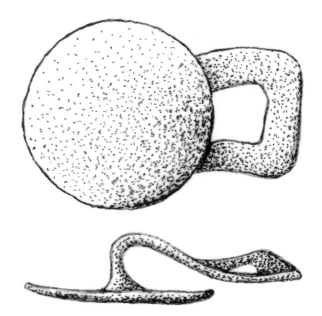

Figure 119 *Button-and-loop fastener of copper alloy. Drawing: A. Smadi, Arch Institute University of Cologne*

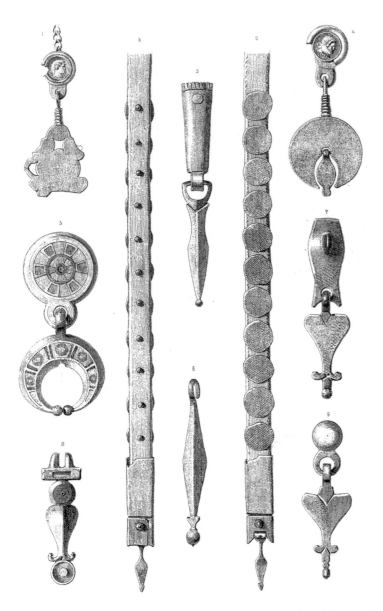

Figure 118 *Apron strap, leather and copper alloy from Mainz (after Lindenschmit 1870)*

Buttons of a similar form, which were either fixed or joined by a hinge to the decorative fittings of the military belt, served the same function. Identical, but larger buttons were used for suspending *gladii*. Here however, those button-and-loop fasteners, which were not directly attached to belt fittings, were designed with double loops.[46] In one case, at Vindonissa, it is clear that even a single, larger button-and-loop fastener was sufficient for the sword suspension, and this also seems to be the case at the new grave site of Ilok in Croatia, where a Mainz-type *gladius* with belt fittings has also been found.[47] From the East, so far only the piece published from Dülük Baba Tepesi[48] is known. It has a size that would be expected for dagger suspension, which is also true for a find from

Mons Claudianus in Egypt.[49] Similarly, the late Augustan and Tiberian double-looped button-and-loop fasteners of non-ferrous metal with glass medallions (Boschung 1987) must have served for sword suspension and were not just decorative *phalerae*.

From the middle of the 2nd century AD, frogs on belt fittings and button-and-loop fasteners fell into disuse, replaced for swords by the baldric (*baltei*), but for daggers by other features (Fischer 2011). The latest known occurrences so far are the specimens on the belt from Chichester (Figs 120, 121). An interim solution is found on a silver belt set of the Neuburg-Zauschwitz type from Constanza on the Black Sea (Romania), which probably originates from a burial: here fungiform studs for dagger suspension are riveted to panels with openwork decoration, which in turn were attached to the belt leather with rivets.[50]

Enamel-decorated *cingula* – From the Flavian period onwards, belt fittings decorated with enamel emerge, continuing to be made until the middle of the 2nd century AD (Fig. 122).[51] The complete set of fittings from grave 251 in Chichester is of particular importance here (Down and Rule 1971). It was associated with a coin of Faustina I, with a *terminus post quem* of AD 144. The Central Gaulish samian from the tomb also dates to about the middle of the 2nd century AD. The Chichester belt has a kind of intermediate position between the belts of the early Imperial type and the belts from the Antonine period in the second half of the 2nd century AD: it is the last known military belt, which still has frogs for dagger suspension and the first which, like the later *cingula*, has an additional suspension (in this case a loop) on a decorative fitting (see below).

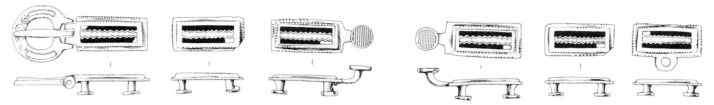

Figure 120 *Belt from a burial of the middle of the 2nd century AD from Chichester (after Down and Rule 1971)*

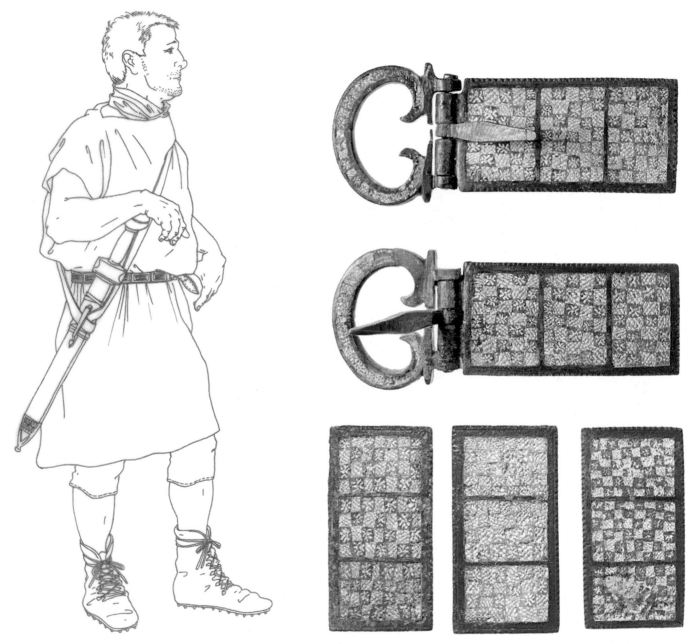

Figure 121 *Reconstruction drawing of a legionary without armour, with Chichester* cingulum *and* gladius *on* balteus. *Drawing: B. Burandt*

Figure 122 *Belt fittings with millefiori inlay (unprovenanced, privately owned). Photo: Ph. Gross, Arch Institute University of Cologne*

Figure 123 *Belt fittings from the second half of the 2nd century AD from a Roman cremation burial at Neuburg an der Donau (after Hübener 1957). Drawing: A. Smadi, Arch Institute University of Cologne*

CINGULA OF THE LATE 2ND AND THE 3RD CENTURY AD

The *cingulum* finally lost its function as a sword belt after the infantry had begun to replace the *gladius* with the *spatha*. It became a simple belt, gathering the tunic and used for attaching purses, knives, or other objects. *Cingula* still served as weapons belts only in the case of the suspension of daggers. However, these now had to be mounted in a different way, since suspension in the form of belt-mounted frogs or button-and-loop fasteners disappeared in the second half of the 2nd century AD at the latest.

From the second half of the 2nd century AD, other types of belt appear among metal fittings. The fastening of the belt now consists of a buckle plus one or two metal tongues. In addition, the belt now had a permanently mounted suspension point, for the attachment of a knife or purse and so on. The oldest such suspension point is on the enamel decorated belt fittings set from Chicester (Fig. 120). The older rectangular or square belt mounts are now replaced by the new, rectangular and long fittings decorated in openwork. The development of the belt can also be better assessed than was previously possible because of the special archaeological circumstances in the middle of the 2nd century AD: complete or almost complete sets of fittings from military belts now increasingly appear in burials, mostly cremations, particularly in Raetia and the adjoining Danubian provinces to the east.[52] The addition of weapons and military equipment as grave goods was an un-Roman custom at this time, but became very common in cremation and inhumation graves in the Germanic regions (Madyda-Legutko 1983). If we check the precise dating of these grave finds with the help of belt fittings from Roman cemeteries, we get to the period of the Marcomannic Wars at the earliest. This would coincide with the *Historia Augusta* mentioning that the Roman army was increasingly reinforced with Germans from the period of Marcus Aurelius (AD 161–80) onwards (*HA, Marc Aurelius* 20.7).

Buckles – The buckle frames were mostly oval and peltate, terminating in volutes. They were no longer connected to the first mount on the belt strap with a hinge. Now the connection was via a rectangular loop on the back of the buckle and a rectangular piece of sheet connected to the first belt mount and inserted through the loop.[53] Buckles with hinges, also with a rectangular buckle strap, remained in use.

Decorative fittings – The number of decorative fittings now increased, openwork items mainly being found, often additionally decorated with enamel, and embossed sheet metal, or contrasted with sheet metal in different colours set behind the openwork. They are often tinned and mostly have an elongated, rectangular shape. However, there are also other forms, for instance those in a Celtic style or – as a special form – letter-shaped fittings (see below).

Suspensions – Characteristic for the belt in the second half of the 2nd and the 3rd centuries AD are eyelets or moveable rings mounted on fittings, both serving as suspensions for a variety of objects. These were still present in the Late Roman period (see below). Combined with various belt types are round, openwork plates, which served as mounts for suspension devices. They either had a hole in the middle through which a split pin was inserted, upon which a movable ring was mounted, or they had a ring cast in one with the plate. This belt component and the VTERE FELIX-belts (see below) are equipment components which occur mainly in the Danube region. However, they are not the only weaponry and equipment elements of the later 2nd century AD that seem to be concentrated in the more limited region of the Danube army. Research has only just begun here.[54]

Military belts with openwork fittings with an elongated rectangular shape (the Neuburg-Zauschwitz type) – This type of belt from the second half of the 2nd century AD, complete sets of which can usually be found in burials, can certainly be further subdivided typologically. For now, I have grouped them together as the Neuburg-Zauschwitz type, although the two eponymous grave finds look quite different. Grave 10 from Neuburg on the Danube (Bavaria) is well dated by a Reginus bowl of Dragendorff type 37 into the period after the middle of the 2nd century AD.[55] The belt from Neuburg (Fig. 123) consists of four openwork fittings with voluted decoration. One of them includes a buckle with a rectangular loop for attaching the first mount. A double hook made of metal represents an unusual suspension device, mounted on the belt by means of rivets. The cremation burial from Zauschwitz, in the district of Borna in Saxony,[56] was a Germanic burial from far outside the Roman Empire. Besides Germanic grave goods, it contained a complete Roman belt set of copper alloy (Fig. 124), which had been damaged in the fire of the pyre. In addition, an iron Roman sword scabbard runner was discovered. On the belt were five almost identical, long rectangular fittings with rectangular openwork, to which a circular plate was fitted

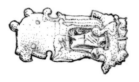

Figure 124 *Belt fittings of the second half of the 2nd century AD from a Germanic cremation burial at Zauschwitz in Saxony (after Coblenz 1960). Drawing: A. Smadi, Arch Institute University of Cologne*

Figure 125 *Belt set of the Neuburg/Zauschwitz type in copper alloy from the second half of the 2nd century AD, probably from a Roman inhumation burial (unprovenanced, privately owned). Photo: A. Pangerl*

on one side, which in turn was decorated with five attached roundels. The rectangular part of the fittings formed a moulded frame, fitted with an embossed plate on which a lion leaping to the right is shown. One of these fittings is constructed as a buckle plate, which was attached by a hinge to an oval buckle frame with volutes.

A long, rectangular openwork fitting forming the word 'IOVIS' in a frame probably did not belong to this set of fittings, but to a baldric. A similar belt type was also found in a cremation grave from Romula in Romania.[57] Lately, more sets of belt mounts from such belts made of copper alloy (Fig. 125) and silver (Fig. 126, 127), which probably originated from the middle to lower Danube region, have appeared in private ownership.

Klosterneuburg type belt – Sets of fittings of the Klosterneuburg type also belong in the second half of the 2nd century AD and lasted into the first half of the 3rd century AD. They consist of various types of buckles and

decorative fittings in a free arrangement of the Celtic style (Reuter 2001). In addition to the eponymous set of fittings from Klosterneuburg, these belts are known from, for example, cremations in Faimingen (Fig. 128), Carnuntum, and in Romania.[58]

In the eponymous cremation burial VIII/10 from Klosterneuburg, three decorated fittings, a suspension attachment, and a moulded strap end were discovered. The belt set from cremation grave 292 from Faimingen contained a buckle and four decorative mounts of different shapes and that from cremation grave 26 in Carnuntum consisted of an ornamental mount, a buckle with a rectangular loop for attaching the first mount and two strap ends. The grave goods in cremation burial 174b from Carnuntum included a decorative mount, a buckle with a rectangular loop and, as a numismatic *terminus post quem*, a *denarius* of Alexander Severus for Orbiana, minted between AD 225–7. Finally, cremation grave 2 at Romula in Romania contained a buckle and a strap end. The only two reasonably complete sets of fittings of this belt type that I know of are made of silver and, because of their completeness, probably come from inhumations. One is apparently complete, but unfortunately without provenance, and is privately owned (Fig. 129, 285, 286). It is shown here for the first time. The other comes from Constanza on the Black Sea.[59] It only lacks the strap end(s) and the suspension attachment.

All other sets of fittings of the Klosterneuburg type mentioned so far (Fig. 130) are known from cremations and are often decimated and damaged by fire. With the increase in inhumation burials by AD 200, the number of complete and intact fitting sets of military belts in the Danube region also increases. Outside this region, the custom of including military belts in burials is seldom found – with exceptions only proving the rule!

VTERE FELIX belt – The so-called VTERE FELIX belt was a special Danubian variant form. Here we have

Figure 126 *Belt set of the Neuburg/Zauschwitz type in silver from the second half of the 2nd century AD with opus interrasile decoration, including the inscription Γ. ΦΙΛΙΡΡΟΥ and four suspension loops. Probably from a Roman inhumation burial (unprovenanced, private ownership, after Spier 2010)*

COSTUMES, WEAPONS, AND EQUIPMENT OF THE ARMY FROM ORIGINAL ARCHAEOLOGICAL FINDS

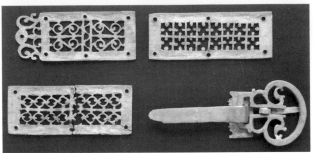

Figure 127 *Belt set of the Neuburg/Zauschwitz type in silver with opus interrasile decoration from the second half of the 2nd century AD from an inhumation burial (unprovenanced, privately owned). Photo: A. Pangerl*

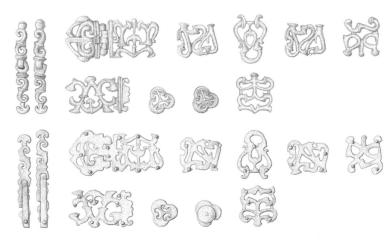

Figure 129 *Silver belt fittings, probably from a Roman inhumation burial (unprovenanced, privately owned). Drawing: A. Smadi, Arch Institute University of Cologne*

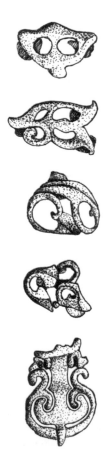

Figure 128 *Belt fittings of the Klosterneuburg type in Celticising style from cremation burial 292 at Faimingen (after Müller 1999). Drawing: A. Smadi, Arch Institute University of Cologne*

Figure 130 *Belt fittings of copper alloy of the Neuburg and Klosterneuburg types from the second half of the 2nd century AD from belts (unprovenanced, privately owned). Photo: A. Pangerl*

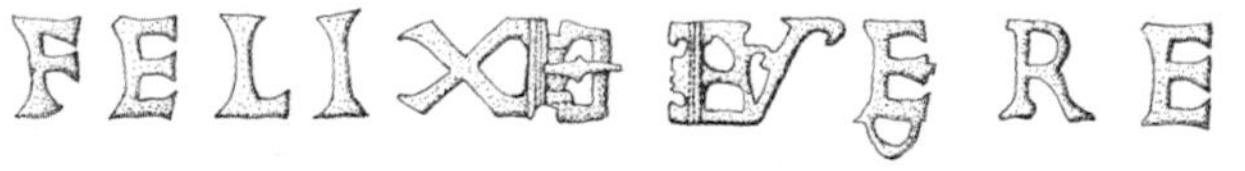

Figure 131 *Belt with fittings of copper alloy in the form of letters with the inscription FELIX VTERE. From an inhumation burial at Lyon (after Hoss 2006). Drawing: A. Smadi, Arch Institute University of Cologne*

Figure 132 *Belt with silver fittings in the form of letters with Greek inscription MNHMΩN. (unprovenanced, privately owned; after Hoss 2006)*

Figure 133 *Solid silver belt fittings with the inscription 'LEONI', and two eye-shaped double studs (unprovenanced, privately owned). Photo: A. Pangerl*

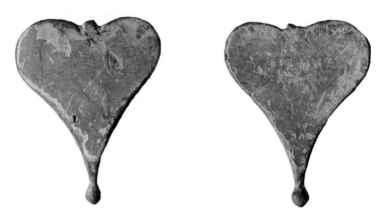

Figure 134 *Balteus fitting in copper alloy, inlaid in silver with 'LEONI' (unprovenanced, privately owned). Photo: A. Pangerl*

a complete finds assemblage that can be precisely dated due to both numismatic and historical considerations. A grave from the region of Lyon and well-dated by coins with a belt set (Fig. 131) and a *spatha* with its scabbard fittings can be related to the decisive battle of the year AD 197 between Septimius Severus and the usurper Clodius Albinus.[60] The copper-alloy belt fittings take the form of letters that make up the slogan 'VTERE FELIX'. The rectangular-framed buckle is connected via a rectangular loop with the letter 'X', while an 'E' of the VTERE FELIX belt carries a suspension loop pointing downwards. The belt from Lyon was found far outside the usual distribution area of this belt type in Noricum and Pannonia.[61] It seems probable that the deceased had been a soldier in the army of the victor in this battle, Septimius Severus (AD 193–211). He was proclaimed emperor by the Danube army while governor of Upper Pannonia in Carnuntum on the Danube and his rule was initially based primarily on troops from this area.

Further belts with letters – A set of silver belt fittings, the components of which form the Greek inscription MNHMΩN ('Remember') (Fig. 132), was published by S. Hoss (2006). It is unprovenanced, but probably comes from the middle to lower Danube region. This also applies to the set of fittings of a belt made of solid cast silver, which will be discussed here for the first time: the assemblage is only known to me from a photograph. It has a buckle with a rectangular frame, which is connected by a hinge

to a fitting with two mounting holes. This is combined with four fittings in the form of ornate letters with tendrils (Fig. 133). The fittings together form the Latin inscription 'LEONI' ('for the Lion'). The last fitting forms a ligature of the letters N and I. An interpretation of the right part of this last fitting as a Christian cross is the first reaction, but it can be rejected for objective and chronological reasons: this would require a dating at the earliest of the 4th century AD. However, no parallels exist for either buckles of this form or belt sets with this sort of decoration in late antiquity (see below), let alone in the Byzantine period (Schulze-Dörrlamm 2009; 2009a)! This belt can be dated unequivocally to the 3rd century AD and therefore cannot be Late Roman or Byzantine.

A different theoretical possibility is to read the inscription in Greek as 'LEONTI', but the content would be the same. According to information from W. Eck (Cologne), this is not necessary. This is also confirmed by a similarly unprovenanced leaf-shaped fitting made of bronze (Fig. 134), which in silver inlay bears the Latin inscription 'LEONI' (with the last letter 'NI' as a ligature, but not designed for the purposes of a cross-shaped decoration). This massively cast piece will have sat at the terminal strap end of a baldric, connected to a matching

Figure 135 *Representation of Roman emperors (Gordian III. And Valerian I.) with frame-buckle belts on a Sassanian rock relief at Bishapur (after Hermann 1983). Drawing: A. Smadi, Arch Institute University of Cologne*

fitting by a hinge (now broken off). Similar baldric fittings from the Upper German-Raetian Limes area[62] and the leaf-shaped terminal of a leather baldric from Thorberg confirm this interpretation.[63]

The forms of the buckle and of the letter fittings with their ornamentation with tendrils are a good match with the dating to the time of Caracalla proposed here (see below)! The belt also includes two fittings with stylized representations of eyes, for which there are currently no parallels. Their function is clear: they may be interpreted as frogs for securing the dagger on the belt (Fischer 2012).

To interpret this belt, Welwei (1992) has already discussed the literary source of the epitome of Cassius Dio (79.6.1):

> Indeed, the emperor had Scythians and Germans around him, free men as well as slaves, which he had taken from their masters and mistresses and provided with weapons, in whom he imbued obviously greater trust than his own soldiers; among other honours, he also awarded them by appointment to the centurionate and called them his 'lions'.

So from the text there was clearly a bodyguard of Caracalla, comprising centurions of barbaric origins and given the honorary title 'The Lions'. They were provided with weapons by the emperor. I would therefore like to relate both the silver LEONI belt and the baldric fitting directly to the bodyguard of Caracalla, which consisted of Goths and other Germanic tribesmen.[64] Leoni is the dative case and this term 'for a lion' could be interpreted in the sense of dedication and/or a gift of the emperor to a guardsman. Thus, the belt would be very closely datable to the later years of the sole reign of Caracalla, from AD 211–17. After the death of Caracalla, the belt could scarcely have been worn publicly any more.

The material of the silver belt fittings may give cause for further considerations: if my suggestion is correct,

the wearers of these belts held the rank of centurion. This supports the view expressed by me a few years ago that the silver belt sets of the Roman military belt in the 3rd century AD may have been a privilege of higher ranks (Fischer 1988).

S. Hoss has listed some letter fittings that do not belong to the letter belts discussed so far.[65] The ring-buckle belt with the inscription LEG III CYR can also be allocated to this group. It can be concluded that there were more inscriptions on letter belts. They belong to belts with fastenings without buckles.

In the 3rd century AD, the Roman army adopted belt fasteners that functioned without the previously conventional buckle with loop and tongue. The so-called ring- or frame-buckle belts now became particularly common. Why this custom started and where it originated is still poorly understood, with von Schnurbein considering a Germanic or Sarmatian origin for ring-buckle belts.[66] Another possibility may be illustrated by the representations on the Iranian triumphal relief at Bishapur (Fig. 135). It depicts the vanquished Roman emperors Gordian III and Valerian I, wearing rectangular frame-buckle belts, while the Persian soldiers wear ring-buckle belts.[67] Thus an eastern Iranian origin for this belt form is also possible. Research has not yet progressed far here. I do not share the opinion of von Schnurbein, that large numbers of civilians also wore ring-buckle belts (von Schnurbein 1995); the bulk of the evidence – whether representational or archaeological – is clearly from military contexts. The frame-buckle belts and belt sets of the Regensburg-Großprüfening type, however, should be seen as being original Roman developments. H. Ubl has associated the introduction of the ring- and frame-buckle belts with a proposed equipment reform under Caracalla, and finds from burials do at least not contradict this dating.[68] However, theories about so-called 'equipment reforms' in the Roman Empire should generally be treated with considerable scepticism! Certain special forms of frame buckle belt sets made from silver occur with a striking frequency in the Danube region. However, this may have more to do with the local burial customs than being a reflection of ancient reality.

Just as suddenly as this belt without regular buckles appeared in the 3rd century AD, so it abruptly and without trace disappeared at the end of that century. So far as it is currently possible to tell, belt sets without a buckle formed a significant share of the belts of the 3rd century AD, but they were not able to completely displace the conventional belt with a buckle fastening.

Belts of the Regensburg Großprüfening type – Among archaeological material of the late 2nd and 3rd century AD, two associated rectangular openwork plates made of copper alloy with rivet holes are found. Each set can be connected together by means of T-shaped hooks on one plate fitting into T-shaped openings on the other plate (Fig. 136). These fittings

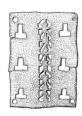

Figure 136 *Belt of the Regensburg-Großprüfening type in copper alloy. 1–3: cremation burial 74 from Regensburg-Großprüfening (Fischer 1990). Drawing: A. Smadi, Arch Institute University of Cologne*

Figure 137 *Frame-buckle belt fasteners of copper alloy (unprovenanced, privately owned). Photo: A. Pangerl*

were already identified by J. Oldenstein as belt buckles, even though no contexts appropriate to this interpretation were known at the time. S. James on the other hand, attributed the specimens from Dura-Europos to horse harness.[69] Cremation grave 74 from Regensburg-Großprüfening[70] contained such a set together with a round openwork plate with a suspension split-ring, which clearly indicates that this is a belt closing system and J. Oldenstein's identification was correct. This belt type is possibly identical with the closed 'buckle-plate belt' of H. Ubl on 3rd century AD gravestone representations of the Danube region.[71] Ubl's opinion, that this form of military belt was reserved for officers and NCOs, is not supported by the archaeological evidence.[72]

Ring- and frame-buckle belts – These very frequent 3rd century AD belt sets are made of copper alloy and often tinned, while examples from bone are rare.[73] They consist of a closure (the ring or frame) through which the leather belt is pulled back on either side and fastened with adjustable double-ended fungiform studs (Fig. 137).[74] Gravestone depictions show that one end could finish in a long strap, which was occasionally split into two, with each end terminated by a strap end (Fig. 138). This strap could be draped around the belt in several ways. There are, however, no temporal differences nor differences in military rank of the wearer in these various styles.[75] These are at best individual fashion trends. Even double fungiform studs by themselves are not diagnostic of either ring- or frame-buckle belts, as they are found used elsewhere, for instance in horse harness.[76] Because of the nature of the fastening, S. von Schnurbein therefore refers to them as button or stud belts.[77] These ring- and frame-buckle

Figure 138 *Strap terminal of copper alloy, probably by a ring- or frame-buckle belt, with inset, coloured enamel inscription VTERE FELIX (unprovenanced, privately owned). Photo: A. Pangerl*

belt sets could have decorative fittings of various types and devices for the suspension of various things[78] as well as belt tongues in a variety of forms, but often in the form of two-part hinged strap terminals.[79] Since the bulk of the sets come from cremations, reasonably undamaged and complete sets of ring- and frame-buckle belt fittings are very rare.

The ratio of 3rd century AD ring- and frame-buckle belts to each other is marked by a strange contradiction: on gravestones, representations of the ring buckle clearly outweigh those of frame buckles, while in the archaeological material ring buckles are very rare, with only a few known, such as the set from cremation grave 39 at Regensburg-Großprüfening (Fischer 2000, Tab. 98D, 1) or the belt set of *legio III Cyrenaica* from the Middle East (Fig. 139). By contrast, frame buckles dominate the archaeological finds. These usually have decorative elements within the frame, mostly in the so-called Celtic style (cf. Reuter 2001). The rarity of the rings from ring-buckle belts among archaeological finds may be because these rings were made of metal or bone and can only safely be identified as belt components in grave contexts. As individual finds in settlement contexts, they might have been used for other purposes, for instance on horse harness, or for other functions.

The scale of our ignorance in these matters is shown by a belt set for a copper-alloy ring-buckle belt in a private collection in England (Fig. 139). It is supposed to have come from Israel, which the inscription, formed by the set of letter-shaped mounts, at least does not contradict. This set of mounts consists of a moulded bronze ring, two strap ends with central rings,[80] and letters that make up the inscription 'LEG (io) III CYR(enaica)'. *Legio III Cyrenaica*, previously in Egypt, is attested in Bosra (province of Arabia, present-day Syria) at least since the reign of Hadrian. The 'Y' of this belt has a suspension loop cast as one on the

LEG Ⅲ ◯ C Ⴤ R

Figure 139 *Copper-alloy set of fittings from a ring-buckle belt with components in the form of letters from the inscription LEG III CYR. Probably from a Roman inhumation burial (unprovenanced, privately owned). Photo: private*

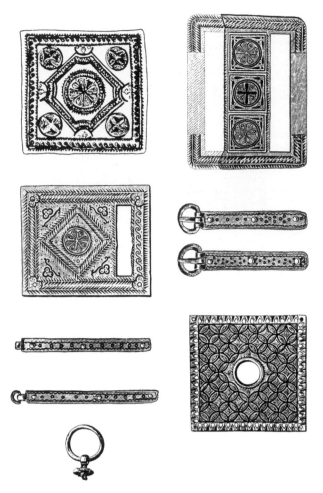

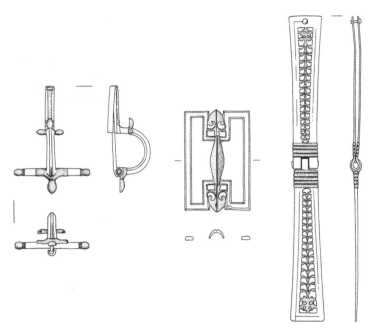

Figure 140 *Frame-buckle belt, elaborately designed in silver with associated brooch with a long hinge arm, probably from an inhumation burial (State Archaeological Collection in Munich, after Fischer 1988)*

Figure 141 *Frame-buckle belt, elaborately designed in silver with niello decoration, from a Roman inhumation burial in Budapest (Fischer 1988)*

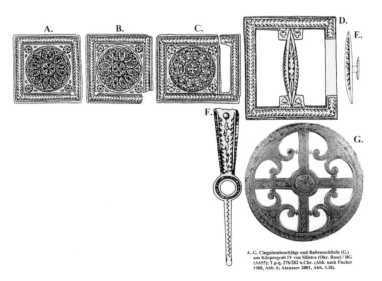

A.-G. Cingulumbeschläge und Balteusschließe (G.) aus Körpergrab IV von Silistra (Okr. Ruse) / BG (A655); T.p.q. 276/282 n.Chr. (Abb. nach Fischer 1988, Abb. 6; Atanasov 2001, Abb. 3.28).

Figure 142 *Frame-buckle belt, elaborately designed in silver with niello decoration, from a Roman inhumation burial in Silistra (after Miks 2007)*

Figure 143 *Frame-buckle belt, elaborately designed in silver with niello decoration with balteus fitting from a Germanic inhumation burial in Sackrau (Fischer 1988)*

end of the Y pointing downwards, as was usual for belts of this period. All letter mounts have cast shanks on the back. A mount or pendant in the shape of a composite bow and an openwork mount (both of copper alloy) must also have belonged to the set, as their patination is visibly the same. Both find parallels in Dura-Europos.[81] What this set of fittings lacks are the studs to fasten the belt and/or frogs to suspend a dagger from the belt.

Intricately detailed versions of ring- and frame-buckle belts – Richly decorated silver sets of ring- and frame-buckle belts can be seen on especially splendid variants of essentially the same type. They were mainly found in the middle and lower Danube region (Fig. 140–2), but also in 'Barbaricum' (Fig. 143). They are dated to the last third of the 3rd century AD.[82] In recent years, such splendid belts have increasingly surfaced in the art market, unfortunately without any archaeological context (Fig. 144). However, it seems very likely that they too originated from the middle and lower Danube region. An extremely opulent variant made from partially gilded silver with rich *opus interrasile*

Figure 144 *Fitting from a frame-buckle belt, elaborately designed in silver with niello decoration and gilding (unprovenanced, privately owned). Photo: A. Pangerl*

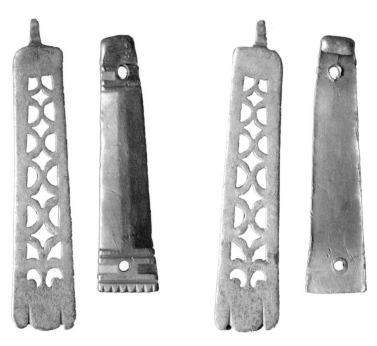

Figure 147 *Hinged strap terminals, probably from frame-buckle belts, elaborately designed in silver and gold (unprovenanced, privately owned). Photo: A. Pangerl*

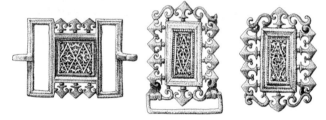

Figure 145 *Set of fittings from a frame-buckle belt, elaborately designed in silver with opus interrasile decoration and underlaid gold sheet from Cologne (Fischer 1988). Drawing: A. Smadi, Arch Institute University of Cologne*

Figure 146 *Strap terminals from frame-buckle belts, elaborately designed in silver with opus interrasile decoration and underlaid gold sheet (unprovenanced, privately owned). Photo: A. Pangerl*

Figure 148 *Annular brooch made of silver, with niello decoration and detachable foot like that of a crossbow brooch (unprovenanced, privately owned)*

decoration comes from Cologne (Fig. 145), another such fitting recently appearing in private ownership (Fig. 146).

In these magnificent sets, often decorated with niello inlay or gilding, the double fungiform studs are replaced by those in the shape of a boat. The strap ends are very large and elaborately worked, mostly in the form of hinge-shaped strap terminals with or without openwork decoration. A golden example is even known from private collections, which allows conclusions to be drawn about the nature of the remaining fittings in the set (Fig. 147).

Ring-buckle belts or omega brooches? – J. Oldenstein has postulated that certain forms of omega brooch were belt fasteners of the late 2nd and 3rd century AD.[83] Now there is a (regrettably unprovenanced) omega brooch of niello-inlaid silver from a private collection (Fig. 148) that clearly contradicts this assumption. This brooch is combined with a faceted foot typical of early crossbow brooches of Keller type 1 (see below). The unique structural affinity with a typical cloak brooch proves that the omega brooches in question should be viewed as brooches for cloaks, and not as belt fasteners or a special variety of ring-buckle belt.

THE LATE ROMAN BELT

Towards the end of the 3rd century AD, the Late Roman army reintroduced a belt which was invariably closed with a buckle with a loop and tongue, rapidly replacing the ring- and frame-buckle belts. These new belts were rich with decorative metal fittings, mostly of copper alloy. However, there were also belts decorated with silver and gold fittings, which were associated with crossbow brooches of the same material. These differences in the value of the metal used definitely reflect differences in the ranks of the wearers.

Origin – There is thus no unbroken continuous development of the soldiers' belts of the Roman army in the period around AD 300. Instead, development is characterized by the sharp break and rapid change between the buckle-free ring- and frame-buckle belts to the reintroduction of belt fastenings in the form of buckles with tongues. So the inspiration for these new Late Roman belt forms may not have been a resumption of older Roman traditions, but instead may have come from outside.

Prototypes for these Late Roman military belts can be found in the Germanic regions of central and northern Europe in the 3rd century AD.[84] There, weapon belts with buckles and multipartite decorative fittings, often made of precious metals, developed independently of direct influences from the Roman Empire. Particularly impressive examples are known from northern Germany and southern Scandinavia, but also from central Germany: plenty of bronze and silver fittings from weapon belts were found at the moorland votive sites of Illerup-Ådal[85] (around AD 200), Nydam (Rau 2010), and Thorsberg[86] (c. mid-3rd century AD). In Tombs 3 and 7 at Neudorf-Bornstein in Schleswig-Holstein and in the votive moorland deposit at Ejsbøl itself, decorative belts of members of the upper classes were found which were decorated with ornamental fittings made of silver, with embossed plates of gold and with blue glass inlays (von Carnap-Bornheim 2003). These belts date to the second half of the 3rd century AD, and therefore belong to a period in which the ring- and frame-buckle belt was dominant in the Roman army. The form of the decorative fittings clearly anticipated later Roman military belt propeller stiffeners of the 4th century AD (Figs 149–50). This also applies to the silver-plated, copper-alloy belt fittings from the inhumation burial at Berching-Pollanten in Bavaria (Fischer 1984). Also dating to the last third of the 3rd century AD, the belt in the royal burial at Gommern in Saxony-Anhalt,[87] in its width and

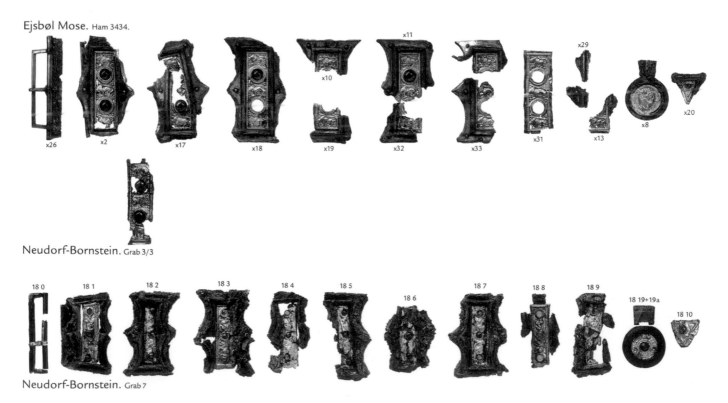

Figure 149 *Germanic ceremonial belt of copper alloy and gold with glass inserts from chambered tombs at Neudorf-Bornstein and Ejsbøl (after v. Carnap-Bornheim 2003)*

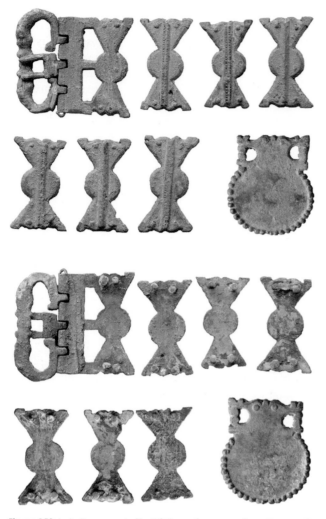

Figure 150 *Late Roman set of belt fittings of copper alloy with propeller fittings made of copper alloy (unprovenanced, privately owned). Photo: A. Pangerl*

Figure 151 *Late Roman buckle with strap terminal, silver gilt (unprovenanced, privately owned). Photo: A. Pangerl*

numerous metal fittings, anticipates features of 4th century Roman weapon belts. So I think it very likely that Germanic weapon belts of the 3rd century AD from the northern German-Scandinavian region and central Germany were the direct forerunners of Late Roman military belts, not internal Roman developments.

Fittings that have suspension attachments are typical for all of these Germanic belts, from which a knife, a firelighter (flint and firesteel), a purse, and other things could be suspended.[88] Germanic influences can also be seen in the fact that Late Roman military belts become more frequent as grave goods not only in the Danube region, but also in Britain, Gaul, and the Rhineland. This is due to the fact that Germans who, when in Barbaricum, usually followed the practice of including belts and weapons in burials, now served in the Roman army in large numbers (Böhme 1986a; Fischer 2009c). For the Late Roman belt there are several synthetic studies with different emphases by A. Riegl (1927), H. Bullinger (1969), E. Keller (1971),

H.-W. Böhme (1974 and 1986), M. Sommer (1984), and Bishop and Coulston (2006),[89] but it is still impossible to gain a satisfactory overview of this category of finds as yet. There is still no study in which Late Roman military belts have been treated in a truly adequate manner. The starting point for such an overview would be far more favourable than for the Roman military belt of earlier periods, since Late Roman belts are indeed found in large numbers in Late Roman burials as complete sets of fittings. The following brief remarks are therefore indicative of an inadequate state of research.

From the beginning of the Late Roman period onwards, simple belts are found among grave goods, consisting of only a buckle, at the most in combination with a strap end of non-ferrous metal or silver (Figs 150–2). From the time of Constantine in the 4th century AD, belts with propeller stiffeners appear, mostly of copper alloy (Fig. 153), less often in silver, occasionally even in gold.[90] These belts also include disk-shaped, heart-shaped, amphora-shaped, and

Figure 152 *Late Roman silver buckle with niello decoration (unprovenanced, privately owned). Photo: A. Pangerl*

Figure 154 *Late Roman copper-alloy buckle (unprovenanced, privately owned). Photo: A. Pangerl*

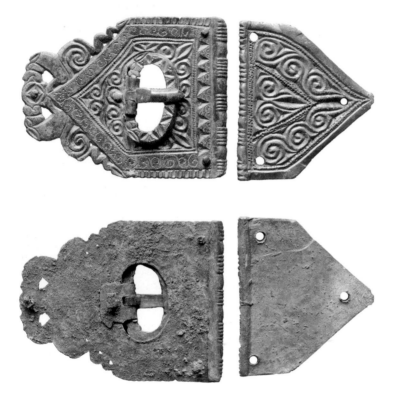

Figure 153 *Late Roman set of copper-alloy belt fittings with chip carving (unprovenanced, privately owned). Photo: A. Pangerl*

Figure 155 *Late Roman copper-alloy chip-carved set (unprovenanced, privately owned). Photo: A. Pangerl*

other types of strap end (Figs 156–7). In the second half of the 4th and in the early 5th centuries AD, wide belts are found, decorated with richly decorated, non-ferrous metal or silver fittings with chip carving (Fig. 154, 155).[91] They are often combined with one or more rosette fittings with suspension attachments.[92] These belong with rectangular, lancet-shaped, and other strap ends.

From the first half of the 5th century AD, in addition to multipart belts with notched fittings, other belt fittings were in use, namely those with just a buckle without fittings and those with a buckle plate.[93] These types then mark the transition towards the Byzantine belts of the eastern part of the Empire. Among burial finds, such as those from the fort cemetery at Krefeld-Gellep (Pirling and Siepen

2006), belt fittings are mostly combined with crossbow brooches (Figs 158–60). Such combinations also occur in gold (Figs 161–3), for instance in the hoard from Ténès in Algeria (Heurgon 1958).

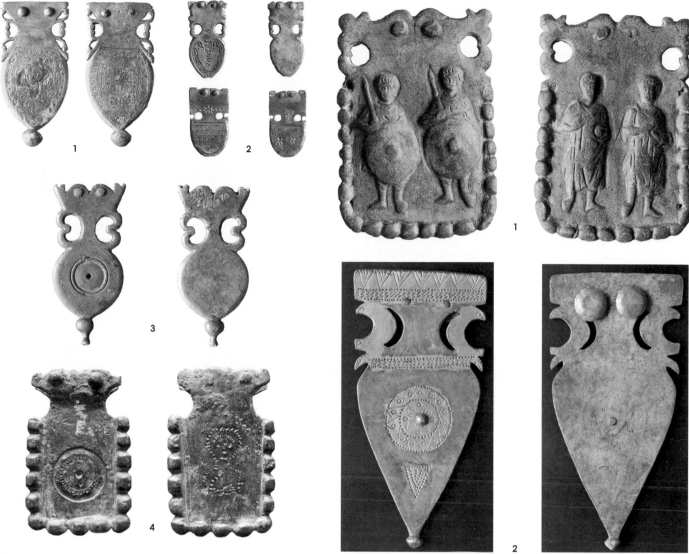

Figure 156 *Late Roman strap ends in silver (1 and 2) and copper alloy (3 and 4; unprovenanced, privately owned)*

Figure 157 *Late Roman strap ends in silver and copper alloy. 1: cast from copper alloy. On the front, two soldiers, on the back officials; 2: partly gilded silver with punched decoration (unprovenanced, privately owned)*

Cloaks

For the Roman period, a confusingly large number of different types of cloak are recorded literarily (*e.g. abolla, birrus* or *burrus, lacerna, laena, paenula, paludamentum, pallium,* or *sagum*).[94] It is still not possible to associate them with particular examples of types of cloak in the representational sources or even in actual finds, especially as these cloaks apparently often differed less in shape than in material and colour.

Cloaks are among the typical job-specific garments of Roman soldiers, because they were obliged to spend long periods of time outdoors, in bad weather and the cold, in contrast to most civilians.[95] Cloaks were worn on the march, on duty, or used as a sleeping mat or blanket. In battle, they were mostly not worn. In the Roman army there

were different types of military cloaks in textile or leather,[96] which were also subject to changing fashions over time.

PAENULA

For the *paenula*, a kind of poncho with a hood, there is a comprehensive general study by F. Kolb, H. Ubl having discussed the military *paenula* in detail.[97] This cloak was made of various materials, such as a fulled woolen fabric (similar to the later Loden cloth of the Alpine regions) or leather. Martial mentioned a *paenula scortea* (14.130), a leather rain cape, which was perhaps worn by the military. The *paenula* was the largest and heaviest cloak for Roman soldiers. It was of a semi-circular, broad cut, had an opening for the head, and was provided with an integral

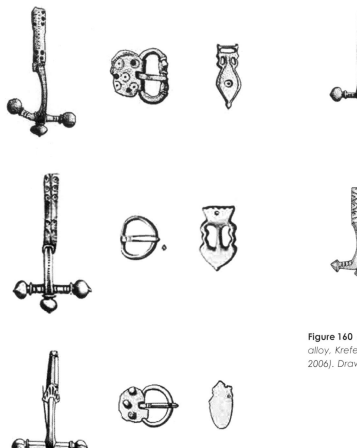

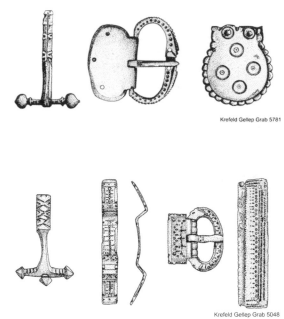

Krefeld Gellep Grab 5781

Krefeld Gellep Grab 5048

Figure 160 *Late Roman belt fittings and crossbow brooches of copper alloy, Krefeld-Gellep burials 5781 and 5048 (after Pirling and Siepen 2006). Drawing: A. Smadi, Arch Institute University of Cologne*

Figure 158 *Late Roman belt fittings and crossbow brooches of copper alloy, Krefeld-Gellep burials 3093, 2872, and 4586 (after Pirling and Siepen 2006). Drawing: A. Smadi, Arch Institute University of Cologne*

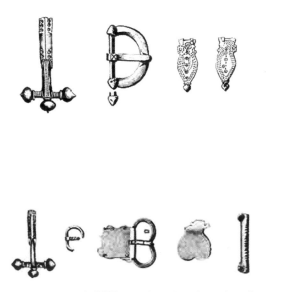

Figure 159 *Late Roman belt fittings and crossbow brooches of copper alloy, Krefeld-Gellep burials 2832 and 2942 (after Pirling and Siepen 2006). Drawing: A. Smadi, Arch Institute University of Cologne*

Figure 161 *Crossbow brooches of the Keller 6 group and belt fittings of gold. Ténès in Algeria (after Heurgon 1958)*

Figure 162 *Belt fittings of gold. Ténès in Algeria (after Heurgon 1958)*

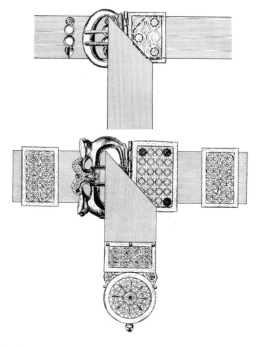

Figure 163 *Reconstructed belt with fittings of gold. Ténès in Algeria (after Heurgon 1958)*

hood. It was slipped over easily with only about one third of the front of the *paenula* stitched up, a fastening with brooches not being necessary. One could, however, reduce the front opening with brooches. To ensure freedom of movement for the arms, the *paenula* could be rolled up, folded, or the hem thrown back over the shoulder. In this, the *paenula* resembles the modern burnus in North Africa. In the military, as well as for the Praetorians, it was probably already in common use in the late Republic, but certainly from the Augustan period to the end of the 2nd century AD without any apparent change in shape. The latest known representations of the *paenula* come from a relief from Croy Hill in Scotland, which dates to the time of Antoninus Pius (AD 138–61) (Coulston 1988a), and Pedestal Relief 16 (Fig. 165) on the Arch of Septimius Severus in Rome.[98]

F. Kolb sees the *paenula* primarily as a raincoat for the military, which was worn along with the *sagum*.[99] This must be treated with some scepticism, because the *sagum* – if it consisted of appropriate material – could also be used as protection from the rain. How else could it replace the *paenula* as a military cloak?

SAGUM

The *sagum* was often considered typical for the army; its name at least seems to come from the Celts. This cloak consisted of a rectangular, later a semicircular woolen piece of fabric, fastened on the right shoulder by brooches with a correspondingly high bow (cloak brooches). The right arm – the 'sword arm' – was not covered by the cloak, remaining free. Brooched cloaks are known in the Roman army from the late Republic onwards. The rectangular- and semicircular-cut *sagum* were apparently in use at the same time in the 1st and 2nd centuries AD but, according to H. Ubl, only the semicircular form was in use in the 3rd century AD, the *paenula* having already been completely replaced among the army at the end of the 2nd century AD.[100] However, the rectangular *sagum* definitely still appears in murals at Dura-Europos in the 3rd century AD.[101]

The *sagum* is testified for both legionaries and auxiliary soldiers, and among the cavalry. Perhaps differences in rank were denoted by the *sagum* colour; in the 3rd century AD, there were some especially splendid variations in Dura-Europos: white *sagum* with purple-dyed fringe on the tribune Terentius (James 2007 XXV, Plates 1 and 2).

PALUDAMENTUM

Officers from the *optio* and above, generals, and emperors wore the general's cloak, the *paludamentum*, derived from the Greek *chlamys*, originally a short riding and travelling cloak. The principal differences between the *sagum* and *paludamentum* are largely unclear. A highly visible distinction could be made with the help of the materials used, the quality of the workmanship of the fabric, and the dyes. It seems that, as with the *sagum*, there were rectangular and semi-circular cut *paludamenta*.[102]

There were certain peculiarities in the way that it was worn, as is shown on cuirassed statues. On the one hand, the *paludamentum* was held together on the right shoulder with a brooch, typically a round plate brooch. It then fulfills a practical purpose as a cloak and is no different from the *sagum*. On the other hand, among the representational sources it is commonly worn about the hips, in other words it was only loosely folded, wrapped around the body, and sometimes loosely draped over the left arm. A brooch was not required for this, the cloak now taking on the function of a pure rank insignia and no longer serves any practical purpose. This method of wearing it can be observed from the late Republic into late antiquity. Murals and Egyptian mummy portraits give an indication that blue shoulder cloaks were common among centurions.[103]

Brooches

In the Roman army, brooches with high bows were direct related to the military cloak. Such cloak brooches made of copper alloy, less often from iron or precious metal, are found at Roman military bases in large numbers. This alone makes clear that they belonged to the standard equipment of the Roman military. However, that does not mean that these so-called military brooches were not also sometimes worn by civilians. A correspondingly high and wide bow is recognisable on these cloak brooches, to include the greatest possible amount of coarse cloak fabric.[104]

In terms of construction, hinged forms predominate, brooches with springs being less well represented. Brooches were used in the military even in regions and times where, in the civilian population, brooches had long since fallen into disuse as a functional component of clothing (Gechter 1984). In the early Imperial period, military brooches were predominantly of bronze and brass, iron or silver pieces being very rare. With brooches of precious metal (silver, gold) increasing in the late 2nd century AD, the difference in material and thus value obviously marking grades of rank.

In the Augustan period, sprung brooches of the Alesia type occur in military contexts as do their successors, the Aucissa brooch. Aucissa brooches are sprung brooches in construction and are considered the embodiment of early Imperial military brooches. With their high bow, they were suitable for accommodating even coarser material and served, as an example, for fixing the military cloak on the right shoulder. Random occurrences in civil contexts, such as women's or children's graves, do not disprove this principle.[105] These brooches are found with a research-related focus in the Rhine and upper Danube provinces, all round the Mediterranean.[106] They usually consist of copper alloys (bronze, brass), very rarely of silver. Iron examples are also rather rare in the north-western provinces, but this is mainly due to their poorer chances of surviving, because smaller iron objects are generally heavily corroded in soil and are often overlooked during excavations. An exception is the piece from Dülük Baba Tepesi.[107] They are common finds at Haltern, where they were probably made. Their very complicated production technology has also been studied there in particular detail.[108] In addition, brooches of Gallic or Germanic origin with a high bow, such as eye brooches, can be found among auxiliary troops of the early Imperial period in use to fix the cloak. The knee brooches, with their different variants originating in the Danube region, became fashionable in the second half of the 2nd century AD and was also mainly worn by the military.[109]

DISC BROOCHES

While most disc brooches are found in both civilian and military contexts from the second half of the 2nd century and the first half of the 3rd century AD,[110] some pieces depict a subject or have a distribution that point towards their being mostly worn by soldiers. Among them are unique pieces like the ones depicting a helmet (Fig. 185) or a sword (Fig. 259).[111] Swastika brooches were also military brooches, as can be seen from their high concentration on military sites from the Upper German-Raetian Limes to the whole Mediterranean, including Dura-Europos.[112]

BROOCHES WITH LONG HINGE ARMS

Late cloak-fastening brooch types, like the brooches with a long hinge arm from the second half of the 2nd and the 1st half of the 3rd century should also be regarded as soldiers' brooches. Typologically, these represent a prototype of the crossbow brooch. Their variants occur in copper alloys – mostly tinned – and silver.[113]

CROSSBOW BROOCHES

The so-called crossbow brooches were the standard military cloak fastening from the late 3rd century, or rather the Tetrarchic period, employed by the military throughout the Roman Empire (Fig. 164). They derive their German name (*Zwiebelknopffibeln* = onion knob brooch) from the three onion-shaped knobs on the head. There are simple examples of this type in copper alloy as well as magnificent pieces with inscription and gilding. There are also massive silver or even gold specimens with inscriptions belonging to senior officers, for example. E. Keller has divided these brooches into six types, the latest belonging in the 5th century, their absolute chronology being refined by Ph. Pröttel and M. Gschwind.[114]

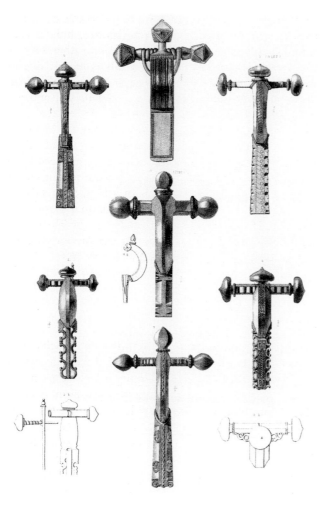

Figure 164 *Crossbow brooches (after Lindenschmit 1881)*

Figure 165 *Soldier with paenula from the Arch of Septimius Severus (after Brilliant 1967). Drawing: A. Smadi, Arch Institute University of Cologne*

Scarves

The scarf (*focale*) was equally good against heat and cold, helping against sunlight and sweat, but also protecting against wind and cold. Furthermore, it also offered some protection for the neck region of the soldiers in action. D. Richter has pointed to some literary evidence that the *focale* could be made of wool.[115]

Cummerbunds

On reliefs, mainly on gravestones, there is a kind of cummerbund (*fascia ventralis*) – similar to the sash of pirate movies – that would prevent chafing by the heavy weapons belt (*cingulum*). H. Ubl said that, in addition, small objects could be stored in this sash.[116]

Headgear

In the early and middle Imperial period, with the exception of the hoods on military cloaks, there was no standardized headgear for the Roman military other than the helmet. Yet it has to be assumed that, at least on the march in hot regions and seasons, soldiers actually knew to protect themselves from exposure to the sun for purely practical considerations. However, we have no sources for this. In a reconstruction drawing, G. Sumner depicted a legionary in a straw hat,[117] but this is pure fantasy. There must have been textile military headgear, however, if the information provided by Vegetius, who reported that earlier soldiers had worn headgear (Vegetius 1.20), is to be believed. However, little is known about this before the Late Roman period. A neat, textile skull cap shown on the gravestone of Aurelius Alexianus from Athens from the first half of the 3rd century AD remains an isolated case and does not necessarily represent standard military headgear.[118] Whether the remains of some textile multipart and multicoloured caps from Dura-Europos, or some from Mons Claudianus or elsewhere in Egypt, really belonged to soldiers is by no means clear.[119] In the period of the Tetrarchy, the fur field cap of the Pannonian army, the *pilleus Pannonicus*, was introduced into the Roman army, right up to the Emperor (Ubl 1976, Fischer 2006).

Shoes

Caligae, those well-known strap sandals with nailed soles, were the typical Roman military footwear of the early Imperial period. They are not only attested in literary and representational sources, but they are also found repeatedly

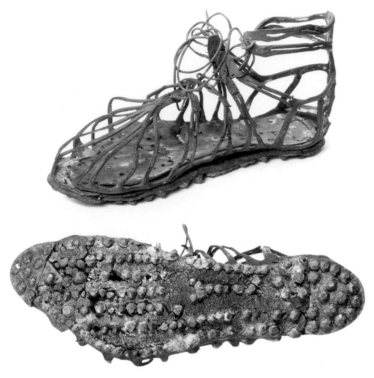

Figure 166 *Caliga (sandal with nailed soles) from Mainz. Photo: RGZM*

in damp soil layers of, for instance, wells. In these original finds, cowhide is always noted as the material. As expected, it was discovered that nailed *caligae* are relatively common in troop garrisons, such as in Mainz (Fig. 166) and Vindonissa.[120] Lately, those using metal detectors often find the characteristic iron hobnails which were lost on the march. Even these inconspicuous finds can be used for chronological purposes. With early Imperial hobnails that were obviously forged with a die, cross-shaped ribs and four dots can be made out on the bottom of the pyramidal, faceted head, which are absent in later shoe nails. Iron hobnails are often found in cremations and also en masse in the ballast of Roman roads. Moreover, footprints with iron hobnails are often found on bricks from military brickworks.

Caligae were the footwear of ranks below the centurionate, hence the term *caligatus miles*, *caligatus*, or just *caliga* to refer to the common soldier.[121] In Judea, *caligae* were such symbols of the hated Roman military that, in Jewish law, a ban on nailed shoes was enacted.[122]

In modern experiments (marching in full kit with reconstructed Roman armour), it turned out that the *caliga* were quite comfortable footwear – except on asphalt and concrete streets (which, indeed, the Romans did not come into contact with). In summer, they were worn with no socks. Furthermore, it was found that during the winter, foot wrappings were enough to withstand the cold. A papyrus from the year AD 81 reported that the soldier was issued with three pairs of *caligae* per annum, so the wear

was therefore quite considerable.[123] In the 2nd century AD, there is less evidence for *caligae*, but rather closed, although still nailed, boots now came to the fore.[124] These *calcei* were also used by the higher ranks and officers, and were – with suitably elaborate designs – part of the official dress of *equites* and senators.

Socks

While the military usually went barefoot in military sandals or wore footwraps, in winter there were puttees to protect the legs (*tibialia*; Richter 2010, 200). Even Roman socks (*udones*) are known.[125]

Defensive weaponry

From Bronze Age beginnings to the present battle tanks, defensive weaponry has, in principle, comprised a relentless search for a compromise between two largely irreconcilable opposites: total protection by complete invulnerability on the one hand and completely unrestricted freedom of movement on the other. It seems the Roman army always understood how to find a good compromise between the two extreme positions. During the Imperial period, only the opponents of Rome seem to have taken recourse in defensive weaponry of such massive proportions that they brought ruin upon the wearers. On the one hand there were the Gallic Aedui in the failed uprising of Sacrovir against Nero in AD 68, apparently borrowing heavily from gladiatorial equipment: Tacitus mentions here the so-called *crupellarii* or 'iron men' who used extremely heavy armour and were unable to move to fight, but were invulnerable to the cut and thrust of the Roman offensive weaponry. Since the Roman legionaries could not harm the iron men with their *pila* and *gladii*, they made short work and simply knocked them down, as they could no longer get up on their own. Others hacked unceremoniously at the armour, including striking at the men within using axes (*secures*) and mattocks (*dolabrae*), with the unfortunates unable to defend themselves.[126] Another example where too much armour brought ruin to its wearers was an episode involving armoured cavalry (*cataphraktarii*), which Tacitus described from a battle in the year AD 69 between the Romans and the Sarmatian tribe of the Roxolani (Tac., *Hist.* 1.79).[127] These had invaded the Roman province of Moesia and their armoured cavalry, in which man and horse were heavily protected by scale armour, had a powerful effect upon the Romans. Fortunately for the Romans, a thaw began. The heavy armour finally brought down the horses and, with their mobility hampered by the over-heavy armour, riders could no longer get up on their own. Thus, the initial superiority of *cataphraktarii* was reversed and the Romans were victorious.

In addition to avoiding extremes, the nature of defensive armament is always subjected to other changing factors: the armament and fighting methods of the enemy, the availability of materials, as well as cost-benefit considerations. Roman body armour, that is the body armour and helmets, was, according to all we know, always made of metal. Leather armour or helmets for the use of regular troops have so far not been attested in the original material. Some curious individual cases from Egypt do not change that: helmets of raw hide from turtles and crocodiles have been found at Wadi Harara[128] or an ensemble of a helmet and body armour, made of crocodile skin, from Manfalout.[129] In these cases it is highly questionable whether these defensive weapons, if they date to the Roman Imperial period, really were the equipment of regular troops.

M. Junkelmann has rightly pointed out that the repeated attempts to identify the two Latin words, *cassis* and *galea*, with the difference between metal and leather helmets, cannot be proven. He counters that leather helmets were definitely not used as regular military equipment in either Antiquity, the Middle Ages or the early Modern Period. As plausible support for his thesis, he can cite experimental evidence: an experiment with replica leather gladiator helmets (sole leather 5–10 mm thick!) brought the result, 'that against blunt impacts and shocks, they were passably effective, against sharp blows moderately effective, and against stabs very inferior, and were hopelessly inferior when compared to metal helmets with a sheet thickness of 1 mm' (Junkelmann 2000, 349).

Helmets

By now, a substantial number of original finds of Roman helmets or parts of them are published, so that a good overview is possible for the Roman era from the late Republic to late antiquity. Nevertheless, fundamental, and important issues remained unaddressed for a long time. The division of Roman helmets of the Imperial period into infantry and cavalry helmets, for example, which in the specialist literature has so far proved very difficult and contradictory. The confusion was fuelled by H. R. Robinson, whose typology, based on the ideas of other researchers on Roman infantry and cavalry helmets, created great confusion.[130]

By systematically identifying every elaborate ornate cavalry helmet not as a regular cavalry helmet, but as parade armour, there remained hardly any regular cavalry helmets for the 2nd and especially for the 3rd century AD.[131] This gap was then filled arbitrarily with 'cavalry' helmets selected from variants of the Niederbieber infantry helmets. Unfortunately J. Garbsch then perpetuated Robinson's misinterpretations in his standard work on parade armour and thus consolidated them in German-speaking countries for a long time (Garbsch 1978). Robinson's arbitrary allocation of infantry helmets to legionary or auxiliary troops also occurred without any plausible justification.

Of course, the easiest way to assign helmets to service branches of infantry or cavalry is when unambiguous owner inscriptions confirm it. Thus the – unfortunately rather rare – inscriptions mentioning legions or cohorts or the membership of their owners in a century can clarify the status of infantry helmets unequivocally. This also applies to the mention of *turmae* on cavalry helmets. Representations on gravestones can also provide clarity in singular instances.

On the basis of grave finds from Ostrov and Tell Oum Hauran, Petculescu and Fischer have pointed out, that decorated helmets do not automatically belong to parade armour, because these assemblages each contained two ornate helmets: one with a face-mask and one without a mask. It seems logical that the latter was the piece for everyday use and combat.[132] This indicates that ornamentation alone is not enough to assign a helmet to parade armour, but that a face-mask is. However, there are opposing views even to this opinion (Junkelmann 1999).

EARLIER HELMET TYPOLOGIES

Metal helmets of the late Republic and the Empire changed their shape over time. Periods of longer stability can be differentiated from those of fast and thorough change. For example, helmets of the Montefortino type in the later Republic endure with only slight changes over three centuries, while Hagenau-type helmets were produced for hardly more than half a century.

Since it is generally the case that helmets were durable items of equipment, they often lasted across several generations of owners. This can be seen from multiple, occasionally overlapping, ownership inscriptions, which are usually inscribed on the neck protection.

Like many archaeological finds, the Roman helmet was subject to gradual evolution, with many newer examples displaying elements of earlier forms. It is thus ideally possible to employ the typological method and – with certain limitations – draw up a consistent developmental series for Roman helmets and determine from this typological sequence a relative chronology.[133] I do not consider the negative assessment of this typological method by Bishop and Coulston justified.[134] The confusion these authors complain of mostly arises from various uncoordinated systems of classification. And these never derive from the material alone, but are always formulated subjectively.

This eventually led to two competing systems: the typology of H. R. Robinson, introduced in 1975 in Great Britain, and all the other classification systems in the rest of the world. M. Junkelmann has recognized this and commented critically upon it. He was not content with the criticism, however, but countered the typology of Robinson with his own system, based on that of G. Waurick.[135] Robinson's typology has also rightly been criticized by Bishop and Coulston: his typological system is very inflexible and would require a linearity of development which never existed.[136] One can only agree because, in fact, Robinson subdivided his system too much, so that its types are often represented by only very few copies, or just a single piece. And often it is also baffling how one type according to Robinson is so different from another, that it is necessary to allot it to its own type. One gets the impression that Robinson neglected two important factors in the preparation of his classification system:

- Ancient helmets do not represent industrially mass-produced artefacts, but are – in spite of there sometimes being a strong resemblance – products individually manufactured by hand. In certain stages of experimentation, such as the beginning of the development of Weisenau-type helmets, singular transitional forms can occur, which are hard to squeeze into a typological scheme.
- The quantity of helmets known to us, which happen to have come down to us through a strongly filtered tradition, biased towards certain areas, time periods, and find circumstances (finds in water!), represent only a tiny fraction of the Roman helmets that once existed. That Robinson's typology is of little use, can easily be judged by the difficulty with which its rigid and closed system adapts to new discoveries or even a large body of new material, such as the Guttmann Collection. There is also an arbitrary and clearly erroneous approach to the classification of the material into infantry helmets, legionary helmets, auxiliary infantry helmets, cavalry helmets, and sports helmets.

In a critical appraisal of Robinson's typology, M. Junkelmann rightly states: 'What one must avoid is a typological straitjacket, into which anything and everything has to be squeezed, and a misconceived Darwinism which knows nothing but logical development lines and suggests an inescapable stylistic or functionally based consistency'.[137]

His typology proposals return to the classic 'continental' helmet typology, as established by P. Couissin and further developed by H. Klumbach and G. Waurick.[138] This is based on a very broad and therefore also flexible scheme of types that can integrate deviating new discoveries without major problems. Modelled upon Couissin's specification of its main types according to the localities from which complete, preserved pieces were first published, he called variants 'subtypes', which are also named after localities. For infantry helmets, Junkelmann maintains the Montefortino type, which he divided into the Talamone, Canosa, Cremona, Rieti, and Buggenum subtypes. The Mannheim and Hagenau types were not further subdivided, while he split

the Weisenau type into the Nijmegen, Verdun, Mainz, Hebron and Niedermörmter subtypes, followed by the Niederbieber type.

For cavalry helmets, Junkelmann differentiated between pseudo-Attic cavalry helmets of the Weyler/Koblenz-Bubenheim type and the pseudo-Attic cavalry helmets of the Guisborough/Theilenhofen type, with the Heddernheim/Bodegraven subtype. However, he sometimes also retains incorrect identifications, calling the Niederbieber type, Heddernheim variant, a cavalry helmet.

A PROPOSAL FOR A NEW TYPOLOGY

A typology which can sensibly be used long into the foreseeable future should have several properties. It should help with dividing the known material into logically comprehensible groups, both by form and chronology, which – if at all possible – should show a development over time. Equally, it should be open and flexible enough that new material can be incorporated without possible contradictions – perhaps with the help of new types which are easy and logical to insert or versions of existing types.

As with most typologies in archaeology, there will always be a residue of pieces of individual form design which do not neatly fit into the system and could theoretically be placed at several points within a typology. However, one must be careful not to force such problematic pieces into a typological scheme.

After the appearance of H. R. Robinson's work, a whole series of new finds of helmets emerged, which present many details in the existing typologies in a whole new light. Therefore a new classification seems essential. In order to get rid of the massive inconsistencies previously existing in the allocation of infantry and cavalry helmets and to take into account the latest research findings, I propose a new typological classification of Roman helmets that differs in large parts from Robinson's typology. It is mainly based on what I believe is the considerably more plausible typology of M. Junkelmann. His helmet typology has developed these older systems in line with the actual assemblage of finds. An essential role in the large and unexpected increase in material is played by the Guttmann Collection. I have somewhat adapted Junkelmann's system, especially by replacing the (in my opinion) somewhat unfortunate term 'subtype', by the more flexible term 'variant', which Waurick had sensibly already used. Also, I have clearly identified and justified the differences between infantry and cavalry helmets of the later 2nd and 3rd centuries AD. In distinguishing between them, many insoluble contradictions had crept in, primarily originating from Robinson and Garbsch, but in some cases also from Junkelmann.[139]

MONTEFORTINO TYPE

This extremely long-lived type of helmet undoubtedly goes back to Celtic iron helmets (conical helmets with a knobbed crown), which were soon acquired by the Etruscans and Romans with the emergence of the Celts around 400 BC in the Po Valley in Italy and produced in a non-ferrous metal alloy (bronze).[140] The eponymous pieces were found in the cemetery at Montefortino in Ancona, on the Adriatic coast in northern Italy. It is difficult to distinguish in each individual case between Etruscan and Roman helmets, especially among the early examples, since the Romans in particular, but also other ancient Italian peoples, seem quickly to have adopted the Etruscan model.

While the knobbed crown was made separately for the Celtic helmets and then attached to it, with the Etrusco-Roman copies, the knobbed crowns were cast in one piece with the helmet bowl. The form of the cheek pieces can also provide evidence of their origin: Celtic helmets have trefoil cheek pieces, where the decorative sheet bosses are riveted to the underlying plate, whereas with Etruscan examples, they are soldered.[141] Later Etruscan and Roman models possess anatomical cheek pieces after the Hellenistic model: the front edges follow the contours of the human face, especially the cheek bone. This kind of cheek piece is retained until the end of the Middle Empire. Schaaff and Waurick forego finer typological and chronological subdivision of the Montefortino type, describing that as needing more research, however.[142]

Robinson's typology was especially confusing for this helmet: for one part of Montefortino helmets he has seven different types, for another part he includes his jockey cap or Coolus-type helmet, subsuming helmets of the Hagenau type within the latter.[143]

Based on the works of Schaaff and Waurick, M. Junkelmann has divided the helmets of the Montefortino type (Fig. 167) into five 'subtypes' (see above), which include non-Roman types. I have here ignored Junkelmann's typological classification for pre- and non-Roman helmet types and retained the Cremona, Rieti, and Buggenum subtypes definitely connected with the Roman military as variants of the Montefortino type (Fig. 169a):

- **Montefortino type, Cremona variant (Fig. 168, 1a–c; Fig. 170, left)** – The oldest helmet securely attributed to the Romans (because of an inscription) comes from Pizzighettone near Cremona.[144] The style of lettering dates it to the 2nd half of the 3rd century BC. Helmets of this variant have a shape that resembles an onion rather than being truly hemispherical, with a cabled border, a small neck guard, and heavy border decoration, with a tab with two riveted rings on the underside of the neck guard to attach the neck strap, which would be tied at the front on the cheek pieces.

- **Montefortino type, Rieti variant (Fig. 168.2)** – Later, mostly Roman, variants of helmets of the Montefortino type from the 2nd and 1st century BC are distinguished

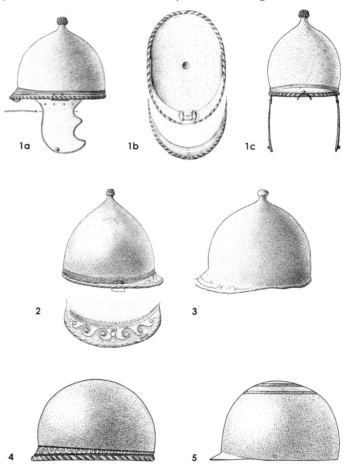

Figure 168 *Helmets of the Montefortino type: 1 a–c Cremona variant, 2 Rieti variant, 3 Buggenum variant (Robinson 1975), 4 and 5 helmets of the Mannheim type in copper alloy from Vielle-Toulouse (after Waurick 1988). Drawings: A. Smadi, Arch Institute University of Cologne*

Figure 167 *Helmet of the Montefortino type in copper alloy (unprovenanced, privately owned). Photo: A. Pangerl*

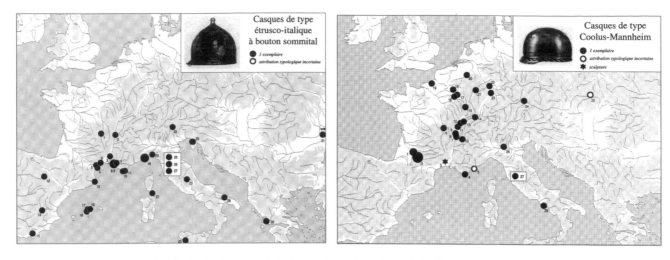

Figure 169 *Distribution maps of the helmets of the Montefortino and Mannheim types (after Feugère 1994)*

Figure 170 *Helmets of the Montefortino (left) and Mannheim (right) types (after Lindenschmit)*

from older forms by sinuous vine decoration on the (now broader) neck guard. A piece from Rieti has the stamped Roman manufacturer inscription Q COSSI Q. It dates from the first decades of the 2nd century BC and is the second oldest definitely Roman helmet.[145]

• **Montefortino type, Buggenum variant (Fig. 168.3)** – This comprises helmets, usually made of bronze, representing

a further development of the late Republican Montefortino type, described by U. Schaaff as the Buggenum variant.[146] The only slightly conical helmet has a crest knob cast in one with it. The reinforced edge remains unadorned or has a slightly deepened decoration, whose origin as the cord pattern of older Montefortino type helmets can barely be discerned. The neck guard, previously angled obliquely, now tends almost to the horizontal and so heralds the transition to helmets of the Hagenau type. Helmets of this variant can be found in Portugal, Italy, Spain, Mallorca, on the coast of southern France, and finds from water in Slovenia and the Lower Rhine. For the dating there are two indications: the example from Slovenia bears the punched inscription of the commander SCIP (io) IMP (erator). G. Waurick demonstrated that, out of the many Scipios, it may well have referred to P. Cornelius Scipio Nasica, who took the title of *imperator* in 49 BC and participated on the losing side in the battle of Pharsalus in 48 BC and then fled to Africa.[147]

However, even in the early Imperial period, this type of helmet was still in use. This is indicated by their distribution along the Lower Rhine and the fact that a helmet from Wardt-Lüttingen has an early Imperial period owner's inscription and the eponymous piece from Buggenum in the Netherlands bears an inscription of the 13th Legion Gemina.[148] Their presence in the Augustan period has not been established for this region, but they were probably involved in the quelling of the Batavian revolt in AD 70. Thus, this helmet was in use from the time of Caesar until the early Flavian period.

MANNHEIM TYPE (FIG. 168.4–5)

By comparison with the Montefortino helmets, the Mannheim type[149] helmet represents a largely independent form. It has a hemispherical bowl without a crown knob and a narrow, horizontal neck guard. As with Montefortino helmets, the edge can be smooth and simple or thickened and decorated. No cheek pieces have so far been found with Mannheim type helmets. However, there are holes where they could be fixed (Fig. 170, top right). Cheek pieces must be assumed here, too, because there is no plausible reason why such a long-standing protective item should suddenly be dispensed with.

H. R. Robinson held this helmet type to still be Celtic and it was therefore not mentioned by him in his standard work of 1975. U. Schaaff was the first to recognize it as Roman, from the time of Caesar's Gallic Wars. An important argument for this dating, and the attribution to the Roman army, is the distribution (Fig. 169), focused on Italy and central and northern Gaul.[150] Otherwise, the find contexts are mostly undated (river finds!). The earliest datable piece comes from a Roman archaeological context, namely from the shipwreck off the French Mediterranean coast of Madrague de Giens, dated to around 70 BC.[151] The other finds from this context include late Republican oil lamps, 35 coins with a *terminus post quem* of 75 BC, and a helmet of the Montefortino type, occurring contemporaneously with the Mannheim type in the 1st century BC.

HAGENAU TYPE (FIG. 171.1–5; 172)

The further development of the form ultimately descended from the Montefortino helmets, with a broader neck guard,

is traditionally named after a river find from the Rhine in Alsace as the Hagenau type,[152] which Robinson assigned to his 'Coolus' types.[153] It has a simple, hemispherical bowl and a neck guard, which is at its broadest on the example from Burlafingen. Normally, the neck guard has a hole in the middle in which two things can be inserted: on the underside a ring for fastening the helmet strap, and on the upper side a ring or hook in order to affix the crest. In addition, these helmets always had cheek pieces. These types of helmets ultimately harked back to Italian prototypes, such as the Buggenum variant of the Montefortino type.

Helmets of the Hagenau type are made (wrought not cast) from copper alloy, as a rule. The only exception are the iron fragments from the camp of Oberaden on the Lippe, dated to 11–8 BC, and lost during the Second World War. Despite corrosion, the only surviving photo allows a clear interpretation of the helmet as of the Hagenau type, because one can still see a rivet for the browband. The helmet was not restored and examined more closely, resulting in a lack of details that precludes the naming of a specific variant. The view expressed by Waurick – that it was likely a Weisenau type helmet – is, I believe, incorrect.[154]

In the Augustan period, helmets of the Hagenau type (with the exception of the Cremona variant) adopted the substantial brow guard from infantry helmets of Celtic origin of the Weisenau type. They were not quickly replaced by those of the Weisenau type, as older research has claimed.[155] Rather, both types were used in parallel for nearly a century. It was only towards the end of the 1st century AD that the Hagenau-type helmets disappeared from the equipment of Roman infantry. However, it seems that occasionally a demand was nevertheless seen to adapt this type of helmet – perhaps perceived as 'old fashioned' – to the more 'modern' Weisenau form. This at least is shown by an example from the Rhine near Eich (Rhineland-Palatinate, Fig. 177), in which ear cut-outs were subsequently incorporated to 'modernize' it (Oldenstein 1990).

HAGENAU TYPE (FIG. 171.2; 172)

The eponymous helmet was dredged from the Rhine near Hagenau in Alsace in the 19th century.[156] It has a hemispherical bowl with a wide neck guard, with laterally protruding edges ('mezzaluna-shaped neck guard', according to Junkelmann 2000, 67). There is also a substantial browband, cheek pieces, conical crest knob and occasionally tubes on either side for more helmet decoration (*e.g.* plumes).

- **Hagenau type, Haltern variant (Fig. 171.1)** – This type has a hemispherical bowl, with a neck guard, which does not protrude at the side, but sticks out at the back of the helmet bowl in a curving arc (a 'crescent' neck guard, according to Junkelmann ibid.). In addition, it boasts a

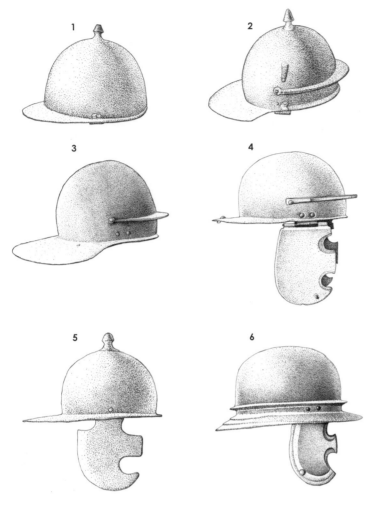

Figure 171 *Copper-alloy Hagenau-type helmets: 1 Haltern variant (Neuss, after Waurick 1988), 2 Hagenau, 3 Burlafingen variant, 4 Schaan variant, 5 Cremona variant (Robinson 1975), 6 Agen type iron helmet (after Connolly 1989). Drawings: A. Smadi, Arch Institute University of Cologne*

Figure 172 *Eponymous helmet from the Rhine at Hagenau (after Lindenschmit 1911)*

massive browband, cheek pieces, a conical crest knob and occasionally tubes on either side for further helmet adornment (*e.g.* plumes). The eponymous piece is dated by its provenance to AD 8 to 9.[157]

- **Hagenau type, Burlafingen variant (Fig. 171.3)** – The eponymous helmet was salvaged as a dredged find from Danube gravels near the Claudian fortlet of Burlafingen, used for only a few years. Perhaps there was a direct relationship with this.[158] Its neck guard, justifying identification as a separate variant, is extremely wide, extending to either side of the bowl in a rounded arc (a 'crescent' neck guard, after Junkelmann ibid.). It has a massive browband, cheek pieces, and a crest knob on the apex (now lost from the eponymous helmet). Three ownership inscriptions on the neck guard indicate a long period of use for the helmet. There is also a stamp with a palm branch on it, probably a maker's mark.

- **Hagenau type, Schaan variant (Fig. 171.4)** – Two helmets of this eponymous type were found in a forest in 1887 about 150 metres above Schaan in Liechtenstein.[159] These helmets have a neck guard, which forms an arc around the bowl (a 'crescent' neck guard, following Junkelmann ibid.) and a browband, but no crest knob or other suitable means to attach a helmet crest.

- **Hagenau type, Cremona variant (Fig. 171.5)** – A river find from the Po at Cremona is very close to the helmets of the Hagenau type, lacking only the browband. Its broad neck guard forms an arc around the bowl ('crescent' neck guard, after Junkelmann ibid.) and is continued in a narrow band, which also runs around the helmet sides and front. At the front it thus had a protective function similar to the browband.[160] The bowl has an integral conical crest knob at the top. Following Robinson, it is suggested that this is not a Montefortino variant from the late Republic, but a piece of armour that – like the Weisenau type (Cremona variant) helmets – was deposited in the river in connection with the battle of AD 69.

PORT TYPE (FIG. 172)

Roman military equipment scholars are unanimous that late Celtic iron helmets similar to the Port type (Pernet 2010, 112–15) served as defensive equipment for the Celts during Caesar's era, which the Romans encountered during the Gallic Wars. They promptly adopted these too, which they then progressively transformed through the Augustan period into the Roman helmets of the Weisenau type. Strangely enough, Robinson has assigned these quite different helmets to a common Agen/Port type, but then divided them into Agen and Port subtypes (A and B),[161] an approach that in its logic is barely comprehensible. By contrast, U. Schaaff provides a better, and also currently still viable, solution. He split the late Celtic iron helmets into three groups: the West Celtic, East Celtic, and Port types.[162]

In the West Celtic ('Agen type') pieces, bowl and neck guard are made in one piece (Fig. 171.6; 179.1). A prominent encircling ridge separates the bowl from the protruding brim, which broadens towards the rear as the neck guard. The projecting front brim could be interpreted as a typological and functional precursor of the brow guard of Augustan helmets. The cheek pieces now assumed the curved contours of the cheek area along the front edge, adapting the forms of Hellenistic helmets from the Mediterranean. This type was used in Gaul and the western Alps.

With East Celtic helmets, the bowl is in three parts: the actual bowl, a projecting rim to the front, and a drawn-down neck guard. The latter are riveted to the bowl. Between the front part and the neck guard, a characteristic gap is left that is replaced in the later Weisenau type helmets by the ear cut-out, usually with an attached ear guard. The cheek pieces largely correspond to the West Celtic pieces. Archaeologically, this type of helmet is concentrated in Slovenia, but this only reflects local burial customs, because the available evidence comes from burials. An overall distribution across the eastern Alpine region is likely to be a more realistic inference. A grave find from Poland has very probably come there from the eastern Alpine region.[163]

Helmets of the Port type largely correspond to the eastern variant, the only difference being that the neck guard is now made separately and riveted to the bowl. Like the East Celtic helmets, the neck guard was pulled down a bit, but differs from them by its ribbed profiling. At the front, a two-part, symmetrical, wing-shaped ornament was embossed (Fig. 173.2). It is – in a somewhat changed, and curlier shape – interpreted in later Weisenau-type Roman helmets as 'stylized eyebrows'.

Usually the ear cut-out is not yet present, with the helmet from the burial at Mesnil-sous-Jumièges in Normandy being an exception.[164] The Port type forms a link between the two areas, in which, according to the current state of research, we have a concentration of late Celtic helmets: it is found in both Gaul and Slovenia.

Helmets from the Port type and its variants are sometimes combined with riding accessories in grave finds in a Gallo-Celtic context, like a piece from Thür in Vulkaneifel, for example.[165] This is also true of cremation burial 3 from Trier-Olewig, assigned to a Treverian warrior of the nobility, which might have been the burial of a mounted warrior. It contained among other things a Mannheim-type Roman infantry helmet made of bronze,[166] so the question arises whether there was ever a strict distinction between infantry and cavalry helmets among the Gauls.[167]

The naturalistic figures on the weapons metopes on the Tomb of Munatius Plancus in Gaeta, dated to the years around 20 BC, prove that helmets of the Port type (with no apparent typological differences) were not only worn by Gallic warriors, but also by Roman legionary infantry

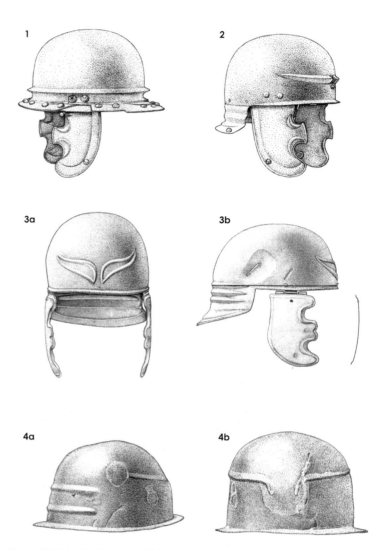

Figure 173 *1 iron helmet from Giubasco (after Connolly 1989), 2 iron helmet from Port (after Connolly 1989); 3 helmet made of copper alloy from 'Heddernheim' (after Fasold 1995), 4 helmet made of copper alloy. Drawings: A. Smadi, Arch Institute University of Cologne*

during the Caesarean to early Augustan periods.[168] The helmets shown on the monument are depicted in seven cases as individual examples on a metope, but on four metopes they occur alongside typical Roman *gladii*.[169] This is proof that the depictions on the tomb of Gaeta do not show captured Gallic weapons, but belong, like the *scuta*, *gladii*, and *coronae murales* shown, to the world of the Roman military. Moreover, in this period and because of their connection with the *gladius*, they most likely are legionary infantry helmets.

Now, if the early forms which a little later emerge as helmets of the Weisenau type were used as defensive equipment for Roman infantry,[170] doubtless legionary infantry, then this also applies for helmets of the Weisenau type itself! This eliminates the opinion repeatedly put forward that such pieces of weaponry were initially worn exclusively by auxiliary soldiers, especially by auxiliary cavalry.[171] In my opinion, since its introduction among the Roman troops, the Port type belonged to the equipment of infantrymen, whether they served in the legion or with auxiliary troops.

TRANSITIONAL FORMS BETWEEN THE PORT AND WEISENAU TYPES

There are some specimens made from copper alloy, which show that Roman troops already wore transitional forms of the helmets between the Port and Weisenau types. This material is considered to be typical of Roman helmets from Italy. One example alleged to have come from Frankfurt was purchased by the Museum for Pre- and Early History of the City of Frankfurt a. M. (Museum für Vor- und Frühgeschichte der Stadt Frankfurt a. M.) (Fig. 173.3). However, P. Fasold doubts its provenance.[172] The piece has characteristics which show it should be assigned an intermediate position between late Republican Roman Italian helmets and late Celtic helmets of the Port type: the material – bronze – and the cable decoration found on the front rim of the helmet correspond with Roman helmets of the Montefortino-Mannheim types. The stepped-down neck guard, the stylized eyebrows on the front, and the lack of a brow guard and ear cut-outs locate the piece among helmets of the Port type, but here the neck guard did not follow the Celtic model – attached separately – but in the Roman tradition was made in one piece with the bowl. With such a hybrid single piece, one should refrain from creating a separate 'Frankfurt' variant of the Port type, so as not to end up back at Robinson's 'single-helmet typology'.

Another intermediate piece, so far typologically unique, has unfortunately no indication of its provenance.[173] Made of bronze, its form is a strange mixture of helmets of the Port and Weisenau types. On the front, there are stylized eyebrows, while at the rear are the ribs which are intended to reinforce the neck guard (Fig 173.4). Now this helmet has neither ear cut-outs nor neck protection, consisting only of a bowl with a narrow brim. However, it cannot be an unfinished example of a Weisenau type helmet because the rim at the back, where the neck guard should then have been worked out of, is much too narrow. It also originally had soldered ornamental elements that would be unthinkable on an unfinished helmet.

WEISENAU TYPE (FIGS 174–6; 178)

Research has unanimously and correctly shown that helmets of the Weisenau type are derived directly from the helmets of the Port type. For reasons that are not quite clear, there is still a debate whether these defensive pieces would have been exclusively reserved for auxiliary soldiers or even cavalrymen in the early Imperial period.[174] However, there are already good reasons (see above) why the preceding Port type was already (also) used by legionaries, and therefore we can assume that this was the same for helmets of the Weisenau type. There is

Figure 174 *Iron helmet of the Weisenau type (after Lindenschmit 1911)*

even more tangible evidence: if the finds of helmets or helmet components (mostly fragments or helmet crest forks) from early Imperial sites, where the presence of legionary soldiers is mainly to be expected, are taken into account, it is striking that iron helmets, *i.e.* above all pieces of Weisenau type (a small proportion of iron pieces of Port type here would theoretically still be taken into account), clearly predominate here against bronze helmets. In chronological order, the camps of Dangstetten (Fingerlin 1986 and 1998), Augsburg-Oberhausen (Hübener 1973), Haltern (Müller 2002, 38, Tab. 2) and Vindonissa (Deschler-Erb 2007, 81) and the battlefield of AD 9 at Kalkriese can be compared here.[175] It must be remembered that, in principle, iron helmets have a lower chance of survival in the soil than bronze helmets due to severe corrosion. However, the latter are more easily recycled by melting and in this manner escape the archaeological record.

With rough equal chances of retrieval, the result of this comparison, with all due caution, suggests the dominance of iron helmets, of which the vast majority probably belonged to the Weisenau type: in Dangstetten (15–9/8 BC), there were seven records of iron helmets, but none for a bronze helmet; in Augsburg-Oberhausen (approximately 10 BC–c. AD 15), there are four documented iron helmets compared to one bronze helmet. In Haltern (1st decade BC–AD 9), seventeen iron helmets were found, against three bronze helmets; in Kalkriese (AD 9), there are the remains of eleven Weisenau helmets and fragments of four bronze helmets. The later legionary camp of Vindonissa, occupied between the Tiberian and Trajanic periods, sees

Figure 175 *Helmets of the Weisenau type: 1 Gutmann variant made of copper alloy (after Junkelmann 2000), 2 a–c Nijmegen variant in iron (Robinson 1975), 3 a–b special shape with extremely large neck guard of copper alloy (unprovenanced, privately owned). Drawings: A. Smadi, Arch Institute University of Cologne*

Figure 176 *Helmets of the Weisenau type, special forms in copper alloy, 1 a–c Ossario helmet (after Bennett 1988), 2 Hagenau helmet, 3 a–c Eich before and after modification (after Oldenstein 1990). Drawings: A. Smadi, Arch Institute University of Cologne*

iron helmets of the Weisenau type becoming even more dominant: thirty-six iron helmets compared to the remains of five bronze examples.

Helmets of the Weisenau type made from copper alloy and iron[176] were randomly divided within Robinson's typology into 'Helmets of Imperial-Gallic type', usually made of iron, and 'Helmets of Imperial-Italic type', mostly made from copper alloy. The criterion for this classification was the presence or absence of stylized, embossed eyebrows on the front of the helmets. Based on only one characteristic, these seem almost counterproductive, because this arbitrarily ruptures established relationships.[177] Therefore, the more flexible backward-looking typology, based by Lindenschmit and Couissin on the piece from the eponymous Rhine area near Mainz-Weisenau,[178] divided into different variants, is a preferable categorization (Figs 174, 175, 176–9).

Like the Port type helmet, this had a shaped, gradually stepped-down neck guard (made from one piece and not riveted like the Port type), together with the frequently occurring embossed stylized eyebrows on the front, as well as the shape of the cheek pieces. Embossed, stylized eyebrows cannot surely provide a monocausal determining factor for a chronological sequence, such as Robinson proposes,[179] although they admittedly form a tempting, almost 'classical' typological series. However, they do not necessarily have to make a strict chronological sequence (indeed why should they?) and they could even disappear entirely, mostly with copper-alloy examples. However, even copper-alloy helmets were repeatedly provided with stylized eyebrows!

The broad, mezzaluna-shaped neck guard, which was always formed from a single piece together with the bowl, now has a striking, embossed arched profile, which should certainly not be seen as primarily decorative. Rather, it served instead to reinforce the neck guard against sword blows.

An important technical innovation which characterizes helmets of the Weisenau type, but also copper-alloy helmets of the Hagenau type, is a horizontal brow guard

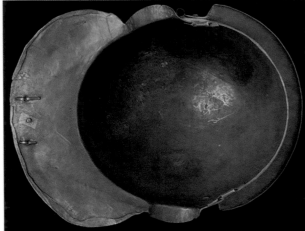

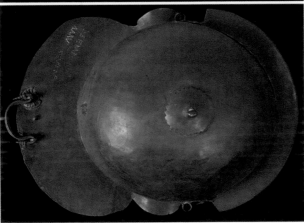

Figure 177 *Hagenau helmet made of copper alloy from the Rhine near Eich, modified into a sort of Weisenau helmet (see Fig. 176.2). Recording: Museum Speyer*

Figure 178 *Iron helmet of the Weisenau type from Straubing, fort IV (after Prammer 2010)*

to better counter the long Celtic swords.[180] This should, however, be examined more critically, because the Celtic longsword, like any cavalry weapon, will typically have struck and damaged the helmet of an opponent more by blows from above. A horizontal browband could offer little protection here! By contrast, the Roman *gladius* should not be viewed as just a stabbing weapon, as it could also be used in confined spaces to chop at the front of a helmet. With this, a browband would have been very useful. Thus this newly invented defensive device, retained for most Roman infantry helmets until the late 3rd century AD, was probably due more to the experiences of the civil wars of the late Republic than to those of the Gallic War.

At the same time, the cut-out for the ears, inserted between the neck guard and the beginning of the cheek piece, became the norm and was increasingly reinforced by riveted ear guards. The latter, however, are sometimes still missing in early pieces of the Guttmann (Fig. 175.1) and Nijmegen (Fig. 175.2) types, for instance. The cheek pieces, which may have certain differences in the detail of their form, always leave the ear exposed. They therefore differ from contemporary cavalry helmets that cover the ear with an embossed metal replica of the ear. Such an ear covering, albeit not in this naturalistic form, also marks the subsequent development of the helmets from the Weisenau type to those of the Niederbieber type.

Not all helmets of the Weisenau type can be unambiguously assigned to the eponymous form or one of its variants, as otherwise there is a tendency towards Robinson's 'single example typology'. One of the helmets that does not fit into a certain typological 'drawer', for example, is the so-called Ossorio helmet, probably from Spain, which is now in the Museo de las Casas Reales in Santo Domingo in the Dominican Republic (Fig. 176.1). It

firmly riveted to the front, undoubtedly an additional reinforcement against downward sword blows. Ultimately they can be traced right back to the West Celtic helmets of Caesar's time. There, a distinctive peripheral ridge separates the bowl from an out-turned rim which broadens towards the rear at the neck guard. The projecting front edge can be regarded as a typological and functional precursor of the browband on Augustan helmets. Robinson and Connolly attributed this browband to the need to be able

is named after its owner, the Mexican General Adolfo Leon Ossario. The peculiar design of the stylized eyebrows in the forehead area, the unique rivets on the helmet brow guard, and the small rectangular cutout for the ear give this helmet wrought from copper-alloy singular detail characteristics (Bennett 1989).

One innovation that occurs in helmets of the Weisenau type are the detachable plume holders with different types of mount on the bowl. Also new were carrying handles fixed with two split pins on the neck guard, similar to box handles. On iron pieces, there were occasionally decorative components made of non-ferrous metals, such as rosettes, sometimes combined with enamel-filled rivet heads, embossed strips, cheek piece and neck guard edging, and figurative and ornamental sheet appliqués.

The Weisenau-type helmets were the most durable standard helmet type of the Imperial period for legionary and auxiliary infantry, whose later variants were still in use in the late 3rd century AD. It seems that it offered ideal protection until the style of fighting of the Romans and their opponents changed so much that other helmet types prevailed.

Until the 60s, the opinion was that the Weisenau type had only emerged in the Claudian period, when it replaced the Hagenau type.[181] That has not proved to be the case: new finds from Augustan camps since the Oberaden level prove their early use. Meanwhile, it is also quite certain that the Hagenau and Weisenau helmet types were used at the same time. There is no more detailed information on the proportion in which these two different types were used. One can also no longer assume that the one type originally predominated in the legions and the other with the auxiliary forces or even that the Weisenau type helmet was originally worn by Gallic auxiliary cavalry. This was possibly the case with a specific variant, where it was combined with the Kalkriese-type mask and will be covered later under cavalry helmets. From a late Augustan level, before the construction of the military camp in Vindonissa, there is a Tiberian iron Weisenau helmet, which was probably deposited in a leather cover, perhaps a recycled shield cover.[182] Another, almost completely preserved iron Weisenau helmet from Vindonissa dates to around the middle of the 1st century AD. The chronology is guaranteed by pottery and a tilestamp of the XXI Legion.[183] Two helmets of the Weisenau type from Krefeld-Gellep (Fahr 2005) most likely come from the context of a marching camp of the year AD 69. One of them is a heavily damaged iron helmet of the Weisenau type, Mainz/Krefeld-Gellep variant. The other example was subsequently modified: the neck guard had been cut off, the visor and cheek removed and it was covered with fur. It has been interpreted as a protection converted for the rebellious Batavians. However, this would presuppose that the Batavians had usually worn similar helmets, of which,

however, we know nothing. Might it not be a standard bearer's helmet, with the neck guard removed in order to fit the wolf's pelt more comfortably?

• **Weisenau type, Guttmann variant** – This type, only known from two privately owned examples,[184] fashioned from copper alloy (bronze, brass), are typologically between the helmets of the Port and Weisenau types (Fig. 175.1). The absence of a browband connects it with the Port type, while the low, horizontal neck guard, which was wrought in one piece with the bowl strongly resembles helmets of the Nijmegen variant. The prominent decorated rivets, partly filled with blood-red enamel, are in the Celtic tradition, the good state of preservation of the two pieces speaking for a possible origin from burials. Therefore these helmets can be dated to the early Augustan period. However, these features might also just be a local (Balkan?) variety and do not necessarily have to be interpreted as chronologically significant, so that the subsequent Nijmegen variant should not necessarily be dated later or earlier. With this type, the riveted protective plate is missing. Otherwise it has the stylized eyebrows (also found in non-ferrous metals!), visor, and cheek pieces. The above-mentioned Ossario helmet, probably originating from Spain (Fig. 176.1) is probably closely related to these helmets. I would classify the piece of unknown origin from a German private collection with these, despite its unusually large and differently shaped neck guard (Fig. 175.3).

• **Weisenau type, Nijmegen variant (Fig. 175.2)** – The Nijmegen variant represents the typologically, and probably chronologically, earliest variant of the Weisenau type helmets. The eponymous iron helmet has now been joined by examples made of copper alloy.[185] The Nijmegen variant is characterized by the fact that the neck guard is not (yet) angled downwards, but is at the same height as the front rim of the helmet. Moreover, the ear cutout is sometimes not reinforced or has just slightly raised edges.

WEISENAU TYPE, SPECIAL FORMS

The eponymous helmet was dredged from the Rhine in the 19th century near the base of the early Imperial troops at Mainz-Weisenau (Fig. 176b). Taking its advanced typological stage of development as chronological evidence, this type then dates later than the 'Guttmann' and 'Nijmegen' variants. However, its presence in the fortress at Oberaden, dated to 11–9/8 BC, is proof that it can hardly be seen as dating much later (Müller 2006). Helmets of this type are wrought from iron and have the stylized eyebrows on the front of the bowl. The neck guard is not as deeply angled downwards as it is with other (later?) examples. The cheek pieces are, like the neck guard, provided with copper-alloy edging. On the lower and rear edges, they are bent slightly

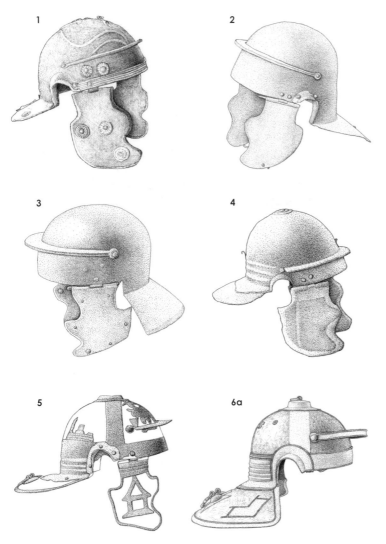

Figure 179 *Weisenau type helmets: 1 Mainz-Weisenau of iron with copper-alloy decoration, 2 Mainz from copper alloy, 3 unprovenanced; privately owned, copper alloy, 4 Cremona variant in copper alloy, 5 Mainz/Krefeld-Gellep variant, Mainz, iron with copper-alloy decoration, 6a unprovenanced; privately owned, iron with copper-alloy decoration, see Fig. 182 (1, 2, 4, 5 after Robinson, 1975; 6a after Junkelmann 2000). Drawings: A. Smadi, Arch Institute University of Cologne*

but this is clearly not borne out.[186] Similarly, a piece of unknown origin from a German private collection can be included here, although it does not have the usual ear cut-outs (Fig. 179.3).

• **Weisenau type, Cremona variant (Fig. 179.4)** – The four known specimens of this type are almost identical in form and technical characteristics. They are made from copper alloy. These helmets were all definitely or probably discovered as water finds from the River Po in the vicinity of Cremona. On the back of the bowl, two ribs are beaten out from the neck guard for reinforcement. On the front and rear are very crudely made bronze hooks with teardrop-shaped base plates for fastening the helmet crest.

These helmets have a brow guard and a circular attachment for fastening the helmet crest holder. There are no stylized eyebrows in the forehead area. There is no separate riveted metal ear guard over a cut-out in the helmet bowl. There is just a recess in the bowl which is turned slightly outwards. The neck guard is on the same level as the front of the helmet. These two features link the pieces with the Augustan Nijmegen type and also warn against using isolated typological features as absolute chronological markers, because, as discussed below, helmets of the Cremona variant belong in the late Neronian period!

At the junction with the bowl, a lunate ornament is embossed on the outside of the neck guard, which indeed also served to reinforce it against blows. All over the bowl, rough traces of work with a raising hammer can clearly be seen. Rivet holes that could have served for fixing the carrying handles of the helmet, which are often found, are missing. The attachment of the cheek piece with the two hinge tabs is unorthodox and somewhat improvised, with a rounded bronze pin, tapering on one side and flattened at the other. The finish of the bowl and neck guard is extremely careless: the edges have only been roughly worked, without reworking and trimming with shears or with a cross pein hammer. The surviving cheek piece has burrs and sharp edges. There is a multitude of such obvious examples of sloppiness in its production, whereas Roman helmets were usually very carefully and precisely finished.

This type of helmet has a peculiarity: there are four examples and the shoddiness of the detail work in completely identical counterparts is only explicable if they originate at the same time and from the same workshop. This is not typical of original finds from the early and middle Imperial period. All helmets – even those described by scholars as belonging to a single type – on closer inspection reveal individual characteristics. These Weisenau-type helmets, Cremona variant, were most likely pieces of equipment from the *legio Classica*, hastily raised under Nero, which had almost certainly been produced in Campania in the area of the fleet at Misenum. This is supported by a number

outwards to deflect lateral sword blows. Around the ear cut-outs there are ear guards made of copper alloy. The front edge of the helmet is reinforced with an embossed copper-alloy brow band and there are decorative, purely ornamental copper-alloy rosettes riveted onto the cheek pieces and on the rivets of the cheek pieces. These rivets were originally decorated in the centre with enamel. A fitting is riveted on to the bowl to attach a crest holder.

• **Weisenau type, Mainz variant (Fig. 179.2)** – This type of helmet largely corresponds to the classical Weisenau type (without the decorative copper-alloy fittings). It is made of copper-alloy (bronze, brass), but does not have the stylized eyebrows in the forehead area. H. R. Robinson wanted to assign these helmets to the auxiliary infantry,

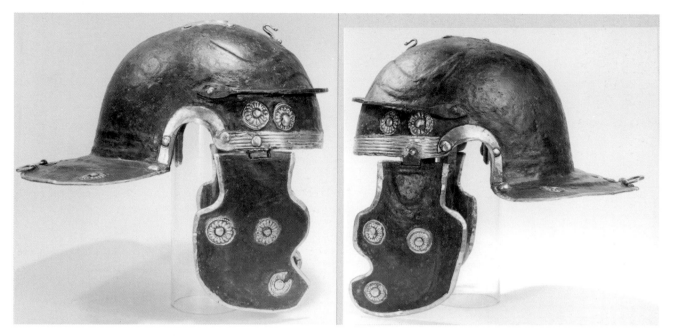

Figure 180 *Eponymous Weisenau-type helmet, RGZM copy. Photo: RGZM*

of common technical characteristics with two fleet helmets from the Vesuvius cities. The troops raised were renamed a little later by Galba as *legio I Adiutrix*. The loss of these helmets may have been connected with the First battle of Cremona on April 14th AD 69 (Fischer 2004a).

• **Weisenau Type, Mainz/Krefeld-Gellep variant (Fig. 179.5–6.)** – This type of helmet is to date represented by three examples: one comes from the Rhine at Mainz, one from Krefeld-Gellep, and an unprovenanced piece with quite strikingly singular features was included in the Guttmann Collection. They are made of iron and feature appliqué decoration of brass sheet which, on the helmet from the Guttmann Collection, is bordered by beaded copper wire. The stylized eyebrows on the forehead are absent. Cruciform strips of brass, which, however, have no protective function, lie over the bowl. So they have nothing to do with the iron cross pieces found in the time of Trajan. On the large, mezzaluna-shaped neck guard, there are also decorative brass sheets and handles mounted.

The helmets have a tin-can-shaped fitting with a cruciform slot for inserting the crest holder. On the helmet in the Guttmann Collection there is a brass split pin with a movable copper ring here. The Mainz piece is adorned with two eagles made from brass sheet, holding victory wreaths in their beaks, on the brow of the bowl. On the rear left side, there is a complete brass sheet metal decoration surviving, in the shape of an *aedicula* with an altar. Only the lower portion of the identical decoration on the right side is intact.

The decoration of the piece from the Guttmann Collection consists of two small discs with intersecting, incised lines and two small mice of brass sheet metal on the rear of the bowl. The helmet from Krefeld-Gellep, damaged in antiquity, was decorated much like the river find from Mainz: similar, crossed, brass-sheet stiffeners and an *aedicula* of copper alloy are still preserved.

The better-preserved helmets have browbands made of brass, that from Mainz resembling in its dimensions the standard Weisenau-type helmets. As for the piece from the Guttmann Collection (Fig. 179.6), the browband is exceptionally large, with openwork decoration which probably led M. Junkelmann to label this helmet as of the Niedermörmter type. However, it seems to me to have more in common with the Mainz piece, even if it is likely to date somewhat later, to around the first half of the 2nd century AD. The Krefeld-Gellep piece, on the other hand, can most likely be connected with the camp of the battle during the Batavian uprising in the year AD 69.[187] Thus, the helmet can possibly be dated to the Neronian to early Flavian period.

• **Weisenau Type, Hebron variant (Fig. 181; Fig. 182.7)** – The crossed iron bars, which first appeared as a field modification by troops against the Dacian sickle swords during the Dacian Wars of Trajan,[188] were subsequently adopted as the standard reinforcement for the helmet bowl. This is the case, for example, with the helmet which was reportedly found in a cave near Hebron (Israel) along with a face-mask helmet and an iron mail shirt. If the find circumstances have been accurately reported, it should have been deposited during the Bar

Figure 181 *Reconstructed Hebron type helmet (iron and copper alloy).* Photo: J. Pogorzelski

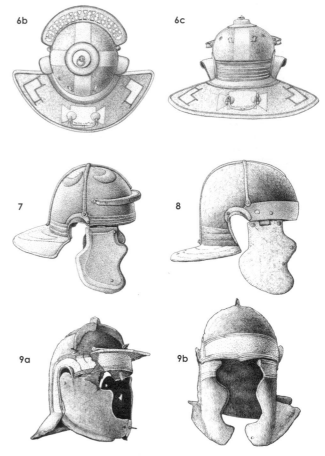

Figure 182 *6b–c Weisenau-type helmet, Mainz/Krefeld-Gellep type, unprovenanced; privately owned, copper-alloy with iron decoration, 7 Hebron variant, iron with copper-alloy decoration, 8 Theilenhofen variant, iron with copper-alloy decoration; Niederbieber type helmet, iron with copper-alloy decoration: 9 Friedberg (6b–c after Junkelmann 2000; 7, 9 after Robinson 1975; 8 after Klumbach and Wamser 1978). Drawings:. A. Smadi, Arch Institute University of Cologne (cf. Figure 179)*

Kokhba revolt under Hadrian (in the years AD 132–5).[189] In this instance, the stylized embossed eyebrows have disappeared from the front of the iron bowl. It has a decorative band of copper alloy on the front rim of the bowl, which is decorated with an olive branch pattern. On top of the bowl, in the quadrants formed by the intersection of the iron crosspiece, there are four appliqué, punctim-decorated *lunulae* of non-ferrous metal in an ornamental pattern.

• **Weisenau Type, Niedermörmter variant (Fig. 184.2)** – This helmet, with its enlargement and enhancement of protective functions (neck guard, ear guards, brow guard) is already anticipating helmets of the Niederbieber type. The neck guard in particular is heavily is drawn forward and sideways over the shoulder, including the wearer's sides. The eponymous piece, a river find from the Rhine near Xanten, is made of non-ferrous metal, with decorative elements from soldered metal sheets, which feature richly engraved figural decoration.[190] On the

front of the oversized brow guard, L. Sollionius Super, a soldier of the 30th Legion from Xanten, is mentioned as the owner. Klumbach wanted to see this type of helmet as a cavalry helmet, so he promoted L. Sollionius Super to the legionary cavalry without any solid evidence at all! Nevertheless, his dating of the piece to the 2nd century AD can be endorsed, as the 30th Legion epithet 'Pia Fidelis', used after AD 197, is missing. It is hard to imagine the production of this helmet in the 3rd century, for since the 80s of the 2nd century AD, helmets of the Niederbieber type dominate.

• **Weisenau Type, Theilenhofen variant (Fig. 182.8)** – This helmet, together with a cavalry helmet of the eponymous type, was probably intentionally buried in the 3rd century AD.[191] It is worked from a piece of iron and still has the reinforcing of the neck guard with three transverse ribs. The helmet has an arcaded profile on the neck guard, but does not have the stylized eyebrows in the

Figure 183 *Niederbieber type helmet (after Lindenschmit 1858)*

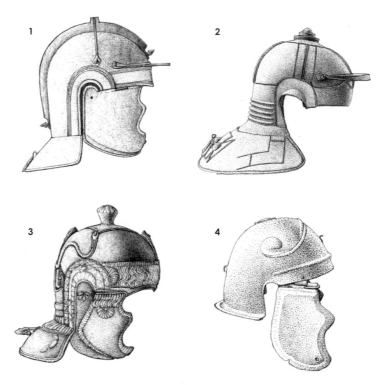

Figure 184 *Iron helmets of the Niederbieber type with coloured metal decoration: 1 Heddernheim variant, 2 Niedermörmter variant, 3 Heddernheim variant; 4 pseudo-Attic infantry helmet (copper alloy) from Pompeii (Robinson 1975). Drawings: A. Smadi, Arch Institute University of Cologne*

area of the forehead. The Weisenau type, Niedermörmter variant, is connected with the Theilenhofen variant by the fact that the neck guard is drawn forward and sideways. The helmet has iron cross pieces and ear guards of copper-alloy sheet metal, and there is a wide strip of sheet metal from the same material that covers the front rim from ear guard to ear guard. It seems that a characteristic feature of this is that there is no brow guard. There are no rivet holes or other indications for attaching it. I cannot tell from his publication from which indicators Klumbach concludes its former existence.[192] The iron cheek pieces leave the ear exposed.

HELMETS OF THE NIEDERBIEBER TYPE (FIG. 182.9; 183; 184.1–3; 185)

Although these helmets have organically developed from the older Weisenau variants, they are so far away from the original Weisenau model that it seems justifiable to treat them as a separate type. One of the key features that sets them apart from the helmets of the Weisenau type are the ever-expanding cheek pieces that now also covered the ear. This feature was previously (1st and 2nd centuries AD) restricted to cavalry helmets. However, their cheek pieces were always decorated and on the part covering the ear also bore an embossed replica of the ear. On one piece (unfortunately

Figure 185 *Silver brooch in the form of a Niederbieber type helmet (unprovenanced, privately owned). Photo: Ph Gross, Arch Institute University of Cologne*

unprovenanced), an interesting element can be seen: the ear plate is perforated for improved hearing (Fig. 189.2.). A similar solution reappeared on the late Roman helmets of the period around the middle of the 4th century AD in Koblenz (Fig. 190). This new ear protection made protruding riveted ear guards unnecessary. They are mostly replaced by slightly protruding edging around the ear cutout. By the end of this development, the cheek pieces cover so much of the facial region that a real visor is produced which leaves just the region of the eyes and nose exposed.

Another characteristic of these helmets is a broad, profiled or otherwise decorated bronze band, in which the ear guard is integrated and that continues behind to the base of the broad, often curved neck guard. Helmets of the Niederbieber type have much more substantial cross-pieces than helmets of the Weisenau type. The previously customary narrow, cast brow guard is absent, but is replaced by a broad, often profiled guard of sheet metal which rises to a point.

Helmets of the Niederbieber type represent the endpoint of a typological development that hardly seems capable of continuation. They offered optimum protection, although they seem to have had certain disadvantages due to their extreme weight and the considerable reduction in their field of view. So it was certainly not just techno-economic reasons which prompted the Romans at the beginning of the Late Roman period to introduce a completely new helmet type.

NIEDERBIEBER TYPE (FIG. 182.9; 183; 184.1)

The eponymous helmet was found in the fort at Niederbieber in Neuwied (Fig. 183). It was allegedly buried together with the metallic components of a standard next to a human skeleton during the violent destruction of the fort in the years AD 259/60. The iron component has a profiled bronze band at the front and at the top of the cheek pieces. The large moulded and pointed rivets with which the cross-strap design and the brow guard are fastened to the helmet bowl are characteristic. The front rim does not run in a straight line, as is the case with all older helmets, but is curved and shaped in the middle into a point. Like the Weisenau type helmet, the cheek pieces are bent slightly outwards below and at the rear to deflect sword blows laterally, extending to the edge of the mezzaluna-shaped neck guard. There are also Niederbieber type helmets in copper alloy, such as the piece from the Guttmann Collection[193] or the well-preserved helmet from Nida-Heddernheim (Fig. 184.1), which was found in the area of the so-called hall building.[194]

- **Niederbieber Type, Hönnepel variant (Fig. 184.2)** – The eponymous piece is a water find from the Rhine near Kalkar-Hönnepel. The helmets of this variant consist of copper alloy or iron (Robinson 1975, 98f. Figs 263–5), *e.g.*

the example from Osterburken,[195] lacking embossed sheet metal strips on the front and around the ear. The edge of the ear cut-out protrudes only slightly and was beaten out from the bowl. Cross-piece construction and brow guard respect the usual Niederbieber form.

- **Niederbieber Type, Heddernheim variant (Fig. 184.3)** – The eponymous helmet was allegedly unearthed in 1927/28 in the so-called hall structure at Nida-Heddernheim, which has for a long time been held to be a military construction from the Late Roman period. According to recent studies by A. Reis, this thesis can no longer be maintained: the 'hall building' seems to have been several strip-houses; the fragmented helmet could originate in a scrap deposit.[196] The helmet is made of iron, and its copper-alloy appliqués (originally tinned brass) are richly decorated. The cross construction design is replaced by massive, copper-alloy snakes, and at the top there is a hollow pommel of ferrous metal for a helmet crest, on a decorated base of rectangular shape with slightly concave edges. Moreover, the surviving cheek piece has ornamental decoration and a representation of Minerva. The front rim, decorated with a copper-alloy metal sheet with a curl pattern, is not straight. It is curved and brought to a point in the centre. Two similar pieces come from Nijmegen[197] and from Musov in Moravia, the latter dating to the period of the Marcomannic Wars (!).[198] There were copper-alloy fittings of two helmets of this type from the German votive site of Thorberg.[199] These richly decorated helmets have repeatedly been called cavalry helmets. They so closely resemble infantry helmets of the Niederbieber type that, for me, their identification as infantry helmets seems certain.

- **Niederbieber Type, Phrygian cap variant (Fig. 186)** – This type of helmet has not yet come to light as an actual find, but so far is only depicted on reliefs from the Arch of Septimius Severus in Rome. There, Roman soldiers are clearly shown wearing helmets with cheek pieces, brow guard, and bowls in the form of a Phrygian cap.[200] From its date, this helmet type would have been a variant of the infantry helmets of the Niederbieber type. On the relief, soldiers equipped in this manner – most likely legionnaires – are to be found close to the emperor and his sons. That is why G. M. Koeppel has already mused if these were the members of specific, specially equipped troops, for instance the Praetorians. Whether these soldiers could also represent members of another guard unit, such as the *legio II Parthica*, is not clear. While infantry helmets in the shape of Phrygian caps have up to now been missing from surviving finds, this original feature is now known from cavalry helmets of the finds of the pseudo-Attic type, Ostrov variant, and the face-mask helmet from Crosby Garrett. Consequently, one should not just dismiss the representations on the Arch of Septimius Severus as pure fantasy.

Figure 186 *Soldiers with Phrygian helmets from the Arch of Septimius Severus in Rome (after Brilliant 1967). Drawing: A. Smadi, Arch Institute University of Cologne*

Figure 187 *Praetorian helmet on the Great Trajanic Frieze. Photo: J. Pogorzelski*

THE PSEUDO-ATTIC TYPE INFANTRY HELMET

This helmet type is far better known from representational sources, such as Trajan's Column, than from actual examples. It has the typical forehead tiara of Attic helmets and has a vertical ring on top of the bowl, which has hitherto never been detected in archaeological finds. The only actual example that exists to date, and is made from solid silver, is a clumsy modern forgery in the Museum of Art in Toledo (Ohio).[201] It is obviously copied from the pieces shown on Trajan's Column; for example, it has the ring on the bowl and also narrow cheek pieces, not based on original finds.

• **The pseudo-Attic type infantry helmet, Pompeii variant (Fig. 184.4)** – From the gladiator barracks of Pompeii there come two copper-alloy helmets with deep neck guards, with a crude diadem at the brow, beaten out from inside and resembling that of Attic-type helmets. The shape and construction of the cheek pieces are similar to those of the Weisenau type, Cremona variant. Like those, they have riveted hooks in the centre at the front and back for attaching a helmet crest, and the tubular plume holder is present.

This type of helmet has been published and discussed by H. R. Robinson and S. Ortisi.[202] Robinson wanted to assign the two copper-alloy helmets to the city watch; Ortisi sees in them an expression of 'classic Italic-Chalcidian form' and assigns them to the fleet. They are likely to have been made in the environs around the fleet at Misenum (Fischer 2004).

• **Pseudo-Attic type infantry helmet, Praetorian variant (Fig. 187)** – On the great Trajanic Battle Frieze, like the reliefs from Arch of Constantine or even the Praetorian Relief in the Louvre,[203] guardsmen wear a kind of dress uniform with richly decorated pseudo-Attic helmets which are topped by a large plume. As we have no possibility to control these depictions with the help of actual finds, there is always the possibility that these pictorial representations were not intended to represent a typical contemporary weapon realistically, but just to give a deliberately archaizing-Hellenistic representation (Waurick 1983).

CONICAL HELMETS

Conical helmets (Fig. 189.3–4), the dome of which has been worked in one piece, are generally associated with oriental archers. This is confirmed by the representations

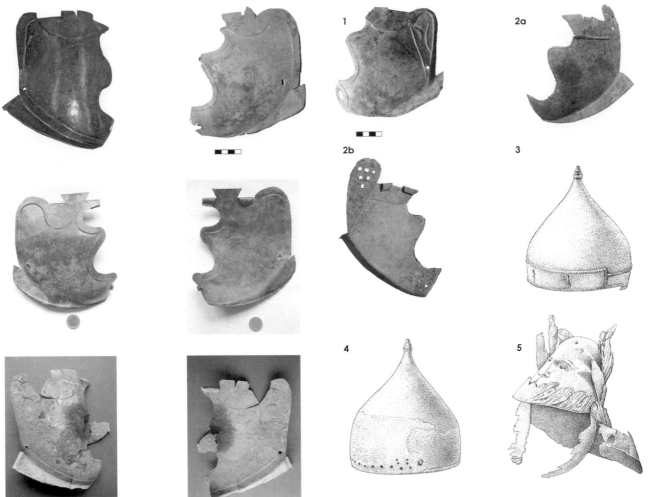

Figure 188 *Copper-alloy cheek pieces from helmets of the Niederbieber type (unprovenanced, privately owned). Photo: A. Pangerl*

Figure 189 *1–2 copper-alloy cheek pieces of helmets of the Niederbieber type (unprovenanced, privately owned). Photo: A. Pangerl; conical helmets made of copper alloy: 3 Dakovo Bosna, 4 Danube at Intercisa, 5 copper-alloy helmet from a statue from Autun (4, after Robinson, 1975; 5 after Szabó 1986). Drawings: A. Smadi, Arch Institute University of Cologne*

on Trajan's Column[204] and the gravestone from the fort of Housesteads on Hadrian's Wall.[205]

A smooth bronze helmet with a profiled point and representations of Victoria, Jupiter, and Mars on a box separated by soldered beading at the front side and a slightly downturned neck guard (Fig. 189.3) comes from the area of Dakovo Bosna.[206] Another specimen came to light from the Danube at Intercisa (Fig. 189.4) in Pannonia.[207] It is beaten out of copper alloy and has a profiled point. The helmet is perforated at the back, probably for attaching copper-ring mail to protect the neck which – with the exception of one copper ring – does not survive. There are holes on the sides for fastening the cheek pieces. On the front side, the border is covered with a beaded strip, around which are two superimposed punctim inscriptions. The lower one reads *T Maxi Constanti(s)*, the upper *T Maxi Macedo*. The helmet was thus worn successively by two soldiers from the *turma* of Maximus in a cavalry unit. A. Mócsy wants to assign the wearer of the helmet to the *cohors I miliaria Hemesenorum sagittaria equitata*, which was a unit of Syrian archers from *Emesa* (Homs).

STATUE HELMETS

Two helmets made of copper alloy, which were regarded as functional, soldiers' helmets in the literature, I would like to interpret as components of statues, probably of cult images for various reasons: from Autun/*Augustodunum* in Burgundy, there is a so far unique pseudo-Corinthian helmet made of copper alloy (Fig. 189.5). It is decorated with a laurel wreath made of gilded bronze sheet, which merges with a sort of neck guard made from acanthus leaves. The front rim is decorated with applied acanthus leaves and the cheek pieces also have this shape.[208]

Figure 190 *Helmets of the Niederbieber type from copper-alloy statues: 1 from a statue of Gobannus (after Pollini 2002), 2 Rainau-Buch (after Imperium Romanum 2005); 3 Late Roman crested helmet with Christogram on a silver medallion of Constantine I. Drawing: A. Smadi, Arch Institute University of Cologne*

Robinson sees in this the helmet of a high-ranking officer, for instance a legate or governor. Upon inspection, in the Musée Rolin in Autun, my impression has been confirmed that – from its shape and size – the piece cannot possibly have been worn by a human, unless he had a very small head of a completely abnormal shape. Rather, I believe that the item formed part of a statue, probably a cult image. E. Künzl is now of the same opinion.[209] Pseudo-Corinthian helmets are particularly common on statues of Mars, but also occur in representations of other gods. This view is supported by the fact that composite statues, whether entirely of copper alloy or as acroliths, were very popular in Gaul from the late La Tène to the 3rd century AD.[210]

Another helmet can probably also be interpreted in a similar way; this is a helmet of the Niederbieber type from a well deposit of the 3rd century AD in the *vicus* of the fort of Rainau-Buch, at the western end of the Raetian Limes (Fig. 190.2). This helmet, because of its extreme thinness, unfinished appearance, and other characteristics, is markedly different from other iron and bronze functional

protective armour of this type. Quoting the description of the excavator, D. Planck:

> It is a relatively thin helmet worked from sheet bronze with a broad neck guard and cruciform decoration on the helmet bowl, which was beaten out of the sheet metal. The two non-matching cheek pieces can be closed at the front on the chin. Some details, such as the unfinished nature of the edges of the neck guard and the differing forms of the decorated cheek pieces, suggest that the helmet was unfinished when deposited in the well. Because of its present so-called 'bog' patina, this shiny, golden helmet is a variant of the Niederbieber type found in the late 2nd and early 3rd centuries. Of particular note are some marks of working on the helmet bowl, which were carried out from the exterior and may indicate that this helmet has been worn in an unfinished state.[211]

It is particularly remarkable that the usually substantial cruciform reinforcing crossing bars (which had a very real defensive function) were only beaten out from the unusually thin metal of the helmet as a sort of 'dummy'. A helmet of this fragile manufacture could never have been worn seriously in combat in my opinion (and certainly not 'in an unfinished state'!). The 'impact points', which Planck says were actual damage from combat, are placed rather strangely regularly and in a rather unusual location. However, the Buch helmet is very similar to the separately cast, naturalistic Niederbieber type helmet from a statue of the Celtic-Roman god of war Gobannus. This originally came from a Gallic temple treasury but, through the art trade, turned up in private ownership in America (Pollini 2002). It may be that this helmet is an essential attribute of a Gobannus cult statue (Fig. 190.1); consequently it may be also found on other statues of this god. We can thus deduce that it is quite likely that the helmet from Rainau-Buch is not a real military helmet, but only the attribute of a life-size acrolith statue of Gobannus in stone or wood. If we assume the latter material, the 'impact points' could be loosely interpreted as mounting sockets.[212]

LATE ROMAN HELMETS

Scholarship has long seen late antiquity as a break in the development of Roman helmets:[213] the general idea was that through the introduction of helmet types originating in the eastern Sassanid region,[214] consisting of a two-part bowl, a comb-like crest, separate, movable neck guard and nasal, an abrupt end came to the production of Niederbieber helmets, as the latest development stage of helmets of the Weisenau type. This break in helmet development has been associated with a profound military and equipment reform under the emperors Diocletian and Constantine I.[215]

However, lately there are certain indications that things were not as simple as that: there are the remains of three iron helmets from Poitiers from a rubble layer dated to the

AD 370s, which according to Ch. Miks, may have been transitional forms between the Niederbieber type and the comb-crested helmets in the 'Late Roman' shape.[216] The find context of an almost complete helmet of the 'Late Roman' type from Augst can be dated numismatically to the period after Tacitus (AD 275–6) and before Constantine. Numismatic evidence had already led B. Overbeck to postulate the possibility of such an early date for the comb helmets in general.[217] All this could help to finally destabilize the theory of comprehensive reforms of military organization and equipment under the emperors Diocletian and Constantine I, as it seems that significant developments in various Late Roman types of weapons (among them the helmets) were already occurring in the pre-Tetrarchic period.

At first glance it seems that in late antiquity, the sharp distinction in shape between infantry and cavalry helmets apparently disappears. On closer inspection, and allowing for the evidence of graffiti and other indicators, helmets of the Deurne/Berkasovo type can be identified as cavalry helmets, and the helmets of the Dunapentele/Intercisa type somewhat more as infantry helmets. A characteristic of the helmets of the Late Roman army is the completely different technical design: instead of, as with the earlier high-Imperial helmet types, bowl and neck protection being worked from one piece, the components were manufactured separately, with even the bowl being produced in two separate parts (left and right halves). The two parts are united into a complete bowl by a riveted band running front to back along the bowl and carrying the helmet crest. This technique facilitates the division of labour for higher production volumes. The crest could be inserted into slots in this comb, but this was not always the case. Ch. Miks believes the ridge crests might have been troop or rank insignia.[218] Another new element is the addition of a nose guard (nasal). The neck guard is now also manufactured separately and connected to the bowl by means of various articulated components. There are different types of cheek piece: some narrow and others broader. Between the two extremes are some specimens from Koblenz with pierced ear protections.[219] In addition to the comb crests (Fig. 195.1), the combs of comb helmets occasionally have fittings attached with a Christogram at the front of the comb (Fig. 195.2 to 5) (Prins 2000), as on a silver medallion of Constantine I in the State Coin Collection in Munich (Fig. 190.3).[220] So far, there is only one Christogram on the nasal of a helmet from the Late Roman fortress of Alsóhetény in Hungary.[221] Only the silver foil coating from this survived. Recent studies of Late Roman helmets have shown with reasonable certainty that evidently most of the known examples of helmets were covered with gilded silver or copper sheet. This eliminates the previously held distinction between those examples finished with a plated surface as the decorated helmets of guards or officers and simple iron helmets for men:[222] Apparently, helmets with plain iron upper surfaces were rare in the Late Roman period.

Based on formal construction elements and important differences in decoration, and following Ch. Miks,[223] the following preliminary and very broad, helmet types can be distinguished:

CRESTED HELMETS

This extremely numerous group is characterized by its two-piece iron bowl with crest and crest holder. The helmets were coated with gilded silver. These helmets have permanent, movable, suspended neck guard and cheek pieces of various types of construction and size, with a variety of methods of attachment. In some pieces, there is a fixed nasal, but there are also helmets without this additional protection device.

- **Dunapentele/Intercisa Type (Fig. 191a; 192.1 to 5)** – These are most likely infantry helmets. They often have ear cut-outs located on the edge that are continued on the relatively narrow cheek guards, the bowl can have perforated ear guards riveted on, and nasals also occur.
- **Deurne/Berkasovo Type (Fig. 191b; 192.6; 193; 194.1)** – These helmets are heavier and of far more complex construction than helmets of the Dunapentele/Intercisa type. Likewise, elaborate decoration with worked stone and glass inserts sets them apart from the others. According to a graffito on the Deurne helmet, which refers to a cavalry unit (*equites stablesiani*), these elaborate helmets belonged to cavalry.[224]
- **Trier type special form** – Miks views a discovery from Trier[225] as a special type of crested helmet: on an iron fragment with ear and eye cutouts, there was some ring mail, which probably formed the neck guard.
- **Bieberwier type special form (Fig. 194.2)** – A curious isolated example is represented by a find from Bieberwier (Reutte district, Tirol, Austria). Here, the iron bowl is beaten out from a single sheet. The crest of this helmet is not technically necessary, representing a purely decorative and protective element. There is no sign of silver plating. A nasal is riveted on to a broad browband, the cheek pieces being riveted together from five transverse iron bands. Iron mail served to protect the neck.
- **Banded Helmets of the Mainz-Bretzenheim type (Fig. 194.3)** – The helmet from the weapon burial of Mainz-Bretzenheim represents a later development of Late Roman helmets of the late 5th or early 6th century AD.[226] While the hemispherical bowl is made of broad iron bands, its quadrants were filled with iron sheets of a matching shape on the inside. There are no remains of a nasal or cheek pieces on this banded helmet. The remains indicate the use of iron mail as neck guard.

Figure 191a *Late Roman comb helmets of the Dunapentele/Intercisa type from Pfersee. Photo: M. Eberlein, Arch Staatsslg. Munich*

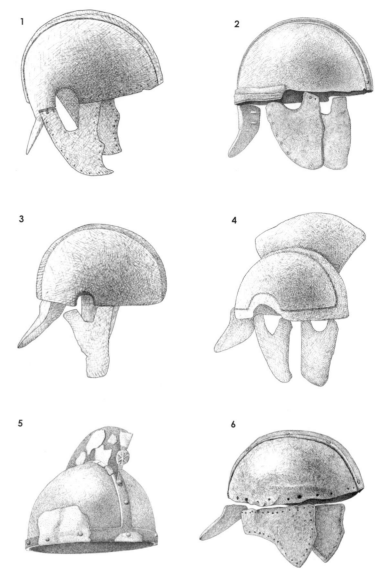

Figure 191b *Reconstructed crested helmet of the Deurne-Berkasovo type with comb plate and Christogram, from a find in Koblenz (after Miks 2011)*

Figure 192 *Late Roman comb helmets of the Dunapentele/Intercisa type, iron with gilded silver plate: 1 Augst, 2 Worms, 3 Dunapentele, 4 Intercisa, 5 Kessel-Hout, 6 Latvus (after Miks 2008). Drawings: A. Smadi, Arch Institute University of Cologne*

SPANGENHELME

In the Late Roman to Early Byzantine period, the conical *Spangenhelme* catch on, the predecessors of which are to be found in the East.[227] Unprovenanced examples such as the helmet from Deir el-Medineh in Egypt (Fig. 194.4) can – in the absence of a context – only be dated typologically (and thus very generally) to the 4th to 5th centuries AD.[228] These helmets will then lead to the early medieval *Spangenhelme* of the Baldenheim type (Fig. 194.5; Vogt 2006).

HELMET DECORATION AND CRESTS

Numerous representational sources of the early Imperial period depict various forms of helmet crests. On Montefortino helmets and related types, there are usually shown as long

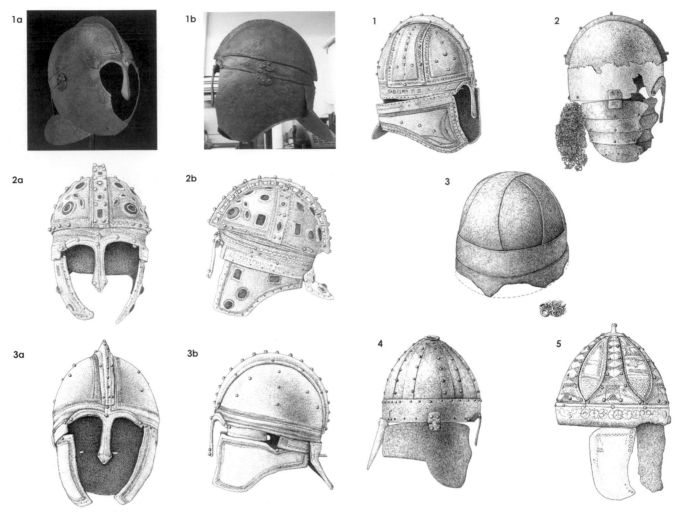

Figure 193 *Late Roman comb helmets of the Deurne-Berkasovo type: 1a and b unprovenanced, private, 2 a and b Berkasovo, 3 a and b Berkasovo (after Miks 2008). Drawings: A. Smadi, Arch Institute University of Cologne*

Figure 194 *Late antiquity comb helmets: 1 Deurne, Deurne-Berkasovo type; 2 Biberwier, Biberwier type; 3 Spangenhelm from Mainz-Bretzenheim; 4 Spangenhelm from Egypt; 5 Spangenhelm from Krefeld-Gellep (1–3, 5 after Miks 2008; 4 after Mackensen 2007). Drawings: A. Smadi, Arch Institute University of Cologne*

tufts, probably of horsehair, secured by means of the appropriate crest knob. However, on Montefortino helmets there are already examples, which have other devices, made from iron for instance, by means of which additional helmet decoration, such as plumes, could be attached.

In the Imperial period, helmets of the Weisenau type had a crest in the form of a front-to-back brush, as was known for Greek helmets. Helmet crest supports made of iron and bronze are plentiful in the archaeological record for helmets of the Weisenau type (Robinson 1975, 46f.) (Fig. 196, 198). Among site finds, they represent the most commonly occurring parts of the helmet. This is also easy to explain: as small pieces of equipment, not permanently attached to the helmet, they were apparently easily lost. The multiple occurrences of crest supports in archaeological contexts are contrasted by only two surviving crests: the piece preserved the best comes from the outer ditch of the earliest of the

three timber forts at Vindolanda/Chesterholm in northern England (Fig. 197). It dates to the period between AD 85 and 90.[229] A holding device made of bronze sheet carries a brush-like bush which surprisingly is not made of animal hair, but from a local moss (hair-moss, Widerton moss *Polytrichum commune*). A crest holder for a brush-like plume (Fig. 198) comes from the rural settlement of Tiel-Passewaaij (Netherlands) in the Batavian region. It is made of tinned bronze.[230]

An unusual type of crest is only preserved in the literary sources, and must have been rather rare: Florus[231] records an apparently somewhat odd centurion named Cornidius from the period of the war against the Moesians in AD 29. Instead of the usual decoration, he wore a burning brazier on his helmet. His movements fanned the flames, giving the impression that his head was on fire. This reportedly spread fear and terror among the enemy and contributed

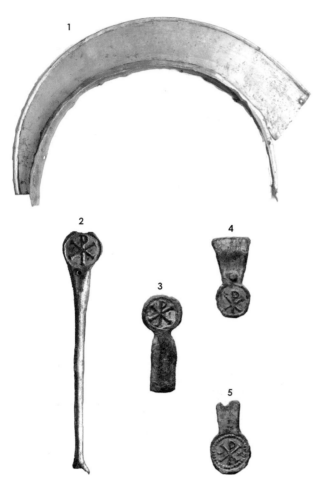

Figure 197 *Crests from Vindolanda (hair moss and copper alloy). Photo: M. Wieland*

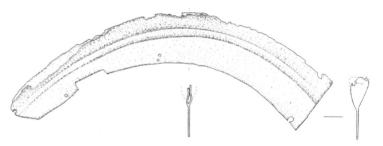

Figure 198 *Helmet crest box of copper alloy from Tiel-Passewaaij (by Nicolai 2007). Drawing: A. Smadi, Arch Institute University of Cologne*

Figure 195 *1 Late Roman comb helmets made of copper alloy, 2–5 Christograms of Late Roman comb helmets (unprovenanced, privately owned). Photos: A. Panger*

Figure 196 *Crest holder of copper alloy (unprovenanced, privately owned). Photo: A. Pangerl*

significantly to the Roman victory. It is still unclear to what extent crests – possibly even in a different colours – marked ranks or special units. On this subject, there are no unambiguous written sources. M. C. Bishop published an attempt towards this by associating the early Imperial helmets with plume tubes on either side, which occur repeatedly, with the *legio V Alaudae*, since crested larks (*alaudae*) are characterized by two such plumes on the head (Bishop 1990). In any event, it is hardly likely the design of the crest can have been left to individual caprice like that shown by curious individual cases such as the centurion Cornidius.

SURFACE TREATMENT

Roman objects of copper alloy (bronze, brass) very frequently show corrosion protection by tinning. This can often be observed on brooches (occasionally mistakenly called 'silvering' in the literature). With copper-alloy vessels, protection from corrosion is particularly important because the so-called 'verdigris', the patina of copper, is highly toxic. This protective coating with tin often disappears when buried, which does not then mean that it was not originally present.

It has to be assumed that this type of protective coating was the rule, particularly as water and bog finds of Roman bronze helmets of the Imperial period are so often tinned.

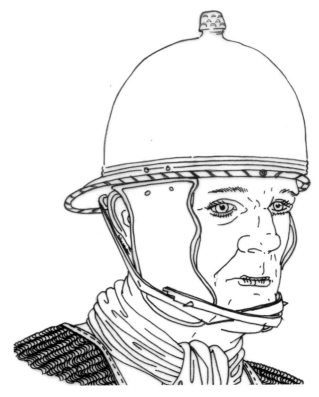

Figure 199 *Helmeted marble bust of Pyrrhus with chin strap (National Museum of Naples). Drawing: A. Smadi, Arch Institute University of Cologne*

Figure 200 *Reconstructed chin strap for the Montefortino type helmet (drawing B. Burandt)*

Consequently bronze helmets were barely distinguishable visually from iron helmets, which also had protective coatings. If we look at iron helmets of the Weisenau type, many have a protective coating made of bronze sheet, such as those from Haltern and Leicester.[232] However, they can also have a protective coating from silver plating, sometimes even gilded, like the Augustan helmet from the River Lech in Augsburg, the early Imperial helmet from the amphitheatre at Besançon,[233] and the Weisenau type helmet of a centurion with *crista transversa* from the river Kupa in Sisak in Croatia.[234]

Theoretically, iron helmets could also have been tinned, but corrosion has usually eliminated traces of such a protective coating. Nevertheless, we should assume this to have been the case as a rule, if only for practical reasons, as bare iron tends to constantly rust, much more than copper alloy. Nevertheless, while most bronze helmets were apparently protected against corrosion with tin, it would have been so much more appropriate for iron helmets!

HELMET LINING AND FASTENING

In order to safely and comfortably wear a helmet, there had to be a cushion or interior lining of textile (fabric, felt) or leather. This liner could either have been firmly connected to the helmet or formed a separate cap. Such a fur cap was found at Dura-Europos, but is not certain whether it really belonged to a helmet.[235] A helmet lining of felt is mentioned by Ammianus Marcellinus for the period around the middle of the 4th century AD (Amm. 19.8.8).

Again and again, organic residues preserved on the inside of helmets are interpreted as the remains of a lining, as was the case with the helmet with the unlikely provenance of 'Kiel', but probably originating from the Po at Cremona,[236] or with the Weisenau type helmet from the amphitheatre at Besançon.[237] The Hagenau type (Haltern variant) copper-alloy helmet from Haltern, displays partially oxydized remains of a woven fabric on the inside, which may come from a protective padding.[238] A leather sheath or a skin bag covered an iron, late-Augustan Weisenau-type helmet from Vindonissa. It is rather unlikely that this helmet is covered with fur in the sense of Künzl's 'hairy helmets' (Künzl 1999; Deschler-Erb 2004).

To ensure a snug fit for the helmet on the head, a special fastening to the head was necessary. This is already proven for the Republican period, thanks to a detailed representation on a marble bust of King Pyrrhus of Epirus (Figs 199–200) held in the National Museum of Naples:[239] a leather strap is fixed below the neck guard and brought to the side of the cheek piece. It is either placed through the rings attached to the inside of the cheek pieces and knotted at the front or it is fastened crosswise across the chin, through rivets mounted on the outside of the cheek pieces. This type of helmet fastening has been convincingly confirmed by the practical experiences of experimental archaeologists.

Armour

The current state of research on Roman body armour is fairly uneven: segmental cuirasses have been published comprehensively in two modern monographs (Bishop 2002; Thomas 2003). But the other types of armour, in other words muscle, mail, scale, and lamellar cuirasses, have been summarized on the basis of older research by Robinson.[240] Modern detailed investigations into these types of body armour are not currently available.

The individual types of armour occur at different times: the muscled cuirasses of senior officers were in use – at least according to iconographic representations – from the Republican to Late Roman periods. Otherwise mail was predominant in the Republic. Mail, segmental, and scale armour then ran in parallel over extended periods from the 1st to the 3rd centuries AD, independent of one another and their numerical ratio is only approximately known. The only thing that is undoubtedly clear is that cavalry never wore segmental or muscled cuirasses. From the later 3rd century, and in the Late Roman period, the segmental cuirass is no longer in use and mail and scale armour predominate. It is still unclear whether lamellar armour found in the East was in fact used by the Roman military. The role of hybrid body armour – composed from the characteristic elements of segmental, mail, or scale – has probably been underestimated.

PROTECTIVE CLOTHING UNDER ARMOUR

H. Ubl has recently summarized the existing state of knowledge on garments made from textiles, leather, or felt worn as a kind of lined protective vest under metal armour. Their ancient name is only recorded very late as *subarmale*, *thoracomachus*, or *peristethidion* (Ubl 2006). These arming doublets were necessary because otherwise the tunic would be worn away quickly while wearing metal armour. They also offered additional warmth in cold weather. Attached to these protective garments were the arm and belly straps and the *pteryges* of muscled cuirasses, which are so common on representational sources. The richly decorated centurion Marcus Caelius, killed in AD 9 in the Varus Battle, wears just such an arming doublet on the representation of his gravestone from Xanten. Apparently, these arming doublets could be worn without armour, if official circumstances allowed the abandonment of the heavy and not very comfortable protective defence. Himmler recently pronounced on the reconstruction of protective clothing under segmental armour through the practical experience of modern experiments.[241]

Figure 201 *Tombstone of Crispus from Wiesbaden (after Lindenschmit 1881)*

LEATHER ARMOUR?

L. Lindenschmit promoted the use of leather armour for the Roman Imperial army by misinterpreting a figural tombstone (Lindenschmit 1882, 6f.; 17; 20). His famous reconstruction of a legionary with leather armour (Fig. 65) drew on a representation of the legionary soldier C. Valerius Crispus of *legio VIII Augusta* on a tombstone from Wiesbaden (Fig. 201). Crispus wears seemingly smooth body armour with epaulettes. However, this is definitely mail, typical of the time, which has been misinterpreted as leather armour on just the basis of this poorly preserved representation. Thus, even now, this long-outdated reconstruction of a legionary occasionally haunts school textbooks in his leather jerkin. However, modern research is fairly unanimous in its opposition to the existence of such leather body armour.

Recently, R. D'Amato and G. Sumner tried to bring Roman leather armour back into the discussion again. Their only evidence is a belt-like strip of leather from the fort of Qasr-Ibsahim in Egypt, dated to the 2nd century AD.[242] However, whether this is part of a cuirass is, I think, highly questionable. In the reconstruction drawing of this armour shown in Pl. V, the front of the chest of the wearer has a laced fastening, which on this highly

Figure 202 *Cuirassed statue of Augustus from Prima Porta with muscled cuirass.*
Photo: Research Archive for Ancient Sculpture, Inst. of Arch. University of Cologne

tombstone of the cavalryman C. Romanius from Mainz Zahlbach[246] which is typical of Roman mail.

MUSCLED CUIRASSES

High-ranking officers, including the emperor, wore the so-called muscled cuirass (Fig. 202), bronze body armour probably mostly embossed, which mimics an idealized male anatomy.[247] The muscled cuirass (*thorax*) consisted of two halves, a plain back and a front part which often bore relief decoration. This front was semicircular at the lower abdomen. To this, hinged, semicircular lappets were then attached, as can frequently be observed on representations. These are often decorated and called *pteryges*.[248] That they could be made of metal is shown by a bronze mould, by means of which *pteryges* could be embossed from bronze sheet.[249] The front and back part of the cuirass were – as the representations and the few original discoveries show – connected by hinges, probably on one side with split pins.[250] Under this cuirass would be an undergarment made of leather or textiles, the hem and sleeves of which ended in fringed strips. These strips are often shown on cuirassed statues.[251] A fabric sash, knotted in a special way, is often worn on the armour as a badge of rank: the general's band (*cinctorium*).

Originals of Roman muscled cuirasses have only rarely been found, only their Greek and Etruscan precursors being known in larger numbers from archaeological finds. Up to now, only three known or putative fragmentary finds of Roman muscled cuirasses exist: the front half of a worked bronze muscled cuirass from the shipwreck at Cueva del Jarro in Almuñécar should be dated to the second half of the 1st century BC, with the date coming from the amphorae found with it.[252] This piece has the same hinge closure on the side as those found on cuirassed statues, mainly from the Imperial period.[253] A review of the amphorae by N. Hanel has, however, revealed that the ship and hence the cuirass date to the first half of the 1st century AD.[254] Fragments of such a cuirass have been found in a Germanic cremation grave (grave 622) in Kemnitz, in the district of Potsdam in Brandenburg, dating to the second half of the 2nd century AD. The front features relief decoration with the labours of Hercules. Again, one of the (at least four) hinges necessary for a muscled cuirass was found.

A fragment of a bronze sheet with a representation of a griffin, which probably comes from the front of an imperial muscled cuirass, has been published by Vermeule. It comes from the British art market and is unprovenanced.[255]

Pictorial representations of muscled cuirasses are common on armoured statues of emperors and generals,[256] as well as on the statues and statuettes of gods wearing an officer's uniform, such as Mars, Jupiter Dolichenus, or representations of Genius.

vulnerable part of the body just leaves a gaping hole! This would not quite be what could be called the best protection and because of that alone the reconstruction is implausible. Instead, this might be a part of the protective clothing for a charioteer, for which there are strikingly similar depictions on iconographic sources.[243] In addition to this highly dubious version of leather armour, D'Amato and Sumner have also uncritically accepted Lindenschmit's misinterpretation of supposed leather armour on the tombstone of the legionary soldier Crispus from Wiesbaden.[244] The leather lamellar armour from Dura-Europos, along with the pieces of crocodile skin from Manfalout in Egypt, do not seem to belong to regular Roman equipment.[245]

The same also applies to the attempt by A. Böhme-Schönberger, who wants to see 'leather jerkins' in the images of mail with shoulder doubling on tombstones of soldiers in the Rhineland. Apart from all the other counter-arguments already mentioned, she overlooks (among other things) the clearly recognisable S-shaped fastener on the

The most common body armour of Roman legionaries in the Republic and the Augustan period was mail, which was acquired from the Celts.[257] Like the others, it is more common on iconographic sources than as actual finds. The earliest evidence on the Aemilius Paulus Monument in Delphi shows iron mail with a straight hem and with the thighs almost completely covered.[258] The soldiers on the so-called Altar of Domitius also still wear such long mail.[259] A weapons relief from Pergamon, which is dated to the 2nd century BC, displays a mail shirt of the defeated Galatians with a crossbar (or leather strap?) serving as a fastener.[260] This forms the functional precursor of the later Roman fastening hook.

As we know from pictorial representations, broad epaulets were mounted over the shoulders for additional protection, as with the sculpture of an early Imperial warrior from Vachères (Basses-Alpes), illustrated by Robinson.[261] This shoulder doubling has not yet been identified in the archaeological material. What have been found more frequently in the early Imperial period until the Flavian period, however, are pairs of S-shaped clasps made of bronze, which held together the mail opening at the top in the front in the early Imperial period (Fig. 203, 204).

In the 2nd and 3rd centuries AD the form of chain mail changed: it was now longer and its construction was easier to manufacture. There were two types: a portion of the armour was cut like a modern T-shirt, so it could simply be slipped over the head, lacking the fastener and shoulder doubling. However, most of them had a fastening made of sheet metal breastplates in the chest area. The mail found at Bertoldsheim near Neuburg an der Donau (Fig. 205), for example, had a single breastplate fastener in the chest region, which could be opened with a mechanism which is not yet fully understood and thus was easier to put on. However, we do not know who wore this mail, which consisted of rectangular, standard prefabricated iron parts, assembled in a 'patchwork' pattern with bronze rings. Both infantrymen – in other words legionaries and auxiliary soldiers – and horsemen have been considered (Garbsch 1984). B. A. Greiner has suggested that the mail rings were manufactured by being in part prepared on the lathe (Greiner 2006).

The cuirasses with ornate fastening breastplates are found from the second half of the 2nd century AD. This is shown by the breastplate with an inscription from Mušov (10th Legion, Vienna) from the period of the Marcomannic wars. It also confirms that these cuirasses were worn by legionary soldiers.[262] If found isolated from armour, these fastening plates cannot automatically be assigned to mail: scale armour had the same method of fastening from the second half of the 2nd century AD onwards (Fig. 206).

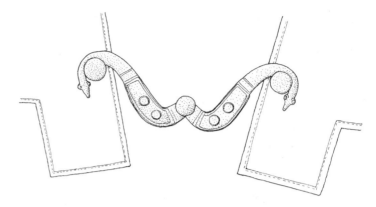

Figure 203 *Fastening hook for mail armour (reconstruction drawing)*

Figure 204 *Copper-alloy fastening hook from mail armour (unprovenanced, privately owned)*

The erroneous view that decorated fastening plates belonged to 'parade armour' goes back to H. R. Robinson, J. Garbsch taking it up, and so this legend lives on unhindered to this day,[263] although it was refuted long ago.[264]

There are one-piece and two-piece closure plates. One-piece plates have trapezoidal panels on the chest, as in the Bertoldsheim and Musov pieces.[265] Most of the pieces occur in pairs, sometimes in iron, more often in copper alloy. They are rectangular with a locking mechanism in the centre and have a rounded cut-out around the neck (Figs 207–8). On Trajan's Column, auxiliary soldiers always wear a short mail shirt with serrated lower edge, to distinguish it clearly from the legionaries in segmental armour. This special type of mail has not been identified in the archaeological record.

SEGMENTAL ARMOUR

As we know from the latest discoveries from Kalkriese and Dangstetten, a newly invented form of body armour was already starting to come into use by the time of Augustus: the segmental cuirass. It consisted of strips of iron plate from which a highly protective articulated cuirass was made for the upper body and shoulders using leather straps and buckles, and hinges and clasps made of bronze. The name *lorica segmentata* for this special form of defence is not ancient, but an invention of 16th-century antiquaries.[266] The representations on Trajan's Column show the segmental cuirass as the predominant body

Figure 205 *Cuirass fastening plate made of copper alloy from Bertoldsheim (after Garbsch). Drawing: A. Smadi, Arch Institute University of Cologne*

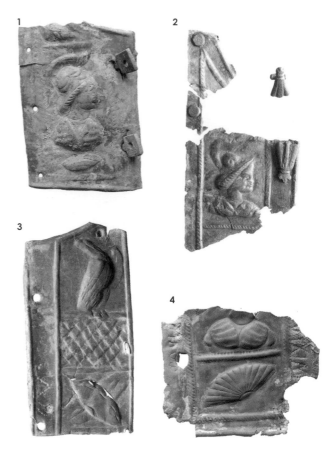

Figure 207 *1–4 Cuirass closure plates made of copper alloy. Note the cicada-like toggle fastener in no. 2 (unprovenanced, privately owned). Photo: A. Pangerl*

Figure 206 *Reconstructed cuirass fastening plates made of copper alloy. Photo: Private*

Figure 208 *Cuirass fastening plates made of copper alloy (1 unprovenanced, privately owned; Photo: private), 2–3 from the legionary camp at Potaissa (by Isac and Barbulescu 2008). Drawings: A. Smadi, Arch Institute University of Cologne*

armour for legionaries. Legionaries are recognisable by it and the rectangular *scutum*, differing significantly from auxiliary soldiers with the short mail shirt, serrated at the lower edge, and the oval shield. However, this cannot be a realistic representation! The contemporary Adamclisi monument provides an entirely different picture with its representations of legionaries (where they can be recognized) on its metopes:[267] here, out of the 24 metopes with representations of legionary soldiers, not a single man wears segmental armour, as there are 12 men with scale armour, and 30 men equipped with mail; similar diversity is encountered among the legionary representations of the column of Marcus Aurelius, which is later by about two generations, although here segmental armour is still relatively common.

Overall, the representations on Trajan's Column form the earliest, and those on the Arch of Septimius Severus the latest, pictorial representations of segmental armour; it is extremely rare on gravestones.[268] A cuirass depicted on the early Imperial honorific pedestal of M. Nonius from Isernia looks like a segmental cuirass.[269] Upon closer inspection, however, it turns out that it only shows the epaulets of segmental armour; the breastplate itself could have been mail. Thus this defence is one of the hybrid cuirasses.

Overall, the iconographic sources are in clear contradiction to the situation revealed by actual finds: we now know of components of the earliest identifiable segmental armour from the Augustan camps of Dangstetten, Oberaden, and Haltern, as well as from the battlefield at Kalkriese from the year AD 9.[270] Consequently, these seem to be an innovation of the Augustan period. M. C. Bishop's attempt to construct a Hellenistic prototype with the help of some fragments of an unprovenanced iron plate cuirass from Pergamon is unconvincing.[271] The Pergamene fragments, deviating as they do from the canonical forms of previously known Roman segmental armour, could equally well represent an unusual Imperial cuirass or a more recent (Byzantine?) one. Meanwhile, fragments and components of segmental cuirasses have been found in many forts and fortresses, but, there is still no find of a complete cuirass. One such might have come to light in the fort of Rißtissen on the upper Danube; unfortunately, it was largely destroyed during recovery. Its discovery was used by G. Ulbert to summarize the existing state of research into segmental armour.[272]

The discoveries of larger groups of several segmental cuirasses from a hoard of the later 1st century AD in the English fort of Corbridge first allowed a secure reconstruction (Figs 209–11). The segmental cuirass is so far the only type of Roman armour to enjoy recent extensive publication in a monograph.[273] Identification of the main components of segmental armour goes back to M. von Groller. He worked on the finds from the Carnuntum weapons store:[274] von Groller differentiated girth hoops, shoulder guards, breast-, and backplates.

Based on the Corbridge discovery, it has been found that in each case a shoulder portion and a girth hoop section were connected together on the back with leather (Raab 2012), with firmly riveted leather straps, the assembly and

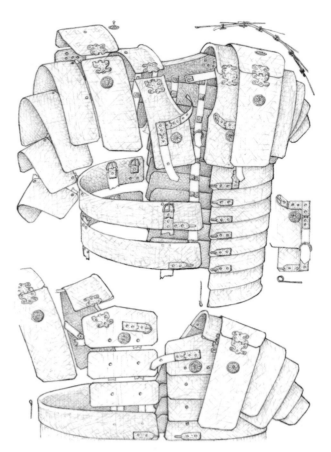

Figure 209 *Reconstructed Corbridge-type segmental cuirass (Robinson 1975). Drawing: A. Smadi, Arch Institute University of Cologne*

Figure 210 *Legionary re-enactors with reconstructed segmental cuirasses of the Corbridge type. Photo: J. Pogorzelski*

connection of the individual elements being carried out using fixed hinges (Fig. 211) or with detachable buckles, fastening hooks, or pin connectors. While the bands were of ferrous sheet, the buckles, hinges and fastening hooks were of copper alloy in the Kalkriese and Corbridge types.

Figure 211 *Copper-alloy hinge from a Corbridge-type segmental cuirass (unprovenanced, privately owned). Photo: A. Pangerl*

These fittings seem to have been subject to high wear and were often lost on fort sites as single items.[275] They also occur on the Newstead type, but on this type fittings of iron sheet were also used, such as on the fragment from the Weinberg near Eining (Fig. 213).

M. C. Bishop listed four types of segmental cuirass, which can be ordered chronologically.[276] Their chronological separation has now also been confirmed by the discovery of segmental armour from Spain (Aurrecoechea Fernandez 2009). Even assuming rustproofing for segmental armour by blueing or tinning, significant problems with rust have occasionally arisen in modern experiments.[277]

- **Kalkriese type segmental armour** – Individual components of this earliest type of segmental cuirass have appeared, inter alia, in Dangstetten, Kalkriese, and Vindonissa, M. C. Bishop believing that, due to the shape of the fittings, two Kalkriese variants can be isolated.[278] The latest evidence for this type come from Claudian deposits in Britain.

- **Corbridge type segmental cuirass (Figs 209–211)** – After the Claudian period, the shapes of the segmental cuirass fittings change. This form is best represented by the hoard from Corbridge in northern England (Allason-Jones and Bishop 1988). It was buried as scrap metal in the first half of the 2nd century AD. It did not contain one complete cuirass, but rather larger articulated portions of six different examples, which were still in use in the first half of the 2nd century AD. Around the middle of the 2nd century, the Corbridge type was replaced by the Newstead type.[279]

- **Newstead type segmental cuirass (Figs 212–14)** – Named after a find from the Scottish fort of Newstead dated to around the middle of the 2nd century AD,[280] it is a new, somewhat simplified type of segmental cuirass. The hinges seem more sturdy, but the turning pin fasteners, also found on contemporary fastening plates of mail and scale cuirasses, are new. The camp of Eining-Unterfeld, which dates between AD 171/2 and AD 179, only produced the Newstead type (Jutting 1995). A find from the fort of Zugmantel in the Taunus, as well as material from the

Figure 212 *Part of a segmental cuirass of the Newstead type, iron and copper alloy, from Newstead (after Curle 1911)*

weapons store at Carnuntum and on the Weinberg near Eining, indicate use until the middle of the 3rd century AD.

A curious find, which is presented here for the first time, confirms this late date: a fragment of an iron plate from a segmental cuirass in private ownership, has had two *denarii* riveted to it in antiquity (Fig. 107). A *denarius* of Domitian (AD 81–96) and one of Maximinus Thrax (AD 235–8), providing a *terminus post quem* for the use of this piece of equipment. We shall never know what prompted the then owner to attach this unique, eccentric decoration to his armour. Soon afterwards, segmental cuirasses fell into disuse.

- **Alba Iulia type segmental cuirass** – This type of cuirass, which is known only from a limestone statue from the Romanian military camp of Alba Iulia,[281] does not necessarily, in my view, belong to segmental armour, but rather represents a previously unrecognized mixture of elements of segmental and scale armour and would be better classified as a hybrid cuirass (see below). I am also not really sure that the statue is in fact a soldier; another

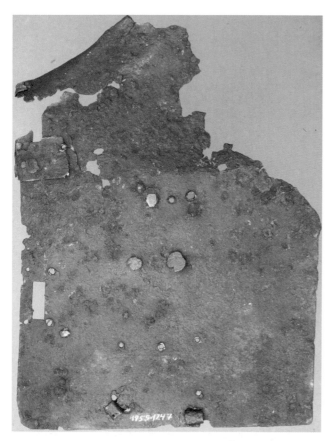

Figure 213 *Part of a segmental cuirass of the Newstead type, iron, Eining-Weinberg. Photo: Th. Fischer*

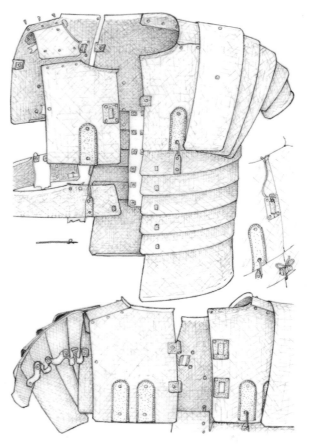

Figure 214 *Reconstructed segmental cuirass of the Newstead type (Robinson 1975). Drawings: A. Smadi, Arch Institute University of Cologne*

possibility would be a gladiator. Whether a copper-alloy breastplate decorated in relief, up to now only known on scale or mail cuirasses, really belongs to an Alba Julia type cuirass, as has allegedly been suggested for a find from Santa Marina/San Albito in León in Spain, has not yet been definitively clarified (Aurrecoechea Fernandez 2009).

SCALE ARMOUR

Unlike segmental armour, Roman scale armour (Figs 215; 216) has not yet been examined in a modern synthetic work. Robinson's work from 1975 is still the standard, followed by the information in Bishop and Coulston (2006) and local publications.[282] Scale armour originated in the Middle East, where its origins date back to the Bronze Age.[283]

So far, no clear indications of scale armour from Augustan deposits (*e.g.* Oberaden, Haltern, Kalkriese) have been found, although remnants of segmental and mail armour occur in some quantities. This could mean that scale armour only appeared in the military equipment of the Empire after a certain delay. With its undeniably Eastern origins, this may mean that it came to the West with Eastern auxiliary cavalry and was then introduced

Figure 215 *Copper-alloy armour scales from Newstead (after Curle 1911)*

COSTUMES, WEAPONS, AND EQUIPMENT OF THE ARMY FROM ORIGINAL ARCHAEOLOGICAL FINDS

Figure 216 *Examples of copper-alloy armour scales with a stamped bust of Minerva on the scales (unprovenanced, privately owned). Photo: Private*

into the armament of the Roman army in the post-Augustan period.

While earlier forms had individual scales of various sizes and shapes attached to each other at the sides with wire and then fastened flexibly to an organic backing, a different form of construction appeared in the middle of the 2nd century AD: the scales were now fixed to each other on four sides with wire, resulting in a much more rigid construction which, when it was actually used for a complete cuirass, is likely to severely have restricted the mobility of the wearer. In the absence of relevant finds, it is not yet possible to be certain whether this rigid system perhaps only protected certain parts of the body, and the cuirass was made in a more flexible manner elsewhere.[284]

Scale armour made of copper alloy – A complete scale cuirass has not yet been found. More detailed, comprehensive studies on these types of armour are, as I said, not yet available. At the moment it is just possible to say that there are considerable differences in the shape, size and type of the fastening holes of the scales. These are mostly made of bronze, more rarely of iron. A good example of this diversity is presented in the illustration of finds from the Carnuntum armoury.[285]

In the east of the Roman Empire, copper-alloy scales occasionally exhibit a central ridge, like those from Masada, Dülük Bebe Tepesi, or Dura-Europos.[286] At Masada, larger sections of such a scale cuirass have been found, with alternately coloured individual scales (tinned and brass coloured), arranged decoratively. From the context of the finds, this armour can more likely be attributed to the Jewish defenders than to the Roman attackers.

Unique is thus far a cuirass with silvered, copper-alloy scales found at Mušov in Moravia, dating to the Marcomannic Wars of the 60s and 70s of the 2nd century AD.[287]

Scale armour made of iron – The finds from Pannonia are striking because large iron scales from scale cuirasses often appear which are (up to now) unknown from Raetia, the German provinces, or Britain. Large armoured scales are also depicted on representations of legionaries from Adamclisi and later on the Marcus Column, assuming they are indeed to be viewed as accurate. Sarmatian influences are likely to be present in these large iron armour scales that occur in the middle Danube region from the time of the Marcomannic Wars, as in the examples from the 'weapons store' from Carnuntum.[288] However, here, as at other sites, both large and small iron scales are found together. It can therefore be assumed that such iron scale cuirasses were made in a combination of both scale sizes, thus ensuring sufficient flexibility for the wearer.

Iron scale armour may have been protected against corrosion by coatings of tin or other metal; at any rate, tinning was identified on armour scales from Sagalassos in Pisidia dated to the Late Roman–Early Byzantine period.[289] Occasionally, there were also scale cuirasses where scales of iron and copper alloy were combined because of the colour contrast, as at Eining and Urspring.[290]

LAMELLAR ARMOUR

Lamellar armour (Fig. 217) seems to have been an invention of the Assyrians.[291] In Roman times, it is represented in depictions of Palmyrene gods and in an original piece from Dura-Europos, but this armour is of leather. In the West, lamellar armour is completely absent, with the exception of some elongated scales from Corbridge (although, these unusually long pieces could also be from a scale cuirass[292]). This raises the question of whether the Roman army ever used lamellar armour in the Early and Middle Imperial period. The pieces from Dura-Europos could also derive from the equipment of the Palmyrene units stationed there or from the Persian enemy.

'HYBRID' ARMOUR

MAIL AND SCALE CUIRASSES WITH SEGMENTAL SHOULDER GUARDS

We know of body armour where added shoulder guards of iron plates like those of segmental cuirasses were combined with mail and scale cuirasses from the iconographic sources and a few original finds, including an early Imperial relief from Arlon in Belgium on which a group of cavalrymen wear such mail with shoulder guards; Bishop has virtually reconstructed this form of armour, but actual finds have so far not come to light.[293]

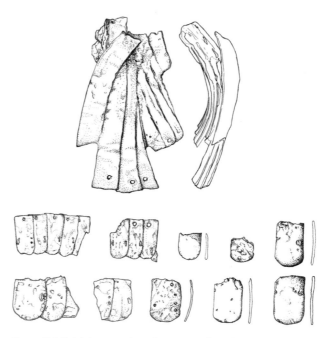

Figure 218 *Hybrid armour from the cavalry fort of Rusovce/Gerulata (after Varsik 1996)*

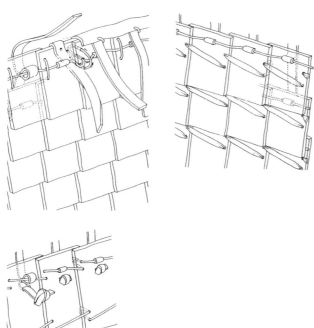

Figure 217 *Lamellar armour made of leather from Dura-Europos (after James 2004)*

However, fragments of an iron scale cuirass, found together with iron shoulder guards (Fig. 218) are known from a late Flavian burnt layer in the Slovakian cavalry fort of Rusovce-Gerulata.[294] The so-called Alba Julia type segmental cuirass[295] should not be included among segmental cuirasses, but rather represents a hybrid mixture of elements of segmental armour in the area of the torso and the scale armour on the shoulders.

As only small fragments of mail and scale armour are often present, the question arises of whether armour with a hybrid construction were not far more common in the Roman army than was previously thought, especially if we consider that the finds of shoulder regions of mail and scale cuirasses are quite rare in the find spectrum. This finding is more easily explained if we assume segmental armour components for this area.

COMBINED MAIL AND SCALE CUIRASSES (FIG. 219)

Early Imperial pieces of a very special style and in good condition are known from Augsburg and Vize in Bulgaria.[296] These have fine bronze scales mounted on mail. This type of armour has been assigned a Thracian origin. A fragment of body armour is known from Dülük Baba Tepesi, where strips of iron mail links are replaced with such copper-alloy scales.[297] This piece does not come from a dated context. M. Wijnhoven has published other examples of combined Roman mail and scale armour (Wijnhoven 2011).

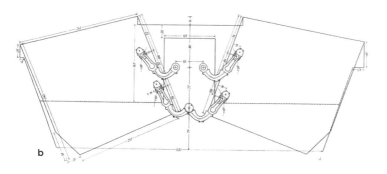

Figure 219 *Hybrid armour (mail with copper-alloy scales) from a) Vize and b) Augsburg (after Künzl 2002)*

Figure 220 *Iron strips, probably from an armguard (manica) from Newstead (after Curle 1911)*

Greaves

Roman infantry greaves, which were made of iron or bronze, are known today mainly from representations, such as those on the triglyph metope frieze of the tomb of Lucius Munatius Plancus in Gaeta, dated to around 20 BC.[298] Original finds are rare. Iron greaves are only known from an example in the hoard from Künzing, which comes from the burned material from the armouries.[299] This piece, made from thin iron sheet, has probably only survived due to the patina that formed during burning, which suggests that most examples of the defensive weapon, both the older and the more recent examples, have largely been destroyed by corrosion or have been rendered unrecognisable and thus are not represented among original finds. They may well have been much more widespread. In contrast, a group of greaves made of bronze sheet exists, which may or may not be sports armour. If they are decorated, they are predominantly associated with cavalry, especially if they have knee guards.[300] Simple examples made of sheet bronze might be assigned to cavalry or infantry, as with pieces from Dura-Europos or Hebron. The textile lining of a greave has also been found at Dura-Europos.[301]

Armguards (manicae)

The armguard (*manica*) consisted of overlapping strips of plate which are similar to segmental cuirasses in construction. According to Jörg Pogorzelski (Cologne; pers. comm.), who has reconstructed *manicae* from different materials (iron, bronze, brass), brass has been shown to be best because of its elasticity. *Manicae* were probably taken from gladiatorial armament.[302] Throughout the 1st century AD there are neither depictions (apart from gladiatorial representations) nor original finds. They then appear on the legionary reliefs on the metopes of the victory monument at Adamclisi; however, here the *manica* was only worn on the right (sword) arm, which was unprotected by the shield.[303] A probable Hadrianic piece comes from Carlisle at the western end of Hadrian's Wall.[304] Somewhat later finds come from Newstead and Carnuntum.[305] A new find of 2011 from the newly discovered fort of Steincheshof on the lower Rhine[306] has not yet been dated (Fig. 220, 221).

Figure 221 *Copper-alloy manica (in situ discovery from 2011, from the newly discovered (2009) fort at Steincheshof near Till-Moyland, Kleve district). Photo: M. Brüggler*

Shields

An important part of the defensive armament of the Roman army was the shield (Figs 222–32). Again, the Romans made their own improvements based on borrowings from opponents: the original curved, oval, legionary shield with its spindle-shaped shield boss came from the Celts;[307] while the Imperial-period oval and round shields with their round shield bosses have Germanic elements: the round shield boss itself probably was a Germanic invention of the 1st century BC.[308]

CURVED OVAL AND RECTANGULAR SHIELDS (SCUTA)

The curved, oval shield, which gradually transformed into the rectangular shield from the late 1st century BC, was a piece of equipment that identified legionaries with some certainty. However, there were also auxiliary units – *cohortes scutati, cohortes voluntariorum* – which were equipped with the *scutum*.[309] From the late Republic onwards, the legionary soldier carried the robust, almost man-sized oval or rectangular *scutum*, which consisted of a distinctly semi-cylindrical body of wood-leather-felt/fabric, which was glued together with a core of lath-like strips to form a kind of plywood. Apart from metal fittings, actual finds of this type of defence are very rare. A shield of late Republican or early Imperial date, which is made of birch wood is known from the Fayum in Egypt (Fig. 226.1). Since there are no birches in Egypt, the piece must have been brought to Egypt from somewhere to the north.[310]

The earliest representation of a rectangular shield, which then became predominant over the oval *scutum* during the 1st century AD, is on the weapon metopes of the Tomb of Lucius Plancus in Gaeta, which is dated to around 20 BC.[311] On metopes nos 7, 41, 55, 81, and 115 curved, rectangular shields can be seen. In addition to round shields, oval,

Figure 222 *Rectangular scuta from the time around the middle of the 2nd century AD from the relief from Croy Hill (after Coulston 1988a). Drawing: A. Smadi, Arch Institute University of Cologne*

Figure 223 *Shield covered from leather (reconstruction). Photo: J. Pogorzelski*

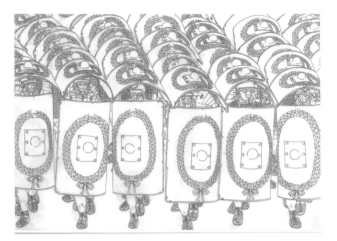

Figure 224 *Testudo formation with rectangular scuta (reconstruction drawing B. Burandt)*

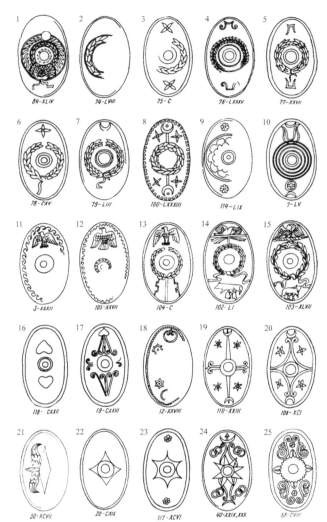

Figure 225 *Oval shields on Trajan's Column (after Richter 2010)*

pelta-shaped, figure-of-eight-shaped forms, and other forms of shield appear here, even long, oval, curved *scuta* (metopes nos 29, 37, 42, 54, 67, 79, and 93). (Fig. 224). Relatively early depictions of rectangular *scuta* can also be found on a *sestertius* RIC 32 of Gaius (Caligula; Fig. 28), minted in Rome in the years AD 37/38.

The metal components of a shield (copper-alloy or iron) included the edging of sheet metal, a spindle-shaped or round shield boss, and a handle, the shield grip.[312] Ornamental metal fittings are often discussed, but in practical terms they are so far only found on the rectangular shield from Doncaster, South Yorkshire[313] and fragments from Kalkriese. The former, excavated *in situ*, probably belonging to a British auxiliary (note the vertical handle!) from the middle of the 1st century AD, had decorative elements of sheet bronze and numerous small ornamental nails. With the exception of the finds from Dura-Europos, coloured components of organic material, painted with the insignia of units among other things, have not been found.[314] On the battlefield at Kalkriese, there was an area where, among other things, pieces of copper-alloy shield binding were concentrated. These numerous small decorative nails and rivets have copper-alloy and silver heads.[315] In addition, there are partly gilded fragments of silver plate, which are designed to look like lightning.[316] Thunderbolts are among the most common (probably only painted) decorative elements on Roman Imperial *scuta*, which is how they are depicted on Trajan's Column (Richter 2010).

In the case of Kalkriese, A. Rost is of the opinion that at the place with the concentration of finds of metal shield fittings, Roman shields had been 'scrapped' after the battle by the Germanic victors;[317] in other words, the valuable metal was removed from the wood and leather components of shields and collected for re-melting, because the great Roman shields were completely unusable for the mobile fighting techniques of the lightly armed Teutons, but the metal was most welcome. The numerous small copper-alloy and silver nails and rivets from Kalkriese could also be shield components like those of the Doncaster Shield as well as the gilded silver, lightning-shaped appliqués, which conform to the iconographic sources. However, these decorative elements made of gilded silver were certainly not mounted on the standard-issue shields of the average Augustan legionary soldier. It seems more likely that these are the elaborately decorated defensive weapons of a prominent elite unit. The epigraphic evidence proves the presence of such an elite unit on the battlefield at Kalkriese: the first cohort (*cohors prima*) of an unspecified legion.[318] A. Nabbefeld and A. Busch have now noted legitimate doubts over the widely accepted opinion that the rectangular *scutum* was the standard shield of the Roman legions from the Augustan to the Severan periods.[319] The oval shield, proven for the legions from the time of the Marcomannic Wars onwards, may have been introduced even earlier.

1

2

Figure 226 *1 Oval scutum from the Fayum (after Nabbefeld 2010), 2 rectangular scutum from Dura-Europos (after Nabbefeld 2010)*

comprises the second example of this shield shape so far.[320] What the background of that special form is, whether only special units were equipped with this shield, or whether it offered advantages in combat, are all as yet unclear.

BUCKLERS (*PARMA*)

The name *parma equestris* was used for the small round shield of the cavalry of the city of Rome, which was disbanded in the late Republic in favour of auxiliary cavalry regiments.[321] In Imperial times, pictorial representations of such small round shields focus on standard-bearers. An original find is from a grave from Feudenheim, Mannheim city, on the Neckar in Swabia.[322] Similarly, a leather shield cover from Castleford, West Yorkshire, indicates the existence of such a shield.[323] In Germany, larger round shields are familiar from the early Imperial period onwards. There are complete shields from Thornberg.[324] Round shields were later adopted by the Late Roman army.[325] Finds of colourful leather components of round shields painted with ornamental and figurative hunting and battle scenes (Fig. 227) dated to the Late Roman period come from Egypt and lack a precise context.[326]

ROUNDED OVAL SHIELDS

The most common Roman shield shape was the rounded oval shield. They are depicted on iconographic sources from the 1st century AD onwards for auxiliary soldiers (infantry and cavalry); from the Marcomannic Wars onwards, they also occur in representations of legionary soldiers; from the period around AD 200 they then replace the rectangular *scutum*.[327] Whether this impression is indeed true is undecided because it is only based on the iconographic sources. It has recently undergone a critical revision.[328] The only surviving Roman examples of oval shields come from Dura-Europos (Fig. 228) and are dated to around the middle of the 3rd century AD. They are brightly painted with geometric, vegetal, and figurative representations; there is even a leather shield facing with the representation of a map.[329]

HEXAGONAL SHIELDS

Hexagonal shields are only known from pictorial representations, such as cavalry gravestones from the 1st to 2nd century AD. There are no original finds, apart from appropriately shaped shield-edge binding, for example a piece from Aislingen, which possibly belonged to a hexagonal shield.[330]

SHIELD FITTINGS

As a rule, only the metal fittings have survived from Roman shields. Unlike the Germanic finds where plain wooden shields are known – the shield from Hjortsprung (Denmark), for example[331] – there is no evidence of shields

Similarly, H. Ratsdorf has now critically reviewed the theory that the leather-covered wooden parts of the shields always had flat or smooth surfaces (the semi-cylindrical, rectangular *scutum*) (Ratsdorf 2009). From his background as an experimental archaeologist, he has demonstrated in detail on the basis of iconographic sources, the angles of inclination of the edges of bosses, and his own experiments, that ancient wooden shield boards probably mostly had curved cross sections and were not flat.

TRAPEZOIDAL SHIELDS

On a Republican relief from Estepa near Seville in Spain, Roman soldiers are depicted with a trapezoidal shield flattened at the top and bottom, with a spindle-shaped shield boss. A late Augustan find from the Hunerberg in Nijmegen, also with a spindle-shaped shield boss,

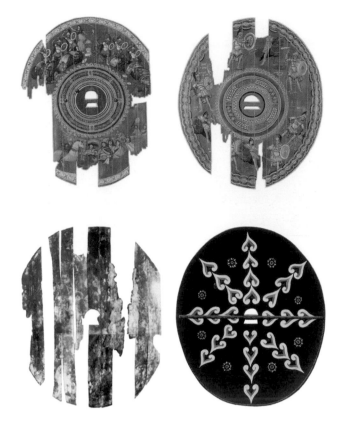

Figure 228 *Wooden painted oval shields from Dura-Europos (after James 2004)*

Figure 227 *Fragmentary Late Roman shield leather from Egypt with artist's reconstruction (after Junkelmann 1996)*

without metal fittings from the Roman Empire. S. James is convincing when assigning the shields from Dura-Europos made from wooden sticks and rawhide to the Persian invaders, not to the Roman defenders.[332]

BOSSES

Like Celtic and German shields, Roman ones possessed an iron or copper-alloy boss placed at the centre over an opening in the shield board.[333] The shield handle was mounted horizontally on the back of this opening. The boss had the task of protecting the hand. While barleycorn bosses derived from Celtic traditions predominated among the long, oval *scuta* of the late Republic and the early Empire,[334] rectangular *scuta* had a hemispherical shield boss on a rectangular base plate. However, finds of these are strikingly rare.[335] Round and oval shields had round shield bosses with forms of dome (Fig. 230, 231) which came from German traditions.[336] The ratio of iron to bronze shield bosses is unknown, due to the nature of the sources, whereby bronze objects are more likely to survive. For Upper Germany and Raetia, M. Gschwind established that there had been a lot more iron than bronze pieces.[337]

SHIELD GRIPS

Horizontally positioned iron or copper-alloy shield reinforcers, which are located beneath the shield boss, formed handles for Roman shields. This is often just the framework for a wooden handle, which would probably have been additionally padded with fabric or leather. The rectangular shield from Doncaster, with its horizontally set

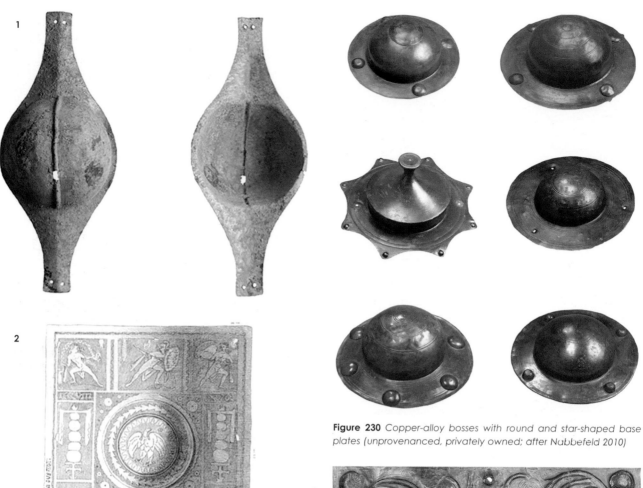

Figure 230 *Copper-alloy bosses with round and star-shaped base plates (unprovenanced, privately owned; after Nabbefeld 2010)*

Figure 229 *1 Spindle-shaped shield boss of copper alloy (unprovenanced, privately owned). Photo: A. Pangerl; 2 shield boss with a rectangular base plate made of copper alloy naming the Leg VIII Augusta from the River Tyne (after Lindenschmit 1881)*

Figure 231 *Rectangular decorative shield boss of copper alloy with depiction of Dionysus (unprovenanced, privately owned; after Nabbefeld 2010)*

grip (South Yorkshire),[338] is a notable exception which can probably be attributed to British auxiliaries.

Unlike Greek shields, Celtic, German, and Roman shields were carried with the left hand using the horizontal hand grip.[339] There is no evidence for additional support to relieve the hand, such as a shoulder strap attached to the shield, which is sometimes discussed in re-enactment circles.

Greek shields, however, did not have a handle with a shield boss in the center, but a shield band, through which the arm was placed. The fist then held a grip at the

Figure 232 *Copper-alloy shield nails with incised representations of a Minerva and b Ganymede (unprovenanced, privately owned). Photo: A. Pangerl*

edge. It is a characteristic feature of archaising, unrealistic representations in Roman art, like those on the Marcus Column, or on some battle sarcophagi, where a completely inaccurate method of carriage for shields is shown: Roman oval shields with shield bosses are depicted there in an unrealistic Hellenized style with shield band and edge grip, as on the Ludovisi battle sarcophagus.[340]

SHIELD EDGING

Finds from Imperial sites from the Augustan period onwards (Oberaden, Kalkriese) include copper-alloy shield binding, seldom iron. These are divided into segments of U-shaped cross-section and have perforated semicircular tabs, with which they are riveted to the wooden shield board. Based on the shape, especially of the corner pieces, round, oval, rectangular, and hexagonal shield forms can be identified. Remarkably, the preserved shields from Dura-Europos have no metal shield fittings but in some cases have a narrow opening. Here, the shield binding was apparently sewn leather or rawhide, which is not otherwise found among the archaeological evidence. Logical considerations and modern experiments demonstrate that metal edging is subjected to extreme wear on the upper part of the shield in action. M. Junkelmann, who told me about his practical experience in mock gladiatorial demonstrations, pointed out that metal fittings are often cut on the top of shields. These produced sharp, protruding edges that can be as dangerous to the user under certain circumstances as the enemy. He has therefore changed over his Gladiator group to shields, especially *scuta*, which have rawhide edging.

SHIELD COVERINGS (TEGIMENTA)

Since shield boards, leather, and felt or textile components held together with water-soluble bone glue were very sensitive to moisture, such as rain, shields were protected on the march with a well-greased leather cover (Fig. 223), remains of such leather cases having been found, for example, in Oberaden or in the midden at Vindonissa.

They often bear devices in the form of a name plate (*tabula ansata*) with the name of the unit of the owner in embroidery or sewn perforated leather.[341]

SYSTEM OF CARRIAGE

In the rare cases where complete shields have survived or could be identified by careful examination of appropriate contexts, metal rings found on or with shields may indicate a carrying device employing leather straps.[342] From practical experience, in re-enactment circles it is discussed[343] whether the shield was carried on the back with straps like a backpack, or if it was strapped with a cross belt on the march. This may have something in it, and some practical considerations are against it, but this is not proven for antiquity. Some re-enactment groups have solved the problem pragmatically so that they have secured the support straps to the shield covers, with which the *scutum* was strapped to the back on the march (Himmler 2012). This is relatively comfortable according to experimental evidence, especially as it could then also support the marching pack attached to the baggage pole (*furca*).[344]

Offensive weapons

Offensive weapons are traditionally thought to include edged or bladed weapons (swords, daggers), polearms (spears), and missiles (javelins, *pila*, arrows, sling bullets, and artillery projectiles).

Swords

Writing about the year AD 50/51, Tacitus describes a battle between the Romans and the Britons under their chief Caratacus. He clearly distinguished between the *gladius* of the legionary troops and the *spatha* of the auxiliary soldiers, by which he probably meant cavalry (Tac., *Ann.* 12.35; Miks 2007, 19). Here, the 'classic' Roman short sword is meant by *gladius*, the longer bladed weapon by *spatha*. This terminology, nowadays generally customary in research, was by no means so clearly and unambiguously fixed for the Romans in antiquity between the Republic and Late Roman period: the term '*gladius*', although usually meaning 'short sword', can also mean 'sword' in general. In Vegetius (Vegetius, *Epitoma rei militaris* 2.15.8) there is a definition 'Such was heavy armament, as the heavily armed had: greaves, shields, large *gladii*, which they describe as *spathae*, and other smaller examples called *semispathae*'. As Vegetius briefly discussed, the *semispatha* should not be equated with the *gladius* in the sense of a short sword, but as a third type of sword.[345]

Christian Miks has tried to differentiate the length of the sword blades of *gladii*, *semispathae*, and *spathae* using

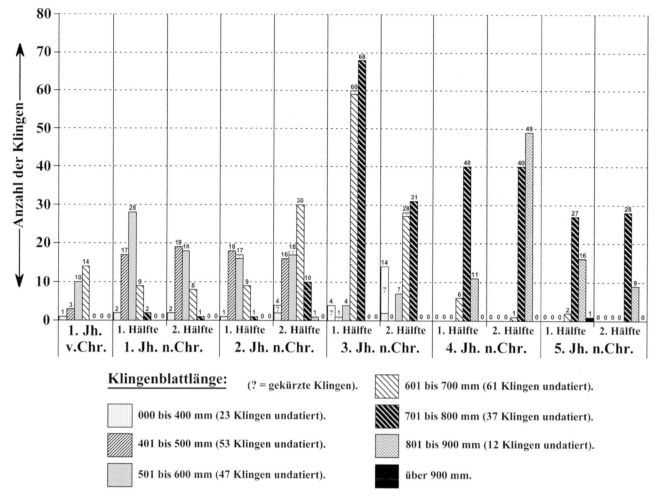

Figure 233 *Statistics for Roman Imperial swords: number of blades dated to (1st/2nd half) centuries AD. The different shading indicates length classes in millimetres with the number of undated examples in parenthesis (after Miks 2007)*

statistical methods (Fig. 233). With *gladii* and *spathae* of the 1st and 2nd century AD, this presents no problem. There were two clear groupings: cutting blade lengths between 476 and 550 mm define the *gladius*, and those between 601 to 825 mm the *spathae*. At the latest, there is a change in the early 3rd century AD: blade lengths below 550 mm disappear, excluding broken and then provisionally reforged short swords as weapons from these considerations. From this time, blade lengths between 551 and 600 mm testified in the literature by Vegetius as the *semispatha* can actually be defined; those with blade length more than 600 mm would be termed *spathae*.[346]

SHORT SWORDS (*GLADII*)

GLADIUS HISPANIENSIS

The most important bladed weapon for Roman legionaries, normally fighting in close formation, from the Republic up to the 2nd century AD was the classic, double-edged Roman short sword, the *gladius*. However, as emphasized

above, it is a convention in modern research only to employ the name *gladius* for this weapon, when in ancient parlance any sword could sometimes be meant by *gladius*. According to written sources (Polybius, *Hist* 6.23; T. Livius, *Ab urbe condita* 31.34) this weapon was adopted from opponents during the Second Punic War in Spain (218–201 BC) as the *gladius Hispaniensis*. After thorough investigation by Christian Miks, this origin does not seem so clear archaeologically. Although Spanish short swords of the Iron Age (Fig. 234) were fairly similar to the waisted blade of the Augustan Mainz-type *gladius*, the archaeological material has not as yet bridged the yawning time gap in the development of the sword. Above all, the fact that – compared to the amount of finds from the Imperial period – there are hardly any sword finds safely attributable to the Roman military of the Republic plays a part. Even the few representational sources offer little by way of alternative in the discussion of these issues.

Overall, the development of the early Imperial *gladius* seems to have been more diverse than current research

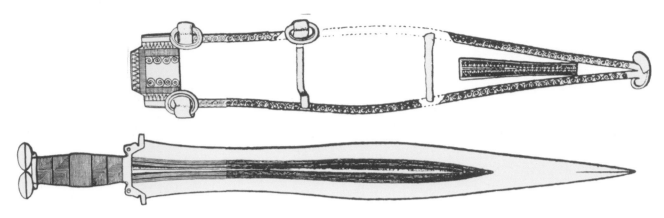

Figure 234 *Spanish short sword with curved blade and frame scabbard made of copper alloy. 2nd century BC (After Miks 2007)*

based on the archaeological evidence of the *gladius Hispaniensis* was able to convey. Thus Miks traces *gladii* back initially to the Greek short sword of the 7th to 5th centuries BC, the *xiphos*. This sword form emerged in the 4th century BC in northern Greek tombs and in depictions on Roman *aes signatum* ingot currency from the first half of the 3rd century BC, so its use by the Roman Republican army may be assumed (Miks 2007, 30–8; 435). The extent to which the Romans modified this sword form for their own use is still unclear. Miks comments on the incomplete current state of research with this remarkable passage:

> Based on sword representations on Italo-Greek and Roman monuments of the 2nd and 1st century BC, starting from classic *xiphos* shapes, the emerging trend is that it is entirely conceivable that both a typological derivative of the blade formats, but also individual handle and sheath elements, were based on an Italo-Greek sword tradition. Nevertheless, the testimony of the written sources (Suidas *sv* Machaira; Polybius, fragment 179.96) counters that the Roman army adopted a sword equally suitable for cut and thrust from Celtiberian weapons during the Second Punic War (218–201 BC). Subsequent literary clarifications of this weapon significantly point to the short sword originating from Gallic La Tène *spathae* in terms of quality and handling (*ibid.* 435).

In fact, the Celtiberian short sword – separated as it was by a significant gap in the archaeological material – seems to have had an influence on the development of the Roman sword, because early Roman Iron Age weapons of the Mainz type, both in terms of blade shape, as well as in details the scabbard construction (a scabbard frame with hinged suspension rings on cross-pieces), have obvious similarities to Celtiberian swords of the 3rd century BC (*ibid.* 39–51, 435f.).

MAINZ-TYPE GLADIUS

In a seminal essay, G. Ulbert (1969a) divided early Imperial *gladii* into the older Mainz type and the later Pompeii type. With this type series in particular, he dated the Pompeii type blade and sheath to the Flavian-Trajanic period as a whole.

As more evidence is found, there are now also transitional forms where 'Mainz' blades occur together with 'Pompeii' sheaths. This cautions against considering the blade and scabbard of a sword together in typological studies. Hence Miks has demonstrated that, for a typological-chronological sequence of swords, the material is better managed by just considering the individual components of a weapon separately, in other words blades, sheaths, and also occasionally handles (Fig. 235) (Miks 2007). This has in fact been done by W. Menghin, in studying early medieval swords (Menghin 1983).

- **Blades** – 'Mainz'-type blades are curved more or less along their cutting edges and have no kinks in a long solid tip which is often thickened for use as a thrusting weapon (Fig. 236). The Mainz-type blade (up to 60 cm long) is divided into six variants by Miks. Chronologically distinct types can even be observed with sheaths: the waisted blade of the Mainz type *gladius* is theoretically derived from Spanish parallels of the Middle and Late Iron Age and thus from the *gladius Hispaniensis* mentioned in the literature, but so far, as I said, the 'missing link' is absent from the archaeological record. It is primarily the blade variant of the Augustan to the Claudian period – especially in the region of Germany – dating up to the early 2nd century AD.
- **Hilts** – The handles of the various types of *gladius* consisted of wood or bone and even ivory (Figs 237–8). In some cases they were studded with metal nails or even covered with silver foil. They were terminated with a large spherical or disc-shaped pommel. In the early Imperial period, in other words on Mainz-type swords, wooden handle components still predominated. In the case of the Rheingönheim sword (Fig. 239.3), the manufacturer L. Valerius and the weight of silver are listed on the silver foil coating of the hilt. It weighed *pondo semiunciam scripula VII*, or 21.6 grams.[347]
- **Scabbards** – The scabbards of the Mainz type *gladius* (Fig. 241) changed faster than the blade shapes. In

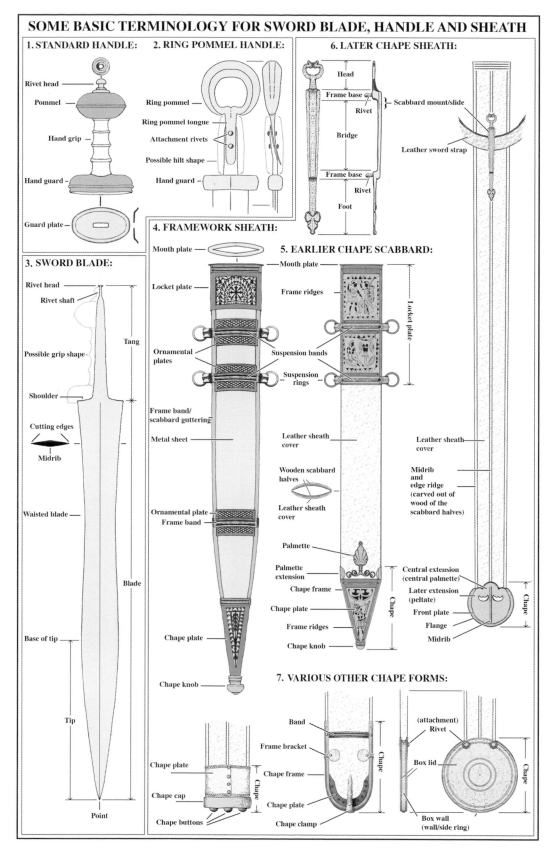

SOME BASIC TERMINOLOGY FOR SWORD BLADE, HANDLE AND SHEATH

1. STANDARD HANDLE:

Rivet head

Pommel

Hand grip

Hand guard

Guard plate

2. RING POMMEL HANDLE:

Ring pommel

Ring pommel tongue

Attachment rivets

Possible hilt shape

Hand guard

6. LATER CHAPE SHEATH:

Head

Frame base

Rivet

Scabbard mount/slide

Bridge

Frame base

Rivet

Foot

Leather sword strap

3. SWORD BLADE:

Rivet head

Rivet shaft

Tang

Possible grip shape

Shoulder

Cutting edges

Midrib

Waisted blade

Blade

Base of tip

Tip

Point

4. FRAMEWORK SHEATH:

Mouth plate

Locket plate

Ornamental plates

Frame band/ scabbard guttering

Metal sheet

Ornamental plate
Frame band

Chape plate

Chape knob

5. EARLIER CHAPE SCABBARD:

Mouth plate

Frame ridges

Locket plate

Suspension bands

Suspension rings

Leather sheath cover

Wooden scabbard halves

Leather sheath cover

Palmette

Palmette extension

Chape frame

Chape plate

Frame ridges

Chape knob

Leather sheath cover

Midrib and edge ridge (carved out of wood of the scabbard halves)

Central extension (central palmette)

Later extension (peltate)

Front plate

Flange

Midrib

Chape

7. VARIOUS OTHER CHAPE FORMS:

Chape plate

Chape cap

Chape buttons

Chape

Band

Frame bracket

Chape frame

Chape plate

Chape clamp

Chape

(attachment) Rivet

Box lid

Box wall (wall/side ring)

Chape

Figure 235 *Basic terms for Roman sword blades, hilts, and sheaths (after Miks 2007)*

COSTUMES, WEAPONS, AND EQUIPMENT OF THE ARMY FROM ORIGINAL ARCHAEOLOGICAL FINDS

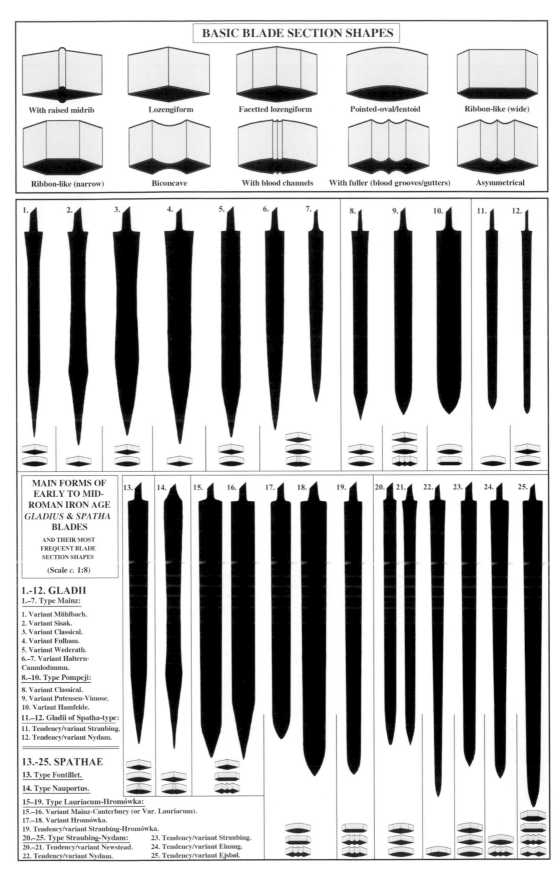

BASIC BLADE SECTION SHAPES

With raised midrib · Lozengiform · Facetted lozengiform · Pointed-oval/lentoid · Ribbon-like (wide)

Ribbon-like (narrow) · Biconcave · With blood channels · With fuller (blood grooves/gutters) · Asymmetrical

MAIN FORMS OF EARLY TO MID-ROMAN IRON AGE *GLADIUS & SPATHA* **BLADES**

AND THEIR MOST FREQUENT BLADE SECTION SHAPES

(Scale *c.* 1:8)

1.-12. GLADII

1.–7. Type Mainz:

1. Variant Mühlbach.
2. Variant Sisak.
3. Variant Classical.
4. Variant Fulham.
5. Variant Wederath.
6.–7. Variant Haltern-Camulodunum.

8.–10. Type Pompeji:

8. Variant Classical.
9. Variant Putensen-Vimose.
10. Variant Hamfelde.

11.–12. Gladii of Spatha-type:

11. Tendency/variant Straubing.
12. Tendency/variant Nydam.

13.-25. SPATHAE

13. Type Fontillet.

14. Type Nauportus.

15–19. Type Lauriacum-Hromówka:

15.–16. Variant Mainz-Canterbury (or Var. Lauriacum).
17.–18. Variant Hromówka.
19. Tendency/variant Straubing-Hromówka.

20.–25. Type Straubing-Nydam:

20.–21. Tendency/variant Newstead.
22. Tendency/variant Nydam.
23. Tendency/variant Straubing.
24. Tendency/variant Einang.
25. Tendency/variant Ejsbøl.

Figure 236 *Blade types of Roman swords (after Miks 2007)*

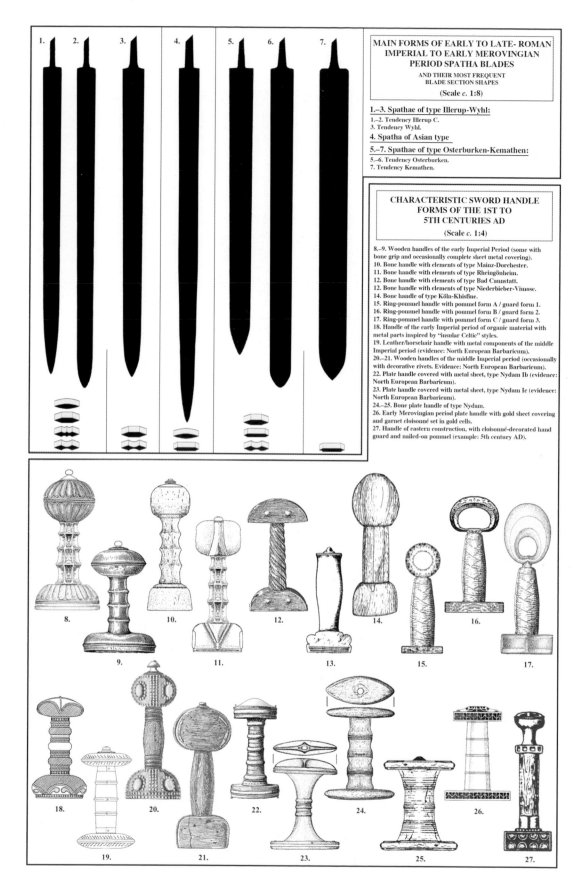

MAIN FORMS OF EARLY TO LATE- ROMAN IMPERIAL TO EARLY MEROVINGIAN PERIOD SPATHA BLADES

AND THEIR MOST FREQUENT BLADE SECTION SHAPES

(Scale *c.* 1:8)

1.–3. Spathae of type Illerup-Wyhl:
1.–2. Tendency Illerup C.
3. Tendency Wyhl.
4. Spatha of Asian type
5.–7. Spathae of type Osterburken-Kemathen:
5.–6. Tendency Osterburken.
7. Tendency Kemathen.

CHARACTERISTIC SWORD HANDLE FORMS OF THE 1ST TO 5TH CENTURIES AD

(Scale *c.* 1:4)

8.–9. Wooden handles of the early Imperial Period (some with bone grip and occasionally complete sheet metal covering).
10. Bone handle with elements of type Mainz-Dorchester.
11. Bone handle with elements of type Rheingönheim.
12. Bone handle with elements of type Bad Cannstatt.
12. Bone handle with elements of type Niederbieber-Vimose.
14. Bone handle of type Köln-Khisfine.
15. Ring-pommel handle with pommel form A / guard form 1.
16. Ring-pommel handle with pommel form B / guard form 2.
17. Ring-pommel handle with pommel form C / guard form 3.
18. Handle of the early Imperial period of organic material with metal parts inspired by "insular Celtic" styles.
19. Leather/horsehair handle with metal components of the middle Imperial period (evidence: North European Barbaricum).
20.–21. Wooden handles of the middle Imperial period (occasionally with decorative rivets. Evidence: North European Barbaricum).
22. Plate handle covered with metal sheet, type Nydam Ib (evidence: North European Barbaricum).
23. Plate handle covered with metal sheet, type Nydam Ic (evidence: North European Barbaricum).
24.–25. Bone plate handle of type Nydam.
26. Early Merovingian period plate handle with gold sheet covering and garnet cloisonné set in gold cells.
27. Handle of eastern construction, with cloisonné-decorated hand guard and nailed-on pommel (example: 5th century AD).

Figure 237 *Blade and hilt types of Roman swords (after Miks 2007)*

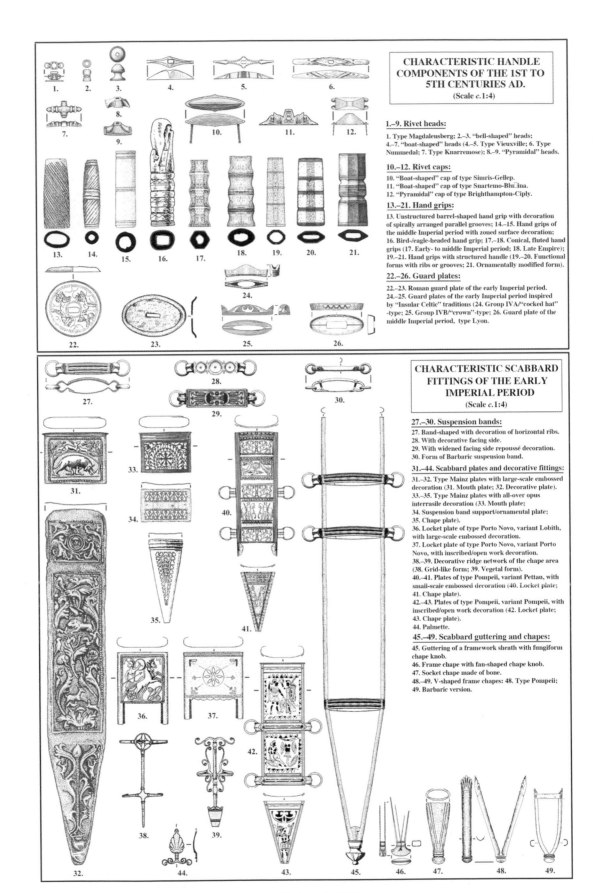

CHARACTERISTIC HANDLE COMPONENTS OF THE 1ST TO 5TH CENTURIES AD.
(Scale c.1:4)

1.–9. Rivet heads:

1. Type Magdalensberg; 2.–3. "bell-shaped" heads; 4.–7. "boat-shaped" heads (4.–5. Type Vieuxville; 6. Type Nummedal; 7. Type Knarremose); 8.–9. "Pyramidal" heads.

10.–12. Rivet caps:

10. "Boat-shaped" cap of type Simris-Gellep. 11. "Boat-shaped" cap of type Snartemo-Blu̇ina. 12. "Pyramidal" cap of type Brighthampton-Ciply.

13.–21. Hand grips:

13. Unstructured barrel-shaped hand grip with decoration of spirally arranged parallel grooves; 14.–15. Hand grips of the middle Imperial period with zoned surface decoration; 16. Bird-/eagle-headed hand grip; 17.–18. Conical, fluted hand grips (17. Early- to middle Imperial period; 18. Late Empire); 19.–21. Hand grips with structured handle (19.–20. Functional forms with ribs or grooves; 21. Ornamentally modified form).

22.–26. Guard plates:

22.–23. Roman guard plate of the early Imperial period. 24.–25. Guard plates of the early Imperial period inspired by "Insular Celtic" traditions (24. Group IVA/"cocked hat"-type; 25. Group IVB/"crown"-type; 26. Guard plate of the middle Imperial period, type Lyon.

CHARACTERISTIC SCABBARD FITTINGS OF THE EARLY IMPERIAL PERIOD
(Scale c.1:4)

27.–30. Suspension bands:

27. Band-shaped with decoration of horizontal ribs. 28. With decorative facing side. 29. With widened facing side repoussé decoration. 30. Form of Barbaric suspension band.

31.–44. Scabbard plates and decorative fittings:

31.–32. Type Mainz plates with large-scale embossed decoration (31. Mouth plate; 32. Decorative plate). 33.–35. Type Mainz plates with all-over opus interrasile decoration (33. Mouth plate; 34. Suspension band support/ornamental plate; 35. Chape plate). 36. Locket plate of type Porto Novo, variant Lobith, with large-scale embossed decoration. 37. Locket plate of type Porto Novo, variant Porto Novo, with inscribed/open work decoration. 38.–39. Decorative ridge network of the chape area (38. Grid-like form; 39. Vegetal form). 40.–41. Plates of type Pompeii, variant Pettau, with small-scale embossed decoration (40. Locket plate; 41. Chape plate). 42.–43. Plates of type Pompeii, variant Pompeii, with inscribed/open work decoration (42. Locket plate; 43. Chape plate). 44. Palmette.

45.–49. Scabbard guttering and chapes:

45. Guttering of a framework sheath with fungiform chape knob. 46. Frame chape with fan-shaped chape knob. 47. Socket chape made of bone. 48.–49. V-shaped frame chapes: 48. Type Pompeii; 49. Barbaric version.

Figure 238 *Hilts and scabbard fittings of Roman gladii (after Miks 2007)*

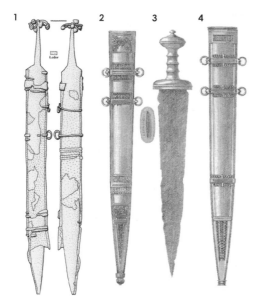

Figure 239 *Republican gladius from Delos (after Miks 2007), early Imperial Mainz-type gladii from Mainz and Rheingönheim (after Lindenschmit)*

Figure 240 *Early Imperial Mainz-type gladii from Strasbourg, Vindonissa, and Bijlandse Waard (after Miks 2007)*

Figure 241 *Mainz gladius (original and reconstruction RGZM). Images: RGZM*

general, only the metal fittings from leather-covered wooden sheaths survive. They consisted of bronze and brass but, as the discoveries at Kalkriese show, they were occasionally of silver. As for construction, these were frame sheaths with terminal knobs, two moulded suspension bands with hinged rings, a frame band, and a mouth plate (Fig. 238).

The earliest variant consists of a frame scabbard with decorative ridges. Next come framework sheaths, which are decorated with ornamental plates in an openwork technique, so-called *opus interrasile* (Fig. 239.2,4). Beneath, to provide a colour contrast, there was either a metal sheet or coloured leather. Then, in the late Augustan-Tiberian period, a form of decoration appears

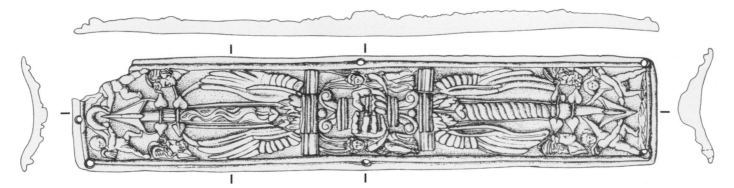

Figure 242 *Copper-alloy die from Nijmegen for the production of embossed plates for the decoration of gladius sheaths (after Miks 2007)*

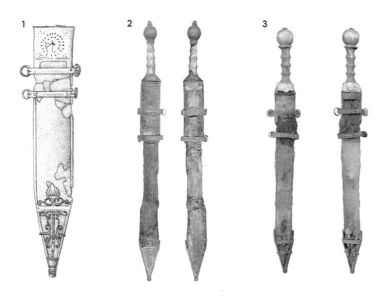

Figure 243 *Pompeii-type gladii from Porto Novo (after Miks 2007) and Pompeii. Photo: S. Ortisi*

Figure 244 *Gladius from the Rhine at Eich with preserved wooden handle (unprovenanced, privately owned). Photo: Museum Speyer*

– often a thunderbolt and tendrils – from large-scale embossed bronze plates (Fulham type), which dominated until the Claudian period (Fig. 238, Fig. 240). A massive cast bronze relief from Nijmegen with thunderbolt motif and mounting holes (Fig. 242) should probably be interpreted as a punch for mass production of such embossed plates.[348]

POMPEII-TYPE GLADIUS

• **Blade** – G. Ulbert described the blades, named after the findspot, as follows: 'The blade has straight edges, which meet with a sharp angle to form a short stubby

tip'.[349] Christian Miks distinguished three variants here, disregarding the long forms that are attributable to *spathae*.[350] The 'traditional' blades were in use from the early Flavian period to about the middle of the 2nd century AD; the 'Putensen Vimose' and 'Hamfelde' variants were – especially around Germany! – in use up to AD 200 (Fig. 236, Fig. 243, 244).

• **Hilts** – Technically, the hilts of Pompeii-type *gladii* are similar to those of the Mainz type, but hilt components made of wood are significantly less likely than those of bone.

• **Scabbard fittings** – The bronze fittings of the leather-covered wooden sheaths were quite characteristic for the Pompeii-type *gladius*, so they often can be identified from tiny fragments (Fig. 238, 243, Fig. 245). Ch. Miks has divided the *gladius* sheaths of the Pompeii type into two versions, the earlier, transitional 'Porto Novo' type and a later 'Pompeii' type.[351] It is typical for both types of scabbard that the whole scabbard is not now surrounded by a continuous frame, but that there are separate mouth and chape plates, with decorative fittings on the leather-covered wooden scabbard.

For the 'Porto Novo' type, the moulded suspension bands for the four suspension rings were still separately attached to the leather-covered wooden scabbard (Fig. 243.1). The locket plate bore geometric or figural patterns in openwork and inscribed styles. With the classic Pompeii type, the moulded bands for the four suspension rings were no longer separately attached to the leather-covered wooden scabbard, but integrated into the locket plate (Fig. 243.2–3; 245). On the locket plate, there are two zones of victory openwork, which may also refer specifically to the Jewish War of Vespasian.[352]

The lower ends of the guttering of the locket plate, with the multiple-line decoration of *spatha* sheath fittings of the Pompeii type, may be terminated with downward-facing, stylized palmettes. The V-shaped frame chapes of Pompeii-type *gladii* are also finished on the sides with the characteristic stylized palmettes, with openwork plates in the chape, but also with vegetal decoration, inserted;

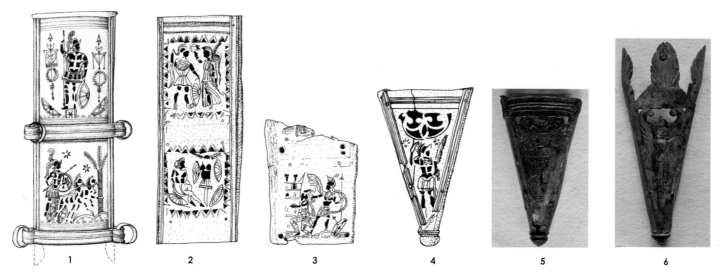

Figure 245 *Pompeii-type gladius sheath and chape plates (after Miks 2007; unprovenanced, privately owned). Photos: A. Pangerl*

the relatively small chape knobs were cast in one with the frame.[353] In the centre, above the chape, there is a characteristic decorative palmette.

These Pompeii-type scabbards must date from the Flavian period to the end of the reign of Trajan. From the time of Hadrian different forms of decoration and construction appear.

CARRIAGE

Up to the end of the 1st century AD, the *gladius* was usually worn on the right side on the *cingulum*, the metal-plated weapons belt. Only centurions wore the short sword on their left. The sword either hung on a separate belt, crossed with a dagger belt (cowboy fashion), or on a single belt, together with the dagger. The weapon was attached with four suspension rings made of bronze (Fig. 247). It could thus either hang straight or diagonally. However, this is never depicted realistically on the tombstones of soldiers from the Rhineland. The only representations we know of that are realistic are depictions of gods from Palmyra (Fig. 246.1).

From the Flavian period, the suspension of *gladii* on the *cingulum* slowly goes out of fashion and is replaced by attachment to the *balteus*, a baldric. Early *baltei* consisted of narrow leather straps, the characteristic metal fittings having not yet been identified.

OTHER DECORATIVE ELEMENTS ON *GLADIUS* SHEATHS

S. Ortisi has recently pointed out another decorative element that could be attached to early High Imperial *gladius* sheaths in addition to the actual decoration of the scabbard (Ortisi 2009b). On the front of the Pompeii-type *gladius* from the beach at Herculaneum, Ortisi could identify additional decorative elements attached

1

2

Figure 246 *Early Imperial gladius suspension on reliefs from Palmyra and Pula (after Miks 2007)*

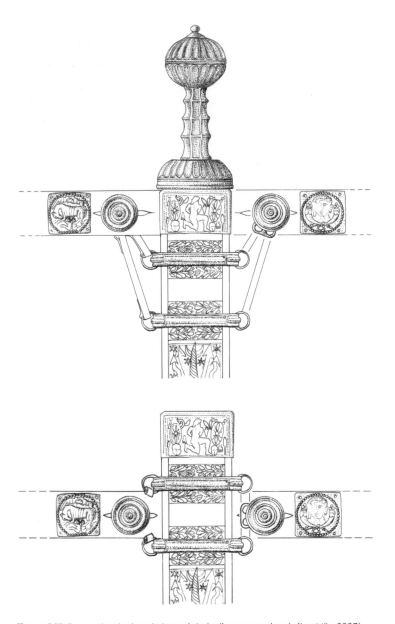

Figure 247 *Reconstructed early Imperial gladius suspension (after Miks 2007)*

The swords of the 2nd century, after the demise of weapons of the Pompeii type, are far more difficult to assess, for now the evidence from the Roman Empire becomes scarcer. There are hardly any dated finds of complete *gladii* with scabbard fittings. So we are increasingly dependent upon studying blades in material from German *barbaricum*, present there in graves and sacrificial bogs in large quantities.[357] Variants of the Pompeii-type blade currently cease at the end of the 2nd century.

One should also take into account that, during the transitional period from short to long swords among the Roman infantry, daggers increased in size quite drastically that they almost reached the size of *gladii*. These phenomena should therefore be seen together: they suggest that up to the middle of the 3rd century AD, a need for short sword-like weapons still existed. Whether this provides a context for the '*semispatha*' mentioned in Vegetius remains unclear.

While the development of the sword blades can thus be assessed reasonably well, the development of the scabbard fittings is still rather vague: while there are isolated dated pieces, in individual cases it is hardly possible to distinguish between the fittings of *gladii* and *spathae*. We know of pointed scabbard chapes with Hadrianic-Antonine dates, which are partly decorated with enamel (Fig. 258.2) – corresponding to belt fittings. Sword suspension had completely changed by being combined with the *balteus*: the characteristic four suspension rings of the early Imperial period had disappeared completely by the post-Trajanic period. During the 2nd century AD, however, the number of *spathae* increased, which then evolved from an exclusively cavalry weapon into the standard weapon for infantry and cavalry with no discernible difference. How this change to the longsword and the decline of short swords is to be explained is an ongoing topic of discussion. However, it must have had something to do with a changed style of fighting, quite likely due to the increasing occurrence of enemy cavalry.

DIGRESSION ON THE DECORATION OF SCABBARDS AND SWORD BELTS IN THE EARLY IMPERIAL PERIOD

In the late Republic and early Empire, the decoration on belts and scabbards – if they had any – is dominated by geometric decorative elements. In the early Imperial period, some additional figural decorations related to each other turn up on some Mainz-type scabbards and sword belts connected to the army on the Rhine (Fig. 248). To a large extent their representations have to be seen in the context of propaganda statements: they were supposed to reinforce the dynastic succession of the Julio-Claudian imperial dynasty.[358] However, up to

to the scabbard, consisting of a silver chain (*catellae*) with medallions, which he connected with the *catellae* mentioned by Pliny (Pliny, *Nat. Hist.* 33.31). The latter generally criticized the use of silver in the equipment of soldiers as extravagance. Medallions eventually associated with such chains as elements of scabbard decoration were already used at Kalkriese, the site of the Varus Battle of AD 9. Pliny's *catellae* would then have been already in use in the late Augustan period.[354] The Claudian tombstone of Annaius from Bingerbrück also clearly depicts this additional decoration on the scabbard.[355] It may be possible to observe this custom up to the 2nd century.[356]

Figure 248 *Ornamental embossed copper-alloy plates of the Mainz-type gladius sheaths: 1–2 Vindonissa, 3 Bonn (after Miks 2007). Drawings: A. Smadi, Arch Institute University of Cologne*

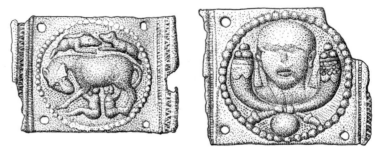

Figure 249 *Cingulum plates with figural decoration*

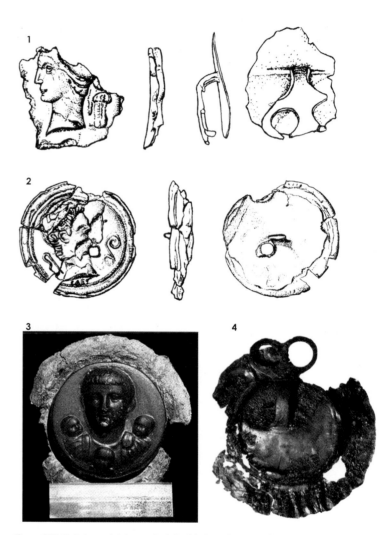

Figure 250 *Early Imperial decorated double-loop fasteners (from gladius suspension). From copper-alloy, silver, and lead: 1–2 Kalkriese (after Harnecker and Franzius 2008); 3 with glass medallion, unprovenanced (after Harden et al. 1988); 4 With glass medallion (rear face) Rheingönheim (after Ulbert 1969)*

now only the decorated scabbards and belt plates have been seen in a functional relationship while the double-loop sword suspension frogs with glass medallions having been interpreted so far as *phalerae* in the sense of military awards. These figural decorated weapons components are:

• Sword scabbard decoration: among the figural decorated scabbard plates of Mainz-type *gladii*, representations of the emperor and his family predominate. The overarching logic behind it is securing the dynasty.[359] The famous 'Sword of Tiberius' from Mainz belongs in this context.[360] Some motifs on excavated sword scabbards

found in the region around Vindonissa were attributed by Künzl to the suppression of the uprising of Sacrovir in Gaul in AD 21 dated to AD 22/23.[361]

• Belt plates: similar images (for example, the bust of Tiberius, the representation of the Roman wolf, crossed cornucopias with busts of Germanicus Gemellus and

Tiberius Gemellus) also appear on embossed belt plates, hinting at their production in the area around Vindonissa (Fig. 249).[362]

• Double-loop sword suspension frogs with glass medallions (Fig. 250): D. Boschung collected this category of finds and analysed their representational content (Boschung 1987). They are distributed across the reigns of the Emperor Tiberius (AD 14–37), Caligula (AD 37–41) and Claudius (AD 41–54). These images were also intended to convey the assurance that the dynasty would continue.[363] Their back consists of a double-looped shank, which corresponds exactly to the structures of simple double-looped frogs decorated with circular grooves with which Mainz-type *gladii* were attached to the belt in two sealed finds of swords and belt fittings. Likewise, their size is the same.[364] Such copper-alloy and lead double-looped frogs with portraits of Augustus have already been found on the AD 9 battlefield at Kalkriese.[365] Because of the shank buttons, I therefore consider these, as well as the *phalerae* with glass medallions, to be fastenings for *gladii* to the *cingulum* (Fischer 2013a).

A conspicuous feature of all these individual elements is a largely shared geographic distribution which alone speaks for closer links between the pieces. The distribution maps published by E. Künzl in 1996 clearly show this.[366] Because of the close functional similarities (among other things), I look upon the three assemblages as originally belonging together (swords, along with supporting sword belts), which were issued to legionaries for a special purpose. These decorated weapons could be interpreted as awards for special services, for example, given to individual soldiers or to whole units as donatives, because of the successful completion of particular campaigns.

DECORATED SCABBARD PLATES FROM POMPEII-TYPE GLADII

Scabbard mouth plates of Pompeii-type *gladii* also have figural representations in larger quantities. These are manufactured in a mixed technique of openwork and engraving, with the coloured leather of the scabbard showing through in the former.[367] Most of the representations are connected to the war and victory gods Mars and Victoria and are therefore broadly based on military virtues. However, there are also clear references to the first Jewish War in images of palm trees or prisoners in oriental dress depicted on a scabbard plate from Nijmegen, which also shows what has been named with good reasons the oldest depiction of Jerusalem (Fig 245.3).[368] The new Flavian dynasty took advantage of this war, which ended in AD 70 with the capture of Jerusalem by the 'crown prince' Titus, for the propagation of their military prowess (*virtus*). No similar representations of specific wars are known from the

time of Trajan (AD 98–117), when *gladii* of the Pompeii type were still in use.

EMBOSSED STUDS

G. Ulbert and M. Feugère have catalogued embossed studs dated to the Flavian period decorated with victories and imperial busts which were used for a range of functions.[369] In the rather blandly executed Emperor portraits, E. Künzl sees primarily Vespasian and Titus, Domitian less so.[370] These studs were mainly used on the apron attached to the *cingulum*, but are also known as components of *catellae* or decorative attachments to scabbards (Ortisi 2009a).

DECORATED SCABBARDS AND BELTS IN THE 2ND AND 3RD CENTURY AD

With the decline of Pompeii-type *gladii* and the end of the *cingulum* as a sword belt, figural decorations on these elements stop. An exception is a silver chape from Leiderdorp in Holland with a silver medallion which shows Hadrian on the front and Trajan on the back.[371] Now what little figural decoration there was shifted to baldrics and box chapes.

LONG SWORDS (*SPATHAE*)

SPATHAE IN THE REPUBLIC AND THE EARLY TO LATE IMPERIAL PERIOD

Unlike the *gladius*, research into the origin of long slashing swords (*spathae*), which, in the early and middle Imperial period especially, were used by auxiliary cavalry, is on somewhat firmer ground. *Spathae* were probably only really added to Roman armament on a large scale when non-Roman cavalry auxiliaries of non-Italian, Celtic origin were permanently incorporated into the Roman army. This happened under Caesar at the latest. Thus it is not surprising that, even in the early Imperial period, the Celtic longsword is closely linked to Roman *spathae* and a truly 'Roman' weapon cannot be identified as such (Fig. 251, 252). The bulk of later *spatha* blades of the later 2nd to 5th centuries AD were not found within the territory of the Roman Empire, but come instead from burials in Germany and from bog deposits in northern Germany and Scandinavia. They are usually combined with Germanic hilt and sheath components.

During the Late Roman period, grave finds in the territory of the Roman Empire that included longswords increased again. Among blade and sheath fittings, a smooth developmental transition can be seen into the long sword of the early medieval period (Menghin 1983).

• **Blades** – Christian Miks has classed the early Roman *spatha* blades which show signs of early to middle la Tène-period forms into the 'Fontillet' and 'Nauportus' types.[372]

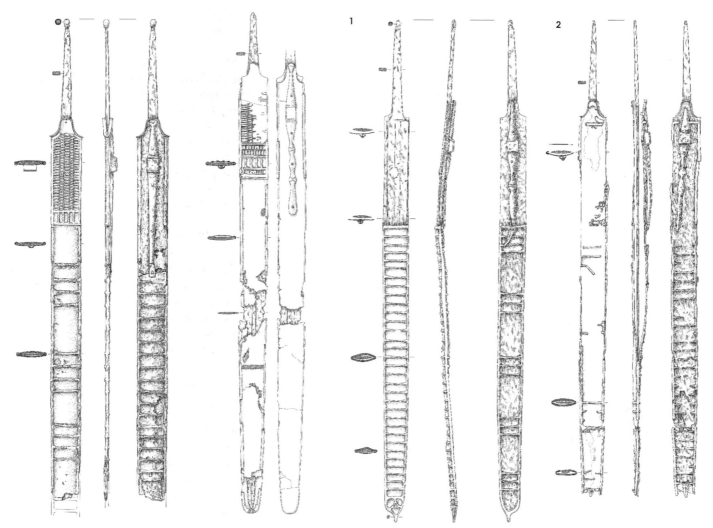

Figure 251 *Early Imperial spathae of late La Tène type from the Ljubljanica River and Bela Cerkev (after Istenic 2010)*

Figure 252 *Early Imperial spathae from late La Tène type from Verdun burial 37 (1) and Verdun burial 131 (2) (after Istenic 2010)*

It is also very likely that late la Tène-period slashing swords, whose sheaths with *opus interrasile* decoration were made of copper alloy and especially brass and show Roman influence, were also used by Celtic and Germanic auxiliary cavalry of the early Imperial period (Istenic 2010).

Only in the mid-1st century AD, with the introduction of a *spatha* form which, as it were, was an extended version of the Pompeii-type *gladius* (Fig. 253), did a truly Roman development of cavalry slashing swords begin.[373] These longswords have a length of at least 67.5 cm.[374]

During the later Imperial period, numerous variants of the *spatha* blade appeared. Following Ulbert (1974), Miks called weapons of the 2nd and 3rd century AD with slender blades tapering towards the tip and a short, rounded tip (Fig. 254) the 'Straubing-Nydam' type, and those with broad, parallel-edged blade with a triangular

or short, ogival tip the 'Lauriacum/Hromówka' type. Miks designated a mixed form of these types from the 3rd–5th centuries AD, with clear influence from the Sassanid region, as the 'Illerup-Wyhl' type and a heavier, Late Roman version as the 'Osterburken-Kemathen' type. The latter continue until around AD 500. The narrower and longer form of the 'Asian type' represents a weapon of the late 4th and early 5th centuries AD influenced by Central Asiatic, Hunnic weapons.[375] *Spatha* blades frequently feature maker stamps or logos and copper-allloy inlay, (Fig. 255) with representations of Victoria and/or Mars.[376]

• **Spatha hilts of the early and middle Imperial period** – The grips of Roman *spathae* of wood or bone in the 1st to the 3rd centuries AD were essentially the same as those of *gladii*: a hand guard and a spherical or disc-shaped pommel on either side of a smooth or ribbed hand

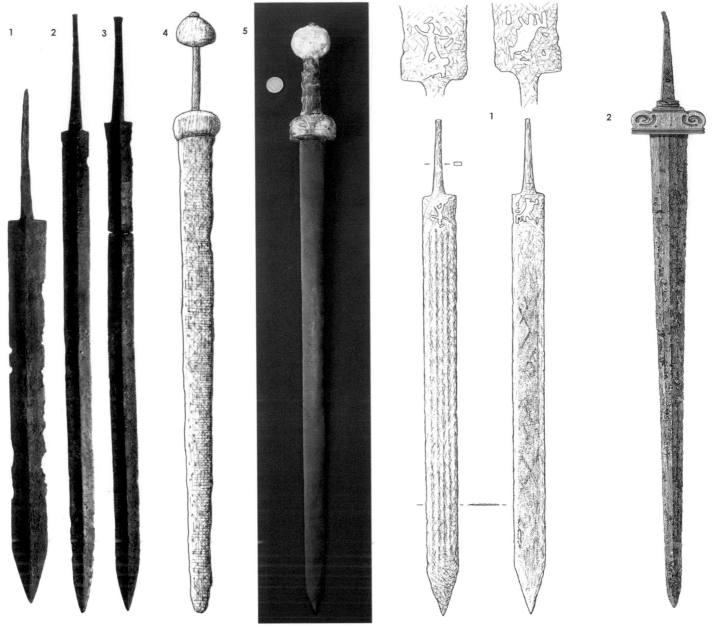

Figure 253 *Pompeii type gladius and spathae: 1–3 Newstead (after Curle 1911), 3–4 unprovenanced, privately owned. Photo: private, drawing: A. Smadi, Arch Institute University of Cologne*

Figure 254 *1 Straubing-Nydam type spatha from Sisak, 2 Lauriacum-Hromówka type spatha from Vimose (after Miks 2007). Drawing: A. Smadi, Arch Institute University of Cologne*

grip. During the same time, there was a rising tendency to use bone rather than wooden grip components. The hilt fittings were pushed over a long tang and often held in place with moulded bronze or silver rivet heads. In Britain, there was an unusual development with metal hilt components based on Celtic traditions.[377] In Barbaricum, Roman blades were very often fitted with their own hilt forms, for example from wood, leather, and horsehair.[378] Ring-pommel swords are treated separately.

• *Spatha* **hilts of the Late Empire** – Among Late Roman swords, the hilt components changed significantly in the middle Imperial period: the tang was shortened considerably, because the emerging hilt fittings were shorter overall. Hand guard and pommel now consisted of very similar, flat wooden or bone plates of a long, lenticular, oval-shaped basic design. They sandwiched a handle made of wood or bone that was frequently ribbed. These new sword hilt types could occasionally be covered with metal (*e.g.* silver sheet). When slightly conical hand grips with

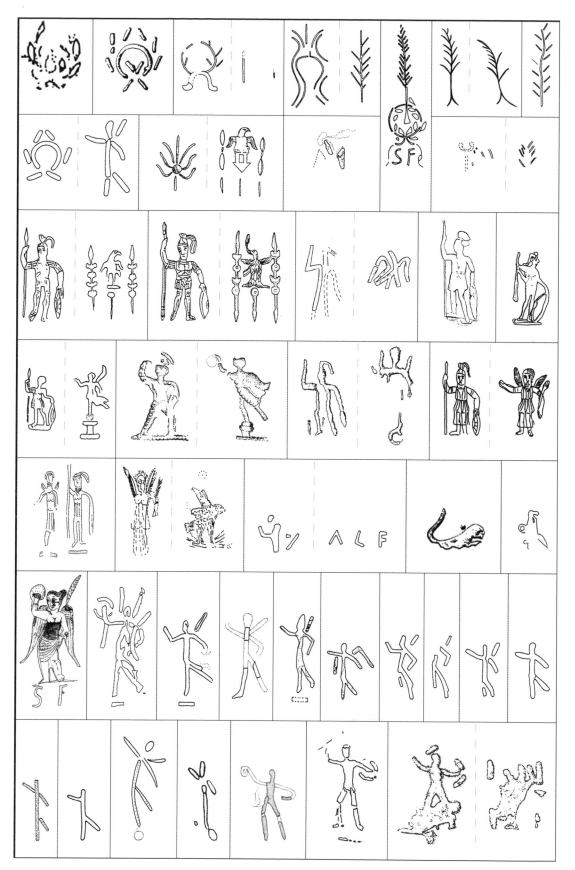

Figure 255 *Copper-alloy inlay in high Imperial spatha blades (after Miks 2007)*

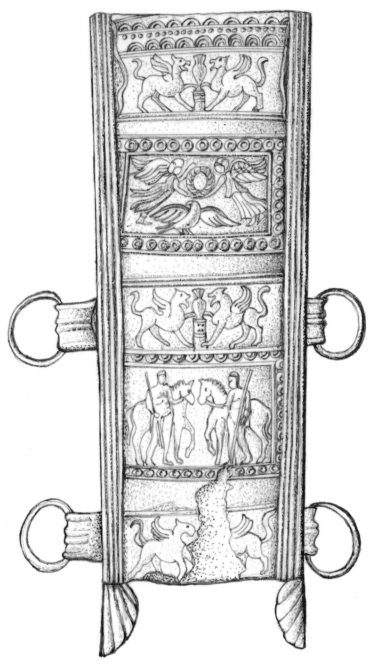

Figure 256 *Spatha scabbard fitting of the Pettau type from Ptuj (after Miks 2007). Drawing: A. Smadi, Arch Institute University of Cologne*

suspension bands, but to the guttering of the scabbard frame. It is very probable that these represent fittings from the Pompeii-type *spatha* scabbard.

From the 2nd century AD, sword suspension changes fundamentally (Fig. 257): the weapon is no longer attached to the belt using the four rings on the sheaths and the belt loses its function as a sword belt. With the adoption of the *spatha*, a broad shoulder strap called the *balteus* is introduced instead for Roman infantry as well. Now the infantry sword is no longer worn on the right, as was the rule with the *gladius*, but exclusively on the left with the *balteus*.

On the *balteus*, the sheath is suspended by means of bone or metal (copper-alloy and iron) scabbard slides. Here, too, a wide spectrum of types was developed in the region of Germany, differing from Roman types.[381] To attach swords to the *balteus*, Miks has offered new proposals that complement those of Oldenstein.[382] A similar solution also seems to be shown on the Iranian rock relief at Bishapur.[383] This new type of sword suspension was apparently adopted by contact with barbarian enemies in the Danube region during the Dacian and Marcomannic Wars. It is ultimately related to eastern forms, which can be traced as far as China.[384]

Spatha sheaths of the 2nd and 3rd century AD consisted of wood covered with leather and no longer have edge fittings. The only metal or bone mounts are scabbard runners and chapes, scabbard mouth plates being absent.[385]

The chapes of the 2nd century AD used V-shaped pieces of the 'Nijmegen-Doncaster' type that belong between the Pompeii type and pelta-shaped chapes (Fig. 258.1). These British-Celtic-influenced forms date to the early 2nd century.[386] From around the middle of the 2nd century AD to the middle of the 3rd century AD, different variants of peltate chapes in copper alloy, iron and bone were preferred (Figs 258–262), with individual pieces recorded into the second half of the 3rd century.[387] Box chapes made of different materials (silver, copper alloy, iron, bone, and ivory) date from about the middle of the 3rd century AD to the time around 300. There were simple, undecorated forms as well as magnificently decorated pieces of inlaid iron or niello-inlaid silver.[388] Disc chapes, which were common from the first half of the 3rd century AD to the time around 300, were more often of bone than copper alloy (cast in one piece) and iron (welded together from several components and inlaid). They represent transitional forms to the Late Roman plate chapes of the 'Gundremmingen-Jakuszovice' type, Miks seeking their origin in the Near Eastern or Parthian region.[389]

• **Sword scabbard fittings of the late Imperial period** – While an abundance of sword hilts and scabbard fittings were preserved in German Barbaricum in graves and bog finds, this find group is far less well represented in both

transverse grooves and a flat, multi-facetted cross-section arrive in the early 5th century AD, their decorative variants can be found in the gold-handled *spathae* of the early Medieval period.[379]

• **Scabbard fittings of the middle Imperial period** – Miks has defined a 'Pettau' variant, distinct from Pompeii-type scabbard fittings (Fig. 256). This has warlike mythological content in cross-hatched decoration.[380] In this variant, the four suspension rings of the scabbard are attached not to

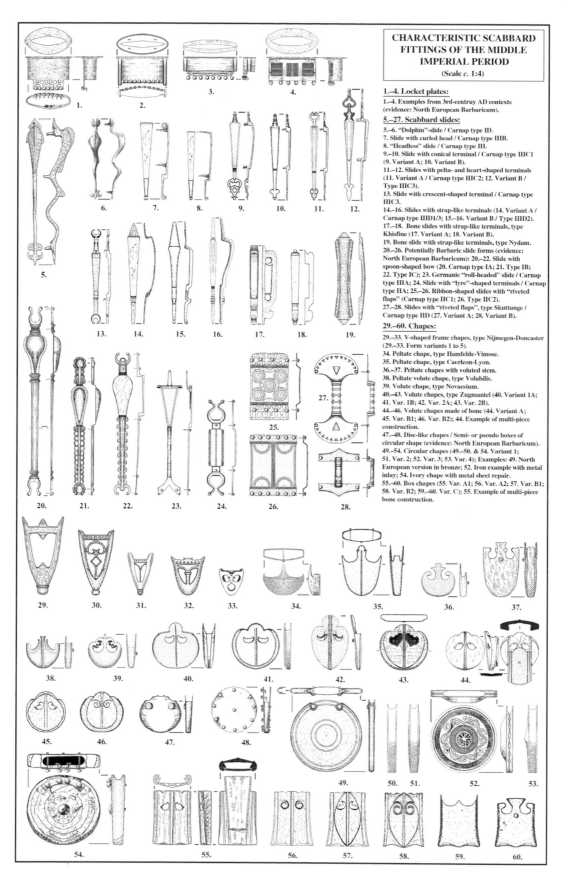

CHARACTERISTIC SCABBARD FITTINGS OF THE MIDDLE IMPERIAL PERIOD
(Scale *c.* 1:4)

1.–4. Locket plates:

1.–4. Examples from 3rd-centruy AD contexts (evidence: North European Barbaricum).

5.–27. Scabbard slides:

5.–6. "Dolphin"-slide / Carnap type ID.
7. Slide with curled head / Carnap type IIIB.
8. "Headless" slide / Carnap type III.
9.–10. Slide with conical terminal / Carnap type IIIC1 (9. Variant A; 10. Variant B).
11.–12. Slides with pelta- and heart-shaped terminals (11. Variant A / Carnap type IIIC2; 12. Variant B / Type IIIC3).
13. Slide with crescent-shaped terminal / Carnap type IIIC3.
14.–16. Slides with strap-like terminals (14. Variant A / Carnap type IIID1/3; 15.–16. Variant B / Type IIID2).
17.–18. Bone slides with strap-like terminals, type Khisfine (17. Variant A; 18. Variant B).
19. Bone slide with strap-like terminals, type Nydam.
20.–26. Potentially Barbaric slide forms (evidence: North European Barbaricum): 20.–22. Slide with spoon-shaped bow (20. Carnap type IA; 21. Type IB; 22. Type IC); 23. Germanic "roll-headed" slide / Carnap type IIIA; 24. Slide with "lyre"-shaped terminals / Carnap type IIA; 25.–26. Ribbon-shaped slides with "riveted flaps" (Carnap type IIC1; 26. Type IIC2).
27.–28. Slides with "riveted flaps", type Skuttunge / Carnap type IID (27. Variant A; 28. Variant B).

29.–60. Chapes:

29.–33. V-shaped frame chapes, type Nijmegen-Doncaster (29.–33. Form variants 1 to 5).
34. Peltate chape, type Hamfelde-Vimose.
35. Peltate chape, type Caerleon-Lyon.
36.–37. Peltate chapes with voluted stem.
38. Peltate volute chape, type Volubilis.
39. Volute chape, type Novaesium.
40.–43. Volute chapes, type Zugmantel (40. Variant 1A; 41. Var. 1B; 42. Var. 2A; 43. Var. 2B).
44.–46. Volute chapes made of bone (44. Variant A; 45. Var. B1; 46. Var. B2); 44. Example of multi-piece construction.
47.–48. Disc-like chapes / Semi- or pseudo boxes of circular shape (evidence: North European Barbaricum).
49.–54. Circular chapes (49.–50. & 54. Variant 1; 51. Var. 2; 52. Var. 3; 53. Var. 4); Examples: 49. North European version in bronze; 52. Iron example with metal inlay; 54. Ivory chape with metal sheet repair.
55.–60. Box chapes (55. Var. A1; 56. Var. A2; 57. Var. B1; 58. Var. B2; 59.–60. Var. C); 55. Example of multi-piece bone construction.

Figure 257 *Scabbard fittings from Roman and Germanic swords of the 2nd and 3rd centuries AD (after Miks 2007)*

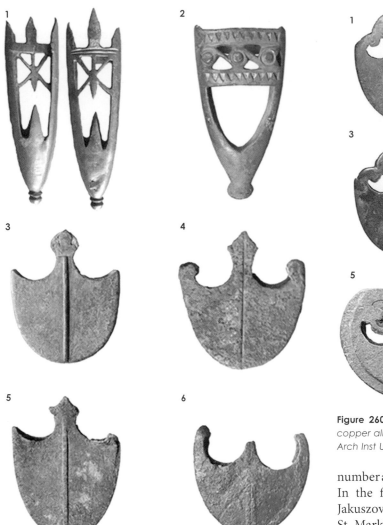

Figure 258 *Openwork, pointed, and peltaform chapes of the 2nd century AD of copper alloy (unprovenanced, privately owned). Photos: Ph. Gross, Arch Inst University of Cologne, A. Pangerl*

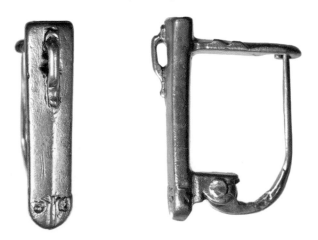

Figure 259 *Silver brooch in the form of a sword sheath with scabbard runner and peltaform chape (unprovenanced, privately owned). Photos: Ph. Gross, Arch Inst University of Cologne*

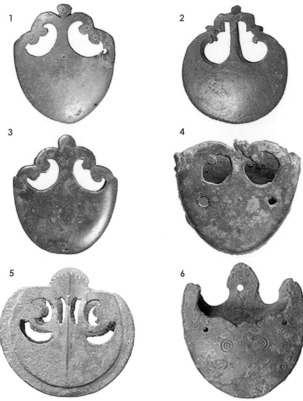

Figure 260 *Peltaform chapes of the 2nd and 3rd centuries AD of copper alloy (unprovenanced, privately owned). Images: Ph. Gross, Arch Inst University of Cologne, A. Pangerl*

number and amount of different types in the Roman Empire. In the first instance, chapes of the 'Gundremmingen-Jakuszovice' type are found on the Tetrarch relief at St Mark's in Venice (originally from Istanbul) for the period from AD 300 (Fig. 263, 264), but the type continues into the early 5th century. Unlike Barbaricum, where the variety of metal scabbard fittings rather increased during the 4th and 5th century, the variability of this find group within the Roman Empire decreased, apart from scabbard slides made of metal, which also occur in pairs (Fig. 265). In the early 5th century, scabbard mouth plates reappear in Roman contexts (Fig. 266) after disappearing in the middle Imperial period. They were often of silver and bore chip-carved decoration. Towards the end of the 4th century AD, U-shaped frame chapes were also used. From the mid-5th century onwards, weapons richly decorated with cloisonné appear under Hunnic-Pontic influence, culminating in *spathae* with golden hilts (Fig. 266.3), which mark the onset of the early Medieval period.[390]

THE BALTEUS IN THE MIDDLE IMPERIAL PERIOD

After Trajan's Dacian Wars, the wide sword belt (*balteus*) worn over the right shoulder, together with scabbard slides made of bone or metal, (Fig. 267), became the general standard for Roman sword suspension. The belt

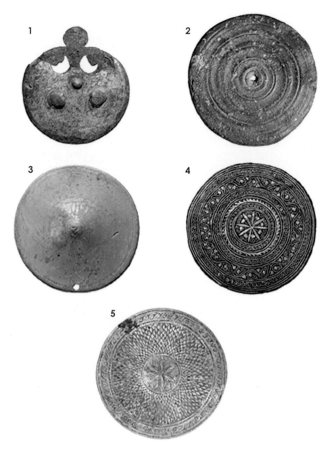

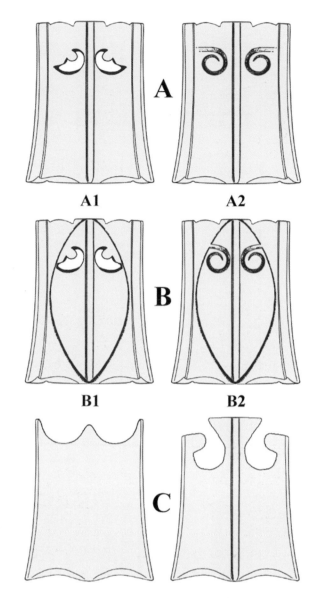

Figure 261 *Disc chapes of the 3rd century AD of copper alloy and inlaid iron (4–5) (unprovenanced, privately owned). Images: Ph. Gross, Arch Inst University of Cologne, A. Pangerl*

Figure 262 *Box chapes of the 3rd century AD (after Miks 2007)*

consisted of a wide leather strap, narrowing considerably at one long, drawn-out end. These sword belts often appear in the iconographic sources, such as Danubian gravestones of the 2nd and 3rd century AD. In Roman archaeological contexts, there are hardly any complete sets of sword sheaths and baldric fittings. Exceptions include a burial from Silistra[391] and a finds assemblage from a house in Palmyra (Ployer 2010). Both assemblages are dated to the last third of the 3rd century AD by the circular chapes and other objects found with them. As for original discoveries of Roman *balteus* straps, the only known specimens come from Germanic sacrificial bogs in northern Germany and Denmark (Thorsberg, Illerup Ådal, and Vimose). These baldrics are made of double stitched leather with embroidery and/or openwork decoration (Graef 2009; Fig. 268). The *balteus* normally included solid or openwork metal fastenings, usually disc-shaped fittings (Fig. 269). These were made of copper alloy or occasionally silver (Fig. 270.1,5,6). A separate group is formed by copper-alloy or silver baldric fasteners (Fig. 271.3,4) in the form of so-called *beneficiarius* lances (Ubl 2001).

Balteus fittings have an eyelet on the back, which was adjustable by being inserted through one of several slots in the leather. On the back, they could be tied with the narrow end of the baldric, which had been attached to the scabbard slide. In this way, the *balteus* was adjusted for length and adjusted to the body size of the wearer, because it was not unfastened every time the weapon was taken off, but remained fastened. It was put on and taken off just by putting it over the shoulder.

In addition, metal terminals for the broad strap end, often comprising two parts with a hinge, could be used. As the bog finds show, the wide belt end is viable even without metal fittings. Then it was simply decorated by cutting it into a decorative form. Occasionally one finds sets of matching baldric fasteners and decorative fittings, such as the so-called NVMERVM OMNIVM fittings.[392]

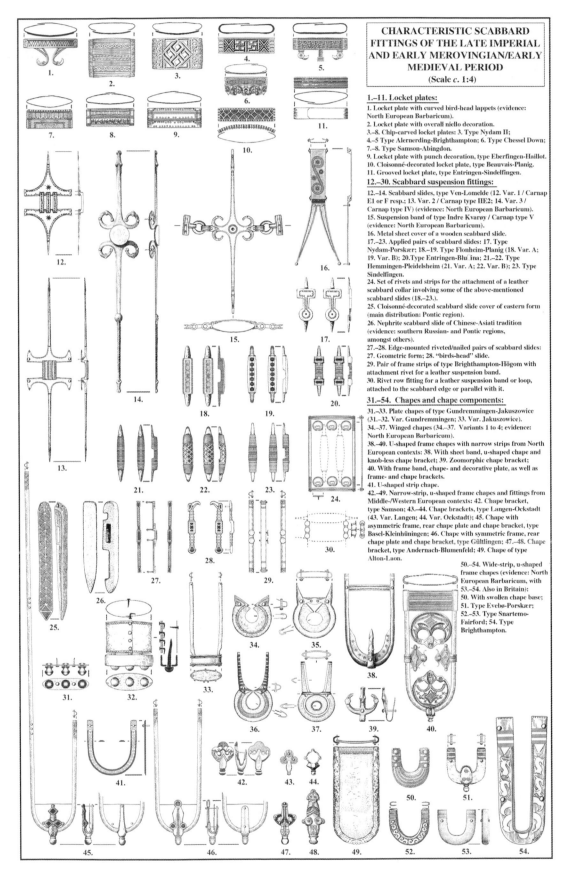

CHARACTERISTIC SCABBARD FITTINGS OF THE LATE IMPERIAL AND EARLY MEROVINGIAN/EARLY MEDIEVAL PERIOD
(Scale *c.* 1:4)

1.–11. Locket plates:
1. Locket plate with curved bird-head lappets (evidence: North European Barbaricum).
2. Locket plate with overall niello decoration.
3.–8. Chip-carved locket plates: 3. Type Nydam II;
4.–5 Type Alernerding-Brighthampton; 6. Type Chessel Down;
7.–8. Type Samson-Abingdon.
9. Locket plate with punch decoration, type Eberfingen-Haillot.
10. Cloisonné-decorated locket plate, type Beauvais-Planig.
11. Grooved locket plate, type Entringen-Sindelfingen.

12.–30. Scabbard suspension fittings:
12.–14. Scabbard slides, type Ven-Lomelde (12. Var. 1 / Carnap E1 or F resp.; 13. Var. 2 / Carnap type IIE2; 14. Var. 3 / Carnap type IV) (evidence: North European Barbaricum).
15. Suspension band of type Indre Kvarøy / Carnap type V (evidence: North European Barbaricum).
16. Metal sheet cover of a wooden scabbard slide.
17.–23. Applied pairs of scabbard slides: 17. Type Nydam-Porskær; 18.–19. Type Flonheim-Planig (18. Var. A; 19. Var. B); 20.Type Entringen-Bluͤina; 21.–22. Type Hemmingen-Pleidelsheim (21. Var. A; 22. Var. B); 23. Type Sindelfingen.
24. Set of rivets and strips for the attachment of a leather scabbard collar involving some of the above-mentioned scabbard slides (18.–23.).
25. Cloisonné-decorated scabbard slide cover of eastern form (main distribution: Pontic region).
26. Nephrite scabbard slide of Chinese-Asiati tradition (evidence: southern Russian- and Pontic regions, amongst others).
27.–28. Edge-mounted riveted/nailed pairs of scabbard slides: 27. Geometric form; 28. "birds-head" slide.
29. Pair of frame strips of type Brighthampton-Högom with attachment rivet for a leather suspension band.
30. Rivet row fitting for a leather suspension band or loop, attached to the scabbard edge or parallel with it.

31.–54. Chapes and chape components:
31.–33. Plate chapes of type Gundremmingen-Jakuszowice (31.–32. Var. Gundremmingen; 33. Var. Jakuszowice).
34.–37. Winged chapes (34.–37. Variants 1 to 4; evidence: North European Barbaricum).
38.–40. U-shaped frame chapes with narrow strips from North European contexts: 38. With sheet band, u-shaped chape and knob-less chape bracket; 39. Zoomorphic chape bracket; 40. With frame band, chape- and decorative plate, as well as frame- and chape brackets.
41. U-shaped strip chape.
42.–49. Narrow-strip, u-shaped frame chapes and fittings from Middle-/Western European contexts: 42. Chape bracket, type Samson; 43.–44. Chape brackets, type Langen-Ockstadt (43. Var. Langen; 44. Var. Ockstadt); 45. Chape with asymmetric frame, rear chape plate and chape bracket, type Basel-Kleinhüningen; 46. Chape with symmetric frame, rear chape plate and chape bracket, type Gültlingen; 47.–48. Chape bracket, type Andernach-Blumenfeld; 49. Chape of type Alton-Laon.
50.–54. Wide-strip, u-shaped frame chapes (evidence: North European Barbaricum, with 53.–54. Also in Britain): 50. With swollen chape base; 51. Type Evebø-Porskær; 52.–53. Type Snartemo-Fairford; 54. Type Brighthampton.

Figure 263 *Scabbard fittings of Late Roman and Germanic swords (after Miks 2007)*

Figure 264 *Eagle-headed sword with sword hilt and Gundremmingen type chape from the Tetrarch relief in Venice (after Miks 2007)*

RING-POMMEL SWORDS

In the 2nd and 3rd century, both swords and daggers with a very heterogeneous blade shape appear which terminated with an iron ring as the pommel. The pommel is often inlaid and occasionally is made of copper alloy (Fig. 272). Almost invariably the ring pommel was riveted to the reforged tang of the blade afterwards. In research terms, these swords have been treated as 'ring-pommel swords' in the sense of a distinct sword type. Christian Miks was the first to correctly point out that the 'ring pommel sword' does not exist as a type. Instead, a ring pommel was secondarily attached to quite different blade shapes, common in the Roman army. This tradition derives from Sarmatian contacts during the Dacian Wars, while the fashion for ring pommels can ultimately be traced to China.[393] What lies behind the preference for ring pommels is unclear. Could they have designated a participant in the heavy fighting in the middle Danube region and thus a particularly battle-hardened veteran? Or were ring pommels lucky amulets?

EAGLE-HEADED SWORDS

Swords with a handle in the shape of the head of an eagle have so far almost exclusively been represented iconographically during the Roman period. There are numerous examples, especially on the cuirassed statues of Roman emperors (Fig. 273). However, eagle-headed swords can already be found among Hittite, Greek, and Hellenistic iconographic sources. By contrast, there are virtually no actual finds from either the Roman or earlier periods. For the Roman period, Miks can only cite one copy of an eagle-headed sword, allegedly from Spain, in a

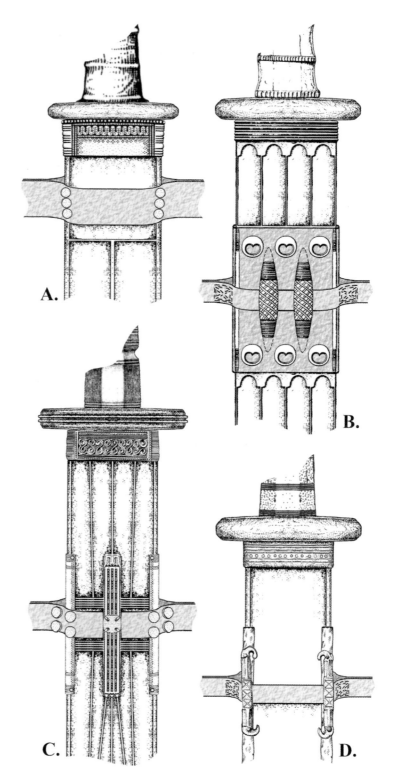

A.

B.

C.

D.

Figure 265 *Late Roman spatha suspension (after Miks 2007)*

private collection in the United States, and he could give no clear opinion on its authenticity. In addition, there is a fragmentary ivory handle from the Museum of Adana in Turkey.[394]

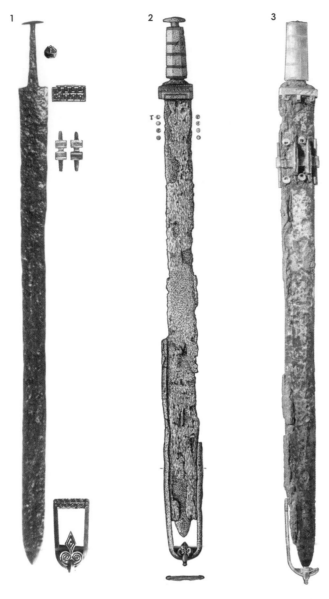

Figure 266 *Late Roman spathae (3 golden-handled spatha after Miks 2007)*

Figure 267 *Sword hilt from the representation of the captured weapons from the relief on the base of Trajan's Column (after Miks 2007)*

In his publication of militaria from the Vesuvius cities, Salvatore Ortisi has now presented a whole series of eagle-headed swords with copper-alloy handles, some of which had been fastened rather carelessly to their blades. Because of their fragile construction, these do not give the impression of real weapons (Ortisi 2009a). Their findspot offers no evidence of military use. He sees in these pieces a kind of sword of honour, which would be awarded in connection with public or religious offices at the city level. The final record of this hilt form can be found in the porphyry relief of the tetrarchs, originally from Constantinople (Fig. 264). Today, the statues are located at the south-west corner of St Mark's in Venice.[395]

Parazonia

If Salvatore Ortisi's interpretation of the eagle-headed swords from the Mount Vesuvius cities was correct, it is possible that these pieces are the *parazonia* testified in the literature, which have not yet been identified with actual finds. These may be considered as short weapons between a dagger and the *gladius*, which were worn by military tribunes and senior officers on the *cingulum* as a kind of sword of honour.[396]

Hewing knives

From Pompeii there are hewing knives with curved blades, which have copper-alloy scabbard fittings, resembling those of the Pompeii-type *gladii*. Because of this similarity, Salvatore Ortisi has concluded[397] that these hewing knives were not military but carried by paramilitary troops (town guards and so on) (Fig. 274).

Daggers

As a secondary sidearm, Roman infantry soldiers, both legionaries and auxiliary, wore the dagger (*pugio*). Like the *gladius*, perhaps, this weapon was also adopted from Celtiberian opponents in Spain under the late Republic (Kavanagh de Prado and Quesada Sanz 2009; Casprini and Saliola 2012). However, here the history of its origins

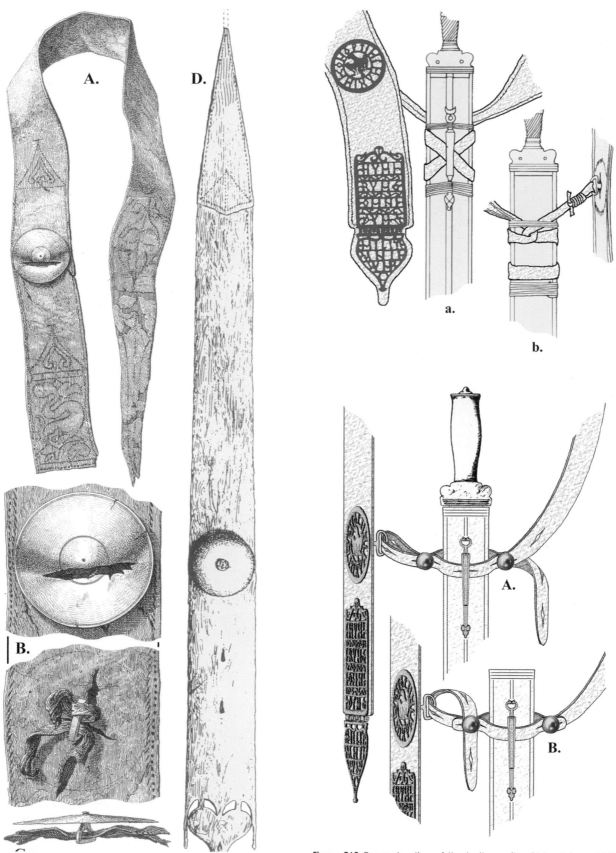

Figure 268 Baltei from Vimose and Thorberg (after Miks 2007)

Figure 269 Reconstruction of the balteus after Oldenstein and Miks
a. front view; b. rear view (after Miks 2007)

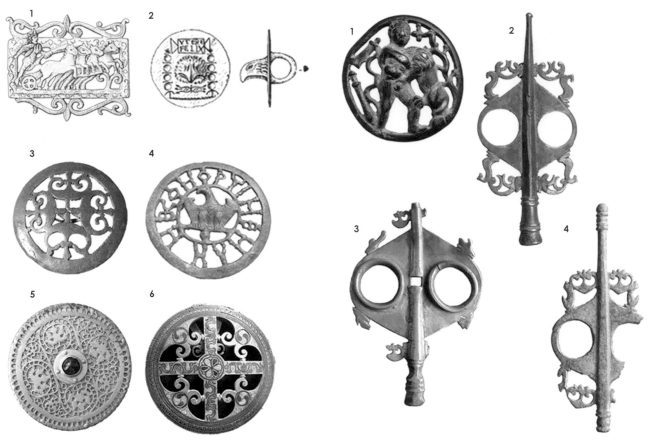

Figure 270 Balteus *fittings of silver and copper alloy (unprovenanced, privately owned). Photos: Ph. Gross, Arch Inst University of Cologne, A. Pangerl; Drawings: A. Smadi, Arch Institute University of Cologne*

Figure 271 Balteus *fittings (round and in the form of a beneficiarius lance) of silver and copper alloy (unprovenanced, privately owned). Photos: Ph. Gross, Arch Inst University of Cologne, A. Pangerl*

is clearer than for the *gladius*: Polybius, who writes about the period before 146 BC, did not mention the dagger, unlike the *gladius*. Archaeological research thus assumes the weapon to have been known to the Romans from the Numantine Wars onwards, but the more general adoption of the dagger by the Roman army is only likely to have occurred in the 1st century BC,[398] because archaeological finds of double disc daggers from the Spanish camps at Numantia (195–133 BC) and Cáceres el Viejo (80 BC), could theoretically have been pieces that were captured from the enemy or lost by local auxiliary forces. They do not inevitably have to have been Roman weaponry.[399] The dagger was certainly adopted as part of Roman armament from the time of Caesar: on the one hand, there is a dagger dated to the year 52 BC found in the siege works at Alesia and, on the other, realistic depictions of military daggers decorate *denarii* of Caesar's assassin Marcus Junius Brutus minted in the years 43/42 BC.[400] On this first depiction of Roman daggers, both a double-disc dagger and a dagger with a cruciform hilt but no central expansion can be seen (Fig. 275).[401] Furthermore, a dagger and sheath are depicted across the belt of the centurion Minucius of *legio*

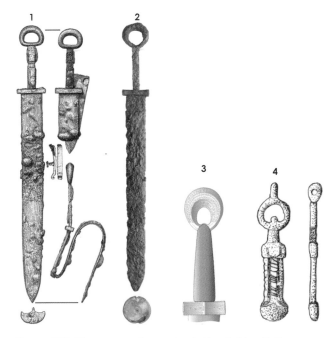

Figure 272 *Ring-pommel swords: 1 Hamfelde, 2 Pevensey, 3 reconstructed grip from the ring-pommel sword from Mainz, 4 copper-alloy pendant in the shape of a ring-pommel sword (after Miks 2007, 2008a)*

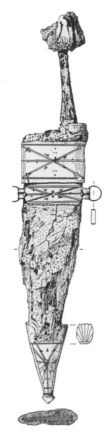

Figure 275 *Daggers with a cruciform hilt and double-disc hilt (denarius Sydenham 1301 approximately 43/42 BC). Photo: A. Pangerl*

Figure 273 *Eagle-headed sword from a bronze statue in Murrhardt (after Imperium Romanum 2005)*

Figure 274 *Hewing knife from Pompeii (after Miks 2007)*

Martia on his tombstone from Padua, which is dated to the period around 42 BC.[402]

Daggers in the strict sense, *i.e.* short, double-edged stabbing weapons, were never standard equipment for Greek or Hellenistic armies. However, they often occur among finds assemblages from the Iron Age in the Iberian Peninsula, whence the Romans directly adopted this weapon.[403]

Characteristic for the daggers from the early Imperial period were their strongly curved edges with a pronounced midrib and two-part handle made of sheet iron with a central expansion. At the end of the handle – following earlier Spanish models – there could be a disc-shaped pommel, or a differently shaped, for example cruciform, terminal (Fig. 276).[404] Daggers of the early Imperial period still clearly show their descent from Spanish weapons of the Republican era. This is also the case with the frame scabbards. In addition to these forms, decorated iron sheath plates, which are original Roman developments, occur from the Augustan period onwards. Here, both the handles and the sheaths of the early Imperial pieces often exhibit identical decorative techniques, mostly inlaid. This

is proof that both weapon and scabbard were produced together individually.

Early dagger sheaths, like those from Oberammergau (Fig. 277) [405] and Auerberg[406] in Raetia, could be richly decorated with inlay and niello, enamel inlay also being found (Fig. 278). However, at the same time, there were also more modest specimens with simple framework sheaths, like the piece from Titelberg in Luxembourg.[407] What the percentage of the two types is in relation to each other is difficult to judge. Dagger scabbards, like early *gladii*, had four metal rings for suspension.

J. Obmann divided early Imperial decorated scabbards into two types: an older and more powerful, stocky Mainz type (Fig. 279) and a later, slimmer and more graceful Vindonissa type (Fig. 280, 281), the latter being found from the middle of the 1st century AD onwards (Obmann 1999a). He distinguished four groups of decoration, based on the material and decorative motifs, dating between the Augustan and Flavian periods. Daggers were usually fastened to the belt by frogs, either looped or integrated into the belt (Fig. 282).

From the middle of the 2nd century AD (the exact date is unclear) to about the middle of the 3rd century, a much larger form of dagger was probably already in use (Fig. 283, 284), which can almost be seen as a functional replacement for the missing *gladius* and which is referred to as the Künzing type after the well-known hoard (Hermann 1969; Reuter 1999a). The handles on late daggers were

Figure 276 *Dagger with a cruciform hilt (unprovenanced, privately owned). Photo: Ph. Gross, Arch Inst University of Cologne*

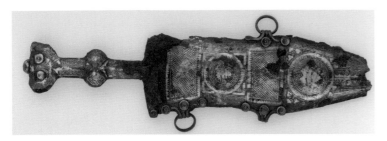

Figure 277 *Dagger from Döttenbichel at Oberammergau. Photo: M. Eberlein, Arch Staatsslg. Munich*

Figure 278 *Dagger from Mainz with silver inlaid decoration and inscription of the leg. XXII PRIMI (genia) on the iron scabbard (after Lindenschmit 1892)*

Figure 279 *Mainz-type dagger with brass and silver inlay, Alphen aan den Rijn (privately owned); photos: Ph. Gross, Arch Inst University of Cologne*

made of organic material – in other words, as with most swords, only the tang is present in metal. Other handles, like early examples, were made from two-part iron sheet with central expansions. The sheaths were made of sheet iron with rectangular openings left at the front, terminating with a moulded knob. Like their older predecessors, they still had four moveable suspension rings. As decoration, the scabbard occasionally had a simple line of beading. Other forms of decoration have not survived, but the leather that covered the wooden sheath under the iron sheet was probably dyed at the openings or decorated with embossed patterns. There is a hitherto unpublished example, allegedly from the Middle East or Asia Minor, where older embossed scabbard plates, probably from a Claudian *gladius* sheath, were fitted in the openings as a makeshift (Fig. 74).

While the dagger was often worn on its own belt on the left in the early Imperial period, this changed to the right side of the body with the advent of the *spatha* being suspended on the left. Since frogs for dagger suspension, either independent or attached to the belt as decorative fittings, disappear around the middle of the 2nd century (the latest known example comes from a grave in Chichester, Fig. 120), there must have been a

Figure 280 *Vindonissa-type dagger with silver inlay, Alphen aan den Rijn (privately owned). Photos: Ph. Gross, Arch Inst University of Cologne*

Figure 281 *Vindonissa-type dagger (unprovenanced, privately owned). Recordings: Ph. Gross, Arch Inst University of Cologne*

different method for attaching the dagger to the belt from the second half of the 2nd century AD. They were most likely suspended with leather straps from the belt. Double studs were used to fasten them adjustably. A very nice silver belt fitting of the Klosterneuburg type now, designed as a trefoil combined with double studs, shows this very clearly (Fig. 285, 286).

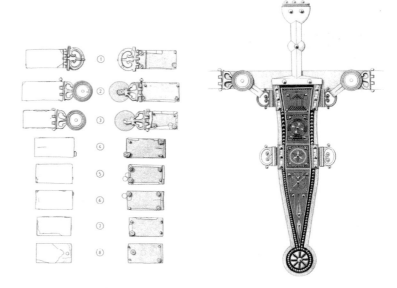

Figure 282 *Mainz-type dagger from Velsen with belt and suspension fittings. Probably deposited in the Frisian Rebellion in AD 28 (after Morel and Bosman 1989)*

Figure 283 *Künzing-type dagger (unprovenanced, privately owned). Photo: Ph. Gross, Arch Inst University of Cologne*

Figure 284 *Künzing-type dagger (unprovenanced, privately owned). Photo: Ph. Gross, Arch Inst University of Cologne*

Shafted weapons

Among the Roman armament under the Republic and the Empire, as well as the weaponry of all opponents, there was a wealth of different specialized shafted weapons (spears and lances) which were suitable for thrusting, fencing, and for throwing. They consisted of an iron tip, a shaft made of a wooden pole of different lengths, and of an iron spear butt. As a rule, only the iron components of these weapons – the spearheads and butts – are found. These iron components of shafted weapons exhibit purely functional types, which had soon found their ideal shape and barely changed even over long periods and larger geographical areas. Therefore,

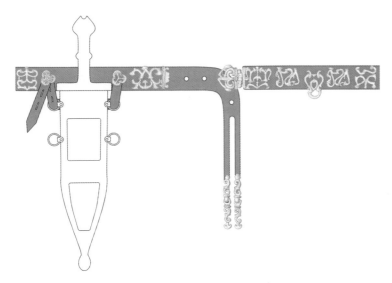

Figure 285 *Reconstructed dagger suspended from a silver Klosterneuburg-type belt (unprovenanced, privately owned). Drawing: A. Smadi, Arch Institute University of Cologne*

Figure 286 *Soldier with reconstructed dagger suspended from a silver Klosterneuburg-type belt (as Figure 285; Drawing B. Burandt)*

these weapons parts can very often not be attributed to either the Romans or their Celtic or Germanic opponents, if the armament cannot be assigned to a clear find context.[408] However, the case of a characteristically Roman variant of the throwing spear, the *pilum*, is unambiguous.

Overarching analyses of javelin and spear points from Roman border regions or provinces exist for Dacia (Gudea 1994) and Britain (Scott 1980; Marchant 1990), without really significant results or differences emerging geographically or temporally. Only in the last third of the 3rd century AD does the introduction of Germanic barbed spearheads make a clearly definable change here.

An overarching study on Roman polearms is still awaited, and one must for now be content with the more general remarks of Bishop and Coulston.[409]

PILUM

The *pilum* was one of the national Roman weapons. It was a throwing spear with a lethal punch, with a particularly refined construction: a wooden shaft with an iron butt was joined – using a range of different junctions – to a roughly equally long iron shank which had either a barbed or a pyramidal tip. While the tip was hardened, the rest of the shank was of soft iron (Figs 287–9).

A terrifying effect could be achieved with this combination of features with a close-range volley of *pila* thrown at the beginning of the attack: either the weapon pierced an armoured opponent with great force, or at least his shield. The tip punched a hole in the shield and bent below the head under its own weight. This created a double effect: on the one hand the weapon could not be pulled out because the point was bent in the hole; on the other hand, even if successful, the bent and thus unusable weapon could no longer be thrown back.

There are a few literary references to the effectiveness of the *pilum*, the most famous testimony coming from the *Gallic War*, where Caesar describes the nature of the action in the battle against the Helvetii in 58 BC thus (Caesar, *BG* 1.25):

> His soldiers hurled *pila* from above and easily broke through the enemy's front line. As this was fragmented, they went in with drawn *gladii*. The Gauls were extremely disadvantaged during the fighting in the following way: several of their shields were pierced by individual *pila* and were fixed to one another, because the iron head had bent over. The enemy could not pull them out, nor fight properly with their left side encumbered. Therefore, at length, many took off and discarded the shield after attempting to shake them off, and fought with an unprotected body.

ORIGIN

There are two theories on the origin of the *pilum*.[410] On the one hand, the *pilum* may have developed from a similar weapon from Spain, the *soliferrea*. This javelin has certain similarities with the *pilum*, but consists entirely of iron

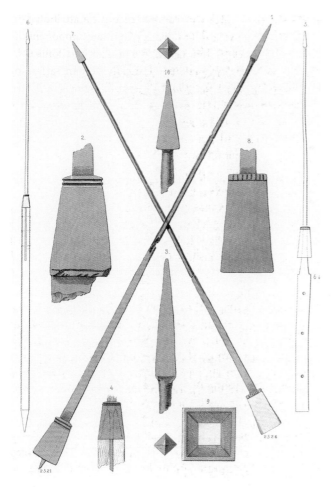

Figure 287 *Pila (after Lindenschmit 1881)*

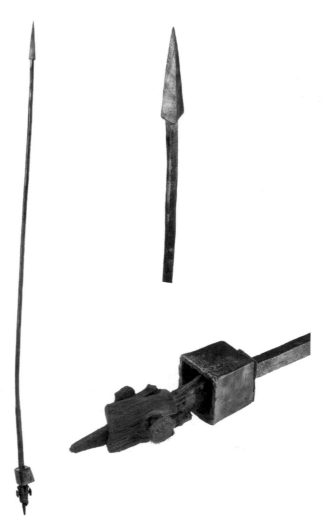

Figure 289 *Tanged pilum with shaft collet, 1st century AD (unprovenanced, privately owned). Photo: A. Pangerl*

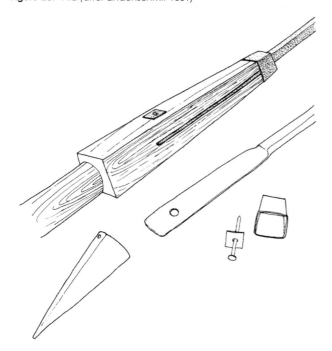

Figure 288 *Hafting of a tanged pilum (after Radman-Livaja 2004). Drawing: A. Smadi, Arch Institute University of Cologne*

and does not have a wooden shaft. *Soliferrea* are found in graves from the Iberian Peninsula and south-west France from the 6th to 4th centuries BC. Stary rejects them as a precursor of the *pilum*, because they overlap in time with them and possess differing geographical distributions.[411]

The theory of a Spanish origin contrasts with the opinion that the *pilum* was a genuinely Italian invention. As evidence of the so-called tanged *pilum*, M. Luik cites among others the discovery from Pomarico Vecchio in Basilicata from around 400 BC. He sees this as the most important evidence of the Italian origin of this weapon. As for the socketed *pilum,* which he considers to be older, he sees the question of its origin as still unresolved.[412]

However, the inhabitants south of the main range of the Alps, who were influenced by the Celts in their weaponry, in the 4th century BC also possessed socketed javelins with an extremely long iron shank resembling the *pilum*. This is shown by specimens from the hoard from the Gailtal in East Tyrol dated to around 300 BC.[413] The two examples from the Gailtal and from Spain demonstrate that we must assume that other peoples independently developed and used similar weapons to the *pilum* in the Republican era.

The most effective use of the *pilum* was in the close-order battle formations of the Roman legions, because even in the Imperial period, there are many indications suggesting that the *pilum* was mainly used by the legions and hardly at all by auxiliary troops. Thus, on the occasion of a description of a battle between the Romans and Britons, Tacitus distinguishes clearly between the *gladii* and *pila* of the legionary troops and the *spathae* and *hastae* of the auxiliary soldiers (Tac., *Ann.* 12.35).

There are some written sources on the *pilum* from the time of the Republic, some of them with very detailed information. However, these have brought more confusion than clarification to the field of study. So there is still no agreement on the extent to which Polybius' (6.23.9) traditional division into a light and a heavy *pilum* is recognisable among archaeological material.[414] Furthermore, Plutarch reports that Marius introduced a technical improvement of the *pilum* when fighting the Cimbri: he had one of the two iron rivets which fastened the tanged *pilum* to the wooden shaft replaced with a wooden dowel. This wooden rivet then broke upon impact and made the weapon useless to an opponent. Neither actual finds nor experiments have so far managed to confirm this action or to demonstrate their practical use (but see now Grab 2012).

Three types of *pilum* can be distinguished from the method of attaching the iron shank to the wooden shaft: the socketed *pilum*, the tanged *pilum*, and the *pilum* with a spike tang. With tanged *pila*, the junction was secured with iron rivets. During the Republic, the very broad tang was also bent around the wooden shaft at the junction with the rectangular-sectioned tang. In the Imperial period, the attachment of narrow tangs was effected by introducing a slightly pyramidal, square-sectioned iron ferrule.

A special form of the *pilum*, as an incendiary missile, is up to now only known from the Republican era hoard from the hillfort of Grad near Šmihel.[415] The hoard is dated between the end of the 3rd and the first half of the 2nd centuries BC. There is an ring-shaped opening forged near the top of a socketed *pilum,* which served to hold combustible material (Fig. 77.8).

During the long period of its use in the Roman army, the *pilum* changed its form significantly. The earliest crudely forged weapons with relatively short shanks and barbed tips grew longer from the late Republic on, so that they could reach a shank length of up to one metre in the early Imperial period (Fig. 77). These tended to be very precisely manufactured weapons which were then almost always provided with a pyramidal tip, being more varied again later.

Although the *pilum* in its several variants occurred from the early Republic right up to the Franks of the Merovingian period, it is represented very differently among the iconographic sources and actual finds. The Cologne Master's thesis of A. Bongartz has, for example, revealed that pictorial representations of the *pilum* are rather biased towards the 1st century AD. The evidence of actual finds is similarly distributed: they occur most frequently during the late Republic and the early Imperial period. However, this has less to do with historical reality, but is merely a reflection on the various filters to which material in the archaeological record is generally subjected.

After the 1st century AD, archaeological evidence for *pila* gets less frequent. However, this does not mean that this classic weapon entirely fell into disuse from the 2nd century AD onwards (Fig. 290). So we have, for example, Arrian recording in his *Marching Order Against the Alans* the use of the *pilum* for the year AD 132 in the fight against the Alans in the area of modern eastern Turkey. In the book it is not directly referred to by its Latin name, but is still described by its distinctive peculiarities:[416]

> The first four ranks will be equipped with spears that have long thin iron points. The men in the front row holding their spears ready, so that they can hurl the iron points at the horses when the enemy advance, especially at their breasts. The second (?), third, and fourth ranks stand ready to wound the horses with spears and kill the riders, if possible. If the spear has penetrated the shield or protective armour, they will bend, as the iron is soft, and the rider be unable to fight.

However, from Hadrianic times onwards, not all of the battle line of legionary soldiers seems to have been equipped with *pila*, apparently using a combined *pilum* and spear formation. K. Strobel assumes that the first four rows in the battle against the Alans used the *pilum* and the back rows spears.[417] However, the passage of Arrian's description is not entirely clear on this: he speaks of '*lanceae*' when the description clearly implies *pila*.

Although actual discoveries of *pila* become more scarce in the 2nd century AD, they are still present in the iconographic sources, as on the relief from Croy Hill in Scotland (Coulston 1988a) dating to the time of Antoninus Pius (AD 138–61). Moreover, the weapons store at Carnuntum, doubtless dating to the later 3rd century AD at the earliest, still contained tanged *pila* with ferrules.[418] The last archaeologically documented socketed *pilum* comes from a destruction layer in the fort at Krefeld-Gellep dated to the year AD 275 (Reichmann 1994; 1999). It seems clear that during this period, the *pilum* had largely faded into the background in comparison with spears, just as the differences between legionary and auxiliary soldiers in weaponry and methods of fighting may also have largely disappeared.[419]

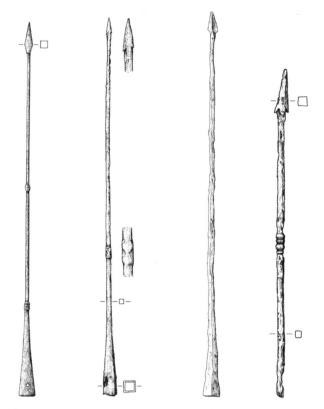

Figure 290 *Pila of the 2nd and 3rd centuries AD: 1 Lobith in the Netherlands (after Nikolay 2007); 2, 4 Eining and 3 Markt Berolzheim (the bent piece straightened in the drawing) (after Gschwind 2004). Drawings: A. Smadi, Arch Institute University of Cologne*

Figure 291 *Antoninianus of Probus RIC 560 Var. dating back to AD 276/282 with a depiction of a javelin and plumbatae with barbed tips. Photo: A. Pangerl*

Perhaps influenced by the *pilum*, javelins with long iron shanks that possessed unusually shaped barbed tips arrived in the region of northern Germany in the later Imperial period.[420] These were then also soon introduced into the Roman army with the increased employment of Germanic soldiers in the army. While it was believed this only happened in the Late Roman period,[421] there was always clear, well-dated evidence for the earlier introduction of throwing weapons with barbed tips into the Roman army, which has been overlooked until now. On the obverse of coins of the Emperor Probus (AD 276–82), spears and javelins with barbed tips clearly appear (Fig. 291). It is most clearly shown on the obverse of the *Antoninianus RIC* 560 (Var.), minted in Ticinum: here the emperor, wearing scale armour and round shield, is represented as supreme cavalry commander to demonstrate his *virtus*: probably as supreme leader of the mobile cavalry force founded by Gallienus. While on coins he usually carries only one shafted weapon with a barbed head, here there are three: a spear with a larger head in his right hand and two smaller javelins in his left hand with the shield. It is precisely these light javelins which are known as typical cavalry weapons. It may be that these were *plumbatae* or *mattiobarbuli* (Estiot 2008).

Weapons with barbed tips were represented in various sizes up to the arrowhead (see below), their longest examples being functionally equivalent to the *pilum* and probably continuing its tradition seamlessly. Perhaps this weapon is the *spiculum* which, according to Vegetius (*Epitoma rei militaris* 2.15), was what the *pilum* was called in the Late Roman period. Only in the early Medieval period, after the Frankish *ango* of the Merovingian period, the youngest variant of the *pilum*, had fallen into disuse, do records for this ancient Roman 'national weapon' disappear (von Schnurbein 1974).

LANCES

Very long lances, like the *sarissa*, which were in use in the Greco-Hellenistic phalanx, were unknown among Roman infantry in the late Republic and early Empire. However, from the beginning of its confrontation with Hellenistic Macedonian armies, Rome had effective tactics and weaponry to cope with the phalanx in battle. Since the long thrusting spear of the Macedonians had proved to be clearly inferior in these battles, there was thus no reason for Roman infantry to adopt it.

In the Severan period, however, K. Strobel believes the application of phalanx tactics with correspondingly long spears seems to have been used by the Roman army in battles with the Parthians.[422] Archaeological evidence is still pending. In Strobel's eyes, the use of the *pilum* had declined in the legions and other spears would come into use in the early 3rd century AD;[423] the Severan tombstones of *lancearii* from Apamea (Syria) confirm this: by way of

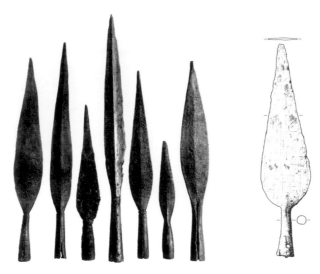

Figure 292 *Iron spearheads from Newstead (after Curle 1911); iron spearhead from Eining (after Gschwind 2004). Drawing: A. Smadi, Arch Institute University of Cologne*

example, there is the soldier Marcus Aurelius of the *legio II Parthica* shown with a kind of quiver containing five short javelins.[424]

The forms of Roman spearheads are quite varied, as is their size (Fig. 292). Occasionally, cross-regional groupings also seem to emerge. For example, larger spearheads of very similar design were found repeatedly in the archaeological material of the Upper German-Raetian Limes of the late middle Imperial period, which had to be parts of larger spears.[425] There is currently no way to decide whether they belonged to the equipment of auxiliaries fighting in a special formation, or what may otherwise lie behind this weapon.

JAVELINS

Smaller iron spearheads with a square or triangular cross-section or shaped like a leaf are usually identified as javelins, although problems of differentiation between javelin heads and catapult bolts frequently occur. Such javelins are known for the cavalry, but they were also present in the infantry, as the representations from Apamea demonstrate.

In late antiquity, there was a special type of javelin (or perhaps throwing dart?), as testified by the archaeological material. It possessed a barbed head, characteristic of the German region, a long iron shank with a socket to which was attached a lead weight (Fig. 293).[426] The names *plumbata* or *mattiobarbulus* are associated with them. Numismatic testimonials already show this weapon in the reign of Probus (AD 276–82), from the period of the Tetrarchy (Estiot 2008).

According to Vegetius (Veg. 1.17), five examples of these missile weapons were secured to the inside of the shield, so that they were instantly available when needed.

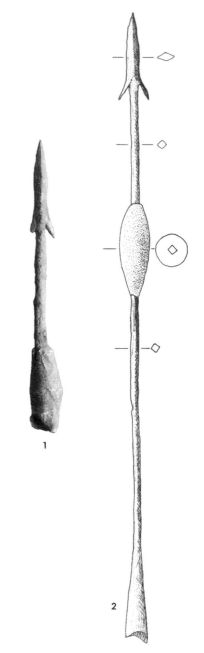

1

2

Figure 293 *1 plumbata (unprovenanced, privately owned; Photo: A. Pangerl); 2 plumbata from Sisak (after Radmann-Livaja 2004) Drawing: A. Smadi, Arch Institute University of Cologne*

Bow and arrow

In the Republican era, there was no tradition of the large-scale use of archery in the Roman army. Only when confronting the Parthians in the 1st century BC, were the Romans given a painful lesson about the importance of this long-range weapon. For, in the year 51 BC, the army of Crassus fell victim to the deadly arrow volleys of the Parthians at Carrhae together with their commander. This insight was at once taken into account: after the occupation of the Middle East by Pompey, units of auxiliary archers with the characteristic composite bows and arrows with trilobate heads were immediately deployed (Fig. 294). In particular, special units recruited from the Syrian tribe of the Ituraeans already played an important role in the late Republic (see Coulston 1985; Ziethen 1997). In the Imperial period, the bow was widespread, not only among special forces from the Middle East. Beyond the epigraphic record, there is frequent archaeological evidence for the armament with bows and arrows. These have been compiled by J. C. N. Coulston and W. Zanier.[427]

Arrows usually occur in archaeological contexts as single arrowheads: assemblages, such as that of a Late Roman archer in Grave 4 at Westendorf near Augsburg, are rare (Czysz 1986). This discovery demonstrates that in the quiver of a late Roman *sagittarius* (probably of Germanic origin), different types of arrow were present: from arrows with bolt-like bodkin heads to those with leaf-shaped heads to arrows with barbs.

BOWS

There were two types of bow in use. Purely wooden bows existed, but due to conservation problems they have not been found within the Roman Empire. By contrast, they are well represented by North German bog finds. They are usually made of yew (Pauli Jensen 2009).

The structurally complicated reflex or composite bows are archaeologically well documented by bone components such as ear laths,[428] like the ones from Oberaden for the Augustan period or from Mušov from the time of the Marcomannic Wars.[429] Similarly, the weapons store at Carnuntum, with certainty dated to the late 2nd/3rd century AD at the earliest, contained, besides trilobate arrowheads, bone components of composite bows.[430] Such

bow components were especially common in the Raetian Danube fort at Straubing/Sorviodurum where a Syrian archer unit, the *cohors I Canathenorum milliaria equitata*, was stationed.[431]

This superior weapon, developed in arid steppes and deserts, had a disadvantage, especially in the more humid areas of central Europe. Its components made from wood, bone, horn, tendons, and rawhide were held together with water-soluble bone glue, and during long periods of rain, there was a risk that the weapon would fall apart. For this reason, composite bows were always kept in a case, of which, as is the case with quivers, only pictorial representations and no actual finds, have been preserved.[432] The only finds come from the Germanic princely burial at Gommern, from the period after the middle of the 3rd century AD, where the silver fittings from a quiver made of poplar and (probably) leather were found.[433] M. Becker has also compiled other archaeological evidence for quivers in the Germanic area.

ARROWS

In the Roman army, various forms of iron arrowhead were used: there were leaf-shaped projectiles and others with barbs. However, often these are indistinguishable from those of Celtic, Germanic, or other opponents.[434] Distinguishing bodkin-headed arrowheads from catapult bolts is difficult; in individual cases the find context is helpful – as with the examples from the quiver of the Late Roman archer from Westendorf near Augsburg.[435] However, the characteristic trilobate arrowheads of Eastern auxiliary troops are found particularly frequently (see below). Special weapons such as incendiary arrows are found less often. The heads of these, with a basket for containing combustible material (such as oil-soaked flat or hemp fibres), have come for example from Straubing and Tilurium (Fig. 295); more than a dozen such heads are known from all over the Empire.[436] In the Late Roman

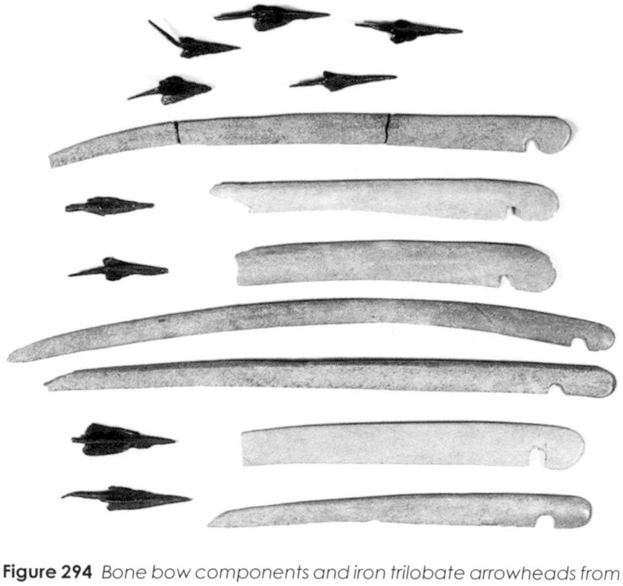

Figure 294 *Bone bow components and iron trilobate arrowheads from Straubing (after Prammer 2010)*

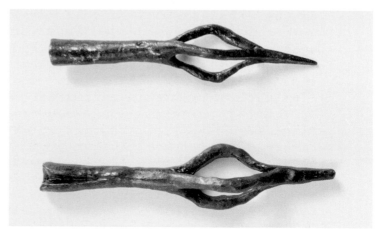

Figure 295 *Iron incendiary arrowheads from Straubing (after Prammer 2010)*

period, Germanic types with barbs representing miniature versions of barbed spearheads are found among the armament of Roman archers.[437]

TRILOBATE ARROWHEADS

Trilobate arrowheads of iron are undoubtedly Eastern in origin. In Imperial-period deposits in the north-western provinces and the Danube region, they serve almost as an 'index fossil' for oriental archers who fought as auxiliaries in the Roman army. These arrowheads, which were shot from the composite bow, have been studied intensively by W. Zanier. He distinguishes between three different types (Zanier 1988, 6). These can scarcely be dated more precisely, as they are attested virtually unchanged from the late Republic into the 3rd century AD and the Late Roman period.

From the Middle East, there are trilobate arrowheads of the 1st and 3rd centuries AD from Masada and Herodium in Israel, from Dülük Baba Tepesi in Eastern Turkey, and Dura-Europos on the Middle Euphrates in Syria. Here there were even a few wooden arrow shafts, some with fore shafts surviving.[438]

Slings

The sling is an ancient pastoral and hunting weapon, the origin of which is suspected to have been south-west Asia (Korfmann 1972). Their use in war is attested from the famous episode of the struggle between David and Goliath in the Old Testament (1 *Samuel* 17, 49–50). The evidence of their use in the Roman army is summarized in Völling and Bishop and Coulston.[439]

Slinging was already being mentioned in Roman Republican literature as the weapon of light infantry. In the ancient tradition, there is a distinction between three types of sling, as in the sling catapult invented by the Macedonians during the Third Macedonian War against Perseus, the staff sling, and the most common form, the hand sling.[440] In the beginning, the bullets were naturally occurring pebbles of a suitable form and size. However, in the archaeological record, these stone bullets are often barely distinguishable from naturally occurring pebbles, unless clearly non-local stones are found in conspicuous amounts in Roman layers.

With the invention of the biconical or acorn-shaped lead slingshot (*glans*), the sling is increasingly found on archaeological sites. In the late Republic and early Empire these occasionally bear cast inscriptions ranging from curses for the addressee to the names of generals and legions.[441] These inscriptions assume opponents able to read and understand the Greek or Latin language. During use against illiterate barbarian enemies, as in Germania or Britain, the inscriptions on lead slingshot cease of course.

Völling has divided lead slingshot into six groups by shape; they principally appear in deposits in contexts from the late Republic and the early Empire. This is certainly related to the fact that they were often inscribed and thus datable examples. In the middle Imperial period they seem – with some exceptions in Britain – to decline; they are then only sporadically found in the Late Roman period and spherical slingshot predominate.[442]

D. Baatz published ballistic calculations on the extent to which Xenophon's assertion (*Anabasis* 3.316–17) from around 400 BC – that bullets made of lead had a greater range than stone – would correspond with the facts (Baatz 1990). The result confirmed the details of Xenophon in full: lead slingshot were most efficient at a distance of approximately 100 m and were still effective up to about 200 m. Stone shot were effective to about 85 m and were hardly effective at all at distances over 100 m.

Projectiles of baked clay also occur in Roman archaeological contexts.[443] Caesar's (*BG* 5.43.1) description of how the northern Gallic Nervii used red-hot clay shot against the thatched roofs of a Roman camp is not otherwise proven for the Romans, but has to be accepted as a possibility. In the middle Imperial period, unlike lead bullets, clay sling bullets are still found in military camps.

The effective use of the sling requires intensive exercise from childhood onwards. So slingers (*funditores*) in the Roman army are mainly described as originally being members of pastoral peoples, for example residents of the Balearic Islands or Cretans.[444] However, unlike archers, there were no specialized, independent, traditional auxiliary units of slingers from the early Imperial period. Archaeological evidence for slingers can be found in the Imperial period in units of all kinds; perhaps there were smaller groups of specialists within legions and auxiliary units that could be used accordingly.[445]

2. Cavalry

Cavalry recruited from the Roman population itself only played a major role in the early days of Rome; in the later periods of the Republic, the cavalry were increasingly provided by allies of Rome or by mercenaries. Caesar in particular, during the Gallic War and later in the Civil War, opted for Celtic cavalry, including Noricans and mounted Teutons from the right bank of the Rhine. Apparently Augustus initially continued this tradition for ethnically homogeneous auxiliary cavalry with largely indigenous armament and equipment. This could be the reason that weapons and specialist pieces of equipment that can be attributed to national, uniformly equipped Roman cavalry for the cavalry only appear from the Tiberio-Claudian period onwards (Fig. 296). Therefore

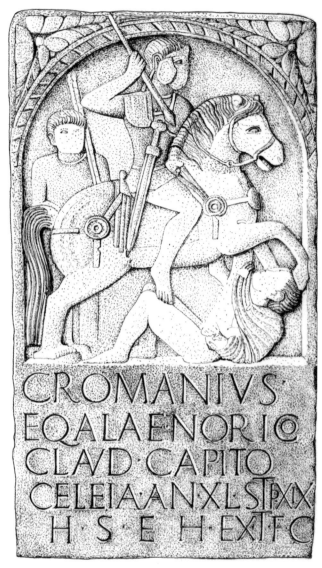

Figure 296 *Cavalry tombstone of C. Romanius of Ala Noricorum from Mainz, after Selzer. Drawing: A. Smadi, Arch Institute University of Cologne*

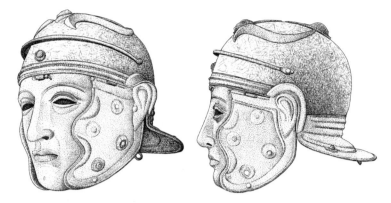

Figure 297 *Kalkriese/Weisenau-type cavalry helmet of iron with copper-alloy decoration (unprovenanced, privately owned). Drawings: A. Smadi, Arch Institute University of Cologne*

it can be assumed that, up to the Augustan period, these riders fought with their native armament. This assumption is supported by Gallo-Celtic horse gear pendants from Dangstetten, Thracian *phalerae* from Oberaden, or Dacian bridles from Augsburg-Oberhausen. This circumstance may also be responsible for the fact that no Roman cavalry helmets are known from the Augustan period which are as clearly different from infantry helmets as would become customary later. In the Augustan period, the helmets of the Weisenau type, combined with Kalkriese type masks and provided with cheek pieces with representations of the human ear, are the best candidates for cavalry helmets (Fig. 297). Distinctively Roman cavalry swords (*spathae*) were also not yet known in the earliest Imperial period. Among

the archaeological material of the late Republican-Augustan period, the only long swords are of the late La Tène tradition, and were worn by Celts, 'Romans' (that is, auxiliary cavalry), and Germans (Istenic 2010). A uniformly armed and equipped Roman auxiliary cavalry was first formed in the post-Augustan period, mainly mixing Celtic and Greco-Thracian equipment, initially wearing the eastern Greek-derived Weyler/Koblenz-Bubenheim-type helmet in addition to the Celtic *spatha*.[446] After the middle of the 1st century AD, the first truly 'Roman' cavalry swords then appeared with the long version of the Pompeii-type blade.

Members of the Roman cavalry were the best-paid Roman auxiliary soldiers. Accordingly, their equipment was often more elaborately worked and considerably more splendidly decorated than that of the infantry. However, they differed little from them in clothing, except for wearing half-length (leather?) breeches under the tunic from the beginning and metal spurs on the boots. For body armour, mail apparently predominated over scale armour. The long sword acquired from the Celts, the *spatha*, was worn on a belt, which was not decorated with metal fittings in the early and middle Imperial period to the same extent as the infantry belt. The dagger, compulsory among the armament of infantry up to the 3rd century AD, does not appear among the cavalry.[447] In combat, cavalrymen carried spears, the heads of which, however, cannot be distinguished from those of the infantry among the archaeological finds. At the same time, until the later Imperial period, there was special armament associated with ethnically homogeneous cavalry, the archaeological evidence for which, however, is not always available: the javelins of Numidian cavalrymen testified to in literature are hard to identify in the archaeological record. This also applies to the thrusting spear (*contus*) and armour of cataphracts. The same iron arrowheads and bone bow components occur in finds assemblages for mounted archers of Eastern origin as are customary among bow-and-arrow-armed infantry.

Clothing

Tunic, cloaks, leggings

In the case of tunics and cloaks, the Roman auxiliary cavalry under the Empire were barely distinguishable from infantry by clothing. At least, there is no evidence for it in the sources. Theoretically, there could have been differences in colour or decoration. Likewise, cavalry cloak brooches cannot be differentiated from those of the infantry.

In pictorial representations (tombstones!), cavalry soldiers from the early Imperial period onwards always wear half-length leggings which are repeatedly referred to in the archaeological literature as being made of leather[448] – without any substantive evidence for that. A supposed example of Roman leather leggings, in the form of a fragment from Vindonissa, is questionable.[449]

Belt

On soldiers' tombstones of the 1st century AD, cavalrymen always wear narrow, undecorated belts with simple buckles (Hoss 2009). They thus stand in stark contrast to the infantry, for whom narrow and wide belts, richly decorated with metal fittings, are attested in pictorial representations and among actual finds. A narrow belt buckle of a cavalryman decorated with enamel, from a weapon burial with a *spatha* from the fort of Koblenz-Niederberg, is proof of this for the early 2nd century AD.[450] From the reign of Caracalla onwards, cavalrymen also adopted ring- and frame-buckle belts, as is proved by depictions on tombstones.[451]

Spurs

Spurs of non-ferrous metals and iron were attached to the closed boots of cavalrymen. Distinctive eyelet spurs (with eyelets for receiving straps to secure them) can be distinguished from riveted head spurs (with the straps attached by riveted heads), which appear by the 2nd century AD. These were then used into the Late Roman period and also influenced the development of spurs under the Teutons (Giesler 1978). Unlike in Germany, where spurs were firmly integrated into cavalry riding boots (Tejral 2002), Roman examples were always removable.[452]

Defensive weapons

Cavalry helmets: the various types and their variants

The remark by Polybius, that the Roman cavalry during the Republic were equipped like the Greeks, can be taken seriously with regard to helmets, based on the iconographic sources.[453] This is the case, for example, in the representation of riders on the monument of Aemilius Paulus at Delphi, or the so-called Altar of Domitius in Rome. Unambiguous archaeological finds of original, late Republican cavalry helmets are still missing, as is a 'missing link' for the Augustan period. Almost all Roman cavalry helmets known from the Tiberio-Claudian and later periods are derived from Greco-Hellenistic helmet types. An exception is the Pompeii type helmet (Fig. 298), of which only a single piece was ever found – if this piece can indeed be identified as the richly decorated variant of the Montefortino type helmet and if it was intended for cavalry.

For the Augustan period, there are no clearly defined Roman cavalry helmets, which would qualify as predecessors for the helmets of the Weyler/Koblenz-Bubenheim type, first introduced slightly later. However, Augustan cavalry – whether of Celtic, Germanic, or Thracian origin – must have worn helmets. That these have been missed because of bad luck in archaeological excavations until now seems unlikely. They must therefore be sought and located among existing finds.

These Augustan cavalry helmets are most likely found in the special variants of helmets of the Weisenau type that occur combined with Kalkriese-type masks, where ear protection occurs in the form of an embossed metal human ear on the cheek piece (Fig. 297). With their removable masks, they could be used either as battle helmets or sports helmets. Their ear protection, in the form of an embossed metal human ear on the cheek piece, continues to be found on later cavalry helmets up into the 3rd century AD as one of the main features distinguishing it from the infantry helmet. These cheek pieces can be either non-ferrous metal sheet or formed from sheet iron, provided with a decorated copper-alloy overlay.

Cavalry helmets were generally richly decorated and already differed in this from infantry weapons, at least in the early and the beginning of the mid-Imperial periods. It was not until the end of the 2nd century AD that infantry helmets were also decorated, mostly in the form of copper-alloy metal fittings on iron helmet bowls.

In the archaeological record, examples from the 1st and 3rd centuries AD are numerous. It is more difficult with cavalry helmets of the 2nd century. Some specimens have been identified as dating to this period based more on typological considerations and less because they are dated by context. Thus, for example, although some of the characteristic decorated cheek pieces of cavalry helmets are found in assemblages dated to the Marcomannic Wars in the 60s and 70s of the 2nd century AD, the types of helmets themselves remain unclear.

The following proposed typology of Roman cavalry helmets differs significantly from those of Robinson, Garbsch, and Junkelmann, because they have confused to an unacceptable degree – at least for me – regular cavalry helmets with infantry helmets on the one hand and sports helmets on the other.

KALKRIESE-TYPE CAVALRY HELMETS

These early Imperial cavalry helmets are characterized by removable masks that mimic or cover only the front part of the face. To achieve full protection for the face, cheek guards were still needed to fill the gap between the mask and helmet bowl. Such masks – named after the famous discovery from the battlefield at Kalkriese – have been catalogued by N. Hanel; technological and scientific investigation was also undertaken (Hanel *et al.* 2000; 2004). The masks are made of copper alloy or iron. Iron specimens were covered with silver plate. These types are distinctive in that they only show the front part of the face, with neither ears nor hair. They also have a forehead hinge which allows for the removal of the mask from the helmet or for it to be turned up, at least.

Whenever this type has been found combined with a helmet, so far, then for one thing it is with the Weisenau helmet which, in contrast to the other forms of this type, has cheek pieces with moulded ear depictions, like cavalry helmets.[454] Along with other authors, I am inclined to think these helmets, which are actually a variant of the Weisenau type with a removable mask, were cavalry helmets. This could be worn in combat without a mask and for sports with a mask.[455] An example in the Guttmann Collection is combined with a helmet bowl decorated in repoussé work, which is close to the basic shape of helmets of the Weyler/Koblenz-Bubenheim type, but without the ear cut-outs and without the characteristic representation of hair.[456] However, the possibility has also been discussed, following some representations on tombstones, of attributing infantry helmets with face masks to standard bearers wearing face-mask helmets under the head parts of their characteristic animal skins (wolf pelts and so on).[457] Kalkriese-type masks represent the earliest known examples of Roman cavalry and sports helmets, and the (now lost) piece from Haltern[458] is likely to belong with them. They date from the period before AD 9. Whether they were in use until the second half of the 1st century AD is less well documented (Junkelmann 1997).

POMPEII-TYPE CAVALRY HELMET

An ornate helmet made of copper alloy (Fig. 298) was found in Pompeii and identified as a cavalry helmet by Salvatore Ortisi.[459] It consists of a bowl with a narrow neck guard wrought from the bowl, and closely resembles infantry helmets of the Montefortino type. The piece is unparalleled, either in iconographic sources or among the archaeological material. Ortisi's interpretation as a cavalry helmet relies on just the rich decoration, executed in repoussé work, but

Figure 298 *Pompeii-type cavalry helmet (?) of copper alloy. Photos: S. Ortisi*

not upon any other formal features that might suggest an interpretation as a cavalry helmet.

CAVALRY HELMET WITH HAIR TYPE

Under this type and its variants I am including all cavalry helmets, which have ear cut-outs with riveted ear guards, a lower neck guard, and decorated cheek pieces with embossed representations of the ear as common characteristics. Their bowls are decorated in various techniques to look like a human hairstyle. Furthermore, these helmets can have diadems of various designs on the front, including examples that are similar to Attic helmets. They also share the development of the helmet bowl as a hairstyle,[460] which justifies their inclusion into one type. The presentation of the hair can be done in several ways.

THE CAVALRY HELMET TYPE WITH SEPARATELY EMBOSSED SHEET HAIR, WEYLER/KOBLENZ-BUBENHEIM VARIANT

These pieces have a separate decorated bowl forming the hair, made from copper alloy or silver foil and fixed on a smooth iron bowl. While the piece of Koblenz-Bubenheim can only be considered as a scattered deposit, probably from a destroyed burial,[461] the example from a cremation burial in Weyler can be dated to the Claudian period with its accompanying ceramic and glass finds.[462] The separate decorated bowls of these helmets, wrought from copper alloy, are riveted to an iron helmet underneath. For reasons of stability, an organic filler (pitch?) must be assumed in between the two bowl surfaces. In the early helmets a tiara or similar decoration is missing. Here, only the front edge is finished with a moulded copper-alloy band, like early examples of infantry helmets of the Weisenau type.

An especially opulent example comes from the Rhine near Xanten-Wardt (v. Prittwitz and Gaffron 1991) (Fig. 299). It has an iron bowl underneath upon which is mounted the decorated bowl with partly fire-gilded silver sheet depicting pronounced curly hair with an olive wreath. A tiara is absent; above the forehead there is an *imago clipeata* with the bust of a cuirassed young man with a baldric, probably to be identified with the Emperor Claudius (AD 41–54).

Figure 299 *Weiler/Koblenz-Bubenheim-type cavalry helmet from Xanten-Wardt, iron, copper alloy, and gilded silver. Photos: Rheinisches Landesmuseum Bonn*

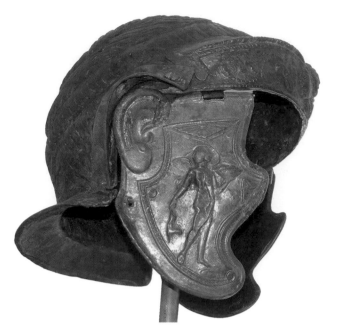

Figure 300 *Iron cavalry helmet with hair (Bassus variant) and decorative bronze plating (unprovenanced, privately owned). Photo: private*

The example of this helmet type, which is typologically probably the latest, came from a deposit from Vechten in the Netherlands.[463] Over an iron bowl, a decorated copper-alloy bowl is located which no longer has the three-dimensionally moulded curly locks of hair in shallow repoussé work so typical of early helmets, but has only a straggly, highly stylized hairstyle. The diadem on the forehead, ear guards, and cheek pieces are missing.

CAVALRY HELMET TYPE WITH A WORKED REPRESENTATION OF HAIR DIRECTLY ON THE BOWL, BASSUS VARIANT

These helmets have no distinction between the helmet bowl underneath and the decorated bowl; the hairstyle is beaten directly from the iron bowl. The only complete example known so far from this type is in a private collection and of unknown provenance (Fischer 2008a). The bowl consists of iron, which depicts the characteristic imitation hairstyle in repoussé work (Fig. 300). On the top, this is done skilfully and realistically, but at the back it is rather flat and stylized. The overlay of the neck guard, the roughly riveted ear guards, and the moulded brow diadem of the Attic type (so far unique in its form) are of copper-alloy plate. It is similar to that on the helmet of T. Flavius Bassus (see below) and is richly decorated with embossed serpents, masks, and other designs which have certain echoes of the votive plaques of the so-called Thracian or Danubian riders.

From a cursory examination of the published material, the surviving right-hand cheek piece with the embossed ear represents an exception with its figural decoration (Busch 2009a). Framed by punched dot-and-triangle motifs, ending in a volute beneath, it depicts a winged Eros, who carries in his right hand a dead hare probably and in his left a basket of fruit. In this figure, one can see an allegory of autumn, the time for hunting and harvesting. However, what such a portrayal is doing on a piece of armour, where martial motives are usually found, remains unclear. The upper end forms a triangular frame, which resembles a kind of undulating conch (a sun motif?). When compared with dated representations on tombstones, such as that of T. Flavius Bassus from Cologne,[464] a date for the piece in the second half of the 1st century AD, more precisely in the late Flavian period, is certain.

CAVALRY HELMET TYPE WITH REAL HAIR, XANTEN VARIANT

These helmets have a glued wig-like hairstyle of real hair (with a hairnet or cap) on a smooth iron bowl (Fig. 300).[465] The helmet shape is thus closely connected to mask helmets of the Homs-Nijmegen type. It was thanks to coincidence that the similarly constructed mask helmets from Nijmegen (Fig. 328) were discovered shortly before the Xanten piece. Thus, during the restoration of the Xanten helmet, the first ever real hair covering was found, recognized, and preserved. Against this background, it is possible that cavalry helmets with a smooth iron bowl discovered a long time ago, probably had similar remains of a glued-on hairstyle removed undetected, from the

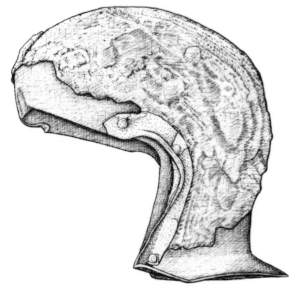

Figure 301b *Iron bowl of a Weiler/Koblenz-Bubenheim-type cavalry helmet from Newstead (after Curle 1911)*

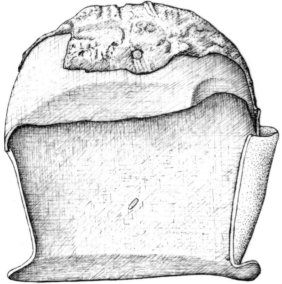

Figure 301a *Cavalry helmet made of iron with real hair overlay from Xanten (after Schalles and Schreiter 1993). Drawing: A. Smadi, Arch Institute University of Cologne*

Figure 302 *Reconstructed Butzbach-Dormagen-type cavalry helmet. Photo: private*

specimen from Newstead (Fig. 301b) in Scotland for example.[466] The surviving copper-alloy ear guard of the Xanten helmet was covered with silver foil. Due to the fact that no fittings have been detected in the forehead area to attach a mask, these helmets should be viewed as cavalry battle helmets. Forehead diadems have not been observed on this type of helmet.

CAVALRY HELMET TYPE WITH A SMOOTH CAP AND FOREHEAD TIARA

Typologically these helmets belong between the Koblenz-Bubenheim/Bassus cavalry helmet variants, with an iron bowl and copper-alloy decoration, and the pseudo-Attic copper-alloy helmets of the Guisborough/Theilenhofen type. They also seem partly to fill the chronological gap in the 2nd century AD between the helmets with a hair style and the helmets of the Guisborough/Theilenhofen type, although their dating is not so far confirmed (Fig. 302).

A unique helmet of iron and copper alloy from Witchham Gravel in England also belongs to this group, which – with its small, inset bowl and its decoration of attached bosses – makes a strange 'un-Roman' impression.[467] It is still dated to the period around the middle of the 1st century AD.

Not to be confused with these helmets are iron cavalry helmets, from Newstead, for example,[468] which

Figure 303 *a) Butzbach-Dormagen-type cavalry helmet (unprovenanced, Mougins Museum of Classical Art)*

Figure 303 *b) Butzbach-Dormagen-type cavalry helmet (unprovenanced, Mougins Museum of Classical Art; after Junkelmann 2011)*

are obviously the underlying bowls of either Koblenz-Bubenheim or Xanten variants, either lacking the embossed metal hairstyle or where traces of human hair hairstyle have been eliminated by old 'restoration'.

CAVALRY HELMET TYPE WITH A SMOOTH DOME AND A STRAIGHT FOREHEAD DIADEM, BUTZBACH VARIANT

This cavalry helmet made of copper alloy, the brow diadem of which has a characteristic feather pattern, has never been satisfactorily restored or published. It was found in the extramural settlement of Kastell Butzbach in the Wetterau in Hessen (Fig. 302). Marcus Junkelmann dated it to the 2nd/3rd centuries AD and assumed there was a (now lost) iron bowl underneath, which would connect the piece with the older helmets of the Weyler/Koblenz-Bubenheim type in construction. The cheek piece of a cavalry helmet from Dormagen am Rhein has a similar feather pattern and probably belonged to a similarly late piece.[469] The straight brow diadem of the Butzbach helmet differs significantly from the pointed tiaras of Attic or pseudo-Attic helmets.

Another more richly decorated example of this helmet type with an iron bowl underneath and copper-alloy decoration exists from the Guttmann Collection.[470] Even though its diadem is missing, the completion of the crown decorated with laurel leaves and a laurel wreath only leaves room for a straight terminal to the forehead diadem, as on the piece from Butzbach (Fig. 303a, b).

Figure 304 *Cavalry helmet from Tell Oum Hauran (Robinson 1975). Drawing: A. Smadi, Arch Institute University of Cologne*

CAVALRY HELMET TYPE WITH A SMOOTH BOWL AND WREATH OF LEAVES, NIJMEGEN VARIANT

Two helmets with smooth iron bowls and a diadem in the form of oak (?) leaves and a bust made of copper alloy mounted in the centre[471] come from the river Waal at Nijmegen.

CAVALRY HELMET WITH DECORATED DOME WITHOUT BROW DIADEM FROM TELL OUM HAURAN

This unique piece (Fig. 304), which was found in a burial of the southern Syrian Hauran along with a similarly decorated mask helmet, a shield boss of Germanic type, and ring-pommel swords, is dated to the 2nd century AD. The decoration of its bowl is in keeping with the rear part of the bowl of a mask helmet from Antinoupolis in Egypt.[472]

PSEUDO-ATTIC CAVALRY HELMET TYPE

These later cavalry helmets are beaten out of bronze sheet, replacing the iron helmets with a copper-alloy decorated bowl some time after the middle of the 2nd century AD. When datable contexts are present, then these helmets continue to around the middle of the 3rd century AD and, like the eponymous piece from Theilenhofen, they even occur beyond the middle of the 3rd century AD in the cleared Raetian Limes area (Reuter 2007). A corresponding piece of dating evidence is also a coin portrait of Gallienus (AD 253–68), wherein the emperor is wearing a pseudo-Attic helmet. His successors from Claudius II (AD 268–70) onwards, however, already preferred pseudo-Corinthian helmets. H. R. Robinson and, following him, J. Garbsch too, did not consider these later cavalry helmets of copper-alloy sheet to be battle helmets, because of their supposedly much lower protective value, but rather parade equipment.[473] However, there are some very weighty arguments against this: theoretical considerations and practical tests have shown that these helmets provide good protection, especially as they were reinforced by linings of fabric, felt, or leather.[474] Apart from this, there is also the question of whether these helmets were primarily needed for protection at all, such as when fighting against infantry. Or would they rather have created a psychological effect by their bizarre and striking enhancement of the wearer? And, moreover, how should grave finds such as Tell Oum Hauran or Ostrov be explained where, in addition to a bespoke sports helmet with a mask, an additional, richly decorated combat helmet of copper-alloy sheet was also included?

And a fourth, very pragmatic argument ultimately speaks for identifying these helmets as regular cavalry helmets: if it is supposed, along with H. R. Robinson and J. Garbsch, that they belonged to sports equipment, then there would simply be no regular helmets left for the cavalry for the late 2nd century AD and the whole 3rd century AD. To solve this dilemma, as Robinson and Garbsch did in the tradition of previous researchers, by completely arbitrarily declaring some types of later infantry helmets to be cavalry helmets, makes little sense in the current state of affairs. Because then we would have an overwhelmingly high number of sports and cavalry helmets for this period, but we would have a lack of infantry helmets that could hardly be explained in a logical manner!

PSEUDO-ATTIC CAVALRY HELMET TYPE, WORTHING/
THEILENHOFEN VARIANT

The bowls of these copper-alloy helmets are beaten out from a single piece and richly decorated (Fig. 305), the brow

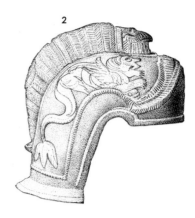

Figure 305 *Pseudo-Attic cavalry helmets of the Theilenhofen type: 1 Theilenhofen. Photo: M. Eberlein, Arch Staatsslg. Munich; 2) from the River Wensum at Worthing (Robinson 1975). Drawing: A. Smadi, Arch Institute University of Cologne*

diadem with one or more peaks on top being particularly noteworthy. The ear guard around the ear cutout, normally applied separately, was here also beaten out of the bowl. A characteristic of this variant of pseudo-Attic helmets is the fact that an often fantastically frilly plume is also beaten out of the bowl. The helmet from Worthing comes from the River Wensum,[475] and the helmet from Theilenhofen from a hoard in the extramural settlement of the fort (Klumbach and Wamser 1978; Fischer 2002a).

PSEUDO-ATTIC CAVALRY HELMET GUISBOROUGH-CHALON
TYPE

The bowls of these copper-alloy helmets are beaten out from a single piece and richly decorated, the forehead diadem with the tapering peak being particularly noteworthy. The ear guard around the ear cut-out, normally separately applied, was beaten out of the bowl. A characteristic of this variant of pseudo-Attic helmets is the lack of a crest (Fig. 306). At most, the bowl is crowned with small representations of eagles or snake heads, as with the helmet from Gerulata/Rusovce in Slovakia (Krekovic and Snopko 1998) or the river find from the Saône at Chalon.[476]

PSEUDO-ATTIC CAVALRY HELMETS OF THE OSTROV TYPE

The eponymous piece is finished in the shape of a Phrygian cap and thus resembles Phrygian-type Hellenistic helmets. However, there is no direct unbroken line of development from these helmets to this defensive weapon. The thickened, forward-leaning 'peak' of the Phrygian cap is here replaced by an eagle head. The upper edge of the forehead diadem is formed by snakes. At the front, in the centre, there is a depiction of Mars flanked by Victories. To the rear there is a representation of Medusa. The helmet and the cheek pieces, on which the Dioscuri are displayed together with horses, bear a characteristic scale or feather design. There is no neck guard; to the sides and at the rear there are merely holes

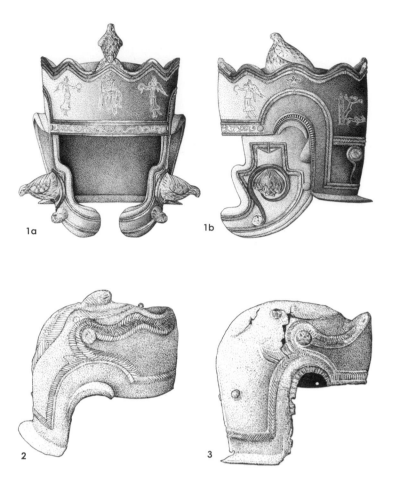

1a   1b

2   3

Figure 306 *Pseudo-Attic cavalry helmets of the Guisborough-Chalon type. 1 a and b Rusovce/Gerulata (after Krekovic and Snopko 1998) 2 Guisborough, 3 Chalon (after Robinson 1975). Drawings: A. Smadi, Arch Institute University of Cologne*

Figure 307 *Pseudo-Attic cavalry helmet of copper alloy of the Phrygian cap type from Ostrov. Neck guard of armoured scales (unprovenanced, Mougins Museum of Classical Art, after Junkelmann 2011; Fischer 2013c)*

for attaching a separately produced protective device.[477] A mask helmet of the Pfrondorf type was found together with this helmet.[478]

A very well preserved specimen has appeared on the art market recently and is in private ownership (Fig. 307). It is now on display in a private museum in Mougins (Provence).[479] The helmet has so many parallels to that from Ostrov that it can be assumed that it came from the same workshop. The cheek pieces are decorated with Mars and Minerva and the characteristic scale or feather pattern found on the helmet from Ostrov. The neck guard was not beaten out from the bowl, as is usual in Imperial helmets. Rather, its rear edge bears holes where a mail guard could have been attached. On the privately owned example, bronze scales (modern additions!) are attached at this point, which are identical to those of a scale cuirass. Whether or not this find is truly ancient cannot really be clarified for certain in the absence of information about the circumstances of its discovery. However, such a technical solution would be at least conceivable. There is a good dating clue for this rare type of helmet: on the so-called Ludovisi sarcophagus, there is a realistic

representation of this piece of equipment[480] with an eagle's head and scale or feather decoration (Fig. 308). E. Künzl recently dated this sarcophagus to the time around the middle of the 3rd century AD which would then also apply to these helmets.[481]

PSEUDO-CORINTHIAN CAVALRY HELMETS

PSEUDO-CORINTHIAN CAVALRY HELMETS OF THE HEDDERNHEIM TYPE

This type of helmet is at first glance closely related to mask helmets of the Pfrondorf type because the cheek pieces have been united, so to speak, to form just a single 'visor'. It retains a narrow opening in the area of the eyes and nose. Theoretically, it would have been possible to provide an insert with eyes and nose here, which transformed the helmet into a real closed mask helmet. However, the fittings for attachment of such items seem to

Figure 308 *Illustration of a pseudo-Attic cavalry helmet of the Ostrov type on the Ludovisi battle sarcophagus (after Künzl 2010)*

Figure 309 *Eponymous pseudo-Corinthian cavalry helmet from Heddernheim (after Lindenschmit 1892)*

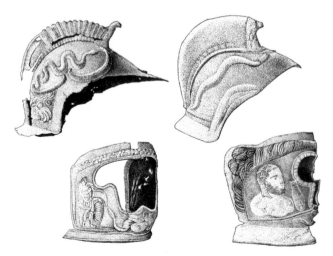

Figure 310 *Pseudo-Corinthian cavalry helmets (bowls and visors) of the Heddernheim type from the Danube at the Iron Gates, from Brigetio, from the River Wensum in Worthing, from Rodez (Robinson 1975). Drawings: A. Smadi, Arch Institute University of Cologne*

be missing from the relevant helmets. However, distinctive of this type are helmet bowls which quite obviously mimic a 'classical' Greek helmet, the Corinthian-type helmet (Pflug 1988).

The only complete example is the eponymous tinned copper-alloy helmet from Nida/Heddernheim (Fig. 309).[482] A. Reis has now established a possible late dating to the period after the middle of the 3rd century AD, *i.e.* the time of the abandonment of Heddernheim/Nida.[483] This helmet has the typical, tapering, pointed brow guard which clearly projects over the visor. A comb-like crest, the front terminating in an eagle head, is beaten out of the bowl. On the visor, eyes, nose, and mouth have been embossed, reminiscent of the Corinthian helmet. On the visor, curly hair with long sideburns has been depicted by embossing. This similarity to mask helmets with a similar manner of hairstyle representations is the main reason why the helmet has been misinterpreted as a sports helmet for so long.

The other helmets of this type are only represented by separate bowls (with images of faces on the brow guard) (Fig. 310). Examples come from Brigetio and the Danube Region in the area of the Iron Gates.[484] There are also separate visors, like the pieces from the River Wensum at Worthing, from Rodez and the Aschberg near Dilligen.[485] In order to avoid an exaggerated typological fragmentation, I have also grouped the bowl of a cavalry helmet[486] and the strange 'eagle helmet' from the Guttmann Collection,[487] with the Heddernheim type; although on both of these examples of the eye, nose, and mouth representations as typological vestiges of Corinthian helmets are absent on the point of the browguard.

- **Models** – Here a Corinthian helmet is obviously being imitated, but only the 'third stage' of the Corinthian helmet after Pflug,[488] which occurred from the mid-6th century BC. The cheek pieces are rigidly beaten out from the bowl running down closely together, thus forming a sort of tip. This helmet can be worn in two ways: firstly, elegant and casual, in a kind of 'resting position', in which the helmet is pushed back so that cheek pieces and nasal lose their actual protective effect and together form only a type of brow guard. This manner of wearing is known from the depiction of Ajax from the west pediment of the temple of Aegina.[489] In the other, the actual battle position, the helmet is pulled forward down so that the nasal actually protects the nose and cheek pieces can also fulfil their intended protective function in full.

However it seems that it was the western Greek development of the Corinthian helmet, worn between the end of the 6th century BC to the 4th century BC, which in the 3rd century AD, influenced a new type of Roman cavalry helmets: the Apulian-Corinthian helmet (Bottini 1988a). The above-mentioned 'resting position' of the Corinthian helmet was converted in the sense that it now was the only possible wearing position and could also simultaneously exert a protective function. Thus the nasal and eye apertures lost their function, as with the later Roman cavalry helmets of the Heddernheim type, and withered – as a kind of typological remnant – into a decoration. In this case, the eye openings could even be transformed into functionless small slits or even into depictions of eyes, in repoussé or inlaid, such as on the helmet from Ruvo di Puglia in Bari Museum.[490]

- **On the dating of pseudo-Corinthian cavalry helmets of the Heddernheim type** – Under Gallienus there is a very interesting change in coin portraiture of the Roman emperor which, as far as I am aware, has never been deemed worthy of a comprehensive and thorough investigation: from this time onwards, Roman emperors are depicted in varying frequencies with helmets, or, more accurately, with cavalry helmets (Figs 311–13). Undoubtedly, this was a new stylistic device to underline their military prowess or *virtus* (Estiot 2008). A marked change is observed in the helmet types worn by emperors, which is of great typological and chronological significance for actual finds: while Gallienus still wears a pseudo-Attic helmet, the emperors up to and into the Tetrarchic period are shown with pseudo-Corinthian helmets.

However, the engraver was always required to compromise in reproducing the helmets: cheek pieces and visors were always omitted in order not to partially

Figure 311 *Coin portraits of emperors with a pseudo-Attic helmet of the Theilenhofen type (1) and pseudo-Corinthian helmets of the Heddernheim type (2–8): 1 Gallienus (AD 253–68), Siscia Antoninianus RIC 580; 2 Claudius II Gothicus (AD 268–70), Antoninianus (not RIC); 3 Probus (AD 276–82), Rome aureus RIC 142; 4 Probus (AD 276–82), Siscia Antoninianus RIC 818; 5 Probus (AD 276–82), Siscia Antoninianus RIC 817; 6 Probus (AD 276–82), Antoninianus Siscia RIC 634 Var.; 7 Carus (AD 282–3), Antoninianus Lugdunum RIC 12; 8 Constantine I (AD 305–6), Antoninianus Trier RIC 272 (Var.). Photos: A. Pangerl*

conceal the portrait of the emperor. This phenomenon of intentionally scaled cheek pieces is indeed seen even earlier in Roman art, such as on Trajan's Column. Again, the representation of the individual was given preference over a realistic depiction of the helmets.

Since Imperial coins are always closely datable, the representations of dated portraits with helmets provide the opportunity to also use them for the dating of these helmets.[491] Thus we can establish that the pseudo-Corinthian helmets of the Heddernheim type with their decorated versions can be seen as the latest group of cavalry helmets during the late 3rd century AD. Helmets

Figure 312 *Coin portrait of Probus (AD 276–82) with pseudo-Corinthian rider helmet, armour, shield, barbed spear and Victoria. Aureus Ticinum RIC 308. Photo: A. Pangerl*

Figure 313 *Illustration of a pseudo-Corinthian cavalry helmet from the Ludovisi sarcophagus (after Künzl 2010)*

of this type can be dated from their occurrence on coin portraits from the emperor Gallienus, through Claudius II Gothicus and Probus, up to coins of Constantine I well into the last third of the 3rd century AD. They are particularly frequently depicted on coins of Probus (Figs 311.3–6; 312). On most of these helmets, rich decoration is indicated, but it cannot be seen in detail because of the small image size.

There is another, matching indication of the date on an iconographic source: on the Ludovisi battle sarcophagus, which can be dated to the middle third of the 3rd century AD,[492] a richly decorated pseudo-Corinthian cavalry helmet[493] is shown (Fig. 313), although Künzl has unjustly dismissed this helmet as pure fantasy.

It is important to establish why cavalry helmets current in the period after AD 260 suddenly appeared on emperor portraits: in the various battles of the second half of the 3rd century, the mobile cavalry established under Gallienus had proven particularly useful. The commanders of this mounted mobile army grew rapidly in power and thus also political importance, and some became emperors, for example Claudius Gothicus, Aurelian, or Probus.[494] It was apparently so important to highlight this fact for propaganda purposes that the emperor was now sometimes represented on coins as a fully armed cavalry officer. This was indeed true to reality, because these emperors were often themselves actually present at the head of the mobile army in numerous theatres of war.

This pseudo-Attic helmet, which had also been introduced for troops up to commander, was thus for a while (without the cumbersome visor which obscured

the individuality of the portrait) one of the attributes on depictions of the emperor on coin portraits. Since the emperors were also shown in other respects heavily armed as generals and cavalry commanders (helmets, scale armour, shield, *paludamentum*, spears and lances with barbed heads), the aim was, as mentioned above, to demonstrate their *virtus*, or military prowess (Estiot 2008). Indeed, the military virtues of the emperors were in particularly strong demand in these turbulent times.

DECORATED CHEEK PIECES

With the exception of pseudo-Corinthian helmets, all Roman cavalry helmets were equipped with often richly decorated cheek pieces (Busch 2009a). The opportunity will be taken here to show some newly discovered finds. A comprehensive analysis of the images on these cheek pieces would certainly be very rewarding, but it has yet to appear (Fig. 314).

Armour

The armour which the cavalry wore had to be more flexible than that of the infantry. Thus mail and above all scale armour had been preferred since the early Imperial period. Segmental cuirasses, however, were only worn by the infantry. In the 1st century AD, cape-like shoulder doubling regularly appears on cavalry representations, in which it is often barely distinguishable whether mail or scale armour is intended. This cape-like shoulder doubling appears relatively infrequently with mail in the 2nd and early 3rd centuries AD, and then it appears again on the

Figure 314 *Decorated cheek pieces from copper-alloy cavalry helmets (unprovenanced, privately owned). Photo: A. Pangerl*

helmeted and armoured coin portraits of emperors from Claudius II (see Fig. 312).

MAIL ARMOUR

On cavalry tombstones, mail is often very naturalistically depicted with a cape-like shoulder doubling and fastening hook. While these shoulder protections are seldom found as actual artefacts (except the finds from Augsburg and Vize, Fig. 219), the fastening hooks are found relatively frequently. Neither the iconographic representations nor the archaeological material make it possible to distinguish the particular types of mail of the cavalry or infantry.

SCALE ARMOUR

The same is true of scale armour, which is recorded for cavalry on iconographic sources. Neither the iconographic representations nor the archaeological material make it possible to distinguish the particular types of scale armour of cavalry or infantry.

'HYBRID' ARMOUR

From iconographic sources and a few actual finds, a body armour is known that combines the shoulder plates of overlapping iron laminated iron plates (corresponding to segmental armour) with mail and scale armour: an early Imperial period relief is known from Arlon in Belgium, where a group of cavalrymen wear mail like this with plate shoulder guards. M. Bishop has discussed this form of armour with the help of this iconographic source and reconstructed it virtually.[495] Actual finds of such armour are as yet unknown. Fragments of iron scale armour that were combined with iron shoulder guard plates are known from the Slovakian cavalry fort of Rusovce/Gerulata, found in a burnt, late Flavian layer (Fig. 218).[496]

Shields

Cavalry shields were similar to the oval shields of the infantry.[497] Hexagonal shields, known from reliefs and from appropriately shaped edge binding made of bronze sheet,[498] were only used by the cavalry.

Offensive weapons

Spathae

From the beginning, cavalrymen carried a long slashing sword, the *spatha*. This was in contrast to the infantry who, in the early Imperial period, always used the short stabbing sword, the *gladius*. Ch. Miks has summarized early Roman *spatha* blades showing hints of early to middle La Tène-period forms into the 'Fontillet' and 'Nauportus' types.[499]

It is very likely that the slashing swords developed in the late La Tène – the sheaths of which were decorated with *opus interrasile* made in copper alloy, especially brass, and exhibit Roman influence – were still used by Celtic and Germanic auxiliary cavalry in the early Imperial period (Istenic 2010). After all it was only around the middle of the 1st century AD that a tangible, truly Roman development begins to be visible among the finds with the introduction of a *spatha*, which represented, as it were, the extended version of the Pompeii-type *gladius*.[500] These *spatha* blades were about 67.5 cm long.[501] In the course of the 2nd century AD, the infantry also gradually began to adopt the *spatha*, so that from then on no distinction can be made between infantry and cavalry swords.

Christian Miks distinguished a 'Pettau' variant with multiple fields of decoration with embossed martial and mythological content (Fig. 256) from the sheath fittings of the Pompeii-type *gladius*. The attachment rings are not attached to suspension bands, but to the guttering. Perhaps the 'Pettau' variant is more suitable for the longer blade variant of the Pompeii type as a cavalry sword (*spatha*). The *spatha* is always worn on the left-hand side on the belt. In representations on tombstones, where the rider rides to the right, it is often wrongly depicted on the right. This inaccuracy is explicable as the intention of the sculptor to ostentatiously display the *spatha* as an important weapon.

Spears

In other respects the cavalry carried spears and various types of javelins, the iron heads of which cannot be clearly distinguished from the armament of the infantry or from that of Celtic-Germanic opponents.

Bow and arrow

Eastern mounted archers had reflex or composite bows made of wood, sinew, and bone, and arrows with trilobate heads, like those known for *sagittarii* fighting on foot.

Horse harness

For the reconstruction of the Roman horse harness there are two main groups of sources. On the one hand the 1st century AD (mostly) Rhineland cavalry tombstones, which M. Schleiermacher compiled and M. C. Bishop has discussed in detail, can be used.[502] For the later period, such as on Trajan's and the Marcus Columns, such realistic iconographic sources, corresponding to actual finds, are no longer available;[503] there is no summary of the archaeological material for this period. On the other hand, harness fittings, mostly made of copper alloy, come in large numbers from virtually every military find context. These fittings from military sites, by themselves, cannot be distinguished from the fittings of civilian riding and draft horses.

Harness components can be identified in early Augustan deposits, for example a bridle from Augsburg-Oberhausen,[504] two *phalerae* from Oberaden,[505] or a comb-shaped amulet pendant of Celtic origin from Dangstetten,[506] which can be assigned to specific riders of certain regional or ethnic origin; in this manner, cavalrymen and horses from Dacia, Thrace, and Gaul are known.[507] Soon, however, regular unified types of equipment with Empire-wide distributions

were developed, which cannot really be regarded as having a definite local origin.

For a long time in research, metal finds from the harness and bridle of riding and draft animals (horses, mules) were automatically expected to be 'militaria', especially, if they were found in camps and forts (Deschler-Erb *et al.* 1991; Deschler-Erb and Unz 1997). Behind this lay the expectation – usually unspoken – that there would have been in addition to the military, a separate different-looking civilian harness and bridle for riding and draft animals. Here, E. Deschler-Erb adopted a different position.[508] He stressed that many military and civilian harness fittings could not be distinguished, so it is often unclear whether a particular item belonged to the harness of a horse or a draft animal. He thinks he can create three criteria under which one could recognize 'military harness'. Namely, when the objects in question:

- can be identified on ancient representations of Roman cavalry;
- come from finds assemblages that are in a military context;
- are so uniformly designed and widespread, that only the military can be considered as a distributor.

When processing the rich material from the Vesuvius cities, S. Ortisi has now shown that practically no difference can be seen between military and civilian equipment of horses and mules, for harness similar to those types classified by Deschler-Erb as 'military' came from purely civilian contexts in the Vesuvius cities.[509] There is still no summary of work on harness of the Roman Empire for all time periods, M. Junkelmann providing an overview.[510] A study by M. C. Bishop only is on the material of the 1st century AD (Figs 315–16) (Bishop 1988). For harness of the late 2nd and the 3rd centuries AD (Fig. 316), there are important works by S. Palagyi, M. Gschwind and M. Schleiermacher.[511] Late Roman horse harness has not yet received a synthetic treatment.

Whole sets of fittings for horse riding have been preserved under special circumstances, as at Pompeii. There is an assemblage of Claudio-Neronian horse harness fittings from Xanten with a *phalera* bearing the punched inscription PLINIO praef(ecto) EQ(uitum). This probably does not refer, as has sometimes been suggested, to the harness of the horse of the Elder Pliny himself; it is known that he was *praefectus alae* on the Lower Rhine in the period in question (Fig. 317). Rather, this punched inscription just identifies him as the commander of the *ala* in which the former owner of the horse harness from Xanten served.[512]

A river find from Doorwerth in the Netherlands also contained the larger components of Flavian horse harness (Brouwer 1982). Enamel decorated harness fittings from the Scottish fort of Newstead (Curle 1911) can be dated

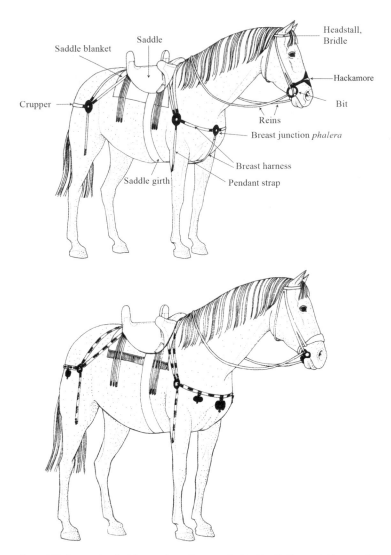

Figure 315 *Reconstructed Roman horse harness: 1 after the Gallic model (according to Bishop 1988), 2 the Tiberio-Claudian period (after Bishop 1988). Drawings: A. Smadi, Arch Institute University of Cologne*

The labels on Figure 315 (top left horse):
- Saddle blanket
- Saddle
- Headstall, Bridle
- Hackamore
- Crupper
- Bit
- Reins
- Breast junction *phalera*
- Breast harness
- Saddle girth
- Pendant strap

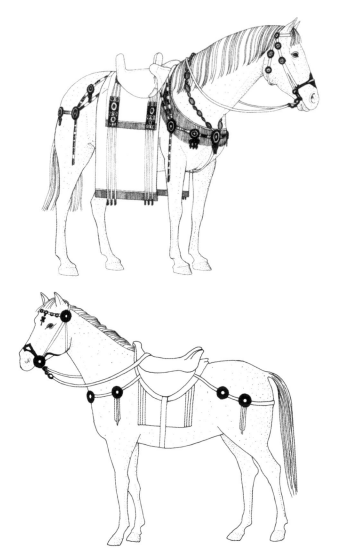

Figure 316 *Reconstructed Roman horse harness: 1 the Flavian period (after Bishop 1988), 2 the middle third of the 3rd century AD (Schleiermacher 2000). Drawings: A. Smadi, Arch Institute University of Cologne*

to the middle of the 2nd century AD (Fig. 318). From the middle third of the 3rd century AD, there is a hoard from the area of the fort of Zugmantel containing the entire metal components from riding horse harness. This was largely reconstructed by M. Schleiermacher. As for the silver horse harness fittings from the so-called Esquiline Treasure from Rome,[513] from the late 4th/early 5th centuries AD, it is not entirely clear to me whether they come from a riding horse or a draft animal.

Components of horse harness

The components of horse harness from the early and middle Imperial period are found in large quantities in military sites. Even in those cases where no violent destruction has led to excessive deposits of metal objects. This shows that, even in normal, everyday military life,

fittings or pendants were detached in large quantities from their mounts and lost inadvertently. This includes *phalerae*, pectoral fittings, amulet pendants, buckles, belt fittings and strap junctions.[514] These were normally tinned and provided with punched decoration; between the Tiberian and Flavian periods, there were also copper-alloy fittings with niello decoration (Figs 320, 321).

BITS

The many bits found could be made of iron or copper alloy or of both materials. Three main forms can be distinguished, which can occur in different variants: the ring snaffle with a single- or two-piece mouthpiece developed from Celtic models (Fig. 319), the Thracian-Italic lever bar bit (a variant of the curb), which today is perceived as very brutal, and hackamores or cavessons.[515]

Figure 319 *Iron bridle with copper-alloy cheek pieces (unprovenanced, privately owned). Photo: A. Pangerl*

Figure 317 *Niello-inlaid, copper-alloy horse harness fittings from Xanten naming the Elder Pliny (after Jenkins 1985). Drawings: A. Smadi, Arch Institute University of Cologne*

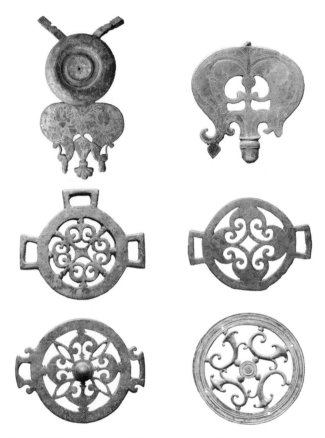

Figure 320 *Horse harness fittings of copper alloy (unprovenanced, privately owned). Photo: A. Pangerl*

Figure 318 *Horse harness fittings from Newstead decorated with enamel (after Curle 1911)*

PHALERAE

In addition to simple discs, strap junctions can also often have decorated discs (*phalerae*) of copper alloy or silver, like those known from bronze equestrian statues.[516] A *phalera* of copper sheet and a particularly complex decorated example of a partially gilded silver sheet, which are of Thracian origin, are known from Oberaden (Fig. 478.13–14). On the first *phalera*, there is the head of

a woman (?) in embossed and punched work and a canine animal is depicted on the second.

PECTORALS

An extraordinarily opulent example of a pectoral fitting is here presented in greater detail (Fig. 322). It is one of a number of metal fittings of Roman horse harness made of copper alloy, probably brass, which once probably belonged together and today are privately owned. The pieces date to the second half of the 1st century AD and were recovered as river deposit (probably from the Rhine). With the exception of the magnificent pectoral fitting, which has been artificially patinated by a previous owner, they still have the gold-coloured water patina.

Figure 321 *Horse harness fittings of copper alloy (unprovenanced, privately owned). Photo: A. Pangerl*

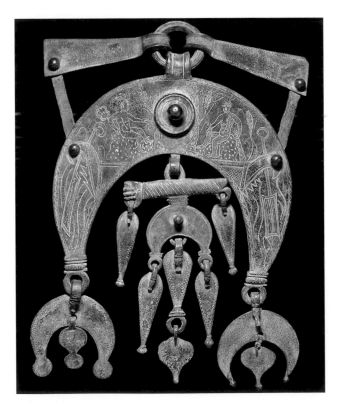

Figure 322 *Copper-alloy pectoral fitting from Flavian-period harness, probably from the Rhine (unprovenanced, privately owned). Photo: Private*

Above all, the riding harness fitting from a horse puts everything ever known in the shade in terms of size and decoration. This symmetrically structured pectoral fitting combines different pendant shapes in a unique manner that are more often found on a lesser scale and used individually on harness and which are interpreted as symbols of good luck or apotropaic magic: on a massive ring hangs a large crescent moon (*lunula*), which is decorated with incised decoration. At the top left sits the god Mercury, to the right opposite the hero Hercules. In between, a stud decorated with a spiral is attached. Below them is the steering oar, a popular symbol of Fortuna, the goddess of luck. This *lunula* is additionally connected by two metal strips with triangular brackets which extend from the upper ring. In the centre, hanging under the *lunula* from a loop, there is a transverse fitting that ends on one side in a phallus, and on the other side in a hand making an obscene gesture (*fica*). At the ends of it are respectively lanceolate pendants with terminal knobs. Under the transverse fitting, a smaller *lunula* with a decorative stud is centrally mounted, and lanceolate pendants with final knobs hanging from the terminals. In the middle of the smaller *lunula,* a leaf-shaped pendant with a final knob is attached. The smaller *lunula* and the pendant have punched decoration. The ends of the large *lunula* terminate in loops that are bordered by transverse bars. In turn, smaller *lunulae* are suspended, terminating to the left in discs, to the right in decorative studs. Beneath these hang leaf-shaped pendants, the ends of which correspond to the associated *lunulae*.[517]

STRAP JUNCTIONS

The usually circular junctions, with multiple straps converging to the rear, are also decoratively designed, mainly in the form of *phalerae*. These cover mounting loops for leather straps attached to the back. The decoration encompasses simple profiling as well as niello decoration or even figural motifs in repoussé work. They occur on the breast harness, the bridle, and the breeching.

STRAP FITTINGS

Strap fittings in various forms can be purely decorative mounts, but there are also pieces to fasten a strap connection. Their fastening mechanism could consist of a loop or a toggle.

RIBBED MELON BEADS OF QUARTZ CERAMICS

This form of decoration is mainly found used in harness, starting in the Claudian period up to the 3rd century AD. Principally found in the Claudian to Trajanic periods in the iconographic sources, as well as among actual finds,[518] ribbed melon beads are made of quartz ceramic. Their manufacturing technique originated in the East or Egypt; their production is attested in the fleet base at Köln-Alteburg.[519]

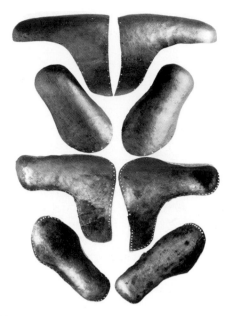

Figure 324 *Fittings from saddle straps made of copper alloy (unprovenanced, privately owned). Photo: A. Pangerl*

Figure 323 *Copper-alloy fittings from two saddles ('saddle horns') from Newstead (after Curle 1911)*

SADDLES

Usually only the metal components, the so-called saddle horns, decorative fittings, and girth buckles are found from the Roman cavalry saddle, which was designed as a saddle pad with high horns. The horn- or pad-saddle was apparently softly padded and had two metal stiffeners inside the horns to the front and rear which offered the rider a secure seat.[520] This was also necessary because the Romans still had no stirrups, which today guarantee a firm seat in the saddle. There is an unresolved controversy to this day over the detailed design of Roman saddles between P. Connolly and M. Junkelmann.[521] This involves the question of whether Roman cavalry saddles possessed a solid wooden inner structure, a so-called saddle tree, as Connolly believed, or whether they would only have had a form of seat cushion without a solid interior structure, as M. Junkelmann says. Both tried to prove their point of view with practical tests. The so-called saddle horns made of copper alloy strengthen the four horns of the saddle under the saddle leather from the inside (Fig. 323). So far as they can be dated, they can be assigned to the Augustan to Flavian periods.[522]

Rectangular decorated plates for straps that hang down from the saddle, covered with openwork or boss ornamentation, can be found on the very naturalistic images of the horse of early Imperial cavalry tombstones.[523] They are often found among original material of the Augustan to Flavian periods (Fig. 324).[524] M. Bishop has also compiled saddle girth buckles of copper alloy or iron.[525] Isolated finds of saddle leather are currently not sufficient to reconstruct the Roman saddle completely unambiguously (Groenman van Waateringe 1967; Winterbottom 1989).

STIRRUPS AND SHOEING – A NEGATIVE RESULT

Compared with later periods, some essential details in the equipping of Roman riding and carriage horses were absent in antiquity.[526] Thus the stirrup, which, coming from central Asia, only arrived in central Europe in the 6th century with the armoured cavalry of the Avars. It was then immediately adopted everywhere.[527] Likewise, fixed shoeing in the form of the horseshoe first appeared in the Middle Ages.[528] In ancient times, there were only detachable iron hipposandals, probably meant especially for pack animals,[529] which were used for dangerous tracks or hoof diseases.

Parade weapons

For tournament-like equestrian games, which served both for military training as well as a spectacle for onlookers, Roman cavalry had their own parade armour, which is described by the term 'parade armour' in the literature.[530] It is still to some extent the subject of scholarly debate as to which individual items of equipment are to be classified as parade armour and which as combat equipment. In many cases, the so-called 'cavalry treatise' of Flavius Arrianus written in AD 136 gives clear instructions on this. Here, the essential components of parade armour are mentioned and described,[531] so that they can easily be matched with the archaeological material. Arrian mentions:

- gilt helmets of iron or bronze, which protect the face (with openings for the eyes) and bearing plumes;
- so-called 'Cimmerian robes' as body armour (a kind of *linothorax*?);
- lightweight shields;
- horse chamfrons;
- dragon standards.

Researchers have assumed that the existing metal components of parade armour were distinguished from combat equipment by particularly rich decoration. This is undoubtedly the case with face-mask helmets, horse chamfrons, greaves, and *phalerae*. Here, particularly martial goddesses, gods, and heroes, as well as specific military symbols, are found in repoussé work. Minerva, Mars, Victoria, Hercules and Dioscuri, the eagle of Jupiter, snakes, sea dragons (*ketoi*), dolphins and lions are known, for example. In addition to the rich repoussé work, the decorative effect is enhanced by gilding, silvering, and tinning. E. Künzl has collected these decorative motifs and statistically ordered them based on their frequency (Künzl 2004). Numerous new discoveries, which have since come to light, make it seem advisable to review these statistics.

One can assume that two teams would have been clearly distinguished by clothing and equipment at the tournaments. If this depended upon colour or type of garments, then it is no longer detectable. With face-mask helmets, by contrast, the differences in the form of 'male' and 'female' helmets are clearly visible (see below). Theories that the two teams mentioned by Arrian as fighting each other in exhibition fights were Greeks and Trojans have not really been verified.

In discussion of parade armour, it has repeatedly been overlooked that – especially from the second half of the 2nd century AD – there are also cavalry helmets and fasteners of mail and scale cuirasses manufactured and decorated in a similar way to parade armour. For this reason, decorated operational equipment of infantry and cavalry were completely indiscriminately declared to be parade armour.[532] The assertion that it is also possible to distinguish parade from combat equipment by the considerably thinner metal sheet used, are unsustainable.[533]

Oriental migrant craftsmen were occasionally postulated for the production of the components of parade armour, for example, in the area of the Raetian limes,[534] but there are indications that there were local workshops that were able to produce parade equipment on all sections of the frontier.[535]

Components of parade armour are particularly common finds in burning and destruction layers or the hoards of the late *limes* from the period around the middle of the 3rd century AD. Pieces of parade armour with known finds contexts were found mainly in the frontier area of the province of Raetia. This is due to the fact that here, in addition to a good excavation record in the region, the frontier defence garrisons were obviously overrun in a surprise attack in the year AD 254, and thus a lot of relevant artefacts were buried (Fischer 1999a; Reuter 2007).

Face-mask helmets

As a rule, face-mask helmets are assigned to the Roman auxiliary cavalry parade armour by researchers.[536] This is confirmed by the information provided in the aforementioned cavalry treatise by Arrian.

There is a proposal by Marcus Junkelmann that face-mask helmets were also useful in combat – at least, the early and more stable forms, such as Kalkriese and Nijmegen

types (Junkelmann 1999). He justifies this with practical tests. Now, even such an experienced battle re-enactor as Junkelmann cannot claim that he has really tested his theory in realistic cavalry battles, because he would have problems with the authorities! Real combat might have brought quite different demands to the reenactment display. Only a small slip of the helmet, for example, from a blow or hit with a projectile, and the rider is blind! If it had really been possible to fight with masks that cover the whole face so easily, then the helmets with removable mask of the Kalkriese type or the Pfrondorf type three-piece face-mask helmets with a removable face insert would have been completely pointless!

Parade equipment includes two-piece mask helmets made of iron or bronze, which consist of a face-mask and bowl. Apart from a clumsy forgery, there have been no purely silver face-mask helmets.[537] The silver part of the Germanic face helmet from Thorsberg Moor[538] was therefore unlikely to be have come from a face-mask helmet but from the silver face part of a figure of a Gallic god.[539]

The face-masks were made of iron or copper alloy and normally beaten out. The almost unique cast copper-alloy face-mask from Dormagen is an exception (Gechter and Willers 1996). Just one other cast face-mask from the early Kalkriese type is known. Face-masks made of copper alloy may be wholly or partially tinned, silver- or gold-plated. On iron face-masks, a coating of silver sheet has so far been detected only on the face-mask from Kalkriese and the helmet from Hama (Syria).

There are helmet bowls of copper alloy, iron, or of iron with overlays of copper alloy. Examples with a brow guard, without a brow guard, with or without a diadem, with male or female hairstyles, and those in the form of Phrygian cap can be differentiated (Robinson 1975; Garbsch 1978; Junkelmann 1997).

On the ownership of parade armour, Jochen Garbsch said:

> As with other pieces of equipment, Roman soldiers have often stated their names and detachments on helmets and other pieces of parade armour with punched or incised inscriptions. Sometimes multiple users are even attested in succession, an indication of the durability and value of the equipment as well as of the fact that they were state property, not personal property.[540]

Such an interpretation can only astonish, because in the case of combat equipment, ownership inscriptions, together with other arguments, are rightly regarded as indications of private property!

The more helmets come into circulation – unfortunately mostly not from properly observed professional excavations – the harder it is to find a typology that is at least fairly reliable, in order to organize them reasonably sensibly. Even more than the battle helmets of the infantry and the cavalry, parade helmets were customized products. So it is about time to deal with this category of finds comprehensively and in detail, in order to work out possible temporal and regional distribution patterns. With only a superficial point of view, recognising these is so far still in its infancy.

ORIGINS

There was already a helmet with a face mask depicting a bearded man's face in the Hellenistic period – such as on a weapons frieze from the Temple of Athena in Pergamon from the first half of the 2nd century BC.[541] On the same relief, a horse chamfron adorned with feather plumes can also be seen covering the entire head of the horse. Otherwise, contemporary Hellenistic types of weaponry are depicted. Cheek pieces representing bearded human cheeks were already in use in earlier Greek helmets, such as a Thracian helmet of the Phrygian type from the 4th century BC, which was found in Bulgarian Kovacevica.[542]

Considering all the theories on the origin of Roman face-mask helmets, whether from the East, from Thrace, or from the Italo-Etruscan region, Junkelmann chose to identify a Hellenistic origin. He cannot explain how far the tradition went back and what the purpose of these full or partial face-mask helmets was in Hellenistic military affairs. Nothing can be added to this in the absence of any pertinent new discoveries or the advent of a new, more plausible explanation.

A strange one-piece copper-alloy helmet is sometimes placed at the beginning of development, decorated with the face and hairstyle of a man with a full beard (Fig. 325). It has no obvious context from Semendria in Serbia and for stylistic reasons is dated from the 1st century BC up to the beginning of the 2nd century AD, although Junkelmann would not rule out an even earlier date.[543] That is hardly a sound basis for detailed chronological discussions on the relationship of the other face-mask helmets to this unique piece![544]

The first really datable examples of face-mask helmets are the iron face-masks of the Kalkriese type from the eponymous locality and from Haltern. Face-mask helmets of various types are now represented in Roman military contexts up to the end of the 3rd century, their proliferation among the assemblages of the 3rd century having less to do with increased use at this time, but rather just with the circumstances in which they were deposited in those turbulent times, and thus they survived until today. Face-mask helmets were no longer in use in the Late Roman period.

TYPOLOGY

In a typology of this group of artefacts, it is important to note that most of the many face-masks were found without associated bowls. The much rarer isolated bowls, as well as the isolated face-masks, cannot automatically be combined into particular helmet types. Instead, the few complete

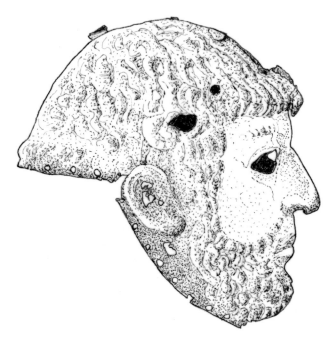

Figure 325 *Face-mask helmet made of copper alloy, Semendria/Serbia (Robinson 1975). Drawing: A. Smadi, Arch Institute University of Cologne*

helmets demonstrate that very similar types of masks can often belong to very different types of bowls, which then often contradict the current thinking. Thus, for example, face-masks with the Alexander hairstyle and the so-called Asian face-masks with the vertically piled-up coiffure of curls have been constructed into the equipment sets of two different teams, who would have faced each other in tournaments as opponents. However, among the face-masks with the Alexander hairstyle, there are both the correct bowls with the appropriate curly hair and those with Phrygian caps, which, as a headgear with an Eastern origin, might rather be expected to belong to the 'Asian' face-masks with curls.

Robinson (1975), Garbsch (1978) and Junkelmann (1996 and 1997) designated all other types of decorated cavalry helmets (pseudo-Attic and pseudo-Corinthian helmets) as parade armour and forced them into a consistent typological scheme together with face-mask helmets. However, this would have the consequence that – apart from all other counterarguments – cavalry combat helmets no longer existed from the second half of the 2nd century.

A sensible helmet typology for face-mask helmets, which is as open as possible, should be based as far as possible on genuine parade equipment and complete helmets and summarize the characteristics of the face-masks and bowls. However, even then it is not always possible to insert the known material in an overarching, clear, and unambiguous typological template. After weighing all of these contradictions and problems, I propose the following grouping of face-mask helmets.

Figure 326 *Kalkriese-type face mask of copper alloy (unprovenanced, privately owned). Photo: Private*

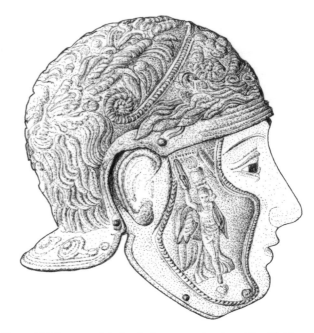

Figure 327 *Face-mask helmet of copper alloy from Vize (Robinson 1975). Drawing: A. Smadi, Arch Institute University of Cologne*

FACE-MASK HELMETS WITH MASKS WITHOUT A MALE HAIRSTYLE

KALKRIESE-TYPE FACE-MASK HELMETS

These helmets occupy an ambiguous position between cavalry and parade helmets. They actually represent a variant of the infantry Weisenau-type helmet with a removable mask. Thus, they should be seen as cavalry helmets that were worn in combat without a face-mask and in parades with a face-mask.[545] Face-mask helmets of the Kalkriese type are characterized by removable face-masks (Fig. 326) which imitate or cover only the front part of the face. Therefore, cheek pieces are needed to fill the gap between the mask and the helmet bowl, if full-scale protection of the face was to be achieved. In visual appearance, they were indistinguishable from face-mask helmets of the Vize type.

VIZE-TYPE FACE-MASK HELMETS

The helmet from Vize represents a peculiarity, which can be considered, so to speak, as a typological transition from helmets with removable face-masks of the Kalkriese type to helmets with permanently attached masks: while its face-mask of a young man has no hairstyle, it does have embossed decorated cheek pieces of a Weyler/Koblenz-Bubenheim type cavalry helmet. With their usual stylized representation of an ear, these replaced as it were the obligatory ear on the mask (Fig. 327).

NIJMEGEN-KOPS PLATEAU-TYPE FACE-MASK HELMETS

These helmets are characterized by face-masks with a forehead hinge, depicting the facial region of a young man with ears, but with no hair style (Fig. 328). The bowl is provided with a coiffure by a glued-on wig from real hair. Helmets of this type from Nijmegen-Kops Plateau date

Figure 328 *Face-mask helmet of iron with human hair wig. Reconstruction after the discovery from Nijmegen, Kops Plateau (after Meijers and Willer 2007)*

to the Claudio-Neronian period.[546] Junkelmann is of the opinion that this type of helmet, like the Kalkriese type, was a defence which, combined with the face-mask, could be worn as a parade helmet, and without the mask and with added cheek pieces, as a battle helmet.

NIJMEGEN-TYPE FACE-MASK HELMETS

These helmets are characterized by face-masks made of copper alloy with a brow hinge and depict the facial region of a young man with ears, but with no hairstyle (Fig. 329). This is combined with a bowl finished in the manner of a richly decorated cavalry helmet with a forehead diadem, ear cutouts, ear guards and embossed hairstyle. The eponymous helmet was found in Nijmegen in the River Waal.[547] The example from the late Tiberio-Claudian burial at Chassenard in France could be assigned to this type of helmet, for example.[548]

Figure 329 *Face-mask helmet of copper alloy from Nijmegen (after Garbsch 1978). Drawing: A. Smadi, Arch Institute University of Cologne*

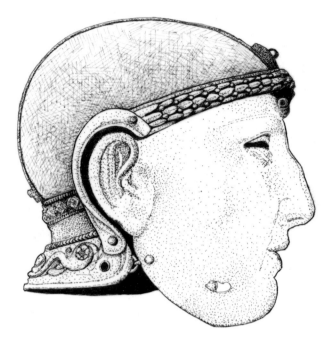

Figure 330 *Face-mask helmet of iron and silver with real hair wig (?) from Homs in Syria (Robinson 1975). Drawing: A. Smadi, Arch Institute University of Cologne*

HOMS- AND PLOVDIV-TYPE FACE-MASK HELMETS

The helmet from Homs[549] has an iron face-mask plated with silver sheet without a hair style. On its forehead there is a diadem in the form of a silver laurel wreath (Fig. 330). It is dated to the first quarter of the 1st century AD. It remains unclear what the textile cover on the iron bowl was for. It might be considered whether the substance should be regarded as the foundation for a wig-like hairstyle.[550]

The helmet from Plovdiv (Bulgaria) also has an iron face-mask plated with silver sheet without a hairstyle.[551] With its dating in the first quarter of the 1st century AD and the silver wreath of oak leaves on the iron bowl, it resembles the helmet from Homs. The iron bowl is here provided with an embossed hairstyle.

FACE-MASK HELMETS WITH MALE FACE AND EMBOSSED HAIR

RIBCHESTER-TYPE FACE-MASK HELMETS

On the Ribchester type, named after an old find from 1796 in England, the face part is that of a young man's head, only the forelocks and sideburns of whose hairstyle are visible (Fig. 331). The rest of the hairstyle is covered by a cavalry helmet, a variant of the Weyler/Koblenz-Bubenheim type. Its brow diadem is still attached to the face-mask part of the helmet, the rear part being worked like a regular cavalry helmet. At the junction with the face-mask, there is a protruding sheet in the style of a brow guard on the later Niederbieber-type infantry helmet. However, the two cannot be related for chronological

reasons, since the eponymous helmet from Ribchester is dated to at least the turn of the 1st to the 2nd century AD.[552] A complete face-mask helmet in private ownership (Fig. 332) is similarly worked, in which, however, the face-mask does not display a diadem but only the curly hairstyle.

The defining characteristic of this type, the integration of the forehead tiara, which imitates a cavalry helmet, into the face-mask, is still evident on the face-masks from Hellingen in Luxembourg and Hirchova in Romania.[553]

SILISTRA-TYPE FACE-MASK HELMETS

The bowl region is similarly worked like richly decorated cavalry helmet in this type, with ear cutouts, ear guards, and embossed hairstyle, the face-mask bearing a youthful face with curly hair and long sideburns. The helmet diadem is absent.[554] This feature sets this type of helmet apart from the Ribchester type. The Tell Oum Hauran helmet could also be assigned here (Fig. 333).[555]

I cannot understand why Junkelmann claims helmet AG 449 from the Guttmann Collection as one of the helmets of the Silistra type.[556] The rear part of the bowl is not a simulated cavalry helmet, but only stylized curly hair, so would be assigned to the Herzogenburg type when applying the criteria presented here.

HERZOGENBURG-TYPE FACE-MASK HELMETS

On this type of helmet, named after a location in Lower Austria,[557] the face-mask bears a youthful face with curly hair and long sideburns. The bowl, even on copper-alloy

Figure 331 *Face-mask helmet of copper-alloy from Ribchester (from an engraving by Th. Underwood 1799)*

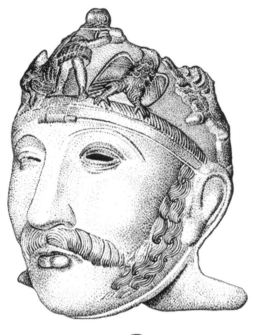

Figure 332 *Copper-alloy face-mask helmet of the Ribchester type (unprovenanced, privately owned). Photo: Private*

Figure 333 *Copper-alloy face-mask helmet of the Silistra type from Tell Oum Hauran (after Robinson 1975). Drawings: A. Smadi, Arch Institute University of Cologne*

helmets, is often made of iron, usually with decorative copper-alloy decorations. Helmets of this type possess an embossed curly hair style, but not ear cut-outs or ear guards. This type of helmet includes for instance the helmets from Newstead and Hebron.[558]

• **Herzogenburg-type face-mask helmets, Crosby Garrett variant (Figs 336–7)** – A previously unknown type of mask helmet from Crosby Garrett in Cumbria (Breeze and Bishop 2013) shows that there can always be surprises from new finds of Roman helmets. This unique piece has a face mask similar to that from Herzogenburg but a bowl in the shape of a Phrygian cap to which a moulded griffin with *kantharos* is attached.[559] A similar helmet bowl comes from Vechten in the Netherlands. Its long, drawn-out tip terminates in an eagle head.[560]

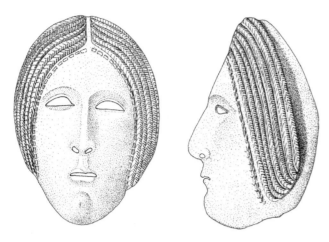

Figure 334 *Iron face-mask helmet of the Resca type from Gilau (after Isac and Barbulescu 2008). Drawing: A. Smadi, Arch Institute University of Cologne*

Figure 336 *Copper-alloy face-mask helmet with the bowl in the form of a Phrygian cap of copper alloy from Crosby Garret (privately owned)*

Figure 335 *Iron face-mask helmet of the Resca type from Straubing (after Prammer 2010)*

Figure 337 *Copper-alloy face-mask helmet with the bowl in the form of a Phrygian cap of copper alloy from Crosby Garret. On top, a cast griffin with kantharos (privately owned)*

• **Herzogenburg-type face-mask helmets, 'Alexander type' variant** – Helmets of this type in iron and copper alloy belong to the so-called Hellenistic type; in other words the face mask emulates a young man with curly hair. The characteristic two central superior locks of hair, the so-called *anastole*, imitates similar representations of the hairstyle of Alexander the Great. It can be assumed that these face masks were consciously imitating him. Some particularly good examples can be found in the Straubing hoard.[561]

FACE-MASKS HELMETS WITH FEMALE FACE AND HAIRSTYLE

RESCA/WEISSENBURG-TYPE FACE-MASK HELMETS

These helmets of iron and copper alloy have feminine features combined with a female hairstyle (Fig. 334). The eponymous copper-alloy types come from the river Olt at Resca in Romania[562] and the hoard from Weissenburg.[563] An iron example was found together with an infantry helmet of the Weisenau type in a pit at Straubing (Fig. 335). On the helmet bowls, the hairstyle is mostly decorated with a kind of diadem and crown. There are also types with a knot hairstyle, from the hoard of Eining, for

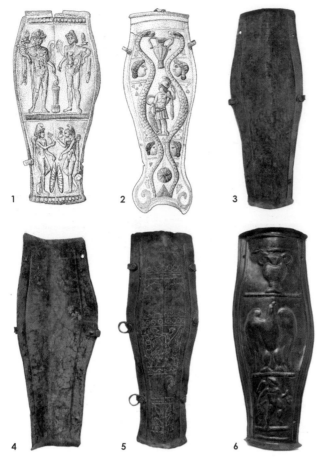

Figure 338 *Copper-alloy greaves with embossed decoration 1) unprovenanced, RGZM (after Künzl 2004), 2) Regensburg-Kumpfmühl (after Garbsch 1978). Drawings: A. Smadi, Arch Institute University of Cologne; 3–6 (unprovenanced, privately owned). Photos: private*

Figure 339 *Copper-alloy greaves with embossed decoration 1–4 (unprovenanced, privately owned). Photos: private*

example.[564] The iron face-mask helmet from the Guttmann Collection[565] which allegedly comes from Bulgaria, is so far the only complete specimen found.

STRAUBING/EINING-TYPE FACE-MASK HELMETS

Face masks with a pointed hairstyle of little curls, which is also sometimes interpreted as a fur cap, have been seen as a so-called Oriental type.[566] There are several from the hoard of Straubing.[567] An example from the Eining hoard[568] has a blue, glass gemstone on the forehead.

THREE-PART FACE-MASK HELMETS WITH REMOVABLE FACE INSERT

PFRONDORF/OSTROV-TYPE FACE-MASK HELMETS

Of these iron and copper-alloy helmets with face-mask and rear bowl component, complete or almost complete examples were found in Pfrondorf in Baden-Württemberg and in Ostrov in Romania.[569] It is characteristic of these helmets that the face-mask consists of two parts: the eyes and nose are fashioned separately and removable. In

Pfrondorf, where the mask is finished as a Medusa (so far without parallel!), it survives complete. However, eyes and nose sections also occur as individual finds.[570]

Greaves

Decorated copper-alloy greaves (Figs 338–9), sometimes provided with removable knee guards, have been attributed to parade armour, although this is not quite so certain, since they could also be used in combat. The simpler, plain style, like that from Eining, are considered parts of combat equipment, because they can be separated from the decorated copies by the use of thicker sheet.[571]

Parade armour?

In the literary tradition, it is explicitly mentioned in Arrian that the Roman cavalry did not wear metal cuirasses for their equestrian games, but only so-called 'Cimmerian robes' (a kind of *linothorax*?). Therefore, it is definitely incorrect to assign scale and mail armour from the late 2nd and the 3rd century AD with decorated fastening plates in the style of parade armour (see above) to parade equipment, as Garbsch and others did.[572] These cuirasses are, instead, combat equipment.

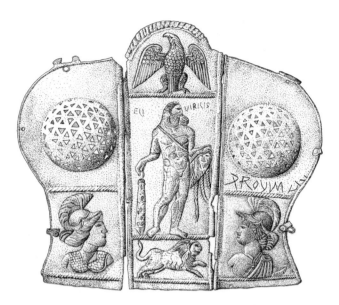

Figure 340 *Copper-alloy horse chamfron from the Eining hoard (after Kellner, 1978). Drawings: A. Smadi, Arch Institute University of Cologne*

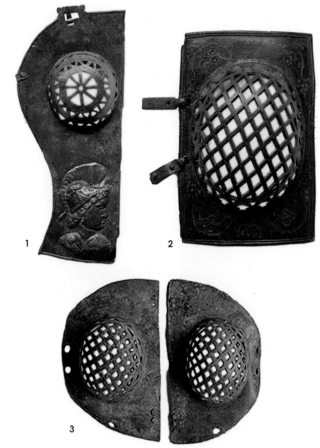

Figure 341 *Copper-alloy horse chamfrons 1–3 (unprovenanced, privately owned). Photos: private*

Parade equipment for horses

Horse chamfrons

The horses for the equestrian games were also splendidly decked out. Both as decoration and for the protection of the animals, they wore richly decorated head guards (chamfrons) of copper alloy, mostly in repoussé work, with perforated eye guards.[573] In the literature, these are unanimously considered to be parade armour. One wonders, however, whether it would not have been useful for the cavalry to wear chamfrons in certain combat situations. In addition to chamfrons made of metal, richly decorated leather specimens are also known, where copper-alloy eye guards were attached, like those from Newstead,[574] Vindolanda (van Driel-Murray 1989a) and Carlisle (Winterbottom 1989).

The all-metal types come in several variants:

- as a three-piece chamfron with central plate (Fig. 340, 341.1), covering the whole head;[575]
- as a three-piece chamfron with central plate (Fig. 341.1–3), only partly covering the head;[576]
- Eye guards without a central plate.[577]

Phalerae

Large *phalerae* provided with repoussé decoration are also considered to be a pectoral ornament for equine harnesses from parade equipment (Fig. 342–3).[578] They are also sometimes interpreted as parade shield bosses.[579] A decision in any given case can be difficult because the distinctive devices for attachment are mostly missing from these *phalerae*. A. Nabbefeld A. (2010) has published a

Figure 342 *Copper-alloy parade shield boss from Miltenberg with representation of Minerva. Photo: Arch Staatsslg. Munich*

Figure 343 *Copper-alloy parade shield boss with Hercules and the Nemean lion (unprovenanced, privately owned). Photo: Private*

particularly sumptuously ornate shield boss of copper alloy with a rectangular base plate upon which Dionysus is represented (Fig. 176). This shield boss is also thought to belong to parade armour.

3. Artillery

It was a characteristic of the legions of the late Republic and the early and middle Imperial period to be armed with bolt- and stone-shooting artillery. These were direct adoptions from the sophisticated Hellenistic artillery, which the Romans had already encountered in the conquest of southern Italy and Sicily. All these were so-called torsion weapons, that is weapons that do not derive their energy from the tension in a bow, but from the tension in twisted bundle of sinew into each of which was inserted a lever arm. Two such sinew bundles, held and clamped in position with washers of bronze and a

metal-studded wooden frame, formed the core of every artillery piece.[580] The missiles were bolts with long or short pyramidal tips and short feathered wooden shafts (Fig. 344), like those found at Dura-Europos,[581] and stone balls of various calibres.

The earliest finds, from the 2nd century BC, come from Spain (Ampurias) and from the fortified farmstead at Ephyra, destroyed in connection with the battle of Pydna, the decisive victory of Aemilius Paulus over the Macedonian king Perseus in 167 BC.[582] In Imperial times, the most important bolt-shooting artillery were called *catapultae* or *scorpiones* (Fig. 345), and the stone throwers *ballistae* (Fig. 346–7).

Moulds for washers from torsion artillery (bolt-shooters) were discovered in the early Imperial settlement of Auerberg in Bavaria.[583] The parts of an artillery piece found in Cremona in northern Italy are dated by means of the named consuls for the year AD 45. It belonged to the *legio IV Macedonica* from Mainz and was probably destroyed and dismantled during the Second Battle of Cremona in the autumn of AD 69. Its metal parts, protective shield, and washers were hidden.[584] Around AD 100, there was a significant change in the construction of catapults: the metal-studded wooden frame was replaced by an iron structure (Fig. 347), which was lighter and more powerful. Here, the sinew bundles were protected by sleeves made from sheet metal.[585]

Research continues to favour the possibility that only legionary troops possessed artillery in the early and middle Imperial period.[586] In the Scottish fort of Elginhaugh, which was occupied only briefly in the late Flavian period, a washer from an artillery piece and an inwardly stepped bronze channel, which was interpreted as part of an artillery piece, have been found (Hanson *et al.* 2007). From the time shortly before AD 100, there is a lead tag naming a IVSTINVS SCORPIONARI (Nuber 1986). One might interpret these cases as legionary artillerymen temporarily assigned to auxiliary units.

In the 3rd century AD, artillery pieces in auxiliary forts at High Rochester near Hadrian's Wall or Rainau-Buch on the Raetian limes can be deduced from the finds. At High Rochester, a '*ballistaria*' is mentioned on an inscription

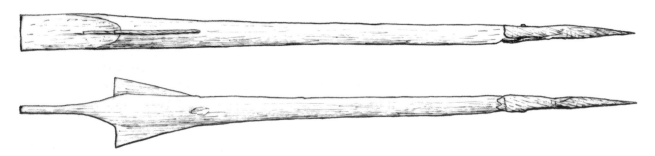

Figure 344 *Artillery bolts from Dura-Europos (after James 2004). Drawings: A. Smadi, Arch Institute University of Cologne*

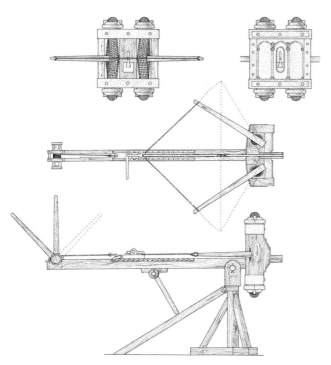

Figure 347 *Reconstructed bolt-shooter of the later type. Photo: J. Pogorzelski*

Figure 345 *Reconstructed bolt-shooting artillery piece (after Baatz 1994). Drawings: A. Smadi, Arch Institute University of Cologne*

Figure 346 *Reconstructed ballista. Photo: J. Pogorzelski*

Figure 348 *Wheeled bolt-shooting artillery piece from Trajan's Column (after Bartoli and Dzur 1941)*

dating from the early 3rd century AD, whatever that might have been.[587]

In Rainau-Buch, a hoard of bolts dating back to the middle of the 3rd century AD was discovered in the *armamentaria* during the excavations of the Reichslimeskommission.[588] Bolts are also found in many other auxiliary forts, although they can also easily be confused with cavalry javelins. Thus it remains unclear for the 3rd century AD to what extent the artillerymen in forts were auxiliary soldiers or detached legionary troops.

Lighter torsion artillery could be shot manually without a mount, as with the so-called *cheiroballistra* of Heron,

which has now been meaningfully reconstructed by Christian Miks (Miks 2001). However, whether the small torsion artillery piece which was dredged from the Rhine gravel near Xanten could be really shot by hand is doubtful. Like J. Schalles, I can better imagine it mounted instead.[589] There were also hand weapons such as crossbows, although normally used only for hunting.[590]

4. Standards and instruments for signalling

Standard-bearers and military musicians were important specialists in the Roman army who both served as non-commissioned officers (*principales*). Together they formed the 'signal corps' of the Roman army and also appeared together on various ceremonial occasions. It is appropriate

Figure 349 *Tombstone of the 14th Legion's eagle bearer Cn. Musius from Mainz (after Alexandrescu 2010). Drawing: A. Smadi, Arch Institute University of Cologne*

their instruments: there were *tubicines*, *cornicines*, and *bucinatores*. They could also be classified as *immunes* only and were thus ranked below the *principales*.

Standard-bearers enjoyed a higher rank than army musicians. They had opportunities for advancement into the centurionate. Both groups maintained their *esprit de corps* in special colleges. Standard-bearers are depicted on tombstones equipped like ordinary infantrymen. However, instead of the *scutum* or oval shield, they often carried small round shields (*parmae*), which could have an animal skin cover.[591]

The task of both groups was varied in functional and representative ways: in battle, the standard-bearers had to hold upright the various standards to clearly mark the position of the individual sub-units. These standards were similar to today's regimental flags, also the core of the unit tradition and proudly carried in front of troops in parades or even in a triumphal procession.

The role of army musicians was to convey the orders of the commander of the troops in battle with the aid of pre-arranged, easily audible acoustic signals. In camp, they also had the duty of marking the hours of the day and the division of military service, such as relieving the watches, with appropriate acoustic signals. They also organized festive marches right up to the triumphal procession with musical performances.

Standards

In many cases, the shape of standards has been supplied by literary descriptions and illustrations, but with little by way of actual finds. All these documents were collected by Alexandrescu in 2010.[592] If the standards of the Praetorians and legions, even individual units, used to be optimistically identified on the iconographic sources, then the latest examination by Alexandrescu painted a rather sober picture that does not always produce clear results.[593] Apparently artistic licence took precedence over the will to produce a factually accurate representation in the depiction of military standards. It is also clear that not all the standards of a unit were used for signalling in battle, some also being for purely representative and ceremonial purposes.[594]

Alexandrescu divides the standards of the Imperial army into two main groups with subgroups.[595] Apparently many standards originally go back to spears or flags on spears, as is also shown by actual finds of stylized spearheads. The distinction between military standards and badges of office or even standards of religious associations is very difficult in some cases.[596] With the exception of *vexilla* and other cavalry standards, all standards probably had an iron spear butt and a kind of one-sided, perpendicular handle made of metal, so they could be safely rammed into the ground.

that they were both presented together in a detailed comprehensive study (Alexandrescu 2010).

The standard-bearers were divided into the eagle-bearer (*aquilifer*), who held the highest rank (Fig. 349) and then came the bearers of the imperial *imagines* (*imaginiferi*), of the *vexilla* (*vexillarii*), and the bearers of various *signa* (*signiferi*). All these ensigns were present in the legions or legionary detachments (*vexillationes*), but for the cavalry only *vexilla* are known. The musicians are named after

Simple standards

LEGIONARY EAGLE

Evidence for the famous eagles of the legions only exists in the iconographic sources and texts. The eagle was the symbol of Jupiter, the standard of the legion, and could represent the Roman military in general. Legionary eagles had existed since the late Republic. They were carried by the first cohort and were under the special protection of the *primus pilus*. The eagle was depicted with outstretched or raised wings, carrying a thunderbolt in its talons. In the Republic, this was made of gold and the eagle of silver. In Imperial times, the eagle was also made from gold. That it was earlier made of silver, according to Pliny (*Nat. Hist.* 10.16), was for a practical reason: so that it was more visible. The legionary eagle was carried on a long shaft, which ended in an iron spear butt. The eagle only left camp when the legion marched out; it also possessed a protective cover that resembled a cage (Stoll 1991), as is shown by a tombstone of the Severan period from Apamea in Syria.[597]

IMAGO STANDARDS

These standards with the image of the emperor (*imagines*) were introduced at the latest in the Tiberian period. However, *imagines* were also mounted on *vexilla* and *signa*, being forcibly removed and destroyed in rebellions.[598] Their appearance has survived on tombstones: a shaft is mounted with a bust of the emperor, shown from the shoulders up. In one case, the bust is located in a kind of protective housing.[599]

ZODIACAL STANDARDS

On tombstones, but also on other monuments, there are standards with animal figures. It is not always possible to relate these to the animal totems of individual units. Another contentious issue is whether these acted as military standards in the field or for solemn ceremonial purposes.[600]

VEXILLUM STANDARDS

The *vexilla* of the Roman army were flags on spears: a crossbar was mounted on a spear below the head, where a colourful flag was fastened. While representations of *vexilla* increased from the 3rd century AD, composite standards declined. It is possible that the *vexillum* was the only form of Roman standard which was kept into the Late Roman period.[601] *Vexilla* were used by both infantry and cavalry, where they formed the only form of field standard. The vexillations or combat groups formed from legionary detachments got their name from the *vexillum* they carried. Moreover, the commander and veteran units also each had their own *vexillum*.[602]

One example of an original *vexillum* survives. It comes from Egypt (Fig. 350) and is now held in Moscow's

Figure 350 *Vexillum from Egypt (after Parlasca and Seemann 1999)*

Figure 351 *Dacian draco standards on Trajan's Column (after Bartoli and Dzur 1941)*

Figure 352 *Roman draco standard on a late Roman copper-alloy box plate, probably from Pannonia (unprovenanced, privately owned). Photo: A. Pangerl*

Figure 353 *Head from a dragon standard of copper alloy, Niederbieber (after Garbsch 1978). Drawing: A. Smadi, Arch Institute University of Cologne*

Pushkin Museum.[603] The rectangular piece of linen fabric (47 × 50 cm) features a red background with painted motifs, partly in gold, with Victoria with crown and palm fronds standing on a globe. At the four corners, right-angled ornaments (*gammadia*) have been painted and the remains of a fringe are detectable at the bottom.

DRACO STANDARDS

This standard type was adopted in the early 2nd century AD by Roman cavalry from barbarian standards, such as the wolf's head Dacian standard (Fig. 351). They were in use up to the Late Roman period (Fig. 352). In the Hadrianic period, Arrian describes their use in parade performances: *draco* standards, such as the find from the 3rd century AD from Niederbieber shows,[604] consisted of a copper-alloy dragon head 30 cm long, with the top gilded and the bottom tinned (Fig. 353). To the rear there were holes for inserting the shaft. *Draco* standards had a textile body with coloured ribbons, which fluttered in the breeze.

Figure 354 *Standards from Niederbieber, iron, copper alloy, and silver (after Lindenschmit 18)*

Composite standards

Standards composed of different elements are particularly frequently represented in the iconographic sources. Crossbars with *imagines* or pendants, *phalerae*, small *vexilla*, *peltae*, images of gods, wreaths, crescents (usually with the tips pointing upwards) and tassels were attached to a shaft, the top of which could be a hand, a wreath, or a lance tip. In addition there are the awards decorating the whole unit, such as the *corona muralis* or *corona rostrata/navalis* or *armillae* (Fischer 1988, 237). Ch.-G. Alexandrescu[605] has divided these composite standards into two groups according to the principal motifs:

PHALERA STANDARDS

Phalera standards had various kinds of tip, such as spearheads with a wreath or a hand. They were adorned with several equally large medallions, which are usually undecorated and only have a boss (*omphalos*) in the centre. Such a medallion is known from an actual find from Novae in Bulgaria. They are found until the end of the 3rd century AD.[606]

STANDARDS WITH *IMAGINES*

Instead of undecorated *phalerae*, these standards have round *imagines* with imperial busts. These field standards are notable for their wealth of (metal) wreaths, which should probably be seen as awards.[607]

ACTUAL FINDS

Chr-G. Alexandrescu has also collected actual finds of standards in her standard work,[608] but the numerous tips formed from stylized spearheads are (conveniently) only represented by a selection. The standard tip from the iron hoard from Künzing from the middle of the 3rd century AD[609] is also depicted as the tip of a shaft on the late Flavian Cancelleria relief (Fig. 29).

The only surviving set of fittings from a *signum* – the remains of a standard of the *cohors VII Raetorum* – come from the fort at Niederbieber.[610] It was found, together with the skeleton of the standard bearer and an iron helmet of the Niederbieber type, in the chapel of the standards of the *principia*. The assemblage was deposited during the violent end of the fort in the year AD 260 (Fig. 354).

The remains of the *signum* comprised an iron tip in the form of a stylized spearhead (ST 2), the left-hand fragment of the bronze base plate of a small rectangular plaque of silver plate (ST 5), 16.5×6.5 cm, bearing the fragments of a unit name (most likely COH V [II Raetorum]). In addition, there was a silver, partly gilded *phalera*, 19 cm in diameter (ST 3). It shows a Roman emperor (probably Tiberius), the triumphant commander in uniform (muscled cuirass, *paludamentum*) standing on a pile of captured weapons. Two Amazonian axes are shown emphasized on its right-

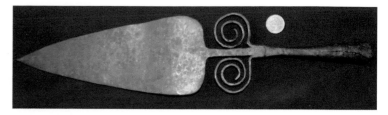

Figure 355 *Iron head from a field standard (unprovenanced, privately owned). Photo: private*

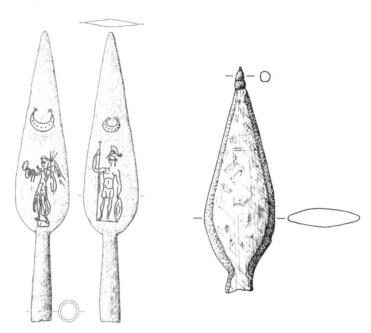

Figure 356 *Iron spearheads from standards from Eining (after Gschwind 2004) and Regensburg-Kumpfmühl (with copper-alloy edging; after Faber 1994). Drawings: A. Smadi, Arch Institute University of Cologne*

Figure 357 *Iron head of a standard with inlay. A collar made of copper alloy on the twisted socket probably served to attach a banner (unprovenanced, privately owned): Photos: Ph. Gross, Arch Inst University of Cologne*

hand side. These weapons go back to the halberds actually used by Raetians in the early Imperial period and – already misunderstood by Horace as Amazon weapons – in Roman iconography symbolize Raetia or the Raetians. The piece shows that such *imagines* were awarded to units at the time of their foundation and apparently were a 'kernel of tradition' of the unit, continued for over 200 years. Add to that a fitting of iron (ST 4), 28.6 cm wide, which Alexandrescu regards as the crossbar from a *vexillum*. More components of standards not listed by Ch.-G. Alexandrescu, such as standard tips or pendants of iron and copper alloy, are presented here (Figs 355–9).

Figure 358 *Copper-alloy standard heads (unprovenanced, privately owned). Photo: private*

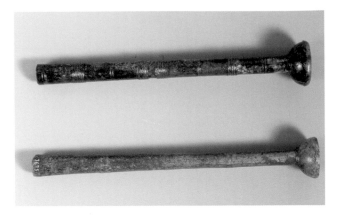

Figure 360 *Mouthpieces of wind instruments made of copper alloy from Straubing (after Prammer 2010)*

Figure 359 *Copper-alloy pendant with the portrait of Nero (AD 54–68) (unprovenanced, privately owned). Photo: private*

Signal and musical instruments

For military signal instruments, a loud, piercing sound, comparable to the fanfare, was especially important in order to penetrate the noise of battle. Various instruments were used to transmit commands in the Roman army. The

ancient descriptions, the illustrations, and the actual finds of military instruments from the Roman period were also collected by Ch.-G. Alexandrescu. To correct a widespread misapprehension from popular 'sword and sandal' films, it should be clearly emphasized here that this only related to wind instruments! The drums and kettledrums so popular in films were completely unknown in the Roman army! They are only found in European military music in the early modern period as a borrowing from the Turks. From the musical instruments of the Roman army, the *lituus*, the *bucina*, the *tuba*, and the *cornu* are known.[611] The most commonly found remains of Roman signal instruments in forts and *limes* towers are the copper-alloy mouthpieces of wind instruments, cast and finished on a lathe (Fig. 360).

Lituus

It is not quite clear whether the *lituus*, a characteristically curved wind instrument, ever played a major role in military music. Pictorial depictions from antiquity relate only to civil festivities such as processions. However, passages in the literarature mention the *lituus* used for military purposes.[612]

Bucina

The appearance of the *bucina*, often mentioned in the literature, remains unclear, because the only *bucinator* depicted on a tombstone is holding a *tuba* on the pictorial representation! Ch.-G. Alexandrescu proposes to see it as an animal horn-like signalling instrument.[613]

Tuba

The *tuba* was a straight, collapsible wind instrument in at least three parts, to which a removable mouthpiece was attached.

Cornu

This ring-shaped, curved large wind instrument is most often found on ancient depictions. It has in its developed

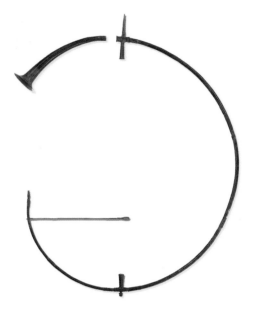

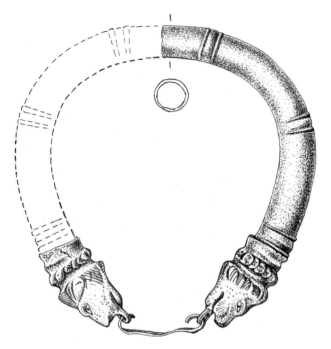

Figure 361 *Cornu made of copper alloy after Alexandrescu 2011 (unprovenanced, privately owned)*

Figure 363 *Torques, copper alloy, from Dambach (after Grabert and Koch 1986). Drawing: A. Smadi, Arch Institute University of Cologne*

Figure 362 *Brooch (2nd–3rd centuries AD) in the form of a cornu from copper alloy (unprovenanced, privately owned). Photo: A. Pangerl*

form a characteristic handlebar (Figs 361–2), some cast and decorated T-junction handle supports surviving.[614] Distinguishing between military and civilian instruments (it was used – among other things – in circus games) is almost impossible.[615]

5.   Awards and decorations

There were various awards and medals for bravery and distinguished service in the Roman army since the Republican era (Maxfield 1981), of which only a selection are mentioned here. Oak wreaths for saving the life of a Roman citizen, or wall and rampart crowns (*corona muralis, corona vallaris*) for the first to climb the walls of an enemy city or camp are known. For bravery in naval warfare, the *corona navalis* was given. Even a *hasta pura*

is mentioned from the time of the Republic. Under the Empire, the *torques, phalerae,* and *armillae* – which are archaeologically attested by actual finds – are of particular importance.

Torques were originally the typical neck rings of the Celtic warrior. Since T. Manlius Torquatus overcame a Celtic chieftain in a duel in 361 BC and took his neck ring from him as a trophy, *torques* have served as military awards in the Roman army.[616] From the *villa rustica* at Treuchtlingen-Weinberghof (Grabert and Koch 1986) and from the *vicus* (Fig. 363) of the fort at Dambach,[617] fragments of *torques* beaten from bronze sheet are known, awards of honour worn on the chest over the armour.[618]

Similarly, *armillae* ('bracelets') with snake-headed terminals are testified among actual material military awards in the Imperial period.[619] They are made of bronze, like the piece from Prutting, Rosenheim district, in Bavaria.[620] We know of silver examples from the strongroom of the *principia* at Aalen and the hoard from Causevo in Bulgaria,[621] with those from Aalen probably coming from a standard of a unit or subunit decorated with *armillae*.[622]

Discs with relief decoration (*phalerae*) were worn several at a time on the chest on crossed straps.[623] Actual finds in silver were discovered from Lauersfort at the Lower Rhine (Figs 364–5) (Jahn 1860), in bronze from Dambach and Regensburg-Großprüfening.[624] Out of the many iconographic sources, I shall only refer here to the Caelius cenotaph from Xanten (Fig. 365).

Figure 364 *The Lauersfort phalerae (after Jahn 1860)*

Figure 365 *Depictions of phalerae on: 1) tombstone of Cn. Musius from Mainz; 2) tombstone of Q. Cornelius from Wiesbaden; 3) tombstone of M. Caelius from Xanten; 4) tombstone of Q. Sertorius from Verona; 5) inscribed block from the tomb of M. Pompeius Asper from Tusculum (see Alexandrescu 2010, 329 P 11; after Jahn 1860)*

6. Pioneer tools, tents, field pack

Typical of the finds assemblages from Roman camps and forts from Augsburg-Oberhausen up to the *limes* forts of the 3rd century AD are all kinds of tools: from bricklayers' and stonemasons' tools to implements for processing metal, wood, leather, and textile. These tools were used by military craftsmen in the camp workshops (*fabricae*). Since they are, in and of themselves, indistinguishable from civilian finds, they will not be considered here in detail, reference only being needed to the standard work of W. Gaitzsch and M. Pietsch (Gaitzsch 1980; Pietsch 1983).

In addition to these military artisan tools, there are also special pioneer tools (Figs 366–7), not used by a soldier in a permanent base, but carried with him on campaign.[625] This is the universal equipment for building roads, bridges, and camps, and for felling wood for fortifications. Their use is primarily illustrated on Trajan's Column.[626]

Digression on the Künzing hoard

The large iron hoard from the armouries of Kastell Künzing on the Raetian Danube frontier has produced pioneer tools in particular large quantities. This assemblage was discovered with burnt weapons and military equipment in 1962 during excavations in the fort in the area of the *armamentaria*, which were part of the central building. With a total weight of 82 kg of iron, the assemblage provides a unique insight into the armoury of a cohort in the first half of the 3rd century AD. Besides weapons and a standard-tip, the hoard includes 7 mattocks, 12 heavy picks, 20 lighter picks, 6 axes, 12 hoes, 34 billhooks, timber nails and tent pegs, and 29 locks with manacles and chains, which should have been sufficient to restrain about 60 prisoners of war.

Figure 366 *Iron pioneer tools from Straubing: entrenching tool, turf cutter, spade iron, dolabra, and tent pegs (after Prammer 2010)*

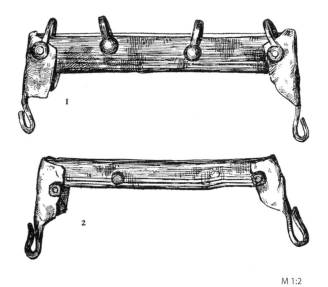

Figure 368 *Sheath fittings from a dolabra of copper alloy from Newstead (after Curle 1911)*

Figure 367 *Pioneer tools of a re-enactment group. Photo: J. Pogorzelski*

These tools have a distinctive feature that has never been properly appreciated: they are pioneer tools, as they have been known since the Augustan era, but those were considerably larger. The pieces from Künzing – *dolabrae*, picks, axes, billhooks – are all designed smaller than the earlier tools. Although they are somewhat restricted in functionality, they have a great advantage: due to their smaller size and weight, they are much easier to carry on the march. One might say they correspond to the military spades of the present, which because of their small size and light weight, can be carried on the man and can be used universally as picks, draw hoes, and spades. This miniaturization was often misunderstood or overlooked in the subsequent literature, for example, when B. Steidl considers the small axes from Künzing to be German battle axes,[627] or D. Richter maintains that the great pioneer axes of the early Imperial era were still present at Künzing.[628]

Tools

Mattock (dolabra)

The *dolabra* – the classic Roman mattock – represents a versatile, all-purpose tool that is found from the late Republic onwards.[629] On the one hand it is designed as an axe, on the other as a pickaxe. According to the depictions on Trajan's Column, it was held with both hands on a long shaft.[630] Numerous references testify to its association with military equipment, a tombstone from Aquileia naming a *dolobrarius*, a *dolabra* farrier who was a member of a *collegium fabrum*.[631] With *dolabrae* from military assemblages, pieces with socket lugs predominate. Whether *dolabrae* without this feature can really be attributable to civilian use, as D. Richter says,[632] remains to be seen. In the early Imperial period the mattock could be up to 40 cm long, but afterwards an average size of about 30 cm length was the rule. *Dolabrae* occur in two variants that affect the pick end: in a first group this is curved and mostly designed as a point; in a second group, a straight or narrowing, rather than broader, pick. Historical developments or regional differences are not observed in these devices.

The axe end of the *dolabra* was sharpened, requiring a blade sheath when not in use. This was made of copper alloy and fastened with rivets mounted on movable side panels which ended in lacing. On this, the blade sheath was attached to the axe blade with thongs (Fig. 368). A leather pad can be assumed, but has not survived anywhere. The blade sheaths were also decorated with leaf-shaped pendants, additionally sometimes being decorated with glass beads.[633]

Trees could be felled with the *dolabra*, walls demolished, and earth excavated, for the construction of a defensive ditch (Fig. 369), for example.[634] However, it was also a potential weapon, as is repeatedly reported (Tac., *Hist.* 3.28; Tac., *Ann.* 3.46).

Pickaxe

The pickaxe, which is very similar in principle to the *dolabra*, served primarily for tillage or dealing with scrub and roots.[635]

Figure 369 *Legionaries engaged in construction work with pioneering tools on Trajan's Column (after Bartoli and Dzur 1941)*

Figure 370 *Possible applications of double-ended stakes at a reconstructed marching camp. Photo: J. Pogorzelski*

Entrenching tool

This universal tool was on the one hand a hoe; on the other it had a broad blade.[636] This could be used to initially loosen hard earth during excavation of a military ditch, for example, and then drag the blade sideways and fill baskets. Modern military folding entrenching tools are also to some extent adjustable as draw hoes.

Turf cutter

This device is similar to smaller leather knives, with its crescent-shaped blade, the other side straight with a socket in the middle.[637] With a stem which corresponded to a spade, they served to precisely cut the turf used to build a turf rampart.

Axe

Large axes with socket lugs should also be counted as engineering equipment, even though they are indistinguishable from civil or military felling or carpenter's axe.[638] They served for tree felling and for finishing wood for storage or bridge construction or other purposes.

Billhook

The billhook with grip plates or sockets for handles are used for lopping branches for road or camp construction on the one hand, and on the other also for the production of leafy branches as animal feed. They seem to have been of some importance, because with 34 examples they are particularly well represented in the Künzing hoard.

Baskets (cophini)

Actual finds of woven baskets for moving earth for entrenchments or transport baskets for weapons and equipment only very occasionally survive (Gaitzsch 1986).

By contrast, their meaning is strongly emphasized by representations of entrenchments on Trajan's Column and passages in written sources.[639]

Timber nails

There are also particularly large timber nails in the Künzing find. These were carried for the construction of wooden structures (towers, warehouses, bridges), but also of vessels (boats, ferries) on campaign.

Palisade stakes

Double-ended, pointed rectangular-sectioned wooden stakes with handles in the centre, found in Oberaden and at Welzheim, have long been misunderstood as so-called *pila muralia*, throwing weapons for the defence of fortifications. J. Beeser sees them as augers for drilling post holes. However, they were probably used for the erection of temporary palisades in marching camps (Fig. 370) or, with several tied together in the middle as barriers similar to the 'Spanish rider'.[640] In any case, centurial inscriptions, like the ones on the Oberaden pieces, suggest that they were frequently used equipment, carried on campaign.

Shackles and 'crow's feet'

Iron chains were also found in the Künzing hoard, coupled with lockable manacles and shackles that were used as fetters for prisoners. These were also important items on campaign. Among other things, this is supported by the representation on pedestal relief No. 16 of the Arch of Septimius Severus in Rome,[641] in which a Roman soldier leads a captive Persian in such chains.

When describing his siege works at Alesia, Caesar reports (*Bell. Gall.* 7.73) on various defensive obstacles, including iron caltrops (*stimuli*). These could in part be identified in the archaeological record at Alesia; in addition to the so-called crow's feet (*tribuli*), [642] which were mainly used against cavalry. Crow's feet are small iron objects welded together radially from four spikes, with a tip always pointing upwards. [643] These timeless, insidious devices are still in use today by gangsters and terrorists, against the tyres of pursuing police cars, for example.

Tents

The equipment of Roman troops included leather tents (*papiliones*, Figs 371–2). On campaign, the troops were housed in them ('*sub pellibus*') in marching camps. Roman military tents are very rarely found, but can be reliably extrapolated from the relatively frequent finds of iron tent pegs since the Republic. [644] However, these were also made from wood. [645] Iron tent pegs existed in two types: an older type, which was current in the Republic and the early Imperial period, consists of a perforated and sharpened stake with a movable ring through its opening. [646] The tent guy ropes were fastened to this ring. In the later version, as represented in the hoard from Künzing, [647] the upper end of the peg was not pierced. It had instead been forged to form a loop, where tent ropes could be attached.

The appearance of these tents is illustrated by the iconographic sources, [648] such as the representations on

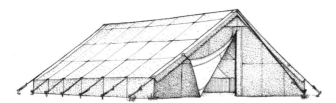

Figure 371 *Leather tent (reconstruction drawing). Drawing: A. Smadi, Arch Institute University of Cologne*

Figure 372 *Reconstructed leather tents of a re-enactment group. Photo: J. Pogorzelski*

Figure 373 *Tents on Trajan's Column (after Bartoli and Dzur 1941)*

Trajan's Column (Fig. 373): these are tents with a gable roof and straight side walls, in which one could stand. These tents were sewn together from smaller square and triangular pieces of leather. If we were dealing with fabric, such as canvas tents, larger tent tarpaulins could have been produced in one piece. Actual finds from the early and middle Imperial period confirm this, the preserved remains showing that the tents of the Roman military consisted of greased goatskin.

The tents were privately owned by the soldiers: in a papyrus from Egypt discussed by J. F. Gilliam, it is reported that, in addition to the arms of a deceased auxiliary soldier, a share of a tent was also acquired by the unit, the money then being given to the mother (Gilliam 1967). It may be concluded that every member of an eight-man *contubernium* had a share of tent, which together with the shares of the seven other companions, produced a complete tent (*papilio*) for the *contubernium*. [649] This scheme had the advantage that every soldier in a *contubernium* was responsible for his part of the communal tent, and that the social pressure of his comrades also placed great importance on keeping his tent tarpaulin functional, for instance greased, so it remained watertight. No archaeological evidence for tents is known from the Late Roman period, but they must have existed according to the literary evidence.

Marching pack

In pictorial representations, especially on Trajan's Column, marching soldiers are shown with their marching pack (Fig. 375). Additionally, Josephus (Jos., *Bel. Iud.* 3.115 f; 5.47 *et seq.*) and Vegetius (Veg., *Mil.* 3.6.13) supply more detailed information on the order of march. [650] The information from ancient authors about the weight of the baggage to

Figure 374 *Hypothetical method of scutum carriage on the march. Photo: J. Pogorzelski*

Figure 375 *Marching pack on Trajan's Column (after Bartoli and Dzur 1941)*

Figure 376 *Reconstructed marching pack with furca. Photo: Ch. Miks*

be carried on the march by the individual soldier (about 40 kg) is certainly exaggerated. Here, modern experiments provide more realistic information on the basis of empirical data.[651] Thus the load of the soldiers is estimated to have weighed between 18 and 25 kg. This includes (calculated for the 1st century AD) the following weapons and items of equipment: tunic, cloak, *caligae*, segmental armour, two belts, sword and dagger (each with a sheath), helmet, shield, and *pilum*.

Now there are certain contradictions. While Richter argues that the shields were loaded on mules or carts during marches in non-acute circumstances,[652] most reenactment groups practise wearing the shields on their backs.[653] To do this, straps are attached to the leather cover of the shields (not attested in antiquity!) and they were worn like a backpack (Fig. 374). Modern 'legionaries' have always emphasized in my conversations with them that this is a very convenient solution and also has the advantage that the *furca*, the carrying pole with the marching pack, can be supported on the upper edge of the shield (Fig. 376), which is a considerable relief for the shoulder.[654]

Josephus (Ios., *Bell. Iud.* 3.95) also states that every soldier carried a saw, a basket, a bucket, a chain, leather straps, a sickle, and a mattock (*dolabra*). However, it seems unlikely that this – together with weapons, shovels,

axes, and additional tools as well as palisade stakes – was personally carried by the soldiers. These things were surely carried on mules and wagons,[655] as well as food supplies beyond iron rations, reserve clothing, tents, and other items of equipment.

The marching pack (*sarcina*), which was carried on a wooden carrying pole with a cross-bar (*furca*), is only shown on the reliefs of Trajan's Column.[656] This is said to have been introduced by Marius (Frontin., *Strat.* 4.1.7). In addition to a leather bag (*pera*) for iron rations[657] and essential bits and pieces (knife, strike-a-light, and so on), a carrying net and a canteen, there were copper-alloy vessels (sieve/scoop, pans, buckets) and a wineskin (*uter*) attached to it. In experiments, this marching pack weighed between 16 and 18 kg. I have already pointed out the possibility of the *furca* being supported on the shield strapped to the back, which is not supported by the ancient sources, however.

Notes to Part III

1. Ubl 2013, 476–81; Fahr and Miks 2001; Bishop and Coulston 2006, 253f; Hoss 2010, 115f.
2. See Marquart 1986 II, 550–72.
3. Paetz gen. Schieck 2010, 93 and 2011.
4. Sumner 2002, 2003 and 2009; Böhme-Schönberger 2009; Wild 2010.
5. Ubl 2013, 484; Bishop and Coulston 2006, 110f.
6. On the tunic generally: Marquart 1886, 550–2; Pausch 2003; for the military tunic Ubl 2013, 481–534; Richter 2010, 37ff.
7. Ubl 2013, 483–92.
8. Ibid., 492–509.
9. Ibid., 493.
10. Ibid., 498.
11. Ibid., 517–34. Pausch 2003, 197.
12. On under tunics Pausch 2003, 143–51; two tunics are clearly visible superimposed with the soldiers on the Hadrianic relief at Chatsworth, for example (Boschung *et al.* 1997, 77ff, No. 76; Plates 67–9.); Paetz gen. Schieck 2010, 94).
13. For instance in numerous representations on Trajan's Column (Richter 2010, 148–51); see also some soldiers on the Hadrianic relief at Chatsworth (Boschung *et al.* 1997, 77ff, No. 76; Plates 67–9).
14. Speidel 1999; Paetz gen. Schieck 2010, 92f.
15. Fuentes 1987; Obmann 1999, 192,
16. Himmler 2010, 32.
17. Ubl 2013, 578–98; Richter 2010, 46f; Bishop and Coulston 2006, 111.
18. Bishop and Coulston 2006, 41.
19. James 2004, Pl. 1 and 2.
20. On these, the defeated Roman emperors usually wear military uniforms with ring- or frame-buckle belts and long trousers. See Girshman 1962, Figs 204–5; Ubl 1969, 591.
21. Richter 2010, 399; 401f.
22. *Tab. Vindol.* II.346; Sumner 2002, 42; Richter 2010, 46.
23. Müller 1873; Sommer 1984, 83–119; Deschler-Erb 1996, 84; Richter 2010, 40–6; Bishop and Coulston 2006, 106.
24. Müller 1873, 8; Hoss 2010, 124; Suetonius, *Augustus* 24.
25. Fischer 1990, 77.
26. Ulbert 1984, 69.
27. Bishop and Coulston 2006, 57.
28. Pernet 2010, 61, Fig. 27.
29. Müller 2002, 39; Bishop and Coulston 2006, 67f.
30. Ulbert 1968, Fig. 16.
31. Ulbert 1969, 9; 44f; Tab. 32.
32. Bishop and Coulston 2006, 106–10.
33. Deschler-Erb 1999, 43.
34. Deschler-Erb 1991, 22ff.
35. Ibid., 40ff; Müller 2002, 39ff.
36. Deschler-Erb and Peter 1991, 22, n.104.
37. Trumm 2001, 112ff; Jütting 1995, 193; Fig. 6, 34.
38. Müller 2002, 42; Deschler-Erb and Peter 1991, 28, esp. n.151.
39. Deschler-Erb and Peter 1991, 28, esp. n.151.
40. Deschler-Erb 1999, 44; 2000.
41. Deschler-Erb 1999, 43f.
42. Franke 2009, 20f.
43. Unz and Deschler-Erb 1996, 38; Tab. 46f.
44. C. M. Hüssen, K. H. Rieder, and H. Schaaff, 'Der Forschungsbericht. Römerschiffe an der Donau', *Archäologie in Deutschland* 1/1995, 6–10, esp Fig. p.10.
45. Wild 1970; Oldenstein 1976, 185f; Unz and Deschler Erb 1997, 37f; Franke 2009, 21; the latest example of the belt from Chichester (see above).
46. Deschler-Erb 1997, 28; esp. n.75; Miks 2007, 244f.
47. Deschler-Erb 1997; Miks 2007, 245, Fig. 44; Radman-Livaja 2010, 245.
48. Fischer 2011, 109f.
49. Maxfield and Peacock 2001, 402; 415, Pl. 14.1, 33.
50. D'Amato and Sumner 2009, 100, Fig. 100 below.
51. Bateson 1981; Deschler-Erb 1999, 41. The dating to the second half of the 2nd and early 3rd century AD proposed by Flügel *et al.* 2004 is certainly too late.
52. Thus, for example, in cremations from Neuburg on the Danube, Regensburg, Regensburg-Großprüfening, and Künzing in Raetia, and Klosterneuburg in Noricum. See Fischer 1990, 77–80.
53. Oldenstein 1976, 213–16; Nos 1009–25.
54. Fischer 1995, 342.
55. Hübener 1957, 76f, 87, Fig. 11; Hübener 1963/64, Fig. 4; Oldenstein 1976, 132–6 (where the W-shaped suspension is not taken into account); Fischer 1990, 77f.
56. Coblenz 1960; Hübener 1963/64; Oldenstein 1976, 133–5; Fischer 1990, 77f.
57. Petculescu 1995, 124f.
58. Cf. Neugebauer and Grünewald 1975, 143–66, esp Tab. 13; Fischer 1990, 80; Müller 1999, 132, Tab. 51,1–5; Ertel *et al* 1999, burial 26; 174b; Romula: Petculescu 1995, 124f.
59. D'Amato and Sumner 2009, 100, Fig. 100o.
60. Hoss 2006, 247.
61. Gschwind 2004, 159.
62. Oldenstein 1976, Nos 217–20.
63. Engelhardt 1963, pl. 11, 48.
64. Welwei 1992; Strobel 2007, 279.
65. Hoss 2006, 239, Fig. 2.
66. Schnurbein 1977, 87–91. On Germanic ring-buckles see Schach-Dörges 1998, 628–32. Particularly interesting in comparison with the Roman belt fittings is the reference to the Elbe-Germanic woman's grave from Erlbach from the second half of the 3rd century and related finds assemblages where belt rings were each combined with two strap ends (as in the Roman belts!).
67. Hermann 1983, Tab. 2, Triumph of Shapur, central scene.
68. Ubl 2013, 227–39; Fischer 1990.

69. Oldenstein 1976, 221; Nos 1070–1; James 2004, 100; See also the review by M. Gschwind of James 2004 in *JRA* 20, 2007, 622.
70. Fischer 1990, 78; Tab. 108B, 1–3.
71. Ubl 2013, 239–42; Oldenstein 1976, 233, Fig. 14, 1.
72. Ubl 2013, 241.
73. Obmann 1997, 55.
74. Oldenstein 1976, 222f; von Schnurbein 1977, 87; Gschwind 2004, 164–70.
75. Oldenstein 1976, 232f; Fischer 1988, 187.
76. Gschwind 2004, 169f.
77. Schnurbein 1977, 87.
78. Thus, for example, in Regensburg grave 284, grave 664 (Schnurbein 1977, Taf 56; 82); Mangolding grave 7 (Fischer 2000, Tab. 126B, 1–3).
79. Fischer 1988, 185f.
80. Cf. Oldenstein 1976, Nos 339–40; James 2004, Nos 147–9.
81. James 2004, 101; 96ff.
82. Fischer 1988; Quast 2009, 37; Fischer 2013.
83. Oldenstein 1976, 218f.
84. For central European Barbaricum see for instance Madyda-Legutko 1983, 104–12 or the belt from Gommern of around the middle of the 3rd century AD; Becker 2010, 79–88). Sackrau grave I: Quast 2009, 36; Stráže: Quast 2009, 36–8.
85. Ilkjær 1993. These findings are from a time when ring- and frame-buckle belts had not yet been introduced into the Roman army.
86. See. K. Raddatz, *Der Thorsberger Moorfund. Gürtelteile und Körperschmuck*. Offa Bücher 13 (Neumünster 1957). Here, however, parts of horse harness and *baltei* are listed as belt components.
87. Becker 2010, 79–88.
88. Best documented and processed at Illerup-Ådal (Ilkjær 1993).
89. Bishop and Coulston 2006, 218–24.
90. On propeller fittings of silver, see Keller 1971, 67; Böhme 1986a; Bishop and Coulston 2006, 220. In gold: Heurgon 1958, 48–50; pl. 5,1; A. Yeroulanou in: Daim and Drauschke 2010, 339, Fig. 2.
91. Böhme 1974, 1986b; Bishop and Coulston 2006, 220–4.
92. Bishop and Coulston 2006, 223.
93. Schulze-Dörrlamm 2009, 6–35 has divided the buckles without fittings into 15 different types, the buckle plate fittings (ibid., 36–83) into 20 types. They run up to the end of the 6th century AD and mark the transition from Roman to Byzantine and early medieval Germanic belts. The latter are then represented by the buckles with cloisonné lashing fittings of the second half of the 5th and the early 6th centuries AD (ibid., 84–145).
94. Ubl 2013, 535; Kolb 1973.
95. Bishop and Coulston 2006, 111.
96. Ubl 2006, 266, esp. n.39; 271f.
97. Kolb 1973; Ubl 1969, 536–48.
98. Brilliant 1967, Pl. 55a.
99. Kolb 1973, 110.
100. Ubl 1969, 548–70.
101. James 2004, Pl. 1 and 2.
102. Ubl 2013, 570–8.
103. Speidel 1999; Paetz gen. Schieck 2010, 92.
104. Martell 2001, 249.
105. From the rich literature see for instance Ulbert 1959, 67f; Müller 2002.
106. It is of course impossible within the confines of this contribution to fill the lacunae from assembling a full collection of Aucissa brooches outside the North-Western provinces. So only a few examples will be mentioned here: Olympia: H. Philipp, 'Bronzeschmuck aus Olympia' in A. Mallwitz (ed.), *Olympische Forschungen* 13 (Berlin 1981), 328–34 (also mentioning other examples from Jerusalem and Greece: Dodona, Karapanos, Aigion, Delphi, Corinth, Athens, Eitresis, Thessaloniki); Troy: three copies in H. Dannheimer and W. Menghin (eds), *Schliemann und Troia*, Ausstellungskat. Prähist. Staatsslg. 21 (Munich 1992) 111f; Dura-Europos: Ulbert (see n. 5) 68, note 68; North Africa: M. Mackensen, 'Eine augusteische Hülsenscharnierfibel aus der Provinz Africa Proconsularis', *Germania* 79, 2001, 143–50.
107. Fischer 2010, 106f.
108. E. Müsch and S. Pechtold, 'Beobachtungen zur Herstellungstechnik eiserner Aucissafibeln aus Haltern', in Müller 2002, 85–108.
109. Böhme 1972, 17–22.
110. Ibid., 36–46.
111. Bishop and Coulston 2006, Pl. 8a and b.
112. Böhme 1972, 45f; Fundlisten 45/46, 69f; Tab. 30–1; Fischer 2011, 107.
113. Böhme 1972, 29f; Fischer 1988, 167ff.
114. Keller 1971, 171ff; Pröttel 1988; Gschwind 2004, 190–8; esp. n.824.
115. Ubl 2013, 481; Richter 2010, 39f; Paetz gen Schieck 2010, 93; Löffl 2012.
116. Ubl 2013; Richter 2010, 45f.
117. Sumner 2003, Tab. C1.
118. Cowan and McBride 2008, 27.
119. Sumner 2003, 38; Pritchard 2004; James 2004, 108f; 144f; Mannering 2006, 153–9.
120. Göpfrich 1986, 16–50; Gannser-Burckhart 1942.
121. Richter 2010, 49–54.
122. Hoss 2010, 120, esp. n. 46.
123. Richter 2010, 51; 102; Bishop and Coulston 2006, 111ff.
124. Van Driel-Murray and Gechter 1983, 16–24; Richter 2010 51f; Himmler 2012a.
125. *Tab. Vindol.* II.346; Sumner 2002, 38 and 2003, 35f; Richter 2010, 53f; Bishop and Coulston 2006, 113.
126. Iron men with heavy armour: Tac., *Ann.* 3.43; 44ff.
127. Harl 1996, 602; Coulston 2003.
128. Bottini *et al.* 1988, 541f., No. 120f.
129. In the British Museum (London). There is a C14 date in the 3rd century AD. Sumner 2007, 117; Glad 2009, 46, esp. n.207; 146, Fig. 6, 5.
130. For example, going back on the ideas of Klumbach 1974, 45–54; even the bronze Weisenau-type helmet, Niedermörmter variant, is interpreted by him as belonging to the legionary cavalry, despite its ownership inscription from the 30th legion (Klumbach 1974, 39). Waurick 1988a, 361 also still represents the opinion that Niederbieber helmets were worn by the cavalry. This view ultimately derives from Lindenschmit 1911, 121.
131. Waurick 1988a, 359 has already seen this correctly.

132. Petculescu 1990, 848; Fischer 1991, 130f.

133. Still useful for the typological method: Eggers 2004, 88–105; see also Eggert 2001, 133–42; 181–200.

134. Bishop and Coulston 2006, 100f.

135. Junkelmann 2000, 45–92; Waurick 1988a.

136. Bishop and Coulston 2006, 104.

137. Junkelmann 2000, 46. This basically correct critical remark on pseudo-Darwinian development models, however, does not prevent Junkelmann from giving his graphically translated helmet typology in Foldouts I and II, a design characterized by quasi-vegetal motifs. Here a 'classic Darwinist' representation suggests a consistent and straightforward development. A 'box scheme' like that Waurick 1988a created in Appendix 2 would have been better and more consistent.

138. Couissin 1926; Klumbach 1961, 1973 and 1974; Klumbach and Wamser 1976/77; Waurick 1988a.

139. I have thought such a renaming necessary for some time. I had earlier named the newly discovered helmet purchased by the Römisch-Germanisches Museum Cologne as Weisenau type, Cremona variant. At the time there seemed little sense in undertaking a fundamental review of all the existing helmet typologies in the publication of a single helmet find, even though I already had considered the ideas of a reclassification of the material presented here. See Fischer 2004, 70, esp. n.18.

140. Schaaff 1988, 318; Junkelmann 2000, 52–65; M. Mazzoli in Schoenfelder 2010, 38–41.

141. Schaaff 1988, 318f; M. Mazzoli in Schoenfelder 2010, 40.

142. This is only to be agreed. However, this basic work cannot be done in the present book. A more comprehensive study on Italian helmets with crest knobs and their derivatives is currently being undertaken by M. Mazzoli (Mainz).

143. Robinson 1975, 13–41.

144. Junkelmann 2000, 60.

145. Ibid., 60ff.

146. Schaaff 1988, 324–6, esp 324 map Fig. 9; Junkelmann 2000, 62–5.

147. Waurick 1988a, 351f.

148. Klumbach 1974, 20f.

149. Junkelmann 2000, 66.

150. U. Schaaff in Bottini et al. 1988, 324 Fig. 8; Waurick 1990; Feugere 1994, 43.

151. Feugere 1994, 43f.

152. The designation as a Hagenau type (type de Haguenau) goes back to Couissin 1926, 329. He was referring to Lindenschmit 1911, 5 Tab. 34.

153. Robinson 1975, 26–41.

154. Oberaden 1942, 161, No. E 105a. Pl. 53. Unfortunately, this unique helmet was never restored, being lost in the bombing campaign. Following Albrecht, three rivets were visible on the centre of the inside of the bowl, probably from a device for fastening the helmet crest. Correct description at Robinson 1975, 28f., Pl. 45 and especially at Müller 2006, 300f; described as a Weisenau-type helmet at Waurick 1988a, 327, esp. n.3.

155. Thus still Klumbach 1974, 12.

156. Robinson 1975, 39ff; Figs 84–7; 49.

157. Ibid., 30f, Fig. 46, 47; Müller 2002, 34, 181, pl. 39f., No. 430.

158. For this helmet and its find history, see A. Radnoti, 'Ein Legionärshelm aus Burlafingen, Landkreis Neu-Ulm' in *Aus Bayerns Frühzeit. Friedrich Wagner zum 75. Geburtstag* (München 1962) 157–73; Robinson 1975, 36f, Figs 77–80 ('Coolus type G'); 40, Fig. 48; Mackensen 1987 119–25; on the circumstances of deposition L. Pauli, ibid., 298–302.

159. Robinson 1975, 28ff; Figs 41–3 ('Coolus type G'); Overbeck 1983, 112.

160. Robinson 1975, 22–5, 34–6, Tab. Fig. 30.

161. Ibid., 42f.

162. Schaaff 1990, 302–11.

163. M. Jazdzewska, 'A Roman legionary helmet found in Poland', *Gladius* 17, 1986, 57ff.

164. Connolly 1989, 227; 223, Fig. 3.

165. Von Berg 2006. This iron helmet already has embossed 'stylized eyebrows' on the front, which became typical of the Roman helmets of the Weisenau type; the ribbed neck guard, however, was still manufactured separately and riveted to the bowl. The piece comes from the cremation grave of a member of the Treveran aristocracy, and is dated by the excavator to around the mid-1st century BC. It contained weapons, riding equipment, and writing implements (!).

166. Miron 1984. The unobserved and probably not completely recovered grave contained, besides ceramics, an iron razor and two iron shears, iron spearheads and a long iron cavalry sword with bronze scabbard. This weapon could suggest that the deceased fought as a cavalryman.

167. From the helmets among Celtic armament, Conolly 1989, 227, wanted to make an infantry helmet of the Agen type helmet, and a cavalry helmet from the Port type helmet. I think this is very problematic, because both types are not concurrent throughout (Port type lasts longer!) and the Weisenau type infantry helmet undoubtedly developed out of the Port type helmet.

168. Fellmann 1957, 31; 43; Fig. 15, Nos 3, 11, 18, 34, 47, 59, 71, 84, 104, 111, 119; the drawings of the helmets are not always correct when, compared with the photos; there are better pictures (photos) in D'Amato and Sumner 2009, 23, Fig. 11, 1st, 2nd and 5th row.

169. Fellmann 1957, Fig. 15, Nos 18, 84, 104.

170. Junkelmann 2000, 73 and Waurick 1988aaa, 352f suspected this without being able to prove it conclusively. Waurick, however, assumes its use by just auxiliary troops, while the legionary troops at the same time were using the Bugenum type.

171. Most recently Deschler-Erb 2004, 6.

172. Fasold 1995, 88. Now that the very similar helmet from Thür has appeared in close proximity to the alleged location of Frankfurt, the place of origin no longer seems quite so far-fetched.

173. It is originally from the Guttmann Collection and was for sale at the 60th auction on 13.10.2010 in Munich by the Hermann-Historica company as Lot No. 2190.

174. Most recently Deschler-Erb 2004, 6.

175. Harnecker and Tolksdorf-Lienemann 2004, 58, Plate 3, No. 794; Plate 4, No. 909; Harnecker and Franzius 2008, 8f., Pl. 10, 93–100.

176. The designation as a Weisenau type (type de Weisenau) goes back to Couissin 1926, 331. He was referring to the eponymous piece shown at Lindenschmit 1911, 5, Tab. 22.

177. Robinson 1975, 45–81. This is also rightly criticized by Junkelmann 2000, 72; he counters Robinson's view with his own typology (Weisenau type with 'subtypes' named after findspots).
178. Couissin 1926, 331f.
179. Robinson 1975, 45.
180. Ibid., 26. Connolly 1991.
181. Klumbach 1961, 100f.
182. Deschler-Erb 2004; esp. 10f.
183. Hartmann 1982. 9.
184. Junkelmann 2000, 138–41; No. AG 501 and 600.
185. Without location at Junkelmann 2000, 124f; 129; No. AG 292. A bronze helmet from Nidda/Heddernheim should also be included: Robinson 1975, 38f, Fig. 88 (a single example of 'Coolus type H'!); 41, Fig. 50.
186. Robinson 1975, 84, no. 235.
187. Fahr 2005, 123–6.
188. Used by the helmet from Berzovia/Berzobis in Romania; see. D. Protase and L. Petculescu, 'Coiful roman din Berzovia', Banatica 3, 1975, 85ff.
189. Robinson 1975, 70ff; Tab. Nos 175–8. In Robinson's rigid typology the piece embodies the only specimen of the type Imperial-Italic G.
190. Klumbach 1974, 37–40; Robinson 1975, 72f.
191. Klumbach and Wamser 1978, 45.
192. Ibid., 53f.
193. Junkelmann 2000, AG 534, pl. 18; 158.
194. Reis 2010, 171; Tab. 65.
195. Robinson 1975, 104f., Fig. 125f.
196. Ibid., 100f, No. 273–6; Rice 2010, 83; 171f; 224f; Tab. 52f.
197. Ibid., 100f., 277–82.
198. Unpublished; pers. comm. B. Komoroczi (Brno).
199. The chemistry of this moor has decomposed the iron components completely. Meanwhile, the helmet is newly reconstructed and copper-alloy fittings of a second specimen were found (pers. comm. researcher S. Matesic).
200. Brilliant 1967, 203f; Tab. 81; Koeppel 1990, 23; 25.
201. Vermeule 1960 (there taken for genuine!).
202. Robinson 1975, 65, Nos 150–1; Ortisi 2005, 144–7.
203. Koeppel 1985, 177, Fig. 16; 195, Fig. 25.
204. Robinson 1975, 86f.
205. Coulston 1985, 341, Fig. 26.
206. Robinson 1975, 85, Pl. 237.
207. Szabó 1983.
208. Robinson 1975, 136–9; M. Pinette (ed.), Ville d'Autun, Autun Augustodunum. Capitale of Eduens. Exhibition Catalogue 1985 (Autun 1985), no. 515, 251ff.
209. Künzl 2010, 88, Fig. 12.
210. Fischer 2008, 111–16.
211. Planck 1983, 142–4, Fig. 101.
212. Fischer 2008, 114–18.
213. Klumbach 1973; Bishop and Coulston 2006, 210.
214. Miks 2008, 5f. and 2011.
215. For example, even with Fischer 2006, 126ff.
216. Miks 2008, 6f. and 2011, 449; Miks 2011. These have now been identified as gladiator helmets.
217. Overbeck 1974, 219f.
218. Miks 2011, 476ff.
219. Miks 2008, 24ff.
220. Ibid., 52ff; Miks 2011, 456.
221. Kocsis 2008a, 256f, Taf 12/13,1; 267–70.
222. Miks 2008, 21f; Mackensen 2009, 289.
223. Ch. Miks is currently preparing a larger work on late Roman helmets. For the time being, I am referring to Miks 2008.
224. Klumbach 1973, 60f; Mackensen 2009, 292f. If Mackensen's hypothesis for the occurrence of such helmets in Pfaffenhofen is accepted, then the proof of equites stablesiani iuniores for this place (Notitia Dignitatum Occ. XXXV, 15) would be an indication of the designation of this type of helmet as a cavalry helmet.
225. Miks 1985, 13.
226. Behrens 1950, 24, Fig. 43, 1f.
227. Miks 2008, 5.
228. Mackensen 2007, 620; 622, Fig. 7; 625, n. 40.
229. Birley 2009, 47f; 49, Fig. 17 – For photos and notes I thank M. Wieland (Cologne).
230. Nicolay 2002, 364f; Figure 9 and 2007, Tab. 6E, no. 242.4.
231. Florus 2.26: Non minimum terroris incussit barbaris Cornidius centurio satis barbarae, efficactis tamen apud tales homines stoliditatis, qui foculum gerens super cassidem, agitatum motu corporis, flammam velut ardenti capite funditabat.
232. Gschwind 2004, 135.
233. Klumbach 1961, 103f.
234. Robinson 1975, 56, Tab. 121; Radman-Livaja 2004, Tab. 26, no. 127, pl. 14f.
235. James 2004, 108f.
236. Fischer 2004, 68f.
237. Klumbach 1961, 104.
238. Müller 2002, 181.
239. Robinson 1975, 15.
240. Ibid., 147–94. See now also Sim and Kaminski 2012 and Travis and Travis 2012.
241. Himmler 2010, 30f.
242. D'Amato and Sumner 2009, 91, Pl. V., 143f; Fig. 191.
243. Ibid., 90f; 143f. For protective clothing of charioteers see Ch. Jandes, Le Cirque Romain (Toulouse 1990), 86, No. 41, the terracotta figurine of a charioteer from Utica (Tunisia); 87, bronze statuette of a charioteer of unknown origin, both from Paris, Musée du Louvre.
244. Ibid., 68f., Pl. III.
245. In the British Museum (London). It produced a C14 dating to the 3rd century AD. In front. Sumner 2007, 117; Glad 2009, 46 esp. n.207; 146, Fig. 6,5.
246. Böhme-Schönberger 2009, 30f. – Selzer et al. 1988, Titelbild, dust jacket, 72, Fig. 48;. 156, No. 87. CSIR II, No. 5, 31.
247. Robinson 1975, 147–52.
248. Stemmer 1978, 2, esp. n. 11,.
249. Found in Kerch, preserved in the archaeological collection of the John Hopkins University (Baltimore, Maryland, United States). See. Treister 1994, 97f; Tab. 2 above.
250. Fischer 2004a, 133.
251. Vermeule 1959/60; Stemmer 1978.
252. A. J. Parker, Ancient Shipwrecks of the Mediterranean & the Roman Provinces. BAR Int. Ser. 580 (Oxford 1992) 156; D'Amato and Sumner in 2009, 42, Fig. 29; ibid. 2009a, 212.
253. Fischer 2004a, 133.
254. I thank N. Hanel (Cologne) for his expertise.

255. Vermeule 1959–60, 82.
256. For cuirassed statues in general, see Vermeule 1959/60 and Stemmer 1978.
257. Robinson 1975, 164–73; Bishop and Coulston 2006, 63f.; 95f.; 139.
258. Robinson 1975, 165, Fig. 160.
259. Ibid., 166f., Fig. 463–7.
260. Ibid., 164, Fig. 459.
261. Ibid., 164f., Fig. 461.
262. Tejral 1992, 396, Fig. 12, 2. Pfahl 2013.
263. Robinson 1975, 160f; Garbsch 1978, 7f; Borhy 1990; Flügel 2004.
264. Fischer 1991, 137f.
265. Garbsch 1984; Tejral 1992, 394, Fig. 11, 2.
266. Richter 2010, 25.
267. Florescu 1965, 417–72; Figs 179–232.
268. Bishop and Coulston 2006, 5f; Richter 2010, 25f.
269. Lohr and Trunk 2008, 143, Fig. 2, 4.
270. Richter 2010, 26 still represents the older view that the segmental cuirass was introduced in the Roman army during the second quarter of the 1st century AD.
271. Bishop 2002, 18f.
272. Ulbert 1970, 12–16; Tab. 4–6.
273. Robinson 1975, 174–86; Bishop 2002; Thomas 2003; Bishop and Coulston 2006, 95–100; 171ff.
274. Von Groller 1901, 95–113.
275. Ulbert 1970, 16.
276. Bishop 2002, 23–65.
277. Himmler 2010, 31.
278. Bishop 2002, 23.
279. Ibid., 31–45.
280. Curle 1911, 104–39; Robinson 1975, 179–86; Bishop 2002, 46.
281. Bishop 2002, 62–5.
282. Robinson 1975, 153–61, 164–73; Künzl 2002; Bishop and Coulston 2006, 95, 100, 139ff., 170–3.
283. Robinson 1975, 153; for incorrectly dated modern scales see Henrich 2013.
284. Bishop and Coulston 2006, 139f; Gschwind 2004, 128.
285. Von Groller 1901, Tab. 15.
286. Stiebel and Magness 2007, 1f; Fischer 2011, 107f; James 2004, 120f.
287. Tejral 1992, 393–6.
288. Von Groller 1901, Taf 15, 1–8; 10–19; 22–6; 28–35, 37; I–IX.
289. Van Daele 2005, 238f.
290. Gschwind 2004, 128f.
291. Robinson 1975, 153.
292. Ibid., 162f; James 2004, 122–5.
293. Bishop 2002, 73f.
294. Varsik 1996, 556ff.
295. Bishop 2002, 62–5.
296. Wamser 2000, 91, Fig. 69; Künzl 2002, 135; 138ff; Driehaus (†) et al. 2010.
297. Fischer 2011, 108; Pl. 27, 2.
298. Fellmann 1957, Fig. 15.
299. Robinson 1975, 188f; Fig. 510.
300. Gschwind 2004, 125f.
301. James 2004, 125f.
302. Junkelmann 2000a, 83f.
303. Bishop 2002, 68–72; Bishop and Coulston 2006, 97, Fig. 53, 2.
304. Bishop and Coulston 2006, 98–101.
305. Ibid., 141.
306. Brüggler et al. 2010; Brüggler et al. 2012. I thank M. Brüggler and M. Drechsler (Arch. Inst. of Univ. of Cologne) to be allowed to include the find here.
307. E. Künzl has described the change from the Celtic oval shield to the Roman scutum in detail from the early beginnings (Künzl 2003, 285–91). It is quite incomprehensible to me, however, that he stressed that it was a Hellenistic form, adopted by Celts and Romans. Without wishing to enter into a larger debate here, I see it differently. The original Celtic oval shield was taken over by the Romans through northern Italian contacts, and in the Hellenistic regions from Celtic or Galatian mercenaries.
308. Zieling 1989, 379.
309. Bishop and Coulston 2006, 92.
310. Nabbefeld 2008, 18.
311. See D'Amato and Sumner 2009, 23, Fig. 11, 2nd row left, 8th row left.
312. Bishop and Coulston, 2006 61–3; 91–4; 179–82; Nabbefeld 2008, 17–20; Richter 2010, 75–98.
313. Nabbefeld 2008, 220f; No. 483, Tab. 51.
314. Ibid., No. 682, Tab. 101.
315. Harnecker and Franzius 2008, Taf 5–8; 41f; Varusschlacht 2009, 65, Fig. 23.
316. Harnecker and Franzius 2008, Tab. 8; Varusschlacht 2009, 58, Fig. 4.
317. A. Rost in Varusschlacht Katalog 2009, 111; Varusschlacht 2009, 64f.
318. R. Wiegels in Schlüter et al. 1992, 383–96; Harnecker and Franzius 2008, Tab. 11; 22.
319. Nabbefeld 2008, 44f; Busch 2009.
320. Nabbefeld 2008, 20f.
321. Ibid., 14.
322. Ibid., 21f; No. 54, Tab. 10.
323. Ibid., No. 501, Tab. 62f.
324. Ibid., Nos 410–16. Tab. 42–6.
325. Bishop and Coulston 2006, 216–18; Nabbefeld 2008, 24; Nos 3–5; Tab. 2ff.
326. K. P. Goethert in Junkelmann 1996, 115–26.
327. Nabbefeld 2008, 24.
328. Ibid., 44f; Busch 2009.
329. Nabbefeld 2008, 33–41; Nos 672–6; Nos 684–5; Tab. 97–102.
330. Ibid., 23; No. 133, Tab. 15.
331. Ibid., no. 14. Tab. 7.
332. James 2004, 186f; 242.
333. Plain wooden or wicker bosses were also traditional for Germanic shields. See. Zieling 1989.
334. Stary 1985; Künzl 2003, 285–91.
335. Nabbefeld 2008, 44f.
336. Ibid., 30f., 43–7.
337. Gschwind 2004, 132.
338. Nabbefeld 2008, 220f; No. 483, Tab. 51.
339. Ibid., 50f.
340. Künzl 2010, 89, Fig. 121.
341. Junkelmann 1986, 177f; Bishop and Coulston 2006, 46; 92–4; Nabbefeld 2008, 32; 53f; Koepfler 2012; Raab 2012; Schmalhofer 2012.

342. Nabbefeld 2008, 22, esp. n.27; Himmler 2012.
343. Junkelmann 1986, 176f; Fuentes 1991, 83–8; Himmler 2012.
344. Junkelmann 1986, 202; Fuentes 1991, 86–8.
345. Vegetius, *Epitoma rei militaris* 2.16.1; Miks 2007, 20. The date of the introduction of the *semispatha* is difficult because, although Vegetius writes towards the end of the 4th century AD, he nevertheless extensively refers to older literature.
346. Miks 2007, 20–3.
347. Ulbert 1969, 44f.
348. Miks 2007, 241, Fig. 41.
349. Ulbert 1969a, 119f; Ortisi 2006.
350. Miks 2007, 66–71.
351. Ibid., 258–82.
352. Ibid., 262–80.
353. Ibid., 230; Mackensen 2002.
354. Ortisi 2009, esp. n.16.
355. Ibid., Fig. 3.
356. Ibid., 542f.
357. Miks 2007, 442.
358. Boschung 1987; Künzl 1996; Miks 2007, 241–56.
359. Künzl 1996, 400.
360. Ibid., 402–6.
361. Ibid., 411f.
362. Ibid., 406–11.
363. Boschung 1987, 234–43; Künzl 1996, 412–15.
364. Deschler-Erb 1996, Fig. 6, 8; Miks 2007, 245; Grave 5 from Ilok in Croatia: Radman-Livaja 2010, 244f.
365. Miks 2007, 244.
366. Künzl 1996, 399, Fig. 9; 407, Fig. 11; 413, Fig. 14.
367. Ibid., 426–33, Miks 2007, 282–99.
368. Künzl 1996, 430 Fig. 20, 4. Miks 2007, 274.
369. Ulbert; 1971; Feugère 1985.
370. Künzl 1996, 433f.
371. Ibid., 434f; Miks 2007, 835, No. B159; Tab. 213.
372. Miks 2007, 77–80.
373. Ibid., 71f; 115.
374. Ibid., 20–3.
375. Miks 2007, 77–134.
376. Ibid., 135–47.
377. Ibid., 161–4.
378. Ibid., 148–211.
379. Ibid., 455ff.
380. Ibid., 262–9.
381. Oldenstein 1976, 95–109; Carnap 1991; 1994; Miks 2007, 284–319.
382. Miks 2007, 284–9.
383. Hermann 1983, Tab. 2, Triumph of Shapur, central scene, kneeling Roman emperor to right.
384. Miks 2007, 284; 311f.
385. Oldenstein 1976, 110–23; Miks 2007, 319–37.
386. Miks 2007, 319–24.
387. Oldenstein 1976, 110–17; Miks 2007, 327–45.
388. Oldenstein 1976, No. 138–47, Taf 22–4; Miks 2007, 345–67.
389. Miks 2007, 367–73; 408–11.
390. Menghin 1983, 180–9; Miks 2007, 457–63.
391. Burial IV, Miks 2007, 722f, No. 655 A, 1 and 2; Tab. 72.
392. Oldenstein 1976, 223–6; 229, Fig. 11; 231, Fig. 12.
393. Miks 2007, 177–87.
394. Ibid., 208–11.
395. Bishop and Coulston 2006, 204, Fig. 129; Fischer 2006, 125, Fig. 6.
396. Martial 14.32; *RE* XVIII.2. H., 1416.
397. Ortisi 2005, 147b.
398. Ulbert 1994, 108; Obmann 2000, 14; Bishop and Coulston 2006, 56f.
399. Ulbert 1994, 108; Luik 2002, 87–90.
400. Sydenham 1301; Obmann 2000, 16, Textabb. 1; Bishop and Coulston 2006, 19, Fig. 9.
401. For this late Republican–Augustan dagger type see Mackensen 2001. Since the dagger from Taranto presented here was found with a buckle with a tongue, it is unlikely to date from before the middle third of the 1st century BC (as buckles of this kind did not yet exist then).
402. Bishop and Coulston 2006, 57.
403. Luik 2002, 90; Kavanagh de Prado and Quesada Sanz 2009.
404. Examples from Italy and Oberaden in Obmann 2000, 16; Luik 2002; Mackensen 2001.
405. G. Ulbert locates the production of this particularly richly inlaid weapon in Italy. Ulbert 1962; 1971a.
406. On the Auerberg: Wamser 2000; 318f.
407. Bishop and Coulston 2006, 86; Fig. 86, 1.
408. Fischer 2000a, 70f.
409. Bishop and Coulston 2006, 53f; 76–8; 130f; 151–3; 200ff.
410. Ibid., 52.
411. Stary 1994, 142.
412. Luik 2000, 275; esp. n.26–7, and 2002, 81.
413. U. Schaaff, *Keltische Waffen* 1990, 21, Fig. 10, the specimens 4–6 (counted from the left).
414. See Luik 2002, 81.
415. Horvat 1997 and 2002; Horvat and Bavdek 2009 136, Fig. 8.
416. Arrian, *Acies contra Alanos*, 16–17, translation by Gilliver 2007, 206.
417. Strobel 2007, 277.
418. Von Groller 1901, 126f; Tab. 23, 1–4.
419. Strobel 2007, 277.
420. Schnurbein 1974, 424–8; Ilkjær 1990; Bemmann and Hahne 1994, 408–57.
421. Bishop and Coulston 2006, 200ff.
422. Strobel 2007, 277.
423. Ibid.
424. Sumner 2007, 108.
425. Fischer 1995, 342f.
426. Bennett 1991; Völling 1991; Bishop and Coulston 2006, 200f.
427. Coulston 1985; Zanier 1988; Bishop and Coulston 2006, 58f; 88f; 134f; 164–8; 205f.
428. Coulston 1985, 285–95.
429. Rajtár 1992, 199.
430. V. Groller 1901, 126; 128–31; Tab. 23, 16–24; 24, 22–5.
431. Prammer 2010, III 16.
432. Bishop and Coulston 2006, 168.
433. Becker 2010, 103.
434. See Gudea 1994, 85 Fig. 5; Gschwind 2004, 184f.
435. Czysz 1986, 266, Fig. 5, 12ff.
436. Franke 1998; Radman-Livaja 2010, 57 No. 4; Dörschel 2012.
437. Czysz 1986, 266, Fig. 5, No. 1. Gschwind 2004, 188ff.
438. Coulston 1985, 333 Fig. 8; Stiebel and Magness 2007, 22–6; Stiebel 2003, 216f; James 2001, 91–208; Fischer 2011, 111; Tab. 27, 7 and 8.

439. Völling 1990; Bishop and Coulston 2006, 58f; 88f; 134ff; 164–8; 205f.
440. Völling 1990, 25f.
441. Ibid., 36f.
442. Ibid., 33–7.
443. Völling 1990, 37ff.
444. Ibid., 44ff.
445. Ibid., 46f.
446. Waurick 1988a, 359f; Krier and Reinerth 1993, 60–3, esp. Fig. 41.
447. Corresponding doubts by Franke 2009, I think unjustified.
448. Junkelmann 1992, 125–30; Gansser-Burckhardt 1942, 50, Fig. 31; D'Amato and Sumner 2009, 221; Fig. 310.
449. Gansser-Burckhardt 1942, 50, Fig. 31; D'Amato and Sumner 2009, 221; Fig. 310.
450. Jost 2007, 53f.
451. Ubll 1969, 236f.
452. Giesler 1978; Junkelmann 1992, 98ff; Bishop and Coulston 2006, 70.
453. Polybius 6.25.3ff; Waurick 1988a, 360.
454. In the Shelby White and Leon Levy Collection in New York. The piece is supposed to come from a grave in Bulgaria. Junkelmann 2000, 79f. See cheekpieces AG 546 and AG 547 from the Guttmann Collection at Junkelmann 2000, 165f; Fig. 92; another privately owned piece of unknown provenance is first introduced in this volume (Fig. 267).
455. Klumbach 1976, 13; 41; Junkelmann 2000, 80.
456. Junkelmann 1997, 84–8; Fig. 67.
457. L. Lindenschmit the Elder already suspected this (Lindenschmit 1882; Bishop and Coulston 2003). Upon examining these pieces in Mainz, however, I had the impression that the objects – interpreted as face-masks from a face-mask helmet – are instead rather to be seen as animal heads from the animal skin covering from standard bearers' helmets.
458. Garbsch 1978.
459. Ortisi 2009a, 43ff; Tab. 19.
460. I am not so sure that this hairstyle is really derived from the fur helmets of Alexander the Great as E. Künzl assumes. An animal fur is definitely different from human hair! In addition, the distribution of the 'hairy helmets' to date rather points to Batavians as the wearers, whose special connection to Alexander the Great is not particularly obvious to me (see Künzl 1999).
461. Klumbach 1974, 45f. No. 32; Tab. 32; Waurick 1988, 343.
462. Krier and Reinert 1993, 55–60.
463. Kallee 1989, Fig. 16; Junkelmann 2000, 85; Fig. 24.
464. Schleiermacher 1984, 90ff.
465. Schalles and Schreiter 1993, Mil 16; 191f; Tab. 28; conservation report by J. Kempkens in Schalles and Schreiter 1993, 113–20.
466. Curle 1911, 165, Plate 35, 8; Robinson 1975, 94; Fig. 246.
467. Robinson 1975, 94f; Figs 250–3.
468. Curle 1911, 165, Plate 35, 8; Robinson 1975, 94f; Fig. 246.
469. Junkelmann 1992, 191, Fig. 169, and 2000, 90f; Müller 1979, 126–8; Pl. 21, 12.
470. Junkelmann 2000, No. AG 461, 147, Tab. XIX; 159f.
471. Robinson Auxiliary Cavalry type G; Robinson 1975, 98f; Fig. 269–72.
472. Robinson 1975, 122f; Figs 352–4.
473. Ibid., 107–35; Garbsch 1978, 7.
474. Fischer, 1991, 130f; Gschwind 2004, 134ff; Junkelmann 2000, 29ff.
475. Robinson 1975, 130f; Fig. 384ff.
476. Ibid., 132f; Fig. 394ff.
477. Robinson 1975, 134f; Figs 407–10; Garbsch 1978, No. O. 58; 73; Tab. 32; better photos in D'Amato and Sumner 2009, 189; Fig. 273a.
478. Robinson 1975, 126f; Figs 370–3; Garbsch 1978, No. O. 56; 56; Tab. 27; better photos in D'Amato and Sumner 2009, 189; Fig. 273b.
479. Antike Welt 4/2011, 4 Fig. 1.
480. Künzl 2010, 90, Fig. 122.
481. Ibid., 85.
482. Robinson 1975, 110, Fig. 130ff; 129, 376–7; Figs 376–7; Garbsch 1978, No. O. 53; 72; Tab. 29.
483. Reis 2010, 225; 236.
484. Robinson 1975, 128f; Figs 378–83; Garbsch 1978, O 54, O 55; 72; Tab. 28.
485. Robinson 1975, 131; Figs 387–90; Garbsch 1978, O 62, O 63, O 64. 74: Tab. 30.
486. Junkelmann 1997, no. AG 451, 51ff; Tab. I–III; 106ff; 193, Fig. 112.
487. Ibid., No. AG 471, 54f; Taf IV and V; 109–13; 195ff., Pl. XXV–XXVII.
488. Pflug 1988, 87–99.
489. Ibid., 93, Fig. 36.
490. Bottini 1988a, 114. Fig. 8.
491. Ubl 1969, 37 has already proposed this with reference to coins of Probus. Strangely, his illuminating hint was never discussed. Rice 2010, 226, who cites this proposal, nevertheless rejects it. He does this by arguing that antiquated portrayals of Corinthian helmets often appear on Roman monuments.
492. Künzl 2010, 85. The sarcophagus is correctly dated from the representation of a ring-buckle belt and a circular chape. The fact that, according to Künzl, 'here, the dominant chape form of the 4th century already is present in the years 250/260' is not correct. In the Late Roman period, the circular chape had long fallen out of use.
493. Künzl 2010, 88. Fig. 119.
494. See: Goltz and Hartmann 2008; Hartmann 2008; Kreucher 2008; Speidel 2008, 677–84.
495. Bishop 2002, 72ff.
496. Varsik 1996, 556ff.
497. Nabbefeld 2008, 24.
498. Ibid., 23.
499. Miks 2007, 77–80.
500. Ibid., 71f; 115.
501. Ibid., 20–3.
502. Schleiermacher 1984; Bishop 1988, 67–91.
503. Bishop 1988, 67.
504. Hübener 1973, Taf 24, 15; Werner 1983.
505. From Schnurbein 1986; Kühlborn 1992, 149; Pl. 34, 75f.
506. Fingerlin 1986, 323 finds location 311, 2; ibid. 1998, 226, finds location 708, 3; 327 finds location 1040, 1; 397 finds location 1343, 1.
507. On Scytho-Thracian elements in Roman harness, Schleiermacher 1995.

508. Deschler-Erb 1999, 49.

509. Ortisi 2009a, 63f.

510. Junkelmann 1992, 76–88.

511. Palagyi 1989; Gschwind 1998 and 2004, 173–7; Schleiermacher 2000.

512. The pieces are now in the British Museum in London. See Jenkins 1985, 154ff.

513. Kent and Painter 1977, 44–9, esp. Fig. 98; Junkelmann 1992, 86f.

514. Bishop and Coulston 2006, 120–3; 145ff; 190ff; 227.

515. Garbsch 1986, 72–5; Taylor 1975; Junkelmann 1992, 11–34.

516. See the representation of *phalerae* on horse head P1 from Cartaceto (Italy), dated to around 30 BC, in Bergemann 1990 50f., Pl. 11 or on the equestrian statue of Marcus Aurelius in Rome P 51, 105–8, Pl. 80.

517. Th. Fischer in Humer and Kremer 2011, 269.

518. For the iconographic sources, see the tombstone of T. Flavius Bassus from Cologne (Schleiermacher 1984, 90ff and 1995, Fig. 2). For actual finds, see A. Böhme in Schönberger 1978, 288; Bishop, 1988, 114f, Figs 30–1.

519. For ribbed melon beads from quartz ceramics, C. Höpken, *Kölner Jahrb.* 36, 2003, 694ff; Hoffmann 2006.

520. Bishop and Coulston 2006, 120f.

521. Connolly 1987; Junkelmann 1992, 34–74.

522. Bishop 1988, 127f.

523. Ibid., 73, Fig. 8; 75, Fig. 10; 76, Fig. 11.

524. Ibid., 130–3; Schalles and Schreiter 1993, 220–4.

525. Ibid., 128f.

526. Junkelmann 1992, 100–19.

527. See von Freeden 1987, 523–31 and 1991, 621–4.

528. In spite of all the alleged Roman horseshoes, the notion that the Romans were not yet aware of horseshoes is still the current understanding. See Drack 1990; Junkelmann 1992, 88–98; Martini 2010, 73–6.

529. In the Austrian Alpine region, there is now evidence of Roman trails detected by mass finds of iron hipposandals along the route. On these trails, alpine salt was transported from the salt mines (partially) situated in the high mountains at Michelhallberg and Hallstatt to the Danube, but also to areas south of the main Alpine ridge. Good evidence for this is the mass occurrence of Roman hipposandals discovered in the body of the roads near Michelhallberg and between Hallstatt and Lake Traunsee in the Salzkammergut. These roads, which also produced other Roman metal finds, were used to transport the salt from its Alpine sites to the Danube and the regions south of the main Alpine crest. See Grabherr 2001, 71–4; M. Pollak 2004.

530. The term 'parade armour' was coined in 1924 by Friedrich Drexel (Drexel 1924). For the history of research into parade armour, cf. Garbsch 1978, 19; Junkelmann 1997, 9f.

531. Garbsch 1978, 35–42.

532. For instance, see Robinson 1975 and Garbsch 1978. With a similar general thrust, Junkelmann 1996 and 1997, who wants to see early face-mask helmets as combat equipment. For alternative viewpoints Fischer 1991, 130–3; 137f; Busch 2009a, 329f.

533. Gschwind 2004, 134ff.

534. Waiter 1978, 41f.

535. Fischer 1991, 155; Waiter and Zahlhaas 1993, 80.

536. Garbsch 1978, 3–7.

537. Junkelmann 1997, 164, Fig. 96.

538. Garbsch 1978, No. O 57.

539. From a figure made from a variety of materials with a silver face (an acrolith statue). See Fischer 2008.

540. Garbsch 1978, 33.

541. Junkelmann 1997, 11 Fig. 1.

542. Junkelmann 1996, 22, Fig. 32.

543. Junkelmann 1997, 12.

544. Robinson 1975, 112, Fig. 309; Garbsch 1978; Junkelmann 1996, 23f., Fig. 33; 66.

545. Klumbach 1976, 13; 41; Junkelmann 2000, 80.

546. Junkelmann 1997, 27.

547. Robinson 1975, 118; Fig. 399f; Garbsch 1978, O 6; 58; Tab. 1963; Junkelmann 1997.

548. Robinson 1975, 118, Fig. 337f; Garbsch 1978, O 10; 64; Junkelmann 1997, 29; Fig. 18.

549. Robinson 1975, 121, Figs 349–51; Garbsch 1978, O 4, 63; Tab. 17; Junkelmann 1997, 24, Fig. 9.

550. Mitschke 2010, 106.

551. Garbsch 1978, O2, 62; Tab. 17; Junkelmann 1997, 28.

552. Robinson 1975, 112f; Figs 310–13; Garbsch 1978, H 2; 58; Tab. 12; Junkelmann 1997, 32–6.

553. Garbsch 1978, O 13; 65; Tab. 19; ibid, O. 27; 67; Tab. 22.

554. Robinson 1975; Garbsch 1978; Junkelmann 1997, 32–6; Fig. 22.

555. Garbsch 1978, N1; Tab. 16; 61.

556. Junkelmann 1997, 90–7.

557. Garbsch 1978, O23; 67; Tab. 21; Junkelmann 1997, 41–4.

558. Robinson 1975, 324; Fig. 318f; Junkelmann 1997, 42, Fig. 28; 43, Fig. 29; Garbsch 1978, L 1; 9; Tab. 14.

559. Auction no. 5488 at Christie's in London on 7.8.2010, Lot. # 176. Breeze and Bishop 2013.

560. Kalee 1989, 207–9; Junkelmann 1997, 66, Fig. 49.

561. Robinson 1975, 176f; Figs 334, 336, 337; Garbsch 1978, B1, B, B3; 47f; Tab. 2; Junkelmann 1997, 43f.

562. Robinson 1975, 125; Fig. 363; Garbsch 1978, O 40; 69f; Tab. 24; Junkelmann 1997, 44–8, Fig. 30.

563. Kellner and Zahlhaas 1993, no. 40; 81f; colour plate 40; Tab. 70–3.

564. Garbsch 1978, A3, A4; 45; Tab. 1.

565. Junkelmann 1997, 102; Figs 73–6.

566. Garbsch 1978, 5.

567. Robinson 1975, 125; Figs 365–6; Garbsch 1978, 5; B5–7; 48; Tab. 2; Junkelmann 1997, 46.

568. Garbsch 1978, A1; 45; Tab. 1; Junkelmann 46; 49, Fig. 38.

569. Robinson 1975, 125; Fig. 363; Garbsch 1978, O 48; 71; O 56; 73; Tab. 26; Tab. 27; Junkelmann 1997, 59.

570. Garbsch 1978, O 49 O 50; 71f.; Tab. 26.

571. Robinson 1975, 187ff; Garbsch 1978, 9–12; Tab. 38f; Junkelmann 1997, 268–71.

572. Garbsch 1978, 7f; Tab. 34–7; Robinson 1975, 161f.

573. Garbsch 1975, 10f; 13f.

574. Garbsch 1978, S 6; 86; Tab. 46.

575. Ibid., 10f.

576. Ibid., 11.

577. Ibid., pl. 45, 1–6; Tab. 77, 1.

578. Garbsch 1978, 11ff; Tab. 40–3.

579. Ibid., 12; Nabefeld 2008, 47–50.

580. Marsden 1969 and 1972; Baatz 1994, 113–283; James 2004, 209–30; Bishop and Coulston 2006, 58–61; 135ff; 168ff; 206ff; Schalles 2010.
581. James 2004, 211ff.
582. Baatz 1994, 146–71.
583. Ibid., 277, 282.
584. Ibid., 185–206.
585. Ibid., 297.
586. Baatz 1966, 194f.
587. Baatz 1994, 118f.
588. ORL B 67, 2f; 8; 13f.
589. Schalles 2010, 68.
590. Baatz 1994, 284–93.
591. Alexandrescu 2010, 183–7; Richter 2010, 284–300.
592. Details also in Bishop and Coulston 2006, 69; 113ff; 144ff; 185–90; 226f and Richter 2010, 284–338.
593. Ibid., 217–21.
594. Ibid., 149–52.
595. Ibid., Appendix 2.
596. Ibid., 234–7.
597. Alexandrescu 2010, 149; 203ff.
598. Ibid., 150; 207f.
599. Ibid., 206.
560. Ibid., 207; 219f; 222–6.
601. Ibid., 206.
602. Ibid., 221.
603. Parlasca and Seemann 1999, 187; Alexandrescu 2010, 379, ST 13.
604. Alexandrescu 2010, 234; 379 ST 16.
605. Alexandrescu 2010, 208–11.
606. Ibid., 208; 378, ST 10, Taf 100; App. 3.
607. Ibid., 207f; App. 3.
608. Alexandrescu 2010, 377–80; Tab. 98–102.
609. Ibid., Pl. 102 top right.
610. Ibid., ST 2–5, 377f; Tab. 99.
611. Bishop and Coulston 2006, 68f; 115f; 144–6; 185–9; 226f; Alexandrescu 2010, 106–45.
612. Alexandrescu 2010, 121f.
613. Ibid., 120f.
614. Ibid., 365f., MI 22, 23, 25ff., Pl. 80ff.
615. Ibid., 116–19.
616. Maxfield 1981, 86–9.
617. Garbsch 1986a and 1992, 80.
618. Maxfield 1981, 88.
619. Ibid., 89ff.
620. Garbsch 1986a, 333f.
621. Fischer 1988, 170ff.
622. Ibid., 172, esp. n.21.

623. Maxfield 1981, 91–5.
624. Garbsch 1992, 80; Fischer 1990, 82.
625. Fuentes 1991, 71–6.
626. Richter 2010, 152–78.
627. Steidl 2000, 57; Fischer 2014.
628. Richter 2010, 154.
629. Bishop and Coulston 2006, 69f; 117f; 185; 187.
630. Richter 2010, 153.
631. Ibid., 153f.
632. Ibid., 154.
633. Bishop and Coulston 2006, 118 Fig. 68, 6–7; Richter 2010, 157.
634. Richter 2010, 157f.
635. Ibid., 160.
636. Bishop and Coulston 2006, 187 Fig. 121, 3; 7; Richter 2010, 161f.
637. Pietsch 1983, 64, Tab. 23, 528.
638. Richter 2010, 158.
639. Ibid., 175ff.
640. Beeser 1979; Bishop and Coulston 2006, 116–18; Friedrich 2010, 36.
641. Brilliant 1967, Pl. 55a.
642. S. Sievers, in Redde et al. 2006, 297f; 229f; Pl. 83, 85; Redde 2006a, 125, 151, 159.
643. Bishop and Coulston 2006, 185; 187; Flügel 2010.
644. Bishop and Coulston 2006, 69f.
645. Ibid., 117.
646. Ibid., 70.
647. Ibid., 187.
648. Groenman-van Waateringe 1967; van Driel-Murray and Gechter 1983; van Driel-Murray 1985 and 1990; Bishop and Coulston 2006, 116f.
649. This is also the case with modern armies. For example, in the German armed forces, each infantryman had a triangular tarpaulin, which could be used as a kind of poncho, four of which tarpaulins make up a tent. However, with these tarpaulins it was also possible to build larger tents for correspondingly more soldiers (pers. comm., L. Riedmeier).
650. Richter 2010, 109–19.
651. Junkelmann 1986, 196–200; Fuentes 1991; Atkinson and Morgan 1987, 105; Richter 2010, 101.
652. Richter 2010, 101.
653. Fuentes 1991, 83–9.
654. Richter 2010, 113; Himmler 2012.
655. Ibid., 102.
656. Ibid., 103–12.
657. Fuentes 1991, 90–6.

IV

THE BUILDINGS OF THE ROMAN ARMY

1. Introduction

Like no other army in antiquity, the Roman army of the Imperial period erected large-scale buildings of all kinds and left them in the form of archaeological remains. These included short-lived installations connected with sieges or campaigns. However, it is the more durable buildings for the accommodation of troops, for infrastructure, and for frontier protection, which are the legacy of the Roman army. These include camps, forts, roads and complex border protection systems along river and land frontiers (*ripae* and *limites*).

In many cases, these Roman military buildings still characterize the landscape in the former frontier provinces of the empire, since remains of these facilities around the Mediterranean, the Rhine and the Danube, and in the UK have survived to this day (Breeze 2011). All of these buildings were planned, built, and used by the military itself. However, the civilian infrastructure of the provinces has also benefited from military building activity, as with the Roman road network, originally military, which soon became the backbone of trade and civilian traffic.

As a distinctive speciality of the Roman military, in addition to the planned camps and forts, the frontier protection systems of the *ripae* and *limites*, hundreds of kilometres long, are one of the defining structures of the Roman army. Their closest parallel is the Great Wall of China.[1]

From early on, the striking remnants of Roman frontier installations fascinated later generations and invited explanation. Thus, in the Middle Ages, there was initially an inclination to look upon the enigmatic trail of the Upper German-Raetian Limes as a work of the devil ('Teufelsmauer' or 'Devil's Wall'), before serious research began in the Renaissance. With the intensification and systematization of research into Hadrian's Wall, the Upper German-Raetian Limes, or in the Augustan military base at Haltern, a special area of research developed from this Roman military archaeology: Roman provincial archeology (Fischer 2010).

The preserved material, which has been excavated by archaeologists, exhibits a clear temporal focus: there are a large number of camps and fortresses from the early and middle Imperial periods, but only a few from the Republican period. The historical reasons for this are easily understandable: Roman troops in the Republic were only on active campaign for longer periods during the summer and wintered at home or in cities. Thus the bulk of the Republican camps are marching camps or short-term winter quarters, which have left only a few, barely recognisable traces in the ground. At that time, Roman camps were occupied for a longer periods (and extended accordingly) only during sieges or wars which lasted a long time. However, even these more permanent Roman military installations only consisted of perishable material: wood or wood-and-earth constructions, dry (unmortared) stones, or unfired bricks. Only city fortifications or Hellenistic fortresses occupied by the Romans were built in solid stone construction with mortared stone or solid masonry.

It is therefore unsurprising that, with the exception of the only very briefly used – but systematically explored – camps and siege works around Alesia, there is little or no knowledge of the many camps of the Gallic Wars of C. Julius Caesar, even though their position has often been precisely described. This is also true of the numerous camps and sieges of the civil wars between Caesar and his internal political opponents attested in the literature, or the clashes between the armies of Caesar and Octavian or Octavian and Marc Antony up to the battle of Actium in 31 BC.

It was only from the Augustan period onwards, when a standing professional army began to occupy long-term camps with permanent buildings in the frontier regions, that the number of Roman camps known to researchers increases. Many of them can still be seen clearly in the landscape today, especially if they have been built in stone. In addition to the erection of camps, forts, and frontier installations of all kinds, infrastructure, such as roads and canals, as well as special buildings, like military baths, were among the responsibilities of the Roman army.

There are differences in the preservation of forts and legionary bases: in regions occupied only briefly by the Romans, for example in Germany between the Rhine and the Elbe, in Britain beyond Hadrian's Wall, in the Upper German-Raetian Limes, or in Transdanubian Dacia single-phase or short-term sites are found, which provide clear ideas about Roman fortification in well-defined periods. In the lower Danube region and in the East (including Egypt), sites of the early and middle imperial period which can easily be assessed are much rarer, because they have often been modified and fundamentally changed from the Late Roman period, through the Byzantine era, to the Islamic Middle Ages.

2.   Roman camps and forts

When the Romans enter enemy territory, they do not join battle before they have set up a permanent camp; but they do not erect it at random and without fixed order (Flavius Josephus, *Bell. Jud.* 3.76)

The quotation from Flavius Josephus from the end of the 1st century AD exemplifies that, out of all of the peoples who waged war in ancient times, the Romans distinguished themselves through the construction of planned camps. There were already military camps among the ancient peoples of the East, namely the Persians, the Greeks, the Hellenistic empires, and the Carthaginians. However, none applied the principle of establishing them on the march, in sieges, and in peaceful areas, on a strictly prescribed scheme, as rigorously as the Romans. Following the motto 'sweat saves blood', it was always and consistently ensured that there was a fortified camp available on the march in enemy territory, before battles and sieges, even if only for a single night.

The origin of this custom of establishing camps with a street grid of roads on a fixed pattern is unknown. However, *coloniae maritimae* were known from the 4th century BC in central Italy, which, in their regular configuration of the defences, streets, and internal buildings, can be compared to Roman military camps known from later times. These first Roman 'filial' towns with their armed Roman settlers with their families secured the first conquests in Italy and gave access to the coast: Ostia, Tarracina, Minturnae, Puteoli, and Pyrgi. They all have a basic square or rectangular shape and a regular road network with streets that cross each other at right angles. H. von Hesberg, who catalogued these *coloniae maritimae*,[2] argues that there are no Italian influences here, but more likely from the Greek cities of southern Italy and Sicily.

However, this does not help with the question of the origin of the Roman camps: did the Romans build early military camps on the model of Greek cities and then convert them into stone as cities in their *coloniae maritimae*, or did they found their first colonies directly according to the Greek model and then adopt these as models for their camps?

For as far as we can look back, Roman camps were carefully planned. This is also the case for marching camps, which Roman armies erected every evening, including ramparts and ditches. In practical terms, it worked like this: an advance guard, which included a team of surveyors, laid out a camp site according to a fixed, rectangular plan and corresponding to the exact number of troops. Without really having to think about it, the soldiers occupied the camp according to the familiar layout, and erected their leather tents in the usual arrangement on the usual camp streets, while others constructed walls and ditches and secured it with the palisade stakes they carried with them.

These camps were always laid out in the same pattern, without regard for the terrain. The first literary reference can be found in Polybius (6.26–32) in the 2nd century BC. He described a camp for two legions in detail: it was rectangular, protected by ramparts and ditches, with a breastwork of palisade stakes on the rampart. The rampart enclosed regularly set out tents (Fig. 377).

In the course of the expansion of Rome, wars shifted to territories outside Italy, to the extent that the necessity arose to erect camps for longer periods of time. A consequence of the Punic Wars in Spain, for example, was that armies had to remain in the same place for several years during sieges. This also had consequences for the shape and amenities of the camp. When, after the establishment of a standing professional army in the early days of the empire, permanent frontiers were established on the Rhine, Danube, and the Euphrates – for the most part riverine frontiers – camp construction proceeded apace. Now the permanent bases for the legions and their auxiliary troops became standard, in which the armies would over-winter, while in the summer they were often on campaign.

With the ultimate introduction of linear frontier defences from the middle of the 1st century AD onwards, legionary camps were built in stone. Auxiliary units, which had previously been closely connected with the legions, increasingly became self-sufficient units, taking over their own auxiliary forts and the frontiers, while the legions were ready for major operations.

On the basis of selected examples, the development of the different types of fortification will be reviewed in this section, so far as they are known archaeologically. However, the conditions for their survival are not equally favourable everywhere, and research has likewise not been uniformly intensive. For example, Republican camps are almost exclusively known from Spain, although they must also have been present in Italy, the Balkans, Greece, and Asia Minor.

One thing that these camps and fortifications of the Republic and early and middle Imperial periods have in common, however, is their purpose: they were not intended as fortresses, in which a numerically inferior force of troops can resist a greater number of opponents. Rather, they served only as relatively weakly fortified barracks, from which the troops could operate offensively and dynamically, at best as a precaution against surprise attacks and as protection for the baggage and the supplies of the troops. H. von Petrikovits has, for good reason, applied an expression from the former Austrian military terminology to Roman camps: they were not fortresses, but 'fortified barracks'.[3]

Camp and fort defences

Most of the elements of Roman fortification were not genuinely Roman inventions. In many cases, the Romans used individual elements from the highly developed system of Greco-Hellenistic fortification, but these elements were often rearranged, so that something uniquely Roman evolved. In particular, the consistent use of camp construction is typically Roman – in an extreme case the daily construction of a marching camp.

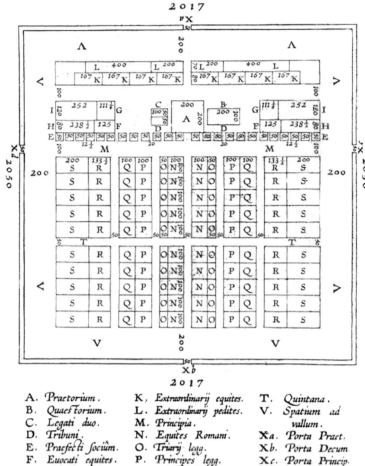

Figure 377 *Plan of a Roman marching camp from the time of the Republic, as described by Polybius (after Lipsius 1598)*

Timber and earth defences

MARCHING CAMPS

In the case of marching and field camps, the simplest form of defence was used. It consisted of a ditch and an earthen rampart. That is, a V-sectioned ditch was dug and the spoil was tipped into the body of the rampart. Experience from experimental archaeology indicates that in regions where this was possible from the natural vegetation, the front side of the rampart and the edges of the V-sectioned ditches were covered with turf so that attacking enemies would slip. The palisade stakes that had been brought along were planted on the ramparts, and these could be connected by lacing. While the enemy could easily tear down this kind of 'fortification', he would lose time and thus the advantage of surprise. The perimeter of a marching camp

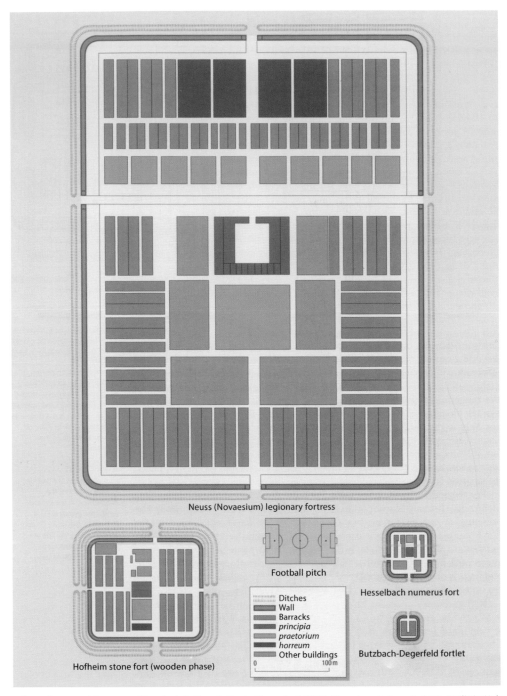

Neuss (Novaesium) legionary fortress

Football pitch

Hesselbach numerus fort

Butzbach-Degerfeld fortlet

Hofheim stone fort (wooden phase)

Ditches
Wall
Barracks
principia
praetorium
horreum
Other buildings

0   100 m

Figure 378 *Comparison of areas of Roman military installations (after to Campbell 2009). Drawing: A. Smadi, Arch. Institute University of Cologne*

was probably divided into work stints by predetermined distances, each of which was supervised by senior ranks, such as centurions. While they were being built, other soldiers erected the leather tents inside the camp. The fact that camp construction was carried out according to well-defined regulations comes from the written sources (*e.g.* pseudo-Hyginus). That the system was also systematically practised is proved by the numerous practice camps.

Of course, such a defensive circuit can hardly be regarded as a fortification. Nevertheless, it protected from a sudden incursion by cavalry and surprise attacks by infantry. Such an obstacle hindered any attempt to form a closed shield wall.

As a rule, the basic shape of Roman marching camps corresponded to the usual forms of contemporary long-term camps when constructed. There are both polygonal shapes, adapted to the terrain, as well as long, rectangular installations with rounded corners (so-called 'playing-card shape'). The rounded corners, Hyginus explained, was related to the integrity of stone camps, in order that it would be difficult to remove stones from the their fabric.[4]

LONGER-TERM CAMPS AND FORTS

In the construction of camps and siege fortifications occupied for longer periods as summer or winter quarters or even as a permanent base, this system was further refined. In addition to substantial fortifications with gates and towers, permanent internal buildings were now provided in place of leather tents. The sites of fixed fortresses and forts were carefully selected, with traffic connections, access to water, wood, grain, fodder, and other supplies, as well as a tactically favourable location.[5] The chosen site was then carefully prepared and, if necessary, cleared and levelled.[6] The construction sites for the defences and the interior were carefully surveyed by specialists (*agrimensores*), apparently using manuals for the correct size of the installation in relation to the intended garrison.[7] In the case of legionary bases, the *praefectus castrorum* was responsible for site management; while for auxiliary forts this could be done by members of the unit, but also attached specialists, such as legionary centurions.[8]

BASIC SHAPE

There were quite different designs for the basic shape of Roman fortresses and forts, which were always – with exceptions – related to their date. During the late Republic and the early Imperial period, polygonal forms, which were adapted to the terrain, predominated. On the other hand, however, there were already quite rectangular structures, but with right-angled corners (*e.g.* Cáceres el Viejo). The first known camp in the playing card scheme, *i.e.* in the shape of a rectangle with rounded corners, is the Augustan base at Obrezje in Slovenia (Mason 2003; Sašel-Kos 2011). Undoubtedly, the Praetorian camp built by Tiberius in the shape of a playing card in the years AD 21–3 also had an important influence on military bases in the frontier provinces.[9] At the latest, this form was established from the time of Nero. However, there could also be variants: square camps and forts or rhomboid bases. Camps could also be diamond-shaped or playing card-shaped, but adapted to the terrain at a particular point.

DITCHES

Broader and deeper V-sectioned ditches, sometimes several of them, were dug around fortresses and forts occupied for a longer period of time.[10] It was important to take care that the distance from the rampart and the angle of slope of the ditches were such that no blind spots were created (Fig. 379), which would protect an enemy concealed in the ditch from shots from the defensive wall. According to Hyginus (*Mun. Castr.* 49), and also confirmed

Fossa fastigata   *Fossa fastigata* with cleaning slot   Fossa Punica

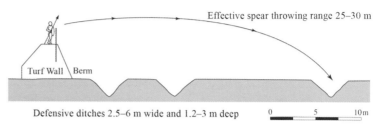

Effective spear throwing range 25–30 m

Turf Wall   Berm

Defensive ditches 2.5–6 m wide and 1.2–3 m deep

0   5   10m

Figure 379 *Various forms of Roman camp ditches and reconstruction of the defences of a camp with a turf rampart (after Johnson 1987). Drawing: A. Smadi, Arch. Institute University of Cologne*

by the archaeological evidence, there were two forms of ditch, the *fossa fastigata* with the symmetrical V-sectioned profile, and the *fossa Punica* with an asymmetrical profile: on the shallow face, opposite to the defensive wall, they were easier to enter, but on the steeper face next to the wall they were more difficult to get out of, especially when encumbered by heavy equipment with armour and a shield.

In the north-western provinces, the *fossa fastigata* often has a small slot, which was apparently used for drainage, for, contrary to a widespread view, the ditches around Roman camps, forts, and towns were not moats, but always kept as dry obstacles.

Ditches occur in widely varying numbers, depending on topography and period, and in the early Imperial period one or two ditches were usually used. On the other hand, more stringent rules were sometimes observed locally: Claudian fortresses on the Rhine and Danube, for example, had two ditches. When reconstructed under Vespasian, after the destruction of the civil war and the Batavian uprising, they only had one ditch.

In case of a particular threat or unfavourable topography, fortifications were often reinforced with several ditches, *e.g.* in Britain or in the Upper German-Raetian Limes, where sometimes five ditches or more are to be found. However, it is often necessary to check whether they were really all in contemporary use or come from different phases. There are frequently different numbers of ditches on all sides of a fort, and they are completely missing on steep slopes.

In the gate area, short lengths of rampart and ditch (*clavicula* and *titulum*) could offer additional protection (Fig. 380). This fortification detail is found from the Republic up to the 3rd century. There were also isolated, rather unusual, offset basic layouts for ditches and ramparts,

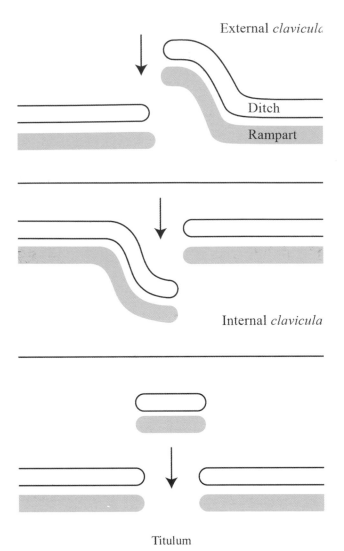

External *clavicula*

Ditch

Rampart

Internal *clavicula*

Titulum

Figure 380 *Tituli and claviculae (after Johnson 1987). Drawing: A. Smadi, Arch. Institute University of Cologne*

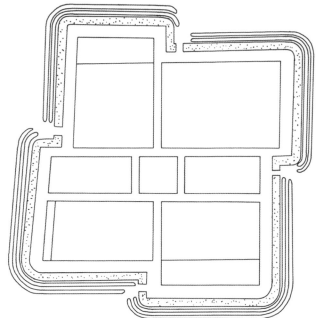

Figure 381 *Newstead fort in its primary phase, around AD 80 (after Johnson 1987). Drawing: A. Smadi, Arch. Institute University of Cologne*

as at Altenstadt, Period 4 on the Wetteraulimes[11] or in the late Flavian phase of Newstead (Fig. 381) in Scotland.[12]

In the case of siege- and permanent camps, there were further obstacles in front of or even in the ditches, such as the spiked entanglement (an equivalent to modern barbed wire!), pitfalls and man traps.

RAMPARTS

For longer-term use, timber-and-earth camps were not confined to simple earthen ramparts and a loose breastwork of palisade stakes, but rather were constructed more substantially. For example, one- or two-sided turf ramparts were erected, especially in Britain, which in wetter areas were often protected from the damp ground by a timber corduroy placed on the surface, and sometimes by broken, unmortared cobblestones. The outer faces consisted of turf blocks stacked like bricks, mostly battered at an angle, but there were also vertical faces (Fig. 382). Inside, they were

filled with soil from the excavation of the ditches, often reinforced by a stabilising timber structure.[13]

In one excavation in Tulln/*Commagenis*,[14] on the Danube frontier in Noricum, unfired mud bricks have also been discovered as a building material for walls, in this case with wooden fixtures. This type of construction (without wooden fittings) was often used for camps and forts in the Mediterranean and the East, where it originated.

Since turf ramparts and defences made of unfired clay bricks were more vulnerable in the wetter climate of the north-western provinces, one could reasonably debate whether they were roofed. However, this has not yet been demonstrated.[15] In the Mediterranean, dry walls consisting of broken, unmortared stone are often found in temporary camps. In the north-western provinces, on the other hand, this type of construction has only been identified, for instance, in the earlier stages of the Saalburg fort or Zugmantel.[16] In addition, there are various timber-and-earth constructions of defensive walls in the north-western provinces,[17] especially in the early Imperial period. There are simple wooden faces, made of vertically secured beams and transverse timbers, with an earthen fill upon which the walkway sat. However, even more complicated, earth-filled, box constructions with wooden tie beams could be used for the defences. All these walls of perishable material also had a wooden breastwork with battlements, which, together with the defences, have usually been simply reconstructed as open to the elements. The walkway may also have been covered (see above). With the breastwork, these walls would have reached a maximum height of 4–5 m. To the

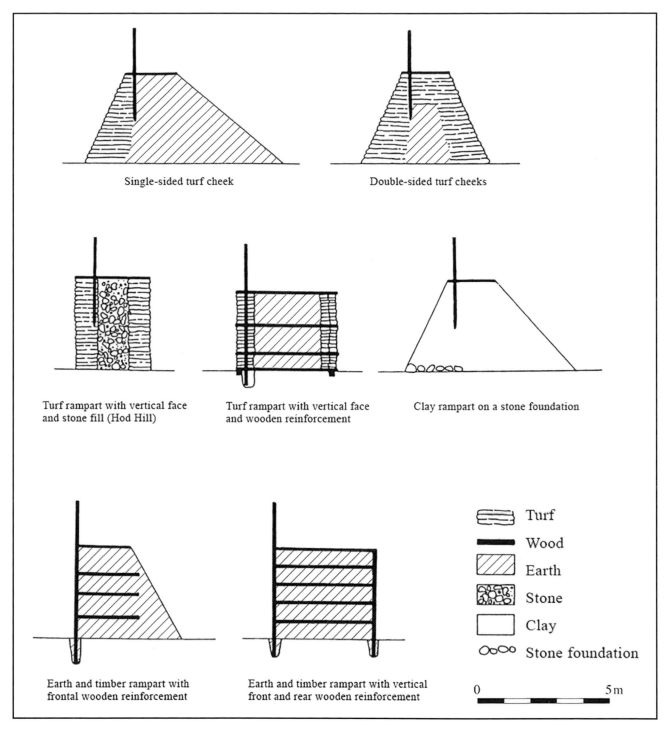

Single-sided turf cheek

Double-sided turf cheeks

Turf rampart with vertical face and stone fill (Hod Hill)

Turf rampart with vertical face and wooden reinforcement

Clay rampart on a stone foundation

Earth and timber rampart with frontal wooden reinforcement

Earth and timber rampart with vertical front and rear wooden reinforcement

Turf
Wood
Earth
Stone
Clay
Stone foundation

0   5 m

Figure 382 *Turf and earth-and-timber ramparts (after Johnson 1987). Drawing: A. Smadi, Arch. Institute University of Cologne*

rear, ramps or wooden staircases were installed at several points, in order to allow for rapid manning of the walls in the case of an alarm.

TOWERS

Towers were often used, with corner and interval towers on the different types of rampart construction,[18] of which only the postholes for the upright posts are recorded during excavation (four in the case of interval towers, five to six in the case of corner towers). Wooden towers were always embedded in the wall, that is, they never project in front of the wall. Their height is to be assumed to have been at least three storeys. According to depictions on Trajan's Column, they were often constructed as an open scaffolding with open, crenelated platforms. This was certainly not the case for most long-term bases. For defensive reasons, and in view of the climatic conditions in the north-western provinces, closed towers (boarded or wattle-and-daub) with pent or gabled roofs have to be reckoned with.

GATES

Most of the fortresses and forts had four gates flanked by towers. In the centre of the narrow front side facing the enemy was the *porta praetoria*; opposite that was the *porta decumana*. The two gates on the longer sides were mostly not central, but offset a bit towards the *porta praetoria*. These lateral gateways were called the *porta principalis dextra* and *porta principalis sinistra*. On Hadrian's Wall, there are special cases: where forts with the front part, including the *portae principales*, projected over the Wall into enemy territory, there were occasionally other gates in the *retentura*, the *porta quintana dextra* and/or *sinistra*.

There are various wooden structures at the gateways, all of which have in common that their outer face did not project far from the front of the defensive wall. In the openings through the defensive circuit, there were pairs of single or double four- and six-post structures, which can be reconstructed into flanking gate towers. Between these towers were bridges with walkway and breastwork. In the earlier Imperial period, on the basis of Republican precursors, gateways with recessed gates were used, which, like the so-called pincer gates (*Zangentore*) of late La Tène *oppida*, formed an enclosed gate courtyard that could be shut from both sides. If an opponent broke through the outer gate, he then fell into the trap at the inner gate and could be shot at from all sides. The gateways had either one or two passageways. Here, too, reconstructions of the gate towers should assume them to be closed structures with a pent or gabled roof.

Stone construction

Defences of drystone walling, mud bricks, or timber-and-earth constructions could be erected quickly and needed no special infrastructure. On the other hand they were of limited durability and not as stable as stone buildings. However, a certain infrastructure was necessary for the construction of these buildings in the north-western provinces, where there had been no pre-Roman stone buildings. This was only available after a certain period of consolidation of Roman culture, infrastructure, and economy. One only needs to think of quarries, lime kilns, and extended transport routes. Therefore, it took some time for military buildings to be constructed with mortared stone walls. While, for example, in the area of military and civilian centres in the Rhineland (Mainz, Cologne), there were occasional stone buildings in the Augustan period, stone construction was only adopted for military

architecture in the Neronian period with the double-legion base of Vetera I.

DEFENSIVE WALLS

The earliest curtain wall and interior buildings of a military camp in solid stone construction are found in the Praetorian Camp in Rome, built under Tiberius in the years AD 21–3.[19] Here, bricks were used for the outer face of the defensive circuit constructed in *opus caementitium*, and the Praetorian Camp was the very first (archaeologically proven) brick-built structure in Rome.[20] In its first phase, the defensive walls were only about 5 m high (with battlements).[21] In the northern border provinces, locally available material was used, and brick walls were unknown there. In the case of the double-legion base of Vetera I in Xanten, for example, the tuff and greywacke stone was imported from a more southerly range of hills, and stone construction was then gradually established as standard for permanent legionary bases (Fig. 383a). From the Flavian period onwards, stone defences appeared for auxiliary forts as well, all of which had been built using timber and earth before that. There were also cases where a stone-faced masonry wall was inserted in front of a still standing timber-and-earth rampart, as at Kastell Urspring,[22] in the region of Lonsee in Baden-Württemberg. This process of upgrading to stone proceeded slowly: it was not until the middle of the 2nd century, under Antoninus Pius (AD 138–61), that most forts had stone curtain walls, gates, and towers (Fig. 383b).

The curtain walls consisted mostly of masonry walls with a stone breastwork and battlement, behind which an earthen bank (*agger*) was located to carry the walkway. However, there are also examples of walls without *aggeres* which had wooden structures, often supported by buttresses, for the walkway.[23] Masonry walls were generally plastered and painted white with red dummy joints, simulating ashlar masonry.[24] Only rarely were there truly substantial ashlar walls, as at *Reginum*/Regensburg, the base of *legio III Italica*.[25] Ashlar facing for concrete is also occasionally found, at least in the case of gates and towers. Similarly, for stone walls, there were numerous stairways (*ascensus*), mostly integrated into the *agger*.

A moulded cornice along the exterior of the defensive walls, at the height of the wallwalk, seems to have been compulsory. Pieces of it are therefore frequently found at forts in the north-western provinces. This cornice, consisting of four layers of brick, is still preserved *in situ* on the early Imperial wall of the Praetorian Camp in Rome, which was incorporated into the Aurelian city wall.[26] Elsewhere, this cornice can also be seen, for example, in the well-preserved fortification of Gheriat el-Garbia in Libya, or in the collapsed fort wall at Wörth am Main.[27] The battlements, which were broader in antiquity than in the Middle Ages, had semicircular-sectioned caps of worked

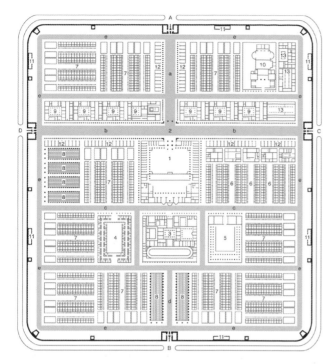

Figure 383a *Idealized reconstruction of a legionary base of the early 2nd century AD (design S. Hoss and J. Schamper). Drawing: A. Smadi, Arch. Institute University of Cologne*

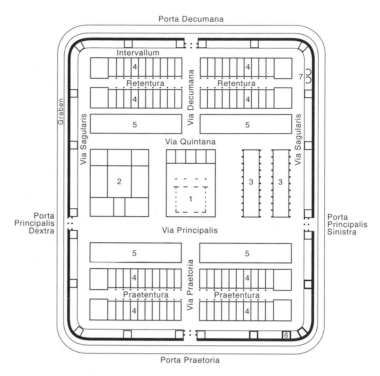

Figure 383b *Idealized reconstruction of an auxiliary fort (after Johnson 1987). Drawing: A. Smadi, Arch. Institute University of Cologne*

stone.[28] The heights of these walls are only rarely revealed by actual examples. They were about 5–6 m in legionary camps, and roughly 4–5 m in auxiliary forts.[29]

TOWERS

As with wooden towers, stone corner and interval towers were also integrated into the *agger* in legionary camps and auxiliary forts, and either did not project beyond the front of the outer face of the wall, or just a little. This means, on the one hand, a direct continuation of the timber building tradition where, for technical and constructional reasons, towers could only be placed within the wall without falling down. In Greco-Hellenistic walls and in the Late Roman periods, towers usually protrude beyond the front of the wall, in order to be able to enfilade along the walls from the flanks with archers and bolt-shooting artillery. The fact that this is not seen in forts of the early and middle Imperial period corresponds with the assumption that auxiliary units did not yet have artillery at this time. The first fort in which the towers protrude beyond the wall is the late *limes* fort of Niederbieber (Fig. 445), built around AD 200.[30] No tower of a legionary base or an auxiliary fort is completely preserved, so its height can only be inferred indirectly from models or depictions (Fig. 424) as three- or four-storey.[31] A building inscription from North Africa confirms this by mentioning four-storey towers.[32] In most attempts at reconstruction for early to mid-Imperial camps

and forts, the heights of the gate, corner and interval towers have been underestimated.

Finds of worked stone confirm arched windows and embrasures in fort towers, probably with wooden shutters. The relatively frequent occurrence of roofing tiles in the interior of fort and camp towers proves that in the north-western provinces such towers had pitched or gabled roofs with tiles and not crenelated platforms. Lead roofs might also be conceivable, but they are only confirmed for the Late Roman period, at the *burgus* of Engers in Rhineland Palatinate, for example.[33]

GATES

In the case of stone camps and forts, the layout of the four gateways was generally retained: *porta praetoria*, *porta decumana*, *porta principalis dextra*, and *porta principalis sinistra*. The exceptions on Hadrian's Wall with the occasional occurrence of *portae quintanae* have already been mentioned. The gates of legionary camps could be very elaborate and have several passages (Fig. 384). Their basic forms often correspond to contemporary city gates. Gateways were often very different in design at the same facility, at both legionary camps and auxiliary forts, without any identifiable rules. Some were polygonal flanking towers, as at Vindonissa or Mainz, some of which had recessed gates. At *Reginum/Regensburg*, the *porta praetoria* has flanking towers with semi-circular, protruding gate towers on either side of two passages. However, simple rectangular or square flanking

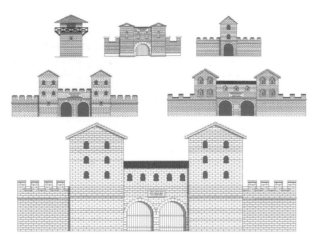

Figure 384 *Comparison of gates of Roman military installations, design T. Fischer. Left to right: limes tower, numerus fort, fortlet, cohort fort, ala fort, legionary fortress. Drawing: A. Smadi, Arch. Institute University of Cologne*

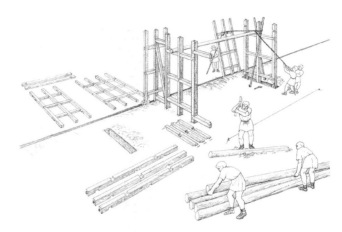

Figure 385 *Erecting the basic framework of a half-timbered building. Design by T. Fischer (after Scholz 2009). Drawing: A. Smadi, Arch. Institute University of Cologne*

towers are very common. Camp and fort gateways often formed barbicans or outer courtyards with two gates, in which opponents who had passed the outer gate were then caught before the inner gate.

Occasionally the basic forms of gateways of legionary fortresses were adopted by auxiliary forts of the same province, such as the *porta praetoria* of Regensburg and the north gate of the *ala* fort of Kastell Weißenburg.[34] The *portae principales* of Lambaesis,[35] with its bevelled corners on the outer faces of the flanking gate towers, were imitated in the forts of Bu Njem and Gheriat el-Garbia, in which vexillations of *legio III Augusta* from Lambaesis were stationed.[36]

Auxiliary forts could have gateways with either single or double passageways. There is no definite rule here, but rather a tendency: forts with cavalry, that is, installations in which *alae* or *cohortes equitatae* were stationed, frequently have gates with two passages, especially at the *portae praetoriae*.[37] It has repeatedly been observed that, in the later building phases, gateways with two passageways had one of them subsequently closed, in order to be able to control and defend the fort more easily during periods of crisis. Stone inscriptions, partly lettered with bronze, were built into the wall at all four gates of legionary camps and forts. In England, wooden building inscriptions are also attested at timber-and-earth forts.[38]

Internal buildings of legionary camps and auxiliary forts

In short-term camps of the early and middle Imperial period, buildings made of drystone walling, mud bricks, or half-timbered structures were preferred, depending on the region. In the case of long-standing fortresses and forts in the north-western and northern provinces, timber-

framed structures were predominant in the beginning (Fig. 385). These were then gradually replaced by stone walls, complemented by architectural decoration in worked stone such as cornices and columns. Up to the 3rd century AD, some buildings, for example barracks, were built half-timbered on masonry footings.

The framework of half-timbered buildings was not intended to be seen, but plastered in white. Occasionally red-painted dados in the lower part of the walls have also been found on these half-timbered structures.[39] However, in the case of half-timbered barrack buildings on stone footings, the officers' quarters with baths and hypocaust heating were built entirely of substantial stone masonry.

Streets

Inside, a continuous road ran behind the defences, the *via sagularis*. A street grid divided the interior. The principal axis was the *via principalis*, which connected the *porta principalis dextra* and the *porta principalis sinistra*. This divided bases into two areas, usually unequal in size: the smaller front part was the *praetentura*, the larger rear the *retentura*. The *via principalis* met the *via praetoria* in front of the main entrance of the central building. However, there are also forts with a 'transverse' internal layout, whereby the *retentura* is absent and the *principia* has the *via sagularis* or the defences immediately to the rear: Valkenburg (Fig. 386) in the Netherlands or Eining/*Abusina* in Bavaria are examples of this. Neither a spatially nor temporally meaningful pattern is discernible in the distribution of these exceptional installations in the frontier provinces at present.[40] The road leading from the rear gate, the *porta decumana*, to the inside of the camp was called the *via decumana*. Apart from these main streets, there were also lesser streets in fortresses and forts. The water and sewage pipes of wood and stone were buried within the gravelled and cobbled streets.

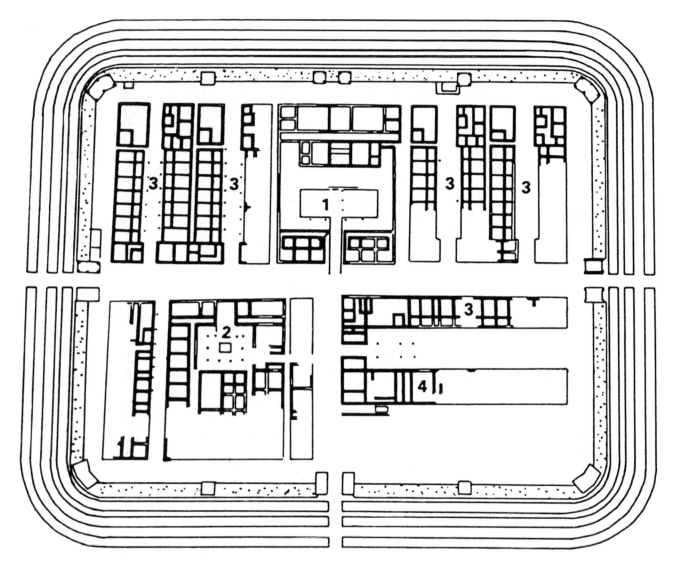

Figure 386 *Valkenburg fort (after Johnson 1987). Drawing: A. Smadi, Arch. Institute University of Cologne*

Principia

Under the Republic, the general's tent, called the *praetorium*, was erected in the centre of the camp. Before its main entrance lay the *groma*, the main surveying location for the camp. The standards were also planted there. In front of the *praetorium*, commanders used to give their speeches to the troops and offer sacrifices. The general lived and performed his duties in the *praetorium*.

In temporary and permanent bases of the early Imperial period, the accommodation of the commander and the rooms where he performed his duties were separated. Archaeological discoveries in bases reveal a spatial separation into two different buildings, the *praetorium* and the *principia*, for the first time in the Augustan period. When exactly this division of the former general's tent into *praetorium* and *principia* took place is currently unclear. In the case of the central structures of the Scipionian siege camps in Numantia

in Spain, built with drystone walls and dating to the year 134/133 BC, such a division did not yet exist, and we know nothing of the interior of Caesarean camps.

From the Augustan period onwards, the *principia*, a large building complex around an inner courtyard, lay at the centre of the camps, fortresses, and forts.[41] Its origins in the forum of a civilian city are undeniable. According to building inscriptions and literary testimony, this building was called the *principia*, linguistically a *plurale tantum*. The term 'camp forum', proposed by H. von Petrikovits,[42] for the *principia* has not been used by researchers for a good reason: no other name should be introduced for an ancient structure where the ancient designation is known for certain (Fig. 387).

This central structure retained its basic form throughout the Imperial period, but underwent a certain development in the course of time.[43] The main entrance of the *principia* was on the *via praetoria* in the area of the *groma*. The

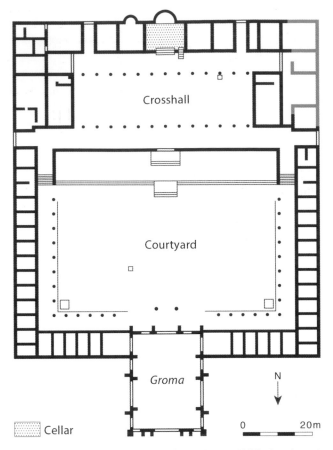

Crosshall

Courtyard

Groma

N ↓

Cellar

0   20m

Figure 387 *Lambaesis principia (after Johnson 1987). Drawing: A. Smadi, Arch. Institute University of Cologne*

entrance to the *principia* was architecturally emphasized in various ways; in the legionary camps of *Lambaesis* and Budapest/*Aquincum*, for example, *tetrapyla* are known, four-sided arched monuments above the camp *groma* on the *via principalis*. This type of architecture also finds parallels in urban architecture (see Kader 1996).

The rear portion of the *principia* consisted of a row of rooms with a transverse hall (*basilica*) in front. Similar to the *basilica* of *fora*, there was also a *tribunal* or speaker's platform inside, as well as altars, and emperor statues. The middle room of the rear range of rooms in the *principia* underwent a particularly interesting development:

In Augustan camps, there was always a passage to the *praetorium* at this point, which was separated from the *principia* by a street. Obviously, in this phase, the *praetorium* still had the character of an official administrative building, and the standards were probably still kept there. At least this can be inferred from the fact that the passage through the back of the *principia* was replaced by the *sacellum*, the shrine of the standards, in the post-Augustan period.

Depending on the method of construction of the whole building, a wooden or stone cellar could be found in this shrine of the standards, used as an *aerarium* or strongroom for the unit funds. From the Flavian period onwards, the

shrine of the standards was emphasized architecturally in comparison to the rear facade of the *principia*, whether as a rectangular structure or as a semicircular apse in legionary bases, as well as vexillation fortresses and auxiliary forts. Altars and other inscriptions, as well as sculptures of gods and emperors, were also concentrated at the rear of the *principia*. O. Stoll has catalogued these for the auxiliary forts of the Upper German and Raetian Limes (Stoll 1992).

The rooms adjoining the shrine of the standards can be identified as libraries, archives, or other administrative areas, and from the 2nd century AD onwards often were also heated. Then, from the second half of the 1st century AD, a series of rooms was found to the side, behind the porticos, some of which were identifiable by inscriptions or by pertinent finds as *armamentaria* or armouries. In the side ranges, additional office and archive rooms of the military administration might also be found. The *officia* of the legionary legate, the senatorial and equestrian military tribunes, and the *praefectus castrorum* are, for example, epigraphically recorded in the legionary base at *Lambaesis* in Algeria from the area of the *principia*. *Scholae*, that is, assembly and cult spaces for certain grades or ranks of service, are recorded in inscriptions from the *principia* in Imperial legionary bases, without it being possible to identify specific rooms. In the case of auxiliary forts, the *principia* in the *latera praetorii*, as a rule, housed the most important functional structures, such as the *praetorium*, *horrea*, *fabricae*, or *valetudinarium*.

Praetorium

In the Imperial period up to the 3rd century, the *praetoria* of legionary camps were reserved for legionary legates, who came from the top echelon of the nobility, from the senatorial order. Accordingly, a level of residential comfort can be expected in their quarters – at least in well-built, multi-year permanent bases – which did not differ very much from what this group of people was accustomed to in their home country. Indeed, R. Förtsch (Förtsch 1995) has shown for the *praetoria* of the great early Imperial-era bases with legionary garrisons, that these buildings followed the basic concepts of sophisticated architecture according to Italian models. As a plausible reason for this, he pointed out that generals such as Drusus or Tiberius were lodged in these palaces, who, as high-ranking members of the Julian-Claudian imperial family, did not want to give up a certain level of comfort even when in the field. *Praetoria*, located beside or behind the *principia*,[44] had an abundance of rooms and several courtyards; dining rooms (*triclinia*) and bathing facilities can be identified. Their decoration (architectural ornamentation, wall paintings, and so on) also demonstrates expensive taste. This can even be seen in the much more modest facilities of the auxiliary forts (Fig. 388). A discovery at Ladenburg also shows that the *praetoria* in auxiliary forts were significantly higher than had been imagined so far: the fallen wall of a half-timbered

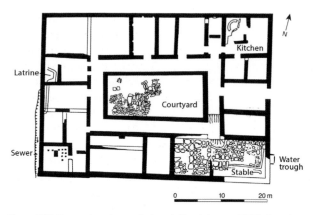

Figure 388 *Housesteads praetorium (after Johnson 1987). Drawing: A. Smadi, Arch. Institute University of Cologne*

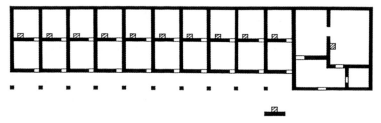

Figure 389 *Idealized reconstruction of a barrack building (after Johnson 1987). Drawing: A. Smadi, Arch. Institute University of Cologne*

building with rich painting and high-set windows allowed for a room height of at least 5.5 m high. This suggests that this was a particularly representative unit of rooms.[45] The findings could also indicate that those parts of the building that served for less official purposes were two-storeyed.

Tribunes' houses

The houses of the military tribunes, the senatorial *tribunus laticlavius*, the five or six equestrian *tribuni angusticlavii*, and probably also the *praefectus castrorum*, represent, albeit in a much more modest form, modifications of the Italian town-house.[46] These tribunes' houses were traditionally located in the *scamnum tribunorum* in the *praetentura* on the *via principalis*, where the tents of the tribunes in fact stood in the marching and field camps of the Republic.

The form and position of the tribunes' houses are most obvious in the Scottish legionary base at Inchtuthil, from the time of Domitian.[47] Apart from their location in the *scamnum tribunorum*, these are also clearly identifiable by their construction as buildings with an inner courtyard and several ranges of rooms. So far there is no other legionary camp in which the tribunes' houses can be seen quite so clearly in relation to each other, as at Inchtuthil. Occasionally, special buildings also occur, such as a *mithraeum* being found in a tribune's house at Budapest/*Aquincum*.[48]

Barracks

A legion consisted of 10 cohorts, which – probably only from the Flavian period – comprised the first cohort (*prima cohors*) of about 1000 men and the *cohortes* 2–10 of about 500 men. Each of cohorts 2–10 consisted of six *centuriae*, each of 80 men, commanded by a centurion. These *centuriae* were again divided into ten *contuberia* (sub-units of 8 men each), which were housed together in quarters in the barracks. The *prima cohors* consisted of five *centuriae* each of 160 men. To these infantry units were added 120 legionary cavalrymen. The centurions were ranked according to the *centuria* commanded by them, and the

highest rank that could be given to a non-commissioned officer below the level of the senators and *equites*, was that of the *primus pilus*, i. e. the centurion of the first *centuria* of the first cohort. These hierarchies were also reflected in the accommodations of men and centurions: this can best be understood at Inchtuthil.[49]

The soldiers in legionary camps and auxiliary forts were housed in elongated barracks buildings (*centuria*) with porticos to the front, which had developed from the tents in Republican marching camps and field camps (Fig. 389). They have no precursor in civilian architecture.[50]

In the infantry barracks, each *contubernium* had two rooms available, the rear sleeping and living room with four bunk beds (?) and a hearth. This dwelling was called the *papilio*, in front of which was a storage room for weapons and equipment, which was called the *arma*. These terms were derived from the Republican tradition, inasmuch as *papilio* actually means tent, and the *arma* was originally the forecourt in front of the tent, where weapons and baggage were deposited. In the *papiliones*, hearths and fire-places are found, which are moreover regularly absent from *armae*. It is assumed that the smoke was carried away from a clay and wood fireplace with a clay chimney in the roof.

Up to a few years ago, researchers were unsure whether the horses of cavalry units were housed in separate stables or not.[51] Recent excavations, like those at Ladenburg, Wallsend on Hadrian's Wall, or at Heidenheim,[52] have clearly shown that cavalry units lived under the same roofs as their horses, so the accommodation of the men was arranged differently here. There was a (heated) living room for three riders and next to it a stable for three horses. The reserve horses were probably placed outside the forts,[53] the *calones* ('stable lads') presumably in an upper storey above the stables.[54]

Depending upon the period, about 25 to 40 m² were available for a *contubernium* in an Imperial legionary base, and about 10 to 40 m² were available in an auxiliary fort (Davison 1989 passim). These calculations include cavalry barracks and assume the premise that Roman barracks only had residential and utility areas on the ground floor. However, there are indications that two-storey structures existed (*e.g.* the Praetorian Camp in Rome[55]). Currently the limited discoveries in the north-western provinces, where most camps have been excavated, usually do not provide an answer to the question of whether or not the

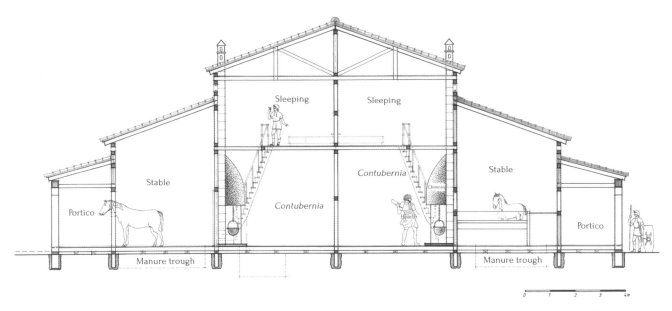

Figure 390 *Reconstruction of a two-storey cavalry barrack from Heidenheim (after Scholz 2009). Drawing: A. Smadi, Arch. Institute University of Cologne*

barracks were single-storied or two-storied one way or the other. In Heidenheim, however, the discoveries from the double barracks are extremely suggestive of a two-storey arrangement,[56] which might possibly also apply to other fortresses and forts (Fig. 390). The likely two-storey nature of the *praetorium* at Ladenburg can also be cited as a supporting argument.

The centurions inhabited the so-called officers' quarters at the end of the barracks, which offered a much higher level of comfort. Here, for example, baths, underfloor heating, or wall paintings, as well as several living and sleeping rooms were often situated. In some camps and forts, there were also larger areas at the other end of the barrack. These buildings may have housed the junior officers – the *optio*, as well as the *tesserarius* and the *signifer*. They also contained offices.

From the Augustan period onwards, it is noticeable that centurions' quarters were constructed in a very different way from the rest of the barracks. Thus, the officers' quarters were built as more substantial wooden or stone buildings, contrasting with the lightweight design of the *contubernia*, which for instance were built in half-timbered construction.

The officers' quarters were usually placed at that end of the accommodation for each of cohorts 2–10, which lay next to the defences, and thus closest to the enemy. In the event of an alarm, the centurions were apparently responsible for their centuries manning the section of the defensive walls or other emergency stations assigned to them. In the first cohort, the centurions' quarters fronted on to the *via principalis* and lay next to the *principia*. As a sort of bodyguard for the legionary commander, they were obviously responsible for his security, or constituted a tactical reserve under his direct command. This distinction can again best be observed in Inchtuthil. Here the centurion's

houses of the first cohort not only stand out because they differ from those of the other centurions in their location: they are also much larger and more comfortably built, but are still smaller than the tribunes' houses. However, there were also clear differences within the first cohort: the house of the *primus pilus*, with its pillared courtyard, was the largest and most beautiful of all five.[57]

As seen above, the structure of the accommodation of Roman legionary soldiers in their barracks can be seen with unique clarity in the base at Inchtuthil. Nevertheless, things are generally not quite as clear as they might seem. There are still some details under discussion: here, as in many other camps, the barrack blocks have 14 or more *contubernia* instead of the allegedly standard 10. On closer inspection, however, there also seem to be hardly any of these alleged 'standard barracks' in other bases, most barracks offering rooms for 11–14 *contubernia*. However, this not only means that more soldiers, such as troops in transit, could be accommodated, but that they might also be considered to have been additional storage rooms, office space, or workshops. Likewise uncertain, for example, is where the legionary cavalry were quartered or where the accommodation for the *immunes* were situated, if these were not also housed within the *centuria*.

Tabernae

Along the main roads of the legionary fortresses, as was the case at Inchtuthil for instance,[58] lay rows of simple buildings, which are probably the *tabernae* of the literary and epigraphic sources.[59] These were probably the accommodation for the baggage train, stable lads, muleteers, and the carters for the transport wagons. However, they also provided orderly offices, and stables for draft and pack animals, as well as sheds for wagons and the artillery. A letter from Vindonissa shows that the *tabernae* were numbered – that is, easy to find – and that in one of them a woman of indigenous origin ran a tavern.[60] However, such *tabernae* have not been identified in every base, the state of research possibly having a role in that, as well as the fact that less substantial timber structures have not always been recognized consistently in excavations. At Inchtuthil, 141 *tabernae* have been found, while at Novaesium, there were probably 106 *tabernae*.

Baths

Even in the early Imperial period, it can be assumed that soldiers from the Mediterranean area did not renounce their customary hot bath in the field. However, heated bath buildings are inevitably connected with stone architecture, so they are missing in the early timber-and-earth camps. However, it must be assumed that there were bathing possibilities in tubs and vats of wood and metal in buildings, which have not been identified from their floor plans as bath-houses. Military bath buildings in camps are constructed from the Neronian period onwards, as soon as camps were built in stone.[61] Their position within the camp at first varies quite a lot, but then a regular location in the *praetentura* on the right is adopted.

In contrast to the fort baths of auxiliary units, nearly all of which are of the same sequential type (*Reihentyp*), there is no standardized design for legionary baths. They have individual ground plans that were derived from urban baths.

From the Flavian period onwards, bath buildings were also indispensable for auxiliary forts. The baths of auxiliary units are only in exceptional cases within the fort (*e.g.* Niederbieber). As a rule, they are located outside in the fort *vicus*.[62] Fort baths were usually laid out according to the *Reihentyp* form, with the rooms for the most important bathing activities arranged sequentially: *frigidarium* (cold bath), *tepidarium* (warm bath) and *caldarium* (hot bath). They do not quite reach the level of urban bath buildings, but wall paintings and locally produced statues are sometimes attested. As stone and brick buildings, there are often abundant finds of stamped brick, indicating that the legions frequently supplied the forts situated in their field of operations and jurisdiction with building materials. Moreover, building inscriptions often record specialists, such as centurions detached from legions, who were deployed as leaders of building parties in order to build such technically demanding buildings as baths.

The size and also the quality of the facilities of fort baths depended on the size of the units near whose fort they lay; the size and importance of the fort *vici* seem also to have played a role. In the 3rd century AD, it can occasionally be noted that baths on the Upper German-Raetian Limes were reduced during reconstruction work, which allows corresponding conclusions to be drawn about the dwindling strength of the troops on this sector of the frontier – at Rainau-Buch fort on the western Raetian Limes, for example.[63] In Britain parts of the *vici* have been preserved with important structures, such as the bath buildings, in the form of the so-called annexe fortifications, which connect directly to the defences of the fort.[64]

Exercise halls

Exercise halls, where cavalrymen and infantrymen could practise fencing and shooting in the dry, are testified for legionary bases in literary sources, but are largely absent among archaeological discoveries.[65] At Inchtuthil, such a building was suggested to the left of the *praetentura*, but it is more likely to be a commercial building.[66] With the exception of Birdoswald on Hadrian's Wall (Wilmott 1997 and 1997a), no exercise hall has as yet been recognized for an auxiliary fort.

Grain storage (horrea)

One of the most important tasks for military logistics is the provision of sufficient food for soldiers. As the ancient sources show, the food given to the legionary soldiers of Rome was, above all, in the form of unground wheat, which had to be ground by the soldiers themselves with a hand mill. From this, each received at least 650 grams per day (Kehne 2004). In addition, there were bacon, cheese, vegetables, oil, and sour wine, which when mixed with water was the standard drink of the legionaries, *posca*. Other food, especially beverages, had to be purchased by the soldiers with their own money from the retailers (Junkelmann 2006). Central camp or field kitchens were unknown, meals being prepared by the soldiers themselves in the *contubernia*. Discoveries of hand mills with inscriptions from *contubernia* prove this.[67] In addition to bread, the main foods were cereal (*puls*) with various ingredients (Junkelmann 2006).

It is clear from all of this that the main task of military logistics in Roman times was to provide large quantities of grain in the bases. If we learn that, as was the case for Britain, for example, the annual consumption of a force was kept in stock in the camp (this corresponds to about 2,000 tonnes in the case of a legionary base), it is not surprising that there were numerous *horrea* (grain stores) in legionary camps and auxiliary forts.[68] Since the grain was obviously not stored in sacks, but rather as bulk material on floor boards, these *horrea* have a very distinctive method of construction. The floors were raised and thus set above ventilated spaces, which ensured a continuously dry storage.[69] In the case of wooden structures, *horrea* are recognisable from closely placed sill beam construction (Fig. 391, 392) for the foundations of these structures, while for stone buildings they were designed as pillars or closely placed parallel lengths of walling. On the short sides of the *horrea*, there

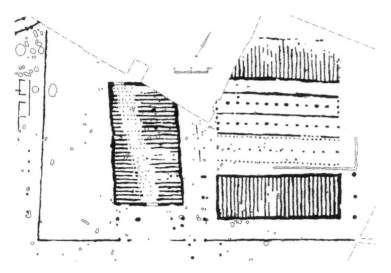

Figure 391 *Anreppen Augustan base, eastern area with horrea (after Fischer 2009a). Drawing: A. Smadi, Arch. Institute University of Cologne*

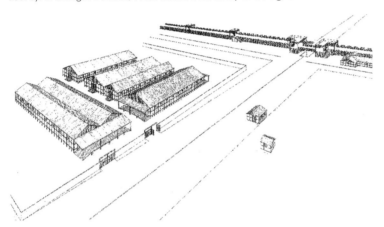

Figure 392 *Anreppen Augustan base, reconstruction drawings of horrea (after Fischer 2009a). Drawing: A. Smadi, Arch. Institute University of Cologne*

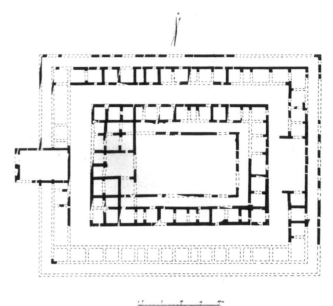

Figure 393 *Vetera I valetudinarium (after v. Petrikovits 1975). Drawing: A. Smadi, Arch. Institute University of Cologne*

were loading platforms. In the case of stone buildings, buttresses were always attached to the walls which bore the thrust against the outer walls from the grain. Corresponding supports may also have existed for the wooden buildings, but they cannot normally be identified from ground plans.

Horrea were always constructed near the camp gates, in order to provide short distances for transport by wagon. A special form of *horrea* was found in the late Augustan base camp at Marktbreit, never used, which was intended for the logistics of the short-term campaign against the Bohemian Marcomannic kingdom of Maroboduus in the year AD 6. Here, a grain-drying kiln was placed in the vicinity of a *horreum* to protect the grain, which had become damp during transportation, from being destroyed during storage.[70]

Hospitals (valetudinaria)

According to E. Künzl's studies, *valetudinaria* were an invention of the Augustan period, which were not derived from civilian models of hospital buildings in the Mediterranean

area. They are evidently based on the invention of a brilliant military architect who had to take account of the fact that the climate of the north-western provinces and fighting with the Germans led to a higher incidence of sick and wounded.[71] Thus, in legionary camps, a four-sided building complex was built around a peristyle courtyard with a garden (Fig. 393), which was in the Mediterranean tradition in a more general sense. One side served as an entrance area and contained operating rooms, storage rooms, possibly also kitchens or rooms with other function, the other three wings having corridors opening on to small wards on both sides, as well as rooms for nursing staff. All in all these *valetudinaria* are surprisingly modern. It might almost be thought that they were the model for modern hospital buildings. However, there is no indication of continuity, examples of *valetudinaria* of the form just described no longer being found even in the Late Roman period.

Hospital buildings are assumed for auxiliary forts as well, but the problem is that these have not yet been identified as clearly.[72] Buildings in the *latera praetorii*, mostly corridor buildings, which are certainly not *fabricae*, are often referred to as *valetudinaria*. This is especially the case when there is a second, similar construction, which can safely be identified as a *fabrica* because of furnaces, finds of slag, or the like. In none of these postulated *valetudinaria* in an auxiliary fort, have inscriptions, surgical instruments, or other finds been found up to now which would confirm such an assertion.

Workshops (fabricae)

Further building complexes consisting of smaller units of rooms grouped around a courtyard or corridor are often encountered in legionary fortresses and auxiliary forts. They frequently contain water tanks or ovens of various types and sizes. Slags, moulds, and semi-finished products sometimes make it clear that these are *fabricae* or workshop buildings, mainly for metal processing.[73] These *fabricae* were mainly found during the early occupation of an area, and as soon as a civilian economic infrastructure was formed, much of the supply for the troops shifted to the private sector. Therefore the evidence for the production and repair of weapons and military equipment accumulated in the *canabae legionis* and the fort *vici*.

Storage and other rooms

In addition to the *horrea* and *tabernae*, a whole range of buildings of different forms are found in camps and forts, the function of which is unclear. They are often referred to as storage and store rooms, but it is not impossible that these were smaller, specialized workshops.[74] Armouries (*armamentaria*) are recorded in legionary camps and auxiliary forts in the side ranges of the *principia*, but also in separate buildings, as for example at Carnuntum and Rainau-Buch.[75] In the case of the fort at Künzing, it was possible to prove that it contained not so much the fighting arms of the soldiers as old stocks, reserve and surplus weapons, parade armour and tools for the pioneers (Fischer 1991). *Armamentaria* have also been proved to have existed in cities (Eck 1990).

Ovens

Occasionally, ovens are found built into the *agger* (rampart) of a fortification, on the edge of the *via sagularis*. At the Saalburg, in particular, entire kiln batteries have been excavated which, of course, were not all in use at the same time, but were replaced over time.[76]

Water supply and latrines

The supply of fresh water and provision for sewerage were a matter of course for legionary camps and auxiliary forts of a more permanent nature. Accordingly, camps and forts seldom had wells, except for a well in the *principia*.[77] Water tanks (for fire-fighting water), baking ovens, or latrines were frequently integrated into the rear of the earthen ramparts of the defensive circuit, on the *via sagularis*.[78]

Infrastructure and facilities

Exercise and training sites (campus)

An exercise ground (*campus*) should be expected to have existed at every camp and fort too, but in fact such sites are rather rare. At Hardknott Castle fort in northern England, a *campus* of about 1.3 ha is recognisable in the landscape, for example, but they are also known from altars dedicated to the *campestres*, the tutelary deities

of the *campus*. A *campus* has now also been identified near the cavalry fort at Heidenheim.[79] Round pens or enclosures, such as those found in the *vici* of some forts, like Virunum in Noricum,[80] were also used for the training of horses and for cavalry games. Just such a '*gyrus*' was laid out within the Neronian fort of The Lunt at Baginton in southern England.[81]

Civilian settlements in the area

A civilian settlement grew near every Roman garrison of troops that had existed for a while. In the case of legionary camps, the term *canabae legionis* has survived (von Petrikovits 1981). These *canabae* were under military control and had no administration of their own, although they could resemble a town.

Civilian settlements around auxiliary forts were considerably smaller, although they were equipped with temples, *fora*, amphitheatres, and bath buildings (Sommer 1988; Moneta 2010). The latest survey results on Hadrian's Wall or on the Upper German and Raetian Limes clearly show that most of the fort *vici* have been underestimated in terms of their size and facilities (Mischka *et al.* 2010). Fort *vici* were planned together with the fort by specialists from among the troops and laid out according to the same system of measurement, the resulting regular parcels on the planned streets and squares then being developed by civilians who had followed the troops.[82] Among these were craftsmen, innkeepers, prostitutes, and traders, as well as the families of the soldiers.

The distinctive quality of the fort site, its favourable road traffic, and later a densely populated hinterland, were the reasons why most of the *vici* in the north-western provinces continued to exist after the relocation of garrison and the complete withdrawal of the troops. They not only remained as settlements, but sometimes blossomed into impressive towns in the wake of economic development.

3. The most important types of camps and forts

In a proper marching camp the soldiers are safe day and night, even if the enemy is at the gates. It is as if they were in a mobile fortress, which they carry with them everywhere (Vegetius, *Epitoma rei militaris* 1.21).

Marching camps without internal buildings

The term 'marching camp' means very short-term fortifications, often occupied only overnight. The Roman military, at least on the march through enemy territory, built one every evening. Defences of a turf wall with earthen rampart and ditches were built around the camp, reinforced by the palisade stakes carried by the troops. Inside, there were the customary leather tents to house the soldiers and baggage of the Roman army, not permanent buildings. Such installations are normally only indicated archaeologically by their ditches. In the interior, baking ovens, waste pits, or latrines can be found as archaeological features. As a rule, finds are scarce or even non-existent, which is not exactly conducive to more precise dating.

Republican marching camps

The best evidence for the emergence of marching camps, as they are so appropriately characterized by Vegetius, is based on literary, not archaeological sources. At the very beginning, there is the description of a marching camp (Fig. 394) by Polybius (6.26–32): this camp was designed for two legions and auxiliary troops, a total of 16,800 infantry and 1,800 cavalry. It was a square with each side 2,017 Roman feet (around 600 m) long. The surveying team first marked out a cruciform axis, the intersection of which was called the *groma* after the surveying device placed there. Behind the *groma*, the site for the *praetorium* was marked with a white flag. From this cruciform axis, the whole camp interior was now set out and the places for the individual units and functional areas marked with coloured flags.

In front of the *praetorium*, but still within the *retentura*, the tents were set up for the 12 legionary tribunes, six for each legion. In front of these tents was the principal camp road, the *via principalis*, which connected the *porta principalis dextra* with the *porta principalis sinistra*. Its centre was called the *principia*, a designation which was to

be passed on to the headquarters building in the Imperial period. Another transverse road, the *via quintana*, ran across the storage area in front of the *praetorium*, in the *praetentura*. The *via sagularis* usually extended right round the defences. In specific cases, this area, the *intervallum*, could be particularly broad to accommodate cattle and booty and to keep the tents out of reach of enemy missiles. The road from the *praetorium* to the gate facing it, the *porta praetoria*, was called the *via praetoria*, the rear gate the *porta decumana*.

In the *praetentura*, on either side of the *via praetoria*, lay one legion, along with the accompanying cavalry, which was formed from allies. In the 2nd century BC, the legions were still divided into different parts from those after the Marian army reforms: the maniple, consisting of two centuries, was still the smallest tactical unit of the legion, each legion having 30 maniples. It was only with the reform of the army that the *centuria* became the smallest tactical unit, the legion thus being more flexible to lead. These maniples were arranged in battle in three equally strong ranks: in front were the light-armed troops (*hastati*), then fully armed men (*principes*), and then the veterans, the *triarii*. The soldiers of the legion also occupied their tents within the camp in this formation. The *equites*, the cavalry, were situated directly on the *via praetoria*, so that they could leave the camp as quickly as possible, the auxiliary infantry being located at the sides, facing the encirclement. On the side of the *praetorium* were the *quaestorium*, the camp treasury, and the *forum*. These were, in turn, flanked by the bodyguard of the general, in this case one of the two consuls, the *pedites* and *equites extraordinarii*. Behind these were other *extraordinarii* as well as other allied troops.

Imperial-period marching camps

Marching camps from the Republic are extremely scarce as archaeological monuments, while those of the Imperial period are still being discovered with relative frequency. Research into these is particularly good in Britain, since the onset of aerial photography in the 1920s enabled the discovery of many of these installations. So far, more than 200 marching camps are known in the UK, with several camps often being found in one place. It is also often the case that in a place where marching camps were concentrated during the occupation phase, permanent bases were later built (Welfare and Swan 1995). Usually only the backfilled ditches are known from these marching camps, or, in rare cases, the remains of the rampart. Traces of interior buildings are, of course, hardly ever present, because they consisted only of tents.

In recent years, since aerial archaeology has become possible in the former Eastern Bloc countries following the fall of the Iron Curtain, numerous marching camps of

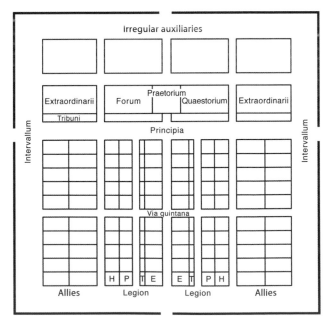

Figure 394 *Plan of a Roman marching camp from the time of the Republic, as described by Polybius (after Johnson 1987). Drawing: A. Smadi, Arch. Institute University of Cologne*

various sizes have become known in the area north of the Danube frontier in Pannonia. They are usually from the Marcomannic Wars of the second half of the 2nd century AD (Komoróczy 2009). As examples of marching camps, only a few more recently studied examples are mentioned here, connected with the German campaigns under Augustus (Fig. 395).

HEDEMÜNDEN IM WERRATAL (GERMANY)

At Hedemünden, in the region of Göttingen in Lower Saxony, a number of Roman camps were discovered in the valley of the Werra, which here in fact forms the upper course of the Weser.[83] It is an oval camp of 2 ha, probably occupied on a long-term basis, as well as two other facilities, probably marching camps, located at a ford on the Werra (Fig. 396). The material published to date belongs to the Oberaden Horizon.

HOLSTERHAUSEN (GERMANY)

In Dorsten-Holsterhausen, eight Augustan marching camps have been discovered and excavated since 1952 (Fig. 397). The larger camp of two is situated on the north bank of the Lippe, occupying an area of about 900 × 500 m and, at 50 ha, is only slightly smaller than the base at Oberaden (54 ha). The defences consisted of a V-sectioned ditch approximately 4 m wide and 2.5 m deep, as well as a turf rampart with no wooden buildings. Gateways were located on three sides. There were no permanent internal timber buildings, with only a few waste pits and ovens set into the ground being found. More recent investigations about 200 m west of this camp were carried out and over an area of 15 ha, the ditches of five other marching camps being discovered (Ebel-Zepezauer 2003; Ebel-Zepezauer et al. 2009). The eight camps known so far from Holsterhausen are more likely to belong to the time of Drusus' offensive, as is evident from the sparse small finds, with occupation in the time of the Haltern Horizon also being indicated.

Practice camps

Sometimes, aerial archaeology in the vicinity of legionary camps, such as at Xanten and Bonn, repeatedly results in the discovery of large concentrations of camp ditches of different sizes, which lack internal structures and do not really seem explicable as marching camps. Many of them have just lengths of ditch or corners, but not complete enclosures. One has to assume these are practice camps. Practice camps usually consist only of backfilled ditches and no finds. Examples can be found in the Xanten area (Vetera I and II). Aerial photographs from Britain and from Straubing-Hofstetten on the Raetian Danube Limes show that such practice camps also existed in the vicinity of auxiliary forts.[84]

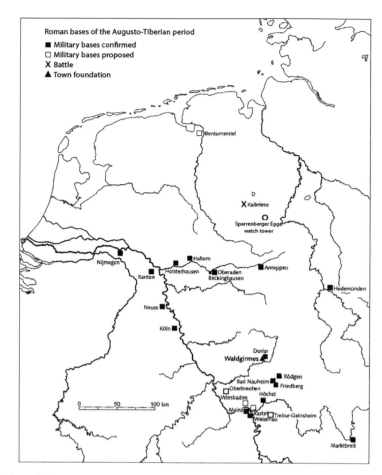

Figure 395 *Roman military bases and civilian settlements between the Rhine and the Elbe in the Augustan to early Tiberian periods (after Fischer 2009a). Drawing: A. Smadi, Arch. Institute University of Cologne*

Permanent camps with internal buildings

Semi-permanent Republican camps

While marching and practice camps lack internal buildings and are virtually free of finds, the so-called semi-permanent camps, which were built as winter quarters or siege camps, have internal buildings and finds, which are frequently suitable for extremely accurate dating independent of any historical tradition. The internal structures were mostly rudimentary designs, which changed according to the geographic location. In the arid areas of Spain or Palestine, these buildings were built from drystone walling and covered with wood. In the more temperate zones, such as in Gaul, buildings of just wood or, at best, wattle and daub were erected.

CÁCERES EL VIEJO (SPAIN)

This strictly rectangular camp with sharp-edged corners was excavated by Adolf Schulten during 1910–1930 and published by Günter Ulbert (Ulbert 1984). It was provided

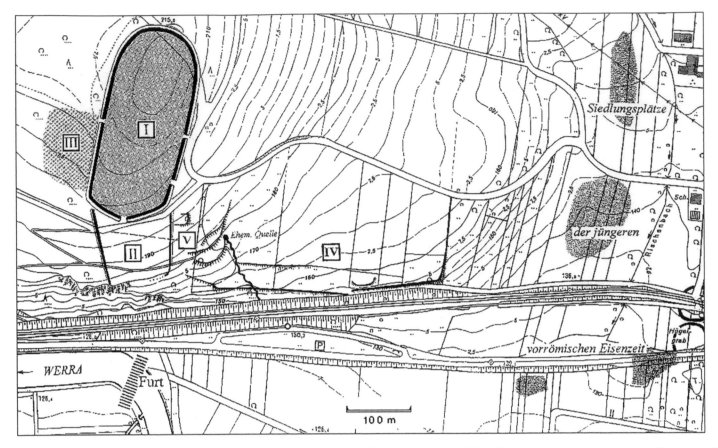

Figure 396 *Augustan camp near Hedemünden. I: permanent camp with Annexes. II and III; IV–V: presumed camp; shaded: settlements of the Later Iron Age, east of which are two large burial mounds (after Fischer 2009a). Drawing: A. Smadi, Arch. Institute University of Cologne*

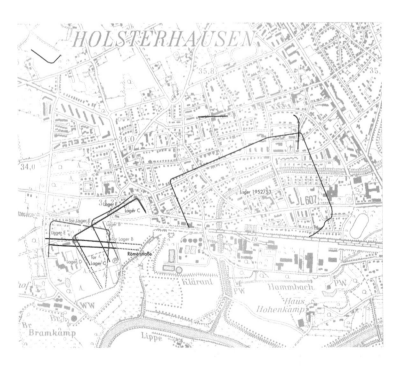

Figure 397 *Augustan marching camp 1952/53 and excavation areas 1999–2002 in Holsterhausen (after Fischer 2009a). Drawing: A. Smadi, Arch. Institute University of Cologne*

with sturdy internal buildings of stone, was occupied only briefly, and ended with a burnt layer rich in finds (Fig. 398). Cáceres was most likely Castra Caecilia of the Roman general, Caecilius Metellus, mentioned in the sources, destroyed during Rome's wars against the renegade commander Sertorius in 79 BC.

Siege works of the Republican and Imperial periods

NUMANTIA (SPAIN)

In the bitter and changing wars of Rome with the Celtiberians of Spain (154–133 BC), the northern Spanish city of Numantia played a particularly important role as the core of Spanish resistance. The conquest of Numantia was attempted several times by the Romans and ended in catastrophes for the besiegers. Only Scipio Aemilianus the Younger, the adopted son of Scipio Africanus, successfully captured the northern Spanish town of Numantia after an eight-month siege in the years 134/133 BC. The city was surrounded by an 8.9 km-long wall and ditch, including six large camps. Numantia capitulated in 133 BC. These camps were examined and published by the ancient historian Adolf

Schulten from Erlangen in the years 1906–1908 (Fig. 399) and even today represent an important milestone for provincial Roman military archeology.[85]

ALESIA (FRANCE)

During Caesar's Gallic War, the Great Gallic Uprising under Vercingetorix took place in 52 BC. The insurgents gathered in Alesia, the *oppidum* of the Mandubiii. Caesar had the city surrounded with a 16 km-long fortification. This consisted of a line of obstacles facing the city, and a 21 km-long line of contravallation, which was a successful defence against the attacks by the Gallic relief army (Fig. 400). This circumvallation incorporated seven large military camps, which, following the first excavations under Napoleon III, have been investigated and published by a Franco-German research project (Reddé and von Schnurbein 2001; Reddé *et al.* 2006; Reddé 2006). Some Roman, Celtic, and probably also Germanic weapons were found, mainly in the ditches of the siegework around Alesia. Other Caesarian camps are known to some extent there and elsewhere, but have not yet been systematically explored.

DURA-EUROPOS (SYRIA)

The Persian siege works in the area of the city wall of Dura-Europos on the Euphrates dated to around AD 256/7.

Camps, fortresses and forts of the early and middle Imperial period

During the reign of Emperor Augustus (27 BC–AD 14), the conditions for the garrisoning of Roman troops changed fundamentally. After the end of the civil war and the final pacification of Spain, no major concentration of troops was needed inside the empire, apart from the Imperial guards and some units with a police function in Rome. The territorial expansion to the Rhine, Danube, and Euphrates had given Rome fixed frontiers, which were threatened by dangerous enemies. Thus it was only logical to station the military on these focal points for active or threatened conflicts. Since Tiberius revised the plans of Augustus to make the Elbe the frontier of the empire in AD 16, the Rhine frontier gained in importance as a naturally stable river frontier. This finally led to the establishment of fixed garrisons of troops, which then lasted for many years. This fixed garrisoning of troops on the frontier was soon followed by an ever-growing military and civilian infrastructure. In addition, there was a civilian settlement system that was closely related to the military and its huge economic potential. Under Claudius, auxiliary troops, which had previously been closely bound to the legions, gained

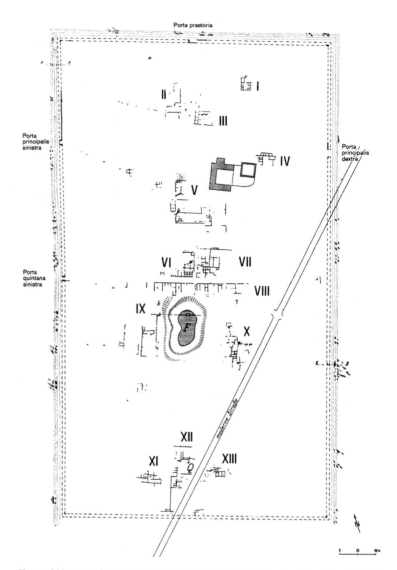

Figure 398 *Plan of the camp at Cáceres el Viejo in Spain (after Ulbert 1984). Drawing: A. Smadi, Arch. Institute University of Cologne*

greater independence. This was due to the fact that they were increasingly used for frontier protection. The basic form and interior construction of the now increasingly common group of auxiliary forts looked to legionary fortresses. From the middle of the 1st century, at the latest, Roman fortifications were presented as uniformly standardized installations with a mostly elongated, rectangular basic form with rounded corners ('playing card shape'). As a rule, these fortifications were built at first with a timber-reinforced earthen fortification and with internal buildings made of wattle and daub. Once the appropriate infrastructure was available in the Neronian period, they were converted into stone, starting with the legionary fortresses.

Double legionary bases in chronological order

TRIER-PETRISBERG (GERMANY)

The oldest Roman camp in Germany (30/29 BC) stretched over at least 50 ha on the Petrisberg on the steep eastern bank of the river Moselle, above the later Trier (Löhr and Trunk 2008). It offered space for two legions and auxiliary troops (cavalry). Geophysical prospection and rescue excavations under H. Löhr have taken place since 2001. The elongated oval base had defences comprising a turf rampart and two V-sectioned ditches. Only the north gate has been found so far. Inside the single-phase, densely built camp, roads, the *praetorium* (?), wells, latrines, and cavalry barracks were found. Ceramic finds already discovered in the 1930s, combined with the coin series from the recent excavations and a dendrochronological date from the spring of 30 BC, connect the camp with the literary account from 30–27 BC of the suppression of the revolt of the Treveri under Nonius Gallus. The camp at Petrisberg was probably the short-term winter camp of Nonius from 30/29 BC.

NIJMEGEN/*BATAVODURUM* (NETHERLANDS)

Cassius Dio (54.32) reports that in 12 BC Drusus led his army over the *insula Batavorum* against the Germanic tribes of the Usipetes and Sugambri. A large Augustan camp of about 42 ha on the Hunerberg in Nijmegen can be directly connected with this action. There were two legions and auxiliary troops here (Fig. 401). The camp has the typical polygonal form of the early period, which is well adapted to the terrain. The camp was surrounded by a turf rampart, hardly visible during excavation, in front of which ran a double V-sectioned ditch. The east and the west gates (25 × 9 m), as well as towers 3 × 3.6 m and 24 m apart, have so far been detected. Out of the internal timber buildings, the *principia* (?), *praetorium* (?), tribunes' houses, and the barracks and the centurions' quarters are partly known so far. This camp was soon abandoned, but a legionary base, the camp of *legio X Gemina*, was erected in the Flavian period. The brief period of occupation begins with a deposit which predates the beginning of Drusus' offensive of 12 BC.[86]

To the east, on the Kops plateau, contemporary with the large camp on the Hunerberg, an Augustan oval-shaped fortification of almost 3.5 ha and with an unusual internal

Figure 399 *Numantia with the surrounding Roman siege works (after Luik 1997). Siege works of the Republic and the Imperial period at Numantia (Spain)*

Figure 400 *Reconstruction of the Caesarian siege works at Alesia (after Reddé 2006a). Graphic: P. Connolly*

layout was created.[87] Inside, there was a remarkably large and luxurious wooden *praetorium* (Fig. 402), as well as several officers' houses, but hardly any accommodation for troops. The *praetorium*, which in many details corresponded to that of contemporary legionary camps, is a building with a floor plan clearly related to the top-quality residential architecture of the Augustan period in Italy, according to investigations by R. Förtsch.[88] From this, Förtsch concludes that the inhabitants were from the top echelons of society, perhaps Drusus himself. The theory that the headquarters of Drusus and other generals during the first Germanic offensive was on the Kops Plateau thus has much in its favour.

OBERADEN (GERMANY)

At Oberaden, a seven-sided camp of about 56 ha was built entirely of timber.[89] The sides measure about 840 × 680 m. The 2.7 km-long wall cleverly used the lie of the land, hence the remarkable, seven-sided form. The defences consisted of a V-sectioned ditch, 4–5 m wide and 2–3 m deep, and a 3 m-wide, double-shelled timber-and-earth rampart (Fig. 403). Four gateways have been found, with the construction of the east gate apparently being secondary. Towers have been detected every 25 m. In the modern excavations of the internal buildings, parts of the *principia* and *praetorium*, as well as accommodation for the troops, have been examined.

Finds of weapon and equipment point to legionary and auxiliary troops, including cavalry. For the earliest date, dendrochronological data are available: the wooden components of the defences at Oberaden are made of green oak, felled in the late summer of 11 BC. This date is in perfect agreement with the passage in Cassius Dio (54.33.4) where Drusus, retiring to winter quarters, built a camp as a bulwark against the Sugambri at the confluence of the Lippe and Elison. The dating of the final withdrawal from the camp is based on numismatic and historical considerations. In the year 8 BC, Tiberius, after the death of his brother Drusus the year before, stopped all Roman activity east of the Rhine. Some 40,000 Germans, especially Sugambri, were deported to the region to the west of the Rhine. Thus the main task of Oberaden, namely to keep the Sugambri in check, was gone. The camp was apparently rendered unusable, the larger buildings being burnt down. Similarly, the wells were systematically poisoned with faeces, animal carcasses, and kitchen waste, to prevent the enemies of Rome from using the site.

MARKTBREIT (GERMANY)

One of the most spectacular new finds of Roman archaeology of recent years is the large Roman timber-and-earth camp on a bend in the Main near Marktbreit in the Franconian region of Bavaria (Fig. 404). It was discovered by aerial photography and explored by magnetometer survey and

VIA PRINCIPALIS

0   100   200m

Figure 401 *Nijmegen, the Augustan double legionary base on the Hunerberg (after Fischer 2009a). Drawing: A. Smadi, Arch. Institute University of Cologne*

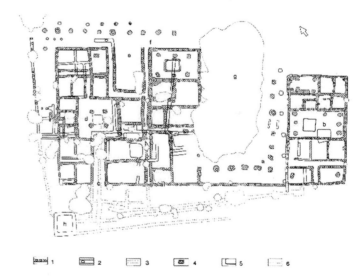

1   2   3   4   5   6

Figure 402 *Nijmegen, the praetorium of the Augustan base on the Kops plateau. 1: posts in foundation trenches; 2: posts in foundation trenches – rebuild; 3: drainage channels; 4: hearth; 5: cellar; 6: rubbish pit; a: peristyle courtyard; b: central room with cellar; c: entrance; d: atrium; e: room flanked by a narrow corridor; f: north-east portico; g: modern disturbance; h: cistern (according to Fischer 2009a). Drawing: A. Smadi, Arch. Institute University of Cologne*

excavation under the direction of Martin Pietsch up to 1993.[90] Over an older, smaller camp, a 37-ha base was built, with an area of 760 × 480 m and a defensive system of 2.3 km in length, which could accommodate two legions with their auxiliary troops. The fortification consisted of a timber-and-

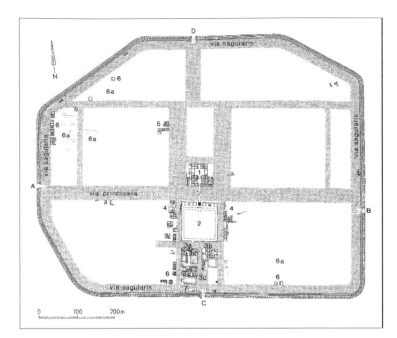

Figure 403 *The Augustan double-legionary base at Oberaden. 1: praetorium; 2: principia; 3 larger residential buildings; 4: houses and tabernae; 5: buildings of unknown function; 6: officers' quarters; 6a: barracks; 7: structure at the south gate; A: porta principalis dextra; B: porta principalis sinistra; C: porta praetoria; D: porta decumana (after Fischer 2009a). Drawing: A. Smadi, Arch. Institute University of Cologne*

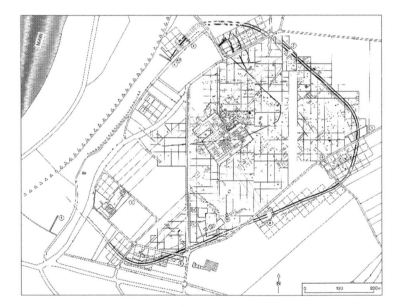

Figure 404 *The Augustan base at Marktbreit. 1; 3; 4; 5; 6; 7; excavated areas of defences with south and north-east gates; 2: barrack and storage building; 9; 13; 15: central buildings; 10; 11: officers' quarters; 16: principia (after Fischer 2009a). Drawing: A. Smadi, Arch. Institute University of Cologne*

earth wall (2.80 m width) and a double V-sectioned ditch. In the interior, the buildings were in part placed close to each other and included a *principia, praetorium*, officers' accommodation, and a timber *horreum*. However, there were also large open spaces. The few finds belong to the Haltern Horizon. The camp was obviously never occupied by troops and was deliberately burnt down by the Romans after a short time in which it had stood empty. There are various options for placing the camp at Marktbreit into a historical context, but, after weighing all possibilities, the most likely interpretation seems to be a connection with Tiberius' campaign against the Bohemian empire of Maroboduus of the Marcomanni in the year AD 6.

XANTEN/*VETERA* I (GERMANY)

In connection with Drusus' offensive, a first camp was erected around 13/12 BC on the Fürstenberg, a push moraine dominating the landscape at Xanten near the mouth of the Lippe, the name of which Tacitus has preserved as Vetera Castra. For the oldest camp, Enclosure B, the 18th Legion, which was defeated in the battle against Varus of AD 9 AD, is assumed to have built it, its presence being indicated by the tombstone of the centurion, Marcus Caelius. *Legio V Alaudae* and *legio XXI Rapax* are attested as the garrison of Vetera for the year AD 14 by Tacitus, then, around AD 46 the 21st Legion was replaced by the *legio XV Primigenia*. From the Tiberian to early Claudian period there was a polygonal double-legionary camp of about 45 ha on the Fürstenberg. The 56-ha rectangular Neronian double-legionary camp then replaced this. It was the first camp on the Rhine to be built in stone (Fig. 405) and possessed one *principia*, but two *praetoria* and a *valetudinarium*. There was a civilian settlement, the *canabae legionis*, belonging to the camp, of which a wooden amphitheatre is still visible in Birten as a depression in the landscape (Hanel 1995; Hanel and Song 2007).

Legionary camps in chronological order

From the Augustan period there were two types of fortress in which legionary troops were based. On the one hand, there are very large permanent camps (up to 56 ha), which are designated as double-legionary camps, and also included the auxiliary units assigned to the legions. The other are vexillation fortresses (well below 20 ha), in which parts of legions and auxiliaries, mostly cavalry and archers, could be found. The 'classic' legionary bases, in which a complete legion (initially together with their auxiliary troops) was based, only began in the Tiberian period with the base at Vindonissa. From the time of Claudius, auxiliary troops become increasingly self-sufficient and received their own forts, but there are also exceptions (*e.g.* Bonn) where, until the end of the 3rd century, they

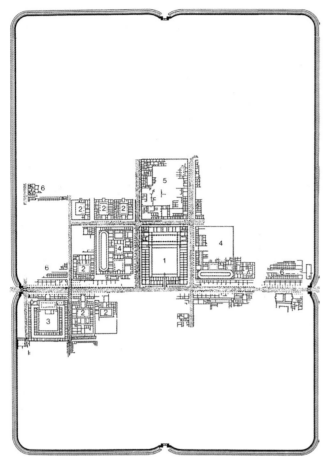

Figure 405 *The double-legionary fortress of Vetera I (after Petrikovits 1975). Drawing: A. Smadi, Arch. Institute University of Cologne*

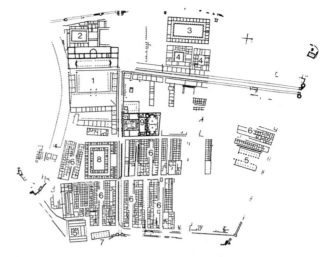

Figure 406 *The legionary fortress of Vindonissa (after Petrikovits 1975). Drawing: A. Smadi, Arch. Institute University of Cologne*

remained in the legionary fortress (von Petrikovits 1975; Campbell 2006).

WINDISCH/*VINDONISSA* (SWITZERLAND)

In Windisch in the Swiss canton of Aargau, where the legionary base of Vindonissa had been since AD 16/17, a garrison of the Roman occupation army lay beneath the later camp. This small force probably did not have any offensive tasks, but was rather assigned to secure supply lines.

Under Tiberius, the 13th Legion was stationed in Vindonissa in a permanent earth-and-timber structure from AD 16/17 onwards (Fig. 406). The fortress lay on a high gravel terrace between the Aare and Reuß, and overlay a small Augustan military post. The fortress was related to important long-distance routes that led from the Rhône to the upper Danube or via the upper Rhine and the Bünde passes to Italy. The exact size and position of this earliest fortress are not yet known, but it is certain that there were also auxiliaries in the base. Around AD 45, the 13th Legion was transferred from Vindonissa to Pannonia and replaced by *legio XXI Rapax*. They constructed the fortress

in the form of an irregular, seven-sided stone construction covering 23 ha. It contained the *principia*, *praetorium*, tribunes' houses, bath buildings, a *valetudinarium*, store buildings and *horrea*, a temple of Mars, barracks, and – outside the fortress – a *forum* and an amphitheatre. Since the 21st Legion had made itself unpopular during the turmoil of 69/70 by triggering and suppressing a revolt of the Helvetii in this region, it was sent by Vespasian to Bonn in the year 70. The 11th Legion arrived at the fortress. The archaeological evidence here confirmed, as in Mainz, the information from Tacitus that Mainz and Vindonissa were the only fortresses on the Rhine which were not destroyed in the upheaval following the death of Nero. Under Trajan, the 11th Legion was withdrawn to the middle Danube, the fortress being abandoned and released for civilian development (Hartmann 1986).

NEUSS/*NOVAESIUM* (GERMANY)

The legionary base of the Claudian to the Trajanic period was largely excavated and published by Constantin Koenen in 1988–1900 (Fig. 407). This so-called Koenenlager was for a long time regarded as the most excavated Roman legionary fortress. Today, this excavation still leaves many questions unanswered. With a size of 570 × 420 m (22.8 ha), the oldest wooden building phase of the fortress of *legio XVI* was already built in the form of a playing card, which was retained by the two (?) subsequent stone building phases. Following destruction in the Batavian revolt, *legio VI Victrix* rebuilt the fortress. After their withdrawal to the lower Danube area in the early 2nd century AD, the fortress was evacuated. Around the middle of the 2nd century, an unknown *ala* built its fort in the centre of the old legionary fortress. It measured 187 × 165 m and covered 2.7 ha.[91]

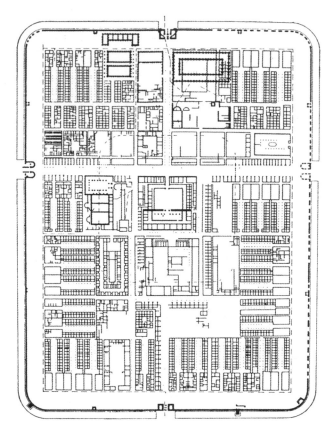

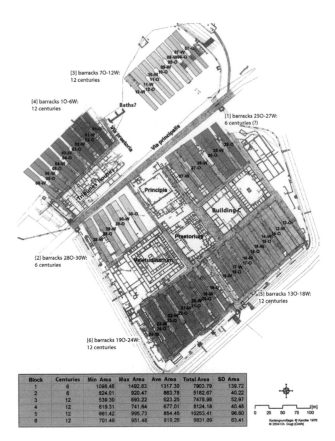

Block	Centuries	Min Area	Max Area	Ave Area	Total Area	SD Area
1	6	1098.46	1492.83	1317.30	7903.79	139.72
2	6	824.01	920.47	863.78	5182.67	40.22
3	12	539.30	693.22	623.25	7478.98	52.97
4	12	619.31	741.64	677.01	8124.18	40.48
5	12	661.42	995.73	854.45	10253.41	96.60
6	12	701.49	951.48	819.28	9831.09	63.41

Figure 407 *The legionary fortress of Novaesium (after Petrikovits 1975). Drawing: A. Smadi, Arch. Institute University of Cologne Carnuntum (A)*

Figure 408 *The legionary fortress of Carnuntum (after Gugl 2007a)*

CARNUNTUM (AUSTRIA)

From the Claudian period onwards, various legions were based in the fortress at Carnuntum in Lower Austria: *legio XV Apollinaris* until AD 62, then *legio VII Gemina*, *legio X Gemina* and *legio XXII Primigenia*. After 72, *legio XV Apollinaris* returned, until it was replaced by *legio XIV Gemina Martia Victrix* under Trajan. This remained there until the end of the Roman frontier at Carnuntum. Apart from the legions, various auxiliary units are epigraphically documented, and the *classis Flavia Pannonica* also had its main base in *Carnuntum*.

Since the legionary base at *Carnuntum* was excavated extensively before the First World War by M. Groller von Miltensee, the results are, by today's standards, fraught with many problems. At virtually no point were natural deposits reached, the building traces of all periods being drawn together in an undifferentiated manner, and there was hardly any separation of finds and features according to their stratigraphy. In 1968–1977, a stratigraphic excavation of limited size in the north-east of the fortress yielded seven construction periods from the Claudian period to the 8th century AD.

The fortress forms an irregular polygon, the north side of which has fallen victim to erosion by the Danube (Fig. 408). Its length is still 490 m, the width varying between 334 and 391 m. At only about 17.7 ha, Carnuntum is well below the usual size of legionary fortresses (about 20 ha). This could explain the perceived absence of fortress baths. Two unexpected details are a kink in the line of the defences to the north of the *porta principalis sinistra* on the one hand, and on the other an indentation in the defences at the *porta principalis dextra*. There was a double ditch around the fortress, which, however, at a point south of the east gate was replaced by a single ditch. Despite the unusual outline of the fortification, the internal structure of the stone building phase largely reflects the classic fortress layout: the *principia*, *praetorium*, tribunes' houses, and the barracks, the fortress bath buildings seemingly missing.

According to the available evidence, the fortress was built in the Claudian period (AD 41–54), using timber-and-earth constructions. Soon afterwards, rebuilding in stone began, probably only completed under Trajan. In the late 4th and 5th centuries, the remaining civilian population seems to have moved into the fortress. When barracks became dilapidated in the 5th century, they were in part replaced by Germanic post-built constructions. Destruction could not be verified for the late period, the fortress seeming to have slowly decayed in the course of the early Middle Ages (Gugl and Kastner 2007; Gugl 2007a).

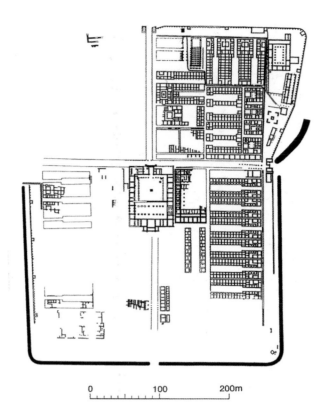

Figure 409 *Nijmegen, Flavian legionary fortress (after Petrikovits 1975). Drawing: A. Smadi, Arch. Institute University of Cologne*

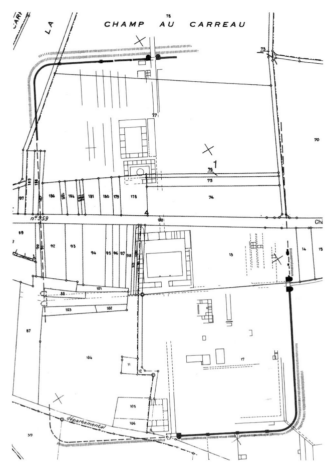

Figure 410 *The legionary fortress of Mirebeau (after Goguey and Reddè 1995), Mirebeau (F)*

NIJMEGEN/*NOVIOMAGUS* (NETHERLANDS)

In Nijmegen, Vespasian had a 17 ha legionary base built on the Hunerberg on the site of the Augustan double-legionary fortress, abandoned much earlier. This was rebuilt in stone under Trajan (Fig. 409). In the years AD 70–1, *legio II Adiutrix* occupied the fortress, replaced by *legio X Gemina*. This legion was then moved to Transylvania for the Dacian Wars around AD 104, afterwards being stationed in Budapest/*Aquincum*. After the withdrawal of *legio X Gemina* around AD 104, a vexillation of *legio XXX Ulpia Victrix* from Xanten (Vetera II) seems to have maintained a military presence here as a caretaker garrison. It is possible that around 121 under Hadrian, *legio IX Hispana* from Britain was in the fortress for a short time before moving to the East. By AD 125 at the latest there was no longer any garrison in Nijmegen, but to the west of the fortress, the civilian *municipium Ulpia Noviomagus* flourished.[92]

MIREBEAU (FRANCE)

Following first the discovery of brick stamps and then aerial photography and excavations, it became apparent that *legio VIII Augusta* had for a short time occupied a legionary base at Mirebeau in Burgundy in the second half of the 1st century AD, and not, as had until then been assumed, returned to Strasbourg. The fortress lies on the road from Geneva to Langres in modern Burgundy, where a road leads from Autun to Dijon. In this location, a concentration of brick stamps of *legio VIII Augusta* had long been known (Fig. 410).

This means that it did not return to Strasbourg at the time of the restoration of the frontier defences under Vespasian (AD 69–79), but instead only shortly before AD 100. One reason for this is the fact that the uprisings in Gaul, which took place in the course of the year of three emperors and the uprising of the Batavians, made it advisable for the Romans to station a legion in this uncertain territory. The finds indicate Mirebeau was occupied for a period from the 50s to the 90s of the 1st century AD (Goguey and Reddé 1995).

INCHTUTHIL (GREAT BRITAIN)

The most northerly Roman legionary fortress was that at Inchtuthil in Scotland, which served as a base for the short-term Caledonian offensive of Agricola attributed to the 20th Legion. It was most probably only in use between AD 83 and 86. It is therefore well dated and closely too, and

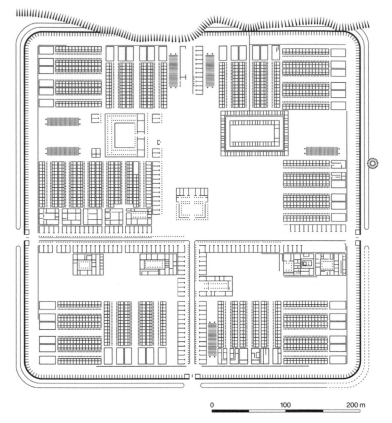

Figure 411 *The legionary fortress of Inchtuthil (after Petrikovits 1975). Drawing: A. Smadi, Arch. Institute University of Cologne*

six large *horrea*, the place for at least two more having been left free. A building identified by the excavator as a *basilica exercitatoria* stood in the eastern *praetentura*, in front of the *scamnum tribunorum*. The building, measuring 25 × 50 m, was built around a gravelled courtyard, but its function is controversial.

The barracks for the 10 cohorts of the legion can be seen more clearly, the first of which with about 1000 men was twice as strong as the rest. The officers' quarters for the centurions of cohorts 2–10 were built at the end of the barracks, those of the first cohort being oriented towards the *via principalis*, next to the *principia*. However, not only the differing position separates the centurions' buildings of the first cohort from those the other centurions: the former are also much larger and more comfortably built, but still have smaller dimensions than the tribunes' houses. However, there were also clear differences within the first cohort: the house of the *primus pilus* with its pillared courtyard was the largest and most beautiful of all the five. As for other structures usual for a Roman legionary base, water and sewerage pipes, latrines, and ovens were found.[93]

CAERLEON/*ISCA* (GREAT BRITAIN)

This 20.5 ha fortress was constructed in timber in the shape of a playing card in the years AD 74/75 for the control of southern Wales (Fig. 412). It replaced the earlier legionary base at Usk. The rebuilding in stone around AD 100 is connected with the arrival of *legio II Augusta*. The

moreover represents one of the very few legionary bases which, due to their short period of occupation, remained single-phase and without modifications to the interior, with only the wooden defences being quickly replaced in stone. Gates, towers, and internal buildings, however, were still timber structures (Fig. 411).

The base at Inchtuthil has numerous features typical of fortress construction in the Flavian period, but also some anomalies. These include the fact that obligatory buildings such as the *praetorium* are missing, while there is a lot of free space in the camp, which would be densely built up in a normal camp.

The defences of the almost-square legionary camp at Inchtuthil encompassed 21.8 ha. It was surrounded by a V-sectioned ditch of about 6 m width and 2 m depth. The *principia* at Inchtuthil lies in the centre of the camp behind the *via principalis*. At 45 × 42 m, the headquarters building is only slightly larger than those in most auxiliary forts, which is much too small for a legionary fortress. The *valetudinarium* was located in the *retentura*, both its construction and its size lying within the standard range. The *fabrica* was likewise built around a courtyard, but with three-aisled halls on three sides and one side with single rooms and the entrance. In the fortress there were

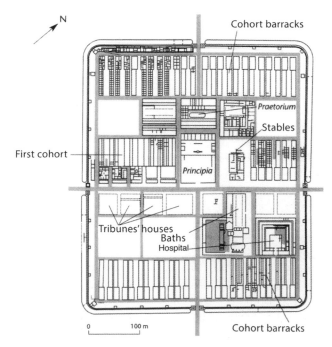

Figure 412 *The legionary fortress of Caerleon (after Campbell 2006). Drawing: A. Smadi, Arch. Institute University of Cologne*

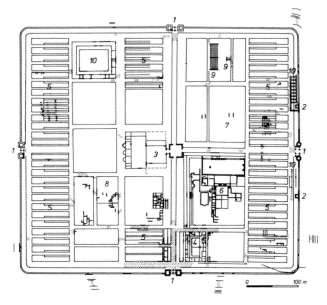

Figure 413 *The legionary fortress of Budapest (after Polenz 1986). Drawing: A. Smadi, Arch. Institute University of Cologne*

internal buildings are related to those at Inchtuthil, but here a large bath building was added in the *praetentura*. Up to AD 260, *legio II Augusta* remained in the camp until it was withdrawn under the British usurper Carausius (287–93).[94]

BUDAPEST/*AQUINCUM* (HUNGARY)

As a result of the wars against the Quadi and the Dacians, a legion was stationed on the middle Danube in Budapest/*Aquincum* under Domitian: *legio II Adiutrix*. Its timber-and-earth base was first constructed around AD 89 in the form of a trapezoid, the later fortress only partially overlapping it (Fig. 413). However, the troops were soon withdrawn for the Second Dacian War and Trajan's Parthian campaign, and was replaced by *legio X Gemina Pia Fidelis* from Nijmegen between AD 105 and 118. When *legio II Adjutrix* returned to remain until the end of the Roman Empire, the *legio X* was transferred to Vienna/*Vindobona*. The stone fortress was built at the beginning of the 2nd century. It existed throughout the 2nd and 3rd century AD and had an area of 476 × 570 m (27.1 ha), with the *porta praetoria* facing the Danube. While on the western side, there was only one ditch, three ditches ran around the other sides. Some of the internal buildings are known: the *principia* with tetrapylon over the *groma*, tribunes' houses, one with *mithraeum*, fortress baths, *valetudinarium*, *fabricae*, and a *horreum*.

Around AD 330, that is, under Constantine I (AD 306–37), the old fortress was abandoned and replaced by a newly built Late Roman fortress, which adjoined the western wall of the former fortress.[95]

VIENNA/*VINDOBONA* (AUSTRIA)

The legionary fortress at Vienna was built under Domitian (AD 81–96) when the *legio XIII Gemina* was moved from Ptuj/*Poetovio* to the Danube. This is interpreted as being in the context of the German Wars of AD 89–93. It was then soon replaced by *legio XIIII Gemina Martia Victrix*. After AD 114, the *legio X Gemina* remained in Vienna until the 5th century AD. The size of the fortress, which was first built in wood and then in stone, is unclear, since its northern extent was washed away by the Danube in post-Roman times (Fig. 414). In addition to a plethora of minor separate observations, larger excavations have mainly occurred in the *latera praetorii*.[96]

TURDA/*POTAISSA* (ROMANIA)

Around AD 170, a legionary fortress was constructed within sight of the gold-rich mountains of the Transylvanian highlands and near the salt mines of Turda, in order to better get the area under military control. The camp of *legio V Macedonica* was built on the site of the *vicus* of *Potaissa*, already mentioned under Trajan, the name of which passed to the fortress and its civilian settlement (Fig. 415). The legion was moved to Dacia Porolissensis from the province of Moesia Inferior on the lower Danube. After the evacuation of the province of Dacia under Aurelian (AD 271–4), the troops also returned. So far, only small parts of the camp have been uncovered and preserved. The camp was laid out as a regular rectangle, 573 × 408 m, which corresponds to an area of 23.37 ha.

The excavated parts are portions of the defensive wall with gates (*porta decumana* later closed by masonry) and (two-phased!) corner towers, with a ditch in front of it. Of the internal buildings, the *principia* has been completely excavated, and the baths have been identified, just as parts of the accommodation for the *prima cohors*, other barracks, and a *horreum*.[97]

LAMBAESIS (ALGERIA)

The construction of the first fortress by *legio III Augusta* took place around AD 129 under Hadrian. The legion was disbanded and demobilized in AD 238 as a punishment, because it had committed itself to the wrong side in the civil war of that year. It was reformed under Valerian in AD 253, so a new fortress was built (Fig. 416). This existed until the time of the tetrarchy around AD 300. With the establishment of French colonial rule, the extremely well-preserved fortress was at first used as a quarry for a prison, with excavations starting in 1866. The *principia* and the *groma* in front of it are particularly well preserved.[98]

REGENSBURG/*REGINUM* (GERMANY)

The building inscription (*IBR* 362) confirms the completion of the defences of Regensburg legionary base in the year

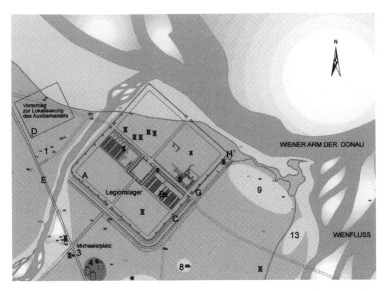

Figure 414 *The legionary fortress of Vienna and probable location of the auxiliary station (D) (after Kronberger 2007)*

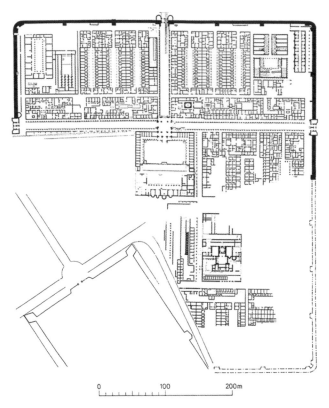

Figure 416 *The legionary fortress of Lambaesis (after Petrikovits 1975). Drawing: A. Smadi, Arch. Institute University of Cologne*

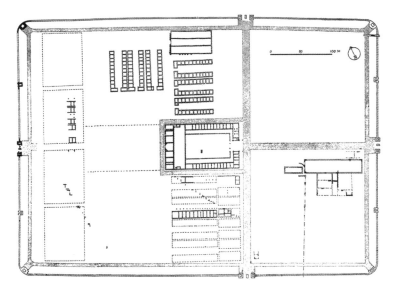

Figure 415 *The legionary fortress of Potaissa (after Barbulescu 1997). Drawing: A. Smadi, Arch. Institute University of Cologne*

AD 179. The 3rd Italica legion, which was only raised at the beginning of the Marcomannic Wars, is established as the garrison. This legion remained in its fortress in Regensburg, where it is attested to have been almost to the end of the Roman rule in Raetia in the early 5th century AD (Fig. 417). On the south bank of the Danube, opposite the mouth of the Regen, a fortress was completed within a few years of construction which, with its dimensions of 542 × 453 m (*c.*25 ha), clearly exceeded the area of about 20 ha necessary for a legion. So far, however, there is a lack of evidence for any auxiliary unit that may have been located within the fortress. After phases of destruction in the 3rd century AD, the unit was reduced in the Late Roman period and possibly occupied a smaller fort within.

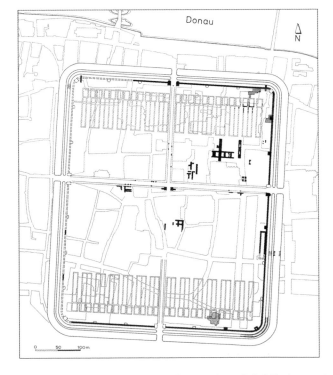

Figure 417 *The legionary fortress of Regensburg (after Fischer and Rieckhoff-Pauli 1982). Drawing: A. Smadi, Arch. Institute University of Cologne*

The rest of the area of the fortress offered space for the civilian population after the *canabae legionis* had been given up (Dietz and Fischer 1996).

LORCH-ENNS/*LAURIACUM* (AUSTRIA)

In the late 2nd century, the *legio II Italica Pia Fidelis* built the legionary fortress of *Lauriacum*, after abandoning the old base at Albing, and remained there until the Roman frontier was abandoned in the Late Roman period. The lie of the land here is responsible for a strange anomaly in the street grid, namely that the north-east to south-west and north-west to south-east oriented axes of the legionary camp do not cross at right angles, resulting in the ground plan of the fortress having the shape of an oblique-angled diamond (Fig. 418). The length of the legionary base was 539 m, its width 398 m, resulting in an area of approximately 21 ha. The defensive wall was 2.1 m wide at foundation level and secured by 30 towers in total (one tower at each corner, between which there were seven on the long and six on the narrow sides). In front of the wall was a 15 m-wide and 4 m-deep ditch, which is still visible in some stretches. Of the four gates, the *porta principalis dextra* was completely recorded, while the remainder was only partly recorded or not at all. A little bit of a problem arises with the internal buildings because, due to the older excavations, several phases from the early 3rd century to the Late Roman period have been drawn on the ground plan together. We know the following details of the internal structure: the *principia*,

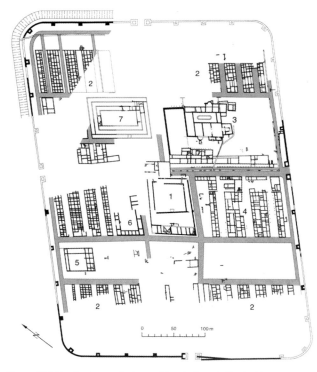

Figure 418 *The legionary fortress of Lorch-Enns (after Petrikovits 1975). Drawing: A. Smadi, Arch. Institute University of Cologne*

barracks buildings for 10 cohorts, the accommodation of the *prima cohors* (first cohort) to the right of *principia*, bath-buildings, *fabricae*, and the *valetudinarium*.[99]

Vexillation fortresses in chronological order

Numerous detachments from legions, which were assembled from units for a limited time for campaigns or other special tasks, are known from literary and epigraphic sources (Saxer 1967). Often, legions were not sent into a theatre of war as complete units, but acted in the form of ad hoc detached subunits, the *vexillationes*. Together with auxiliary units, especially cavalry, these formed independent tactical units for a limited time, which were then disbanded after completion of the task and returned to their original units. We also know of some exceptions, where vexillations were garrisoned for longer periods separated from their original units, for instance in North Africa.

In Great Britain especially, archaeological research has identified fortresses which were evidently occupied by legionary troops, but are too small for a whole legion. As a rule, their size corresponds to half a legionary fortress (about 10 ha). In addition, there are also indications of auxiliary troops, especially cavalry, in these fortresses. Such bases have lately also been found on the Rhine and the Danube. These fortresses occur with particular frequency in the Augustan period on the Rhine and Lippe and in England during the period between Claudius and the Flavian dynasty. They are referred to as vexillation fortresses in publications.

It seems that, contrary to popular notions, vexillation fortresses were the norm in the early phase of the occupation of an area or in war, while double and normal legionary bases were the exceptions. For the Augustan period in Germany, for example, we know of no fortresses for a whole legion, with only double-legionary bases or vexillation fortresses known. It was not until the consolidation of Roman domination and the establishment of the Rhine border in the Tiberian period, that the sequence of classic single-legion sites began with Vindonissa. In Britain, during the occupation phase up to the Flavian period, vexillation fortresses outnumber legionary bases.

DANGSTETTEN (GERMANY)

The largest military base of the early occupation period is the camp discovered in 1967 at Dangstetten north of the upper Rhine.[100] The camp was an elongated oval in shape with a re-entrant south-east corner. It originally measured about 420 × 300 m, thus having an area of approximately 12 ha. It was protected by a timber-and-earth rampart in the form of a 3 m wide wooden, earth-filled box rampart of more than 1.3 km in length and with two V-sectioned ditches. Wooden towers were uncovered every 40 m; out of

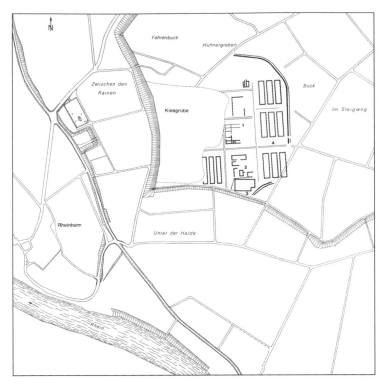

Figure 419 *The vexillation fortress of Dangstetten (after Filtzinger et al. 1986). Drawing: A. Smadi, Arch. Institute University of Cologne*

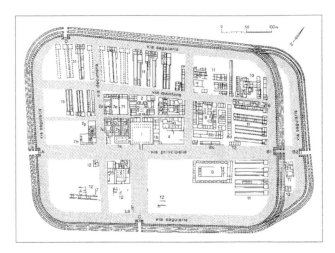

Figure 420 *The vexillation fortress of Haltern, main base (Hauptlager): 1 principia; 2: praetorium; 3, 5–7: residential buildings for officers; 4: building of unknown function; 8 fabrica with sheds; 9: valetudinarium; 10: building of unknown function; 11 barracks; 12 building of unknown function; 13 horrea; A: porta principalis dextra; B: porta principalis sinistra; C: porta praetoria; D: porta decumana (after Fischer 2009a). Drawing: A. Smadi, Arch. Institute University of Cologne*

the presumed four gates (Fig. 419), the *porta praetoria* and two further gates were located and excavated. Among the poorly preserved wooden internal buildings, the *principia*, *praetorium*, workshops, and *horrea* could be identified. Similarly, accommodation for the troops, partly for cavalry, was confirmed.

The interior of the camp had enough room for at least half a legion, and the finds also confirmed the presence of legionary infantry and Gallic (and Germanic?) auxiliaries. An equipment identification tag made of bronze sheet names the 19th Legion. The sigillata finds, as well as other indications derived from the material, suggest the possibility that the camp at Dangstetten was occupied from the time of the Alpine campaign (15 BC), its abandonment dating to the years 9 or 8 BC, thanks to the complete absence of more recent coins, which were found in large numbers in camps occupied slightly later. This means that Dangstetten, along with the camp at Oberaden on the Lippe, is one of the most accurately dated and, at the same time, earliest Roman establishments on German soil.

HALTERN/*ALISO* (?) MAIN CAMP (GERMANY)

Above the valley of the Lippe, the so-called main fortress was constructed over the slightly older and smaller so-called field camp in the time around the birth of Christ.[101] The defences of the roughly rectangular main base consisted of two V-sectioned ditches, *c.*6 m wide and *c.*2.5 m deep

with a 3 m wide timber-and-earth rampart (Fig. 420). The main fortress at Haltern had a short axis, the *porta praetoria* being aligned to the south-eastern long side facing the Lippe. The *porta principalis dextra* and *sinistra* lay at the respective ends of the *via principalis* on the narrow sides, the *via decumana*, quite unusually, in the west corner of the camp. At an unknown point in time, the camp was extended by 55 m to the east and thus increased in area from 16.7 to 18.3 ha. Approximately 75% of the interior area has been archaeologically examined or destroyed unobserved. The main road network can be reliably reconstructed.

Haltern main camp, with its 16.7 and 18.3 ha size, was a vexillation fortress with a mixed garrison of legionary and auxiliary infantry, as well as auxiliary cavalry. The garrison may have had a maximum of six to seven legionary cohorts, along with auxiliary units (cavalry and oriental archers). Parts of the 19th Legion can be identified as based at Haltern from an inscription on a lead bar as well as from a graffito. The camp at Haltern was burnt down in the year AD 9 after the battle in the Teutoburg Forest. It is possibly identifiable as the site of *Aliso*, attested by various ancient writers.[102]

In the main fortress at Haltern, there is evidence of structural changes and of installations, such as pottery kilns, which have not been found in other Augustan camps in this form. For example, barracks were replaced by workshops, and the base had an unusually large number of well-appointed buildings, which are attributed to officers. Similar residential buildings, and a possible temple were later added from time to time, and were most unusually built in part on fortress streets. The provision of a water supply is demonstrated by lead pipes. The far-reaching development of this infrastructure is very unusual for a military camp planned for the short-term. From all this, S. von Schnurbein concluded that these were the signs of an ongoing process of transformation in the main base at Haltern, changing it from a purely military base to a more civilian town centre. This is in line with the testimony of the ancient sources that in this last phase of Roman presence in Germany east of the Rhine, the establishment of a province also led to the accelerated establishment of civil centres.[103]

LONGTHORPE (GREAT BRITAIN)

The camp at Longthorpe near Peterborough in the south-east of England was discovered and examined by S. S. Frere and J. K. St Joseph (Frere and St. Joseph 1974). It was made up of two superimposed fortresses using timber-and-earth technology. The larger camp, at 10.9 ha, was a typical vexillation fortress for legionary infantry and auxiliaries, with defences of a turf rampart and two V-sectioned ditches (Fig. 421). The *principia, horrea*, and various barracks for legionary infantry and cavalry were recognisable among the wooden internal buildings. The camp offered space for about 2,000 legionary infantry and around 1,000 cavalry. The smaller base, 4.4 ha in size, overlay the larger, so it was later. Its defences featured an (established) turf rampart and a V-sectioned ditch. Internal buildings were not identified. It offered space for *c*.1,000 cavalry. The finds indicated that it dated to the Claudio-Neronian period. Longthorpe is one of the few Roman military camps to be linked directly to a historically recorded episode (Tac., *Ann.* 14.32): after the insurrection against Roman rule of the year AD 61, led by Boudicca, queen of the Iceni. Petilius Cerialis, the commander of the *legio IX Hispana*, was defeated by the insurgents when he came to the aid of the oppressed colony of *Camulodunum/* Colchester. His legion (or better: legionary vexillation) was completely wiped out. He had saved himself and his cavalry by fleeing back to his original fortress, retiring into it and refortifying it. The fortress of Longthorpe can now be regarded with certainty as the camp of Petilius Cerialis, which he had left with his vexillation of legionary infantry from the 9th Legion plus auxiliary cavalry. This corresponds to the larger, older camp (10.9 ha). After the infantry had been wiped out, Cerialis returned with just the cavalry and entrenched himself in his old fortress for the rest of the war in a base that was reduced to the size of the force. This base can undoubtedly be equated with the later, smaller camp (4.4 ha).

EINING-UNTERFELD (GERMANY)

A large base was located on the Unterfeld field near Eining in Bavaria thanks to casual finds and the surviving remains of ditches. Excavations in the 1960s, as well as aerial photographs, which were published in 1979, today reveal a camp of 328 m in length and 320 m in width with an area of *c*.10.6 ha, the north side of which was washed away by the Danube. In the centre of the camp is a stone *principia* with a semi-circular apse forming a chapel of the standards; at the highest point in the eastern *retentura*, there was a building with two apses, which were connected by a corridor (Fig. 422). These comprised the stone components

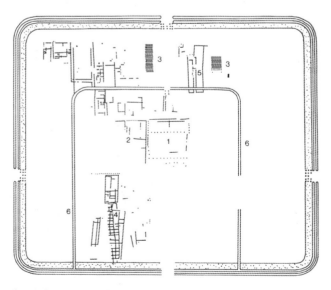

Figure 421 *The Longthorpe vexillation camp (after Johnson 1987). Drawing: A. Smadi, Arch. Institute University of Cologne*

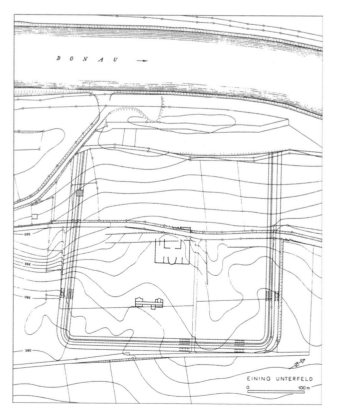

Figure 422 *The vexillation fortress of Eining-Unterfeld (after Christlein and Fischer 1979)*

of an otherwise wooden *praetorium*. Stray finds suggest a workshop for the processing of copper alloy. Numerous finds confirm the dating of the Eining-Unterfeld fortress, which was only in use for a short period, during the time of the Marcomannic Wars between AD 171/2 and 179.[104] The base at Eining-Unterfeld was a vexillation fortress in which the finds (brick stamps, small finds) indicate legionary infantry (about half of the *legio III Italica*) and auxiliary cavalry were located temporarily. With the completion of the Regensburg legionary base in AD 179, the camp at Eining-Unterfeld was abandoned.

Vexillation forts

This designation was proposed in 2010 by M. Mackensen in the publication of his excavations at Gheriat el-Gharbia in Libya (Mackensen 2010). These are sites which, at 1.15 ha (Bu Njem) or 2.25 ha (Gheriat el-Garbia), for example, are similar in size and construction to cohort forts. However, there are enough inscriptions to demonstrate, for example, a legionary unit from the *legio III Augusta* outposted from Lambaesis as garrison at Bu Njem/*Gholaia* in Libya. Their strength of about 200 men is based on calculations from the excavated troop accommodation (Figs 423–4). After the disbandment of *legio III Augusta* in the summer of AD 238, this unit is downgraded and now bore the name *vexillatio Golensis*. In addition, there were also some

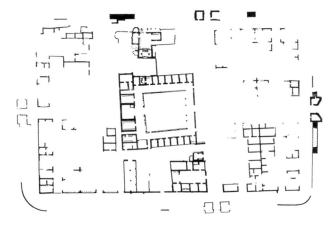

Figure 423 *The Bu Njem vexillation fort (after Mackensen 2008)*

Figure 424 *The Bu Njem vexillation fort, graffito of a fort (after Mackensen 2008)*

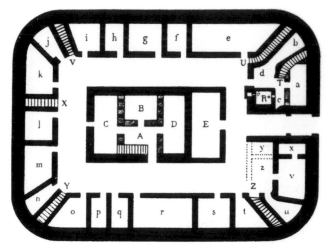

Figure 425 *Rhilane vexillation fort (after Mackensen 2010)*

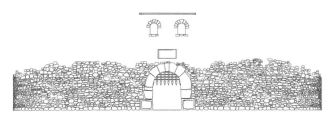

Figure 426 *The vexillation fort of Rhilane, gate (after Mackensen 2010)*

cavalry who were drawn from a larger unit (Mackensen 2008). At Geriat el-Gharbia/*Myd (...)* in Libya, a *vexillatio* of the *legio III Augusta* from *Lambaesis* was also recorded epigraphically for the period AD 201–38, but as the internal buildings are unknown, we have no indication of their strength (Mackensen 2010a). The exceptionally well-preserved, 0.09-ha small fortlet of Ksar Rhilane/*Tisavar* in Tunisia (Figs 425–6) should also be classified as a vexillation fort, since a garrison of a *vexillatio* of *legio III Augusta* from *Lambaesis* can be assumed here (Mackensen 2010).

The fort of Hod Hill in southern England can also be attributed to this type of fortification (Fig. 427). This fort (4.4 ha), which was only occupied for a few years, was built during the course of the Claudian conquest of southern England by incorporating parts of the surrounding fortifications of a fortified British settlement ('hillfort') into the defences of the fort. Therefore, the layout has a slightly different form from the usual 'playing card shape'. From the remains of buildings and from the finds, a garrison of legionary infantry and auxiliary cavalry can be confirmed (Brailsford 1961; Richmond 1968).

Supply bases

ANREPPEN (GERMANY)

A peculiarity among the Augustan military camps in Westphalia was the wooden base at Anreppen south of

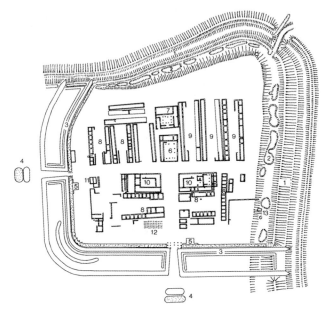

Figure 427 *The vexillation fort of Hod Hill, 8 auxiliary barracks; 9 legionary barracks (after Johnson 1987). Drawing: A. Smadi, Arch. Institute University of Cologne*

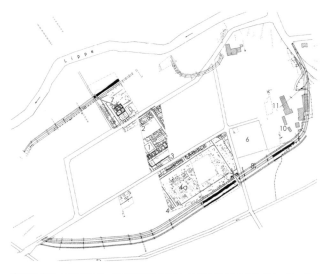

Figure 428 *Anreppen, Augustian base. 1: praetorium; 2, 3: residential and service buildings; 4 officers' quarters; 4a: barracks; 5: porta principalis dextra; 6, 11: horrea; 7 bath building; 8: structures on the side of the gates; 10: barracks (after Fischer 2009a). Drawing: A. Smadi, Arch. Institute University of Cologne*

Delbrück. It is situated on level ground immediately on the southern bank of the Lippe (Fig. 428), without taking advantage of higher ground or an elevated bank. The camp was designed in the form of an irregular oval of about 750 × 330 m in size and about 23 ha in area. It was thus still 5 ha larger than the main fortress at Haltern. A re-entrant in the defences on the bank of the Lippe has been explained with good reasons as a riverine harbour, which was thus directly under military protection. The

eastern part of the camp was recently excavated south of this port, where several *horrea*, some of which were separated from the rest of the camp by palisades, have been found.[105] Consequently, Anreppen can be seen as a hitherto unknown combination of an encampment for troops and a supply base for a larger campaign. The *praetorium*, with its 3,375 m², was far larger than the *praetoria* of the other Lippe camps (Oberaden 2,420 m², Haltern main fortress 2,120 m²). This largest of all known *praetoria* is also very unusual in its layout. R. Förtsch concluded from this that Tiberius was the erstwhile builder and inhabitant of this building,[106] for which there is further evidence (see below).

From the size of the camp, a legion, including auxiliary troops, could have been accommodated. Finds suggest the presence of legionary soldiers and auxiliary troops (oriental archers and cavalry). Apparently, the camp was abandoned by the Romans after a short period of time and deliberately burnt down. A first, cursory examination of the finds indicates a dating within the Haltern Horizon, in other words the first decade AD. Since coins with Varus counterstamps are missing from the now immense coin series, it ended before AD 7, the year when Q. Varus took over the governorship of Germany.[107] It is thus with good reason that the camp of Anreppen can be seen as the winter camp of Tiberius, dating from AD 4/5, attested to by Velleius Paterculus (2.105), when Tiberius personally took command of the '*immensum bellum*' in AD 1 and finished it victoriously.

RÖDGEN (GERMANY)

The Augustan supply base at Rödgen in the Wetterau is a unique facility up until now. It was excavated on a large scale by H. Schönberger.[108] The polygonal shape of the fortification is based on the local topography. Around the base ran two V-sectioned ditches, of which the inner was up to 3 m deep. A 3 m-wide timber-and-earth rampart consisted of a front and back wall filled with earth. It encompassed 3.3 ha and had wooden towers at regular intervals (Fig. 429). As for the gates, the main gate is recorded as having features typical of the period; two further gates are extrapolated just from the narrowing of the ditches and seem only to have been sally ports. The south gate is only suspected. The wooden interior of the camp at Rödgen completely disrupts the regular pattern of Roman military bases: in the centre is a sort of administrative building with a large court which has little to do with a conventional *principia*. Here, the *praetorium* seems to have been integrated into a kind of residual *principia*. The most important buildings are three large *horrea* (Buildings A, B, and C9), which were 47.2 × 29.5 m, 29.5 × 33 m, and 35.5 × 30.7 m. The function of a two-room building is unclear. About 1,000 men could theoretically have been accommodated in six barracks with officers' quarters. A large part of the base was only equipped with light buildings or not built upon. Without doubt, the

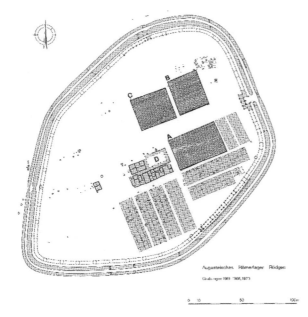

Figure 429 *The Augustian supply base of Rödgen. A–C: horrea; D: principia (according to Fischer 2009a). Drawing: A. Smadi, Arch. Institute University of Cologne*

fortification at Rödgen was not a base for troops, but rather a heavily guarded supply base for campaigns or the supply of other camps. In addition to cereals, for example, horses, draft animals, and cattle could have been accommodated there. The small finds clearly show that the camp at Rödgen belongs to the Oberaden Horizon, that is, from about 10–8/7 BC, perhaps within the framework of the Drusus offensive. Then the camp was vacated as planned.

SOUTH SHIELDS (GREAT BRITAIN)

The fortified supply base at South Shields, near the eastern end of the Hadrian's Wall, is characterized by a highly complex architectural history (Fig. 430). Here, grain from the south of England, which had been brought by ship, was stored in order to carry it further to supply the frontier troops and for campaigns. In the late 2nd and 3rd centuries AD, extensive structural changes were carried out in the fort: a smaller camp was developed under Septimius Severus (AD 193–211) into a supply base with 24 *horrea* to prepare for his campaigns in the north of Britain. In the years AD 222 and 235, even the old *principia* was transformed into *horrea*. In exchange, a new *principia* and troop accommodation were created in the former *retentura*. Between 273 and 318, the barracks in the *retentura* were replaced by a large residential building, probably a *praetorium*. A part of the *horreum* built into the former *principia* was restored into its old function. The last occupants of South Shields, according to the *Notitia Dignitatum*, was a *numerus barcariorum Tigrisiensium*, which replaced the previous garrison of the *cohors V Gallorum* (Bidwell and Speak 1994; Allason-Jones and Miket 1984).

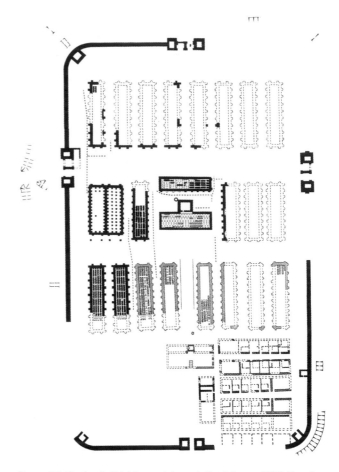

Figure 430 *The South Shields supply base (after Johnson 1987). Drawing: A. Smadi, Arch. Institute University of Cologne*

Auxiliary forts

From the time of the Claudian period and during the second half of the 1st century AD, a blueprint for the construction of auxiliary forts developed, which, complemented by various individual peculiarities, lasted until the end of the 3rd century AD. From the time of the Flavian era, most of the forts were laid out in the 'playing card shape', borrowing heavily from the structure and design of legionary fortresses, but they were naturally smaller in line with the size of the garrison. For a 500-strong infantry unit (*cohors quingenaria*) up to a 1000-strong cavalry unit (*ala milliaria*), the space needed was between *c.*1.5 and *c.*6 ha. However, we are less and less inclined to take the size of the fort as proof for the type of unit in occupation. Increasingly, the evidence suggests that, besides the garrison unit, detachments of other units could also occur in auxiliary forts (Johnson 1987; Campbell 2009).

Ala forts

Cavalry forts were designed for either an *ala quingenaria* or for an *ala milliaria*. An *ala quingenaria* was made up of 480 cavalrymen, each divided into sixteen *turmae* of 30 men, the leader of the *turma* being the *decurio* (not to be confused with the title of a city councillor of the same name). A *praefectus alae* from the equestrian order served as commander of an *ala*. From the Flavian period onwards, an *ala milliaria* consisted of 1008 cavalrymen, divided into 24 *turmae* of 42 men. *Ala* forts were each about 3.1 to 4.2 ha in the case of an *ala quingenaria*, *alae milliariae* being accommodated in forts of around 5.2 to 6 ha.

For a long time, there has been discussion as to whether stables and barracks were structurally separate in cavalry forts. By now, new excavations, for example in Ladenburg, Oberstimm, or in Wallsend in northern England, showed that stables and the men's quarters were accommodated in common barracks buildings. Another unanswered question was the problem that not all of the horses, including the remounts, could be accommodated within any cavalry base. This was solved by only stabling one horse per rider in the camp, while the remounts were kept in paddocks outside the fort.

ALA QUINGENARIA

CARNUNTUM (AUSTRIA)

The fort of approximately 4 ha was founded under Domitian (AD 81–96) and rebuilt under Hadrian (AD 117–38) by the *ala I Thracum Victrix* (Kandler 2007). The fort was thus reduced to about 3.65 ha. As a peculiarity, the fort baths were located within the facility (Fig. 431). Used as a kind of

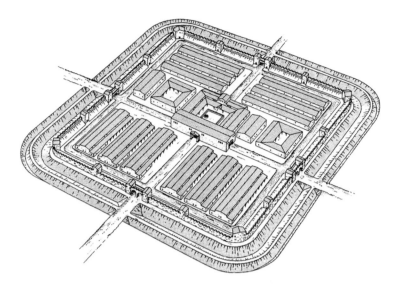

Figure 432 *Ala fort at Weißenburg (after Fischer and Riedmeier-Fischer 2008) Weißenburg/Biriciana (Germany)*

supply base during the Marcomannic Wars, the *ala* fort at Carnuntum existed until the 3rd century AD (ibid. 2007).

WEIßENBURG/BIRICIANA (GERMANY)

The fort of *ala I Hispanorum Auriana* was built in timber-and-earth around AD 90. It was about 175 × 179 m large and enclosed about 3.1 ha area. In a second construction phase around the middle of the 2nd century, the rebuilt stone fort had almost the same size (Fig. 432). In the second half of the 2nd century, the north gate, which was modelled on the *porta praetoria* of Regensburg legionary base, was rebuilt with semi-circular projecting towers. The *principia*, the *praetorium*, and a *horreum* as well as stone rooms from larger half-timbered structures are known out of the interior buildings following the excavations of the *Reichlimeskommission*. Extensive levels of burning with many finds and a hoard of coins put the violent destruction of the fort close to AD 254.[109]

ALA MILLIARIA

HEIDENHEIM/AQUILEIA (GERMANY)

One of the most archaeologically explored forts of an *ala milliaria* is currently Kastell Heidenheim in western Raetia. It lay in the Brenztal at an important junction in the area of the Ostalb. An older timber-and-earth fort was replaced in the early days of Trajan by the stone fort of *ala II Flavia milliaria*. This fort of the largest and most distinguished unit in the province of Raetia covered about 5.6 ha (Fig. 433). In addition to the defences, the *principia* is known. The other functional buildings in the *latera praetorii* have only been investigated to a limited extent. The barracks in the *praetentura* (six double barracks and four single barracks) and the *retentura* (four double barracks) are now known through the excavations of M. Scholz

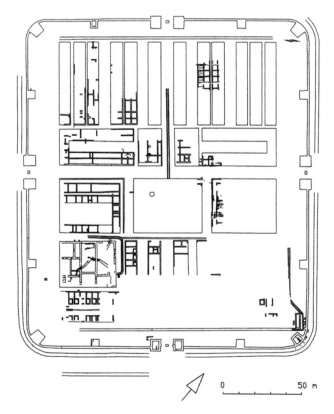

Figure 431 *Ala fort at Carnuntum (after Kandler 2007). Drawing: A. Smadi, Arch. Institute University of Cologne*

0   50 m

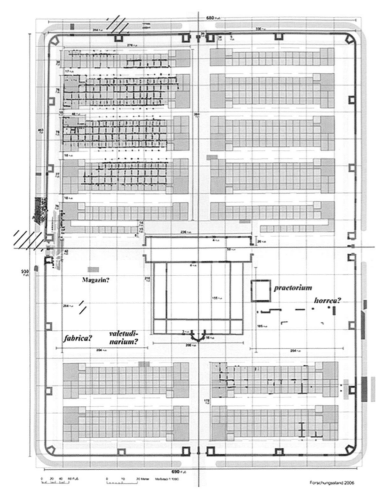

Figure 433 *Fort of ala II Flavia milliaria at Heidenheim (after Scholz 2009)*

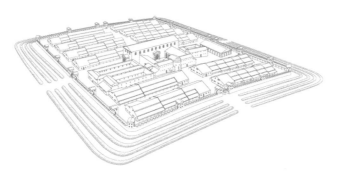

Figure 434 *Reconstruction drawing of the fort of ala II Flavia milliaria at Aalen. Drawing: A. Smadi, Arch. Institute University of Cologne*

Cohors equitata *forts*

Forts with mixed units of infantry and cavalry, the *cohortes equitatae*, are relatively frequent. A *cohors quingenaria equitata* of about 500 men (the exact strength is uncertain!) consisted of six *centuriae* and four *turmae* and a staff, the equestrian commander being the *praefectus cohortis*. With a *cohors milliaria equitata* of 10 *centuriae* of 80 men each and 10 *turmae* of 24 riders each, the title of the commanding officer was *tribunus cohortis*. The size of the forts of a *cohors quingenaria equitata* varies from 2.1 to 3.3 ha, while those of a *cohors milliaria equitata* range from 2.1 ha to 3.1 ha.

COHORS QUINGENARIA EQUITATA

HOFHEIM, TIMBER-AND-EARTH FORT (GERMANY)

This polygonal timber-and–earth fort with double V-sectioned ditches and turf rampart of 1.9 ha existed from the late Tiberio-Claudian period up to the Neronian and early Flavian period (Fig. 435). It was destroyed in the Batavian uprising of 69/70. Traces of burning and numerous metal finds, particularly weapons and unburied skeletal remains, suggest combat. It is assumed the garrison was a *cohors equitata*. In the early Flavian period, the fort was once again repaired (single V-sectioned ditch), then replaced in the early Vespasianic period by the stone fort, some 90 m to the east. The plan shows the mostly wooden interior. Most finds from the Hofheim timber-and-earth fort belong to the Claudio-Neronian period with the main focus close to the destruction horizon of 69/70. This so-called 'Hofheim

Figure 435 *Fort of a cohors equitata: Hofheim, earth-and-timber fort (after Johnson 1987). Drawing: A. Smadi, Arch. Institute University of Cologne. 1 = principia, 2 = praetorium, 3 = horrea, 4 = barracks*

(Scholz 2009). The evacuation of the fort took place around AD 150. The unit moved to Aalen with the advance of the Upper German Limes, in order to erect a somewhat larger fort of 6.07 ha (Fig. 443). According to Scholz, the difference in the area is due to the fact that Heidenheim lay on a plain, whereas Aalen was on a slope. As a result, the internal buildings had to be terraced, which led to an increase in space requirements to some degree.

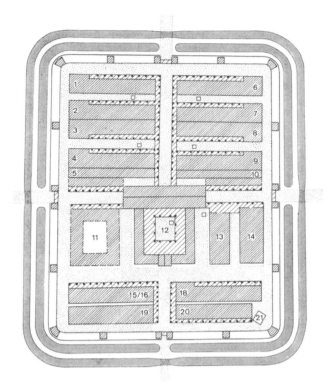

Figure 436 *Fort of a cohors equitata:* Künzing, *Phase 1 (after Johnson 1987). Drawing: A. Smadi, Arch. Institute University of Cologne*

horizon' is of considerable significance for the chronology of the 1st century AD (Ritterling 1912).

KÜNZING/*QUINTANA* (GERMANY)

The founding of the fort at Künzing took place around AD 90, obviously as a successor to the early Flavian fort of Moos-Burgstall, which was only occupied for a short period. The excavations were able to detect four phases of defences, two timber-and-earth phases and two in stone. The size of the fort remained approximately the same in all building periods at 132.5 × 165.5 m (2.25 ha). In phase 1 (*c.* AD 90–120), the fortification consisted of a wooden front wall with an earth rampart and a V-sectioned ditch in front of those (Fig. 436). In phase 2 (120–35) the construction changed: in front of a wall formed from an earth-filled wooden box with wooden front and back faces there were now two ditches. In phase 3, between AD 140 and 150, the first stone fort with up to five ditches was built, which was destroyed by AD 200. The next stone fort of phase 4 had only one ditch, falling victim to a Germanic attack around the middle of the 3rd century.[110]

WALLSEND/*SEGEDUNUM* (GREAT BRITAIN)

Wallsend is the easternmost fort on Hadrian's Wall. Built in Hadrianic times with stone defences and internal buildings partly of timber, at 1.6 ha it had room for a *cohors quingenaria equitata* (Hodgson 1999). In the *retentura*, which had a simple *porta quintana* on the western side instead of an

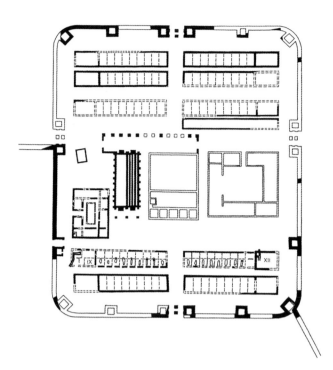

Figure 437 *Fort of a cohors equitata:* Wallsend *(after Hodgson 1999). Drawing: A. Smadi, Arch. Institute University of Cologne*

interval tower, there was room for four *turmae* (Fig. 437). In two of these barracks, nine *contubernia* for three men and three horses (with soakaways!) were found in each during recent excavations, so that each barrack held 27 riders, plus decurions and further junior officers, *i.e.* 30 men, the regular size of a *turma*. Six centuries of infantry were housed in the *praetentura*. This division was retained even after a rebuilding phase towards the end of the second century (ibid.).

COHORS MILLIARIA EQUITATA

STRAUBING/*SORVIODUNUM* – EAST FORT; FORT III (GERMANY)

In the first half of the 2nd century AD, the *cohors I Flavia Canathenorum milliaria sagittariorum equitata* constructed a 3.1-ha fort, first as a timber-and-earth site, then as a stone fort. This was destroyed after AD 170 in the Marcomannic Wars, but soon rebuilt. Of the internal buildings, the *principia* is known from aerial photographs, as are further stone buildings in the *latera praetorii*, and cavalry barracks (Fig. 438). The fort was destroyed in the 3rd century AD, probably in AD 254, and was not rebuilt.[111]

Cohors peditata *forts*

A *cohors quingenaria peditata* possessed six centuries of 80 men or 480 men plus staff under the guidance of a prefect or *praepositus cohortis*. The size of the forts ranged from 1.4 to 2.5 ha. However, regular *cohors quingenaria peditata* forts have seldom been completely excavated. The size of a *cohors milliaria peditata* is not known for certain; it had

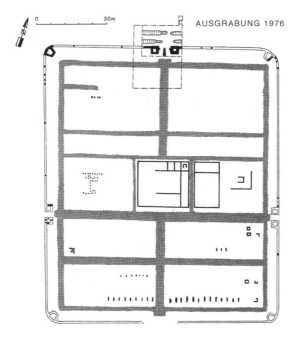

Figure 438 *Fort of a cohors equitata milliaria: Straubing (after Prammer 1976). Drawing: A. Smadi, Arch. Institute University of Cologne*

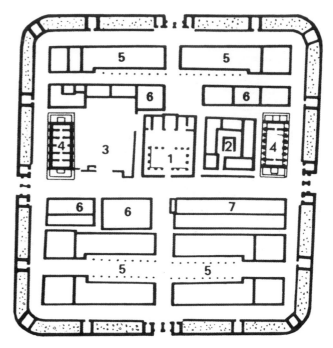

Figure 439 *Fort of a cohors quingenaria: Gelligaer (after Johnson 1987). Drawing: A. Smadi, Arch. Institute University of Cologne*

10 centuries, but this would mean only 800 troops. Their commander was the *tribunus cohortis*. There are no typical examples for the size of the forts.

COHORS QUINGENARIA PEDITATA

GELLIGAER (GREAT BRITAIN)

This fort in Wales was built in stone around AD 110, its Flavian predecessor being adjacent to it (Fig. 439). A building inscription shows that the fort was built between AD 103–11 by a *vexillatio* of *legio II Augusta*. It had six barracks for *centuriae*, which indicates a garrison of a *cohors quingenaria peditata*.[112]

COHORS MILLIARIA PEDITATA

DROBETA (ROMANIA)

According to F. Marcu, the 1.69-ha fort at Drobeta in the province of Dacia Superior, with its barracks for 10 centuries, could be considered as intended for a *cohors peditata milliaria* (Fig. 440). In the 3rd century AD, this would most likely have been *cohors I sagittariorum*.[113]

Forts for mixed garrisons

Occasionally the overview literature gives the impression that most of the Roman camps and fortifications of the Imperial period can be easily pressed into a clearly defined scheme. However, with the increasing knowledge of the individual forts, fortresses and camps, this becomes increasingly less so, especially in the case of auxiliary forts. Many of the forts, even those for which the garrison is known from inscriptions and tile stamps, often exhibit considerable departures from

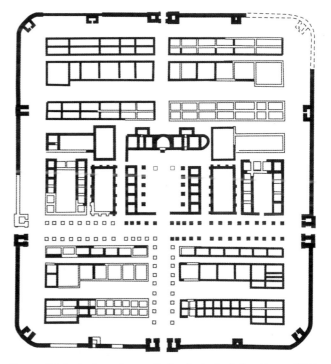

Figure 440 *Fort of a cohors milliaria: Drobeta (after Marcu 2009). Drawing: A. Smadi, Arch. Institute University of Cologne*

the 'norms' for their size and internal structure, without there being an immediate explanation. It seems that a large number of forts were not occupied by a single, complete unit. The range of possibilities extends from the accommodation of several smaller units, through legionary vexillations to units not matching the anticipated nominal strength. This

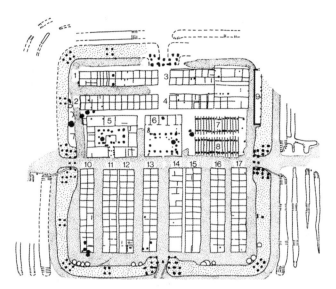

Figure 441 *Elginhaugh (after Johnson 1987). Drawing: A. Smadi, Arch. Institute University of Cologne*

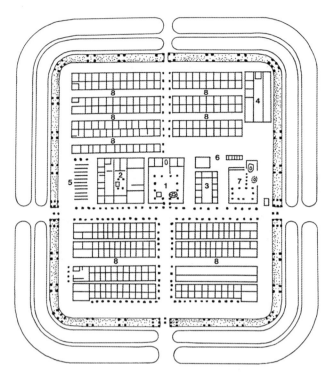

Figure 442 *Hofheim stone fort (after Nuber 1986). Drawing: A. Smadi, Arch. Institute University of Cologne*

Figure 443 *Lead tag naming a scorpionarius (after Nuber 1986). Drawing: A. Smadi, Arch. Institute University of Cologne*

may even have been the case in forts, which, from their size seem at first sight to have been occupied by 'normal' auxiliary units. It almost seems as if a paradigm shift has recently taken place in this field of research, if for instance W. S. Hanson writes, 'It has become increasingly evident, and is now more widely accepted, that forts constructed for single units were the exception rather than the rule'.[114] However, before making sweeping statements, one would have to distinguish between short-term campaigns and phases of occupation on the one hand, and long-term stable installations for frontier protection on the other.

ELGINHAUGH (GREAT BRITAIN)

This fort, only held briefly during the offensive of Agricola in Scotland around AD 83–6, has 12 centurial barracks, which does not correspond to any known pattern for the accommodation of an *auxilia* unit (Fig. 441). In addition, the finds material confirms the occupation of the fort by a mixed garrison. In any case, parts of a bolt-shooting artillery piece point to legionary soldiers (Hanson 2007; Hanson *et al.* 2007).

HOFHEIM, STONE FORT (GERMANY)

The early Flavian wooden predecessor of the Hofheim stone fort (Nuber 1986) had an area of 2.1 ha. So, according to conventional ideas, the garrison would be a *cohors quingenaria peditata* (Fig. 442). However, it has 14 barracks instead of six barracks for *centuriae*. In addition, a small inscription for a *scorpionarius* indicates an artillery detachment of legionary soldiers at least (Fig. 443). So here too a mixed garrison of unknown composition should be assumed.

POMET/*POROLISSUM* (ROMANIA)

This exceptional complex was the most important and largest fort on the Dacian Limes in the province of *Dacia*

Porolissensis. The base on the hilltop at Pomet protected an exceptionally important pass from Transylvania to the valley of the Tisza (Fig. 444). The 230 × 300 m large stone fort of the early 3rd century, at 6.9 ha, was preceded by a slightly smaller timber-and-earth fort, which was occupied in the first decade of the 2nd century AD. In the stone fort, an abundance of units are attested epigraphically, of which a temporary garrison (complete or only in vexillations) is assumed for *Porolissum*. These are: the *cohors I Ulpia Brittonum*, the *cohors I Aurelia Brittonum milliaria Antoniniana*, the *cohors I Hispanorum quingenaria*, the *cohors V Lingonum*, the *cohors VI Thracum*, the *cohors III Dacorum*, the *cohors III Campestris*, the *cohors I Ituraeorum*, a *numerus Palmyrenorum Porolissensium*, and detachments from *legio III Gallica Felix, IV Flavia Felix, legio VII Gemina*, and *legio XIII Gemina*.[115]

NIEDERBIEBER (GERMANY)

With an area of 5.24 ha, the stone fort at Niederbieber was one of the largest forts on the Upper German Limes. It was

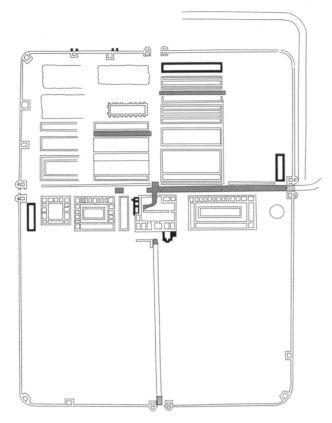

Figure 444 *The fort of Porolissum (after Marcu 2009). Drawing: A. Smadi, Arch. Institute University of Cologne*

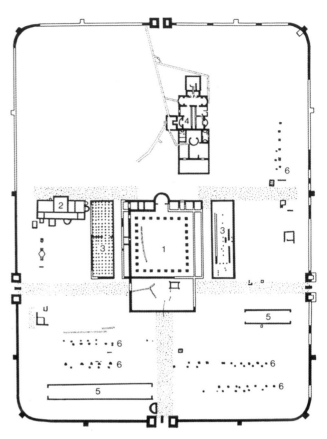

Figure 445 *The fort of Niederbieber (after Johnson 1987). Drawing: A. Smadi, Arch. Institute University of Cologne*

built around AD 200 and most probably replaced the older fort of Heddesdorf. Its garrison is unusual, as we know of two units, a *numerus Brittonum* and a mounted *numerus exploratorum Germanicorum Divitiensium*. This unit must have been unusually strong because their prefect was a Roman equestrian, T. Flavius Salvianus, who belonged to the *quarta militia*, a pay grade which was otherwise only held by the commander of an *ala milliaria*. This late fort was also characterized by a number of peculiarities: the towers protrude beyond the wall and the baths are located within the fort (Fig. 445). The fort was violently destroyed with a burnt deposit rich in finds and human skeletal remains. This destruction took place around 259/60, which is proved by three coin hoards, the eponymous iron helmet of the Niederbieber type, and parts of a field sign of the *cohors VII Raetorum equitata*, which were found with one skeleton. Recent investigations show that this troop had not come to their aid from the neighbouring fort of Niederberg, as has hitherto been assumed. On the contrary, Niederberg had already been evacuated earlier, probably after the invasion of AD 233, and the Raetian cohort belonged to the regular garrison in the last decades of Niederbieber.[116]

Garrison within a city

DURA-EUROPOS (SYRIA)

Dura-Europos was a Hellenistic city founded around 300 BC and under Parthian rule for a long time. It lay on the southern bank of the Middle Euphrates on the edge of the desert. In AD 195, the city was conquered by the Romans under Septimius Severus and given a permanent military occupation. In order to accommodate this garrison, the northern part of the city was cleared of civilian population and remodelled as a military camp. The area was separated from the civilian city by a wall. The military buildings known there are a *principia, praetorium,* baths, and an amphitheatre, as well as barracks, consisting of converted residential buildings (Fig. 446). In addition some temples, including a *mithraeum*, were now mostly used by soldiers. The 3rd century garrison of Dura-Europos probably included legionary vexillations from *legio IV Scythica* and *legio XVI Flavia Firma*, as well as *cohors XX Palmyrenorum*. In the years AD 255/256, the city was besieged and conquered by the Persians. Since then, it has remained abandoned. The remains of this Persian siege are the reinforcement of the western city wall by a provisional mud brick wall on the inner side, a Persian mine and a Roman countermine at Tower 19,

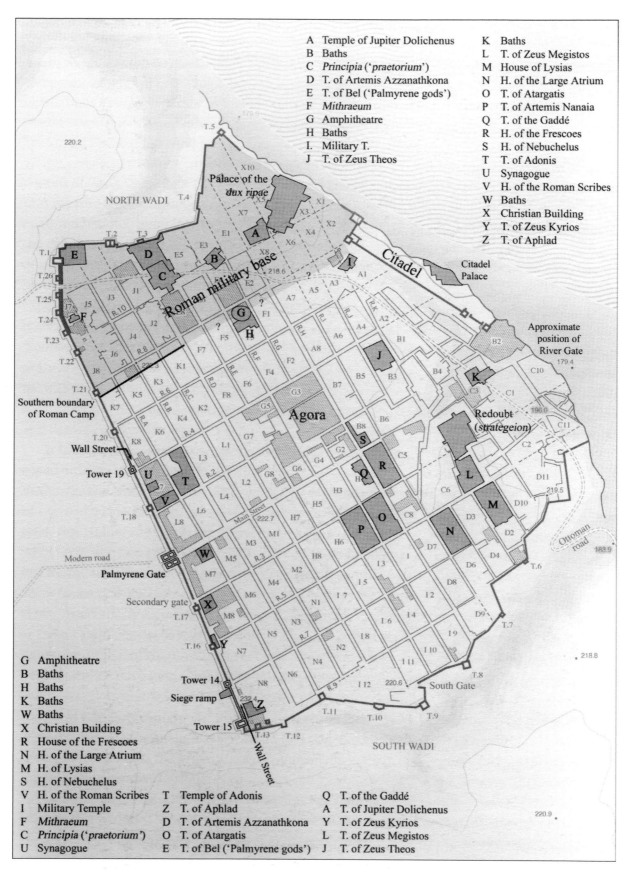

A Temple of Jupiter Dolichenus
B Baths
C *Principia* ('praetorium')
D T. of Artemis Azzanathkona
E T. of Bel ('Palmyrene gods')
F *Mithraeum*
G Amphitheatre
H Baths
I. Military T.
J T. of Zeus Theos

K Baths
L T. of Zeus Megistos
M House of Lysias
N H. of the Large Atrium
O T. of Atargatis
P T. of Artemis Nanaia
Q T. of the Gaddé
R H. of the Frescoes
S H. of Nebuchelus
T T. of Adonis
U Synagogue
V H. of the Roman Scribes
W Baths
X Christian Building
Y T. of Zeus Kyrios
Z T. of Aphlad

G Amphitheatre
B Baths
H Baths
K Baths
W Baths
X Christian Building
R House of the Frescoes
N H. of the Large Atrium
M H. of Lysias
S H. of Nebuchelus
V H. of the Roman Scribes
I Military Temple
F *Mithraeum*
C *Principia* ('praetorium')
U Synagogue

T Temple of Adonis
Z T. of Aphlad
D T. of Artemis Azzanathkona
O T. of Atargatis
E T. of Bel ('Palmyrene gods')

Q T. of the Gaddé
A T. of Jupiter Dolichenus
Y T. of Zeus Kyrios
L T. of Zeus Megistos
J T. of Zeus Theos

Figure 446 *Plan of Dura-Europos with the segregated military area of the 2nd and 3rd centuries AD in the north-west (after James 2004)*

with the remains and equipment of fallen soldiers, and a siege ramp at the south-east corner (James 2004 and 2005).

Numerus *forts*

The so-called *numeri* appeared in the Roman army during the late 1st century. They were included among the *auxilia*. The *numeri* were about 100- to 200-strong guards and reconnaissance units stationed on fixed stretches of frontier. If such units were mounted, they were called *exploratio*. They were under the command of a *praepositus numeri*, often a legionary centurion detached from his unit. *Numeri* were used in addition to the *alae* and cohorts for frontier protection, especially in remote forest areas or for exploring and securing the *Limesvorland* (the area directly in front of the *limes*), as in the Taunus or the Odenwald (Reuter 1999). In contrast to the other *auxilia*, they were apparently always used in the same province and always in the same frontier sector, and were not detached to take part in campaigns. This shows that they were scouts who were especially well-acquainted with a particular frontier section. The forts of the *numeri* were generally less than 1 ha.

HESSELBACH (GERMANY)

This fort was completely excavated and published by Dietwulf Baatz.[117] It was a typical *numerus* fort. The complex had an area of 0.6 ha, three gates and, in the place of the *porta decumana*, only a small gate. The complex was founded at the beginning of the 2nd century, with a fortification in timber-and-earth technique and a V-sectioned ditch. In the second quarter of the 2nd century, the former received a front wall of drystone walling and a retaining wall in the same technique along the *via sagularis*. Around the middle of the 2nd century, the fort defences were finally rebuilt with a mortared stone wall (Fig. 447). The internal buildings

also had three phases, but without exception consisted of half-timbered buildings. Phase 3 belonged to a civilian, post-fort period. The fort at Hesselbach was abandoned around AD 165 as part of the relocation of the frontier. The small *principia* discovered highlights that *numeri* were self-administered tactical units, the *praepositus numeri* inhabiting a larger building behind the *principia*. The approximately 140 men of the garrison were accommodated in small barrack buildings of the contemporary building type; in the *retentura* there were stables, sheds, and a store building.

Smaller *forts*

In the province of Raetia, there are a number of forts which, at under 1 ha, are similar in size to *numerus* forts. The building inscriptions of *numeri*, so common in Upper Germany, are absent here, and if inscriptions are found, they are never related to *numeri*, but rather to auxiliary units and their *vexillationes*.

ELLINGEN/SABLONETUM (GERMANY)

The fort of Ellingen is located about 1.8 km behind the *limes*, just 4 km north of Weißenburg (Fig. 448). The almost complete excavation of the fort took place in the years 1980–2. There was also a completely preserved building inscription in front of the south gate. W. Zanier summarized the results of all research so far (Zanier 1993). The fort was founded either late in the Trajanic era (AD 98–117) or in the early Hadrianic period (AD 117–25).

Figure 447 *Reconstruction drawing of the numerus fort at Hesselbach (after Campbell 2009)*

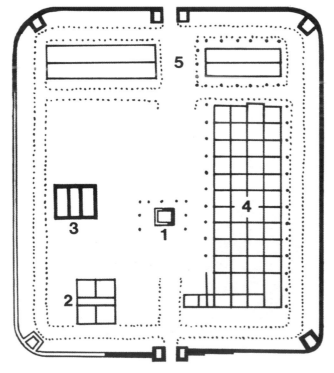

Figure 448 *The fortlet of Ellingen (Fischer and Riedmeier-Fischer 2008). Drawing: A. Smadi, Arch. Institute University of Cologne*

The defences of the fort of *c.* 90×90 m and 0.72 ha in area were in wood at first and then rebuilt in stone in the year AD 182, according to the excavation results and the building inscription. Four corner towers and two gates reinforced with towers were found on the northern and southern narrow sides of the fort. A ditch ran around the fort which was U-sectioned in the south. The older internal buildings consisted of four rectangular timber structures, which seem to have been built during the timber phase of the defensive rampart. With the rebuilding of the fort in stone, the interior was also redeveloped: in the centre, a kind of *principia* reduced to the shrine of the standards in stone with a wooden *peristyle*. Building 4 was a large double barrack of 51×17 m with 24 *contubernia*, while in Barrack 5L, there were ten *contubernia*. Soldiers were probably also housed in Building 5R, while Building 3 was more likely to have been a storage building. Building 2 was interpreted as the residence of the commander of the Ellingen garrison. The garrison of the fort at Ellingen is also known, at least for the time after 182: the building inscription mentioned above names the unit involved in construction as the *pedites singulares* with *c.* 250 men.

Fortlets

From the time of Claudius to the Flavian period, small-scale sites of less than 0.2 ha were found on the Upper Danube and in Britain which were constructed both for a shorter period and for a longer period (Mackensen

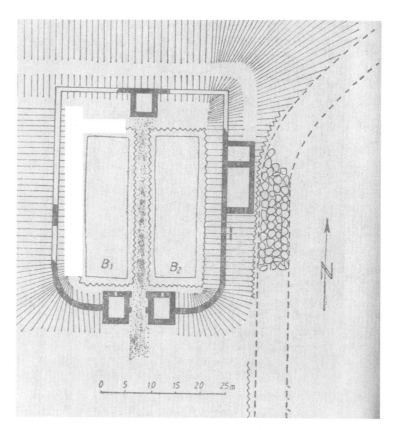

Figure 450 *The customs station at Porolissum (after Gudea 1996). Drawing: A. Smadi, Arch. Institute University of Cologne*

1987 and 1988). These are sites such as Burlafingen and Nersingen (Fig. 449) on the Upper Danube. Mackensen sees them as customs stations rather than military installations.[118]

This function also applied to the milecastles on Hadrian's Wall. A previously completely isolated facility, which looks amazingly similar to the Hadrian's Wall milecastles, was excavated near the Romanian fort of Pomet/*Porolissum* at the Mesec-Limes (Fig. 450). The excavator, Nicolae Gudea, has convincingly interpreted this fortlet, occupied in the 2nd and 3rd centuries AD, as a customs station with the help of inscriptions and finds (Gudea 1996).

Watchtowers

Dietwulf Baatz has summarized the current state of knowledge on watchtowers on the Upper German and Raetian Limes (Baatz 1989). Watchtowers belong with those elements of military construction which the Romans took over from the Greeks. The Latin term *burgus* for watchtowers is derived from the Greek *purgos* (*pyrgos*), but the Latin term *turris* was also used. Solitary towers are already known from the Augustan period, such as the Sparrenburg Egge near Bielefeld (Bérenger 1995), where the circular ditch of a supposed wooden tower has been excavated. The coins probably date to the Oberaden horizon. The first stone

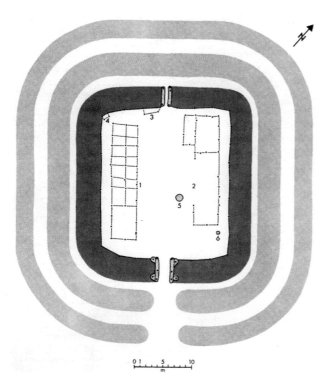

Figure 449 *The fortlet of Nersingen (after Mackensen 1987). Drawing: A. Smadi, Arch. Institute, University of Cologne*

Figure 451 *Watchtower on Trajan's Column (after Lipsius 1598)*

towers, the Walensee towers, are also known from the Augustan period.[119] On the Upper German-Raetian Limes, wooden towers with circular ditches are known (Baatz 1989). A whole chain of such wooden towers secured a late Flavian military road in Scotland known as the Gask Frontier.[120] In the 2nd century, the wooden towers were replaced by stone towers on the Odenwald Limes, the Upper German-Raetian Limes, the Dacian Limes, and also on the river frontiers of the Rhine and Danube. Their appearance (three floors, pyramidal roof, surrounding gallery) are traditionally reconstructed according to the representations on the columns of Trajan or Marcus (Fig. 451). However, other constructions are also possible and documented.[121]

Camps and forts in and around Rome

Most of the camps and forts of the Roman Empire had been erected along the frontiers or in their immediate hinterland, with only a few exceptions, the interior of the empire remaining free from military garrisons. Only the capital, Rome, which was free from the military in the Republic, at least according to the law, had a considerable concentration of soldiers during the Imperial period. A. W. Busch estimates them at up to 40,000 men.[122] Under Septimius Severus (AD 193–211), *legio II Parthica* was transferred from the Danube region to Albano near Rome as an additional force, a clear signal to potentially unreliable forces in the capital (Busch 2010b and 2011). With the best will, it is impossible to say that the buildings of the military have so far been a focal point in

the archaeological exploration of Rome. Actual descriptions of these monuments are correspondingly meagre. In addition, it was very difficult to gain an overview of the military in Rome from the scattered and, in some cases, contradictory literature. The Cologne dissertation published by A. W. Busch, published in 2011, now provides a remedy (Busch 2010).

Castra Praetoria

Under Tiberius (AD 14–37), the Praetorian Camp for the nine Praetorian cohorts (as they were then) was established in the north-east of the city in the years AD 21–3, sending a clear message to the inhabitants of Rome (Fig. 452). The troops had hitherto been garrisoned in a decentralized fashion, partly in the vicinity of Rome.[123] Three urban cohorts as well as smaller special units (*speculatores Augusti*, *statores Augusti* and *evocati*) were accommodated in this base. If we can assume a garrison of about 6,000 men at the start, up to 16,000 soldiers would later be stationed in the base. The first construction phase of about 15.7–16.72 ha was constructed to the playing card shape, with an approximately 5.2 m high *opus caementicium* wall with brick facing, later construction phases strengthening these defences. The possible function of the Praetorian Camp as an example for frontier forts and camps has already been mentioned. Little is so far known of the central administrative buildings, the troops' quarters, being partly built on to the defensive wall, were two-storeyed, and generously furnished with mosaics and wall paintings. It was rebuilt several times, finally being incorporated into the Aurelian city fortification.

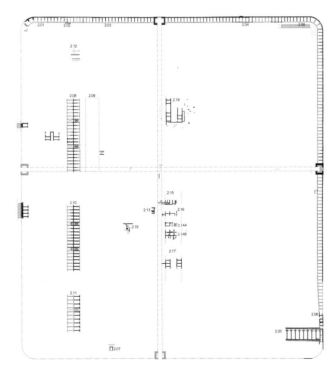

Figure 452 *The Praetorian Fortress in Rome, 1st phase (after Busch 2010). Drawing: A. Smadi, Arch. Institute University of Cologne*

Accommodation for the cohortes urbanae

Before the three units of the *cohortes urbanae* were stationed in the *castra praetoria*, they were probably lodged in *stationes* throughout the city. In the 3rd century AD, when their strength had grown to 6,000 men, they are supposed to have received a single camp under Aurelian. This has not yet been identified, probably lying in the north of the city.[124]

Accommodation for the Germani corporis custodes

This imperial bodyguard, founded by Augustus, consisted of Germans, mainly Batavians. It was dissolved by Galba (AD 68). This unit was mounted and probably possessed the strength of an *ala*. Little is known about their accommodation, apart from the fact that they were likely to have been located in Trastevere in the west of Rome.[125]

Forts for the equites singulares Augusti

With the founding of this guard cavalry unit of 500 or 1,000 men strong under Trajan (AD 98–117), a fort (*castra priora equitum singularium Augusti*) was erected on the south-east side of the city, its size being unknown.[126] When the unit was doubled in strength under Septimius Severus (AD 193–211), the *castra nova equitum singularium Augusti* was added to the south-west.[127] Here, parts of the internal buildings are known, Busch presuming a rectangular site of *c*.2.6 ha.

Castra Peregrina

This camp in the southern part of Rome, on the Caelian, accommodated soldiers who had come from all the provinces, and were residing in the capital for temporary tasks (*peregrini*). The size and shape of the camp are unknown, but among the remnants of the well-equipped interior there was also a *mithraeum*.[128]

Forts for fleet personnel

Personnel from the imperial fleets at Misenum and Ravenna were dispatched to the city, in the Colosseum, for example, to set up and dismantle the awnings. Their accommodation is also suspected near the Colosseum. In Trastevere, in the west of Rome, were stationed fleet personnel from Ravenna, whose help was needed for naval battles (*naumachia Augusti*).[129]

Accommodation for vigiles

In AD 6, Augustus founded a paramilitary urban Roman unit, the *vigiles*, divided into seven cohorts (*cohortes vigilum*). This unit, with its policing function, also acted as the fire brigade. It was distributed in seven stations and 14 watch posts (*excubationes*) throughout the whole city, and later also in Puteoli and Ostia. In the 3rd century AD, the number of *vigiles* had seemingly doubled, and their participation in regular military ventures outside Rome has now been demonstrated.[130]

Legionary base at Albano

Domitian (AD 81–96) built a huge imperial villa in the area of the modern town of Albano Laziale, including today's papal summer residence at Castel Gandolfo. Here, only 20 km south of Rome, the camp of *legio II Parthica* was erected under Septimius Severus (AD 193–211). Its name was *Castra Albana* (Fig. 453). In the process, older buildings and installations of the imperial villa were

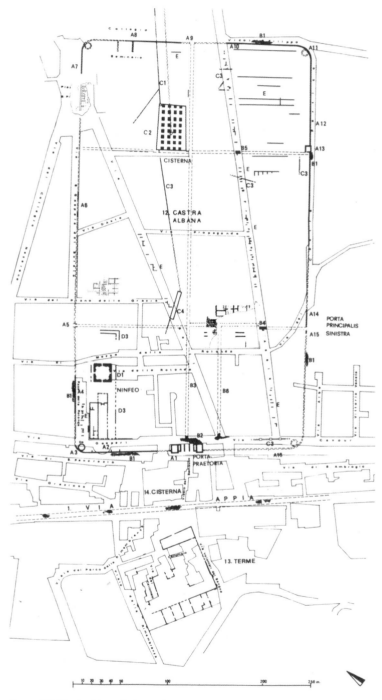

Figure 453 *The legionary fortress of Albano (after Busch 2011). Drawing: A. Smadi, Arch. Institute, University of Cologne Legionary fortress of Albano*

included in the camp. The camp is on a slope above the Via Appia, being internally terraced several times. Its partially well-preserved walls, made of solid tufa blocks, contain a rectangular area of about 9.5 ha. The base was thus only half the 'standard size' of a legionary camp. It is not currently possible to clarify this contradiction. Two-storey barracks in the *retentura* have recently been excavated from among the internal buildings. The camp was only used militarily until the end of the 3rd century (Busch 2010a; 2011).

4. Late Roman fortifications

Forts

The Late Roman period, from the Tetrarchy (*c.* AD 300), with its altered military organization, also brought about serious changes in military and civilian fortifications. The army was divided into stationary frontier groups (*limitanei*, *riparienses*) and a mobile army (*comitatenses*) divided into flexible garrisons. The size of military camps was reduced, since the size of the *limitanei* troops was generally much smaller than that of the earlier auxiliary units of the middle Imperial period.

In many cases, the old camps and forts were repaired, but their defences were often considerably reinforced. On the Danube and Iller in Raetia, on the Upper Rhine, and on the Danube frontier in the province of Moesia Superior, the *limes* fortifications of the Late Roman period had to be completely rebuilt since, after the loss of the Upper German and Raetian Limes or the province of Dacia, the advanced forts were also lost. In the course of constructing the new chain of forts, the new, strongly defended fortifications were placed at naturally defensible sites, like the fortresses of the Middle Ages, for instance at Kellmünz high above the bank of the Iller (Fig. 454). On the Danube frontier in Noricum, on the other hand, the basic form of the older camps was often retained in the Late Roman period and strengthened by just the addition and reinforcement of towers and gates (horseshoe and semi-circular towers) outside the walls.[131]

Troops and the civilian population were frequently accommodated together within the restored walls of the old forts and fortresses from the 3rd century. The military was occasionally housed within its own internal enclosure in the fort, as at Eining on the Danube or Dormagen on the Rhine.[132] Thus Late Roman fortified towns with military occupation often grew out of the purely military camps and forts of the middle Imperial period. A similar development also occurred in the hinterland, especially in Gaul: cities and *vici* were strongly fortified and also received garrisons, more rarely in the form of stationed troops, but often in the form of detachments from the mobile army, which could be quartered in the cities in emergencies or overwintered

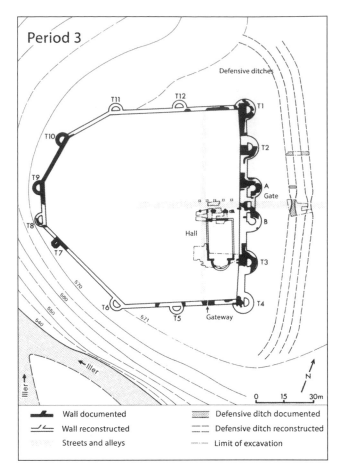

Figure 454 *The Late Roman fort of Kellmünz (after Mackensen 1995)*

there. Finally, there were purely military garrisons, supply bases, and chains of watchtowers formed in the hinterland.

These hinterland military installations do not often differ from the numerous fortified civilian settlements on heights, which were now emerging, if the necessary natural and geographic conditions were available, in the Eifel, the Hunsrück, the Ardennes, Condroz, the Palatinate, Alsace, the Upper and High Rhine Valley and the Bavarian *Voralpenland* to the Eastern Alps and to Upper Italy.[133]

Late Roman fortifications, with their mighty walls, were much more extensively fortified than the older forts had ever been. Late Roman walls, which were apparently often built quickly under great threat, frequently used old architectural fragments or tombstones and other monuments for spolia.

The classic 'playing card shape' was abandoned entirely for the basic form of the fortifications, in favour of entirely different types of structure. The uniformity of military construction, which was so characteristic of the early and especially the middle Imperial periods, disintegrated completely. Depending on the size of the body of men, and in particular according to the topographical requirements, rectangular, square, semi-circular or polygonal, or even irregular groundplans of forts were built, whose walls

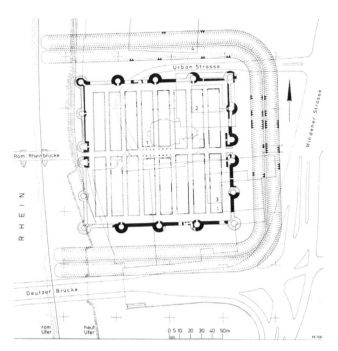

Figure 455 *Constantinian bridgehead fort of Cologne-Deutz (after Horn 1987). Drawing: A. Smadi, Arch. Institute University of Cologne*

were now at least twice as thick and high as in the middle Imperial period. Only the Constantinian bridgehead fort of Cologne-Deutz is discussed as an example here (Fig. 455). The 'tetrapyrgium' shape, that is, quadrilateral layout with four corner towers,[134] was particularly popular from the Tetrarchic period onwards, especially in the East.

In the case of gate, corner, and intermediate towers, which were round, semi-circular, square, or polygonal to fan-shaped, it can be seen that, in contrast to the preceding period, they always projected outside the defensive wall. This can best be explained by the fact that, in the Late Roman period, artillery pieces, the bolts from which are found everywhere in Late Roman fortifications, played a greater part in defence. For with them positioned on the projecting towers, the enemy could be enfiladed from the flank more effectively during sieges and attacks. While many elements of Late Roman fortifications are ubiquitous, the towers occasionally possess regional aspects. For example, the fan-shaped towers at the corners of the fort and horseshoe-shaped interval towers are mainly concentrated on the Danube frontier in the province of Noricum Ripense. In the West, that is, in Raetia, the German provinces, and Britain, they are absent, with very few exceptions. Characteristic of the fortification of the Late Roman period is the now frequent insertion of brick courses into the walls, which were otherwise built of undressed stones, with a curtain wall of dressed ashlars (Johnson 1983 passim).

The internal buildings of most late forts are largely unknown. For there were now no more regular layouts, as in the early and middle Imperial periods: almost every fort

looked different. In principle, it must be admitted that Late Roman defensive architecture on the Rhine and the Danube is something entirely new for the region but still contains no fundamental new developments. Rather, components, such as the basic forms of forts, the types and shapes of towers and gates, were taken from the military architecture of the East, North Africa, or from town defences and combined anew, but almost all of the basic elements were already present in Hellenistic fortifications. However, Parthian and Persian influences were also brought into play in the origin of Late Roman forts.[135]

Burgi

A further development from the frontier towers of the middle Imperial period is the so-called *burgus*. Under this term, which occurs repeatedly in epigraphic and literary sources and is already used for early and middle Imperial watchtowers, researchers jumble together many different things: smaller watchtowers right up to small fortifications laid out to the *tetrapyrgium* scheme, civilian refuges at estates or – especially on the Upper Rhine and the Danube in Pannonia – fortified shipyards. *Burgi* were set along the river frontiers, but also served to ensure security, control, and communication along the main roads (Hock 2001).

5. Military infrastructure

Roads

Undoubtedly, the well-developed system of artificial roads is one of the most important civilising achievements of the Roman Empire. The active role of the Roman military of the Imperial period in road construction can be proved by ancient documents, but in particular by inscriptions on milestones. However, various historical circumstances have led to the fact that the role of the Roman military in road construction has generally been overrated. Not all important, long-distance roads were built by the military; there are also a number of 'civil' roads.[136]

Canals

In order to support logistics for campaigns, Roman troops also dug canals, which were also useful to the civilian infrastructure for a long time after fulfilling their often only short-term military purposes (Hanel 1995). Drusus the Elder, for example, had canals built during the fighting against the Chauci in 12 BC.[137] Similarly, in the struggle against the rebellious Frisians and Chauci in AD 47, general C. Domitius Corbulo had a canal built between the mouth of the Maas and the Rhine, the *fossa Corbulonis*. This probably served as an important trade and traffic route until the Carolingian period.[138]

6.   *Limites* and *ripae*

In the imperial era, the Romans knew better than virtually any subsequent state how to defend their huge empire effectively with a never equalled small number of professional soldiers. The bases for this were the frontier systems (*limites* and *ripae*), monitored by the military, which for a long time were adapted to the local conditions, ensuring the protection and security of the inhabitants of the empire. Beginning in the north-west, Hadrian's Wall and (for a short time) the Antonine Wall protected the island province of Britain. Highly controlled river boundaries from the mouth of the Rhine to the Danube delta were interrupted at only two sections of the frontier by clearly marked, militarily defended land frontiers: the Upper German-Raetian Limes and the Dacian Limes. Naval units patrolled the shores of the Black Sea, and the Euphrates limes protected the frontier with the Parthian and, later, Persian empires. The *limes Arabicus*, military camps in Egypt, and the *limes Tripolitanus* protected the Roman inhabitants of the fertile agricultural areas against the warlike nomads of the deserts beyond the frontiers.[139]

However, the concept of frontiers in antiquity differed quite considerably from what is now understood as a 'border' or fixed 'state boundary': the Roman empire of the Imperial period at the height of its power possessed very clear concepts of what differentiated and separated it (ideologically but also practically) from the peoples outside – the barbarians. Rome and its empire, of course, were, in all respects, the centre of the world and the repository of civilization. Outside its territory there lived only inferior 'savages', the barbarians, with whom concepts such as 'uncouth', 'unsettled', 'traitorous', and 'aggressive' were connected. However, they too had a chance to become 'real' people – as subjects of Rome.

From this clear self-understanding of the Romans, it was only logical that there were no borders protected by a generally recognized international law between Rome and the countries of the barbarians. That would then have meant that they saw them as equal partners. This, however, was a long way off – binding frontier arrangements with peoples outside the empire were at best only temporary. The current needs and the military capabilities of Rome dictated the course of the frontiers. However, these were unilaterally considered as dynamic; in other words, they could theoretically be advanced at any time, at the expense of the barbarian peoples. Thus, the frontiers of Rome were always where the effects of the *gladii* and *pila* of the legions

reached far enough to uphold Roman domination (Cicero, *In Pisonem* 38). With this basic attitude it was also a logical consequence that, for example, every 'good' emperor had a duty to prove his *virtus* by incorporating new territories of Barbaricum into the Roman Empire.

On the other hand, pragmatic military considerations called for these frontiers to be fixed, not because Rome respected the borders of barbarian territories for fundamental reasons, but because the extensive installations necessary for the military control of the borders and the protection of Roman territory, worked best when they were in place for a long time. These roads, frontier barriers, forts, and watchtowers are the ones that are nowadays called the *limes* in modern research.[140]

The terms 'limes' and 'ripa'

The Latin word '*limes*' originally comes from the technical vocabulary of Roman land surveyors. At first, it only meant a road constituting the boundary between two properties or surveying systems. It then developed into a somewhat different meaning during the 1st century AD, namely the term for the militarily controlled frontier of the Roman Empire in the Imperial period. The term '*limes*' comprises the actual frontier marked by an artificially erected barrier construction, for example a palisade, a wall or earthen rampart, and ditches. In addition, there were a system of frontier military roads, and a system of signal towers constructed to be intervisible, as well as a network of larger and smaller forts on the frontier or further back in the hinterland, connected by roads for the control and defensive system of the *limes*. If a river replaced the artificial frontier barriers, the word '*ripa*' ('bank') was used for such frontier sections in antiquity with the same meaning as '*limes*'.

Function

None of these *limites* and *ripae* constituted a rigid military defence and fortification system, which, like modern fortifications, would be able to break attacking waves of larger groups of troops. On the contrary, they served only to control the frontier traffic and to collect customs duties. Furthermore, the *limites* were intended to thwart penetration by smaller robber bands and, as a signalling system, account for and locate more extensive invasions. Such larger attacks from outside had then to be tackled using mobile warfare by larger armies, which were brought from the interior of the province or even from other border sectors. Larger-scale warfare was no longer the task of frontier troops – that was mainly the concern of the elite units of the Roman army stationed in the legionary fortresses along the frontiers: the legions.

Actual frontier guard duty was undertaken by smaller units of lower rank, auxiliary groups (*auxilia*) in their forts and fortlets along the frontiers. The latter were often located in the immediate vicinity of the frontier barrier near crossing points. They were frequently erected at a later stage of the construction of the *limes*, often only in the 3rd century AD. From the late 1st century onwards, the *numeri* were still included among the *auxilia*.

The weakness of the early and mid-Imperial frontier system was that most of the troops were on the frontier without any significant reserves in the hinterland in case of a major invasion. When devastating simultaneous incursions by Germans, Parthians, Persians, and other enemies took place in the north and east, the frontier defence system inevitably collapsed. However, the end only came after it had proven itself for a long time (about 150 years), which cannot be said of any comparable modern military defensive system.

None of these *limites* are mentioned much in the contemporary ancient written sources. For Hadrian, the *Historia Augusta* mentions details, some of which can also be confirmed by archaeology: 'at that time, as elsewhere, he separated the barbarians from the territory of the empire, in many areas where the frontier against the barbarians was not formed by rivers, with artificial barriers formed from a system of large posts, which were driven deep into the ground and attached to each other in the manner of a wall-like palisade' (*HA, Hadr.* 12.6).

If we were only dependent on the ancient written sources on the *limites* and *ripae* around the empire, it would be very difficult to understand the military frontiers of Rome. Most of what is known today is the result of archaeological research, which mainly started in the middle of the 19th century. This information has been acquired during excavations on the monuments of the *limes* itself and is now available in such quantities that it can hardly be grasped in its entirety by a single person anymore. The Imperial Frontier Commission (Reichslimeskommission), founded at the suggestion of Theodor Mommsen in 1892, for a long time did the pioneering work on the Upper German-Raetian Limes in Germany (ORL; Fischer 2010).

Late Roman Frontier Defence

Comprehensive and comparable research on the *limites* of the 4th and 5th century is at the moment mainly found in the north-west and north of the empire, such as in Britain (Maxfield 1989; Breeze and Dobson 2000) and on the Rhine and the Upper Danube frontiers (Bechert and Willems 1995; Cüpers 1990; Garbsch 1988). Likewise, in recent years, research has caught up on the middle and lower Danube (Visy 1985, 2003, and 2003a; Gudea 1997, 2001, and 2005), on the Euphrates and in the deserts of Syria (Konrad 2001), Jordan (Kennedy 2000), and North Africa. However, these frontier sections have not all been equally as well explored as the ones in north-western Europe, although the forts and other defensive systems, for example are much better preserved in the East. Quite often these sites were in use up to the Byzantine period, *i.e.* into the 7th century AD, or even very often into the (Islamic) Middle Ages. It is then frequently very difficult to differentiate the Late Roman phases of the 4th and 5th centuries, let alone older ones.

The Late Roman period, with its modified military organization, also brought about major changes in frontier defences. Artificial barriers were largely abandoned, river frontiers or dense chains of forts and watchtowers (*burgi*) along well-developed military roads being used instead. In addition, there were also defences in the hinterland of the *limes*, especially in Raetia, Gaul, and Pannonia, particularly on important long-distance roads. So Rome moved from a purely linear defensive concept, directly on the frontier, to a defence in depth: along important roads there were now chains of watchtowers and small fortifications (*burgi*). Heavily defended forts and supply bases for the mobile army developed on passes and at nodal points on the road system in the hinterland of the frontier provinces. There were also changes in the course of the frontiers. Where areas had to be cleared in the 3rd century AD, as in the frontier region occupied by the Alamanni in the south and south-west of Germany, or in Dacia, new sections of the *limes* were built in the Upper Rhine and Danube in the Late Roman period, whereby – in part, at least – abandoned defended sites were recommissioned.

The frontier security systems of the Roman Empire

Hadrian's Wall

In AD 122, the Emperor Hadrian visited the province of Britain and personally ordered the beginning of a fortified frontier barrier which, as Hadrian's Wall, is still the best preserved monument of the Roman era in England, (Fig. 456). This can be inferred from the biography of the Emperor in the *Historia Augusta* (*HA* 11.2):

> After he had reformed the army (in Germania) in royal style, he went to Britain; here, too, he made many improvements, and was the first to make a wall over a distance of 80 miles, which was to form a boundary between the barbarians and the Romans.

Hadrian's Wall (Breeze and Dobson 2000) was 76 Roman miles long from Wallsend to Bowness-on-Solway, equivalent to 70 modern British miles or 113 km. Original planning can be distinguished from later modifications. Originally, a defensive curtain wall with a ditch beyond it was provided,

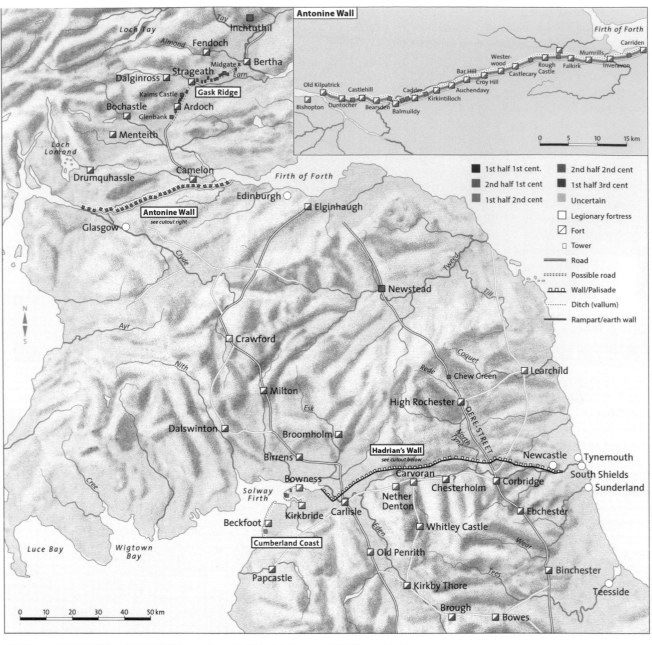

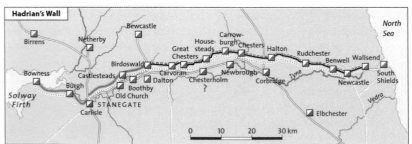

Figure 456 *Hadrian's Wall and Antonine Wall (after Klee 2006, Konrad Theiss Verlag)*

in which there were fixed gateways (milecastles) every mile. In between, there were two turrets. The forts were to be some way behind the wall, along the Stanegate, a military road. The initial plan was then modified so as to move the forts up to the Wall and to link them to it directly. This is clearly reflected by the fact that there are no gaps in the Wall where the forts are today, the newly built Wall having been demolished instead.

The Wall itself initially consisted only of a stone curtain wall in the eastern section, from Newcastle upon Tyne to the river Irthing near Birdoswald. In the western section to Bowness on Solway, it at first consisted only of a turf rampart. Later, the turf wall was replaced in stone, and the fortifications in the east were extended to Wallsend. Likewise, in the west, along the Cumbrian coast, a line of milecastles and towers, in part with palisaded walls, was used to monitor raids from the sea.

The original planning of the Wall in the east still provided for a width of 10 Roman feet (c. 3 m: Broad Wall). In the middle of construction, the standard dimensions were changed and the width was reduced to 7 Roman feet (c. 2.1 m: Narrow Wall). In the east, where the Stone Wall later replaced the Turf Wall, only the Narrow Wall is found. Even narrower are sections of wall with a characteristic white and very hard lime mortar, which are attributed to a restoration under Septimius Severus (AD 193–211).

The height of the Wall is estimated to have been about 4.2 m, with an 8 to 12 m wide V-sectioned ditch located beyond a 6 m wide berm. Behind the wall, the old military road, the Stanegate, ran as a connecting route. In contrast to the Upper German-Raetian Limes, Hadrian's Wall also had obstacles to approaching its rear, to the south. This was the so-called *vallum* of about 36 m in width. It consisted of a ditch, accompanied by two ramparts, which, together with the actual curtain wall, marked a kind of military security zone along which the frontier road ran. It must have been built a little later than the wall, although probably also under Hadrian, because the *vallum* avoided existing Hadrianic fortifications.

Building inscriptions show that construction was divided into sections, which were erected by vexillations from the three legions stationed in Britain (*legio II Augusta* from Caerleon, *legio VI Victrix* from York, and *legio XX Valeria Victrix* from Chester).

Only auxiliaries are recorded as garrison troops for the forts on Hadrian's Wall. Depending on the topography and the presence of important north–south connections, the garrisons consisted of infantry, cavalry, or mixed units (Fig. 457). The defences of the forts on Hadrian's Wall were built in stone, where the Stone Wall had been erected, as well as their inner buildings. Where the Turf Wall existed as the first phase of the Wall, the defences of the forts consisted first of all of a turf rampart, but their inner buildings already were partly built in stone. During the reconstruction of the Wall, the defensive circuits of the forts were also replaced in stone.

As with the construction of the wall, vexillations of the legions stationed in Britain were occasionally involved in the construction of the forts. Seventeen forts, from Wallsend in the east to Bowness-on-Solway in the west, lie on the Wall. Over the course of time, outpost forts were also added: Risingham, High Rochester, Bewcastle,

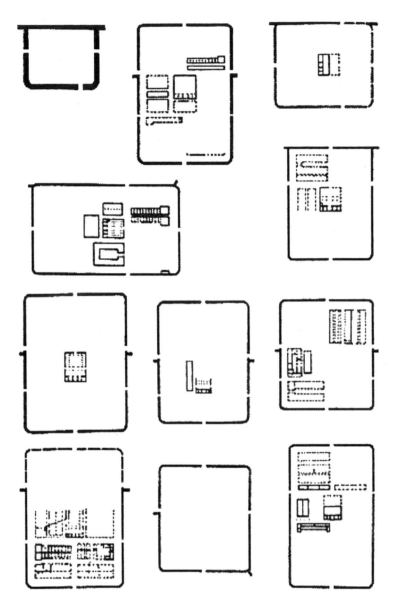

Figure 457 *Forts on Hadrian's Wall (from the upper left to the lower right): milecastle, Birdoswald, Great Chesters, Housesteads, Carrawburgh, Chesters, Halton Chesters, Rudchester, Benwell, Wallsend (after Klee 2006). Drawing: A. Smadi, Arch. Institute University of Cologne*

Netherby, and Birrens. Some of the older forts in the hinterland, on the old Stanegate line, remained occupied (Corbridge and Chesterholm/Vindolanda). On the Cumbrian coast, a line of forts, fortlets, and watchtowers continued Hadrian's Wall. These forts were Beckfoot, Maryport, and Ravenglass.

Between the fortresses, there were 80 fortlets (so-called milecastles) with gates through the Wall and to the rear, and with their interior buildings along the sides. They served as guard and customs posts, their garrisons being commanded by the neighbouring forts. In between, there were towers of stone, which were attached to the Wall, two each between two milecastles. This system was observed without deviation and without regard for the topography. In this, Hadrian's Wall stands in remarkable contrast to, for example, the Upper German-Raetian Limes, the structures of which were very cleverly adapted to the terrain. The reason for this must lie in a rigid system devised, or at least sanctioned, by Hadrian himself, which was then implemented without compromise by the military.

Antonine Wall

Under the Emperor Antoninus Pius (AD 138–61) the Roman frontier policy in the north of Britain changed again. In the years AD 139–41, there were tensions with the neighbouring northern tribes. As a consequence, further areas of the province of Britannia to the north of Hadrian's Wall were incorporated. Therefore, at the narrowest point of the island, on the Forth–Clyde isthmus, the Antonine Wall was built. As later events showed, these plans had, however, been realized on uncertain ground and soon required correction. For as early as AD 155, the Antonine Wall was apparently abandoned and cleared on short notice, but in an orderly fashion. It was reoccupied only shortly afterwards, only to be finally abandoned about AD 163. The line of Hadrian's Wall was restored and maintained until the end of the 4th century (Breeze and Dobson 2000).

At first sight, the Antonine Wall on the Forth–Clyde isthmus had a topographically more favourable position than Hadrian's Wall. At 37 miles long (about 60 km), it was almost half as long as it, with its 113 km. Such a one-sided view is, however, not very realistic, as other and more important factors certainly played a role in the establishment and evacuation of this frontier, such as the behaviour of the indigenous tribes, who do not appear to have been at all comfortable with the advance of the border, or the over-extension of supply lines.

The Antonine Wall differed fundamentally in its construction from Hadrian's Wall: it consisted of a 3 m high turf wall on a 4.5 m wide stone foundation. In front of it lay a 6 m wide berm and a 12 m wide and 4 m deep V-sectioned ditch. Once again, building inscriptions show that the construction of the Wall and forts not only involved auxiliary troops, but also detachments from all three legions stationed in Britain.

There is a greater variety of fortifications on the Antonine Wall than on Hadrian's Wall. There were forts, fortlets, as well as marching camps and other enclosed areas, but no towers. Some of the sites were erected before the Wall was built, but others were erected afterwards. Originally it seems that only six forts were planned, with fortlets every mile of the fortification. However, then there was the need to enlarge the garrison, so that there were fifteen auxiliary forts on the Antonine Wall, with outpost forts at Camelon, Ardoch, Strageath, and Bertha.

Late Roman Frontier Defence of Britain

Since the late 3rd century AD, new enemies had been forming in and around Britain, which now brought to the forefront a completely different kind of threat. The danger now came from the sea: beyond Hadrian's Wall a new, dangerous tribal coalition had formed, the Picts. From the late 3rd century onwards, they not only attacked the frontier, but had perfected a new tactic. In small seagoing ships, they outflanked the defensive line of Hadrian's Wall and devastated Roman territory on the east coast. At the same time, the Scotti from the north of the island of Ireland terrorized western Britain as pirates. Despite these attacks, Hadrian's Wall remained occupied far into the Late Roman period. Meanwhile, it is known that many places remained occupied until the first half of the 5th century (Böhme 1986). Major rebuilding can be found in the forts in Late Antiquity, at Birdoswald the newer excavations even extending its continuous use into the early medieval period (Wilmott 1997).

LITUS SAXONICUM/SAXON SHORE

In the south and south-west of Britain, a new threat occurred in the late 3rd and 4th centuries AD, which is reminiscent of the later Viking attitudes. Here Frankish and Saxon pirates wrought havoc. This permanent threat to essential shipping and unprotected settlements in the coastal area required effective counter-measures and, as a result, a line of coastal fortifications and signal stations were built in the last third of the 3rd century AD which were combined into a regular defensive system, the *litus Saxonicum*. They are still mentioned as a separate military command in a Late Roman troop manual, the *Notitia Dignitatum*, from the early 5th century AD (Fig. 458).

Figure 458 *Saxon Shore (after Maxfield 1989)*

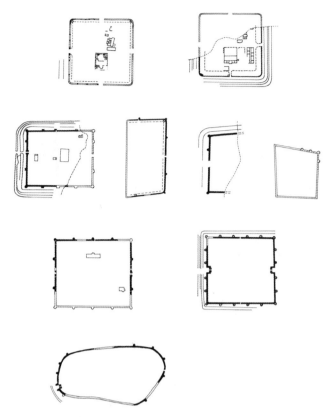

Figure 459 *Forts on the Saxon Shore (from the upper left to the lower right): Brancaster, Reculver, Richborough, Burgh, Bradwell, Dover, Lympne, Portchester, Pevensey (after Maxfield 1989). Drawing: A. Smadi, Arch. Institute University of Cologne*

These fortifications, which are known in British research as Saxon Shore forts (Maxfield 1989), were often enormous installations, some of which are still standing today, as they were used as fortresses in the medieval period. Since this line of fortifications was not all built at once, but during the course of the 3rd and 4th centuries AD, they help to understand the general developments in Roman military architecture. At the beginning, the forts still had the classical Imperial playing card shape and corresponding internal buildings, such as Brancaster, Reculver, or the first phase of Richborough. At the turn of the 4th century AD, the typical, mighty Late Roman installations with strong walls, better adaptation to the terrain, and modified, more individual, gateways and external towers, were introduced (Fig. 459).

Fortresses that also belonged to the *litus Saxonicum* were located on the Gallic side of the Channel. Between the forts of the *litus Saxonicum* and those in the north-east, there were numerous small fortifications, which served as signal stations. These are, for the most part, no longer preserved in the south-east, since they have completely disappeared with the erosion of the coast, which has also damaged a few forts.[141]

The Rhine frontier in Lower Germany (Ripa Rheni Germaniae inferioris)

With the conquest of Gaul by Julius Caesar, the Rhine was regarded as a (provisional) frontier for the Roman sphere of interest. When, in the reign of Augustus (AD 27), Germanic tribes from the regions to the east of the Rhine repeatedly undertook successful raids into the Roman area on the west bank and succeeded in defeating Roman troops, the plan ripened in Rome to extend Roman territory to the Elbe and to organize it as a province of Germania. As starting points for these offensives, large military bases on the Rhine at Nijmegen, Xanten, Neuss, and Mainz were established. The defeat of Quintillius Varus in the Teutoburger Wald in AD 9 (the battlefield has now been located at Kalkriese in Lower Saxony) brought the failure of these plans and the retreat to the Rhine line.

In the years following the defeat of AD 9 and before the foundation of the province under Domitian (AD 81–96), the army of Lower Germany made a decisive change: from an offensive army stationed in winter camps to the west of the Rhine, which conducted operations to the east in the summer, it developed from the Tiberio-Claudian period onwards into a frontier army, whose auxiliary forts formed a linear defence along the west bank of the Rhine (Fig. 460). The legions were based on the Rhine without being directly involved in the guarding of the frontier. In AD 81, during the reign of Domitian, there were four legions in the Lower German army, namely in Nijmegen, Xanten (Vetera II), Neuss and Bonn.

The shifting of the military focus from the Rhine to the Danube under Domitian and Trajan meant a major change. Legionary troops were withdrawn from Nijmegen and Neuss. From about AD 130, there were only two legions in Lower Germany, the *legio I Minervia* in Bonn and the *legio XXX Ulpia Victrix* in Vetera II.

The auxiliary troops in Lower Germany were also reduced over the course of time: under Tiberius there were still eight *alae* and about 20 cohorts stationed there; on the eve of the Batavian uprising there were still at least eight *alae* and 12 cohorts, most of which were raised in Germania or Gaul. During the civil war after Nero's death and the Civilis uprising, at least four *auxilia* units of the Lower German army were completely destroyed, the remainder going over to the insurgents. Vespasian then almost completely disbanded these auxiliaries, so that there was now no longer a single unit formed in Germania based on the Rhine. It is assumed there were six *alae* and 26 cohorts in the Flavian period. In the Flavian-Trajanic period, the auxiliary units were greatly reduced between 83 and 106. In the post-Trajanic period, four *alae* and probably 15 cohorts were located at the Lower Rhine frontier. This force remained largely unchanged until the 3rd century.

Figure 460 *Lower German Rhine frontier (after Klee 2006, Konrad Theiss Verlag)*

The Lower German frontier was hardly affected by military events between the Flavian period and the 3rd century AD. Only in the late Domitianic period or early Trajanic periods were campaigns against the Bructeri on either side of the Lippe mentioned in the literature.

The military installations on the Lower German river frontier consisted of the so-called frontier road, the auxiliary forts on the Rhine, or its delta, and fortlets that had been added over the course of time. Only a few forts lay at the northern section of the hinterland. There seems to have been a complete optical and acoustic signal chain by means of watchtowers, which are rarely explored at the moment. Patrols by the *classis Germanica* were also important for monitoring the river; there must have been many more moorings and bases for the fleet than are known today.[142]

The Upper German-Raetian Limes

The *limes* in Upper Germany and Raetia (Baatz 2000), which acted as a land connection from the Rhine to the Danube as it looked around the middle of the 3rd century AD, shortly before its end, was the result of a development lasting more than 150 years. Since the end of the 1st century AD, Rome had struggled to maintain a militarily controlled line of demarcation under constantly changing conditions (Fig. 461) on this frontier, as well as on other frontiers of the empire.

THE UPPER GERMAN FRONTIER

The river boundary of the Upper German army district on the Rhine was secured by a line of forts during the time of Tiberius (AD 14–37) and Claudius (AD 41–54),

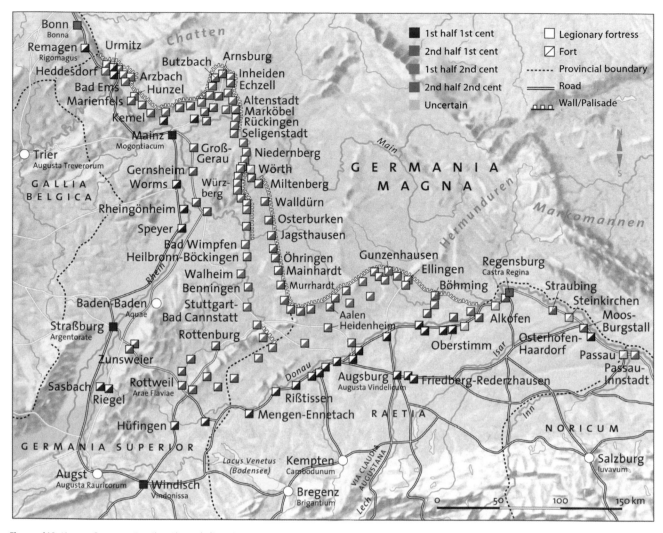

Figure 461 *Upper German-Raetian Limes (after Klee 2006, Konrad Theiss Verlag)*

following the abandonment of offensive plans in Germany. Only in the area to the east of Mainz, around Wiesbaden, had the Romans permanently occupied land to the east of the Rhine since the Augustan period. Military operations during the civil war after Nero's death and the defeat of the resultant Batavian uprising in the years AD 68–9 had clearly shown that the detour which the troops had to take from the Danube region into the Rhineland, via the upper Danube, Lake Constance, and the upper Rhine, was highly impractical. Vespasian (AD 69–79), who had emerged victorious from the civil war, began to change the state of affairs shortly after the first damages of the war had been removed. He had a road built through the Black Forest area, from Argentorate (Strasbourg), across Offenburg and then through the Kinzigtal, to Raetia, and secured it with forts. Nothing is known of any battles while this was done. The most important military base for these enterprises was Rottweil. Under Domitian (AD 81–96), further areas were occupied up to the river frontier on the Neckar, protected

by auxiliary forts from Bad Wimpfen to Köngen. The passes through the Swabian Alp were also militarily secured during this time (the 'Alp *limes*'; Heiligmann 1990). The existing gap between Köngen and the Alp *limes* was closed by the so-called Lautertal *limes*.

Vespasian had also occupied the land on the east bank of the Rhine in front of Mainz in the Wetterau. A larger territorial gain and the initial building of a linear frontier in the Taunus and Wetterau took place under Domitian (AD 81–96) within the framework of the war against the Chatti.

Under Trajan (AD 98–117), an intensive reconstruction of the imperial frontier began, during the course of which the Upper German Limes was created in the sense of a clearly marked and militarily supervised frontier. To continue the Taunus and Wetterau frontier, the Main *limes* was now also constructed. This was followed by a frontier from Wörth am Main to Bad Wimpfen on the Neckar, the so-called Odenwald Limes. During the reign of Antoninus Pius (AD 138–61), the area between the Rhine and the Danube that was protected by the frontier reached its largest extent when the Odenwald and Neckar Limes were abandoned and the front line of the *limes* constructed. This now ran almost directly from the Main to the Raetian frontier at Lorch.

The actual frontier barrier of the *limes* changed its appearance several times over the course of time. First, clearings, which were as straight as possible, were cut through the dense forest in order to mark the border. There was a patrol track within these clearings. At prominent points in the terrain within the linear clearings, watchtowers were built so closely that they were intervisible, and that forts placed to the rear could also see the *limes* watchtowers. This ensured that in the case of enemy raids, it was possible to transmit messages quickly through optical (smoke, fire, flags) or acoustic signals (wind instruments). Around the wooden towers, the ground floor of which consisted of a combination of wood and a drystone (*i.e.* unmortared) construction, there was a ring ditch to drain the tower. In the early 2nd century, the frontier received an additional marker in the form of a massive wooden palisade. The dilapidated wooden towers were not repaired but were replaced by three-storey towers made of solid stonework. With the erection of the forward *limes* line, the forts previously built in timber-and-earth construction were upgraded to stone.

Finally, the Upper German Limes achieved its final appearance with the construction of a wall-and-ditch system. The palisade, which for a long time has been seen as contemporaneous with this frontier barrier, was gone by then according to recent studies. This probably happened around the middle of the 2nd century. Only in a few places was a drystone or mortar wall erected on the frontier as a barrier.[143]

THE RAETIAN LIMES

Raetia was conquered by the Romans in 15 BC, but the Danube frontier was only secured with a line of forts under Tiberius (AD 14–37) and Claudius (AD 41–54), which ended in the east with Oberstimm near Ingolstadt. Between Oberstimm and Linz, a chain of fortlets is gradually being revealed, but larger bases have not been found. The history of the Raetian Limes is closely linked to that of the Upper German frontier. Although both *limites* were, in fact, a single continuous line between the Rhine and the Danube, there were significant differences which show how important the discretion of the provincial administrators was in such construction projects.

The measures undertaken under Vespasian in the western part of Upper Germany also led to a corresponding action further east in the neighbouring province of Raetia. It seems that Vespasian had already sought expansion beyond the Danube north of Augsburg and a further shortening of the frontier with the Rhine. To this end, the first newly founded forts north of the Danube followed at Nassenfels and Kösching.

Under the Flavians, the gap in the linear control of the upper Danube between Oberstimm and Linz, which had existed at this point since the time of the Claudian period, was also closed. As a next step, a frontier line guarded by troops was built in the Raetian part of the *limes* north of the Danube. The frontier line from Eining on the Danube to the Nördlinger Ries was probably drawn here as early as the reign of Trajan. In this manner the connection to the Alp *limes* and to the strongest garrison of the province, the fort of *ala II Flavia milliaria* in Heidenheim/*Aquileia*, was established.

A *limes* line was built between Eining and Ruffenhofen, with its first patrol tracks and the wooden tower signalling system. The route of the frontier line protruding in a bulge far to the north was not due to the constraints of the topography, but instead was apparently dictated by economic considerations. During the time of the Emperor Antoninus Pius (AD 138–61), special measures were taken to improve the defensive strength of the line of the *limes* in many places. Several meandering lengths of the *limes* were replaced by new, straighter and shorter stretches, and marked with the well-known wooden palisade. The defences of the forts erected in timber-and-earth construction were replaced by stone walls with fixed towers and gates, and the wooden *limes* towers by multi-storey stone structures. For the Raetian Limes, the advance from the Neckar to the outer line around AD 150 meant that, in its western part, directly on the outer line of the Upper German Limes, new forts had to be erected in order to close the gap thus created. These are the forts from Schirenhof to Halheim. A few smaller forts were inserted into this line. From the fort at Eining, the land-based Raetian Limes became the 'wet *limes*' (*ripa Danuvii provinciae Raetiae*) on the Danube. On the Raetian Limes, on the other hand, according to the latest research, a *c.*3 m-high stone wall, the Raetian Wall, was erected under Septimius Severus as a final barrier after AD 206/7. After the Marcomannic Wars, Raetia was heavily reinforced with troops by the deployment of *legio III Italica* to Regensburg, there having been no legionary occupation in the province beforehand.[144]

THE END OF THE UPPER GERMAN-RAETIAN LIMES

Since the great invasion of the Germans in the year AD 233, which mainly affected the western part of Upper Germany and the countryside to the east of Mainz (Biegert and Steidl 2011), there was continuous destruction by barbarian incursions and thinning of the frontier troops, which were needed either in the East in the conflicts against the Persians or internally during conflicts of rival emperors. This ultimately led to withdrawal from the Upper German-Raetian Limes. While the eastern part of the Upper German Limes was not lost until AD 260 under Emperor Gallienus (AD 253–68), the Raetian Limes north of the Danube had probably collapsed earlier, under Valerian (AD 253–60) and his son Gallienus. All dendrochronological and numismatic data from other Raetian forts suggest an end to the *limes* just after AD 254, when Valerian withdrew Upper German and Raetian troops to the East.[145]

The Late Roman Danube-Iller-Rhine limes

Due to the loss of the *limes* area, a new defensive line had to be created along the new frontier after AD 260. This would only be achieved after several decades of chaos. In Upper Germany, Rome withdrew to the old line on the Rhine, and in Raetia partly to the old Danube frontier.

Between Lake Constance and the confluence of the Iller and the Danube, Diocletian (284–305) established a new continuous frontier defensive system, the so-called Late Roman Danube-Iller-Rhine limes (Fig. 462). Under the reign of the Emperor Valentinian I (AD 364–75), Rome was once again able to strengthen the frontier fortifications and numerous small fortifications (*burgi*) were now erected. While research had previously assumed that the end of the Late Roman frontier defences began around AD 401, when Stilicho, the army commander in the West, withdrew troops from the Rhine and Danube

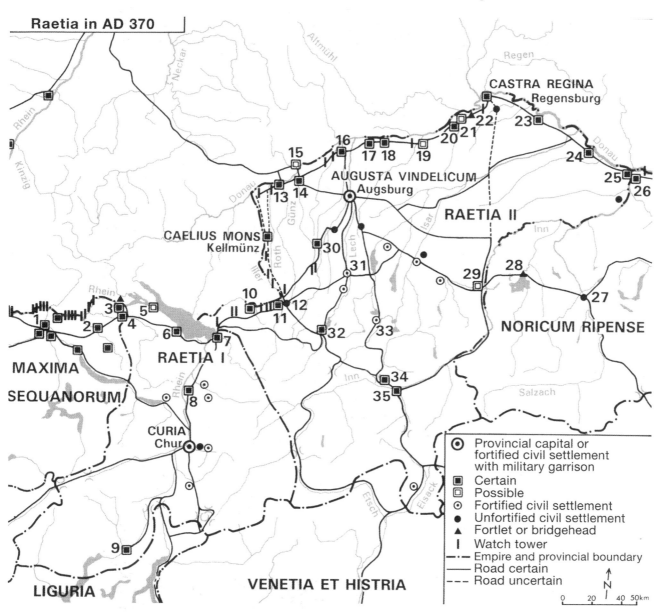

Figure 462 *The course of the Danube-Iller-Rhine limes in Raetia I and II as well as in Maxima Sequanorum: 1 Windisch; 2 Oberwinterthur; 3 Burg bei Eschenz; 4 Pfyn; 5 Konstanz; 6 Arbon; 7 Bregenz; 8 Schaan; 9 Bellinzona; 10 Betmauer bei Isny; 11 Kempten-Burghalde; 11a Kempten-Lindenberg; 12 Kellmünz; 13 Günzburg; 14 Bürgle bei Gundremmingen; 15 Faimingen; 16 Burghöfe; 17 Burgheim; 18 Neuburg; 19 Manching; 20 Eining; 21 Weltenburg; 22 Untersaal; 23 Straubing; 24 Künzing; 25 Passau; 26 Passau-Innstadt; 27 Salzburg; 28 Seebruck; 29 Pfaffenhofen; 30 Goldberg bei Türkheim; 31 Lorenzberg bei Epfach; 32 Füssen; 33 Moosberg bei Murnau; 34 Martinsbühel bei Zirl; 35 Innsbruck-Wilten (after Mackensen in Weber 2000)*

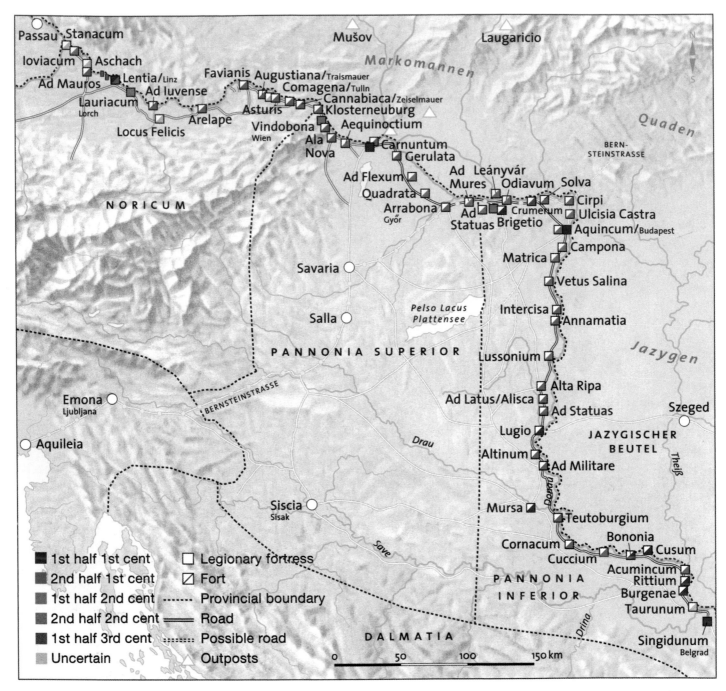

Figure 463 *Danube frontier in Noricum and Pannonia (after Klee 2006, Konrad Theiss Verlag)*

to defend Italy against the Visigoths, new archaeological discoveries together with some historical passages demonstrate that the organized frontier defence on the Rhine and the Danube did not cease until the middle of the 5th century AD.[146]

The Norican Danube limes (Ripa Danuvii Provinciae Norici)

The concept of a river frontier secured with forts only arrived late to Noricum. One reason for this is simply due to the geography of the area north of the Danube: there was hardly any immediate threat from here. In the northern Danube section, the archaeologically attested German settlement zone only extended to the frontier region in the east. In the section stretching from Passau to the Wienerwald, only the Krems region in Lower Austria had a (limited) strategic importance, while Upper Austria was not really exposed to any immediate, serious danger from the uninhabited regions of the Bavarian Forest and the Bohemian Forest beyond it (Fig. 463).

In addition, for a long time a certain degree of protection was provided by the system of client states practised on the opposite bank of the Danube, especially with the Quadi, Marcomanni, and other tribes. For this reason, until the Flavian period, small military bases seemingly had been sufficient on the northern frontier of Upper Austria, but until now, no reliable evidence has yet been established for this, with the exception of *Lentia*/Linz.

It was not until Vespasian (AD 69–79), in the second half of the 1st century AD, that a real linear defensive frontier concept could be perceived for the first time on the entire Danube section in Noricum. Numerous forts were created, mainly where important connecting routes from the north to the Danube had to be directed and monitored. In a first phase of expansion, forts were built in timber-and-earth on the northern frontier section of the Danube. These are the forts of Linz, Traismauer, Mautern, Tulln, and Zwentendorf. Under Trajan (AD 98–117), there was a further consolidation of this dense chain of frontier forts on the Danube. Since, in addition to Carnuntum, a legionary fortress was also set up in Vienna/*Vindobona*, it is possible to conclude from this close proximity of two legions in the area of Vienna, not far from the north-eastern frontier, that these troops would also suffice to protect Noricum in case of emergency, for the province of Noricum did not have its own legionary garrison until around AD 200.

The rebuilding of the older timber-and-earth bases into stone forts can be observed everywhere in the Upper German-Raetian Limes, and also occurred in Noricum. While in the west, this expansion mainly happened under Antoninus Pius (AD 138–61), in Noricum it occurred in the reign of Trajan (AD 98–117) and, above all, his successor Hadrian (AD 117–38).

The few stone watchtowers which have so far been identified on the northern Danube frontier belong to the late 2nd century and are explicable in terms of a build-up of the Norican *limes* after the Marcomannic Wars under Marcus Aurelius (AD 164–80).

In the Late Roman period, the old mid-Imperial forts were considerably reinforced by raising the fort walls and by the addition of horseshoe and fan-shaped towers. The new fort of *Boiotro* in Passau-Innstadt is especially worth mentioning among the new installations. In addition, there were numerous *burgi*. The frontier defence of Noricum remained active in certain parts even after the nominal end of the Western Roman Empire in AD 476.[147]

Pannonian Danube limes (Ripa Danuvii provinciae Pannoniae)

After the end of the great Pannonian insurrection, which began in AD 6, the area on the middle Danube between Vienna and Belgrade was organized into the province of Pannonia. While the three legions of the early Imperial period were situated in the hinterland (*Poetovio*, *Siscia*), one legion was moved to Carnuntum under Claudius (AD 41–54), to protect the March valley with the important Amber Road. Since the end of the 1st century under Domitian, this frontier section was subject to extraordinary pressure by Germans, Sarmatians, and other peoples. Therefore, in contrast to Noricum, there was an unusual concentration of legionary fortresses and auxiliary forts here. Around AD 100, the Pannonian army with its four legions was the strongest of the Empire. The legions were located in Vienna/*Vindobona*, *Carnuntum*, *Brigetio* and Budapest/*Aquincum*, three of them on the northern Danube frontier, opposite the German settlement zone. After the conquest of Dacia in the years AD 106/7, Trajan (AD 98–117) divided the province, with Pannonia Superior (capital *Carnuntum*) having three legions, but Pannonia Inferior (capital Budapest/*Aquincum*) only one legion. It was not until Caracalla (AD 211–17) that the *Brigetio* legionary fortress was included in Pannonia Inferior.

On the enemy side of the Danube in the approaches to the Upper Pannonian *limes*, there were numerous short-term marching camps and military posts built in the Marcomannic Wars (Komoróczy 2009). From Commodus (AD 180–92) onwards at the latest, this frontier section was also secured by stone watchtowers, but an older wooden tower destroyed in the Marcomannic Wars is also known. Several identical *burgus* building inscriptions from the time of Commodus are known, such as *CIL* III, 3385 from Intercisa. This records that the Emperor had the border (*ripam Danuvii*) constructed with towers (*burgi*) and *praesidia* (forts) at 'loca opportuna' (suitable places) to prevent the 'latruncili' ('bandits') from crossing the river from beyond. The Pannonian fleet also patrolled the Danube. In the 3rd century AD, the forts of the Pannonian Danube line were repeatedly destroyed by hostile incursions. In the Late Roman period, the border was strengthened considerably by inland fortifications in the hinterland as well as by building up the forts, constructing bridgeheads and numerous *burgi*. In addition, there was a wall and ditch system in the lands in front of the Transdanubian *limes*, the date and function of which are still being discussed. In this manner, the frontier of the province of Pannonia could be held until the early 5th century AD, when the rule of Rome was replaced by Huns, Goths, and other tribes.[148]

Upper Moesian Danube frontier (Ripa Danuvii provinciae Moesiae superioris)

The province of Moesia was probably established under Tiberius (AD 14–37) as part of the great province of Achaia, Macedonia, and Moesia, after the area had been under Roman control since the time of the late Republic. For the time of Augustus, three legions are assumed to have been stationed there, two after AD 9. This military presence was established with the protection of the

Roman province of Macedonia, which had to suffer repeatedly from incursions by tribes from the territory of the later province of Moesia. However, the early military history of Moesia Superior is largely unknown, since there are still insufficient archaeological data to compensate for the scanty historical tradition. Under Claudius (AD 41–54), Moesia obtained the status of a separate province. Between the legionary fortress at *Singidunum* (Belgrade) at the mouth of the River Sava into the Danube to its delta, Claudius established a frontier control system on the Danube, after the region had two legions stationed there (*legio IV Scythica* and *legio V Macedonica*) since the 20s of the 1st century AD. Whether these legions were already stationed on the river or inside the province is not known.

It is believed there were five legions in the province at the end of the reign of Vespasian (AD 69–79). A military diploma (*IMS* IV, 184) of AD 75 names 11 auxiliary units in the province. When there was fighting against Dacians and other tribes in this region, under Domitian (AD 71–98), the larger province was divided into *Moesia Superior* and *Moesia Inferior* in AD 85/86, each of which initially had two or three legions (Fig. 464). From AD 92 (military diploma *CIL* XVI, 37), a *classis Flavia Moesica* is also named. In *Moesia Superior*, there were two legions at *Singidunum* (Belgrade) and *Viminacium* (Kostolac).

With the formation of the Dacian provinces under Trajan (AD 98–117), the river frontier east of *Viminacium* was interrupted and replaced by the Dacian Limes. After the evacuation of Dacia in AD 275, the Danube frontier in *Moesia Superior* was reinstated and then considerably strengthened in the Late Roman period. During this time, areas from the two provinces of Moesia had been dissolved and organized as the new frontier province, *Dacia Ripense*. Currently, there has not been enough research into the question of forts and watchtowers in this sector of the frontier. In the early 5th century, the frontier defensive system of the province collapsed and was probably only restored in the early 6th century AD under Justinian I (AD 527–65).[149]

Dacian Limes (Limes Daciae)

With the conquest of Dacia under Trajan (AD 98–117), completed in AD 106/107, the area of Transylvania, the Banat and the land between Danube and the Carpathians was organized as a province of *Dacia*. This territory was of particular importance to Rome due to the rich gold, silver, and salt deposits and other mineral resources. It immediately received a strong military presence with auxiliary forts on the frontier line (the details of which are still under discussion) and in the hinterland. At the beginning of Hadrian's reign (AD 117–38), heavy fighting broke out on the eastern frontier of the province, leading

to the partial withdrawal from the territories occupied by Trajan. As a result, the province was divided: *Dacia Superior* (later *Dacia Apulensis*), *Dacia Inferior* (later *Dacia Malvensis*) and *Dacia Porolissensis*.

The *limes* is best understood in the central northern region, in *Dacia Porolissensis*. It ran along the crest of the Mesec mountain range and is known as the Mesec *limes*. In the hinterland, forts, fortlets, and watchtowers are now relatively well known. The most important frontier garrison post is also here at *Porolissum*, near an important pass. In the hinterland of the Mesec *limes*, the legionary bases of *Potaissa* were located in Turda/*Potaissa* and Alba Julia/*Apulum*. The eastern border of Dacia is still inadequately researched: there are forts and towers in front of the Carpathians, where valleys and thus passes from Barbaricum led into the Roman Empire. The eastern *limes* on the Olt (the 'limes Olutanus') is still difficult to understand. Apparently it was withdrawn backwards under Hadrian, abandoning terrain conquered under Trajan. The date and function of the 'limes transolutanus' are unclear: here, there is an earthen rampart with wooden towers and, with one exception, only timber-and-earth forts, the dating of which is largely uncertain. In the 3rd century AD, the eastern frontier of *Dacia Malvensis* was apparently withdrawn. After numerous barbarian incursions into the province, the Emperor Aurelian (AD 270–4) took advantage of a respite after a victory over the Goths and Alans in AD 271, and withdrew from the Dacian provinces north of the Danube. After that the military defences of the Danube frontier were restored.[150]

Lower Moesian Danube frontier (Ripa Danuvii provinciae Moesiae inferioris)

When there was heavy fighting against the Dacians, Germans, and other tribes under Domitian (AD 71–98), the large province of Moesia was divided into *Moesia Superior* and *Moesia Inferior* in AD 85/6. In *Moesia Inferior*, four legionary fortresses were set up, but they were not all occupied at the same time: Gigen/*Oescus* was garrisoned from around AD 100, was abandoned with the establishment of the Dacian provinces, and was reoccupied after the evacuation of Dacia after *c.* AD 275. Svistov/*Novae* existed from the 1st century AD up to the Late Roman period. A legion had been garrisoned in Silistra/*Durostorum* from the 2nd century AD into the Late Roman period, and in Turcoaia/*Troesmis* since the time of Trajan. In addition, there is the late legionary fortress of Arcar/*Ratiaria*, which belonged to the late province of *Dacia Ripense*, formed from regions that had been taken from the Moesian Danube frontier. In addition, more than 40 forts and military stations are known in the area of the Lower Moesian river basin, some of which were also used as a base for operations by

Figure 464 *Frontier on the Lower Danube and Crimea (after Klee 2006, Konrad Theiss Verlag)*

the *classis Moesica*. Several complex systems of earthen ramparts located on the approaches to the Lower Moesian Danube frontier are still being debated.

Under the incessantly repeated barbarian attacks, especially from the Goths and Huns, the Danube frontier in the area of *Moesia Inferior* (or the late-antique province of *Moesia Secunda*) practically collapsed in the 5th century AD. Only after its reconstruction, probably under Anastasius I (AD 491–518), would it be held again until the early 7th century AD, before it was finally overrun by Avars and Slavs.

The frontier defence of the province of *Moesia Inferior* included a control system with fortified ports guarded by the Moesian fleet and vexillations from the Lower Moesian

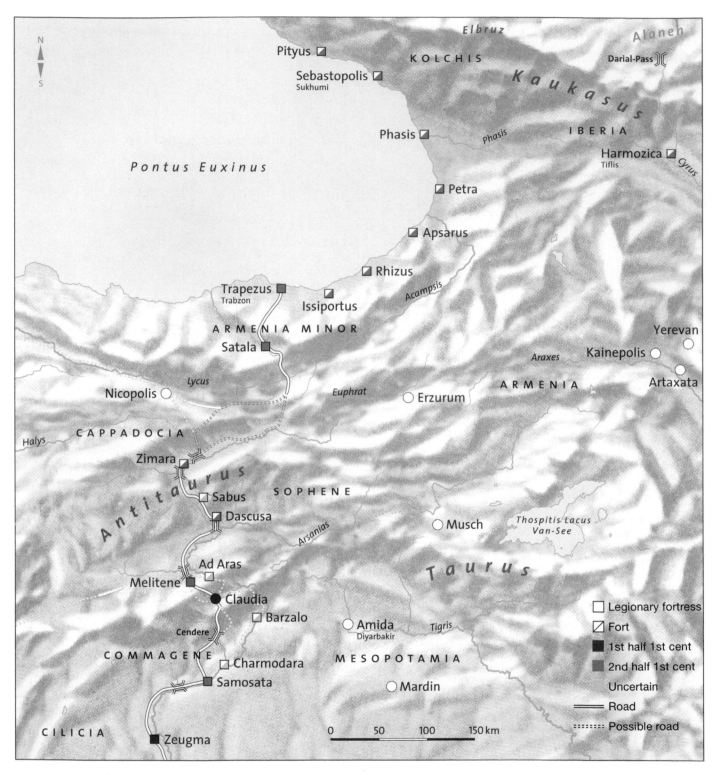

Figure 465 *Frontier in the Caucasus and the eastern Black Sea region (after Klee 2006, Konrad Theiss Verlag)*

legions and auxiliaries. It stretched along the Black Sea coast in the area of the province around the cities of Histria, Tomis and Callatis. Moreover, this coastal protection afforded control of the Black Sea as far up as the Crimea, where the Bosporan kingdom, which was allied to Rome, lay in the 3rd century AD. This military security system was used primarily to secure trade, particularly grain imports from Ukraine and Crimea.[151]

The limes *on the upper Euphrates and in the Middle East*

Compared to the frontiers in Britain and on the Rhine and the Danube, the frontier in this region ran through much wilder and more hostile regions: high mountains, deserts, and only rarely temperate zones with more tolerable living conditions, like those that existed on the northern frontiers. There was also really only one relevant opponent here: the Persian empire, whether it was governed by the Parthians or the Sassanids. The nomads of Syria and Arabia did not really play a role as opponents.

In order to be able to assess these frontiers in the East properly, the numbers of troops must also be compared: in the 1st century AD the Roman troops in the East were only about 50% of the troops in Europe. However, of these troops, 20% were not involved in frontier defence, but controlled the restless population of Syria and Judaea. The garrisons of these troops are still little known, although information about the legionary fortresses in the East has been compiled by S. Th. Parker (Parker 2000). The troops in the East were considerably strengthened, especially in the late 2nd and 3rd centuries, without this resulting in more peace on the frontiers. The long-term conflict with the Persians characterized the frontier policies of the Roman and later the Byzantine empires in the region until the 7th century when, after the Battle of Yarmuk (AD 636) under Emperor Heraclius (AD 610–41), the whole region fell under Arab rule.[152]

Limes *in Pontus and Cappadocia*

The continuation of the fleet-based control system of the western Black Sea coast and the Crimea, organized by the Low Moesian provincial army, can be found in the eastern Black Sea region in the provinces of Pontus and Cappadocia as far as Pythus in the Caucasus. In Trapezus on the Black Sea coast, where the headquarters of the eastern Black Sea fleet lay, a frontier defensive system began across the mountains of eastern Turkey, continuing in the east of Asia Minor and Syria. Here the Euphrates formed a river frontier (*ripa*), which is known as the 'Euphrates *limes*'. In the last few years, excavations have mainly taken place at Zeugma, which was endangered by the construction of the Birecik dam. There were, however, still no clear traces of the legionary fortress, only temporary early Imperial period timber-and-earth camps.[153] Otherwise, the Euphrates *limes* has barely been explored in comparison to the *limites* in Britain, the Rhine, and the Danube.[154]

Limes *in Syria*

In the desert regions of Syria and Jordan, a linear system of roads, towers, forts of various sizes, and legionary fortresses was built on the outer limits between the desert and the fertile land. Its main task was to control the oases, in addition to the important caravan routes into the desert. A major problem in research here is that Late Roman and Byzantine fortifications overlie most of the older forts, and so far many of the latter have not even been located, much less explored. Systematic research has mainly been done on the Late Roman frontier sector in the northern Syrian desert area, between Sura on the Euphrates and the southern line of frontier as far as Palmyra (Konrad 2001).

As a rule, this frontier fairly precisely separated those areas where precipitation still permitted agriculture from those where only pastoralism by nomads was possible. These nomads were also feared as robbers, especially when there was no rain, and therefore had to be excluded from Roman territory (Fig. 466). The *limes* in Syria, which mostly passed through deserts, did not have to be held by a dense line of forts. Forts are known from the Euphrates to Palmyra, but south of them, in the inhospitable desert region, frontier control markedly diminished. The occasionally strong Roman troop presence in the Syrian hinterland and in Judaea (such as the legionary fortresses at *Cyrrhus*, *Raphanae*, or Jerusalem) had less to do with securing the frontier. Their locations were linked to the control of important trade routes and the troublesome provincial population. A *limes* system postulated in the Negev desert in Israel as a frontier system with fortlets is now interpreted as a network of fortified tower farms, occasionally combined with posts to secure the road system. These facilities probably had nothing to do with a regular *limes*, in the sense of a militarily monitored frontier system.[155]

Limes Arabicus

With the conquest of the Nabataean empire in AD 106 by Trajan (AD 98–117) and the establishment of the province of Arabia in the same year, the Syrian *limes* was extended to the Red Sea, and again was fairly densely guarded with forts and watchtowers. In particular, oases or other places where there was water received military garrisons. The task of this frontier was, on the one hand, the control of Arab nomadic tribes, and on the other the control of the caravan trade bringing luxury goods from Arabia (incense!) and from India (spices, silk) into the Roman empire. The backbone of the frontier defences was the *via nova Traiana*, built under Trajan, which led from the legionary fortress of Bosra (*legio III Cyrenaica*) to Aqaba on the Red Sea. It was subjected to a fundamental renewal under Severus. In the Tetrarchic period, the border was reinforced by the legionary fortress at el-Lejjun (Fig. 467).[156]

Limes *in Egypt*

Egypt, which was so important for its production of grain, and also economically very significant for Rome in other ways, had a special settlement structure: the

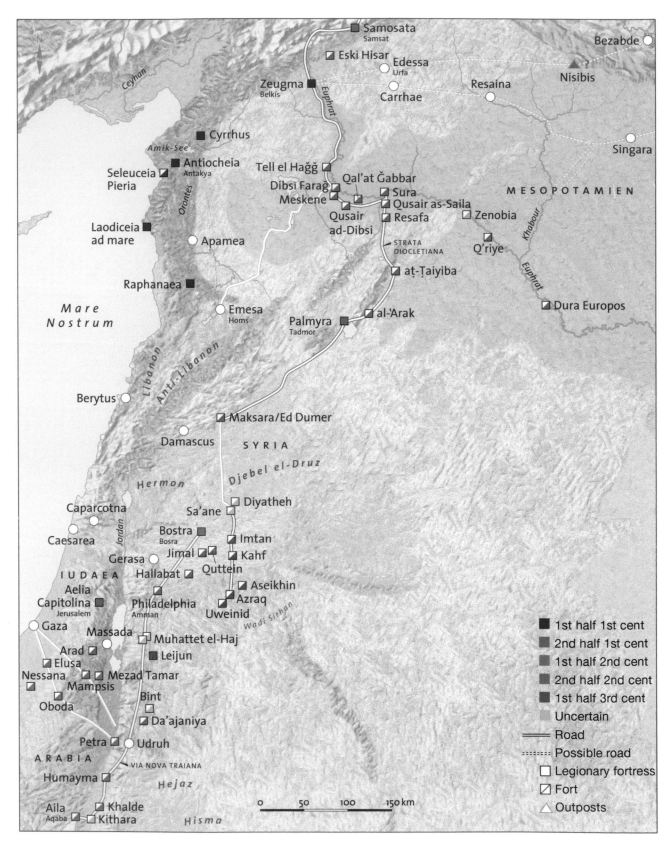

Figure 466 *Syrian and Arabian limes (after Klee 2006, Konrad Theiss Verlag)*

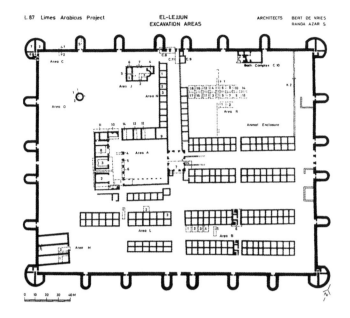

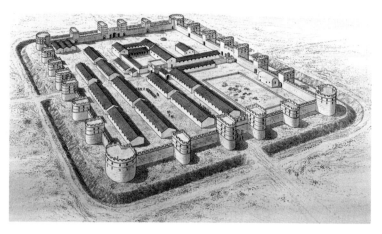

Figure 467 *Legionary fortress of el-Lejjun a) plan b) reconstruction (after Parker 1990; Campbell 2009)*

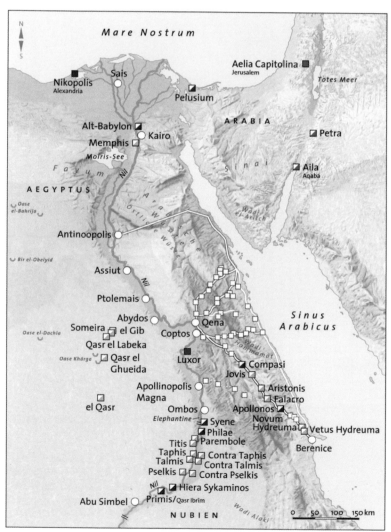

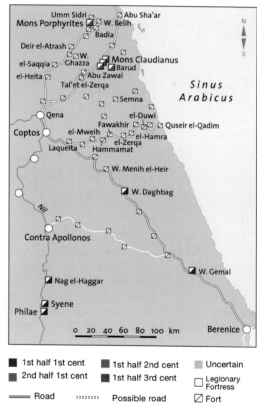

■ 1st half 1st cent	■ 1st half 2nd cent	Uncertain
■ 2nd half 1st cent	■ 1st half 3rd cent	☐ Legionary Fortress
══ Road	⋯⋯ Possible road	⊠ Fort

Figure 468 *Limites and forts in Egypt (after Klee 2006, Konrad Theiss Verlag)*

fertile Nile valley with its delta was accompanied by vast deserts. For a long time, however, exploration of the Roman military and the Roman frontier control was not necessarily the focus of attention in Egypt despite intensive archaeological activity.

Consequently we hardly know of any military sites from the early and mid-Imperial periods, for instance. These will have initially concentrated on the control of the densely populated Nile Valley and the delta with its important export ports. The important quarries and mining areas in the deserts of the country were also under military protection (Fig. 468). It was also important to control the ports on the Red Sea, which served the enormously important trade with India. Here troops were stationed in the ports themselves and secured the routes to the Nile valley with forts and watchtowers along the roads. In the west there were garrisons at the most important oases, because here the marauding nomads from the Libyan Sahara threatened the peace.

In the Late Roman period, the threat to the frontiers increased, in particular towards the south and Nubia, and was countered with the intensified construction of forts. Uprisings in the countryside led to the further expansion

of military installations, also in the Nile Valley and the Delta.[157] In recent years it was mainly the Late Roman forts and fortesses which were archaeologically explored. In addition to the legionary fortress built in a temple (Fig. 469) at Luxor (El-Saghir *et al.* 1986), there were the fortifications at Tell-el Herr (Fig. 470) in Sinai (Valbelle and Carrez-Maratray 2000) and Nag al-Hagar (Fig. 471) in Upper Egypt (Mackensen and Franke 2010).

Figure 470 *Fort of Tell-el Herr (after Valbelle and Carrez-Maratray 2000). Drawing: A. Smadi, Arch. Institute University of Cologne*

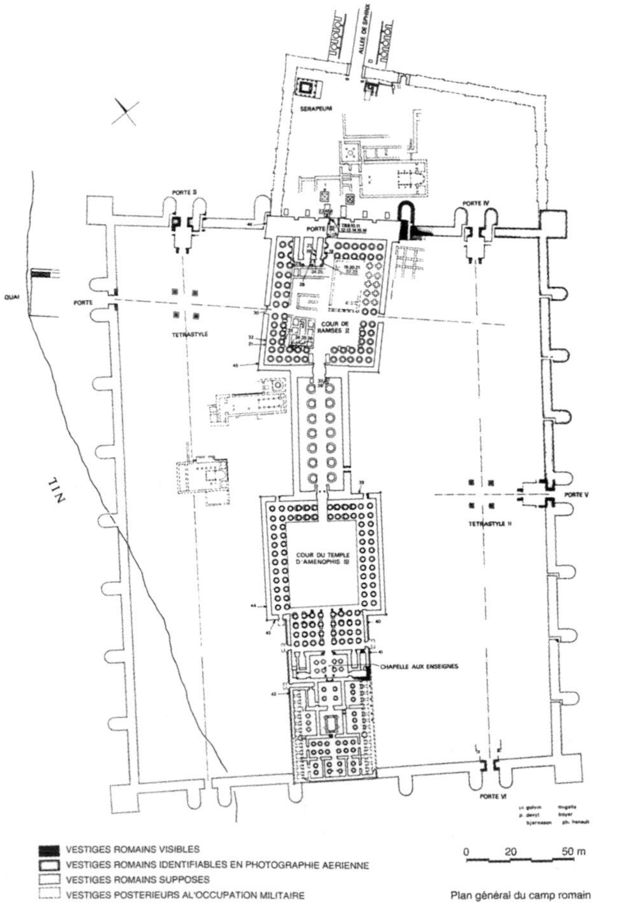

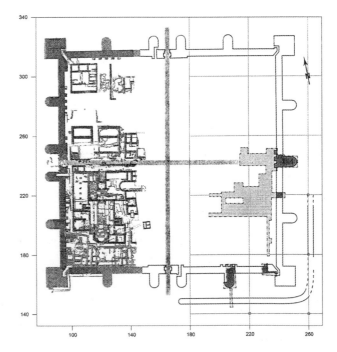

Figure 471 *Fort of Nagal-Hagar (after Mackensen and Franke 2013)*

Figure 469 *Luxor legionary fortress (after El-Saghir et al., 1986)*

The limes in Cyrenaica, Africa Proconsularis, and Numidia

In North Africa, both *Cyrenaica* in Libya and *Africa Proconsularis* and *Numidia* in present day Tunisia and Algeria have a frontier defensive system of about 4,000 km in length, consisting of roads, forts, fortlets, and watchtowers (Fig. 472). For this large region, which was of crucial importance as a granary of Rome, an astonishingly small number of troops was sufficient for a long time: the *legio III Augusta* was first based at Tebessa/*Theveste*, then from Trajan (AD 98–117) onwards in *Lambaesis*, outposting many long-term vexillations in frontier forts. There were only a few auxiliary cohorts and *alae* in addition to it. At the time of the greatest expansion of Roman North Africa under Septimius Severus (AD 193–211), Roman occupation comprised a legion, two *alae*, seven *cohortes*

and two *numeri*. This is all the more remarkable when one compares the forces of Roman North Africa with the enormous concentrations of troops in the provincial armies of Britain and the provinces on the Rhine and Danube! This can only be explained by the fact that, after the civil war under Caesar (49–46 BC) and the suppression of Tacfarinas' revolt under Tiberius (AD 14–37), the period up to the civil wars of the 3rd century AD was relatively peaceful.

The Roman frontier security system in North Africa was concentrated mainly on those regions where there were troublesome tribes on the other side of the frontier, or in the control of caravan routes through the Sahara into central Africa. The oases, with their watering holes, were closely observed.

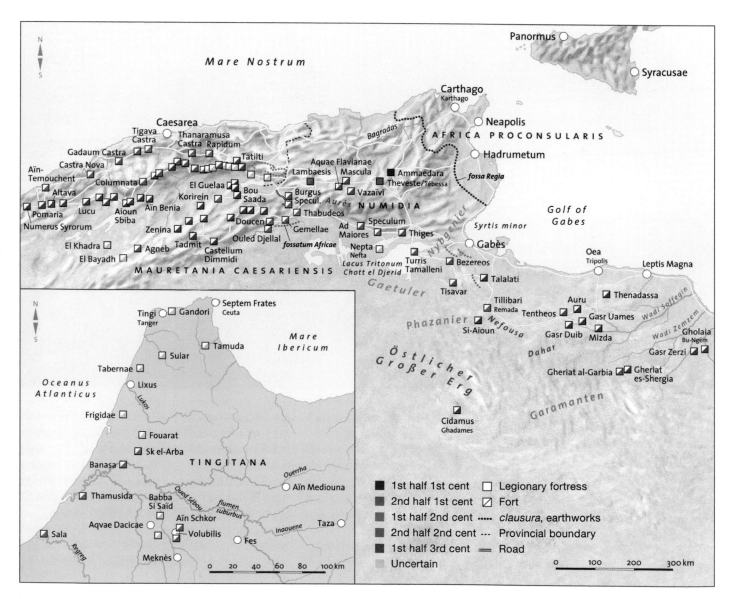

Figure 472 *Limites in North Africa (after Klee 2006, Konrad Theiss Verlag)*

The limes *in the provinces of Mauretania Tingitana and Caesariensis*

The limes system in Northern Africa features a local variation: in the most important valleys of the mountain ranges along the border, which formed access routes into the Sahara, short retaining walls with passing gates were constructed in order to be able to control traffic by nomads and their large herds of livestock. Current thinking assumes that they were denied access before the grain harvest. However, the animals were allowed to graze the stubble fields after harvest (and thus fertilising them at the same time). This example demonstrates that Roman border installations were not always purely military installations in the strictest sense. The border zone also saw the occasional creation of fortified farmsteads which were probably, at least partly, integrated into the military control system. This was subsequently intensified in Late Antiquity. With the Vandal conquest of North Africa (from AD 429 onwards) the Roman frontier defensive system in North Africa rapidly collapsed, the short-term Byzantine reconquest under Justinian I (AD 527–565) only affecting part of the former Roman territory.[158]

The limes *in the provinces of Mauretania, Tingitana and Caesariensis*

The territory of the province of *Mauretania*, established under Claudius (AD 41–54), had been a client kingdom allied with Rome since the late Republic. In the Imperial period there existed a form of political abeyance at first: Augustus (27BC–AD14) instigated the foundation of some *coloniae* without formally annexing the territory. Military protection during the Imperial period was also predominantly focused on the towns. The main objective was the protection of the rich cities on the coast and in the hinterland with their fertile environment from attacks by Mauretanian pirates and warlike mountain tribes. Here, the border ran in mountainous territory which was much more difficult to control than the border with the Sahara. Consequently, there is a much lower concentration of forts along this western border section of North Africa, in present-day Algeria and Morocco, than in the *Caesariensis* further to the east. In the *Tingitana*, the city of *Volubilis*, situated in the hinterland, was under strong military protection. Attacks increased during the 3rd century AD, thus forcing Diocletian (AD 284–305) to abandon the city and further territories in the hinterland and to take back the borders.[159]

Notes to Part IV

1. On similar frontier guards in other areas and times, see M. Pfaffenbichler, Grenzen im historischen Kontext, in: Grenzen 2006, 7–13.
2. v. Hesberg 1985; Johnson 1987, 11; Busch 2010, 55.
3. v. Petrikovits 1975, 33.
4. Hyg., *Mun. Castr.* 54; Busch 2010, 55.
5. Johnson 1987, 49ff.
6. Ibid., 51f.
7. Ibid., 52–6; Baatz 1994, 315–25.
8. Johnson 1987, 56ff.
9. Busch 2010, 31, 107ff.
10. Johnson 1987, 59–67.
11. Baatz and Herrmann 1982, 227f.
12. Johnson 1987, 282.
13. Ibid., 70–81.
14. Fischer 2002, 49; 51.
15. Johnson 1987, 76.
16. Baatz and Hermann 1982, 472; 502; Johnson 1987, 83f.
17. Johnson 1987, 76f.
18. Ibid., 88–93.
19. Busch 2010, 31–72.
20. Johnson 1987, 82.
21. Busch 2010, 54.
22. Johnson 1987, 82f.
23. Ibid., 84.
24. Ibid., 86.
25. Dietz and Fischer 1996, 89–93.
26. Busch 2010, 41.
27. Friedrich 2010, 57–60.
28. Johnson 1987, 86.
29. Friedrich 2010, 57–60.
30. Johnson 1987, 93.
31. Flügel and Obmann 2008.
32. Mackensen 2008, 289.
33. Cüppers 1990, 499.
34. Grönke and Weinlich 1991, 40.
35. v. Petrikovits 1975, Plate 12.
36. Mackensen 2008, 288 and 2010a, 425–48.
37. I am referring here to the undergraduate dissertation of E. Krieger, submitted in 2011 at the Archaeological Institute of the University of Cologne, which focused on the ratio of single and double gateways in the forts of the Upper German-Raetian Limes.
38. Johnson 1987, 17; 111.
39. Ibid., 118.
40. Ibid., Fig. 179; Gschwind 2004, 33, Fig. 11; 43–75.
41. Fellmann 1957/58 and 1983; Blagg 2000.
42. v. Petrikovits 1975, 68–75.
43. Ibid., Johnson, 1987, 123–52.
44. v. Petrikovits 1975, 67; Johnson, 1987, 152–61.
45. Sommer 2002, 51–4.
46. v. Petrikovits 1975, 64–7.
47. Pitts and St. Joseph 1985, 129–41.
48. Visy 1985, 83.
49. Pitts and St. Joseph 1985, 151–71.
50. v. Petrikovits 1975, 36–43; Johnson 1987, 188–98; Davison 1989.
51. Johnson 1987, 198–204.
52. Sommer 1999, 84; Scholz 2009.
53. Sommer 1995, 158–65 and 1999.
54. Sommer 1999, 85; Scholz, 2009, 107–12.
55. Busch 2010, 60.
56. Scholz 2009, 107–12.

57. Pitts and St. Joseph 1985, 161f.
58. Ibid., 179–82.
59. v. Petrikovits 1975, 49f; 58f; 143f.
60. Speidel 1996, n.145; 38.
61. v Petrikovits 1975, 102; Hanel 2000.
62. Johnson 1987, 240–4.
63. Planck 1983, 99–109.
64. Sommer 1984, 18–22.
65. v. Petrikovits 1973, 80f.
66. Pitts and St. Joseph 1985, 123–8.
67. Johnson 1987, 47; 216–22.
68. v. Petrikovits 1975, 82–5.
69. Johnson 1987, 162–79.
70. Pietsch et al. 1991, 292–6.
71. v. Petrikovits 1975, 98–102; Johnson, 1987, 179–82; Künzl 1991.
72. Johnson 1987, 183–8.
73. v. Petrikovits 1975, 89–97; Johnson 1987, 204–9.
74. Ibid., 93–7; Johnson 1987, 209–11.
75. Groller v. Mildensee 1901; v. Petrikovits 1975, 73; Johnson 1987, 18; 210f.
76. Johnson 1987, 221f.
77. Ibid., 223–32.
78. Ibid., 232–5.
79. Scholz 2009, 117–22.
80. Jernej and Gugl 2004, 138.
81. Johnson 1987, 211f; 236–40.
82. Kaiser and Sommer 1994, 388–92.
83. Grote 2006; H. Becker and G. Rasbach in Wiegels 2007, 98f; Moosbauer 2009, 40ff; 68; Grothe 2012.
84. Johnson 1987, 57; 61; Czysz et al. 1995, 520.
85. Luik 2002; 2009.
86. J. K. Haalebos in Trier 1991, 97–107; F. Kemmers in Lehmann and Wiegels 2007, 183–99.
87. H. van Enckefort in Kühlborn 1995, 42–58; J.-S. Kühlborn in Wiegels 2007, 67.
88. Förtsch 1995, 629f.
89. Kühlborn 1992; idem in Kühlborn 1995, 103–24; J.-S. Kühlborn, in Wiegels 2007, 71–7; idem in Lehmann and Wiegels 2007, 201–5.
90. Pietsch et al., 1991; M. Pietsch in W. Czysz et al., 1995, 475–9.
91. v. Petrikovits 1975, 154; G. Mueller, in Horn 1987, 583–6.
92. v. Petrikovits 1975, 152.
93. Ibid., 149; Pitts and St. Joseph, 1985.
94. Boon 1972; V. Petrikovits 1975, 152; Johnson 1987, 291f.
95. v. Petrikovits 1975, 159f; M. Németh in Visy 2003, 99–101.
96. v. Petrikovits 1975, 158; Kronberger 2007.
97. Gudea 1997, 109–11.
98. v. Petrikovits 1975, 160f; Johnson 1987.
99. v. Petrikovits 1975, 157.
100. Fingerlin 1971/1972; 1981; 1986 and 1998.
101. J.-S. Kühlborn in Wiegels 2007, 80–6; Fischer 2009a, 505–9.
102. Velleius Paterculus 2.120.4; Zonaras 10.37; Cassius Dio 56.22; Tac., Ann. 2.7; Claudius Ptolemaios, Geographia 2.11.14.
103. v. Schnurbein 1981, 53–78.
104. Jütting 1995; Fischer and Riedmeier-Fischer 2008, 111f.
105. Schönberger 1985, 428; J. S. Kühlborn in Kühlborn 1995, 130–44; J. S. Kühlborn in Wiegels 2007, 86–93; J. S. Kühlborn in Lehmann and Wiegels 2007, 205–9.
106. Förtsch 1995, 621–6.
107. Glüsing 2000, 120f.
108. Schönberger 1976; J.-S. Kühlborn in Wiegels 2007, 98f; Fischer 2009a, 503f.
109. Fischer and Riedmeier-Fischer 2008, 116–19.
110. In addition, Fischer and Riedmeier-Fischer 2008, 179–81.
111. Fischer and Riedmeier-Fischer 2008, 208f; Prammer 2010.
112. Johnson 1987, 292f.
113. Marcu 2009, 137ff.
114. Hanson et al. 2007, 655.
115. Gudea 1989; Marcu 2009, 88–101.
116. H. H. Wegner in Cüppers 1990; 501ff; Jost 2007.
117. Baatz 1973; Schallmayer 2010, 104ff.
118. Mackensen 1987, 129–35.
119. Zanier 2006, 102–19.
120. Jones and Mattingly 1990, 102; 108f.
121. Fischer and Riedmeier-Fischer 2008, 70.
122. Busch 2010, 13.
123. Ibid., 31–72.
124. Ibid., 94.
125. Ibid., 94.
126. Ibid., 72–5.
127. Ibid., 75–84.
128. Ibid., 84–90.
129. Ibid., 95f.
130. Ibid., 91–4.
131. Johnson 1983 passim; Fischer 2002, 134.
132. Gschwind 2004, 76–86.
133. Overbeck 1973 and 1983; Gilles 1985; Ciglenecki 1987; Steuer 1990; Fischer in Czysz et al., 1995, 366–70.
134. Konrad 2001, 100–4.
135. Ibid.
136. Pekáry 1968; Rathmann 2003, 40f.
137. Suet., Claud. 1; Tac., Ann. 13.53.2; Hanel 1995, 107.
138. Tac., Ann. 11.20.2; Cass. Dio 60.30.6; Hanel 1995, 107.
139. On the limites in general, see Bechert and Willems 1995; Breeze and Dobson 2000; Schallmayer, E. in Fischer 2000, 123ff; French and Lightfood 1989; Friesinger and Krinzinger 1997; Gudea 1997 and 2001; Kennedy 2000; Parker 1987; Ruprechtsberger 1993; Visy 2003; Klee 2006; Grenzen 2006; Breeze 2011; Reddé 2014. For further information on research on the limites of the Roman Empire, see the congress proceedings of the International Congress on Roman Frontiers (Limeskongress).
140. See for example E. Schallmayer in Fischer 2001, 123.
141. Klee 2006, 8–31; Grenzen 2006, 98–104.
142. J. Kunow in Horn 1987, 27–109; Bechert and Willems 1995; Klee 2006, 33–40; Grenzen 2006, 123–32.
143. ORL; Beck-Planck 1980; Jost 2006; Klee 2006, 40–52 and 2009; Schallmayer 2006 and 2010; Grenzen 2006, 112–22; Steidl 2008.
144. Beck-Planck 1980; Klee 2006, 52–9; Grenzen 2006, 112–22; Fischer and Riedmeier-Fischer 2008.
145. Schönberger 1985, 401–24; Reuter 2007.
146. Garbsch 1988; T. Fischer in Czysz et al. 1995, 358–411; Fischer 2009.
147. Genser 1986; Friesinger and Krinzinger 1997; Fischer 2002; Klee 2006, 61–5; Grenzen 2006, 133–9.

148. Visy 1985; Friesinger and Krinzinger 1997; Visy 2003 and 2003a; Klee 2006, 65–71; Grenzen 2006, 133–56.
149. Gudea 2001; Summer von Bülow 2006; Klee 2006, 71–82; Mirkovic 2007.
150. Gudea 1997; Klee 2006, 82–7; Grenzen 2006, 163–8.
151. Gudea 2005; Klee 2006, 78–82; Grenzen 2006, 169–80.
152. Marek 2003, 59–62; Klee 2006, 89–121; Grenzen 2006, 51–61.
153. Speidel 2010, 138–46.
154. Klee 2006, 89–96; Grenzen 2006, 53–8.
155. Konrad 2001; Klee 2006, 101–11; Grenzen 2006, 58f.
156. Parker 1990; Kennedy 2000; Klee 2006, 111–21; Grenzen 2006, 59f.
157. Klee 2006, 123–30.
158. Mackensen 2006; Klee 2006, 130–47.
159. Boube-Piccot 1994; Klee 2006, 147.

(opposite): Remnants of Camp F, one of several legionary camps outside the circumvallation wall around Masada, Israel (photoshooter2015/Shutterstock.com)

THE DEVELOPMENT PERIODS OF ROMAN MILITARY HISTORY

V

1. Introduction

For more precise knowledge of the armament and equipment of the Roman army, we only have relatively secure archaeological sources (iconographic sources and actual finds) from the later Republic, or rather the 2nd century BC onwards. This is the time in which the confrontations with Carthage in the three Punic wars ended. It was only during this period that Roman armies started to remain outside of Italy for longer periods, for example, in the south of France and Spain, where they left behind relevant finds. With archaeological finds of weapons of earlier periods from Italy, there was never any certainty as to whether they really belonged to the Romans or to their Italian allies or adversaries. It is astonishing how few archaeological weapon finds are known to date from this period, which was filled with numerous internal and external conflicts. A considerable increase in the number of iconographic representations, and above all archaeological findplaces and finds, which can provide information about the Roman army, only began with the reign of Augustus (27 BC–AD 14). Throughout the Roman Imperial period, right up to the Late Roman period, this richness of finds persists, although there were considerable fluctuations in the conditions of preservation and survival of Roman militaria. The preservation of militaria depends on the one

hand on the state of research, and on the other directly on the intensity of the military conflicts that Rome had with both external and internal enemies.[1]

At the start of the Imperial period, the necessity of militarily securing stable frontier lines also arose. This was mainly achieved with auxiliary units, which installed and monitored the increasingly developed frontier protection systems (*limites* and *ripae*). It is precisely these sites that provide a wealth of relevant archaeological source material. The development of the frontiers is briefly outlined below, arranged by period. Finally, in chronological order, a selection of dated sites and find complexes particularly important for the research of militaria are summarized. These on the one hand, have produced a large number of important discoveries, while on the other sound dating of Roman weapons and military equipment is only possible with these contexts. However, it must be emphasized that only a selection – admittedly subjective – is presented here.

2. Republic

Military conflicts

At the moment, only a few sites from this period have left clear, unequivocal archaeological traces in the form of military buildings, weapons, and military equipment. The first demonstrable military ventures from which Roman weapons and military equipment are known to be associated include the 1st Punic War (264–241 BC), with combat in Sicily and Spain; the Second Punic War (218–201 BC), with action in Italy, Spain, Southern Gaul, and North Africa; and the 3rd Punic War (149–146 BC) with fighting in Spain and North Africa. In all of these wars, numerous naval battles also took place. Other important military conflicts from the Republic, such as the Jugurthine Wars in North Africa (111–105 BC), the slave revolts in Sicily (135–132, 104–100 BC), the slave revolt of Spartacus (73–71 BC), and the war against the Cimbri and Teutones (113–101 BC), as well as the Social War in Italy (91–89 BC) have not so far really been recognisable among archaeological finds.

The research situation has only consistently improved in Spain, increasingly identifying the locations of military engagements during the period of the Republic from the archaeological finds. One example is the siege of Numantia, where the Roman siege works are among the best studied from the time of the Roman Republic.[2] The camp at Cáceres el Viejo is also well known. Its destruction and burning are associated with the defeat of the Roman commander Q. Caecilius Metellus by Sertorius in 97 BC (Ulbert 1984).

The excavations around Alesia (Reddé and von Schnurbein 2001) are testimony to Caesar's Gallic War, while there is barely any archaeological evidence for the civil war between Caesar and his rivals in Italy, the Balkans, Asia Minor, Egypt, North Africa, and Spain. This also applies to the civil war following the assassination of Caesar in 44 BC between Octavian and Marc Antony against Caesar's murderers in Italy and the Balkans, Octavian's campaigns in Illyria (35–33 BC), and the civil war between Octavian and Marc Antony and Cleopatra.

Armament and equipment

Finds of Roman soldiers' weaponry from the time of the Republic are still very sparse compared to the huge amount of finds from the Imperial period. There are also few contemporary iconographic sources with realistic representations of weapons. Some literary records, such as those of Livy on the *gladius hispanicus* (Polybios, *Fragment* 179 (96)), or Plutarch on the *pilum* (Plutarch, *Marius* 25), contradict the archaeological evidence in some cases.

In general, however, it must be said that from the early Iron Age of central Italy (Stary 1981a) to the Roman armament of the late Republic, hardly any unbroken continuous development can be identified. On the contrary, there was an ongoing development of new products that had no local prototypes. Obviously, the Romans did not develop important parts of their weapons and equipment themselves, but rather took them over from their opponents, once they had recognized their weapons as superior in battle.

As stated above, finds of actual Roman weapons can only be detected in archaeological material once Roman troops were based outside Italy for longer periods – in Spain or Gaul during the Punic Wars, for example. It is noteworthy that most of the weapons and equipment of the period barely progressed from the Punic Wars to the Gallic War of Caesar, at least, if the subsequent relatively rapid and comprehensive change in the Imperial period is taken as a guide.

ICONOGRAPHIC SOURCES

Iconographic sources depicting the armament of Roman soldiers realistically are only available to a relatively small extent from the Republican era. Examples include the following: the Aemilius Paulus monument at Delphi, showing the Battle of Pydna of 168 BC against the Macedonian King Perseus; the reliefs from the so-called altar of Domitius Ahenobarbus in Rome (Fig. 473) from the 1st century BC;[3] and the tombstone of the centurion Minucius from Padua dating to before 42 BC, before the destruction of *legio Martia*.[4]

CLOTHING

Very little is known about the clothing of the Roman military until the late Republic, since iconographic sources are rare and there are no actual finds (Bishop and Coulston 2006). From the beginning, the Roman soldier wore a belted *tunica* under his armour and various types of cloak. Pictorial representations show soldiers barefoot or with shoes that barely merit the term.

BELT

The weapons belts of the Roman army were not fastened by buckles until the time of the late Republic, using instead belt hooks, like those of the Celts and Germans. The invention of the buckle with loop and tongue, developed by the Romans, can be traced back to the middle of the 1st century BC. As a technically superior solution, it subsequently replaced other belt fastenings relatively quickly. The first tongued buckles were found in Cáceres el Viejo,[5] and the last belt hooks were still in use as very old pieces in the Augustan camps in Raetia and on the Lippe.

BROOCHES

The earliest Roman military broochs are from Numantia and Cáceres el Viejo. Middle and late La Tène types with Italian and northern Italian types, as well as Iberian forms, occur among the brooches from Cáceres.[6]

found as archaeological finds in Roman contexts from the 1st century, it is unclear whether the depictions are a genuine representation of reality or the Hellenizing conventions of sculptors.

ARMOUR

The earliest Roman body armour survives in the form of depictions on the Aemilius Paullus Monument in Delphi, erected after the Battle of Pydna in 168 BC. It shows Roman infantrymen with large oval shields, *i.e.* legionaries, in mail cuirasses, under which a *tunica* can be seen. The soldiers wear a belt with an unrecognisable fastening. The shoulder doubling of the mail armour seen in the late Republican period in the depictions on the so-called altar of Domitius Ahenobarbus are not (yet?) identifiable here. The Romans were obviously wearing mail armour adopted from the Celts, who had invented it.

The earliest pictorial representation of (captured) Celtic mail armour can be found in Pergamon on reliefs from the temple of Athena. It was erected on the occasion of a victory by Attalos I (241–197 BC) over the Galateans. However, in iconographic sources, officers also wear Greek linen cuirasses – here the question of authenticity arises. The bronze muscled cuirass, which was common among high-ranking officers up to the Imperial period, was adopted by the Romans from the Greeks via the Etruscans. Older Italian traditions are represented in partial upper-body armour, so-called breast discs, known from Numantia. They may have belonged to Roman legionaries or to soldiers from their Italian allies.

SHIELDS

The oblong shields of the Republic, with their spindle-shaped shield bosses (*scuta*), were also adopted from the Celts. On the Aemilius Paullus Monument in Delphi, erected after the Battle of Pydna in 168 BC, the horizontal handle seen inside the shields – differing from the Greek-Macedonian tradition – was common among the Romans and Celts. From this time too there is a description of Roman infantry shields, the oblong, curved *scuta*, by Polybios. The depictions on the so-called altar of Domitius Ahenobarbus from the late Republic and coin representations on Roman *denarii* are also show the same *scuta*.

SWORDS

From the outset, the most important edged weapon of Roman legionary soldiers fighting in close order during the Republic was the classic double-edged Roman short sword, the *gladius*. According to the literary sources, this weapon was adopted from the enemy as the *gladius Hispanicus* during the 2nd Punic War (218–201 BC) in Spain, but archaeologically it does not now look so clear-cut as a result of detailed investigation by Christian

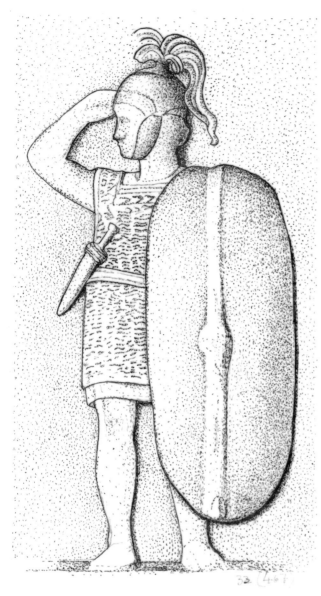

Figure 473 *Late Republican legionary from the Altar of Domitius Ahenobarbus (after Bishop and Coulston 2006). Drawing: A. Smadi, Arch. Institute University of Cologne*

HELMETS

The earliest helmets attributed to Roman soldiers are those of the Montefortino type with its variants, which occur from the 4th century BC. They are made of bronze and have a close typological connection with Etruscan and Celtic helmets. In addition to Montefortino-type helmets, there were Mannheim- and Buggenum-type helmets among late Republican forms of the 1st century BC. With officers' helmets, Hellenistic types occasionally appear on iconographic sources. They show Boeotian, pseudo-Attic, or pseudo-Corinthian helmets, for example, like those on depictions on the reliefs on the so-called altar of Domitius Ahenobarbus. Since these helmet types have not yet been

Miks. While the curved blade of the Augustan Mainz-type *gladius* resembles Spanish short swords of the Iron Age, there remains a large temporal gap in the original material that cannot be bridged.

DAGGERS

As a secondary edged weapon, the legionary carried the dagger (*pugio*) from the time of Caesar onwards. The Romans had become acquainted with this weapon in the 2nd century BC during fighting with the Celtiberians in Spain. Whether the Romans adopted the dagger as a regular sidearm from the beginning is unclear. It is only certain from the middle of the first century. The daggers (*pugiones*) were a new, until then typically Iberian, component of Roman armament, which was unknown to Greek or Hellenistic armies, but also to the Celts and Germans.

PILA

Together with the *gladius*, the *pilum* is considered a Roman 'national weapon'. The earliest documented Roman *pila* are the examples from a pit near the sanctuary of Telamon, destroyed by the troops of Sulla in 82 BC. There were numerous *pilum* irons, which had probably originally been deposited as offerings at the temple. When they had to make room for further offerings, as sacred offerings they could not be disposed of, but had to be buried in a pit (*bothros, favissa*). According to a plausible theory of M. Luik (2000), these may date back to the Battle of Telamon in 225 BC, when the Romans successfully repelled a Celtic invasion. Livy explicitly mentions the decisive role of *pila* in this battle. An obscure passage in Plutarch about technical improvement on *pila* within the framework of the army reform of Marius can perhaps be verified by the finds (Grab 2012). Among actual finds, tanged and socketed *pila* with barbed and pyramidal heads can be distinguished, with markedly larger and smaller pieces.

Armament and equipment of auxiliary units

In the case of infantry and cavalry, such as in Spain or Gaul, there was still no separate equipment influenced by Roman armament. Local armament and equipment are clearly dominant here, indistinguishable from that of Celtiberian, Celtic, or Germanic opponents.

Securely dated weapons and equipment finds (selection)

The important findplace of Ephyra in the north-west of Greece is one of the earliest secure depositions of Roman weapons. Unfortunately, it has not yet been sufficiently published.[7] It apparently was a tower farmstead destroyed in a fight, which probably burned down in 167 BC in connection with the Battle of Pydna, the decisive victory of Aemilius Paullus over the Macedonian king, Perseus. *Pilum* irons (from the Roman attackers) and components from torsion artillery (probably from the Macedonian defenders) were found here. From Spain there are weapons from the 2nd century BC from the Roman siege works around the northern Spanish city of Numantia. Likewise in Spain there is the short-term camp at Cáceres el Viejo, destroyed in 79 BC, among whose finds there are many military items (Ulbert 1984). Roman, Celtic, and probably Germanic weapons were found in the siege works at Alesia, besieged in Caesar in 52 BC (Fig. 474). Other Caesarian camps are to some extent known there and elsewhere, but have not yet been sufficiently investigated (Reddé and von Schnurbein 2001).

Figure 474 *Reconstruction drawing of a late Republican legionary. Drawing: B. Burandt*

3. The early Imperial period from Augustus to Nero

Military conflicts

Augustus (27 BC–AD 14), who defeated Marc Antony and Cleopatra in the naval battle at Actium in 31 BC, founded the period of the Principate with his sole rule. After the civil wars, he reduced the size of the Roman army, reformed it, and stationed it on the frontiers of the empire. The reign of Augustus is characterized above all by military expansion in the north. After the end of the Cantabrian War in northern Spain in 19 BC, troops were now available who could campaign between the Rhine and the Elbe from their strong bases on the Rhine in Germany. The Alpine campaign of 15 BC opened the Alps and the upper Danubian region. The expansion between the Rhine and the Elbe ended in the year AD 9 with the battle in the Teutoburg Forest.

Augustus' successor, Tiberius (AD 14–37), officially decreed the end of the German offensive after the end of the revenge campaigns of Germanicus in AD 16 and ordered the withdrawal of the frontier to the Rhine line. Thereafter, the frontier defences were reinforced on the banks of the rivers Rhine and Danube. In North Africa, the rebellion of Tacfarinas tied up Roman troops between AD 17 and 24.

Under Claudius (AD 41–54) the conquest of Britain began in AD 43 with the occupation of southern England. After the foundation of the province of Noricum, the Danube frontier, including the legionary base at Carnuntum, was also established in Pannonia. In AD 61, during the reign of Nero (AD 54–68), the Romans conquered the island of Mona (now Anglesey) in Britain, the last retreat of the Celtic druids; in the same year the uprising led by the Iceni queen Boudicca led to severe Roman losses. In AD 66, the first Jewish Revolt took place, which could not be ended until AD 70 with the conquest of Jerusalem by Titus under the rule of Vespasian. In AD 68, the revolt of Gallia Lugdunensis' governor, Iulius Vindex, broke out against Nero in Gaul, but he was unsuccessful. However, the uprising of Sulpicius Galba, the governor of Hispania Citerior, against Nero was successful. The emperor was ostracized by the Senate and forced to commit suicide on June 9, AD 68. Now, after Nero's death, a series of civil wars and uprisings culminated in the 'Year of the Four Emperors' in AD 69. The legate of Lower Germany, Aulus Vitellius, and the Rhine armies rebelled against Galba. On January 5 AD 69, Galba was assassinated in Rome and M. Salvius Otho proclaimed himself emperor. Otho was defeated by Vitellius in the First Battle of Cremona on April 1 AD 69, and then committed suicide. On July 1 AD 69, the army in the East proclaimed Vespasian as emperor; he defeated Vitellius in the Second Battle of Cremona, with the support of the Danubian armies.

Securing the frontiers of the empire

After the Roman defeat in the Teutoburg Forest in AD 9, there was the withdrawal to the Rhine line, and from AD 16 the reinforcement of the Rhine line as a frontier was made, renouncing the conquest of Germany between the Rhine and the Elbe by Tiberius. The conquest of Britain under Emperor Claudius in AD 43 resulted in the occupation of the south-eastern lowlands (lowland Britain). This was secured with a large number of vexillation fortresses and fortifications. Under Claudius, the development of militarily secured river frontiers on the Rhine and Upper Danube and the occupation of the approaches to Mainz in the Wetterau also took place. On the Middle Danube, the local reinforcement of the frontier occurred with the foundation of *Carnuntum*.

Armament and equipment

There are extensive iconographic sources for the study of Roman armament and military equipment from the early Imperial period onwards. Actual finds have also increased considerably thanks to material from various types of camps, rivers and battlefields, especially in Germany, the Netherlands, and Britain, and in the Danubian Balkan region. This is due in part to the fact that in this era more weapons and military equipment were being deposited in the ground or the water, but also to the high degree of access to archaeological sites and good research in some regions. This is in contrast to the paucity of information on the Eastern provinces, Egypt, and North Africa, where there should actually be a large number of early Imperial bases, and thus also weapons.

The civil war, with Caesar's assassins at first, and then between Octavian and Marc Antony, led to huge losses in men and matériel in the greatly enlarged Roman army of the late Republic. Through reforms, Augustus transformed the civil war armies into an imperial army and increasingly stationed them along the frontiers in permanent bases. In the course of these efforts, large parts of the Roman army had to be re-equipped to replace the *matériel* lost during the civil war. Therefore, it is possible to see many of the types of arms from the late Republic among the armament of this period, but also a whole series of new forms, some of them new inventions. The heavy losses of the Jewish War and the Civil War following Nero's death, which were replaced by troops equipped with the latest weapon types, also led to a marked change in armament and equipment among archaeological finds.

Figure 475 *The tombstone of M. Caelius from Xanten. Photo: private image sources*

Figure 476 *Military tombstone of the Helvetian cavalryman Licinius of the Ala Hispanorum from Mainz (after Lindenschmit 1858)*

ICONOGRAPHIC SOURCES

For the period between Augustus and the Flavians, soldiers' tombstones offer realistic representations which are particularly rich sources for contemporary armament (Tufi 1988). In addition to a concentration in the Rhineland (Figs 475–6), these gravestones are known from Britain, Northern Italy, and the Danubian Balkan region (see Wieland 2009). There are also depictions of armed soldiers or weapons on larger tombs and monumental arches in southern Gaul, for example (Roehmer 1997). The tomb of Munatius Plancus in Gaeta, which is dated to 20 BC (Fellmann 1957), is particularly noteworthy.

Legionary infantry

CLOTHING

Above all, military garments are now well documented by the iconographic sources. There are various cloaks (*paenula, sagum, paludamentum*) for the belted, sleeveless tunic. Hobnailed boots (*caligae*) are also well documented by the sources and actual finds.

BELT

From the Augustan period to the end of the 1st century, the *gladius* and the dagger were usually worn on the *cingulum*, the metal-plated weapons belt. Occasionally, the sword is carried on the narrow *balteus* (without metal fittings). The metal fittings of the belt (copper alloy, occasionally silver) consist of the buckle, suspension attachments for the dagger and *gladius*, and decorative elements with incised relief, or (from Tiberian to Neronian times) niello decoration. Only isolated Augustan *cingula* were closed with belt hooks in Republican tradition. As a new fashion, an apron was attached to the *cingulum*, which hung on the front of the belt in the form of several metal-studded leather straps.

BROOCHES

Among military brooches, Aucissa brooches in brass and iron predominate in addition to late La Tène forms and local types, such as Germanic brooches, for instance.

HELMETS

The mainly iron helmets of the Weisenau type, which were developed from Celtic helmet types encountered by the Romans during Caesar's Gallic war, were developed in the Augustan period. The helmets of the Hagenau type are a development from variants of copper-alloy Montefortino-type helmets. Both forms of helmet occur together in the Flavian period.

ARMOUR

In addition to the mail inherited from the late Republican period, the newly invented segmental armour arrived in the Augustan period, while scale armour borrowed from the East was only used by the Roman army in the post-Augustan period.

SHIELDS

The rectangular *scutum* appears for the first time on iconographic sources from the early Augustan period, but only begins to eclipse the oval *scutum* (with several intermediate forms) in the Flavian era.

SWORDS

Sword blades and sheaths underwent rapid development in the early Imperial period. It was only with the Mainz-type *gladius* first appearing in the Augustan period, that swords developed from Spanish models (*gladius Hispaniensis*) can be archaeologically attested, even though the literary sources already testify to this process for the 2nd century BC.

DAGGERS

Daggers, which clearly show their Spanish origin, belong to the regular armament of legionaries. As well as specimens with simple frame scabbards, there were also now weapons with iron sheaths exhibiting elaborate inlaid decoration and enamelling.

PILA

For *pila*, long specimens with pyramidal heads predominated. They occur both as tanged and socketed *pila*.

Auxiliary infantry

In the early Imperial period, auxiliary infantry quickly adopted Roman clothing, armament, and equipment following the example of legionary troops. It is still controversially discussed whether segmental armour found in auxiliary forts can be seen as the equipment of auxiliary units, or whether they should be attributed to outposted legionary infantry. Only curved oval and rectangular *scuta* and *pila* were clearly reserved for legionary troops. Auxiliary infantry carried flatter, oval shields and spears. Eastern archers had reflex or composite bows made of wood, sinew, and bone, and arrows with trilobate heads.

Auxiliary cavalry

From the various cavalry units of Celtic, German, and Thracian troops, equipped in the native fashion, the uniformly armed Roman auxiliary cavalry emerged only in the post- Augustan period. In the course of this process of merging, elements of Gallic and Thracian horse gear and weaponry were incorporated to a considerable degree.

HELMETS

For cavalry helmets, which can be safely dated to the Augustan period, only specimens which were variants of the Weisenau type with face masks of the Kalkriesetype are known. From the late Tiberio-Claudian period onwards, Roman cavalry were uniformly equipped, as can be seen in the Weyler/Koblenz-Bubenheim-type helmet. These were decorated and technically very elaborate. They had imitation or real locks of hair on the bowl. The shape of the cheek pieces, which covered the ear with an embossed imitation, was characteristic of cavalry helmets, which did not, like infantry helmets, expose the ear. In addition, most of these copper-alloy helmets were decorated with repoussé work.

ARMOUR

Cavalry soldiers wore flexible mail and (after the Augustan period) scale armour. Some early Imperial period examples, which are probably of Thracian origin, have fine bronze scales mounted on a mail shirt.

SHIELDS

Oval cavalry shields resembled the shields of the infantry. Hexagonal shields, known from depictions on reliefs, and through finds of appropriately shaped edge bindings of bronze sheet, were exclusively used by the cavalry.

OFFENSIVE WEAPONS

From the start, cavalry soldiers used the long *spathae* as their sword, still a purely Celtic model at the beginning of the early Imperial period. The first Roman development of a kind of long version of the Pompeii-type *gladius* was only used as a cavalry weapon after the middle of the 1st century AD. In addition, cavalry soldiers also had spears and various types of javelins, but no daggers.

HORSE HARNESS

Metal finds from the harness and bridle of cavalry horses are common in forts and camps. Saddles were designed as padded saddles with high horns. The numerous bits, amulet pendants, buckles, and strap junctions found from horse harness cannot individually be distinguished from civilian equestrian accessories for riding and driving. Among early Augustan finds, components from halters can be identified, *e.g. phalerae* from Oberaden or amulet pendants from Dangstetten, which can be specifically assigned to cavalry from Thrace or Gaul. Soon, however, there was a widespread homogeneity, loosely based on Celtic horse harness, which can no longer be regarded as distinctly local.

Securely dated weapons and equipment finds (selection)

Sites with larger quantities of well-documented militaria occur from the time and in the region of the Augustan German offensive in particular. These were principally the military camps of Oberaden (Figs 477–8) and Haltern on the Lippe (Figs 479–81), which were only briefly occupied. In addition, there are the sites of Dangstetten[8] and Augsburg-Oberhausen.[9] The site of Kalkriese (Figs 482–3), which dates back to the late summer of AD 9, is particularly important and represents part of the Varus disaster.

The base at Oberaden, which was only used for a short time during 11–8 BC, had, despite its planned evacuation,

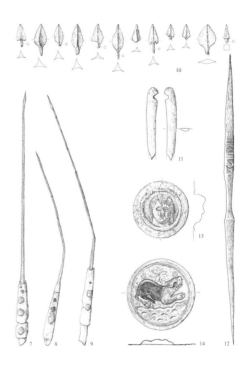

Figure 478 *Militaria from Oberaden: 7–9 Pila with remnants of the wooden shaft, 10 trilobate iron arrowheads, 11 bow stiffener of bone, 12 palisade stake, 13–14 phalerae (after Albrecht 1942, Kühlborn 1992). Drawing: A. Smadi, Arch. Institute University of Cologne*

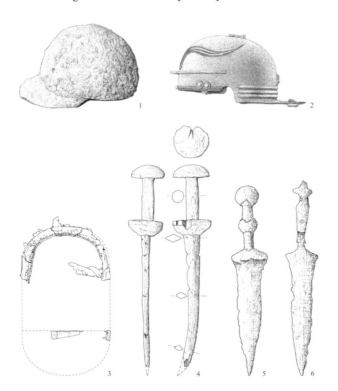

Figure 477 *Militaria from Oberaden: Hagenau-type iron helmet, Weisenau-type iron helmet, 3 leather shield cover, 4 wooden training weapon (sica?), 5–6 daggers with disc pommel and cruciform handles (after Albrecht 1938, Albrecht 1942, Kühlborn 1992, Müller 2006). Drawing: A. Smadi, Arch. Institute University of Cologne*

Figure 479 *Militaria from Haltern: 1 strap fastener made of copper alloy, 2–8 copper-alloy belt fittings, 9 Hagenau helmet made of copper alloy, 10 unfinished Weisenau-type helmet with copper sheathing, 11 copper-alloy cheek piece, 12–13 helmet crest-holder of iron, 14–15 iron shield bosses (after Harnecker 1997, Müller 2002). Drawing: A. Smadi, Arch. Institute University of Cologne*

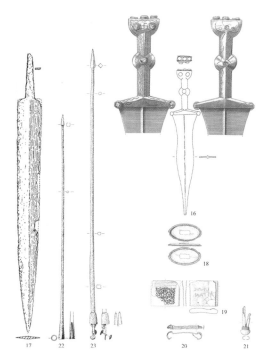

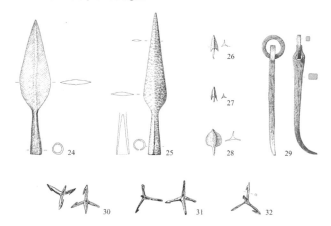

Figure 480 *Militaria from Haltern: 16 iron dagger, 17 iron gladius blade, 18 copper-alloy handguard from the handle of a gladius, 19–21 components from a gladius sheath of copper alloy (after Harnecker 1997, Müller 2002, Miks 2007). Drawing: A. Smadi, Arch. Institute University of Cologne*

Figure 481 *Militaria from Haltern: 24–5 iron spearheads, 26–8 trilobate iron arrowheads, 29 iron tent peg, 30–2 iron caltrops (after Harnecker 1997). Drawing: A. Smadi, Arch. Institute University of Cologne*

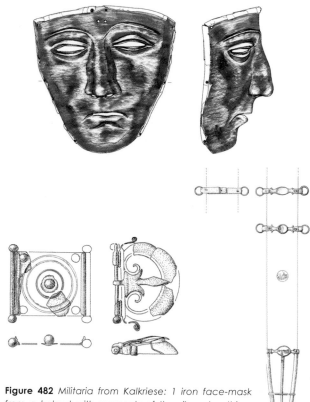

Figure 482 *Militaria from Kalkriese: 1 iron face-mask from a helmet with remnants of the silver sheathing, 2 silver sheath fittings from a gladius with gem stones, 3 silver fittings from the cingulum (after Franzius 1999, Harnecker-Franzius 2008). Drawing: A. Smadi, Arch. Institute University of Cologne*

Figure 483 *Reconstruction of a scene at Kalkriese, late summer of AD 9. Drawing: B. Burandt*

a few finds of weapons and military equipment which had belonged to legionary and auxiliary troops, including iron helmets of the Buggenum and Weisenau types, fragments of mail and scale armour, fittings and leather covers from shields, fragments of *gladii* and a wooden practice sword, daggers, and *pila*. Trilobate arrow heads and components of composite bows indicate oriental archery, and fittings from horse harness Thracian cavalry. Wooden palisade stakes were particularly common finds.[10]

The so-called main fortress at Haltern existed from the 1st decade BC until 9 AD.[11] It was a vexillation base with a mixed garrison of legionary troops from the 19th Legion as well as auxiliary infantry (including Eastern archers). Numerous finds indicate auxiliary cavalry. There are clear indications of metalworking workshops producing weapons and military equipment. The finds include remains of Hagenau- and Weisenau-type helmets, as well as the mask of an iron face-mask helmet of the Kalkriese type, fragments of segmental and mail armour, fittings from *scuta* and oval shields, parts of *gladii*, daggers, *pila*, catapult bolts, and spearheads. Trilobate arrowheads indicate oriental archery. Tent pegs and pioneer equipment were also found in Haltern.

The latest occupation phase of the material horizon in Haltern is reflected in the Roman finds from the battlefield at Kalkriese, which almost certainly represents the remains of the Varus disaster from the autumn of AD 9.[12] The remains of Hagenau and Weisenau type helmets, as well as the mask from an iron face-mask helmet, fragments of segmental and mail armour, fittings from *scuta* and oval shields, parts of *gladii*, daggers, *pila*, catapult bolts, lead slingshot and spearheads. Trilobate-headed arrowheads indicate oriental archery. In Kalkriese, too, tent pegs and pioneer tools were found.

In the Claudian period, it is the early camps of Richborough and Hod Hill in Britain,[13] which provided closely dated material from the time of the invasion. For the Neronian period, there is evidence available in the destruction layers of the Boudiccan uprising in AD 61: *e.g.* the Colchester-Sheepen site (Niblett 1985) or Longthorpe (Frere and St Joseph 1974).

In the Rhineland and on the upper Danube the destruction horizon from the turmoil after Nero's death in the years AD 68/69 is important: large amounts of militaria from the Neronian to early Flavian period were found in military camps, which were deposited during the civil wars after Nero's death or in the so-called Batavian uprising. These include finds from the double-legionary fortress of Vetera I (Hanel 1995), the pre-colonial settlement of Xanten (Lenz 2006), the timber fort of Hofheim am Taunus (Ritterling 1912), Rheingönheim fort (Ulbert 1969), and forts like Aislingen or Burghöfe (ibid. 1959; Franke 2009) on the upper Danube. Since the majority of these are older excavations, the problem often arises that the content of the actual burnt and destruction layers has not been separated from older and later layers.

4. The middle Imperial period from Vespasian to Trajan

Military conflicts

At the beginning of his reign, Vespasian had to cope with the already mentioned Batavian uprising led by the Batavian C. Iulius Civilis in Gaul and Germany during the years AD 69/70. The suppression of this revolt in AD 70 occurred after decisive battles at Trier and Vetera. Afterwards, the Rhine army was reformed, their units having partly gone over to the enemy. In September AD 70, Jerusalem was conquered by Titus, and in AD 73 the conquest of Masada brought an end to the First Jewish Revolt. In Britain, the Romans tried to occupy Cornwall, Wales, and north England with varying degrees of success.

Under Domitian (AD 81–96), there were several wars in Germany: between AD 83 and 85, Rome fought the first war against the Chatti, which ended with territorial gains in the Taunus and the Wetterau. In AD 89, the rebellion of Saturninus, the governor at Mainz, failed. He was defeated by frontier troops from Lower Germany and Raetia. In Britain, Wales and northern England were brought firmly into Roman hands; a victory over the Caledones by Iulius Agricola at the battle of Mons Graupius in AD 84 also brought the Scottish lowlands under the rule of Rome for a short time. However, Domitian ordered a retreat to the Tyne–Solway line (the Stanegate line), since Roman troops were more urgently needed at a new centre of conflict, namely the middle Danube region, fighting against the Dacians under their king Decebalus in AD 85/86. This military confrontation began with several defeats for Rome and the death of the Moesian governor Oppius Sabinus. In AD 87, Praetorian prefect Cornelius Fuscus was killed during an unsuccessful counteroffensive. In AD 89, there were battles with the Marcomanni and Quadi and a compromise peace with the Dacians. The year AD 92 brought an incursion by the Marcomanni, Quadi, and Jazyges into Pannonia and the defeat of *legio XXI Rapax*.

After careful preparations, Emperor Trajan began his First Dacian War against Decebalus in the years AD 101–2. After a series of battles and a peace settlement, the Second Dacian War led to the complete destruction of the enemy and also the suicide of the Dacian king, Decebalus, in the years AD 105/6. The events of these wars are depicted on Trajan's Column in Rome.

In AD 106, Rome intervened in the internal struggles within the Nabataean empire. As a result, this client kingdom was taken over as the Roman province of Arabia. Contest for the throne in Armenia led to Trajan's Parthian campaign of AD 113. It led to the occupation of Armenia and Mesopotamia and to an unsuccessful siege of the desert town of Hatra. The newly conquered provinces of Mesopotamia and Assyria could only be briefly held: revolts by the Jews and a counteroffensive by the Parthians forced the retreat of Rome in AD 117. After Trajan died at Selinus in August AD 117, his successor, Hadrian, organized a withdrawal from the territories in the East occupied for only a short time and the restoration of the status quo.

Securing the frontiers of the empire

Under the Flavians, the extensive conquest of Wales and northern England in Britain up to the Stanegate line was successful. During the campaigns under Agricola, territories conquered in the Scottish lowlands were abandoned again in AD 85.

Under Vespasian (AD 69–79), there was the occupation of further regions to the east of the Rhine: in the Wetterau, the area around the mouth of the Neckar, and the upper Rhine. This was ensured by the provision of forts. The occupation of the Black Forest region as far as the upper Neckar led to the expansion of the military base at Rottweil. A first establishment of the *limes* in the sense of a linear, frontier line, marked out in the Taunus and the Wetterau, took place under Domitian (AD 81–96) within the framework of the war against the Chatti; in south-western Germany, the Odenwald limes and the Neckar line were established. The forts on the upper Danube were in part moved forward to secure the most important passes over the Swabian Alb (the 'Alp limes'). In Raetia, the first forts north of the Danube were built at Nassenfels and Kösching, and the gap was also closed in the occupied line on the upper Danube between Oberstimm and Linz.

Under Trajan (AD 98–117), an intensive expansion of the Upper German limes took place: the Taunus and Wetterau limes were extended through the Main line, then the Odenwald limes from Wörth am Main to Bad Wimpfen on the Neckar. Along the Neckar, the river boundary of the Neckar limes now stretched to the south, secured by larger auxiliary forts from Bad Wimpfen to Köngen. The gap between Köngen and the Alp limes was first closed by the so-called Lautertal limes. A road between Köngen and Heidenheim connected it with the Raetian *limes* to the east. The frontier line from Eining on the Danube to the Nördlinger Ries was built in the early days of Trajan. In addition, the link with the Alp limes and the strongest garrison in the province, the cavalry fort at Heidenheim an der Brenz (*Aquileia*), was established. Between Eining and Ruffenhofen, the line of the *limes* was established which was essentially retained in later stages of development. The building up of the Danube frontier was carried out under the Flavians in Noricum and Pannonia, as well as in Moesia, and continued under Trajan. However, after the end of the Dacian war, many of the units were sent forward from the Moesian territories to the *limes* of the newly conquered province of Dacia. With the conquest of the province of Arabia and the construction of *Via Nova Traiana*, the establishment of the *limes Arabicus* began.

Armament and equipment

This period is characterized by armament which clearly stands out in some particulars from the previous early Imperial period. It is often regarded as the highwater mark of the Roman imperial era, when the armament and equipment of the Roman army were at their most uniform. However, this is less evident after closer examination of the finds: the idea of uniformity is obviously mainly inspired by a fascination with the depictions on Trajan's Column (Coulston 1989). This period is also characterized by a whole series of other seemingly realistic iconographic sources, which have decisively shaped the picture of the Roman army for posterity. In the case of actual finds of militaria, a clear difference to those of the period of the Julian-Claudian dynasty is evident. This difference is the result of the equipment of newly equipped troops, which had to be raised at the beginning of the Flavian period. They came as a substitute for the losses suffered by the Roman army during the civil war after Nero's death, the Boudiccan insurrection in Britain, and the Jewish War. Niello decoration of weapons and military equipment, for example, diminished noticeably, and soon ended completely. The characteristic types of armament and equipment of the Flavian period lasted until the end of the reign of Trajan (AD 98–117). Apparently, the heavy losses of the Dacian Wars and the fruitless campaigns in Mesopotamia led to a massive need for new troops to replace the losses. The outfitting of these new troops with the latest, up-to-date armament can be clearly seen in the finds. This included new features which were only adopted from the enemy during the Dacian Wars or developed from the experiences of these wars.

ICONOGRAPHIC SOURCES

Soldiers' tombstones, especially in the Rhineland, emerge as the main iconographic source of the period. The column base reliefs from Mainz,[14] or the representations of Praetorians on the Cancelleria reliefs in Rome, provide important details. However, the Great Trajanic Frieze, the reliefs on Trajan's Column in Rome, and the metopes of the victory monument at Adamclisi in the Dobrudja (Florescu 1965) provide the best iconographic sources for weapons and military equipment for this period.

Legionary infantry

DRESS

Legionary clothing hardly changed from the previous period, if we discount the first proofs for the long-sleeved *tunica*. However, the harsh climate in the north led more and more soldiers to adopt trousers from the Celts and Germans. Nailed boots (*caligae*) were still in use, but were increasingly replaced by closed types of footwear.

BELT

The metal-plated belts of the early Imperial period were still worn, but the niello and relief decorations declined in favour of decorations with circular motifs or no decoration. The belt still served as both a sword belt and for suspension of the dagger.

BROOCHES

During this period, the Aucissa brooch was falling out of use as the classic soldier's brooch. It was replaced by various types of hinged and spiral brooches (Martell 2001).

HELMETS

Roman bronze helmets of the Hagenau type finally fell out of use towards the end of the 1st century, the Weisenau type helmet, made mainly of iron, taking over as the standard helmet of both legionary and auxiliary infantry. The change in form is only slight, compared to previous decades; the neck guard, for example, is located slightly lower down, and examples with appliqué decoration made from bronze sheet appear. A military adaptation from the Dacian Wars was now universally adopted from the Trajanic period onwards: the sickle swords of the Dacians, with which they attacked and penetrated helmets from above, were a dangerous weapon demanding an appropriate response, which was promptly provided by improvised iron crosspieces. This additional reinforcement of the helmet bowl was adopted by the time of Hadrian at the latest, and from then onwards was a regular feature of newly made helmets.

ARMOUR

Segmental armour appears on a large scale on an iconographic source for the first time on Trajan's Column, about 100 years after its invention and introduction to the Roman army. However – compared with actual finds like those from Corbridge – this was not in a technically correct form. It served to identify legionary soldiers there, while the auxiliary infantrymen always wore short mail shirts with a zig-zag hem. This sculptural convention has often led to the erroneous opinion that, at the beginning of the 2nd century AD, segmental armour was the standard armour of legionary troops. Comparing this with the similar representations on the victory monument at Adamclisi, the latter shows mail and scale cuirasses on unambiguous representations of legionaries (rectangular *scutum*!), but not a single segmental cuirass. Daggers are also completely absent from the depictions on Trajan's Column. This clearly shows how dangerous it is to accept these representations as completely realistic. In reality, the extent to which the individual types of cuirass were distributed to different bodies of troops is unknown.

The pieces from the hoard from the English fort at Corbridge belong to the Flavian period. These are larger connecting components of six different cuirasses of the same type, not complete sets, which were buried as scrap metal in a chest during the withdrawal of troops from the fort. Debate over whether this took place in the Trajanic or Hadrianic period is as yet inconclusive.

MANICA

The increasing use of an articulated armguard (*manica*) on the right (sword!) arm, made of iron or copper-alloy strips, is first documented for the Dacian Wars (Adamclisi). These protective weapons were adopted from gladiators, where, according to representational sources, they also existed.[15]

SCUTA

The curved, oval shield gradually changed from the middle of the 1st century to rectangular. This has usually been assigned to legionary soldiers (however, there were *cohortes scutatae*!). On representations on Trajan's Column, this type of shield predominates (usually with the characteristic lightning bolt decoration). Along with segmental armour, it distinguishes legionary soldiers on the column. On the basis of actual archaeological finds, the reality of this depiction on Trajan's Column cannot really be confirmed or refuted. However, legionaries are always represented with the rectangular *scutum* at Adamclisi, as well as on gravestones and on other reliefs. It seems that in this case, Trajan's Column seems to have come closer to reality in its representation of shields than was the case with body armour.

GLADII

The earlier form of the *gladius*, with a waisted blade and a long, pointed tip – the so-called Mainz type – was replaced after the middle of the 1st century AD by the Pompeii type, which had straight, parallel cutting edges and a short, clearly defined tip. The sword sheaths also had characteristic shapes and fittings.

DAGGERS

From the middle of the 1st century, the slimmer and more elegant Vindonissa variant of dagger became dominant. Its scabbard had a decorated front. From the Flavian period, decorated dagger sheaths slowly disappeared. However, they were still present in a Trajanic burnt layer in the fleet base of Köln-Alteburg. They had rich, inlaid decoration in brass and silver.

PILUM

Chronological developments are not detectable for the *pilum*. The thickening of the pin with an eagle representation on the Cancelleria reliefs belongs to this period, but it is unique and therefore cannot be interpreted as a chronological development.

Auxiliary infantry

The difference between legionary and auxiliary soldiers was now barely detectable in both defensive and offensive armament. Helmets were the same, as were cuirasses, swords, and daggers. The only difference is in the shields, where the flat oval type predominates on Trajan's Column, displaying a distinctly different decoration from the *scutum* of the legionaries. Although *pila* occur occasionally in auxiliary forts, spears still seem to have been more common with auxiliary infantry as shock and long-range weapons.

Auxiliary cavalry

In the Roman cavalry, further developments can be traced in the various types of arms, such as helmets and swords. Flavian-Trajanic horse harness also differs in detail from that of earlier periods.

HELMETS

Weyler/Koblenz-Bubenheim helmets, with their imitation hairstyles on the bowl, developed further. New discoveries from the time around AD 70 from Nijmegen (Netherlands) and from the Rhine near Xanten even indicate that there were smooth iron cavalry helmets to which wigs of real hair were attached. From the Flavian period onwards, brow diadems also beginning to appear. Similarly, locks of hair were now apparently raised directly from iron helmets. Repoussé representations of hair on copper-alloy sheet, which used to be characteristic of Weyler/Koblenz-Bubenheim helmets, now seem to have been declining. However, a more accurate typological and chronological division of Roman cavalry helmets is still a desideratum.

ARMOUR

Cavalry still had mail shirts with a cape-like shoulder doubling and fastening hooks as well as scale armour. Hybrid types of segmental and mail armour also now appeared.

SHIELDS

The oval cavalry shields resembled those of the infantry. Hexagonal shields, depicted on reliefs and documented through appropriately formed edge binding from bronze sheet, only protected the cavalry.

OFFENSIVE WEAPONS

In the case of *spathae*, Christian Miks can show fewer clear developmental tendencies than for the blades of *gladii*. In addition to the extended 'Pompeii' blades, there were other forms. There is not much securely dated material available for the second half of the 1st century. Particularly interesting is a supposed grave from Kastell Niederberg, at the west end of the Upper-German Limes, where a *spatha* was associated with a belt buckle with connected mount, both inlaid with enamel and dated to the early 2nd century AD. This clearly shows that the cavalry carried weapons belts, which did not have metal decorations, but just leather belts with metal buckles, as is also shown on representations on cavalry tombstones.

Securely dated finds of weapons and equipment (selection)

The finds from the Rhine at Xanten-Wardt were almost certainly associated with the Batavian battle of July AD 70 (Figs 484–5) and can thus be dated to the earliest days of Vespasian's rule. There are not many other unmixed, purely Flavian assemblages of finds containing large quantities of weapons and equipment. Short-term forts of this period were mostly evacuated in an organized fashion, leaving behind only a few, small pieces and fragmentary material. See for instance the examples of the early Flavian legionary base at Rottweil 'Fort I' (Franke 2003) or the late Flavian legionary fortresses of Inchtuthil in Scotland (Pitts and St. Joseph 1985) and Mirebeau in France (Goguey and Reddé 1995).

More material, especially of an organic nature, comes from finds from the Jewish War in Judaea. These, however, are not always distinguishable from those of the second Jewish uprising from the time of Hadrian, as at Herodium (Stiebel 2003). At Gamla/*Gamala*, for example, where archaeological discoveries and literary sources can be closely matched with regard to the events of the first Jewish uprising, suitable publication of the material, which by now has been adequately restored, is still a desideratum at the time of writing.[16] On the other hand, the closely-dated material from the fortification at Masada has now been published in an exemplary manner (Stiebel and Magness 2007). This was occupied by the insurgents a few years earlier, and was besieged and taken by the Romans in AD 73. From the cities around Vesuvius, otherwise dominated by the civilian material, buried in the disaster of AD 79, Salvatore Ortisi was able to present an astonishingly large collection of militaria.[17]

SARMIZEGETUSA (ROMANIA)

Under the forum of the colony, a massive burnt layer (burnt deposit 9) was found in the area of the *principia* of the former legionary camp, which contained numerous military items. The latest coins of Trajan, minted in the year AD 102, offer the possibility of connecting the fall of the legionary camp at Sarmizegetusa with the outbreak of the Second Dacian War and the defeat of the army of Pompey Longinus in AD 105.[18] The burnt layer contains cheek pieces, slingshot, and arrowheads, belt components, pioneer equipment, and horse harness (Figs 486–90).

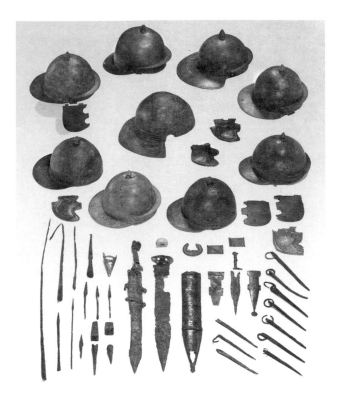

Figure 484 *Xanten-Wardt/Lüttingen, dredged finds from the Rhine from 2005. Legionary weapons (after Müller et al. 2008)*

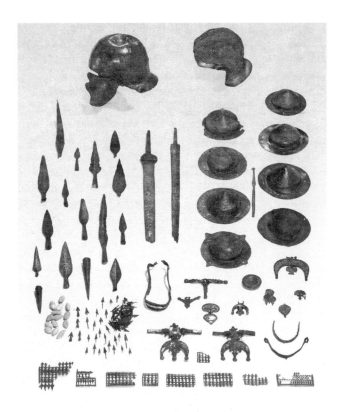

Figure 485 *Xanten-Wardt/Lüttingen, dredged finds of auxiliary weapons from the Rhine (after Müller et al. 2008)*

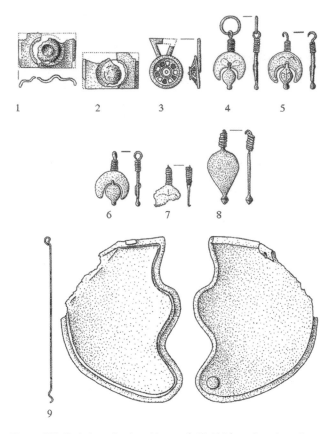

Figure 486 *Finds from the burnt layer of AD 105 from Sarmizegetusa: 1–8 copper-alloy belt fittings, 9 copper-alloy cheek piece (after Éttienne et al. 2004). Drawings: A. Smadi, Arch. Institute University of Cologne*

KÖLN-ALTEBURG (GERMANY)

In the fleet camp at Köln-Alteburg, excavations from the year 1998 revealed two clearly distinct Trajanic burnt deposits in construction phases 5 and 6, which contained numerous militaria: fragments of an iron shield boss, the burned fragment of a bone sword scabbard runner, which is the earliest dated specimen of this type of find, iron spearheads, copper-alloy pendants with silver inlay (embossed sheet metal with a Medusa), a dagger blade and two inlaid dagger scabbards (Fischer 2005).

5. The middle Imperial period from Hadrian to Septimius Severus

Military conflicts

After the death of Trajan, Hadrian (AD 117–38), corrected Trajan's hollow victories against the Parthian empire in the East, and withdrew the surviving remnants of the Roman occupying forces to the initial positions of the Trajanic offensive. The province of Armenia returned to the state of a client kingdom. From then on, Roman expansion

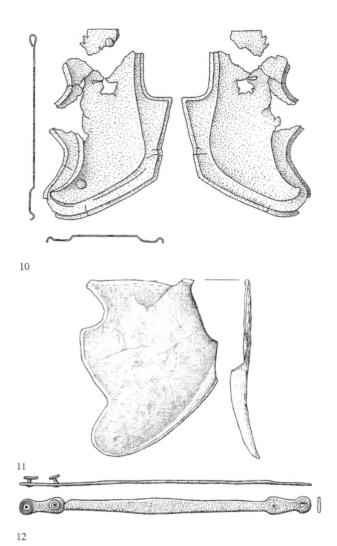

10

11

12

Figure 487 *Finds from the Sarmizegetusa burnt layer: 10 copper-alloy cheek piece that has been shot, 11 iron cheek piece, 12 copper-alloy shield fitting (after Éttienne et al. 2004). Drawings: A. Smadi, Arch. Institute University of Cologne*

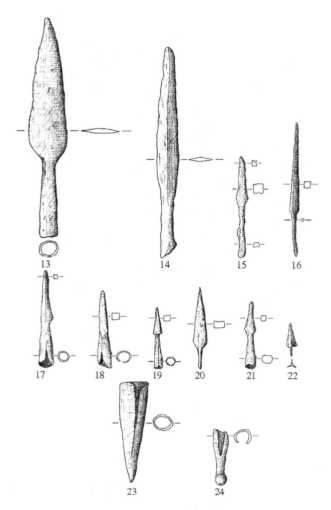

13   14   15   16

17   18   19   20   21   22

23   24

Figure 488 *Finds from the burnt layer from the year AD 105 from Sarmizegetusa: 13–22 iron spearheads, slingshot, and arrowheads, 23–4 iron spear butts (after Étienne et al. 2004). Drawings: A. Smadi, Arch. Institute University of Cologne*

had finally passed its zenith. Apart from minor frontier changes, Roman foreign and military policy was now determined by the preservation of the territorial status quo. At the beginning of the reign of Hadrian, there were several serious battles against the Roxolani and Sarmatians on the lower Danube and Pannonia and major conflicts on the northern frontier in Britain in the years AD 122/3. As a reaction, Hadrian's Wall was built. In AD 134, the Alans invaded Cappadocia; they were repulsed by the governor Flavius Arrianus; his report on this event is preserved. In the years AD 132–5, the Second Jewish Revolt under Bar Kochba brought heavy losses for the Roman army.

The long reign of Hadrian's successor, Antoninus Pius (AD 138–61), on the other hand, was markedly peaceful. The few conflicts and crises in North Africa, the Middle Danube, and Armenia were mainly solved with diplomacy. The short-term advance of the northern frontier of Britain

to the shorter line of the Antonine Wall may have been due to conflicts with the tribe of the Brigantes. The advance of the Upper German-Raetian limes, on the other hand, seems to have been completed without violent clashes.

During the reign of Marcus Aurelius (AD 161–80) and Lucius Verus (AD 161–9), the empire was shaken by costly wars: in AD 162, the Parthians invaded Armenia, Cappadocia, and Syria. After a counter-offensive from AD 163 onwards under Lucius Verus, an infectious disease – historically identified as plague – was transferred in AD 165 to the Roman army. The army was forced to retreat, spreading the plague to Asia Minor and further into the empire, which led to the end of the campaign. In the years AD 166–80, the First Marcomannic War raged on the Danube and in Italy. Rome was now forced into a war on two fronts, in the East and the Danube. One of the drastic counter-measures was the raising of two new legions (the 2nd and 3rd Italic legions) in Italy, the plague now reaching the Danube army.

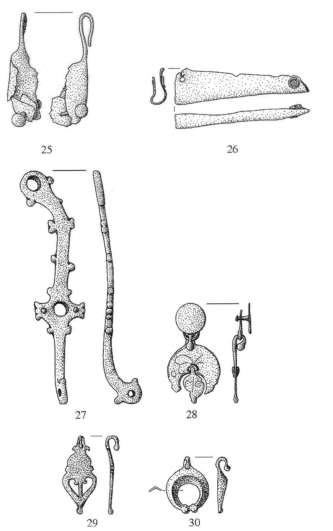

Figure 489 *Finds from the burnt layer from the year AD 105 from Sarmizegetusa: 25–6 copper-alloy* dolabra *sheath fittings, 27 part of a copper-alloy bridle, 28–30 copper-alloy horse harness pendants (after Éttienne et al. 2004). Drawings: A. Smadi, Arch. Institute University of Cologne*

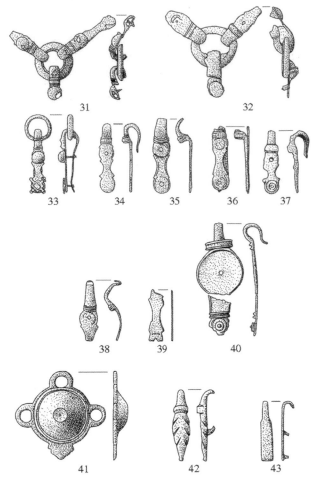

Figure 490 *Finds from the burnt layer from the year AD 105 from Sarmizegetusa: 31–43 Fittings from horse harness made of copper alloy (after Éttienne et al. 2004). Drawings: A. Smadi, Arch. Institute University of Cologne*

In AD 167, the Marcomanni and Quadi broke into northern Italy, Oderzo/*Opitergum* was destroyed, and *Aquileia* besieged. At the same time, there were also conflicts with the Chatti in Upper Germany, and with Germans and Jazyges on the Lower Danube. The Dacian Costoboci crossed the Danube and plundered Greece, including Eleusis, while Moors from Africa invaded southern Spain. In AD 175, a first peace settlement on the Danube ended the disputes, but it did not last long, because in AD 177, the Second Marcomannic War started. It was ended by Marcus Aurelius' son and successor Commodus with a compromise peace in AD 180, the year of the death of Marcus Aurelius.

Commodus' reign (AD 180–92) is marked by internal disturbances ('*bellum desertorum*') in Gaul and Upper Germany and wars in Britain, Dacia, and Spain; these could be dealt with by local forces. Septimius Severus (AD 193–211) and his sons and co-rulers Geta (AD 209–12) and Caracalla (AD 198–211) faced more serious internal and external military situations. The civil war against rival claimants to the throne, Pescennius Niger (AD 193–4) in the East and Clodius Albinus (AD 195–7) in Britain and Gaul, caused serious losses for the Roman army. In particular, the victory of Septimius Severus over Clodius Albinus at the Battle of Lyons on the 19th of February in AD 197 decimated the Roman army. In the same year, there was an attack by the Parthians on the eastern frontier, which led to an immediate counterattack by Rome. In January AD 198, the Parthian royal city of Ctesiphon was conquered, but as during Trajan's campaign, the siege of the desert town of Hatra failed. Invasions and uprisings in Britain led to a Roman offensive in Scotland in AD 208. The Caledonian tribes submitted. Septimius Severus died in York on April 4, AD 211.

Securing the frontiers of the empire

In AD 122, Hadrian visited Britain and ordered the construction of Hadrian's Wall north of the Stanegate line. Soon after its establishment, it was abandoned under Antoninus Pius (AD 138–61). Instead, Antoninus had the Antonine Wall built at the narrowest point of the island, on the Forth–Clyde Isthmus. In AD 155 it was given up, then apparently reoccupied, until it was finally abandoned in AD 163 and the troops retreated to Hadrian's Wall. In Dacia, Hadrian had redefined the frontier line after the loss of territories in the east of the province. Under Antoninus Pius, the Odenwald and Neckar limes in Upper Germany were given up and the frontier advanced to the outer line of the *limes*, which now passed straight from the Main to the Raetian border. In Raetia, this forced the construction of new forts between Lorch and Ruffenhofen, in order to connect the new course of the Upper German limes.

Armament and equipment

The period from the time of Hadrian's reign to the Severan period, is characterized by developments and changes in weapons and equipment, which in part were quite substantial; Bishop and Coulston even speak of the 'Antonine Revolution'.[19] These striking changes were associated with two very costly periods of warfare: the Dacian Wars and the campaigns in Mesopotamia under Trajan, and the Marcomannic Wars under Marcus Aurelius. The Dacian and Marcomannic Wars were centred on the middle Danube region, and the opponents involved in both wars had equipment that was influenced by the Pontic and Central Asian region; indeed influences in the armament can be traced back as far as China! These influences, in turn, also affected Roman armament, with Sarmatian iron scale armour as well as the Eastern ring-pommel swords and scabbard slides being found.

ICONOGRAPHIC SOURCES

There are fewer iconographic sources for this period. There is for instance a dearth of reliefs of armed men on soldiers' tombstones in the 2nd century AD, which only reappear at the end of the century. Hadrianic depictions of soldiers can be found on the Chatworth reliefs (see note 12). Dating to the time of Antoninus Pius (AD 138–61), we have the Croy Hill relief from Scotland (Coulston 1988b), on which three fully equipped legionaries can be seen. Under Commodus (AD 180–92), construction of the Marcus Column was begun in Rome, which was completed under Septimius Severus (AD 193–211). Following the model of Trajan's Column, here too, a spiral-shaped relief frieze shows scenes from the campaigns of Marcus Aurelius in the region of the middle Danube.

Legionary infantry

BELTS

With the advent of the *spatha* at the latest, the *cingulum*, the metal-plated military belt, had finally lost its function as a sword belt, and became a belt used just to gather the *tunica* or to suspend money-bags, knives, or other things. Only in the case of daggers did they still serve for weapon suspension. From the time of Hadrian's reign, the older square *cingulum* fittings with circular decoration are no longer found. Other types are common now, including previously unknown oblong fittings, sometimes with millefiori ornament. From the second half of the 2nd century AD onwards, metal belt fittings were decorated with new types of decorative motifs, mostly in openwork (Neuburg-Zauschwitz type, VTERE FELIX belt, other letter-belts, and belts of the Regensburg-Großprüfening type). Among these are also those with 'Celticising' trumpet patterns (Klosterneuburg type). From the middle of the 2nd century AD, the changing conditions of the archaeological tradition help to better assess the development of belts: under Germanic influence complete sets of military belts appear in burials, especially in the Danube region.

BROOCHES

In the military, knee brooches dominate the other types of cloak brooches during the 2nd century AD. Towards the end of the 2nd century, the brooch with a long hinge arm appears (Martell 2001). Individual examples of silver plate brooches with representations of, for example, weapons are found with remarkable frequency in military contexts.

HELMETS

For legionary helmets, the cross-pieces were now generally used as an additional reinforcement for Weisenau-type helmet bowls. The development of Weisenau-type helmets continued until, under Marcus Aurelius, a developmental leap was made towards helmets of the Niederbieber type. These now offered considerably improved protection, but they were heavier and more uncomfortable to wear.

ARMOUR

The body armour of legionaries also changed during the 2nd century AD. The segmental cuirass was simplified (changing from Corbridge to the Newstead type). In the late 2nd century, legionary soldiers also seem to have increasingly relied on mail shirts for body armour. There were two types: one was cut like a modern t-shirt, so it could easily be removed over the head. Another type had decorative fastenings, which was also worn by legionary soldiers, as is proven by an inscribed example from the time of the Marcomannic Wars found in Mušov that had an inscription of the 10th Legion, which was based in Vienna.

In finds from the Danubian region, large iron scales from scale armour are found, which are unknown in Raetia, the German provinces, or Britain; Sarmatian influences are probably visible in these.

SHIELDS

As before, legionary troops of the 2nd century carried the rectangular *scutum*, as shown on the Croy Hill relief or depictions on the column of Marcus Aurelius. We now also know of shield bosses with decorated rectangular base plates. In the second half of the 2nd century, there was a change: on the column of Marcus Aurelius, rectangular *scuta* were mixed with oval shields and other shield forms in a strange mix for legionaries. One might think of a discord between reality and artistic convention, were it not that the tombstones of legionary soldiers from Apamea in Syria, dated slightly later to around AD 200, only show oval shields, while unambiguously depicting legionaries. This suggests that a smooth change had taken place, in which least some of the legionary troops had adopted the oval shield of the auxiliaries during the Antonine-Severan period and abandoned the rectangular *scutum*.

GLADIUS

The development of the *gladius* in the 2nd century is less clear, because of the dearth of finds, as the differences between *gladius* and *spatha* scabbards mounts have disappeared and dated contexts have become less frequent. In addition, the *gladius* was increasingly replaced by the long sword (*spatha*) in the later 2nd century AD, which had previously only been used by the cavalry. The exact time for this is unknown, but we do know that the *gladius* is still present in deposits from the Marcomannic Wars. However, finds and literary sources show the continued use of a short sword, called *semispatha* by Vegetius, into the 3rd century. Perhaps it was replaced as a melee weapon by daggers, which had become considerably larger.

SPATHA

The *spatha* was now fixed to a scabbard runner of metal or bone, with which the weapon was attached to the *balteus*. The earliest proof for these scabbard runners can be found on Trajan's Column, although not in the Roman armoury, but among captured Dacian weapons on the pedestal of the monument. The *balteus*, from which the sword hung, was now much broader and often had finely decorated metal fittings. As to chapes, in the first half of the 2nd century, box chapes were still in use, followed by peltate specimens which are used far into the 3rd century.

RING-POMMEL SWORDS

From the early 2nd century AD up into the middle of the 3rd century, the so-called 'ring-pommel sword' was in use. The studies of Christian Miks have shown that the ring-pommel sword never existed as a separate sword type. Rather, ring pommels, which were of eastern Sarmatian origin, were being retrofitted to standard weapons – both *gladii* and *spathae* – during or soon after the Dacian Wars of the early 2nd century. We do not know why. It may not have been practical technological reasons that led to this strange custom, but rather it might have indicated that the owners of these weapons had successfully participated in the heavy fighting in the Danube region.

DAGGERS

In the late 2nd century, and up until the middle of the 3rd century, a much larger form of dagger appeared, which could almost be seen as a substitute for the absent *gladius*. The exact time span of this change is not yet clear. The handles of late daggers consisted of organic material or sheet iron plating with central expansions. While the dagger was worn on the left in the early Imperial period, often on its own *cingulum*, it changed to the right side of the body with the advent of the *spatha*, which was worn on the left, and was fastened to the belt with straps and studs. There are also no depictions of daggers on the Marcus Column.

PILA

Other legionary offensive weapons include various types of spear. The number of representations and original finds of *pila* declines markedly in the 2nd century. However, this classic weapon did not completely fall out of use; it is still present on the relief from Croy Hill, for instance. The reason for this is probably to be seen in the fact that the *pilum* was especially useful against an attack of closely ranked infantry, but had little effect on cavalry, which were now the main enemy. However, there are isolated finds of *pila* from the 3rd century.

Auxiliary infantry

With the adoption of the oval shield by legionary troops, it is no longer possible to distinguish between legionary and auxiliary infantry armament and military equipment in the archaeological record: helmets, armour, shields, swords, daggers, and spears were identical.

Auxiliary cavalry

There was some development in the equipment of the cavalry in some areas, especially among helmets and swords. Mail and scale armour with decorated fastening plates also seem to have been adopted by the cavalry.

HELMETS

The development of cavalry battle helmets is difficult to trace in the 2nd century AD. At some point towards the end of that century, the successors of the cavalry helmets of the Weyler/Koblenz-Bubenheim type, such as the Butzbach variant, were replaced by the pseudo-Attic helmets in embossed bronze sheet.

ARMOUR

Scale and mail cuirasses with decorated fastening plates will also have been worn by the cavalry in operations. These cuirasses have long been inaccurately attributed to parade armour.

OFFENSIVE WEAPONS

The cavalry *spatha* also now had the same scabbard fittings as the infantry and was worn on the *balteus*. Distinctions between infantry and cavalry swords, which used to be evident in the finds, were now eliminated. In addition, spears and various types of javelin were used by the cavalry.

Excursion on the 'Celtic Renaissance' in military fittings

Originating with Ramsey MacMullen (1965), there has long been an opinion that there was a revival of Celtic cultural elements in the north-western Roman provinces from the middle of the 2nd century onwards. This was supposed to be mainly observable in the arts and crafts, where late Celtic artistic styles, which had previously only been observed in Britain, suddenly reappeared across all of the north-western provinces. The pelta- and tear-shaped elements appearing especially frequently on military bronzes in openwork, mainly belt mounts, but also components of horse harness from the middle of the 2nd century, were interpreted as a sudden revival of the Celtic style, dormant for a long time under the dominance of Roman decoration. Various theories were derived from this, including 're-establishing Celtic nationalism'. M. Reuter has recently published a critical reappraisal of the complex question of the 'Celtic renaissance' among Roman military bronzes (Reuter 2001). It was already noticed by J. Oldenstein that militaria decorated in the so-called 'Celticising style' from the middle of the 2nd century AD were widely distributed beyond the formerly Celtic-influenced Rhine and Danube regions and Britain, such as in Syria and Morocco.[20] Reuter went further and correctly concluded that there never was a 'Celtic Renaissance' in the comprehensive sense of MacMullen. This is certainly a construct of modern scholarship! The wide-scale adaptation of local, in this case, British, style elements is nothing unusual. It is also possible to repeatedly observe that elements of the local Roman provincial culture spread across larger regions, and are even used empire-wide. Consequently, the 'Celtic Renaissance' cannot be interpreted as an indication of a conscious revival of Celtic self-consciousness or even as a political resistance, but as a simple supraregional trend, which originated in a local fashion.

Securely dated finds of weapons and equipment (selection)

Finds contexts containing exclusively Hadrianic material are rare. Numerous finds, mostly hoards of exceptionally well-preserved weapons from Newstead fort (Scotland), are probably datable to the period around the middle of the 2nd century AD. Among these are cavalry and parade helmets, swords, components of scale and segmental armour, and horse harness. However, these finds are still being discussed in detail.[21] A burnt deposit in the cavalry fort at *Carnuntum* may also possibly date to this time (Jilek 1986; 2005a).

A lot more dated material is available for research from the second half of the 2nd century AD: increasingly, weapons and military equipment come from destruction layers from the Marcomannic Wars (Fig. 491), dating

Figure 491 *Legionary of the 10th Legion from the time of the Marcomannic Wars using finds from Eining-Unterfeld, Iža, and Mušov. Reconstruction drawing: B. Burandt*

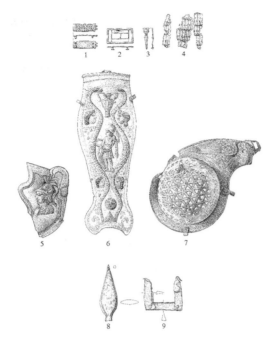

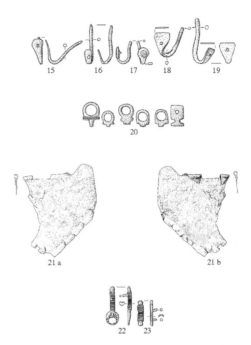

Figure 492 *Finds from the time of the Marcomannic Wars from Regensburg-Kumpfmühl: 1–3 cingulum fittings of copper alloy, 4 copper-alloy armour scales, 5 cheek piece from a copper-alloy cavalry helmet, 6 copper-alloy greave, tinned, 7 eye guard from a copper-alloy chamfron, 8 iron standard tip with copper-alloy binding, 9 copper-alloy dolabra sheath fitting (after Faber 1994). Drawings: A. Smadi, Arch. Institute University of Cologne*

Figure 494 *Finds from the time of the Marcomannic Wars from Eining-Unterfeld: 15–19 fastening hooks made of copper alloy from Newstead-type segmental armour, 20 fastening rings of copper alloy from armour, 21 unfinished cheek piece from a cavalry helmet made of copper-alloy, 22–3 copper-alloy fittings from horse harness (after Fischer 1985 and Jütting 1995). Drawings: A. Smadi, Arch. Institute University of Cologne*

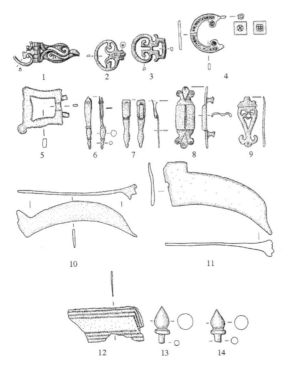

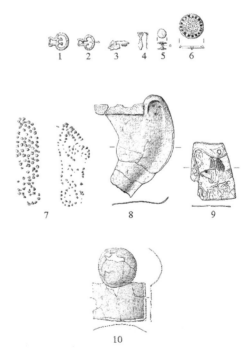

Figure 493 *Finds from the time of the Marcomannic Wars from Eining-Unterfeld: 1–9 fittings of copper alloy from the cingulum (4 enamelled), 10–14 components from Niederbieber-type helmets of copper alloy (after Jütting 1995). Drawings: A. Smadi, Arch. Institute University of Cologne*

Figure 495 *Finds from the time of the Marcomannic Wars from Iža: 1–5 fittings made of copper alloy from the cingulum, 6 round enamelled fittings, 7 iron hobnails from shoes found in situ, 8 iron cheek piece from an equestrian helmet, 9 decorated sheet metal made of copper alloy, 10 iron shield boss with a rectangular base plate (after Rajtar 1994). Drawings: A. Smadi, Arch. Institute University of Cologne*

from AD 165–82.[22] The findspots include the cohort fort at Regensburg-Kumpfmühl, destroyed in the years AD 171/2 (Fig. 492), the vexillation fortress at Eining-Unterfeld (Figs 493–4), occupied in AD 172–9, the bridgehead fort of Brigetio Iža/*Celamantia* (destroyed by AD 180) in Slovakia (Figs 495–7), and the Roman military base at Mušov in Moravia (Figs 498–9).

6. The middle Imperial period from Caracalla to the reforms of Diocletian

Military conflicts

After the death of Septimius Severus in AD 211 in York and the assassination of Geta in AD 212, Caracalla became sole ruler of the empire. He ended the British campaign, which his father had begun. In AD 213, he was forced into a campaign against the Teutones, after the latter had invaded the empire. In AD 214, the campaign against the Dacian tribe of the Carpi on the lower Danube was followed by a campaign against the Parthians, which ended with a Roman victory in 216. However, the Romans could not take advantage of this victory, as the emperor became the victim of a conspiracy by his own generals on the 8th of April 217 in the East.

After a time of confusion, Severus Alexander (AD 222–35) gained the purple. In AD 230, the newly emergent Sassanid empire attacked the Roman army in the East. The emperor withdrew troops from the Rhine and Danube frontiers and began the Roman counteroffensive from AD 231. After costly fighting, there was stalemate. Even during the Persian campaign, Germans invaded the empire in AD 233, with devastating consequences. According to the latest archaeological research, these mainly concerned the approaches to Mainz (Biegert and Steidl 2011).

Severus Alexander concluded an armistice in the East and moved with his troops to Mainz. He was killed there by his own soldiers during preparations for a counteroffensive in AD 235. In Mainz, the army proclaimed an officer, Maximinus I Thrax (AD 235–8), as emperor. He went deep into the interior of Germany with the army of Severus Alexander, where he defeated the Germans. A battlefield from this campaign was only recently discovered at Harzhorn in northern Germany. In AD 236 and 237, Maximinus had to fight against Sarmatians and Dacians on the middle Danube. During the 'Year of the Four Emperors' in AD 238, the Senate appealed for an insurrection against the emperor, which was initiated by unrest in North Africa. Civil war with several pretenders to the throne and the end of Maximinus Thrax were the result. It ended with the

young Emperor Gordian III (AD 238–44) as ruler. Soon there were devastating attacks by the Sassanids under Shapur I. After early successes for Rome, the collapse of the Roman frontier in the East followed in AD 243. In AD 244, Gordian III was killed in combat (or by betrayal?) in Mesopotamia. His successor, Philip the Arab, concluded a compromise peace in AD 244. In the years AD 244 to 247, there were then defensive battles against the Carpi on the lower Danube. In AD 248, a new, long-term enemy threat to Rome appeared on the lower Danube: the Goths. In AD 249, Philip was killed at Verona in battle with usurper Trajan Decius (AD 249–51). However the victor did not find peace: constant inroads by the Goths and Carpi on the lower Danube led to war. In June AD 251, the Goths destroyed the Roman army in marshy terrain near Abrittus in the Balkans. Trajan Decius and his son and co-regent, Herennius Etruscus, met soldiers' deaths on the battlefield. The struggle for the throne and civil war were the result, but the commander Aemilianus was able to destroy the Goths in AD 252, whereupon he was proclaimed emperor by his victorious army. Once again, a struggle for the throne with several usurpers followed.

Valerian (AD 253–60) then had a long reign with a rather unhappy ending. He had dangerously depleted the troops on the Rhine and Danube frontiers during his conflict with his rivals in Italy, which led to German invasions of the *limes* region in Raetia and in eastern Upper Germany in AD 254 (Reuter 2007). Again, attacks by Sarmatians and Goths took place in the Danube region and on the coasts of Asia Minor. Finally, the invasion of Mesopotamia and Syria by the Sassanids and the conquest of Antioch forced the Emperor to intervene in the East. Valerian used his son Gallienus as a co-ruler and moved to his headquarters in Samosata in AD 254. In AD 255/6, the Persians conquered Dura-Europos, one of the most important bastions of Rome on the Euphrates.

The year AD 260 saw the complete defeat of the Roman army in the East, Valerian being the first Roman emperor captured, dying in captivity. The Persians now, almost unhindered, conquered Asia Minor and Syria, only the desert town of Palmyra successfully resisting.

Despite several attempts at usurpation, Gallienus (AD 260–8), the son of Valerian, retained dominion over Rome. However, he had to endure two separate territories separating from Rome: the empire of Palmyra in the East and the breakaway Gallic Empire of Postumus and his successors in the West. The year AD 259/60 was marked by a civil war with Postumus and devastating incursions by the Alamanni and Franks in Upper Germany and Gaul. Goths, Quadi, and Sarmatians invaded Pannonia and northern Italy, and the Franks crossed the Rhine in a thrust that took them into Spain. By no later than AD 260, the

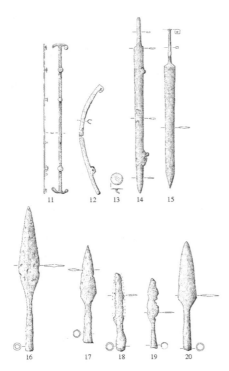

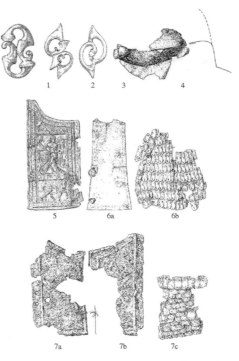

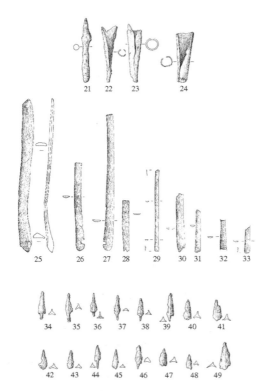

Figure 496 *Finds from the time of the Marcomannic Wars from Iža: 11 iron shield fittings, 12 copper-alloy shield binding, 13 shield nails made of copper alloy, 14–15 iron sword blades, 16–20 iron spearheads (after Rajtar 1994). Drawings: A. Smadi, Arch. Institute University of Cologne*

Figure 498 *Finds from the time of the Marcomannic Wars from Mušov: 1–3 copper-alloy belt fittings of the Klosterneuburg type, 4 fragment of an iron helmet, 5 armour fastening plate of copper alloy with embossed decoration and inscription of the 10th Legion from Vienna, 6a armour fastening plate of copper alloy, 6b silvered armour scales of copper alloy belonging to it, 7a and b iron armour fastening plates, 7c associated iron armour scales (after Tejral 1992 and 1994a). Drawings: A. Smadi, Arch. Institute University of Cologne*

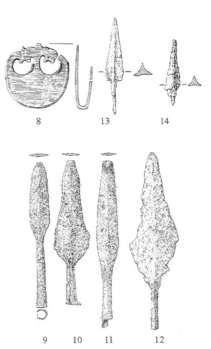

Figure 497 *Finds from the time of the Marcomannic Wars from Iža: 21 iron bolt head, 22–4 iron spear butts, 25–33 bone components from composite bows, 34–49 iron trilobate arrowheads (after Rajtar 1994). Drawings: A. Smadi, Arch. Institute University of Cologne*

Figure 499 *Finds from the time of the Marcomannic Wars from Mušov: 8 peltaform chape of copper alloy, 9–12 iron spearheads, 13–14 iron trilobate arrowheads (according to Tejral 1992). Drawings: A. Smadi, Arch. Institute University of Cologne*

western *limes* area of Upper Germany was lost. A victory altar from Augsburg tells of a Roman victory on 24th April in the year AD 260 against the Juthungi (also known as the Semnones), returning from Italy. In the Danube region and Raetia, barbarian incursions and usurpation attempts against Gallienus followed. In AD 260/61, the emperor achieved a victory over the Alamanni near Milan with the help of Rhenish and Raetian troops. Gallienus then assembled a mounted elite force in Milan, which, of course, additionally weakened the frontier armies. The commander of this group, Aureolus, soon turned against Gallienus. A conspiracy by his officers led to the emperor's death in AD 268 during the siege of Milan.

To succeed him, Claudius II Gothicus (AD 268–70), the commander of the Milanese elite cavalry, was made emperor. He won a victory over the Alamanni in AD 268 on Lake Garda and in AD 269 a victory over the Goths near Naissus in the Balkans. However, in the year AD 270 Claudius II died at Sirmium. Aurelianus (AD 270–5), the commander of the elite cavalry at Milan, was proclaimed emperor after the short reign of Quintillus, the brother of Claudius II. In AD 270, he defeated Juthungi in Raetia and Italy as well as the Sarmatians and Vandals in Pannonia. In AD 271, the Juthungi and Alamanni again invaded Italy, with Roman defensive measures destroying them. In Rome, Aurelian had to put down a revolt by the mint workers with heavy losses for the Roman army. Because of the growing threat to the capital, he ordered the fortification of Rome by means of the Aurelian Wall. The year AD 271 also brought victories over the Goths and Alans in Thrace and Illyria. Thereupon, Aurelian ordered the abandonment of the province of Dacia and the re-adoption of the Danube as a frontier line within the area of the former province. The emperor succeeded in returning both the Palmyrenan and the Gallic breakaway empires under central Roman control. In AD 274, the suppression of internal disturbances in Gaul and a victory over Germans in Raetia followed. For the year AD 275, Aurelian planned a campaign against the Persians, but on the march east the emperor fell victim to a conspiracy by his court and the military.

After an interregnum and the short-term reign of Tacitus, Probus (AD 276–82) became emperor. He also immediately had to fight on all fronts, but almost all of them ended well for Rome: AD 276 victory over the Alamanni and Franks, AD 277 combat with the Germans and Goths, victory over Alamanni and Franks on the Rhine, victory over the Burgundians (in Raetia?), AD 278 victory over the Vandals in Raetia and Illyria, AD 279 victory over the Isaurians in Asia Minor and the Blemmyrs in Egypt and AD 280/1 the squashing of insurrections and usurpations in Gaul and Syria. In AD 282, Probus was murdered by mutineers at Sirmium.

Carus was proclaimed in Raetia as usuper to Probus in AD 282. After his death, Carus became the sole ruler. In AD 283, he gained a victory over the Jazyges in Pannonia. His successful campaign against the Sassanids ended with his death by lightning in AD 283, his sons Carinus and Numerianus taking over the succession for a short time. In AD 284, Diocletian's proclamation as emperor brought his succession in AD 285.

Securing the frontiers of the empire

For the year AD 213, a first barbarian invasion is recorded on the Upper German-Raetian limes. In a pre-emptive war, Caracalla (AD 211–17), who crossed the *limes* from Raetia, defeated the Germans in this year, possibly in the Main area. Twenty years later, under Severus Alexander, a devastating incursion by the Alamanni took place in 233, which by now can be mainly recognized archaeologically in the approaches to Mainz. It represented only the beginning of a long series of raids on the Rhine and Danube borders. The Roman frontier defences were no longer equal to these permanent strikes: in AD 254, the Raetian limes collapsed completely, and in AD 259/60 the Upper German limes under the Emperors Valerian (AD 253–60) and Gallienus (AD 260–8). With the exception of the *cohors III Britannorum* at Eining/Abusina, not a single auxiliary unit stationed on the *limes* is named after AD 260. The loss of the area east of the Rhine had pushed Rome back to the Rhine frontier as in the early Imperial period. Only under Probus (276–82) was it possible to stabilize the borders between the Rhine and the Danube by the year 281. A more sustainable new beginning took place under Diocletian (285–305), with the erection of a new Danube-Iller-Rhine limes.

In the middle Danube region, the province of Dacia was abandoned under Aurelian (270–5) after the year AD 271 and the army retreated to the shorter Danube frontier. After the invasion of the Sassanids and the conquest of Dura-Europos in AD 265/6, there were also short- and long-term losses in the East.

Armament and equipment

Starting a new section on Roman armament with the reign of Caracalla (AD 211–17) can be justified in several manners. Historically, because this is the start of the period of the so-called soldier emperors with quick changes of emperors and massive wars with external and internal enemies in the many crises of the 3rd century AD. Archaeologically, because despite all sorts of other continuity, significant changes in the armament can be identified: the end of segmental armour, the rectangular *scutum*, and the dagger. In addition there is the change of the existing type of belt to the ring- and frame-buckle belts and the introduction of new types of cavalry helmets. In addition, during this period, the German barbed spearhead was adopted by the Roman cavalry. Ubl has even postulated a comprehensive 'across-the-board' equipment reform during the time of Caracalla,[24] a term that should be handled cautiously.

It is becoming increasingly apparent that new types weapons from the Late Roman period, which were associated with an equipment reform by the Emperors Diocletian (AD 284–305) and Constantine I (AD 306–37) by many researchers, had already been developed in the last third of the 3rd century AD.

ICONOGRAPHIC SOURCES

In the late 2nd and early 3rd centuries AD, soldiers' tombstones with pictorial representations (Ubl 1969; Coulston 1987) appear repeatedly in the Danube region and the East (*e.g. Apamea*, Istanbul). With the reign of Gallienus (AD 260–8), emperors appear on coins wearing cavalry equipment that in part is very realistic. In addition to helmets of the Theilenhofen type, but especially the Heddernheim type, their cuirasses are not the usual muscled armour of emperors. Rather, they are depicted in armour typical of the cavalry, that is to say, scale or mail armour. On coins of Probus, barbed spears of Germanic origin and similarly designed missiles (*plumbatae* or *mattiobarbuli*) can be made out (Estiot 2008).

These realistic representations of military equipment, which were supposed to underline the emperor's *virtus* (military efficiency), are connected with the elite shock cavalry founded under Gallienus, whose commanders often became emperor after the time of Gallienus.

Legionary infantry

BELTS

From Emperor Caracalla onwards, ring- and frame-buckle belts dominate in all units and largely replace the traditional belt buckle with tongues. Both a Germanic origin and adoption from the Persian cultural realm are possible for this type of belt. Although the ring buckle is dominant in depictions on tombstones, frame buckles occur more frequently among finds. Decorative silver sets of this type of belt are currently known mainly from the Danube region (Fig. 500).

BROOCHES

Late cloak brooches of the P-shaped type with a long hinge arm led directly to the early types of crossbow brooch. The different variants of these represent the most important military brooch in the Late Roman period (Martell 2001).

HELMETS

The latest variant of the Niederbieber type of iron helmet are the Heddernheim and Niedermörmter variants, which now increasingly had decoration on their copper-alloy fittings. It is highly probable that, in this period, the first examples of ridge helmets were produced following the Eastern model, which would come to dominate the image of Late Roman helmets.

ARMOUR

In the late 2nd century, most legionary soldiers appear to have gone back to mail and scale for body armour. Segmental armour went out of fashion before the middle of the 3rd century AD.

SHIELDS

The rectangular *scutum* was now replaced by the oval shield. The only evidence for a rectangular *scutum* from the time around the middle of the 3rd century AD comes from Dura-Europos and could also have been an old, worn-out piece. The tombstones of soldiers from *Apamea* in Syria, dating to the time of Caracalla, indicate that legionary groups had finally and exclusively adopted the oval shield of the auxiliary troops from the 3rd century AD onwards.

Figure 500 *Officer without armour, with silver frame-buckle belt. Reconstruction drawing: B. Burandt*

SWORDS

The *spathae* of the 3rd century either had a wide blade with parallel edges or were a narrow, rapier-like weapon with a tapering blade. On the blades of the Nydam-Straubing type, representations inlaid in copper alloy mostly show Mars and Victoria, often highly stylized. Its leather-covered wooden sheath had a box chape, often circular in form, in the middle third of the 3rd century AD, occasionally decorated with silver and richly adorned with niello. The piece from Khisfine in Syria even has a scabbard entirely made of ivory (Gogräfe and Chehade 1999). This was followed by trapezoidal chapes with a straight ending of bone and iron, which were probably adopted from the Sassanian East and seamlessly led to the Gundremmingen-type chape of the Late Roman period.

DAGGERS

At some point in the 3rd century AD, but after Caracalla, the dagger was no longer a standard Roman armament and disappeared completely. A plausible reason for this is not yet apparent.

Auxiliary infantry

The archaeological material from this era no longer shows any obvious differences between the armament and equipment of legionary and auxiliary infantry. This can be found, for example, in the standard equipment of legionary and auxiliary soldiers with ring- and frame-buckle belts and *spatha* with box chapes mounted on the *balteus* on Danubian and other gravestones from the period after Caracalla.

Auxiliary cavalry

BELTS

On tombstones, legionary and auxiliary cavalry now adopted ring- and frame-buckle belts from the infantry and were probably wearing them into the Tetrarchic period.[25]

HELMETS

Pseudo-Attic cavalry helmets, such as the Theilenhofen type, were represented until around the middle of the 3rd century (Fig. 501). They are then replaced by the pseudo-Corinthian helmets, like the Heddernheim type, which were worn into the Tetrarchic period.

JAVELINS

A special variant of javelin with bronze heads occurs in Raetia (*e.g.* at Straubing) and in the Danube provinces to the east of it in the 3rd century AD, the Roman units of the Rhine army or in Britain apparently not using these weapons. Javelins with barbed heads are also recognisable

Figure 501 *Cavalryman from the period around the middle of the 3rd century AD. Reconstruction drawing: B. Burandt*

on the coins of Probus (see Figs 291, 311f.), including *plumbatae* and *mattiobarbuli* (Estiot 2008), which were adopted from Germanic armaments. Until now, these weapons were only thought to be a component of Roman equipment in the Late Roman period.

CATAPHRACTS

A special form of cavalry is represented by armoured riders (*cataphractarii* or *clibanarii*) adopted from the East, who mainly fought with the thrusting lance (*contus*). Epigraphic and literary records for these armoured cavalry also appear in the north-western provinces later in the 3rd century AD, although archaeological evidence is still lacking (Harl 1996).

Securely dated finds of weapons and equipment (selection)

From the level of the Alamannic incursions of the year AD 233 onwards, the destruction layers on the Upper German-Raetian limes contain large amounts of militaria. A little later this is also the case on the Danube frontier and in Dacia. In the case of old excavations the problem is to separate the contents of various destruction horizons, as is the case, for example, with the burnt debris from

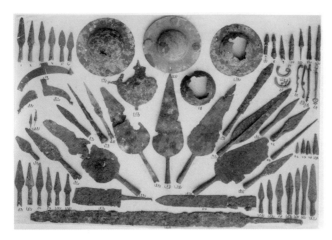

Figure 502 *Weapon finds, mostly from the destruction layer at Kastell Pfünz on the Raetian limes: including helmet components, shield bosses, swords and sword scabbard fittings, and spearheads (historical photo)*

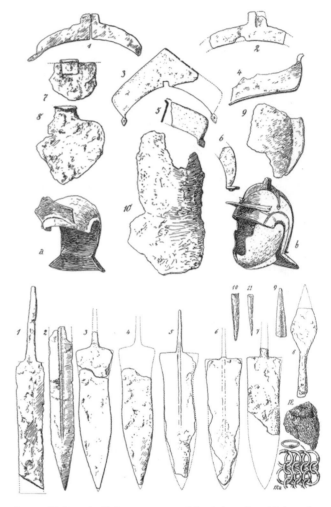

Figure 503 *Hoard with iron weapons of the 3rd century AD from the Mainz legionary base: fragments of helmets of the Niederbieber type, fragments of mail armour, spathae, daggers, spearheads, spear butts (after Behrens 1927)*

the legionary fortress of Regensburg at the Grasgasse site, dating round AD 180.[26] For the time being, the rich finds from Raetia, such as Weißenburg,[27] Pfünz (Fig. 502),[28] and Eining,[29] can more likely be attributed to the destruction of the year AD 254.[30] The material from the final burnt deposits from the Upper German forts of Niederbieber,[31] Zugmantel,[32] and Saalburg,[33] and the *vicus* at Heddernheim[34] probably dates from the time around AD 260. When the large armoury at *Carnuntum* was destroyed during the later 3rd century AD is still completely unclear. Likewise, a more exact interpretation of a collection of iron weapons and equipment from Mainz (Fig. 503) is still awaited.

The two huge metal hoards from Hagenbach and Neupotz, which were retrieved during dredging operations in the Rhine, are testimony to the plundering of Gaul, probably around AD 260. They also contain Roman weapons. It was not so much a case of intentionally deposited votive offerings but rather German plunder, lost in the Rhine by accident or through military actions. The finds are now associated with the incursions around AD 260 under Gallienus.[36]

Around the middle of the 3rd century AD, a number of weapons hoards were deposited, especially in Raetia. Notable among them is the high number of parade weapons. These hoards, for example, the metalwork hoards from Künzing, Straubing, Eining, and Weißenburg, should probably be seen in the context of the great incursion of AD 254.[37]

The newly discovered battlefield at Harzhorn from the time of the Maximinus Thrax (AD 235–8) will probably provide particularly well-dated finds.[38] Finally, the bulk of the Roman militaria recovered from the northern German and Scandinavian bog deposits belongs to this period.[39]

The weapons and other militaria from Dura-Europos on the middle Euphrates are particularly important and abundant. This town was occupied by Roman legions

and auxiliaries in the early 3rd century AD and fell to the Persians after a long siege in 255/6. They abandoned the city and it was never settled again.[40]

7.   Late Antiquity

Military conflicts

In the year 285, Emperor Diocletian appointed the senior soldier Maximianus as his co-ruler. The empire was now divided into an eastern empire and a western empire; Maximianus took over the West as Augustus, Diocletian as Augustus in the East, with in 293 the appointment of two subordinate Caesars (Galerius in the East and Constantinus Chlorus in the West).

Diocletian (AD 284–305) had to survive numerous battles with barbarians who had invaded the empire since the civil war against Numerianus (AD 285): AD 285 against Teutons and Sarmatians, AD 286 repelling the Alamanni and Burgundi on the upper Danube, AD 293 victory over the Sarmatians on the lower Danube, AD 291 repelling an Arab attack in Syria, AD 293 repelling a Blemyr raid in Egypt, and AD 297/8 the suppression of revolts in Egypt and fighting against the Alamanni and Franks.

Maximianus Herculius (AD 286–305, AD 306–8, 310) had won a victory over the Bagaudae in Gaul in AD 286; in AD 287 he defeated the Franks, and in AD 297/8 he put down a rebellion in North Africa.

Caesar Constantinus I Chlorus (AD 293–306) succeeded in recovering Britain after the rebellion of Carausius and Allectus in 296. In AD 305, he defeated the Franks. Galerius (AD 293–311) was involved in battles with the Sarmatians and Jazyges on the lower Danube in AD 294. In AD 295, victories followed over the Goths, Marcomanni, Bastarni, and Carpi on the lower Danube. After a defeat against the Persians in AD 296, he was able to win a great victory over them in the East in AD 298.

In AD 306, Constantine I was proclaimed as a rival emperor in York. Civil war followed: in AD 312, Constantine defeated his rival Maxentius on the Milvian Bridge near Rome. In the years AD 306, 310, 313, and 320, the emperor had to fight against the Franks. He had to fight a civil war against Licinius in the East in AD 316, and against the Sarmatians and Goths on the lower Danube in the years AD 322/3. Only the victory over Licinius in AD 324 ensured Constantine's sovereignty. His son and co-regent Constantine II successfully repelled barbarian invasions: in AD 328, he defeated the Alamanni, and in AD 322 the Visigoths, Taifals, and Carpi on the lower Danube.

After the death of Emperor Constantine I in AD 337, his sons Constantine II, Constans, and Constantius II succeeded, but soon became rivals and fought civil wars. After repelling a Sarmatian incursion in AD 338, the civil war between Constantine II and Constans began. In AD 340, Constantine II fell victim to an ambush. Battles against the Franks and Alamanni followed in the years AD 341/2, and in AD 343, a campaign by Constans in Britain against the Picts and Scots. In AD 350, a revolt by Magnentius broke out in Gaul against Constans, who was murdered. Magnentius moved against Contantius II, but suffered a defeat in the Battle of Mursa in AD 351. The rebellion ended with the death of Magnentius in AD 353. In the years AD 352–5, the Alamanni and Franks invaded the German provinces, Raetia, and Gaul. The Franks conquered Cologne and settled on the west bank of the Rhine, as did the Alamanni on the Upper Rhine. In AD 355, Constantius II appointed Julian as co-ruler (Caesar) and he immediately mounted counter-offensives in Gaul and the Rhine. In AD 357, Julian defeated the Alamanni at the Battle of Strasbourg. He then proceeded to the successful reconquest of Gaul and the Rhineland from the Franks. In

the years AD 357–9, Julian even embarked upon a similarly successful counter-offensive against the Alamanni in the region east of the Rhine.

In AD 358, Constantius II led a campaign against the Quadi and Sarmatians on the lower Danube. Constantius II demanded troops from Julian for the ongoing wars with the Persians, but the latter declined. In AD 361, Julian was proclaimed by his troops as a rival emperor and moved to the East with his army. Before civil war broke out, Constantius II died a natural death. Now Julian II had to fight the Persian War; he was killed in a battle in Mesopotamia in AD 363, his successor Jovian being forced to conclude an armistice with the Persians.

After a brief interlude, Valentinian I (AD 364–75) took over rule in the west. In AD 365, an invasion by the Alamanni into Gaul was repulsed. In the years AD 365/37, riots repeatedly flared up in North Africa. In AD 366, Valentinian I won a victory over the Alamanni at Châlons-sur-Marne. In AD 368, the Alamanni ransacked Mainz, a counteroffensive by Valentinian on the Rhine and Danube frontier leading to intensive expansion of the frontier fortifications. In the years AD 373–5, there followed an incursion by the Quadi in Pannonia; Valentinian died in November 375 at Brigetio.

With Valens (364–78) the ruler in the East, the Huns advanced to the West in AD 375, driving the Goths before them. These were now pushed into the Roman empire or subjugated by the Huns. This led to a war against the Goths on the lower Danube in AD 367/70. Unrest in Armenia from AD 367 onwards led to conflict with the Persians in the years AD 370/1. On the 9th of August AD 378, the Goths completely destroyed the Eastern Roman army in the Battle of Adrianople, and among the countless dead was Emperor Valens. The victorious Goths later became *foederati* and provided a large part of the Roman army in the East. Gratian (AD 375–83), the new ruler in the West, had been prevented from coming to the aid of Valens in AD 378 by a great invasion of Alamanni in Gaul. He had to turn back and won a Roman victory at Colmar in Alsace, before leading the last Roman counter-offensive into the regions east of the Rhine. In the year 383, Magnus Maximus rose in Britain as a usurper, moving to Gaul with the British army, Gratian dying in the ensuing civil war.

In AD 394, Theodosius I, the ruler in the East, took control in the West following chaotic conditions caused by barbarian incursions and successive rulers (Magnus Maximus, Valentinian II, and Eugenius). Under him, Christianity became a state religion in AD 391. In AD 394, Eugenius, the usurper in the West, was defeated by the Eastern army under Theodosius I on the Frigidus between Ljubljana and Gorizia. The death of the emperor in AD 395 resulted in the final division of the empire under the rule of his sons Honorius and Arcadius.

Honorius (AD 395–423), the emperor in the West, fought against the Huns on the lower Danube in AD 395, with the Marcomanni plundering Pannonia and Noricum. In AD 401, Vandals and Alans invaded Raetia and the Visigoths Upper Italy, the *magister equitum* Stilicho expelling them with the aid of Rhenish and Raetian troops. In AD 405 a Germanic invasion under the Ostrogoth Radagais ravaged Italy. It ended with the annihilation of the attackers by Stilicho. In AD 406, Alans, Vandals, and Suebi crossed the Rhine near Mainz, plundering Gaul and reaching Spain in AD 409. Constantine III rebelled in Britain in AD 407, setting forth with his army for Gaul, and remained there until AD 411. The year AD 410 brought a horrendous event: the Visigoths captured and plundered Rome.

Under the rule of Arcadius (AD 395–408), the emperor in the East, Eutropius led a campaign against the Huns in AD 397, and in AD 399/400 the Gothic army commanders Tribigild and Gainas rebelled in Asia Minor.

Under the emperor in the West, Valentinian III (AD 424–55), the Vandals captured North Africa in AD 429. In AD 451, Aetius defeated the Huns under Attila and their allies with a western Gothic-Roman coalition on the Catalaunian Fields in Gaul.

In AD 455, the Vandals again plundered Rome. A long struggle for the throne in the West was the result. The last Roman Emperor in the west, Romulus Augustulus (AD 475–6), was deposed in AD 476 by the German warlord Odoacer. Thus ended the Western Roman Empire. Odoacer now ruled as *rex Italiae*. The Ostrogothic King Theoderich II (AD 471–526) took the diocese of Italy on behalf of the Eastern Roman Empire in AD 488, killing Odoacer in AD 493. In Britain, Gaul, Spain, Italy, and the Danube region, Roman rule ended. It was replaced by Germanic realms.

Securing the frontiers of the empire

In Britain, Hadrian's Wall was retained, the Saxon Shore frontier on the southern and south-eastern coasts of the island being strengthened. The restoration and reinforcement of the Rhine frontier, together with the securing of its hinterland, began with Constantine I (AD 306–37), and under Valentinian I (AD 364–75) the frontier fortifications on the Rhine and Danube were reinforced again, in part quite extensively. After the loss of the Upper German-Raetian limes region, the late Roman Danube-Iller-Rhine limes was constructed under the Tetrarchy, which included securing the most important connections in the hinterland. This *limes* was also reinforced under Valetinian. The continuation of the Danube line, which had been reintroduced after the withdrawal from Dacia, was continually reinforced in the Late Roman period; in Syria a new frontier was built between the Euphrates and Palmyra. In AD 298, the relocation of the frontier to the rapids of the first cataract in Egypt took place.

Armament and equipment

The armament and equipment of Late Roman soldiers had changed at the start of the 4th century AD in comparison with the middle Imperial period (Fig. 504), in some cases considerably. However, compared to earlier phases of the Roman Empire, there is relatively little information from actual finds to study. Moreover, it is often almost impossible to distinguish between cavalry and infantry, or even between *limitanei* and *comitatenses* or *foederates*. Barbarian Germanic weaponry and the equipment of the Roman army (which was now often formed from Germans) became ever more similar.

It is clear that, during the 3rd century AD, some types of weaponry were completely discontinued, for both legionary and auxiliary units. Among them are the curved rectangle *scutum* of the legionary infantry, segmental armour, and the dagger. However, this cannot be linked to a deliberately controlled reform of the armament of the Roman army under the Tetrarchy; these processes seemingly took place earlier, within the framework of the usual organic changes in Roman armament. On the other hand, in the case of individual types of weapons or costumes, it is possible to discern new introductions in the Late Roman period, partly under Germanic influence.

In late antiquity, the Roman army consisted largely of Germans and they were able to rise to the highest positions in the army. If, for instance, the names of the troops in the *Notitia Dignitatum* do not provide direct information on the Germanic origin of a Late Roman military unit, only archaeological sources remain: burial and settlement finds with relevant material regularly provide information on the Germanic origin of Late Roman soldiers and their family members. Anthropology can also provide additional guidance because of the now-prevalent custom of inhumation. On the whole, archaeological evidence for Germanic warriors in Roman service can be found from Britain to the mouth of the Danube and on into North Africa.

The lack of actual finds is a consequence of the fact that pronounced destruction deposits for the Late Roman period are largely lacking. Thus, one often depends upon smaller fragments of defensive and offensive weaponry from forts or in burials, as well as literary and representational evidence.

Figure 504 *Reconstructed Late Roman soldier with ridge helmet, mail armour, spatha, spear, and round shield. Photo: Ch. Miks*

ICONOGRAPHIC SOURCES

Very few figures of armed soldiers are available on gravestones or other private monuments of the Late Roman period.[41] The reliefs on the Arch of Galerius in Thessaloniki or on the Arch of Constantine in Rome provide much more information, for example.

DRESS

The Germanic garment of trousers had already increasingly been adopted by the Roman army in the early Imperial period. Long trousers now became standard clothing for the Roman army. Another novelty in uniform was the adoption by the whole army of a furry cap, the *pilleus Pannonicus*, previously only used by the Pannonian army.

BROOCHES

In the Late Roman period, a standardized military cloak brooch type, the crossbow brooch, with its temporally changing variants are a purely Roman development. Germanic brooch types were also used, but to a lesser extent (Martell 2001).

BELTS

Wide leather belts, which were often decorated with conspicuously splendid metal fittings, were characteristic of the Late Roman uniform. These appear to replace older types of belts, such as the ring- and frame-buckle belts in the period before AD 300. The models for these new belts seem not to be found in the Roman Empire, but rather in elaborate belts in the Germanic regions, such as in central Germany, northern Germany, and Denmark.

HELMETS

Ridge helmets, which had been customary in the Roman army since the time of the Tetrarchy or Constantine I, had been adopted from the Sassanian area, but modified in details. The bowl, which was always made of iron, was of a two-part type, the neck guard being separate, and a new element – a nasal – later being added as a new element. According to the latest research, almost all of the helmets were equipped with a gilded silver sheet overlay. A high crest was occasionally mounted on the helmet, probably as a mark of rank, and a badge with a Christogram could be mounted on the front of it. It can be assumed that this helmet form did not first appear within the framework of a so-called Diocletian-Constantine army reform, as has repeatedly been proposed by scholars, but had already been introduced towards the end of the 3rd century AD, having been adopted from the region of Persia or Mesopotamia.

ARMOUR

There are only a few fragments of scale and mail armour from the Late Roman period. To what extent these differed from older models is unclear. The decorated fastening plates of the 2nd and 3rd centuries AD, however, were no longer used in late antiquity.

SHIELDS

Among shields, Germanic round shields were frequently used. As with helmets, iron shield bosses could be covered with gilded silver plate.

SWORDS

The principal offensive weapon of the Roman army remained the long sword, the *spatha*. It still formed the main weapon of cavalry and infantry in the 4th and 5th centuries AD, and continued as such well into the early Middle Ages. Changes also occurred here under the Tetrarchy, but they were less to do with the blades than the sword scabbards. As an example, the regular circular scabbard terminal fittings – the so-called box chapes – were replaced by (with some intermediate forms) simple straight terminal metal fittings with decorative studs (Gundremmingen-type chapes). At the end of its development, simple U-sectioned metal sheaths led to the sword types of the early Middle Ages.

BATTLE AXES

The increasing barbarization of the Roman army from the later 4th century AD onwards now also brought with it evidence for battle axes in the Roman army in grave and settlement finds. However, I prefer not to call them regular Roman weapons.[42]

SHAFTED WEAPONS

Since the troops had to move quickly and also had to be able to deter mounted opponents, cavalry had become increasingly important. Consequently, the spear and arrow remained important weapons in the Late Roman period; their iron heads, together with catapult bolts, are common finds from all sites of this period. A peculiar weapon of the Late Roman period, which was, however, already recorded from the time of Probus (AD 276–82) onwards, was the spear with long barbed heads adopted from the Germans. Likewise, a special short throwing weapon, which was often provided with a barbed head, the *plumbata* or *mattiobarbulus*, is already found this early (Estiot 2008). It owed its penetrative capabilities to a lead weight around the shank of the iron head.

CAVALRY

While hardly any specific cavalry weapons can be identified among the armament of the Late Roman period, helmets of the Deurne-Berkasovo type can probably be interpreted as typical cavalry helmets. Spurs, which are very similar to types in the Germanic region, are found more often.

Securely dated finds of weapons and equipment

It is true that there are some finds of Late Roman weapons from rivers, settlements, and burials, but so far there are no well-preserved large assemblages, like those found in the destruction layers of the 1st or 3rd centuries AD. An exception is the collection of helmets and shield bosses from Koblenz, deposited around the middle of the 4th century (Miks 2008).

Byzantine weapons – an overview

It was shown above that, along with the enormous increase in relevant archaeological finds of Roman weapons and military equipment, there was also a corresponding increase in technical literature. These range from the study of single finds or groups of finds, through the publication of assemblages, right up to synthetic studies.

Against this backdrop, it seems all the more remarkable that the seamlessly continuing development of weapons in the Byzantine period has not resulted in an equally impressive amount of literature. The commendable summary by T. G. Kolias (1988) was not really based on archaeological finds. This work has not yet been replaced by an adequate synthesis with a stronger emphasis on archaeology – this, while there are by now in fact finds! So far there are only works on individual weapons and pieces of equipment. For example, there are the work by M. Vogt (2006) on *Spangenhelm* helmets and the two-volume monograph by M. Schulze-Dörrlamm (2009 and 2000a) on Byzantine belt buckles which are definitely not all military equipment. The work by W. Menghin (1983) on the swords of the early Middle Ages also contains individual pieces which may perhaps rather belong into a Byzantine context. More recently, some important overviews were added to this (Miks *et al.* 2012).

Notes to Part V

1. In the following, the most important wars of Rome are sketched out, without going into too much detail. The information is derived from summary accounts of Roman history: Krohmayer and Veith 1928; Johne *et al.* 1988; H. Bengtson, *Grundriss der römischen Geschichte mit Quellenkunde. I. Republik und Kaiserzeit bis 284 n. Chr.* Handb. d. Altertumswissenschaft III 5 (3rd ed., Munich, 1989); A. Demandt, *Die Spätantike. Römische Geschichte von Diocletian bis Justinian 284–565 n. Chr.* Handb. d. Altertumswissenschaft III 6 (Munich 1989); K. Christ, *Geschichte der römischen Kaiserzeit* (5th edition, Munich, 2005).

2. Dobson 2008; Luik 1997, 2002 and 2009; Schulten 1927 and 1929.
3. Bishop and Couston 2006, 49, Fig. 21.
4. Keppie 1991; Bishop and Coulston 2006, 30.
5. Ulbert 1984, 69.
6. Ibid., 50–69.
7. Bishop and Coulston 2006, 52; 58.
8. Fingerlin 1971/72, 1986 and 1998.
9. Hübener 1973.
10. Fischer 2009, 499ff.
11. Ibid., 505–9.
12. Varusschlacht 2009; Varusschlacht Katalog 2009.
13. Bushe-Fox 1932 und 1949; Brailsford 1961; Richmond 1968.
14. Bishop and Coulston 2006, 15, Fig. 5.
15. Junkelmann 2000a, 89f.
16. Stiebel 2005, 101–4.
17. Ortisi 2005, 2006, 2009, and 2009a.
18. Éttienne *et al.* 2004; Gazdac 2009.
19. Bishop and Coulston 2006, 128.
20. Oldenstein 1976, 203–7.
21. Curle 1911; Manning 1906.
22. Fischer 2009; Komorócy 2009; Rajtar 2009; Fischer 2012a.
23. Biegert and Steidl 2011.
24. Ubl 1969, 238f.
25. Ibid., 236f.
26. Reuter 2005.
27. ORL B 72 (1906); Fischer and Riedmeier-Fischer 2008, 116–19.
28. ORL B 73 (1901); Fischer and Riedmeier-Fischer 2008, 139–41.
29. Gschwind 2004.
30. Reuter 2007.
31. ORL B 1a (1936); Cüppers 1990, 501ff.
32. ORL B 8 (1909); Klee 2009, 81–4.
33. Jacobi 1897; ORL B 11 (1937); Klee 2009, 103–8.
34. Reiss 2010.
35. Groller v. Mildensee 1901.
36. Bernhard *et al.* 1990; Künzl 1993; Barbarenschatz 2006.
37. Fischer 1991 and 1999; Reuter 2007.
38. Geschwinde *et al.* 2009.
39. Cf. Sieg und Triumpf 2003.
40. Cf. James 2004 und 2005.
41. Bishop and Coulston 2006, 18, Fig. 8; 204, Figs 129–30; 209, Figs 1–4.
42. Cf. Böhme 1974, 104–10.

VI THE ROMAN NAVY

1. Arming and equipping the marines

Organization of the marines

The Roman fleet was divided in its organization and jurisdiction, and a clear distinction was made between the seamen and the marines. This even went so far that each ship had two commanders, a nautical and a military one. The nautical commander on larger ships had the title *nauarchus*, on smaller ones *trierarchus*, these designations quite obviously, albeit with a certain change in meaning, being taken from the eastern Hellenistic area.

The military complement on a ship, in other words the marines, were equated with centuries in land armies. They consisted of combat units of about 80 men under the command of a *centurio*. Therefore, the marine commander had the rank of *centurio classicus*.[1]

Armament

So far, little is known about the subject. The popular work by R. D'Amato and G. Sumner lacks a detailed and secure compilation of the original material.[2] So far, little has been found that would fundamentally differentiate the armament and equipment of marines from that of legionary and auxiliary infantry: the few militaria excavated at Dover[3] offer nothing specific to the fleet, nor do the finds from the naval base at Cologne-Alteburg (Fischer 2005a). The components from body armour, swords, daggers, and shafted weapons found there do not have any special features which would unequivocally connect them with marines. In any case, it could be inferred from the information given by Vegetius (*Epitoma rei militaris* 44) that long-range weapons (artillery, crossbows, bows and arrows, slingshot, javelins, and stone balls) played a greater role in sea warfare than in open field battles.[4]

Only pseudo-Attic infantry helmets from Pompeii might have been specifically assigned to marines. There is also no difference between their clothing and that of other soldiers.[5]

2. Bases of the Roman fleets in the Imperial period

Thomas Schmidts

Introduction

The present article deals with the bases of Roman fleets from the last years of the Roman Republic (40 BC) through to the 5th century AD. The focus here lies on installations that could be characterized as military ports and which were located both on the coast and inland. In the past, as now, naval bases have strongly influenced the layout of port cities. This undoubtedly is also true of the main bases of the Roman fleets, primarily those of the Praetorian fleets in Italy, but also those of the provincial fleets from North Africa to Britain. Our knowledge of the structural organization and the buildings of these bases varies widely. None of the main bases has been fully investigated so far, if we include both the camp structures and the associated port facilities. For now, archaeological finds from the northern provinces of the Roman Empire must illuminate our picture of the camp buildings of the troops and smaller military port facilities.

One difficulty lies in identifying and classifying smaller fleet bases, which temporarily or permanently housed divisions of the fleets. The written sources and, to an even greater extent, the distribution of inscriptions, compel us to study the validity of these sources for the identification of appropriate locations. It is mostly inscriptions of marines and officers up to the commander, which lead to the identification of bases. In addition, brick stamps of fleet units or the depictions of warships on local coinage have been regarded as relevant indications. This has certainly led to mistakes; on the other hand, fleets could have been present in places that do not appear in the literary sources. For a detailed discussion of naval bases and their sources, reference should be made to a chapter from M. Reddé's important work *Mare Nostrum*, published in 1986.[6] The selection of the sites – in some cases differing from Reddé's – taken into account in our distribution maps is the responsibility of the author.

Characteristics of ancient military ports

If one asks what constitutes an ancient military harbour, this seems easy to answer. It is, of course, first and foremost the buildings and structures that enable the deployment

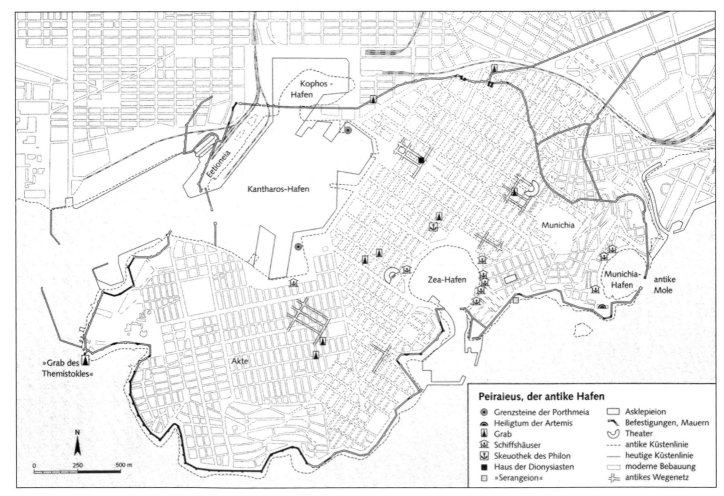

Figure 505 *Topography of Piraeus, showing the location of the various ports (Hafen) with contemporary shoreline (Küstenlinie) and locations of Roman buildings, shipsheds, and graves (Grab), including the 'Grave of Themistocles' (after von Eickstedt 1991, Beil. 1)*

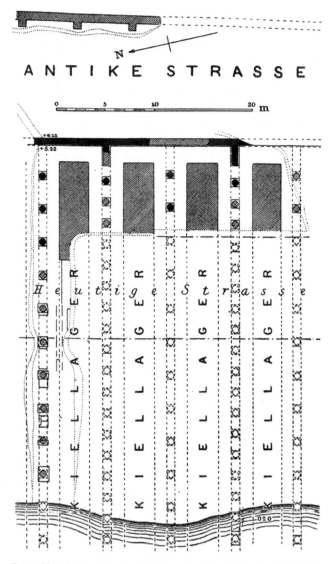

ANTIKE STRASSE

Figure 506 *Piraeus. Shipsheds in the port of Zea (after Judeich 1905, 386 f Figure 43a–b)*

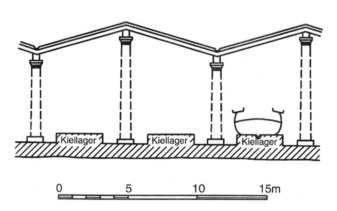

Figure 507 *Cross-section of the shipsheds in the port of Zea (see Fig. 506)*

of ships and boats and their maintenance. In addition, the security of the port must be guaranteed. Up to the end of the Hellenistic period, or, from the Roman point of view, the end of the Republic, port cities with their own fleets are a characteristic feature of settled regions from the Mediterranean to the Black Sea. The size of the fleets differed widely and could range from a few warships to several hundred deployable vessels, like those maintained by Athens, Carthage, or Rhodes. Accordingly, the significance of a fleet is also reflected in the size of its military ports. An important element here is the shipsheds: simple long, rectangular buildings in which the craft could be stored and serviced on land. Because of the immense material value of a warship, it was routine to house it out of the water. The storage of the associated equipment such as oars, sails, and ropes also required its own buildings, which can predominantly be characterized more or less as large arsenals. Access to the shipsheds was generally forbidden for unauthorized persons; in Rhodes, it could even be punished in law by death.

Among the most impressive military port facilities of the ancient world, so far as can be judged from ancient accounts or archaeological finds, were Piraeus as a base for the Athenian and Carthage for the Punic fleets. In Piraeus (Fig. 505), the fleet was housed, in particular, in two separate ports, Zea and Munychia, which were protected against the entry of unauthorized persons by means of walls. Shipsheds, which were also examined archaeologically, lined the shore (Figs 506–7). Similarly,

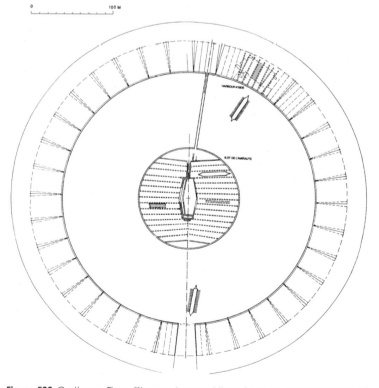

Figure 508 *Carthage. The military port around the middle of the 2nd century BC (after Hurst 1994, 37. Fig. 3.3)*

shipsheds were recorded at least epigraphically in the 4th century BC for the great trading port of Kantharos at Piraeus, so a part of the fleet was kept here too. The large arsenal (*skeuothek*) of the architect Philon, a huge hall that housed 400 warships and had been build around 330 BC, belonged to the Zea harbour.[7] The military harbour of the Carthaginian navy (Fig. 508) also made an impressive picture: a circular artificial basin about 325 m in diameter, with an island, on which admiralty headquarters were located. On the waterfront, shipsheds for more than 200 vessels were lined up.[8]

Both naval ports were destroyed by Roman troops: Carthage in 149 BC and Piraeus in 89 BC. In the Imperial period, the reconstructed port structures were mainly economically important. In Carthage, the fleet no longer played a role. The use of the former military port area for civilian shipping can be demonstrated there archaeologically, as there was now a sanctuary in

the middle of the former admiralty island. At Piraeus, inscriptions suggest a base (thought to be small), but it is unclear whether this was in the area of the former Athenian naval harbours. Roman rule had obviously contributed to a structural change.

Roman naval bases

Overview

The establishment of Roman naval bases (Figs 509–10), as we know them from the Imperial period, was essentially carried out by the Emperor Augustus. The decision to deploy naval units in Italy in the Bay of Naples and on the Adriatic near Ravenna goes back to the final phase of the conflict in the civil war with Sextus Pompey. In the previous centuries, shipsheds for warships had been built in Rome on the Tiber, as well as in Ostia. In addition, further

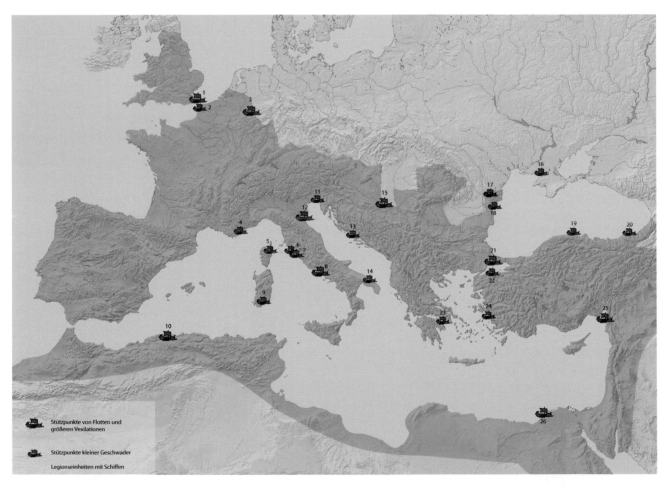

Figure 509 *Roman naval bases from the 1st to the 3rd centuries (design by Th. Schmidts, graphic K. Hölzl, G. Schnorr): red ships: bases for fleets and major vexillations; blue ships: bases for smaller legionary units with ships; 1. Dubris/Dover. 2. Gesoriacum/Boulogne-sur-Mer. 3. Cologne-Alteburg. 4. Forum Iulii/Fréjus. 5. Aleria/Aléria. 6. Centumcellae/Civitavecchia. 7. Ostia. 8. Misenum/Miseno. 9. Caralis/Cagliari. 10. Caesarea/Cherchell. 11. Ravenna. 12. Aquileia. 13. Salona/Solin. 14. Brundisium/Brindisi. 15. Taurunum/Zemun. 16. Chersonesos/Cherson. 17. Noviodunum/Isaccea. 18. Histria. 19. Sinope/Sinop. 20. Trapezous/Trabzon. 21. Perinthos/Marmaraere Iisi. 22. Kyzikos/Erdek. 23. Peiraieus/Piraeus. 24. Ephesos/Selçuk. 25. Seleukeia Piereia/Samanda ı. 26. Alexandreia/Alexandria*

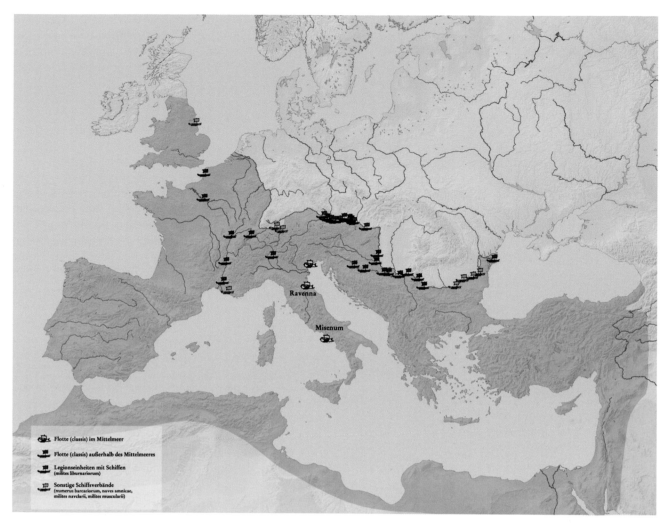

Figure 510 *Fleet bases according to the Notitia Dignitatum (design Th. Schmidts, graphic: K. Hölzl). Ship symbols (top to bottom): naval fleet in the Mediterranean; naval fleet outside the Mediterranean; legionary units with ships/boats; other affiliated naval units*

military bases were used at least temporarily according to military necessity. During the Roman Republic, there was no standing fleet with its own personnel. The establishment of larger Roman fleet units took place according to circumstances, such as the conflicts with Carthage in the 3rd and 2nd century BC, or the fight against the plague of piracy in the 60s of the 1st century. In this, the role of the Roman allies, especially the coastal cities of Southern Italy, cannot be underestimated, since they had nautical experience from the time before the advance of Rome into the Mediterranean.

Before we turn to individual military port facilities, we will briefly explain their distribution and the basics according to the sources. Fleet units have been demonstrated in various parts of the Roman Empire, but they do not occur overal, nor in all seas. The history of the development of the fleet is a separate topic which cannot be discussed here at length. Of course, the expansion of naval bases ultimately reflected the distribution of the units. The

formation of new fleets is a process which began with the founding of the Italian fleets under Octavian/Augustus and then took its course until the late 2nd century with the formation of provincial fleets.[9] While the Mediterranean, the Sea of Marmara, and the Black Sea form areas where military port facilities already looked back on a tradition that had lasted for centuries, the formation of the provincial fleets of the Danube, the Rhine, and the English Channel were something completely new. The distribution of the provincial fleets developed according to the situation on the frontier.[10]

The fleets formed a component of frontier security, and in some cases also a necessary line of communication, as may be assumed in the case of the British fleet. In addition to the regular fleets, which were clearly identified by the designation *classis*, some legions also maintained naval units. For the early and middle Imperial period, the identification of fleet bases and the units stationed there is based on the inscriptions of members of the fleets, as already mentioned. Added to this, of course, are references in the literary tradition, although these give more information on the larger bases. This situation with the sources changes in the Late Roman period. While inscriptions had now almost completely disappeared, we now have an excellent source for the late 4th and early 5th centuries in the *Notitia Dignitatum*, a list of the civilian and military dignitaries in the Roman Empire, its latest edition dating to in the 420s, all fleet units being listed (Fig. 510). This list shows a tendency to divide up the provincial fleets. The stationing of units on inland waters off the frontiers, for instance in Gaul and Northern Italy, was new. In addition, it can also be shown that some of the older fleets no longer existed at this time.[11]

Information on the structural design of naval bases is mainly based on archaeological investigations and

Figure 511 *Rome, Trajan's Column (Scene LXXIX). Representation of a harbour with shipsheds (after Cichorius 1900, plate LVIII)*

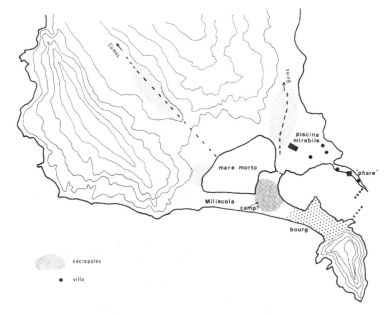

Figure 512 *Misenum. Topography with hypothetical labelling of the fort area (after Reddé 1986, 190 Fig. 12)*

topographical observations. None of the larger sites have so far been fully excavated with both the fort and the associated port facilities. Knowledge of fortifications and barracks comes from excavations in England, France, and Germany, while port facilities are more familiar from the Mediterranean environment. Shipsheds were an indispensable part of a fleet base. In contrast to the older buildings, which were undoubtedly shipsheds, like those known at Piraeus or Carthage, relevant discoveries from the Roman era have recently been hotly debated.[12]

In the iconographic tradition of the Roman Imperial era, which provides ships and coastal landscapes in large numbers, evidence for military port facilities is scarce. For the well-known mosaic from Ravenna (Fig. 513), see the comments on this base below. On other monuments, the problem is that buildings or cities cannot be clearly defined. This also applies to a scene on Trajan's Column (Fig. 511), which depicts the departure of a fleet from a port. Shipsheds with barrel vaults and possibly an arsenal behind them have been identified.[13] Acona, Brindisi, and Ravenna, as well as *Misenum*, have been proposed as the location of the events that probably took place on the Italian section of the Adriatic coast.[14]

A network of larger and smaller bases existed in the Mediterranean, although we can seldom get a picture of the buildings of the bases. It is true that for the large bases of *Misenum* and Ravenna (and for the latter especially for the Late Roman period), conclusions can be drawn about topography, development, and infrastructure, thanks to various sources; the only reliable archaeological evidence for the military camp in question is, however, known from *Forum Iulii*/Fréjus (Fig. 509.4). Recent research in the seaport of *Portus Augusti*, belonging to Ostia up to the 4th century, provided evidence of potential shipsheds of a considerable size. These might have included warships of the larger types, as they were suitable for the voyages of Roman emperors. For other sites, the question arises of the use of older naval bases, which is especially true for Alexandria (Fig. 509.26), where the areas of the Ptolemaic fleet base could be located within the Great Harbour.[15]

In the Sea of Marmara and the Black Sea as well, there is little more than the identification of naval bases themselves, and at most a knowledge of port facilities. Buildings of a clearly military character have not been found yet. Constantinople is a curiosity, for although there is no doubt about large fleet detachments being based there in the Late Roman period, it is not yet possible to locate these unambiguously in one of the city's ports known through literary and now also archaeological sources.[16]

Some of the provincial fleet bases between the Danube delta and Britain are well researched. These include in particular Cologne-Alteburg as the headquarters of the German fleet, Boulogne-sur-Mer as its counterpart for the British fleet, as well as Dover. In addition, Velsen and Vechten were used as military port facilities. However, the identities of the detachments of troops stationed there are unknown because of the lack of epigraphic evidence. There is so far almost no archaeological information on the bases and port facilities of the Pannonian and Moesian fleets, whose headquarters were located at *Taurunum*/Zemun (Serbia) and *Noviodunum*/Isaccea (Romania).[17] A characteristic feature of the provincial fleets is the use of bricks and stamps of these units, which in turn are often used for the identification of fleet bases. However, this can also lead to mistakes, as the example of *Forum Hadriani*/Voorburg-Arentsburg (Netherlands) shows, where bricks with fleet stamps were used in a civilian context.[18] The buildings of the Late Roman fleet bases named in the *Notitia Dignitatum*, which in all probability were quite small and mainly built along the inland waterways, are still largely unknown.[19]

Legions were also able to maintain their own fleets, which required the operation of suitable port facilities and shipyards. Here, two inscriptions of the late 2nd and early 3rd centuries from Mainz are especially important, since they name *optiones navaliorum*, who were NCOs responsible for the operation of shipsheds or wharves.[20] The occasional depictions of warships on bricks of the 22nd legion stationed in Mainz reinforce the assumption that military vessels were actually in operation there.[21] We also know comparable stamps of the 1st Italica legion from the Lower Danube region. This does not mean, however, that there were not already scattered bases for legionary fleets of the 2nd and 3rd centuries, as listed by the later *Notitia Dignitatum* for the Danube.

A selection was made for the following account of naval bases of the Roman Empire, for which literary, epigraphic, or archaeological sources provide information on the structural design and buildings. It does not claim to be complete.

Misenum/Miseno (Italy)

The two most important fleets of the Roman Empire were the Praetorian fleets stationed in *Ravenna* and *Misenum* (Fig. 512), the *classis praetoria Misenensis* surpassing the *classis praetoria Ravennas* in size and importance. A large military harbour had already been in use in the Bay of Naples at *Portus Iulius* around 38 BC, shortly before the basing of the fleet at *Misenum*. For this purpose, the Lucrinus and Avernus lakes were connected by means of a canal at *Cumae*. Moreover, access to the sea was not only possible through Lake Lucrinus, but also through a tunnel that had been bored through the rock.[22] Between the abandonment of this facility, which was probably only used for a short time, and the founding of the military harbour at *Misenum*, which had taken place at an unknown time between 27 and 20 BC, the decision had been made to have a standing fleet, which was to have its most important base here. *Misenum*, like *Portus Iulius*, was greatly expanded by Agrippa. If a minimum size for the Misene fleet of 6,000 to 10,000 soldiers and about 80 ships[23] is assumed, it is clear that this was not only the largest naval base, but that it was also a considerable number of troops, with more men than a legion. However, squadrons from the Misene fleet were also situated in other ports in the Mediterranean, so that the actual presence on the ground did not correspond to the overall strength of the fleet. The remains of the military harbour are now about 8 m below the surface of the water. They had been still visible in the 17th century, so we can at least understand the topography and harbour installations.[24] There were two port basins, connected by a narrow canal, which in turn was covered by a wooden bridge.[25] The inner (Mare Morto) was ideally suited for a military port due to its sheltered position and a shore line of about 3 km. Individual buildings, such as shipsheds, arsenals, or the military camp, have not yet been archaeologically investigated. However, the toponym 'Miliscola' for the harbour basins and land

Figure 513 *Ravenna, Sant'Apollinare Nuovo. Mosaic depicting the harbour town of Classis (after Deichmann 1958, Fig. 100)*

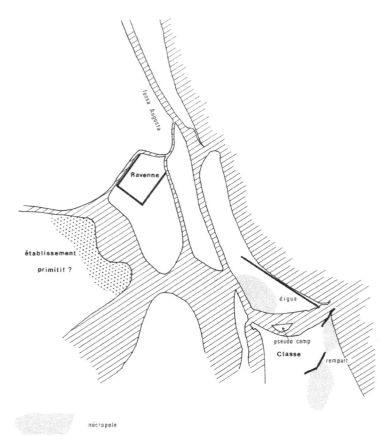

Figure 514 *Ravenna. Topography (according to Reddé 1986, 180 Fig. 11)*

separating them from the sea is a point of reference. It may be derived from the Latin *militum schola*, but this interpretation should not be overstressed.[26] However, the space there is quite limited. If the military camp was placed on the neck of land between the two basins, which seems quite reasonable, a camp with a maximum of 12.5 ha can be assumed, which is clearly below the space requirement for a legion of about 6,000 soldiers (*c*.20–2 ha). Even if the living quarters of the fleet prefects was outside the camp,[27] the question of military buildings must be left to future research. On the southern shores of the outer basin, the buildings of the civilian settlement, which had been raised to the status of a colony, already started, so that there is no further room on this side. A huge cistern (*piscina mirabilis*) on the northern side belonged to the logistics of the military harbour. The two 100 m- and 180 m-long curving breakwaters, which encircled the entrance to the outer basin, are probably the best-known buildings of the complex. Stone tethering rings could be detected on them. Since *Misenum* is mentioned as a fleet base in the *Notitia Dignitatum*,[28] its existence up to at least the early 5th century can be postulated.

Ravenna (Italy)

The base of the *Ravenna* fleet (Figs 513–14) also enjoyed a long period of use. Situated on the Adriatic side of the

Italian peninsula in the Po delta region, it was founded around 38 BC during the battles of Octavian against Sextus Pompey. The heavily forested hinterland, supplying raw material for shipbuilding, will have been one factor in the selection of the site. An important iconographic source representing *Ravenna*'s port city of *Classis* (the Latin term for fleet) dates to the early 6th century AD (Fig. 513). The mosaic in the church of Sant'Apollinare Nuovo shows a city fortified with walls and towers, with two towers at the port entrance that could have served as lighthouses. It must ultimately remain uncertain whether the state depicted on the mosaic is exclusively the result of late building activities or whether it could also depict an earlier state. The area of *Classis* is located outside Ravenna, on a canal (*fossa Augusta*), connected to the Po. It can be unambiguously identified by another early Byzantine church building (Sant'Apollinare in Classe). In its surroundings, the remains of some buildings and moles have also been observed, but their interpretation is still unclear in detail.[29] It is not certain whether the early and mid-Imperial fleet base was also here. However, it is necessary to consider the fact that it was originally situated close to the city of Ravenna.[30]

Forum Iulii/Fréjus (France)

It is known from literary sources that a naval base was established in *Forum Iulii* in southern Gaul after the Battle of Actium in 31 BC with warships and men from the fleet of the defeated Marc Antony.[31] A colony was established there by Octavian for the veterans of the 8th Legion (*Colonia Octavanorum*) which, according to the testimony of Pliny the Elder, was also called *Pacensis et Classica*.[32] The latter designation already refers to the stationing of a fleet. Its strategic importance can be measured by its classification as 'key to the sea' (*claustra maris*).[33] Archaeological investigations have recently been carried out in the area of the fleet fort, which is an exception for a naval base in the Mediterranean. Contrary to earlier speculation, the camp had been located outside the city and away from the well-known harbour. Its area is estimated as *c*.24 ha. The finds, which can clearly be assigned to a military camp, include wooden troop accommodation, remains of a stone building (*principia*?), as well as a large *horreum* and a bath building. The founding date remains uncertain, since possible layers surviving below the water table could not be investigated. The finds from the layers examined do not begin until 10/5 BC. About 20 years later there was a rebuilding phase; around AD 40/50, a change in the use of the area, which was finally abandoned by AD 70, is indicated.[34]

Seleukeia Pieria/Samandag (Turkey)

The expansion of *Seleukeia* (Fig. 515) as a major harbour city in the northern Levant took place – as the name implies – in the Seleucid period. In the first half of the 3rd century BC, it was the residence of the Seleucid dynasty. It owes its strategic importance to the River Orontes, which flows into the Mediterranean south of the city. It could be used to transport soldiers and supplies into the interior of the province of Syria.[35] The port itself, which is now completely silted up, lay inland in the protection of the city walls, and was connected with the sea by a canal and an outer harbour. From the 2nd century onwards, members of the Misene, Ravenna, and Syrian fleets are attested by inscriptions. The latter will probably have had its most important base here. A papyrus document reveals the existence of a camp (*castrum*) with its own barracks for the marines of the Misene fleet.[36] The fort is probably located in the direct vicinity of the port, near the town, judging from the sites of the tombstones.[37] Marine members of a *classis Seleucena* are still mentioned in the year 369/70 in connection with dredging work in the River Orontes. One problem in *Seleukeia* was the permanently threat of silting up in the port and the canal, which was at least partly caused by a mountain stream, which after rainfall flowed through the harbour basin and deposited sediments. To counter this, the water was captured and diverted by means of a dam,[38] a 875 m-long canal with two tunnels, and a cutting through the rock. Inscriptions date these constructions to the Vespasianic period as well as in the middle of the 2nd century, with the work being carried out by legionary soldiers. A renovation of the tunnel, as well as dredging of the silted-up port entrance, fell in the Diocletianic period. Dredging work in the port was still necessary, since the silting up was mainly caused by sediments of the Orontes. Further extensive construction work on the port facilities is also documented under Constantius II around the year 346.

Aliso?/Haltern-Hofestatt (Germany)

The base of Haltern, located on the Lippe, played a central role in the Augustan occupation of the regions to the east of the Rhine. The most important part of this military site is the *Hauptlager*, which is a fortress 18.6 ha in size. It can be dated into the occupation phase from the turn of the century to the Varus Disaster in AD 9.[39] Since it was situated at a distance from the river above the Lippe, a separate base was erected on the 'Hofestatt' (Fig. 516) on the ancient bank, which is no longer on the line of the modern bank due to changes in the river's course. This multi-phase base was archaeologically examined at the beginning of the 20th century. Since the documentation was lost due to the war, only the old reports are available as a source. A re-evaluation of the site as a base for a naval unit was undertaken by J.-M. A. W. Morel.[40] In the first three periods, the complex was each time surrounded by defences of different sizes, triangular or trapezoidal in shape (period 2), while the officers' quarters of barrack accommodation were detectable in the interior

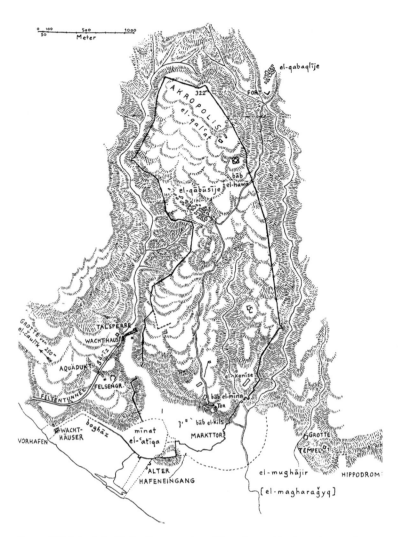

Figure 515 Seleukeia Pieria. *Topography of the city and harbour (according to Honigmann 1923, 1193 f)*

during periods 2–3. In our case, the latest period (4) is of particular interest. The western part of the 1.2 ha camp was occupied by a wooden building *c*.55 × 30 m, which was separated from the rest of the site. The building was subdivided by rows of posts into eight long rectangular units approximately 6 m wide, which, according to Morel, must be shipsheds. This interpretation is strongly supported by the traces of beams, which ran centrally within each of the spaces and which were secured by cross members. This discovery may be interpreted as a slipway on which the ships could be drawn ashore (Fig. 543). The resemblance to Mediterranean shipsheds had already been noted by one of the excavators; however, he had dismissed it because of the comparatively long distance of about 30 m from the shore.[41] More recently, B. Rankov again denied the interpretation as a shipyard.[42] He explained this mainly with the unusually great distance from the water as well as the difficulties that would arise if one wanted to launch a ship into a relatively narrow river. These arguments are quite powerful, but they

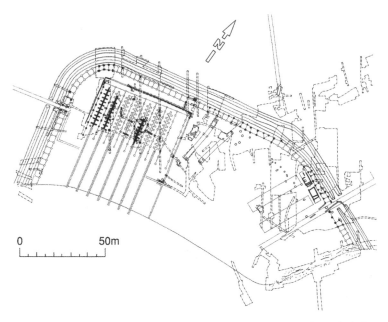

Figure 516 *Haltern-Hofestatt. Plan of the discoveries with supplements (after Morel 1987)*

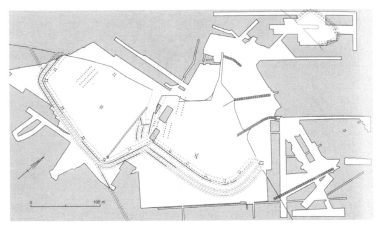

Figure 517 *Velsen. Plan of the discoveries (according to Bechert and Willems 1995, 100)*

also beg the question of the lack of a convincing alternative interpretation for this building complex.[43] In the eastern part of the base, two officers' quarters belonging to barracks were found, so that we can certainly accept it as a military camp – regardless of the possibility of shipsheds. Because of its location, the base was clearly related to the riverbank on which it was built. In the bank area, there were still traces of rows of posts which may have belonged to quays, moles, or piers.[44] In addition, a graffito on a Samian vessel is thought to indicate an Alexandrian ship's crew.[45]

Flevum/Velsen (Netherlands)

As with Haltern (see above), the base at Velsen (Fig. 517) belongs in the context of the early Imperial wars in

Germany. The position of this naval base – in the northern Rhine/Maas delta on an Oer-Ij branch connecting the Ijsselmeer and the North Sea – provided a good starting point for naval actions in the North Sea. The camp was an advanced post in the land of the Frisians. There are two neighbouring early Imperial bases, the older (Velsen I) being the focus of attention due to its state of preservation. Its construction probably took place during the offensive of Germanicus in the years AD 15–16, which also included maritime operations up to the area of the estuaries of the Ems and Weser. The interpretation and presentation of the phases is mainly derived from work on the site by J.-M. A. W. Morel.[46] In addition, there are further discoveries from new investigations.[47]

The size of the base was about 1 ha. The period 1b camp is characterized by its basic triangular shape. On the riverside, there was a platform with two moles about midway on the fort's side. A third mole within the enclosure stood to the east. Thus there was a protected harbour. The moles consisted of wooden formwork/sheathing filled with layers of clay and straw. The eastern bank area was defended to near the platform by an earth-and-timber rampart, which might also argue that civilians had access to the port facilities. In the western half of the fort area, the only archaeologically traceable building was a 20 m-long rectangular post-built structure, which Morel interpreted as a shipshed, but this has more recently been criticized.[48] Wind and current caused silting and floods on the western side of the platform. The western mole and a pier were reinforced to counter this; the end of the central mole was replaced by a pier. Subsequently, the harbour basin was also dredged. The 'shipshed' was also moved inland. In addition, a second 12 × 30 m hall complex has now been excavated, which is interpreted as a double shipshed and could have replaced the aforementioned building.[49]

After an interim abandonment of the site, renewed occupation produced a trapezoidal enclosure this time. The port installations were also changed: the central mole was replaced by a pier and piers were also added to the other two. A new, fourth, pier was added outside the fortification. It is thought this served civilian shipping. To the west of the fort, as well as on the opposite bank, smaller satellite docks have been found, which belong to the final years of use.[50] This base was in use until the year AD 28. It is possible that the site should be identified with the fort of *Flevum*, mentioned by Tacitus, which was defended in 28 against attacking Frisians.[51]

The less well-preserved Velsen II base, which was built about 1 km to the north-west, was temporarily occupied between *c.* AD 39/40 and 47. At Velsen I, we can see a military port at a very early stage in the Roman occupation in the provinces, which, with its shipsheds and the protected harbour basin, contains two elements which are also characteristic of the Mediterranean port construction.

The construction of the port installations in wood cannot only be explained by this being almost exclusively the only building material used at this time; in addition, the material was common throughout the Imperial period for all water-based installations in the northern provinces of Gaul, Germany, and Britain. Stone moles or quays are exceptional in these regions.[58]

Cologne-Alteburg (Germany)

In the presnt-day city of Cologne, a large military camp lay in the borough of Marienburg on the Flur Alteburg (Fig. 518). With its 7 ha of land, it could have accommodated more than 1,000 personnel, when compared to an auxiliary fort where the garrison size is known. The selection of its location had been made with the same thorough consideration as was the case with the *colonia* at Cologne: the fleet base is located about 3 km south of the colony on a 16 ha-large, flood-protected terrace above the Rhine, where it had been adapted to the lie of the land in the basic form of a trapezoid (see Fischer 2005b).

The history of the camp begins with an earth-and-timber base of the late Augustan-early Tiberian period, the finds from which represent a level immediately after the end of Haltern in AD 9. The walls of this first phase might have reached down to the Rhine, an eastern wall having not yet been found. The camp on the Alteburg may have served as winter quarters for a vexillation of the 20th Legion in its early days. From the middle of the 1st century AD, the camp of Cologne-Alteburg can be identified as the camp of the *classis Germanica* from brick stamps and relevant inscriptions of members of the fleet, often of Eastern origin. In late Flavian times, the camp received stone defences, also found on the terraced edge of the eastern side facing the Rhine. Excavations in the years 1995/96 and 1998 resulted in distinct stratigraphies for the barrack accommodation with up to 11 construction phases, although they differed locally. Two burnt layers from the Trajanic period, which follow each other in short succession, contained a large number of easily datable small finds, including weapons. A harbour has not yet been archaeologically identified, but shipsheds and moorings can be supposed between the camp and the Rhine. Among the finds, there are substantial indications of craftsmanship in the camp, including sailmaking. Towards the end of the 3rd century AD, the base was destroyed and abandoned. The numismatic *terminus post quem* for the end of the camp dates to the years AD 270/3.

Gesoriacum/Boulogne-sur-Mer (France)

The main base of the British fleet lay in Boulogne-sur-Mer (Figs 519–20), which until the late 3rd century AD was called *Gesoriacum* and later *Bononia*. The foundation of the British fleet had become necessary after the occupation of

Figure 518 *Camp of the Classis Germanica in Cologne-Alteburg (after Horn 1987)*

southern England by Claudius. The military base was on a hill above the port, located on the estuary of the Liane.[52] Although the earliest archaeological evidence is from the middle of the 1st century AD, the first permanent camp is only dated to the early 2nd century AD. The defences enclose a rectangular military fortification of 12.45 ha. Archaeological investigations in the north of the fort were able to identify four barracks, each consisting of 10 *contubernia* and an officer's building. The course of important fort roads can still be roughly traced in the modern road network, especially since the medieval fortification follows the line of the Roman one. The size of the facility would allow accommodation for up to 4,000 soldiers, which thus shows the importance of the base. Its identification as a base for the British fleet is certain due to numerous brick stamps with the inscription CL.BR [*cl(assis) Br(itannica)*] as well as inscriptions of marines and sailors.[53]

The duties of the fleet in the 1st to 2nd centuries AD will mainly have lain in the maintenance of the connection between the mainland and the province of Britain, while in the third century AD, defence against Germanic pirates played an increasingly important role. The fleet commander Carausius, who ruled Britain and parts of the North Gallic coast as a usurper from AD 286/7 until 293, proved to be quite successful in this. His end was only sealed with the successful siege of *Gesoriacum* by Constantius Chlorus, to whose success the blocking of the harbour with a dam had contributed. In the late 3rd century (according to coin finds after 268/9), the military camp was at least partly

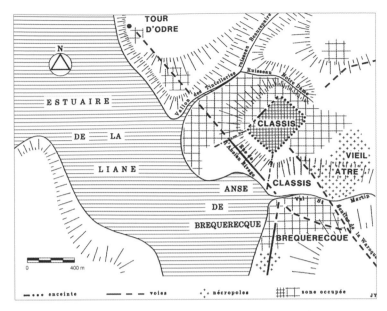

Figure 519 *Boulogne-sur-Mer. Topography (after Seillier 1996, 213)*

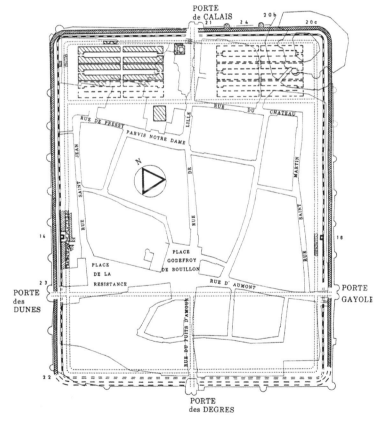

Figure 520 *Boulogne-sur-Mer. Plan of the excavations (after Seillier 1996, 214)*

demolished, levelled, and then rebuilt.[54] However, these measures cannot be dated with adequate precision through archaeology in order to ascribe the new construction to either Carausius or Constantius Chlorus. In the Late Roman period, there are still indications of the use of the

port for troop transportation; evidence for the deployment of a fleet is, however, lacking.[55]

Approximately 1 km north-west of the camp, a supposedly Roman lighthouse dating back to Caligula was located on the basis of descriptions from the 17th century.[56] However, this remains speculative.

Dubris/Dover (Britain)

Dover was predestined for a naval base due to its proximity to the European mainland. In addition, the mouth of the river Dour provided good opportunities for the construction of a relatively protected harbour (Fig. 521). Dover also occupies a special position due to the archaeologically known buildings. In addition to the fort (Fig. 522), the remains of the port facilities are known, and in particular those of a lighthouse.[57] The lighthouse (Fig. 523) has been preserved within a medieval castle and is one of the few archaeologically known buildings of this type from antiquity. There are indications of a second lighthouse on the opposite side of the estuary. The first fort, about 1 ha. in size, was erected around AD 110, but does not appear to have been completed. The next site of 1.05 ha, erected in the same place, dates from *c*. AD 125 to the first decade of the 3rd century, with two phases of reconstruction. At the end of its existence, the camp was demolished and there are also no finds of a later date from the port area. Because of its small area, which is only a fraction of that of the main camp of the British fleet in Boulogne-sur-Mer, only a small, permanently based detachment will have been stationed here. The ground plan of the fort, the defences of which have no corner or interval towers, comprises 10 barrack buildings, each with eight *contubernia*, headquarters buildings, commanding officer's houses, and store buildings. The assignment of the camp to the *classis Britannica* is supported by hundreds of brick stamps discovered there. Around 270, a new fort was built in Dover, which partially covered the older one. According to the *Notitia Dignitatum*, the *milites Tungrecani*, an army unit, were now stationed there.[58]

Conclusion and outlook

Fleet bases of the Roman Imperial era represent a specific form of ancient naval base. While the expansion of a part of the home harbour was customary for the older maritime powers in the Mediterranean, the wide-ranging distribution of the Roman bases alone already demonstrates the wide-ranging missions of the fleets and their mobility. Since professional soldiers also now took on the duties of the seamen, fort buildings, like those known from the Roman army, were probably the rule. The well-known naval bases from the northern provinces give us a good impression of these. In contrast to the Mediterranean and Black Sea, fleets

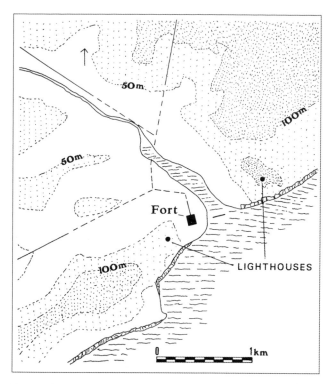

Figure 521 *Dover. Topography (according to Mason 2003, 108 Fig. 41)*

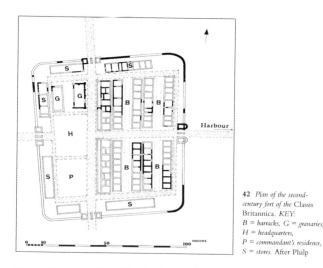

42 *Plan of the second-century fort of the* Classis Britannica. *KEY:*
B = barracks, G = granaries,
H = headquarters,
P = commandant's residence,
S = stores. After Philp

Figure 522 *Dover. Plan of the fort (according to Mason 2003, 110 Fig. 44)*

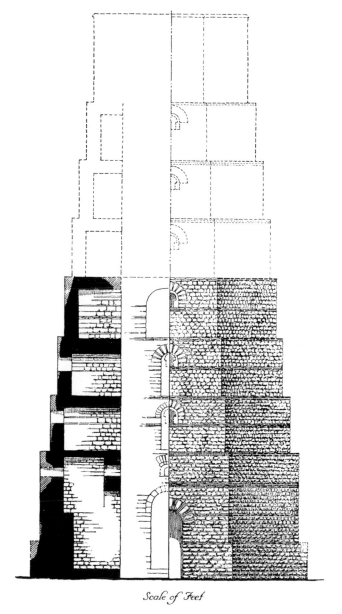

Scale of Feet

Figure 523 *Dover. Lighthouse (after Wheeler 1926, 32 Fig. 2)*

were a novelty in these regions anyway. For the former, we have knowledge that is lacking elsewhere because of the written and epigraphic tradition. The effort involved in the construction and maintenance of port facilities was sometimes immense, but this can also be demonstrated for important facilities for merchant shipping.

The solution of some unresolved questions will be reserved for future research, especially in the eastern Mediterranean. It is ultimately unclear whether or how Hellenistic naval ports like Alexandria continued to be used and which structural changes were brought about

by the stationing of Roman fleets. In the same way, it can only be supposed that smaller fleet bases in the Mediterranean, which are regularly found in existing port cities, were similarly equipped with forts as in the northern provinces. Structural changes in the naval bases that had been used continuously into Late Antiquity cannot yet be demonstrated from archaeological finds. A new development from the 4th century AD onwards is notable in the northern provinces of the empire, where several provincial fleets, after the crisis of the 3rd century, are no longer found. They were replaced by a network of small and very small bases, which were located not only on the frontiers, but also on inland waterways in the hinterland.

3. Roman warships

Ronald Bockius

Warships, small naval units and anciliary vessels

Discussion of the military use of water transport is traditionally based on historical sources; beyond the written tradition, a wealth of contemporary illustrated monuments depict their popularity and significance in society and the state. The Mediterranean and the provincial Roman warship – whether complete vessels, parts, or equipment – are accordingly encountered as stone sculptures and as miniatures made of clay, metal, or glass; more common are relief images on coins and ceramics, including lamps, on intaglios and gems, and less frequently on architectural elements, tombstones, jewellery, and implements. Two-dimensional representations include mosaic scenes, frescoes and individual painted glass, graffiti (Fig. 524) or graffiti on different materials and surfaces.[59] This huge number of monuments of varying qualities is now joined by a considerable number of actual remains. Insofar as the latter go beyond the level of a vaguely reliable identification as military vessels, they have not only influenced our established image of the 'Roman warship' in a provincial context, but also prompted consideration on the forms of tactical use. Thus it must be assumed that the commonly held stereotype of the 'galley' reinforced with a ram as a representative of ancient naval armament applied to only a part of the whole. For two or three decades, a genre of military inland waterway shipping has begun to emerge, whose priorities and most likely also the development of its equipment, seem to emerge in those Roman provinces outside the Mediterranean that were known for their dense river network.

The focus here is on vessels, the strategic value of which is based on operational characteristics and characteristics such as dimensions, crew strength, speed, and armament, as well as those which are considered to be indicative of logistical use, such as troop transports and supplies. Not least because of a highly complex tradition, our knowledge of the waterborne units of Roman fleets and army units is, of course, still incomplete.

It is well-known that the Roman Republic, unlike the Greeks and Phoenicians, cannot be counted among the maritime nations at its beginnings and, consequently, they were not developers of naval ships. The ancient tradition confirms this: even Pliny, who served as a naval prefect in the seventies of the 1st century AD, did not gainsay this (*Nat. Hist.* 7.56.207–8). It was only with the territorial seizure of the Tyrrhenian coast in the 4th century BC, and with the emergence of conflicts and hazards within the framework of a maritime environment dominated by

other states, that Rome had a fundamental need for its own tactical units, which could defend against potential opponents. In the decades around 300 BC, the Republic had just 10 to 20 larger vessels, including triremes. The base of the small fleet was presumably a station on the island of Pontia, but certainly Rome, where, after the demolition of Antium in 338 BC, shipsheds (*navalia*) and, less than twenty years later, naval commanders are mentioned (Livy 8.14:12; 30.4).

Taking a passage in Polybius (*Hist.* 1.20.9–10) literally, Roman shipyards at the beginning of the 1st Punic War were absolutely inexperienced in the construction of larger combat vessels, especially of the class of warships, naval units, and auxiliary vessels, and *penteres/quinqueremes* which were characteristic of that time ('fives', see Fig. 531.1); let alone crews that were familiar with their rowing systems. Only investigation of a captured Punic *penteris* revealed the secret of the way in which they worked. Following this model, 100 'fives' were built which, supplemented by 20 newly launched 'threes', formed the first major Roman fleet. The same passage, for the year 264 BC, concludes that lighter classes of warship, *trieres/triremes* ('threes', see Fig. 530.2) and smaller units, were available for use quite some time earlier, probably from around 400 BC. Sources that go back to the 4th to early 3rd centuries BC seem to confirm this, but they do not furnish information on further details (Diodorus 14.93.7; Livy 5.28.2; 9.26.6; 38.2–3, *Per.* 12). Early coins (*aes grave*) depicting warship prows also indicate this.[60]

In the course of the 1st and 2nd Punic Wars and during the conflicts with Macedonia and Syria, Roman combat vessels were repeatedly replaced after losses. In some cases, they were also supplemented by vessels captured in combat or by allied vessels.[61] In contrast to other maritime powers, especially the Successor states, locked in an internal arms race with their large *polyeres* (among them 'twenties', 'thirties' and greater), but also

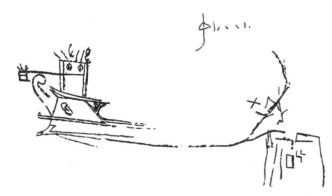

Figure 524 *Alexandria, Egypt. Graffito in a late Hellenistic grave: Warship with ram prow as well as a fighting tower erected at the stern and a fire-bowl hanging from a spar (after A. Schiff, Alexandrinische Dipinti, 1, Leipzig 1905, Plate 1)*

different from those allies, Rhodians and Pergameners, with intermediate classes (up to 'tens'), the quinquereme formed the backbone of the Republican forces in the 3rd and 2nd centuries BC. It was only with the establishment of a standing fleet following the fight against piracy in the 60s of the 1st century BC, that the course was set for the permanent rule of the sea and an independent armaments policy on Roman warships.

Agrippa again built quadriremes, quinqueremes, and *hexeres*, which were specifically designed for offensive operations, due to their size and reinforcement. But manoeuvrable, fast, oared vessels suitable for ramming (Fig. 525), in other words triremes, were also built. At Actium in 31 BC, the armada of Octavian, composed of twos, threes, and fours, supported by quinqueremes and *hexeres*, finally defeated the warships assembled by Anthony in the East, vessels up to the class of decemreme. If the trireme counted among the light classes during engagements, fives up to tens were suitable for loading with defensive equipment and the inclusion of large boarding parties.[62] The greater potential velocity is confirmed by the former, while the quinquereme turned better under oars (Livy 28.30.5–6.11), doubtless because the five was not much longer than the three, but its crew was twice the strength and generated greater thrust with more men on the oars. The quinquereme, like all higher classes of ships, belonged to the covered vessels (*naves tectae* or *constratae*, as opposed to *apertae naves*). Incidental references to the appearance, the architectural peculiarities, the dimensions, and the strengths or characteristics of Roman warships are rare, but there is a quite useful and highly welcome addition to the archaeological sources: *i.e.* boats and ships were painted (Pliny, *Nat. Hist.* 35.31.49; 41.149), partly also with camouflage paint (Vegetius, *Epit.* 4.37). The height above the waterline is reported for a specific class;[63] it is clear from another passage that triremes possessed a draught which was considerably less than the height of a man (Frontinus, *Str.* 2.5.43). Of similar value is information about a Roman trireme captured during the Batavian uprising (Tacitus, *Hist.* 5.22.3), which was towed up the Lippe, and repeated references to 'threes' and even 'fours' going up the Tiber as far as the city limits of Rome in order to be employed in staged battles (*naumachiae*) under Caesar and Augustus (Suet., *Iul.* 39.4; *Res Gestae* 4.43–4). The earliest records of warships brought to Rome date back to the year 338 BC, when contingents were placed in the docks (*navalia*) on the east bank of the river after seizing the fleet from Antium (Livy 8.14.12).[64] In the year 213 BC, a Macedonian fleet of sea-going *lembi* with double banks of oars travelled up the southern Albanian River Seman (Apsus) as far as it flowed through the coast plain to the mountainous region (Livy 24.40.2).

According to these historical records, the draughts of even comparatively large vessels has to be estimated

Figure 525 *Traufsima, terracotta, probably from Central Italy. Relief representation of a ramming attack. (Photo: Chr. Beeck, RGZM)*

as being as small as possible, measurable in centimetres rather than metres. Even with the available information often being very imprecise, they do contain extremely useful information for the assessment of size; with the large crew numbers named in the literature for the oared vessels, either their dimensions tend to be overestimates or unsuitable comparisons with modern steel ships are made. The written tradition – mainly consisting of ancient literature and inscriptions – distinguishes classes of ships according to a nomenclature (Figs 529–32). The structure and numerical graduation of fairly complex oar-powered systems can be deduced from these terms, whose principle of action has only been worked out through a long process of historical research.[65] However, this is by no means enough to provide a three-dimensional picture of the seaworthy Roman warship: among the few archaeological remains of Mediterranean combat ships a few rams (Fig. 526), which are attributed to small- to medium-sized classes of vessel, are important. Their national origin can only be identified using examples from the stylistic derivation of decorations or inscriptions; allocation to actual types of ships, which was attempted according to the size and weight of the weapons, remains quite uncertain. On the basis of comparisons of original rams (*rostra tridentes*) with depictions of them (*e.g.* Figs 539–42), the weapons of Roman warships were not typologically distinguishable from those of other states.[66]

The underwater discovery west of Capo Rasocolmo near the northern tip of Sicily offers evidence from the loss of a small ship, which from the range of coins (34 examples) was

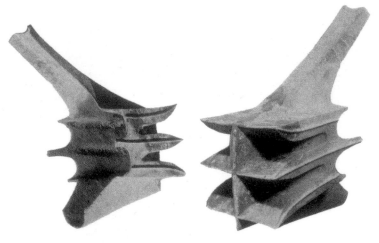

Figure 526 *Bronze ram prow. From the Mediterranean Sea, probably found off the Palestinian coast by trawling (Deutsches Schiffahrtsmuseum, Bremerhaven, Germany). Photograph: R. Müller, RGZM)*

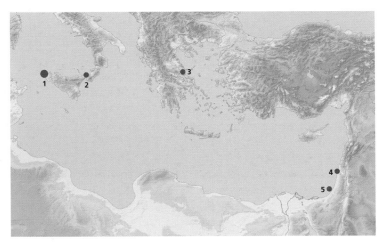

Figure 527 *Distribution of ancient rams of Greek, Punic, and Roman origin (1 = Levanzo, 2 = Acqualadroni, 3 = Cape Artemision, 4 = Athlit, 5 = Gaza naval territory [uncertain])*

destroyed around 36 BC in the civil war. Nothing remained from the ship's hull, which had evidently burned, but melted lead sheathing, fittings, and rigging. Fifteen quern stones with wear marks may be regarded as ballast. Compared to the usual composition of finds from Mediterranean shipwrecks, the absence of any cargo, and especially of inventory, is unusual. No less significant are 100 slingshots, as well as an inscription associated with Gnaeus Pompeius Magnus (106–48 BC). These clues were seen as justifying the identification of the ship as a late Republican oared warship,[67] but there is room for speculation about the nature of the vessel: it may have been a sailing vessel, and even its military nature cannot be regarded as certain. Piracy was never completely eliminated; accordingly, armed traders were the rule rather than the exception, and the vessel now lying in 8 m depth of water may already have been cleared in antiquity.

Since there is no single wreck available that can be identified as the remains of a Roman multiple banked ship, the treatment of the subject must make do with secondary sources. In consequence, when reconstructing warships of superior rank, we have to be content with reconstruction drawings based on comparisons between contemporary representations and information from the historical sources. The occasional technical realisation of warship model replicas, marine vessels, or auxiliary vessels in museums or as experimental replicas is based on marine archaeological knowledge of the constructional features of ancient freighters. On the other hand, some archaeological finds from Imperial Italy and the northern provinces allow for the assessment or justification of the military character of small vessels, as well as illuminating them in a typological and constructive way. Circumstances of preservation often offer excellent conditions for a marine archaeological evaluation, although the historical record and contemporary iconography, with certain exceptions, unfortunately provide little information for this group. It is not worth examining every vessel for military use, because they were not typologically different from others: in its simplest form, such a vessel may be no more than a makeshift or multi-purpose boat, such as an amphora raft or dugout canoe,[68] or could have been a pontoon for a floating bridge, used as a fire ship against enemy forces (Frontinus, *Str.* 4.7.14). Boats designed for tactical or logistical tasks (Fig. 528), or freighters, whether used in the inland waterways, offshore or at sea, must be considered as in civilian use until they were used for military purposes.

It is in the nature of the subject that encountering an actual object close-up, especially if of any constructional and technical sophistication, provides more information than a literary description or overly artistic representation, perhaps also influenced by inferior workmanship. Wrecks can, in favourable circumstances, also reveal organizational background, provide information on the origin of the builders of a destroyed vessel, and even provide solid data on the anatomy of its users. Not least, it helps to gauge the strategic understanding of those who commissioned it.

Roman multi-level ships up to the end of the Republic

In this period, naval forces were composed of very different units: comparatively small vessels were used for reconnaissance, escort duty, outpost and communications boats, barrage breakers or fast troop transports. Among these were boats and light ships with small complements and with a single row of oars (in the sources referred to as *actuariae, celoces, lembi* and λέμβοι, *pristes, scaphae, speculatoriae naves, parva navigia,* and so on). Their tactical advantages were manoeuverability and small draught, so they could reach areas of shallow water. Doubtless, they were available in large numbers and could be quickly replaced after loss. Furthermore, the fleets had ships

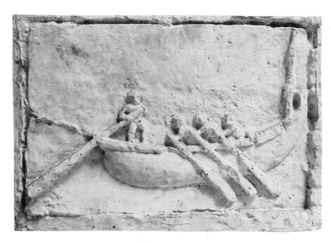

Figure 528 *Ostia, Isola Sacra. Trench construction. 2nd cent. Terracotta plate with relief picture of a towboat*

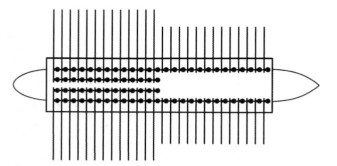

Figure 529 *Schematic representation of the rowing system on a hemiolia (after Meijer 1986, 141 Fig. 9.4)*

that were largely non-combatant or at least not usable offensively: auxiliary and specialist ships, horse carriers, and cargo vessels existed/were used – according to modern parlance marine tenders (*cercuri, hippagogi, onerariae*).[69] We have to imagine these as being requisitioned on an ad hoc basis from the civilian fleet and perhaps refitted, but not really intended for naval warfare. In addition, the Roman Republic used multi-bank ships with the ram, *embolon/rostrum*, as well as other offensive and long-range weapons,[70] along with tactical equipment (for example, turrets and fighting platforms).[71] In the case of the heavier vessels, the four- and five-banked quadriremes and quinqueremes formed the backbone of contingents operating under the Roman flag, while *hexeres/hexaremes* – rarely mentioned in the sources, but a class with 500 oarsmen according to Diodorus (20.112.4) – had been used from the 1st Punic War on as a flagship (Polybius, *Hist.*, 1.26.11; Livy 29.9.8). Large polyremes, like the 'sixteen' taken from Philip V of Macedonia following the Roman victory during the Second Macedonian War in 196 BC, were commonly found in the fleets of allied states or, as in this case, taken as war booty (Livy 33.30.5–6; 45.35.3). Among the lighter warships were the triremes, plus a three-row variant with a shortened oar bank (*trihemiolia* or 'two-and-a-halfer'), as well as vessels of different designs with two banks of oars, including one type with unequal rows and banks of oars (*hemiolia* or 'one-and-and-halfer': Fig. 529).[72]

Warships differed according to their oar systems (Figs 530–2) and usually had sails that were removed before battle, unless all the rigging except for the foremast was stowed away. One reads of open (aphract) and covered (cataphract) vessels, which could be 'armoured' with metal plating. Armour of this kind, as well as the construction of towers, catapults and stone throwers, and sometimes siege devices (Livy 24.33.4–6; 27.15.5, 32.16.10) increased the weight, so that artillery and superstructures on the upper deck could affect the centre of gravity. The former had to be compensated for by the naval architect (*architectus navalis*) when designing the size and shape of the ship's hull for increased buoyancy; the latter required appropriate measures to minimize the unstable trim of a vessel, in particular the risk of capsizing at sea. Both were achieved by broadening a hull relative to its length and/or by changing the profile of the ship's bottom and sides. Compromises in ship design and the compensation in actual construction of the ship for military requirements affected the changing operating characteristics of a vessel, such as a need for more propulsive power, reduced sprint behaviour, and limited manoeuvrability. The tactical advantage of such heavy combat ships were not speed and manoeuvrability, but their superior offensive and defensive armament, making them comparatively unassailable. The only archaeological examples of this type, two vessels representing the appearance, hull shape, and construction of a heavy warship, were provided by two wrecks (Fig. 533) in the lake in a crater near Nemi in the Alban Hills, which unfortunately fell victim to the Second World War.[73] Judging by their equipment, these were the remains of special vessels – one originally carried a luxuriously furnished, stone-built palace, the other a temple probably dedicated to the goddess Isis – built for the emperor Caligula (AD 12–41), regarded as autocratic and lavish, for his pleasure on the lake. One of the vessels (*nave seconda*) was an oared ship with outriggers and multiple oars, each operated by at least two men, according to the surviving remains. On both hulls, lead sheathing had been retained as a means of avoiding bottom-fouling growth.[74] Since this technique is only otherwise seen on seagoing ships, and not inland waterway vessels, the planning and construction of the Nemi ships might have involved a naval dockyard which had experience in the construction of polyremes.[75]

The vessels, over 70 m long, approximately 20 m or 24 m wide, one with elements reminiscent of a warship – the outline of a prow, one row of oars on either side (monoreme system), and outriggers – were not only impressive; as largely wooden constructions, the hulls were

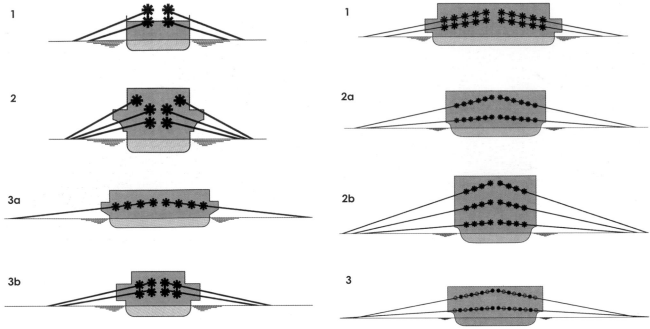

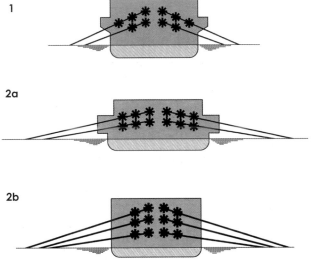

Figure 530 *Rowing systems of ancient warships. Schematic, idealised hull cross-sections with arrangement of sweeps and crew (selection): 1 dieres/bireme; 2 trieres/trireme; 3 one (a) and two-row (b) tetreres/quadrireme.*

Figure 531 *Two-row penteres/quinquereme; 2 two- (a) and three-bank (b) hexeres/hexareme; 3 two-bank okteres/octere*

Figure 532 *1 Two-bank dekeres/decemreme; 2 two- (a) and three-bank (b) dodekeres/duodecimreme; 3 double-rowed hekkaidekeres/sedecimreme with sweeps in each of four groups facing each other (partly after Meijer 1986).*

hulls and their stability and buoyancy in water by means of structural and formative measures: a sophisticated system of supports and longitudinal and transverse members, partly using iron lashing straps to reinforce the carpentry and spread the load and physical forces over the hull. The outer shell had integrated strakes, keel, and side keels. The strong plank skin, fastened together with mortise-and-tenon joints, as well as iron and wooden nails to fix the segmented frames, produced a rigid, torsion-free floating hull. The flat bottom, changing into a rounded chine to relatively steep sides, combined with a small length-to-width ratio for the hull, would have ensured sufficient transverse stability.

Without doubt the Nemi ships were a shipbuilding masterpiece in terms of size and quality of the build, design and construction being adapted to the special conditions of operation and their function: following the tradition of Thalamegos at the time of the Ptolemies,[76] the client burdened the shipyard with extreme requirements,[77] which would neither be militarily nor nautically useful for a seagoing warship.

In the case of a warship, a lighter internal design can be assumed, probably also a hull cross-section with a flat bottom that falls off into a V towards the keel and counteracted lateral drift, and last but not least a narrower design with a significantly longer length-to-width ratio. The 480 rowers of a *hexeres*/hexareme (see Diodorus 20.112.4), housed in 40 units of 2 × 6 men along its length amidships, would find enough space in a hull shorter than that of the

astonishingly long, even compared to shipbuilding as late as the 19th century.

Their designers solved the problem of the weights high above the waterline and the resulting risks for the rigidity of

Figure 533 *Lago di Nemi. Monumental shipwreck from the time of Caligula (AD 37–41). Recovery of Nemi 2 in 1929*

Figure 534 *Experimental replica of the Trajanic crewed boat, Oberstimm 1, during a trial voyage on the Ratzeburger See. Photo: Chr. Schäfer, Trier*

giant ships from Lake Nemi: according to Vitruvius (*Arch.* 1.2.21–4), and underpinned by the technical analysis of oared vessels found on both sides of the Alps, the modular length between oars (*interscalmium*) was a little less than one metre along the length of a vessel.[78] Whether the oars had one or several rowers, or with up to three banks of oars on top of each other, each basic module was multiplied by a factor which produced the number of rowers: *penteres/* quinqueremes with 300 (Polybios, *Hist.* 1.26.8) or 400 men (Plinius, *Hist.*, 32.1.4; Silius, *Pun.* 14.388), had 30 (30 × 5 rowers per ship side = 300 men) or 40 (40 × 5 rowers × 2 = 400) rowing modules. The middle sections of such polyremes were about 26 to 27 or 35 to 36 m long. By comparison, a boat or ship with a single bank of oars, manned with 50 rowers – in other words with the simplest arrangement of a single row of oars on each side – took up 23 to 24 m, a disproportionate amount of the ship's length. On the other hand, with a double module of 12 or 13 oars on top of each other, the rowing section could be shortened to less than 12 m with the same crew size.

In order to minimize collisions between the oar blades moving up and down as well as the mutual obstruction of the rowing benches (Fig. 534), the design engineers allowed for an offset of at least several tens of centimetres longitudinally between the vertical ranks on vessels with two or three banks of oars (Fig. 535). As an extreme case, Pisa Wreck C shows a horizontal offset of an entire length module. The arrangement scheme of thole pins, or oar ports if present, and the necessary technical equipment of oar propulsion (thwarts and foot stretchers) inside the hull were coordinated mechanically as well as biometrically and physiologically for the rowers. It led to a reasonably precise, three-dimensional distribution of men, seating, equipment, and fittings. The method of construction ensured operationally efficient, compact accommodation for the rowers, particularly on lighter, flat-built two- and three-bank vessels with a narrow hull

and a shallow draught. For example, laterally overhanging woodwork structures (outriggers) with thole pins mounted on them helped to separate the rowers using oars with a largely fixed lever ratio within the two to three banks, and avoided clashes in use caused by bodily contact or collisions between the oars. Very broad hull designs, such as heavy combat ships with large numbers of oars, developed without outriggers.

Closer identification of purely Republican warships is extremely difficult. The relative rarity of reasonably meaningful and datable monuments is less problematic than the fact that contemporary representations at best show the number of rows of oars, whereas details associated with the classification are largely unknown. Sometimes contents or details of propaganda images, if they can be referred to a historical event, can indicate the class of ships depicted.[79]

The iconographic tradition does not produce much on the Roman Republican warship. Numismatic representations[80] reflect military successes of the sea, but also demonstrate the typological similarities with Hellenistic and Phoenician warships.[81] It is not surprising that preference was given to vessels of higher classes – indicated by recognizable battlements or other installations.[82] Although details cannot really be identified more closely, on the moneyers' *denarii* minted in the late 2nd century BC, there are tower-like constructions to the fore and aft of the ship, as well as to some extent gallery-like installations amidships.[83] *Aes* coins issued at the time of the Macedonian Wars show various prows with frame-shaped structures,[84] which may be interpreted as symbolic representations of Roman archery weapons or boarding devices (Fig. 536). Other details on the foredeck, recognizable on late *aes grave* and coinage of the early 1st century BC, may also be seen as artillery or boarding equipment.[85]

An undoubtedly Roman monument (only attested numismatically), the *columna rostrata* of Gaius Duilius,

Figure 535 *Experimental replica of an Attic trireme of the 5th/4th century BC. Vertical and horizontal distribution of the rowers (after Morrison and Coates 1990)*

Figure 536 *Republican quadrans (after Hassel 1985, Plate 34)*

Figure 537 *Fragment of a Doric frieze. Warship with single bank of oars, battle structures, and combat crew. Giordani Necropolis, Rome (Museo della Civiltà Romana, copy in the Museum für Antike Schiffahrt Mainz in Mainz). Warships, naval units, auxiliary vessels*

the victor of a naval battle near Mylaie (260 BC), was once set up in the Roman Forum and later lost,[86] naturally only represented the front portions of enemy ships and is only of marginal interest. Reliefs and paintings from the 3rd to early 2nd century BC on Calene ware and Etruscan ceramics[87] depict three-bank vessels with a prow and upper prow, as well as with enclosed outriggers, partly also with oar ports; the former variant resembles the type of Hellenistic warships known in particular from the ship monument of Nike on Samothrace, the Barberini mosaic, and the Isola Tiberiana monument.[88] As a two-banked vessel, the same type appears in the form of a relief of Pentelic marble, dated around 30 BC, in Rome,[89] as a three-banker on the monument to Cartilius Poplicola erected a little later in Ostia.[90] The oval shields with a spindle-shaped rib, which can be seen there above the outrigger defending the crew, recur as a motif on a covered outrigger on a relief on a Doric frieze with historical elements,[91] probably dating from the early Imperial period, from the Giordani necropolis in Rome.

The copy of a Hellenistic painting on the Esquiline is not very useful,[92] any more than the contrasting *naves longae* on a bronze diadem of the 3rd and 2nd centuries BC from

Tarquinia,[93] and similarly the mid-Italian relief depictions on simas and terracotta friezes.[94] Hellenistic-Phoenician ship portrayals from Asia Minor and North Africa[95] are not considered representations of Roman warships, and neither are late Hellenistic graffiti on Delos.[96] Nevertheless, they must be considered as contemporary reference material.

Figure 538 *Fragment of a relief block. Two warships with double banks of oars and combat crew (Naples museum, copy in the Museum für Antike Schiffahrt Mainz)*

This is not true of a relief block dated at the earliest to the 2nd century BC (in the National Museum, Naples[97]), but which may also belong in the 1st century AD from its depictions of helmet and shield forms referencing historic Italic and Roman armament. It shows two-bank vessels with tightly packed armed men (Fig. 538). The outlines of the ships are reminiscent of the later Neumagen type. A motif characteristic of late Republican and early Imperial warships on Central Italian monuments is the mass of marines,[98] who can sometimes be identified as legionaries.[99]

According to their combat equipment, heavy vessels with only one bank of oars, each probably with more than one rower (Fig. 540), in fact also belong here. As with warships of other nations, the ram (Fig. 526), armoured with three horizontal ribs and appearing during the 5th century BC, can be seen as a hallmark of Republican to Julio-Claudian

Figure 539 *Fragment of a pedestal relief from the Temple of Fortuna in Praeneste. Heavy warship with tower construction and two or three banks of oars. The depiction shows an onboard parade. Dating: 30s BC (after Bockius 2007)*

Figure 540 *Relief with a scene from a sea battle (naumachia?). Location unknown (formerly private collection in Seville, photo DAI Rome, after Baatz and Bockius 1997)*

Figure 541 *Fragment of a grave from Mainz-Weisenau. Covered warship with catapults (?). First half of the 1st century (Arch. Denkmalpflege Mainz, copy in the Museum für Antike Schiffahrt Mainz)*

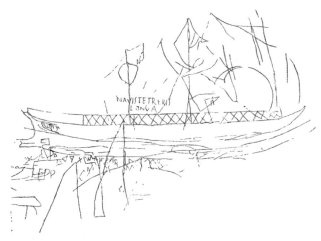

Figure 542 *Graffito on the Temple of Apollo at Alba-Fucens (Albe, Lazio). Depiction of a 'four' with the inscription NAVIS TETRERIS LONGA. Probably Claudian (after M. Guarducci, Notizi Scavi 1953, 120 Fig. 6)*

warship depictions (Fig. 541).[100] This weapon, usually cast from bronze and effective at penetrating the enemy hull planking, became rarer in the 1st century AD, but only appears to have been abandoned in the middle Imperial period.[101]

The depiction of a ship identified by the inscription *navis tetreris longa* as a quadrireme (Fig. 542) is particularly noteworthy. The graffito was discovered on the podium of the Temple of Apollo at Alba Fucens in Abruzzo.[102] The unusual location could be related to the naval battles (*naumachiae*) organized by the Emperor Claudius on the neighbouring Fucine Lake, in which squadrons of triremes and quadriremes are supposed to have fought each other.[103] The outline of the ship from Alba resembles the vessel on the

reverse of a Neronian *as* from Patras, undoubtedly a naval flagship.[104] In the case of a heavier design, its arrangement of rowers can be imagined as a single bank with four to an oar (see Fig. 530.3a); in the case of a narrower version with two banks, two men to an oar (Fig. 530.3b; 546). Depending on the shape and size of the hull, it was not always necessary to have an outrigger to support the oars.[105] Conscious of the Republican history of naval warfare and its iconographic representation, but also bearing in mind the monumental wrecks from Lake Nemi, it can be assumed that Roman naval yards followed the traditions and standards of Hellenistic polyremes.[106]

That the Republican naval shipbuilding programmes did not build imitations of the high-ranking, sometimes mammoth polyremes of Hellenistic princes and kings, but were instead content with a moderate level up to the 'six' and, if necessary, calling upon the assistance of heavier units in Allied fleet operators, marks the sober, pragmatic view of Roman politicians and the military. Exceptions, such as the Liburnian *deceres* commissioned by Caligula, according to Suetonius (*Cal.* 37.2), can be imagined as floating palaces with the oars of a 'ten', perhaps comparable to an Imperial yacht,[107] or as the 'pleasure boats' of a despot's wasteful amusement. The fact that naval battles, which were staged at the end of the Roman Republic for the first time as public spectacles, were becoming a popular means of Imperial propaganda in the early Principate,[108] even allowed the construction of irregular, unseaworthy warships which were suitable only for spectacles of this kind.

Warships of the Roman Empire

As can be inferred from the historical tradition, not least from the epigraphic evidence for Roman fleets, the naval forces of the time of the Principate mainly had biremes and triremes as multi-oared warships; quadriremes and quinqueremes are only recorded in the Italian squadrons,[109] and the only hexareme lay in the Italian base at *Misenum* as a flagship, presumably with the traditional name *Ops*, possibly repeatedly reissued.[110] Thus the types of ships deployed differed from those under the Roman Republic in that the fleets had fewer high-status and more lightweight vessels. In addition, there was a preference for manoeuvrable and fast-paced ships with two banks of oars and about 50 oarsmen (biremes), with which Rome had already become acquainted as pirate vessels in the First Illyrian War of 230/229 BC and whose Late Republican counterpart had contributed to the victory of Agrippa at Actium. As a light, open rowing vessel, the type was referred to in the sources as *lembos* or *liburna* – the latter term later synonymous with the 'warship' par excellence – and was also popular with Cilician pirates. Nobody knows exactly what happened to it in Roman military shipyards.[111] It is true that the warship par excellence of the classical epoch, the trireme, had also changed in the course of naval history. If the flagship of

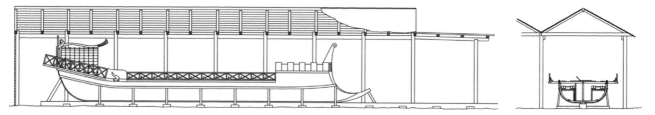

Figure 543 *Haltern-Hofestatt an der Lippe. Suggested reconstruction: shipshed with slipway in timber-framed structure from the excavated remains (see Fig. 516)*

the armed forces in Lower Germany (*praetoria navis*), a trireme (*triremis*) (Fig. 530.2), captured during the Batavian uprising, could be dragged up the Lippe, the (empty) vessel could hardly have had more than a few tens of centimetres in draught. Such vessels are no longer comparable with the Greek warship of the 5th and 4th centuries BC, reconstructed as having a length of more than 30 m at the water line and with a draught of almost 1 m.[112] On the other hand, the shipshed ground plans revealed at Haltern-Hofestatt demonstrate that, in the mid-Augustan period, hulls of up to about 25 m in length could be hauled up (Figs 516, 543), probably vessels of a lighter design and one or two banks of oars.[113] These albeit slight clues are nevertheless appropriate to identify the approximate size and weight of warships used for inland navigation. However, the classification of their arrangement of oars remains problematic. In principle, nonetheless, the existence of two- (biremes) and three-bank (triremes) vessels can be assumed, the design and size of which sufficed for use on inland waters.[114] We learn in passing that a trireme risked capsizing if the weight of its oarsmen shifted (Tac., *Ann.* 14.4.3; 5.2); accordingly such vessels, despite a rowing crew which can hardly have been fewer than 150 men, must have been light and narrow and without many reserves of space or buoyancy. Their construction will have had the minimum necessary for their military requirements, especially speed: a functional oar arrangement as well as a suitable accommodation system for the oarsmen. There was literally no room for facilities for comfort or longer sea voyages. The same may be said for biremes, and for light monoremes nothing else seems possible.

A straightforward chronological list of Imperial warships based on typological criteria can only be provided by numismatics along with comparisons with other iconographic monuments. By and large, no nautical subjects were struck during the early Imperial period, those that were conveying the *pax Romana* at sea to the people. As a coin type, the warship was not prominent until the early 2nd century AD. Nevertheless, it can be assumed that the appearance of late Republican warships did not change markedly until at least the middle of the 1st century AD. Frescoes from the towns around Vesuvius,[115] including the wall painting in the fourth style with the scene of a *naumachia* in the house of the Vettii, show multi-banked vessels with a covered outrigger,

the oars of which emerge below the lateral facings.[116] The rowing sections are completed at the top with an X-pattern balustrade, which seems to mark the edge of a deck area for combatants. A similarly equipped ship on a fresco from Herculaneum also has tall structures or fighting towers,[117] so that the vessel type can be identified as a quadrireme or quinquereme. The vessels with three banks ('threes') depicted on reliefs from Puteoli, however, can be seen as representatives of a lighter design, since their rowers are exposed,[118] so their interpretation as triremes seems likely. Typological changes, such as the more concave shape of the bow, markedly projecting rams without obvious tactical value, as well as the vaulted command shelter (tent) on the poop deck, which are so typical for ship depictions on Trajan's Column,[119] are already found on Neronian provincial reliefs, on the frescoes in the Temple of Isis at Pompeii, as well as on Claudio-Neronian terra sigillata, on relief-decorated Wetterau ware, and on a Cologne tombstone of the 1st century.[120] The *asses* (Fig. 544) issued at Patras on the occasion of Nero's visit (*adventus Augusti*), clearly show reduced forecastles, but also the rowing crew amidships, as far as they were understood by viewers in ancient reality. Both features are also shown on the two two- and three-bank warships depicted in the middle of a relief on Trajan's Column, Cichorius Scene LXXIX, which are differentiated from the vessel depicted in the lower left by their high-boarded nature (Fig. 545). The ship in the middle, which is being steered by the Emperor Trajan, with three banks of oars, the top bank of which is depicted with one man to each oar, can be identified as a 'five' (quinquereme)

Figure 544 *As, issued on the occasion of the visit of Emperor Nero to Patras. Reverse with warship facing left (Schaaff 2003, Cat. No. P16a).*

Figure 545 *Trajan's Column in Rome, Forum of Trajan. Cichorius relief Scene LXXIX: the Roman fleet crosses the Adriatic Sea (copy in the Museum für Antike Schiffahrt Mainz)*

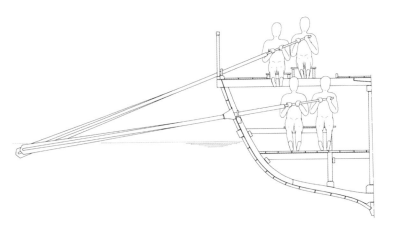

Figure 546 *Reconstruction. Cross-section of a Roman quadrireme, based on the graffito of a ship from Alba-Fucens. Scale 1:80 (after Bockius 1997)*

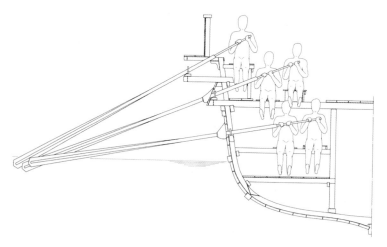

Figure 547 *Reconstruction. Cross-section of a Roman quinquereme, based on the pedestal relief from Praeneste (Fig. 539). Scale 1:80 (after Bockius 1997)*

(Fig. 547), assuming the representation is realistic. However, the arrangement of the oars does not make any sense: the flanking warships, or at least the upper one, have to be understood as high-status vessels. Just as the lead ship was shown with just one man to an oar, but unlike the latter with only two banks of oars, the subordinate vessels would have to be classed as biremes with double-manned oars top and bottom; except for the questionable technical rowing layout combining oars with (top) single and (below) double manning or even a larger crew. If the depiction of the rowers is seen as an artistic concession to how crowded the area depicted is, and allowed for the upper bank of rowers as also being double-manned oars, then the triple-bank vessel in the middle is a hexeres, the upper ship with two banks of oars and architectural forecastle is a quadrireme (Fig. 546) or quinquereme (Fig. 547), and the flat, double-rank ship in the lower field can be interpreted as a quadrireme.[121] For a Roman flagship, the stretched ship outlines on Neronian coin depictions seem more realistic than the column reliefs. Hadrianic coins of different denominations show the same pattern, the vessels either underway with oars and with a spritsail at the bow, or with the mainsail set on the main mast.[122] The series can be traced through coins until the early 3rd century AD.[123]

A distinctive difference to the late Republican/early Imperial period warship is seen in the arrangement of crew and oars: since the later 1st century AD, the crews of multi-bank oared vessels are no longer housed in or behind an outrigger or completely hidden behind gunwales, but divided into divisions within the hull and on the deck, with the upper bank being visible to the observer. The banks of oars partly protrude below the facing of the outrigger or are stretched by railings from the hull, their shafts partly passing through oar ports. This concept results in a relatively low gunwale and a comparatively light design. If this is what was intended, there will have been exceptions, such as the flagship *Ops* at *Misenum*, which is not known from iconographic evidence.[124]

If the iconography of Roman warships on coins of the high Imperial period is compared to representations on contemporary art, doubts about the veracity of the depictions increase quickly. Coins minted under Elagabalus (218–22) still show the rigging dominated by mainmast and spritmast, as well as the conventional shape characterized by a ram and upper ram (Fig. 548.1). The *stolos* (figurehead) and poop, on the other hand, wither into extensions protruding horizontally over the stem fore and aft and forming a horizontal extension of the gunwale, ending in an oversized *aphlaston* (curved stern post) aft. On the poop behind it is a vertical flag staff. The foredeck is depicted unrealistically shortened. Instead of the vaulted shelter on the bridge depicted on the issues of earlier emperors, a helmsman is now forced into the curvature of the S-shaped *aplustre*, looming over the crew depicted on Elagabalus' *denarii*, differing among issues. The identification of an exposed rowing crew – which seems to be the case – rather indicates light ships,[125] but the impression is blurred by the coins of Cilicia and Syria.[126] According to North African mosaic depictions from the 3rd century AD and provincial coins from the period up to the middle of the century, the construction of contemporary warships differs from the previous pattern only in the absence of defences integrated into the hull structure, in particular the forecastle.[127] Nautically useful gunwales, offset vertically from the central section of the ship, pass over into outriggers, so that the flattened appearance of the vessels indicated by the more or less stylized coin representations is closer to reality. Large vessels still have overhanging poops,[128] and for their oar arrangement we can still assume two rows of oars.[129]

The heavily stylized ship depictions of the *aes* and silver coins issued under Postumus (AD 260–9 AD) (Fig. 548.2) seem to be no more informative.[130] The highly extended, towering stern of the ship, the linearly arranged outriggers and geometrically simplified, but distinctive rams and upper rams, show the same pattern of a high Imperial warship as encountered on the representations from Ephesus and Side from the time of Gallienus.[131] A detail in the form of a crozier-like device (Fig. 548.2), understood as an emblematic element,[132] can only be the greatly shortened depiction of the bridge shelter, which is still present in late antique representations.[133] Nevertheless, it must be borne in mind that different types of propulsive system can be concealed behind the iconographic design, although the designation of outrigger constructions suggests a multi-level oar arrangement. At least the dies of the iconographic coin sources under consideration do not give the impression that the lighter models from the fleet, including completely uncovered boats, are intended here.

The motif from the time of Postumus of a picture of a warship reduced to the essentials also characterized the issues of Carausius and Allectus until the nineties of the 3rd century,[134] but lost its highly cipher-like character. The ships' silhouettes were shared by vessels of apparently different sizes and types, but usually show outriggers which were edged with lattice or closed gunwales, sometimes also rows of round shields.[135] Differences in the form of *stolos* and *acrostolion* or the plasticity of the ship's bow and stern indicate a variety of ship types. The crew can nearly always be seen, even armed men standing on deck on the variants *RIC* 55 and 129[136] of the series (Fig. 548.3). Some of the imperial issues under Allectus (AD 293–6),[137] as well as a heavy gold medallion from the Trier mint (Fig. 549), unmistakably invoke the type represented by the so-called Trier (or Neumagen) wine ship. It can be recognized on late-Severan sculpture, as well as on its Late Roman parallels, by means of the sharply separated gunwales leading into an outrigger with lattice railings, through animal-head protomes pointing towards the

Figure 548 *Coins with representations of ships. 1 Denarius of Elagabalus. RIC 188. Reverse with warship facing right (Schaaff 2003, Cat. No. 60a). 2 Antoninianus of Postumus. RIC 73. Reverse with a warship facing left (Schaaff 2003, Cat. No. 61 g). 3 Aes of Allectus. RIC 129. Reverse with a warship facing right, with a combat crew on it (Schaaff 2003, Cat. No. 83a)*

bow, and the vaulted shelter on the poop deck.[138] Similar depictions on the Trier monument, mosaic representations from the middle of the 4th century in the villa at Low Ham, Somerset, and on small objects, like a needle head (Fig. 550),[139] illustrate the transport of supplies packed in barrels by vessels of the navy, presumably carrying out military logistical operations.[140]

The Neumagen type is by no means a variety of Roman warship limited to the north-western part of the empire, but even the eastern Mediterranean region can be considered as its area of use, as indicated by graffiti in the Horologium of Andronikos in Athens.[141] However, the iconographic sources mentioned also reveal the fact that there is no question of uniformity in the classificatory sense. While the use of an outrigger and a double bank of oars can be assumed for the vessels built like the Trier wine ship, the Aeneas mosaic in Low Ham only depicts a single row of oars passed through oar ports, which have to be imagined as

Figure 549 *Gold medallion from the Arras hoard, issued by the Trier mint on the occasion of the re-conquest of Britain under Constantius Chlorus. Obverse with warship of the Neumagen type*

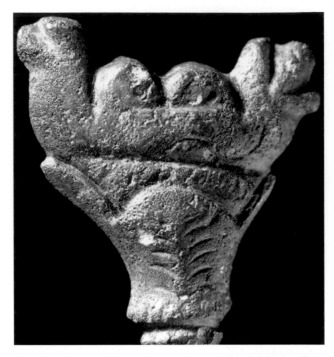

Figure 550 *Fragment of a needle with a bronze figural head from Altrier. Representation of a ship with a cargo of barrels (after F. Dövener)*

being served by a crew located beneath the deck. Depictions contemporary to this on *folles* of Constantine the Great and an issue of Constans I from Antioch[142] likewise show oared vessels with single banks of oars. They are consistent as proof of the single bank of oars, with respect to the fact that the outrigger with the lattice railing[143] can be recognized there, although, because of their high freeboard, seaworthy units are intended.[144] The historical sources on Constantine's fleet seem to contradict the multiple manning of oars of vessels with single banks of oars. Nevertheless, the use of double-bank oared warships is still to be expected in the case of the triconters and penteconters mentioned there, with just 30 or 50 men's helmets; there were even triremes on the side of Constantine's opponent Licinius. Rare issues depicting open boats built with a sharp stern, without a ram, with armed men on board,[145] indicate that the type played an increasing role in the second half of the 3rd century. This is the period to which the older shipwrecks at Mainz belong, our knowledge about their original form being inadequate.[146]

The absence of a working upper ram is a tangible difference between Late Roman iconography and depictions from the high Imperial period. This element, which was originally used when ramming an opponent as a metal-clad deflector, was reduced in the 4th century AD to a functionless vestigial feature. At best one can still recognize the protrusions of fenders projecting beyond the stern, these no longer terminated in a fitting designed to absorb the impact of the force, deflecting it from the

hull of the ship. Similarly, nothing indicates that units had a poop deck. The abandonment of the representation of rowers, which is already characteristic of Constantine coin images, is evidence for a 'cataphract' design, or covered accommodation for the rowers within the hull, without which it might be thought they were special light, small vessels. Last but not least, the class of dromons,[147] which is more clearly defined in the middle-Byzantine sources, suggests that their literarily attested double banks are a continuation of the Late Roman tradition.[148] Bearing in mind that Licinius used triremes against Constantine in AD 324, and the later abandonment of this system of propulsion,[149] the Late Roman war fleet, at the beginning of the second half of the 4th century, must have mainly consisted of single-banked ships and, numerically, scarcely any biremes, a system of operation which continued into the Middle Ages in the Mediterranean. It made sense, especially for coastal boats with a single bank of oars, to have relatively high-sided vessels with more or less concealed crews housed in the hull (see Pisa, wreck C on Fig. 570).

Military boats, ships, and floating craft on inland waters

Transports

Reliefs on Trajan's and Marcus' Columns in Rome show seemingly civilian vessels used by Roman pioneers to construct temporary bridges ('pontoon bridges').[150] These will have been partly or wholly ships, also known as convoy vessels, for the transport of troops, cavalry horses, and military matériel (Fig. 551),[151] which are known to us as civilian or commercial inland ships and lighters (Fig. 552). Their bulbous hulls, pointed at either end, are characterized by a vertically protruding stern and a walkway structure around the aft of the ship. Here the differentiation between a military purpose and a peaceful function is difficult, especially as the iconographically defined type cannot be unambiguously identified from surviving ship remains.[152] Light vessels, probably open boats, were used to cross rivers or to land soldiers.[153] It is unclear whether auxiliary vehicles of this kind were maintained within the fleets or, if necessary, requisitioned or chartered. If need be, they were built by the troops at the site.[154]

The same can be said of the barges from the 1st to 3rd century AD (Fig. 553), excavated on the middle and lower parts of the Rhine, which are characterized by special designs and dimensions. Their transport capacities and attested loads, building material as well as grain, mark them as supply vessels. Due to the fact that the majority of the vessels were found near garrison sites, there might have been at least a temporary use by the military.[155] With at times a length of more than 30 m, and a width of more than 5 m, most of the wrecks found on the Rhine show a construction design only found there, with overlapping planking (lapstrake construction) on the sides (Figs 554–5). Flat-bottomed ships found away from the Rhine, especially vessel remains known from Gaul, differ in their type of planking, being carvel-built (planks fastened edge to edge), which is typical of Mediterranean shipbuilding. Both types of construction sometimes show the conventional mortise-and-tenon plank joints of the Mediterranean or other classical features. Propelled by towing, punting, or sailing before the wind, and downriver perhaps just drifting along with the river current, and aided by oars while manoeuvring in confined spaces, the

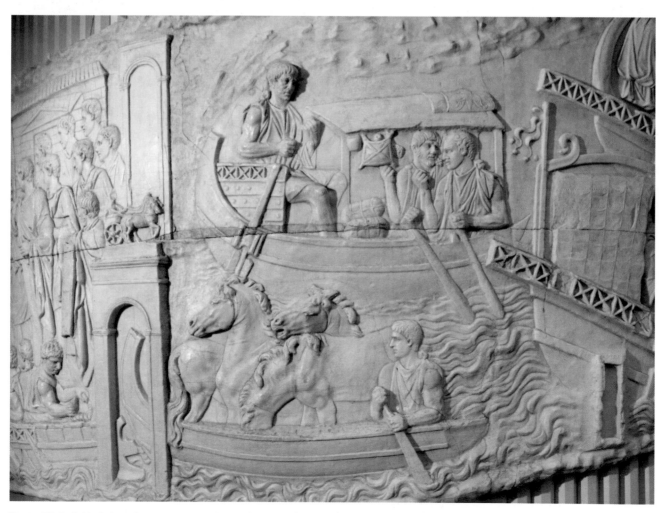

Figure 551 *Trajan's Column in Rome, Forum of Trajan. Cichorius relief Scene XXXIV: convoy of warships (copy in the Museum für Antike Schiffahrt Mainz)*

Figure 552 *Tomb fresco from Ostia. Towed barge ISIS GIMINIANA with a fiscal scene (after Pomey, 1997)*

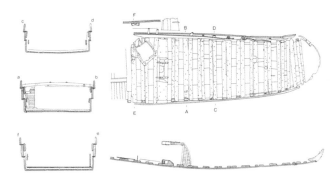

Figure 554 *Woerden, province of Utrecht, Wreck 1. Barge post-dating AD 169, with remnants of a cargo of grain (after J. K. Haleboos 1996)*

Figure 553 *Zwammerdam, province of Zuidholland, Wreck 6. Barge after exposure seen from aft, abandoned around AD 175 (after M. D. De Weerd, Jahrb. RGZM 34, T. 2, 1987, pl. 73.1)*

Figure 555 *Vleuten-De Meern, province of Utrecht, Wreck 1. Barge with partly preserved stern, built around AD 148 (after Jansma and Morel 2007)*

hulls with their blunt, ramp-like ends were suitable for landing on banks.[156]

Due to the design of the barge type, with its shallow draught, its considerable loading capacity, and the fact that potential opponents, at least in the north-west of the empire, had nothing to match them on water, they also offered militarily useful features and benefits. Accordingly, such vessels may have been deployed operationally, at least in the 1st century AD, whether as troop carriers, or

as a fighting vessels armed with artillery and crewed by missile-armed troops.[157] This is formally balanced by the low manoeuvrability and speed of flat-bottomed vessels, and last but not least, the restrictions of their means of propulsion, which did not really allow for easy handling. However, the use of other types of ships, for the historically attested replenishment of the provincial fleets,[158] is not really conceivable for reasons of capacity, at least in the distribution area of the barge types in Gaul and Germany.

Moreover, logistical operations are likely to result in heavier freighters being covered by lighter fighting vessels.

Oared vessels

Original finds of imperial oared vessels are rare. These are often only thought to have been in military service. Sometimes all indications, find circumstances, and historical links, as well as naval technical and constructional evidence, indicate this.

Oared boats of the Oberstimm-Vechten type

The earliest archaeological investigation of a Roman-era wreck of a ship north of the Alps was to be found in a late-Augustan to (early) Tiberian period (Fig. 556) boat, which was apparently well preserved when discovered in late 1892 in the area of the military base at Vechten (*Fectio*), Bunnik-Vechten (NL), excavated and published in 1895.[159] Ignored for decades and hampered by unfortunate circumstances during the excavation, as well as by problematic documentation,[160] the significance of the discovery of the Vechten ship remained unknown to Roman military history for almost a century. Detailed attention was only devoted to it when, in 1986, trenching in the western ditch around the fort in Oberstimm, in the district of Manching, Pfaffenhofen a.d. Ilm region of Germany, established under Claudius or Nero, came across the remains of two boats from the early 2nd century AD.[161] Based on an initially narrowly defined section of the technical examination of the boats, O. Höckmann noted the close constructional relationship between the wrecks and the Vechten boat.[162] In both instances these were oared vessels with approximately comparable dimensions. In addition to equipment- and propulsion-specific similarities, they shared caravel construction, which originated in the Mediterranean, with planking made from softwood (conifers) and ribs normally made of oak or hardwood. In both cases, the circumstances of the find suggest the military character of the boats. A structural feature of the Oberstimm boats also shared by the Vechten boat, the underpinning of the thwarts with central stanchions, was interpreted as an indication of a troop transport, and even as an indication of double-manned oars, but neither of these hypotheses seems reasonable.[163]

Vechten (Netherlands)

Not until after the complete excavation and lifting of the Oberstimm wrecks did further discoveries take place. In the course of their evaluation, an examination took place of several surviving components from the Vechten boat discovery, which was critically re-evaluated on the basis of new data. In doing so, M. D. De Weerd discovered that

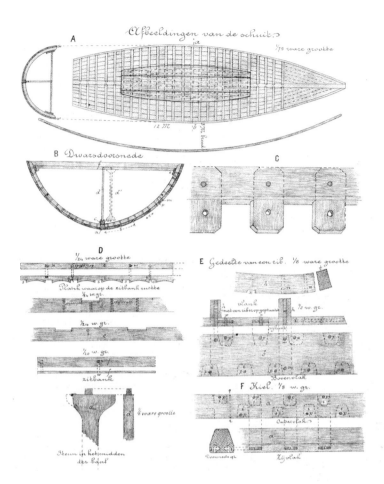

Figure 556 *Vechten, province of Utrecht. Remains of a crew boat of the late Augustan-Tiberian period*

Muller, the excavator of the wreck, did not make accurate drawn records, because the hull, lying deep down, had been damaged by encroaching water. Muller was also inspired by the characteristics of contemporary Dutch watercraft in the reconstruction for his published documentation. Nevertheless, Muller should not be blamed for negligence, for when original relics and drawings are compared, some details, including measurements, are confirmed. Uncertainties over the form of the ship remain. Thus it can be assumed that the boat from Vechten was a vessel 13 to 14 m long, 2.5 to 3 m wide, and amidships up to 1.3 m high, with a pointed bow and stern, a flat bottom, and rounded chine (Figs 557–9). Its crew of oarsmen of probably 16 to 18 men, who were arranged on 8 to 9 thwarts in pairs, was placed at a distance of around 92 cm in the hull, the bottom of which had a closed deck. The differences between the Vechten boat and the much better preserved boats from Bavaria appear to be partly marginal – the type of wood, the shaping and suspension technology of the oar thwarts, as well as the profiling of the keelson – partly serious: the dimensions of the mortise-and-tenon joints in the plank skin and the offset of the ribs are much shorter than on

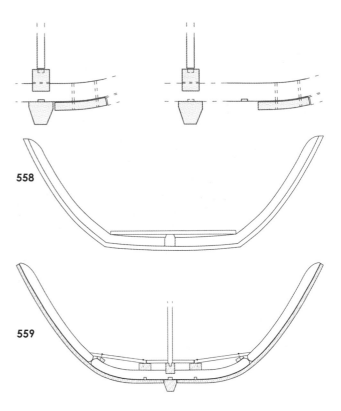

Figure 558, 559 *Vechten, province of Utrecht. Hypothetical layout of a rib fragment (558); theoretical reconstruction (559) (after Bockius 2002)*

Oberstimm (Germany)

The wreckage from Oberstimm (Fig. 560), which was silted up on the banks of an ancient stream running down into the Danube, fulfills a number of criteria which, in short, make the tactical use of boats inevitable.[166]

1. uncovered in the immediate vicinity of the military camp; 2. Mediterranean design with the use of the Roman foot for planning as well as traces of controlled construction of the ship's form with the aid of templates or auxiliary frames (moulds); 3. rowing layout with compressed crew accommodation; 4. combination of primary oar and secondary sail propulsion; 5. relatively high potential pace and well capable of a burst of speed indicative of the parameters of the ship design[167] including a very low power-to-weight ration; 6. shortage of space and buoyancy reserves, which are significant in terms of the accommodation of the crew and their equipment; 7. clues to the participation of shipbuilders from the North Adriatic area.

The boats, built around AD 106 and soon abandoned, can be regarded as the same type, although they differ slightly according to their shape (hull cross-section) and crew number (18 and 20 men at the oars). The reconstruction (Figs 561–2) was based directly on the archaeological findings, with the exception of the design of the bow and individual details of the equipment (stern decoration, dimensions of rigging, oars, and steering oars).

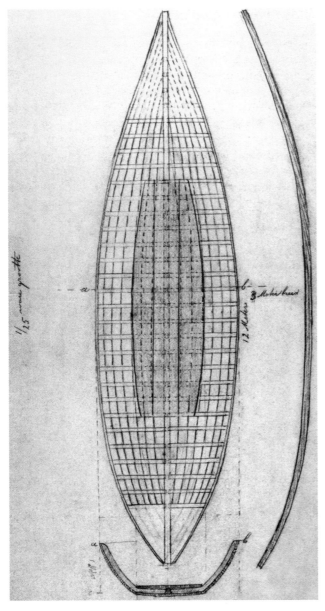

Figure 557 *Vechten, province of Utrecht. Crew boat. Reconstruction drawing by the excavator S. F. Müller, c.1894/95*

the Oberstimm hulls. In addition, with the approximately known main dimensions, the hull appears to have had a relatively high freeboard. For Vechten, all this implies greater structural strength and other proportions, which may be explained by the original function of the vessel. To revise older ideas,[164] the Dutch boat may have been better suited for coastal use compared to the Bavarian finds, without wishing to deny its suitability for inland navigation. The location of the supposed *Fectio* fleet base at Oude Rhijn and near the Utrechtse Vecht,[165] which gave access to the *lacus Flevo* (Zuiderzee), suggests the area where the vessel might have sailed.

Figure 560 *Oberstimm, district of Pfaffenhofen a.d. Ilm. Remains of two crew boats from the late Trajanic period. Excavation photo (after Bockius 2002)*

Oared boat of Mainz type A

The perception of these Late Roman shipwrecks, especially Wrecks 1, 2, 4 and 5, which are recognisable as oared boats, as the remains of military vessels, is based mainly on the assessment of their constructional and propulsion-related workmanship.[169] Due to the nature and extent of their preservation, the research focus has been on the remains of the type 1 and 5 craft from the late 4th century AD, which were in use for several years at the same time, according to the dendrochronological results. Wreck 1 (Fig. 564) is identified as having been the after part of the ship by a support beam for oars on the side piercing the ship's side. Wreck 5 (Fig. 563), which was *in situ*, was still 16.15 m long, barely extends beyond the chine vertically, but is complete up to the onset of a sharply raked stem. The longitudinal orientation of the vessel was determined by the position of a mast pole: the smaller distance between the mast position and the end of the ship coincides with the forward section, indicating the location of the bow.

Mainz 1 and 5, both incomplete hulls, are characterized by a series of boatbuilding, formal, and equipment-related

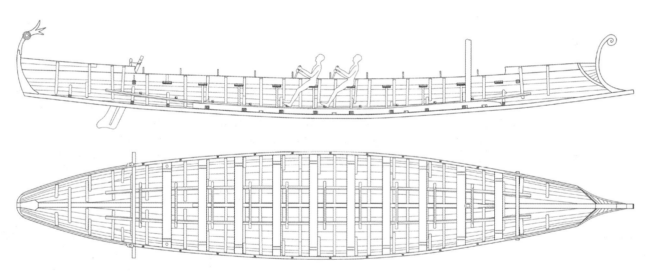

Figure 561 *Oberstimm, district of Pfaffenhofen a.d. Ilm. Reconstruction of a crew boat, based on the evaluation of Wreck 1. Side view and top view. Scale 1:100*

According to their low freeboard and their comparatively light longitudinal and transverse internal reinforcements, these are inland vessels, as is confirmed by the location. Originally a good 15 m or 16 m long and barely 2.8 m wide, there was no space amidships for any crew not rowing, so that only two or three additional crew members can be expected in addition to the rowers and one helmsman. This restricts the offensive nature of the vessel class. However, the features that can be deduced leave scope for a mult-ifunctional military use, essentially monitoring, communication, and convoy coverage (Fig. 551).[168]

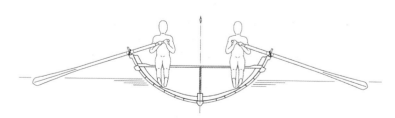

Figure 562 *Oberstimm, district of Pfaffenhofen a.d. Ilm. Reconstruction of a crew boat, based on the evaluation of Wreck 1. Hull cross-section. Scale 1:75*

Figure 563 *Mainz, Löhrstraße excavation 1981/1982. Wreck 5, built AD 390*

Figure 564 *Mainz, Löhrstraße excavation 1981/1982. Wreck 1, built AD 386*

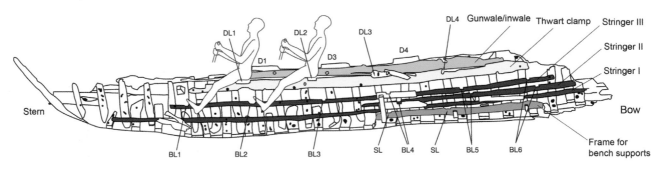

Figure 565 *Mainz, Löhrstraße excavation 1981/82. Wreck 1. Longitudinal section with emphasis on system of propulsion. Key: Scale c.1:50*

similarities. Especially important among these are the design features of a system for seating oarsmen arranged in pairs, less than 1 m apart along the body of the ship. The reconstruction of the single bank of oars is just as certain as the technical design of the hulls and their cross section. Thus, Wreck 1, preserved on the port side up to the gunwale or sheer strake (Fig. 564) showed a section width of a maximum of about 2.6 m and a height of 0.9 m. Cross sections of Wreck 5 can be projected on to the sections of No. 1 both structurally and dimensionally. Including losses and deformation, the original hull width of those vessels was less than 2.7 m amidships. Remnants and indirect traces of complex fittings, which were intended to accommodate a crew of oarsmen, were found in both wrecks. The spaces reserved for the oarsmen were distinguished by a grid of vertical supports arranged in pairs on both sides of the keel at a distance of less than 1 m along the body of the ship. In each case they formed two rows, which were stiffened by longitudinal beams. Banks (thwarts) were originally fitted on these stanchions, and thus were supported from sagging. Crossbeams were laid with one end in the notches in the upper edge of the lowest reinforcing beams, whereas the other end rested on stringers. The beams carried a covering of two to three loosely laid on planks in each case, partly surviving in Wreck 5. They formed a sort of deck in both halves of the ship, which served as platforms between each

of the thwarts and covered the space reserved for the men (Fig. 566.2–3b). The rest of the equipment of the system of propulsion and accommodation is illustrated by the ship's technical features in Wreck 1: the banks of oars, which were stayed on either side of the keel with vertical supports, were inserted into the side walls on a stringer, as can be seen from regularly distributed recesses at its upper edge of up to 20 cm in length. Aft of the mast-frame, the oar benches will have been divided and only extended transversely as far as the pairs of stanchions in order to be able to use the space flanked by the longitudinal fence-like structures above the keel and garboard planking as stowage for the mast and rigging and also to facilitate access to the bilge. As can be seen from the arrangement of small notches cut into the longitudinal beams nailed to the ribs and the stanchions, the footwell of each oarsman was originally traversed by a pair of vertically and longitudinally arranged beams, each of which had its ends inserted into the internal planking of the ship's sides as well as into the longitudinal subdivisions of the bench supports (Fig. 566.3, 2–5). The installation is easy to identify as a foot stretcher system. The sheer plank in the after part of Wreck 1 is completed with a horizontal cover, which was placed on the headers of the ribs as well as a rubbing strake attached to the ship's side, where it was nailed fast. Amidships, the gunwale consists of an oak trunk split lengthways, which was flat in sections and had 35 to

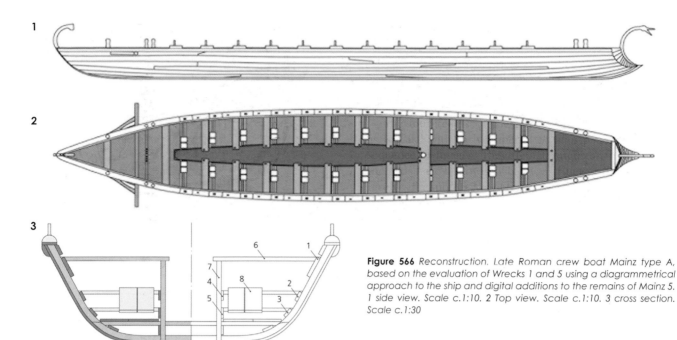

Figure 566 Reconstruction. Late Roman crew boat Mainz type A, based on the evaluation of Wrecks 1 and 5 using a diagrammetrical approach to the ship and digital additions to the remains of Mainz 5. 1 side view. Scale c.1:10. 2 Top view. Scale c.1:10. 3 cross section. Scale c.1:30

40 cm-long semi-circular sections at regular intervals. The elevated segments were used as supports for the oars, each of which was hung in front of thole pins inserted off-centre (Fig. 565–6.1–3).

The crowded accommodation of the rowing crew in modules of less than 1 m lengthwise, but above all the inference of a foot stretcher in the foot area of the rowing crew, provide a clear indication of the intended high-performance rowing, as far as the quasi-rigid system would allow.[170] No less interesting in this context is the crew size. Preliminary reports for the boat type discussed here suggested a total length of 21.0/21.5 m and a 30-man rowing crew.[171] Doubts about the methical approach to longitudinal reconstruction[172] and the insight that Wreck 5 alone can provide information about the original boat length, led to a revision of the excavation documents and quickly brought about a different result.[173] For this vessel, representative of boat type Mainz A, we can assume a total length of somewhat less than 18 m and a crew of 24 oarsmen (Fig. 566.1–2). The assessment of it as military remains unaffected. It is based not least on additional facts and observations: 1. the stem setting found on Wreck 9 constitutes the addition of a bow-construction, which, in its outline is concurrent with representations of late Roman warships; 2. the combination of secondary sail and primary oar power;[174] 3. the extreme utilisation of the hull for propulsion and steering, which at most offers small reserves of space in the short and narrow bow and stern sections; 4. proof of series construction using specific procedures;[175] 5. a power-to-weight ratio of only 260 to 280 kg per oarsman.[176]

What is true of the boats of the same type, Nos 1 and 5, is also the case with Wrecks 2 and 4, which are similarly recognisable as the remains of oared vessels. In both cases, they preserve aft sections with remnants of the steering system. In the case of Mainz vessel 2, which probably dates back to the early 4th century AD, not much more than the ship's body and the traces of torn-out interior elements and fittings could be identified, the arrangement of which suggests short crew modules. On the other hand, Wreck 4 has unusually wide futtock planks with a network of recesses and notches originally used to insert transverse elements – thwarts – which were previously distributed there over the ship's side, as well as suspected foot stretchers and crossbeams for supporting a deck. The distances between the oar attachments in No. 4 are, in some cases, less than 0.9 m, the shortest among the Mainz oared vessels. Wrecks 2 and 4 belonged to boats whose hulls differed in dimension from that of the Mainz A type.[177] Moreover, No. 2 is distinguished by its frame system with half-frames set in pairs, due to the high quality of the boat, and not least because of the quality of the oak used. In addition, the wreck provides the clearest demonstration of the planking method, especially the use of moulds or construction templates. Apparently Wrecks 2 and 4 are variants of Late Roman crew boats.

If some – unfortunately only poorly documented – observations are correct, vessels of this kind were still being built in the second quarter of the 5th century AD. A finds complex (Mainz, S8) that was dendrochronologically dated, but not very well-recorded, consisted of a strong oak plank as well as four thole pins, one of which may still have been nailed to the plank (Fig. 567).[178]

In terms of size, equipment, and crewing of the vessels, which may be described as *naves lusoriae* in the context of contemporary tradition,[179] their military use was limited to

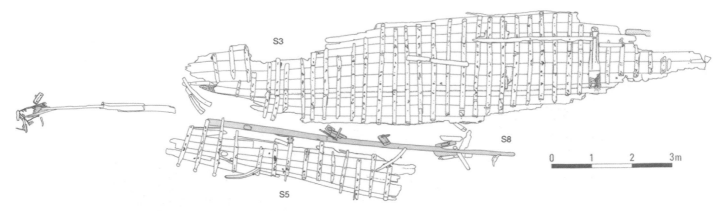

Figure 567 *Mainz, Löhrstraße excavation 1981/1982. Wreck 3, excavation plan, probably early 3rd century*

such tasks which only demanded the moving of relatively small units of men by water. Greater speed replaced carrying capacities, especially the carrying of heavy weapons, equipment or of troops other than the rowers. As a result, the multipurpose capabilities remained the same as those that already distinguished early Imperial *moneres*. Sources from Late Antiquity offer concrete examples of deployment, such as commando raids, the introduction of small amphibious operational army contingents, and the mobile monitoring of a section of the frontier. In particular, incorporation in the section known for the Rhine and Danube Valentinian perimeter defence must be considered for Mainz A type,[180] as well as more general functions of convoying, scouting, and communications.

Mainz type B vessel

The ship find Wreck 3 from Mainz (Fig. 567) is typologically distinct from the oared vessels discussed above. Dated by dendrochronological coring into the latter part of the 3rd century AD at the earliest, it appears to be much older than the three boats, Wrecks 1, 2 and 5.[181] Its poor condition meant that the reconstruction of the vessel leaves questions unanswered. It is possible to reconstruct a hull of 17 to 18 m long and – without its outriggers – 3.6 m wide, with a sharply shaped stern, the central section of which was kept up to 0.4 m flatter than the 1.3 m high stern.[182] However, its completion, in particular the reconstruction of the missing bow, as well as the technical rowing gear, was based on a comparison with a late Roman ship model made of silver-plated bronze. Used as a piggy bank, the piece represents an oared vessel with covered oar outriggers, masts, and a vaulted rear structure (Figs 568–9).

The ship's technical characteristics show that Mainz 3 originally had sails as well as fittings that would have been appropriate to support a deck. The light design, with the two- and three-part segmented ribs as well as the hull proportions, not least the shear line set deep amidships, would suggest propulsion by oars. The constructional

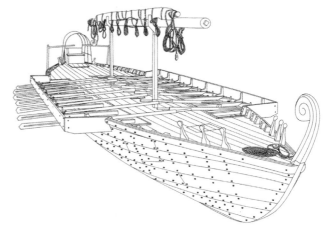

Figure 568 *Reconstruction attempt. Late Roman crew boat of Mainz type B, based on the evaluation of Wreck 3 with the model ship from Rethel as comparison (Fig. 569)*

concept developed for the accommodation is consistent with the data derived from the technical discoveries about the ship, as well as with the iconographic sources. However, in detail it can ultimately be no more than a replica. The same applies to the derivation and shape of the deck as well as to the shape of the bow.

The military use of Mainz 3 is not absolutely certain; it is a case of being content with hints that support the character of the ship as a late Roman warship: the design details on the Mainz boats, such as the indirectly proved support beam for the oars on the side, the light design with the use of prefabricated formers or templates, the relative slenderness of the ship's hull, as well as similarities in the dimensions and design, speak for this; nor does comparison with the model ship from Rethel exclude it. On the other hand, the components and techniques apparent on the wreck – the mast step, a keel that was only a plank, and the nailing technique – are typical of Gallo-Roman shipbuilding and reveal neither the users nor the function of the vessel. Anachronistic-seeming connections with Mediterranean shipbuilding demonstrate the continuing

Figure 569 *Rethel, Dép. Ardennes. Late Roman model ship of silver-plated bronze*

Figure 570 *Pisa, Toscana. Shipwrecks from San Rossore 1999/2000. Wreck C. View of the spur-like prow with metal fittings (according to Bruni)*

importance of Greek-Celtic traditional models. It appears that this style of construction, especially the characteristics of the framing, was cultivated in pre-Roman Gaul and continued there in Roman shipyards.[183]

O. Höckmann can be followed in the assumption that ships of this kind were used as an official means of transport at the time.[184] It is equally conceivable that it was used to carry artillery, or with a different configuration of the ship's deck, as a troop carrier, or even as a freight-carrying support vessel for supplies. However, all of these options have to take into account that while this type of vehicle could be easily manoeuvred, due to its weak system of oars and its far-from-lean design compared to familiar Imperial galleys, it will not have been very swift. A replica, constructed by the Dutch municipality of Millingen aan de Rijn in 2010, may enlighten us as to the characteristics of the ship. The replica, funded by grants, is based on the plans from Mainz and is to be put into operation under reconstructed historical conditions. A second one is under construction at the Archaeological Park in Xanten.

Other boat and ship finds

A military background can be argued, although not conclusively confirmed, for four other vessels. Nevertheless, it seems worthwhile to consider and weigh up the evidence and justifications.

Pisa, ship C (Italy)

The astonishingly well-preserved wreck – not yet published with a sufficiently legible plan, unfortunately – was found together with the remains of several other ships in a dried-up river bed in front of the entrance to an artificial canal,[185] a few hundred metres seaward of the medieval city walls of Pisa. Dated to the late Augustan or Tiberian period, the hull (only incomplete at the stern) was originally about 14 m in length and 2.7 to 2.8 m wide at the most.[186] With the hull almost 1.6 m high amidships, the boat,[187] partly decked fore and aft, looks quite tall (Fig. 571), but there is a reason for it: the vessel had oars for a crew of 12 men, derived from originally six one-man, centrally supported rowing positions. Five of these were doubly occupied, with only one oarsman each sitting on the last rear bench and on the aft edge of the foredeck. Accordingly, the arrangement of six double oars had a longitudinal offset by a full *interscalmium*, a good 1 m. The oars were inserted through the sides of the vessel by means of six rectangular oar ports with rounded corners. There are thole pins surviving, mounted off-centre, behind the openings. From the position of the wooden fittings, it is clear that the boat was propelled with the oars lashed to the thole pins. Traces of nails around the exterior of the openings[188] are evidently due to oar sleeves, attested in the literary and iconographic sources, to seal the apertures (ασκόματα/ *folliculi*).[189] A maststep as well as a mast tabernacle nailed to two thwarts testify to the former existence of a sail which, due to the nature of the tabernacle – the mast (which was attached at the sides to iron chain plates) could be folded aft when necessary – was a secondary form of propulsion. Other interesting details can only be mentioned briefly here: evidence for a name plate with the incised Latin word *Alk [e] do* ('Kingfisher') in Greek letters; a cathead (*epotís*) or a crane beam on the foredeck; bollards located on the elevated bulwarks; traces of red and white external paint with a wax component; and the remains of a bilge pump. Special attention is merited by the shape and design of the bow: a beam of walnut wood, as an extension of the keel, integrated into the 2- to 3 cm-thick outer plank skin made from mortise-and-tenon-joined softwood strakes. This tapers into a wedge-shaped tip at the front, above which there was a rib raked backwards (Fig. 570; 571). The ram-shaped bow segment at its forward edge was covered

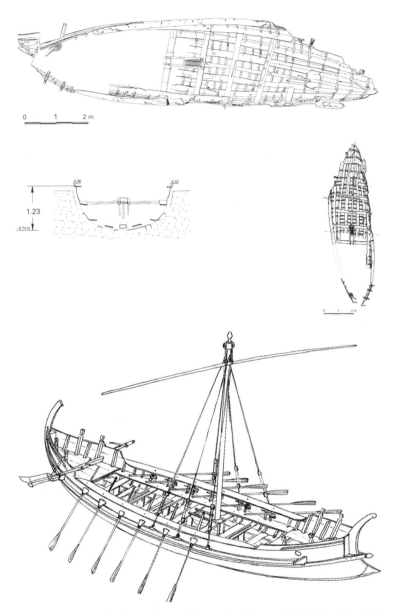

an official crewed boat, probably not in the sense of a vessel for tactical combat, but a boat with a military background, such as a warship's launch, a despatch boat, or an operative vessel with policing duties.[191] Since Pisa definitely played a part in Roman shipbuilding in the early Imperial period (Strabo 5.2; *CIL* XI, 1436: *fabri navales*),[192] the presence of smaller detachments of the Roman fleet, such as guards, bears consideration. According to the information available from preliminary reports and by personal acquaintance of the author, the boat hull can be regarded as comparatively heavy, robust, and stiff. The crew was protected from the chest downwards behind the sides of the ship. There is no doubt that this is a vessel which was at least capable of coastal use, and which could sail into the Gulf of Pisa through the ancient mouths of the Arno and Serchio rivers.

Herculaneum (Italy)

A boat,[193] found on the ancient shore line in Herculaneum, was found with the skeleton of an armed man identified as a soldier.[194] The rowing vessel, smashed and charred as a result of the eruption of Vesuvius on 24/25 August AD 79, and not really well preserved, initially attracts interest from a shipbuilding point of view.[195] The boat hull (Fig. 572) is distinguished by its craftsmanship, particularly by its thin plank skin, which is constructed with mortise-and-tenon joints, which were protected by a longitudinal beam (wale), laterally supplemented by a permanent fender. This may be seen as an indication of frequent mooring against quay walls or ships. The hull – originally 2.4 m wide, probably more than 9 m long, amidships barely 90 cm high – can be attested to have had a comparatively low freeboard and therefore a correspondingly low suitability for rough water. Thus the boat will have been used in sheltered, inshore waters and under moderate weather conditions.

According to the available information, the wreck seems to have been the aft part of a vessel propelled by a rowing crew with at least six thole pins preserved, which are said to have been used with a simple system of oars and several oarsmen seated one behind the other.[196] A square beam piecing the boat skin above the gunwale about 1 m in front of the stem of the boat terminated in rounded outboard sections of over 40 cm length.[197] This device was doubtless used to mount rudders on the side. Duplications in the framing system point to the original presence of a sail rig.[198] The accommodation modules were 92 and 112.5 cm long. These distances do not provide sufficiently clear information about the purpose of the boat.[199] In the face of the overlap in technical equipment with provincial Roman finds, it is extremely tempting to give the vehicle from Herculaneum a military background.

The fact that the boat was apparently laid upside down on the beach (a manner of storing that is still

Figure 571 *Pisa, Toscana. Shipwrecks from San Rossore 1999/2000. Wreck C. above: plan drawings; below: reconstruction based on the evaluation of the wreck (according to Bonino 2006)*

with an iron strip, fastened with bronze nails. The roughly convex-concave contouring of the outline of the bow is reminiscent of the appearance of Hellenistic-Republican warships, and also the iron-plated reinforcement of the prow[190] might speak in favour of an offensive function.

The shape and armour of the bow certainly cannot be compared with the massive rams on contemporary warships, nor are the dimensions of the small vessel comparable. At the same time, the robust wales of the Pisan boat would seem to have reinforced its bow construction, so that a potential use as a weapon cannot be completely rejected out of hand. But even if the metal-clad prow is thought of as a naval emblem, Pisa C will have been

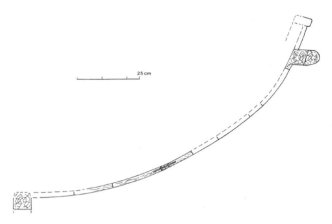

Figure 572 Ercolano, Campania. Charred boat from the beach in front of Herculaneum's suburban baths. Hull half section

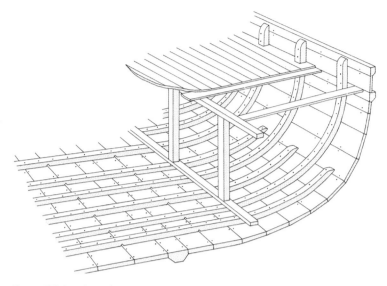

Figure 573 London, River Thames, County Hall. Ship dating to around AD 330, with characteristics of the Mediterranean boatbuilding tradition. Enhanced hull cross-section drawing (after Marsden 1994)

used on the shores of the Mediterranean), perhaps for the purpose of repair, does not rule out a military interpretation. On the other hand, it is of no importance that the ship's hull was found near the remains of an armed man. It is attractive, but ultimately speculative, to link the vehicle to the recorded activities of the Roman navy to save the fugitives from the effects of the eruption of Vesuvius (see Pliny, *Epist.* 6.16). The fact that such open boats, constructed according to Mediterranean principles, were also used by the early Imperial navy as auxiliary vessels does not appear to be at all incongruous. Ancient ship iconography[200] depicts small oared boats in particular as tow boats or pilot boats, although it remains unknown whether assigned by official military or civilian authority.

London County Hall (Great Britain)

The wreck, discovered in 1910 on the southern bank of the River Thames in London, during the construction of County Hall, belonged to a large and unusually constructed ship, built at the end of the 3rd century and foundering after a comparatively short period of time.[201] Being considerably larger than the oared vessels discussed above with more than 5 m at its widest point and around 2 m depth, the round-edged, almost flat-bottomed hull had a deck, which was not necessarily completely closed (Fig. 573). Although the original length could not be reliably determined and hovers between 19 to 26 m, technical indications suggest a rather slender proportion for the ship's hull, the length-to-width ratio of which seems to be greater than usual in civilian vessels. The method of construction was also apparent from the frame – massive oak planks, which were assembled using the mortise-and-tenon method and secured by trenails.

If the wreck is by far the latest evidence of the application of the original Mediterranean shipbuilding technique in the Roman provinces,[202] the use of tangentially cut oak

planking may be due to Gallo-Roman influences, or may have been due to the lack of suitable softwood varieties. There is no conclusive evidence for any sort of official use of the ship. In view of the mobility known for the period, as well as in the knowledge of the amalgam of classical and provincial construction methods, it is not possible to decide whether the construction of the vessel was carried out by personnel familiar with Mediterranean shipbuilding methods or experts from the navy.[203]

Yverdon-les-Bains (Switzerland)

The fact that Roman troops could have used a boat built using hollowed-out oak trunks from two half-shells does not quite fit with our perception of ancient warships. However, arguments can be given which make the discovery of a late Roman rowing vessel from Yverdon-les-Bains II, Vaud[204] (Fig. 574) appear in a different light: nearly 200 m north of the Constantinian fort of *Eburodunum*, the 10-m-long and approximately 1.4-m-wide hull (Fig. 574) provided mounting points for at least five existing thwarts, which had been inserted into the bearing notches on the side walls. In addition, there are structures distributed around the periphery of the ship. large round apertures, which obviously served for tying oars or skulls to the boat's gunwale. The pattern of their arrangement is followed by the distribution of thwarts, positioned from the banks of oars, respectively, at an arm's length. The openings will originally have had frictional spliced grommets to attach the oars. The gunwale could possibly have been protected by the addition of perishable material, such as leather, for there is no mention of wear marks on the wood in the investigation report of the wreck.

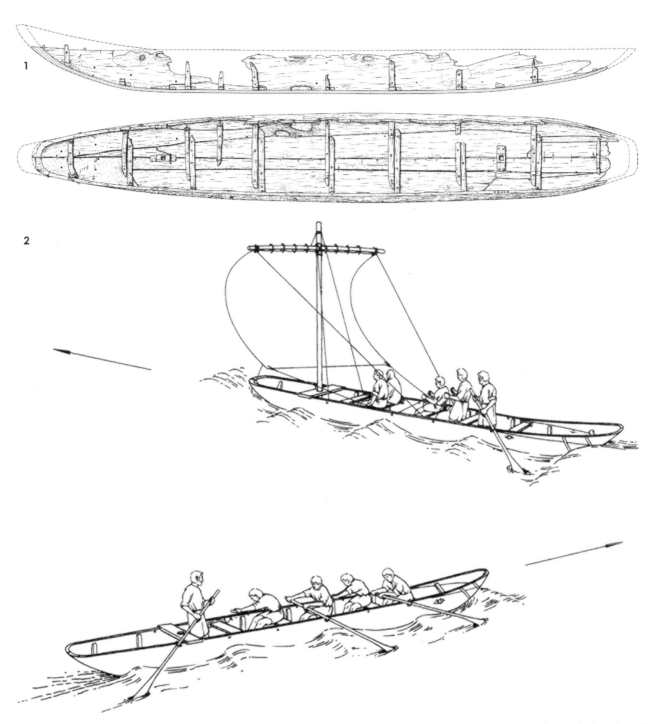

Figure 574 *Yverdon-les-Bains, district of Waadt. 1 oared vessel of the 4th century made from hollowed-out oak logs with repairs. Drawing with minor additions. Scale c.1:60 (after Arnold 1992). 2 Operational reconstruction proposals (after the guide, Musée d'Yverdon-les-Bains, 1997)*

Allowing for it to be equipped with additional fittings, with a sailing rig or a towing post, the hull would have offered space for six rowers lengthwise. These either served three alternating oars to port and starboard, or worked as skulls, which were known in the ancient world.[205] Even paddlled propulsion with up to 12 men is conceivable here.[206] With just 0.7 t unladen weight, the mass of the vessel – with a system

of six oars – of *c.*210 kg, falls some way short of the ratio of displacement to crew size of crew boat Mainz 5. This alone is of course not sufficient to confirm military use, but the hint is all the more obvious since a *classis barcaricorum* seems to have been based in Late Roman Yverdon, presumably a Late Roman body of troops equipped with small vessels, operating on regional inland waterways.[207]

Notes to Part VI

1. Pferdehirt 1995, 74–50.
2. D'Amato and Sumner 2009, 20–34.
3. Philp 1981, 149–73.
4. Baatz and Bockius 1997, 28f.
5. Ortisi 2005, 145f.; D'Amato and Sumner 2009, 16–20.
6. Reddé 1986, 145–319, esp. 145–61 on classification.
7. For Piraeus, see, for example, Lehmann-Hartleben 1923, 248 No. 48; 276 No. 216; Garland 1987; von Eickstedt 1991; Coates 2002; Steinhauer 1996, 471–9.
8. For Carthage see, for example, Lehmann-Hartleben 1923, 258f. No. 126 (with further references); Hurst and Stager 1978; 334–46; The results of the American excavations: Hurst 1992 and 1994.
9. There is an overview of the development up to the Late Roman period in Reddé 1986, 308–19.
10. Konen 2000; Mason 2003 extensively on the development of the northern provincial fleets.
11. However, in the area of the lower Rhine, the former area of the German fleet, there is a failure in the supply, since the corresponding section for the province of Germania II in the *Notitia Dignitatum* is missing. Scharf (2005, 299f.) discussed a removal of a folio due to a mix-up. Alternatively, the end of the frontier guard in Germania II was assumed before the writing of the *Notitia Dignitatum*. See Kunow 1987, 105.
12. Blackman 2008 with a comprehensive overview of Roman shipsheds, which is mainly concerned with literary, epigraphic, and iconographic sources. Rankov 2008 is critical of the archaeological evidence from Haltern, Velsen, Ostia, and Caesarea Maritima, the interpretation of which as a shipshed is rejected or seen as problematic (Ostia).
13. Cichorius, 1900, 11–26 with Plate 58 (Scene LXXIX); in addition Lehmann-Hartleben 1923, 228ff.
14. See Blackman 2008, 24 with note 6 with further refs.
15. *Portus Augusti*: to date, only a short report (Keay 2012) has been published. Further information is available on the homepage of the Portus project <http://www.portusproject.org/>. Alexandria: on topography see Goddio and Yoyotte 2007.
16. Reddé 1986, 265–9; Müller-Wiener 1994, 3–11 to the ancient ports of Byzantion/Constantinople.
17. Reddé 1986, 298–306.
18. Holwerda 1923 identified a fleet base; Bogaers 1972 disagreed, which is also confirmed by recent archaeological excavations (Buijtendorp 2006).
19. The description of such a base in the territory of the Nemetes (near Speyer) in a Panegyricus (Symm., 2.20), written around 370, is imprecise. At least one can see from the text that the ships were placed in a fortified area and this probably had a curved shape on the side towards the water. In Bregenz, which, according to the testimony of the *Notitia Dignitatum*, housed a fleet division, the fortress situated on the shores of Lake Constance near the port facilities occupied an area of only 0.35 ha. See Ertel 1999, 29–32. Höckmann 1986 with an overview of Late Roman fleet supply bases.
20. *CIL* XIII, 6712; 6714. See also Konen 2000, 180–3.
21. Cf. Höckmann 1984. However, the late dating of the Mainz stamp (from the late 3rd century onwards), is too late, in my opinion.
22. For Portus Iulius see Lehmann-Hartleben, 1923, 175; 278 No. 233; Maiuri 1958, 165f.; 168f.; Reddé 1986, 164–71; Döring, 2003, 41–4; Gianfrotta 1995, 37.
23. For personnel strength considerations see Starr 1941, 16f.; Reddé 1986, 551f.
24. On *Misenum* see Lehmann-Hartleben 1923, 176f.; 270, No. 172; Maiuri, 1958, 100–10; Reddé 1986, 164–71; Gianfrotta 1995, 38; Döring 2003, 45f.
25. *CIL* X, 3344 (wooden bridge).
26. A literal translation could be 'School of Soldiers'. A *schola armatur(arum)* is proven by an inscription of the 2nd century AD from *Misenum* (*CIL* X, 3344), which was interpreted as a body of elite soldiers within the fleet. See Hoffmann 1970, 121, note 414. The extent to which the naming can actually be based on this group is, however, uncertain.
27. From the description of the Vesuvius eruption by Pliny the Younger, it can be gathered that the villa of the naval commander was separated from the sea by a court (Plin. 20.4), and the cloud was visible from there, but that Vesuvius was not identifiable as the cause, according to the author (ibid., 16.4f.).
28. *Notitia Dignitatum Occidentalis* 42.
29. Reddé 1986, 177–86 summarising the sources and findings. Reconstruction in Reddé and Golvin 2005, 124.
30. For example, Deichmann 1969, 37f.; Reddé 1986, 185f. Map with hypothetical location of the camp in the eastern part of Ravenna and two military harbours on the *fossa Augusta*: Heucke 2001, 798. Mauskopf Deliyannis 2010, 26–30, summarizes port installations with further refs.
31. Reddé 1986, 171–7 with a critique of the relevant literary and epigraphic testimonies.
32. Plin., *Nat. Hist.* 3.35.
33. Tac., *Hist.* 3.43.1.
34. Publication of the excavations in Goudineau and Brentchaloff 2009.
35. On topography, sources, and strategic importance: Lehmann-Hartleben 1923, 214–16; Honigmann 1923; Van Berchem 1985; Reddé 1986, 237–41; Gebhardt 2002, 68f.; 158–64 with further details. For the results of recent archaeological investigations, see Pamir 2004.
36. *P. Brit. Mus.* 229.
37. Reddé 1986, 238f.
38. Grewe 1998, 108–18.
39. In the course of the controversy surrounding the dating of the site of the massacre at Kalkriese, a later end was also postulated for Haltern.
40. Morel 1987, 221–30; 1988, 358–69; 1991, 161ff. In summary, Konen 2000, 288–94.
41. Dragendorff *et al.* 1905, especially 78.
42. Rankov 2008, 51–5.
43. Ibid., 51–3. See Konen 2000, 292, who explains the distance to the bank with the danger of flooding and referred to the finding of a supposedly 80 m (!) long slipway in Novae/Svištov. If we look at the dimensions of early Imperial

military boats in the northern provinces with the help of the wrecks of Oberstimm and Vechten, ship hull lengths of >12–15.7 m with a width of almost 3 m can be determined. Perhaps accommodation for two such vessels per shipshed segment should be considered.

44. See also Morel 1987, 222f.; Konen 2000, 289 with note 169.

45. Reference to the graffito in Kühlborn 1995, 84.

46. Morel 1986, 1988, and 1991.

47. Bechert and Willems 1995, 99f.; Bosmann 1999, 91ff.; Konen 2000, 280–8 for current research. The new discoveries include a double shipshed from the latest phase and the dock to the west of the camp.

48. Rankov (2008, 51) sees the unusual dimensions of the buildings as problematic, especially in comparison to Mediterranean shipsheds.

49. Konen 2000, 287 with further literature.

50. Morel 1991, 164 sees a predecessor to the late shipyards in the dock on the embankment on the opposite side of the river. See Konen 2000, 286f. for dating.

51. Tac., *Ann.* 4.72–4; Bosman 1999, 92f. for archaeological discoveries that support this thesis.

52. Cl. Seillier summarized the archaeological evidence in several works, *e.g.*, Seillier 1994; 1996 with further references. See also Reddé 1986, 272–9.

53. Reddé 1986, 274 with note 11 summarising these testimonials with references.

54. Information from Seillier 1996, 219.

55. Seillier 1977 for the Late Roman sources and archaeological discoveries. In the relevant section of the *Notita Dignitatum* (*Occ.* 38), no naval unit is mentioned in Boulogne anymore. The location of the *classis Sambrica* mentioned in the *Notitia* is thought to have been Etaples to the south, because of finds of brick stamps.

56. Suet., *Gaius* 46 reports the construction of the lighthouse without any more specific location. For the uncertainty of the allocation see, for example, Reddé 1986, 272f.; Seillier 1994, 219.

57. The findings from the fort were published in detail by Philp 1981. For the port facilities: Rigold 1969. Lighthouse: Wheeler 1923. Conclusion to the fleet location Reddé 1986, 270f.; Mason 2003, 107–11.

58. *Not. Dig. Occ.* 38.

59. The NAVIS II database provides a good, but not exhaustive, overview: <http://www2.rgzm.de/navis2/home/frames.htm>.

60. Basch 1987, 440 Fig. 960; Hellenistic prows, however, cannot be distinguished from them: ibid., 387f. Figs 808–12.

61. For the naval policy of Rome and the naval history of the Hellenistic-Punic countries, see Meijer 1986, 147–236. Lit.; Morrison 1996, 41–172; M. Pitassi, *The Navies of Rome.* Woodbridge 2009.

62. In this sense, for example, Morrison 1996, 163.

63. Orosius 6.19.9. See also Bockius 1997, 45 note 9.

64. On the location, size, and history of Roman state *navalia*, see F. Coarelli, in E. M. Steinby (eds), *Lexicon Topographicum Urbis Romae*, vol. 3, Rome 1996, 330; 339f. s. v. Porta Navalis and Navalia. Iconographic sources at Reddé 1986, 162 Fig. 72. Architectural remains at the foot of the Aventine,

from the second half of the 2nd century BC, see L. Cozza and P. L. Tucci, Navalia. *Arch. Class.* 57, 2006, 175–202.

65. Research history, briefly summarized by Bockius 1997, 41–51. On history and reconstruction in detail Morrison 1996, 255–77; J. F. Coates, Reconstructions, in: Morrison 1996, 285–317; The Naval Architecture and Oars of Ancient Galleys, in Gardiner 1995, 127–41; ibid., Hellenistic Oared Warships 399–31 BC, in: ibid., 66–77; J. T. Shaw, Oar Mechanics and Oar Power in Ancient Galleys, in: ibid., 163–71.

66. Conclusion of the International Symposium on Ship Construction in Antiquity, Hydra 2008. Proceedings (in preparation). For newcomers see Calomino 2011; Tusa and Royal 2012.

67. A. J. Parker, *Ancient Shipwrecks of the Mediterranean & the Roman Provinces*. BAR Internat. Series 580, Oxford 1992, 121f. No. 247.

68. Rafts: *e.g.* Lendle 1983, 176–81 Figs 51–3; Casson 1994, 9f. 6. Military operations of log boats of Hellenistic-Punic operations (Polyainos, *Strat.* 5.23, Polybios, *Hist.* 3.42.2) can be characterized as widespread since the scenarios are not characterized as peculiarities.

69. See also Morrison 1996, 261–6. It is impossible to overlook here that attempts at the reconstruction of the auxiliary vessels failed through poor evidence, in Viereck 1975, 77–88, Figs 76–7.

70. For example, the *corvus* appeared in the 1st Punic War. A vague reference to the Late Roman use of (offensive) boarding bridges, Langner 2001, 68 Cat. No. 1867 (?) 1868. For bolt guns (catapults) in the fleet or as ship's equipment for defence or preparation to board, see Baatz 1994, 127; 130f.; 183f. For the mode of operation, 136–45. Frontinus, *Strat.* 4.7.9 mentions fire grenades being thrown.

71. For the distinction between light and heavy units: Morrison 1996, 256–9. For general and specific boarding equipment: Lendle 1983, 151–79 Fig. 46–7.

72. On classification, characteristics, and equipment, especially Morrison 1996, 255–77; 259 with references to those identified iconographically by the author (to the extent that this is of interest here, with the inclusion of the iconographic sources for pictures from the Principate) [ibid., 205–53, No. 18–50], and reconstructed by J. F. Coates (Reconstructing the Ships, in: ibid., 285–331, Nos 57–72) [= Fig.]). The relevant features are the functionality of the reconstructed propulsion and accommodation systems.

73. G. Rabbeno and G. C. Special, The Roman Galleys in the Lake of Nemi, *Mariner's Mirror* 15, 1929, 333–46; ibid., *Die Forschungen im Nemi-See in ihrer Bedeutung für die Geschichte der Schiffbaukunst. Jahrb. Schiffbautechnischen Ges.* 33, 1932, 248–272; G. Ucelli, *Le Navi di Nemi*, Rome, 1950; M. Bonino, Notes on the Architecture of some Roman ships: Nemi and Fiumicino, in: H. Tzalas (eds), *TROPIS I. Proceedings of the 1 st Symposium on Ship Construction in Antiquity, Piraeus, 1985*, Athens 1989, 37–53; idem. Appeti di tecnica, architettura e cultura navale, in: *IV rassegna di archeologia subacquea. IV premio Franco Papò. Giardini Naxos 13–15 ottobre 1989*, Att. Messina 1991, 113–25; idem, *Un Sogno Ellenistico: Le Navi di Nemi*, Pisa, 2003.

74. The effect as such is naturally known. See the anecdotes on suckerfish (*Echeneidae*) in Pliny, *N. Hist.* 9.79; 32.2–6.

75. Local research now sees the ship finds as the remains of a shipbuilding research workshop of the Roman navy: http://www.dradio.de/dlf/sendungen/forschak/515375/.

76. For the palace ship of Ptolemy IV Philopator: Athen., *Deipn.* 5.204d–206c (after Kallixenos). A Nilotic pleasure craft of much smaller dimensions, but also with a structure resembling terrestrial architecture, can be seen on the Hellenistic mosaic of Palestrina, probably from the late 2nd century BC: B. Andreae, *Antike Bildmosaiken*, Mainz, 2003, 78–109, esp. 78, 80, 96–9, 108.

77. The same applies to special vessels, especially large ships, vessels required for the transport of obelisks up to 32 m long and up to 500 t in weight, from Alexandria to Portus or Constantinople. See also A. Wirsching, How the obelisks reached Rome: evidence of Roman double-ships. *Internat. Journal Nautical Arch.* 29, H. 2, 2000, 273–83; ibid., Die Obelisken auf dem Seeweg nach Rom, *Mitt. DAI Röm. Abt.* 109, 2002, 141–56.

78. Bockius 2000a, 111–125; amendments in Bockius 2012.

79. A prominent example is the relief block from the sanctuary of Fortuna in Praeneste in the Vatican, probably dedicated by a partisan of M. Antonius before Actium: T. Hölscher, Beobachtungen zu römischen historischen Denkmälern, *Arch. Anz.* 1979, H. 3, 342–8 The fact that this is the representation of a heavy warship has never been excluded, irrespective of the controversial precise dating of the relief: cf. *e.g.* Morrison 1996, 229f. No. 29 (reconstructed as a double bank 9). Viereck wanted to see a quadrireme in the relief 1975, 62–64 Fig. 63, while the present author (Bockius 1997, 58–61, Fig. 7, supplement no. 5) calculated on the basis of a different interpretation of a technical detail that it could have been with a three-banked 'five'. See also Casson, 1971, 144f. figs 130; 132 ('probably a quadrireme or larger'). Less productive, but worth mentioning, is the astute identification of a historical painting with a Roman-Punic 'five': Morrison 1996, 244 No. 41b.

80. Höckmann 1996, 61–72. The derivation of vessels with five (sic!) banks of oars on p. 64, Fig. 2, has to be refuted, just as there is no convincing proof of even four-bank oared vessels. See Reddé, Galères à quatre, cinq, six rangs de rames dans l'antiquité. À propos d'un passage de Lucain (*Pharsale* 3.529–37), *Mélanges École Franç. Rome* 92, 1980, 1033–7 for a careful evaluation; Höckmann 1985, 105; 114; 116 with Fig. 98 (drawing from the lost fresco in the Aula Isiaca). Critical of this is Morrison 1996, 242; Bockius 1997, 44f. Note 9.

81. Basch 1987, 419 figs 899–901; Morrison 1996, 205–7 No. 12a–g. Prows on the reverse of *aes grave* series of the late 3rd cent. BC (Hassel 1985, 6f. Fig. 5–8; 15 cat. No. 15–18 Tab. 4–5) only possibly to distinguish from the Punic ones with the help of the *stolos* (Morrison 1996, 215–19, No. 15, 19a–c, 19a). See also Höckmann 1985, 109–12 Fig. 85–6; 90.

82. Basch 1987, 419–22 Figs 899–900; 902; 904; 906; 908.

83. Hassel 1985, 27–9 Cat.-No. 124/1–2; 136/1–2; 138/1.3, Tab. 15–16; Morrison 1996, 224f. No. 24. The multi-storey architecture on an *as* of Octavian (Hassel 1985, 54 Cat. No.

333 Plate 33) and an Augustan sesterce are probable combat structures. See also Morrison 1996, 233, No. 32b.

84. Hassel 1985, 17–19 Cat. No. 34/1–2.4.7–8; 36/5; 44; 47; 52–3; 56, Tab. 8–10; 34.

85. Ibid., 15f .; 33 Cat. No. 20; 21/1; 22/3–4; 171, Tab. 5–6; 19.

86. Viereck 1975, 64; 288; 299 Bild 48; Pekáry 1999, 276f. Rome-M 11 (both with modern reconstruction!). The *columna rostrata* motif is repeatedly present on the reverse of *denarii* after Octavian, for example, *RIC* I, 271. See also the three round altars from the harbour of Antium, with prows projecting from the cylindrical shafts on one side: H. Stuart Jones, *A Catalogue of the Ancient Sculptures preserved in the Municipal Collections of Rome. The Sculptures of the Museo Capitolino.* Rome 1969, 2, 327f. No. 23a; 330f. No. 26a; 27a pl. 80 below.

87. Pekáry 1999, 24 D-36 Anh. XI; 237; 427 Rome-A11 (further Calenic bowl images in Basch 1987, 436–9 figs 947–8, 951–3, Morrison 1996, 216–19, No. 18. Berlin, Antikenslg.: Viereck 1975, 286; 292 notes Bild 17).

88. Basch 1987, 354–9 figs 747–58; 442 Fig. 969A; Morrison 1996, 219ff. No. 20; 226–9, No. 26–7.

89. M. A. Tomei, *Museo Palatino*, Rome, 1997, 65, No. 39.

90. Basch 1987, 436f. Fig. 949.

91. G. Waurick, Untersuchungen zur historisierenden Rüstung in der römischen Kunst. *Jahrg. RGZM* 30, 1983, 290ff., Plate 53.1.

92. Pekáry 1999, 398f. Vat-30a/b.

93. Ibid., 302f. I-T3.

94. For this R. Känel, Eine etruskisch-italische Traufsima mit Naumachieszene in Mainz, *Arch. Korrbl.* 34, H.1, 2004, 51–64 Fig. 1–8.

95. Pekáry 1999, 48–51 DZ-6; 64f. ET-13; 98f. GB-17; 118f. GR-32; 148 IL-18; 346–8 TN-14f; TN-15b; TN-20; 372f. TR7; 378f. T21; T24.

96. Basch 1987, 350 2 figs 737–9; *Recit d'une aventure. Les graffiti marins de Délos. Cat. Musée d'Histoire de Marseille 18 décembre 1992–22 mars 1993*, Marseille n.d., especially 24; 26f.; 44f. with Fig.

97. Pekáry 1999, 184f. I-N49; Morrison 1996, 225f No. 25 (not very convincingly interpreted as large polyremes, 'nine' or more).

98. Pekáry 1999, 82f. F-48 (Boscoreale); 158f. I-E1 (Herculaneum); 202f. I-P4h; 210f. I-P19; 228f. I-P83 (Pompeii); M. Pagano (ed.), *Gli Scavi di Ercolano*, Pompei 2003, 82 with fig. above and 83 with fig. below.

99. Pekáry 1999, 278f. Rome-M19 and 390f. Vat-1 (Palestrina). Fresco paintings from Herculaneum and Pompeii can only be used to a limited extent as iconographic evidence for early Imperial warships due to their Punic characteristics: Morrison 1996, 244f. No. 41b–42.

100. *E.g.* Pekáry 1999, 80f. F-45 (orange); 90f. F-84 (porters); 166f. I-31 (Isernia); 168 f I-N2/N3 (Puteoli); 238f. Rome-A13. Höckmann 1998, 327f. Fig. 7.3 (Mainz-Weisenau); O. Höckmann, in: M. Klein (ed.), *Die Römer und ihr Erbe. Fortschritt durch Innovation und Integration*, Mainz 2003, 91 Fig. 4. Also R. Bockius, A Roman depiction of a war ship equipped with two catapults? in: H. Tzalas (ed.), *TROPIS VI 6th International Symposium on Ship Construction in*

Antiquity, Lamia 1996, Proceedings, Athens 2001, 89–97 figs 1–2.

101. Otherwise L. Casson and E. Linder, in: L. Casson and J. R. Steffy (eds), *The Athlit Ram*. Nautical Arch. Ser. 3. College Station, Texas 1991, 68–71 figs 5.5–5.8, who consider the replacement of the type by other forms of ram or the by the abandonment of metal fittings. Contrary to this, Hadrian's coins, as well as provincial coins from Athens and Kallatis, indicate the use of the three-pronged ram in the second century: Schaaff 2003, 3; 17; 25 Cat. No. 16q; 17g; P3a–b; P55b colour chart. II 16q; 17g and Plate 12, 16q; 13, 17g; 73, P3a–b; 92, P55b.

102. M. Guarducci, *Notizi Scavi* 1953, 120 Fig. 6.

103. For this, see Bockius 2013, 23–4, Fig. 21. The graffito cannot be dated more precisely than 'the centuries around the beginning of the Christian era' (Langner 2001, 15, 68, catalog no. 1847, with the dating of M. Guarducci (note 102). If we wish to follow Tacitus' and Suetonius' notes (n. 21: 6) on the equipping of the *naumachia* with triremes and quadriremes, or only with triremes, the position of the Fucine Lake in Abruzzo at around 660 m above sea level, and the presumed sizes of such vessel classes meant that they were built specifically for the purpose at the lake.

104. Schaaff 2003, 19 Cat. No. 16a–17a Fig. 76. The railing, divided into fields with an X-shaped infill, on a late Republican *as*: Hassel 1985, 54 Cat. No. 334 Plate 33.

105. See the relief fragment of unknown origin in London at Basch 1987, 426 Fig. 918; Morrison 1996, 247f. No. 44.

106. See note 72.

107. So Höckmann 1985, 114 for the Nemi ships.

108. K. Coleman, Launching into history: aquatic displays in the Early Empire, *Journal of Roman Studies* 83, 1993, 48–74. For the forerunners, see A. Trakadas, Athenian naumachiai: Hellenistic and Imperial naval festivals and their contexts, in: H. Tzalas (ed.), *TROPIS X, 10th International Symposium on Ship Construction in Antiquity, Hydra 27 August–2 September 2008* (in preparation).

109. On the origin of the fleets and their military orders, see Kienast 1966. For the dislocation of the ship units, see Reddé 1986, 114–17; 665–71 List I; Morrison 1996, 172–5 List B.

110. *CIL* VI, 3163 (?); 3170 (?); X, 3119 (?); 3560; 3611; XIV, 232 (?). The composition of the Misene squadrons is related in letters of the younger Pliny on the fate of his uncle, who as prefect on August 24, 79, instructs several of the quadriremes stationed at *Misenum* to rescue refugees to Herculaneum: Pliny, *Epist.* 6.16.9 ('*deducit quadriremes*'); Pliny the Elder had earlier used a Liburnian to cross the sea to satisfy his curiosity about natural phenomena: ibid., 16.7 ('*iubet liburnicam aptari*'). For epigraphic records of the classes of ships and their fleets, see Reddé 1986, 665–72, Appendix I.

111. Höckmann 1998, 325 identifies constructional modifications at the stern; Höckmann 1985, 113f.

112. J. Coates, in: J. S. Morrison and J. F. Coates (eds), *An Athenian Trireme Reconstructed*, BAR Internat. Series 486, Oxford 1989, 20; 67f. Fig. 36; Morrison and Coates 1990, 253f. with table; J. F. Coates, S. K. Platis and J. T. Shaw, *The Trireme Trials 1988. Report on the Anglo-Hellenic Sea Trials of Olympias*, Oxford 1990, 2f. (1.1 m at 40 t); 63–4. Fig. 33.

113. R. Bockius, *Jahrbuch RGZM* 44, part 2, 1997, 712–16 and Höckmann 1998, 326–7, Fig. 5 reckon with small biremes.

114. See Tac., *Hist.* 5.22–23.1; See note 158.

115. Basch 1987, 443f. Figs 971B–C; 972–3A. C; 974.

116. Likewise, the fresco in Pompeii, House of the Priest Amandus: Basch 1987, 445 Fig. 977.

117. Basch 1987, 443 Fig. 971B; Pagano loc. cit. (note 98).

118. Ibid., 440f. Figs 962–4.

119. Settis *et al.* 1988, 300f.; 327f.; 397–400; 404 Fig. 44; 69f.; 140–2; 146. The amber ship from the Niessen collection in the RGM Cologne also belongs to this motif. See H. Beck and P. C. Bol (eds), *Late Antiquity, and Early Christianity. Exhibition catalogue. Frankfurt am Main*, Frankfurt 1983, 623f. Cat. No. 212, with fig. and older refs.

120. Schaaff 2003, 18f. Cat. No. P5–6; P16–17 Plate VII and Tab. 74, P5a–b; P6a.c; 76, P16a; P17a; Basch 1987, 444 Fig. 973A. C; B. Andreae, *Odysseus, Myth and Memory*, Mainz 1999, 92 with illustration in the lower left; 384 (relief shawl from Münzenberg); T. Bechert, *Roman Germania Between the Rhine and the Meuse*, Munich 1982, 177 Fig. 21 (graffito from Vechten); in addition, on the age of the plate fragment from Vechten cf. M. Polak, *South Gaulish Terra Sigillata with Potters Stamps from Vechten*, Rei Cretariae Romanae Fautorum Acta, suppl. 9. Nijmegen 2000, 12f. Fig. 1.8 (2nd quarter of the 1st century).

121. Unless the latter were to stand with single-manned oars pars pro toto for light biremes accompanying the squadron. Cichorius 1900, 14f.; 24f. underestimated the classification of vessels.

122. Schaaff 2003, 3; 5, No. 20; 34–6, plates 16, 20a; 38, 34a–36a. See also the motif on a *denarius* of Sextus Pompey: Hassel 1985, 50 Cat. No. 303 Plat. 31. The type is also on a figural brooch, probably a modern fake: M. Prell, Römische Schiffsfibeln (Roman ship brooches), in: L. Bekić (ed.), *Jurišićev zbornik. Zbornik radova u znak sjećanja na Marija Jurišića*, Zagreb 2009, 352 with Fig. 1, C3; 355; 357.

123. See Schaaff 2003, 7f.; 18 Cat. No. 53–5; 57; P11–P12 Plate V and Tab. 46–50; 75.

124. The relief fragment in the British Museum, dated around AD 100, might show a heavy bireme, without a raised foredeck, with oars passing through oar ports, and the upper row curiously divided into compartments. This could also mean a railing against the wash of the sea, which would indicate a rather light, low-decked ship, but not necessarily a bireme. See Morrison 1996, 247 no. 44 for comparisons with monuments approximately one century older. However, the monument remains obscure, because neither a much older date for the relief, nor it being a copy of an older original (such as Morrison 1996, 237f. No. 36) is likely, and declaring it the work of a stonemason using a pattern book could also be used for any other representations.

125. Schaaff 2003, 8 Cat. No. 59–60, Tab. 50–1.

126. Ibid., 2003, 36; 39 Cat. No. P100; P113 Plate IX and Tab. 107; 112.

127. Note 121. See also Yacoub 1995 (note 129).

128. Yacoub 1995, 230f., Figs 116–17a.

129. Due to the illustrated oar outrigger: see Yacoub 1995, 172f. Figs 85–6.

130. Otherwise Höckmann 1983, 428f. Fig. 15, who underestimates size and classification.

131. Schaaff 2003, 31; 34 Cat. No. P84; P92–5, Tab. 100 (Aes, Valerian, with a separate aft bulwark); 103–5.

132. 'Decorated posts': Höckmann 1983, 407f. 10; 426–9 Fig. 15.

133. This had already been considered by Höckmann (1983, 408 note 10), but was rejected. For late antique depictions of such structures, see, for example, Yacoub 1995, 135–7 Fig. 60 (1st half of the 3rd century); 171ff. Figs 85–6 (about 260); 234 Fig. 118 (3rd century); 261–7 Fig. 134a (early 4th century); J. G. Deckers, H. R. Seeliger, and G. Mietke 1987. *Die Katakombe 'Santi Marcellino e Pietro'. Repertorium der Malereien.* Roma Sotterranea Cristiana VI, Rome, Münster 1987), 321–323 No. 67, Plate 49a (4th century AD).

134. *E.g.* Schaaff 2003, 10 Cat.-No. 71 Plate VI and Tab. 60.

135. Ibid, 10 Cat. No. 72g.i.q; 73 Plate VI and Tab. 61; 63. Individual die images in *RIC* 55 (ibid., 10, Cat.-No. 72aa–ab, Tab. 62–3) convey the impression of particularly light units, possibly monoremes: Himmler 2005, 159f. Fig. 5 on the right ('Fig. 5c').

136. Ibid., 10f. Cat. No. 74; 83 Plate VI and Tab. 63; 66.

137. Ibid., 10f. Cat. No. 77–85 Plate VI and Tab. 63–6, especially Tab. 64, 77d. 78b. 79b–d; 65, 80c–d.

138. R. Bockius, Römische Kriegsschiffe auf der Mosel? Schiffsarchäologisch-historische Betrachtungen zum 'Neumagener Weinschiff'. *Funde und Ausgrabungen im Bezirk Trier* 40, 2008, 37–49 with further refs.

139. F. Dövener, Neues zum römischen Vicus von Altrier, *Empreintes-Annuaire Musée Nat. Hist Art* 1, 2008, 62; 64 Fig. 14. The present author thanks Franziska Dövener for her reference to this find, for sharing the information as well as her permission to illustrate the artefact here.

140. As with the coinage shown by Schaaff 2003, 10 Cat. No. 74b, Plate 63?

141. See Damianidis 2011, 86–8, Figs 2–3.

142. Schaaff 2003, 12 Cat. No. 87–8; 95 Plate VI and Tab. 67–8.

143. Ibid., 12 Cat. No. 88, Tab. 67.

144. Himmler 2005, 161f. Fig. 6.

145. Schaaff 2003, 9f. Cat. No. 68a; 74 b, plate 59; 63. In the case of the Roman coins of Constans I, the depictions seem to mean simple, monoreme vessels, which carry shields rigged to the open railing (ibid., 12, No. 90a–91a, Tab. 68).

146. Here, in particular, Wrecks 2 and 3: Bockius 2006, 11f. Table 2; 53–136.

147. J. H. Pryor and E. M. Jeffreys, *The Age of the ΔPOMΩN. The Byzantine Navy ca 500–1204.* The Medieval Mediterranean 62, Leiden/Boston, 2006.

148. R. Bockius, Zur Modellrekonstruktion einer byzantinischen Dromone (*chelandion*) des 10./11. Jh. im Forschungsbereich Antike Schiffahrt, RGZM Mainz, in: F. Daim and J. Drauschke (eds), *Byzanz – Das Römerreich im Mittelalter.* Monogr. RGZM 84, T. 1, Mainz 2010, 456–61, esp. 455 note 20.

149. Zosimos V 20.3. For the new use of triremes under Theodoric, see Kienast 1966, 156 with note 93.

150. Trajan's Column, Scenes IV/V and XLVIII: Settis *et al.* 1988, 264f.; 329f. Figs 6–7; 71–2. Cichorius, 1886, 28–31; 226–30. Marcus Column, Scenes III; LXXVIII–LXXIX; LXXXIV; CVIII; CXV: Coarelli 2008, 115ff.; 273f.; 285f.; 327f.; 346f.

151. Cichorius, Scenes XXXIII–XXXV and XLVI–XLVII: Settis *et al.* 1988, 299–303; 328 Figs 41–5; 70. For this, Cichorius 1886, 155–72; 219–25.

152. See G. Boetto, Fiumicino, 1. Fiumicino, 2, in: Mees, 2002, 126–47; This, The Late-Roman Fiumicino 1 Wreck: Reconstructing the Hull, in: C. Beltrame (ed.), *Boats, Ships and Shipyards. Proceedings of the Ninth International Symposium on Boat and Ship Archeology, Venice 2000,* Oxford 2003, 66–70.

153. See Coarelli 2008, XXVIII 166–7; XXXIV 178–9; LXXX 281–2.

154. See Scene CXXXIII on Trajan's Column: Settis *et al.* 1988, 505 with Fig. 247. Cichorius 1900, 306ff.

155. R. Bockius, Antike Schwergutfrachter – Zeugnisse römischen Schiffbaus und Gütertransports, in: *Steinbruch und Bergwerk. Denkmäler Römischer Technikgeschichte zwischen Eifel und Rhein.* Vulkanpark-Forsch. 2 (Mainz 2000), 122–6. Summarizing lighters idem, Antike Prahme. Monumentale Zeugnisse keltisch-römischer Binnenschiffahrt aus dem 2. Jh. v. Chr. bis ins 3. Jh. n. Chr., *Jahrbuch RGZM* 47, part 2, 2000 (2003), 439–93; idem., Antike Prahme und ihre Rolle in der Binnenschiffahrt der gallisch-germanischen Provinzen, in: K. Brandt and H. J. Kühn (eds), *Der Prahm aus dem Hafen von Haithabu. Beiträge zu antiken und mittelalterlichen Flachbodenschiffen,* Schriften Archäologisches Landesmuseum, Erg.-R. 2 (Neumünster 2004), 125–51; idem., Antike Prahme und ihre Rolle in der Binnenschiffahrt der gallisch-germanischen Provinzen, in: R. Oosting and J. van den Akker (ed.), *Rivierscheepvaart. Inleidingen gehouden tijdens het negende Glavimans-Symposium, Vleuten-De Meern, 16 mei 2003,* Amersfoort 2006, 6–24. For the exquisitely preserved new discovery from De Meern see Jansma and Morel 2007. Regional models: M. Guyon and É. Rieth, The Gallo-Roman Wrecks from Lyon, Parc Saint Georges (France), in: R. Bockius (ed.), *Between the Seas. Transfer and Exchange in Nautical Technology. Proceedings of the Eleventh International Symposium on Boat and Ship Archeology, Mainz 2006.* ISBSA 11 (Mainz, 2009), 157–65. For barge-like vessels in Germanicus' fleet and military use of large flat-bottomed vessels, see also Höckmann 1998, 329–35; 337f.

156. See also Tac., *Ann.* 2.6.2 with details of vessels in the fleet of Germanicus during its third campaign: *quaedam [naves] planae carinis, ut sine noxa siderent, … plures converso ut repente remigio hinc velle illinc adpellerent …*

157. A reference to this is provided by Tacitus, *Ann.* 2.6.2 [cf. 157], although the Roman flat-bottomed vessel, in its traditional form, was not suitable for navigation on the Wadden Sea, due to the usually low freeboard of just one metre. However, part of Germanicus' fleet sank in the rough sea (perhaps confirming the first statement): Tac., *Ann.* 2.23–24.2. On the other hand, the seasonally restricted navigability of the Rhine (Tac., *Hist.* 4.26) will have forced ship-building compromises, and another passage in Tacitus on the Batavian

insurrection (*Hist.* 5.23.2) mentions *... luntrium vis, tricenos quadragenosque ferunt, armamenta Liburnicis solita* (the Batavians).

158. Kienast 1966, 43f.; 111f.; 149f. Note 72; 151; 156.

159. On the history of the foundations, the dating and the older reference, see M. D. De Weerd, *Schepen voor Zwammerdam*, Academic Proefschrift Universiteit Amsterdam, Amsterdam 1988, 184–8; especially Höckmann 1998, 330 note 76 and Bockius 2002, 105 note 172.

160. Explained in detail by Bockius 2002, 105–13.

161. Ibid., 4 Note 10–12.

162. Cited above, 49 Note 54.

163. Cited ibid., 78 with notes 121–2; 120 with note 218.

164. Ibid., 112.

165. The waters are identified at least in section with the *fossa Drusiana*. See, for example, M. Reddé 1986, 294f. fig. 22; in addition to this, K. Huisman, De Drususgrachten. Een nieuwe hypothese, *Westerheem* 44, 1995, 188–94.

166. Bockius 2002.

167. Confirmed by H. Nowacki, Review: Die Römerzeitlichen Schiffsfunde von Oberstimm (Bayern). *Internat. Journal Nautical Arch.* 34, 2005, 351–2. The author casually dismissed the present author's cushions found up calculations on the attained rowing performances, especially the estimated cruising speed of six knots, as well as the theoretical maximum velocity of nine knots. These were also relativized by others (R. Grabert and Chr. Schäfer, in: Aßkamp and Schäfer 2008, 79–92, esp. 89 with debatable performance calculations by Chr. Schäfer and G. Wagener, in: Aßkamp and Schäfer 2008, 93–113. The oar bearings of the experimental replica as well as the shape and construction of the oars did not correspond to the standards of antiquity). It must be said that modern experiments, especially when they are not conducted absolutely uncompromisingly, under the same conditions as in antiquity, literally lag behind the results of ancient reality.

168. Bockius 2002, 119–27. For the possible applications, see also G. Wagener, Die Einsatzfelder der Oberstimm-Schiffe, in: Aßkamp and Schäfer 2008, 118–28.

169. Bockius 2006 with older ref.

170. Whether the sliding cushions found up to the 3rd century BC (Thuycidides 2.93.22, Isocr., 8.48, Plutarch, *Themist.* 4.3, *Papyrus Cairo*, Zenon 59054 – see Casson 1971, 41) were still in use in late antiquity and on such simple vessels is moot.

171. Bockius 2006, 184–7 note 279. The design was used in 1993/1994 for a museum replica in the Museum for Antique Navigation (B. Pferdehirt, Rekonstruktion eines römischen Truppentransporters aus Mainz: Typ Mainz A/Nachbau I., in: Mees and Pferdehirt 2002, 174–83) as well as for an experimental replica in the framework of a project of the Chair for Ancient History of the University of Regensburg (H. Ferkel, H. Konen, and Chr. Schäfer (eds), *Navis Lusoria – Ein Römerschiff in Regensburg*, St. Katharinen 2004; Chr. Schäfer, *Lusoria. Ein Römerschiff im Experiment*, Hamburg, 2008). For the use of the Regensburg reconstruction, see F. Himmler, H. Konen and J. Löffl, *Exploratio Danubiae. Ein rekonstruiertes spätantikes Flusskriegsschiff auf den Spuren Kaiser Julian Apostatas. Region im Umbruch 1*, Berlin 2009. The constructors of this replica seem not to have known or

were indifferent to the archaeological results from the ship to the extent that they have not even adjusted the nail pattern, which is rather relevant to the structural strength. See *Focus* 50, 2003, 109 top left figure.

172. Discussed in Bockius 2006, 184f.

173. Thus for the first time in 1997: Bockius 2000b, 121; 126 note 1; put into perspective by Pferdehirt (note 172) 183. For the justification of the length of the reconstruction of Wreck 5, see Bockius 2006, 184–7; 228; R. Bockius, 'Schiffsgeometrisch-dimensionale Rekonstruktion des spätrömischen Bootswracks Mainz 5', in: F. Brechtel, Chr. Schäfer, and G. Wagener (eds), *Lusoria Rhenana. Ein römisches Schiff am Rhein. Neue Forschungen zu einem spätantiken Schiffstyp*, Hamburg, 2016, 45–58.

174. This is especially true for the Oberstimm type: Bockius 2002, 88; 102ff. It was not possible to calculate the aspect of the secondary nature of the sails on the Mainz Type A, because the reconstruction of the hull of the ship did not offer a viable approach to it (Bockius 2006, 32–52, 177–87). On warship rigging, see Casson, 1971, 235–8.

175. For this see R. Bockius, 'Markings and pegs: clues to geometrical procedures of Roman naval architecture?', in: H. Nowacki and W. Lefèvre (eds), *Creating Shapes in Civil and Naval Architecture. A Cross-Disciplinary Comparison*, History of Science and Medicine Library 11, Leiden/Boston 2009, 73–92.

176. Bockius 2012. The figures are based on weighing a detailed 1:10 scale model (4.2 kg/4200 kg [adding 15% for unforeseen things, such as humidification = 4830 kg]) supplemented by a 2 t weight component of the crew (27 men), divided by 24 for a rowing crew of 24.

177. Bockius, 2006, 85–95; 153–60; 225–8, Fig. 4.3.

178. Ibid., 11 with Table 2; 188ff.; 215 Fig. 45.

179. See, for example, Himmler 2005, 153–79. The author, although firmly convinced of the identification of Mainz Type A with the Höckmann *navis Lusoria*, harbours doubts (ibid., 156f.; 165) as to whether the notion does not imply a class with greater carrying capacity, and also has to capitulate in the face of completely ambiguous terminology such as *naves agrarienses*.

180. Höckmann 1986, 382–415 Table 1, particularly 397–406; Bockius, 2006, 208–15; R. Scharf, Der Dux Mogontiacensis und die Notitia Dignitatum. Eine Studie zur spätantiken Grenzverteidigung. Erg. Vol. *Realexikon Germ. Altkde.* 50, Berlin/New York 2005, 37–44.

181. On dating, Bockius 2006, 10–12 Table 2.

182. Bockius 2000b, 121–6; R. Bockius, Rekonstruktion eines römischen Patrouillenschiffs: Typ Mainz B/Nachbau II., In: Mees and Pferdehirt 2002, 184–95; idem, Antike Schiffahrt. Boote und Schiffe der Römerzeit zwischen Tiber und Rhein, in: H.-P. Kuhnen (ed.), *Abgetaucht, aufgetaucht. Flussfundstücke. Aus der Geschichte. Mit der Geschichte.* Schriften des Rheinischen Landesmuseums Trier, vol. 21, Trier 2001, 131–4.

183. R. Bockius, Spuren griechisch-etruskischen Knowhows im keltischen Schiffbau?, in: H. Kelzenberg, P. Kießling, and St. Weber (eds), *Forschungen zur Vorgeschichte und Römerzeit im Rheinland. Festschr. H.-E. Joachim. Bonner Jahrb., Beih. 57*, Bonn 2007, 253–67, esp. 264–6 figs 11–14;

idem, 'Technological Transfer from the Mediterranean – The Northern Provinces', in: G. Boetto, P. Pomey, and A. Tchernia (eds), *Batellerie Gallo-Romaine. Pratiques régionales et influences Méditerranéennes*. Bibl. Arch. Méditerranéenne et Africaine 9, Aix-en-Provence 2011, 45–59, esp. 55–6 figs 11–12.

184. Höckmann 1985, 141f. 120; 1986, 416; idem, *Arch. Deutschland* 1986, H. 2, 39f., idem, in O. Lixa Filgueiras (ed.), *Local Boats. Fourth International Symposium on Boat and Ship Archeology, Porto 1985*, BAR Internat. Series 438, Oxford 1988, 31; idem, in J. P. Delgado (ed.), *Encyclopaedia of Underwater and Maritime Archeology*, London, 1997, 2 ('conjectural'). In more detail: idem, Römische Schiffsfunde in Mainz, in: U. Löber *et al.* (eds), *2000 Jahre Rheinschiffahrt*, Veröffentl. Landesmus. Koblenz, Koblenz 1991, 50–64 Fig. 2.6; 3.2; idem, *Mainz als römische Hafenstadt, in: M. Klein (ed.), Die Römer und ihr Erbe. Fortschritt durch Innovation und Integration*, Mainz 2003, 99f. Figs 11–12.

185. E. Remotti, in: Camilli and Setari 2005, 30f.

186. Bonino 2006, 21 (length '13.3 m'); Barbagli 2005, 46 ('about 14 m'). With a view of the conservation status of the hull, which is still about 12 m long (Camilli 2002, 22). It is not taken seriously by S. Bruni, Le Navi romane di San Rossore, *Arch. Viva* 18, No. 77, 1999, 45, who claims a length of '10 m' here and '11.7 m' in idem (ed.), *Le navi antiche di Pisa ad un anno dall'inizio delle ricerche*, Florence 2000, 47; 67 figs 36–7. Also see <http://www.navipisa.it/le-navi.htm> – a reconstructed addition of up to 2 m seems justified.

187. Reconstruction design by Bonino 2006, 21–4 with Fig. Photographs of the wreck and its details in Camilli and Setari 2005, 46–53.

188. Camilli 2002, 27 with Fig. 4; Barbagli 2005, 49 with Fig. Further details, 46–51 with fig.

189. Casson, 1971, 83, note 30; 87 Note 52 figs 130; 132. For *folliculi*, see *Thessaurus Linguae Latinae* VI.1, 1014f. s.v. *Folliculus: folliculare appellatur pars remi, quae folliculo est tecta* (Paulus Festus).

190. Barbagli 2005, 51 with illustration in the lower right. Frontal view in Camilli 2002, 27 Fig. 5.

191. Otherwise Bonino 2006, 24, who argues for a harbour or a pilot boat ('barca da diporto' or 'pilotina').

192. Claudianus, *Bell. Gild.* 1.483 mentions *navalia* in the 4th century.

193. *National Geographic* 162, H. 6, 1982, 691 with Fig.; 165, 5, 1984, 571; L. Franchi dell'Orto (ed.), *Ercolano 1738–1988. 250 anni di ricerca archeologica*, Monogr. 6, Rome 1988, 679–80; M. Pagano, *Ercolano. Itinerario Archeologico Ragionato*, Naples, 1997, 26–7; idem (ed.), *Gli Scavi di Ercolano*. Pompei 2003, 110 with figure lower left and 111 with figure above; M. P. Guidobaldi, Schatzgräber und Archäologen. Die Geschichte der Ausgrabungen von Herculaneum, in: J. Mühlenbrock and D. Richter (eds), *Verschüttet vom Vesuv. Die letzten Stunden von Herkulaneum*, Mainz 2005, 22–3, Fig. 6; L. Capasso, A. Di Fabrizio, E. Michetti, and R. D'Anastasio, Die Flüchtlinge am Strand. Die Untersuchungen der Skelette aus den Bootshäusern, in: Mühlenbrock and Richter 2005, 45–6; 50 figs 2 & 6. For stratigraphy, see L. Capasso, I Fuggitaschi di Ercolano. Paleobiologia delle Vittime dell'Eruzione Vesuviana del 79 d. C., *Bibl. Arch.* 33, Rome 2001, 27–30 Fig. 23A.

194. *National Geographic* 165, H. 5, 1984, 572–3 with fig.; T. Rocco, in: P. G. Guzzo and A. Wieczorek (eds), *Pompeji. Die Stunden des Untergangs 24. August 79 n. Chr.*, Publ. Reiss-Engelhorn-Mus. 13, Mannheim, 2004, 62; 70 figs 13–15.

195. Steffy 1985, 519–21 Fig. III 1; 1994, 67; 69; 71 Fig. 3–56; R. Bockius, Die Schiffsfunde von Herculaneum, in: Mees and Pferdehirt 2002, 164 ff. Figs 1–3. Ein weiterer Bootsfund aus Herculaneum: F. Ruffo, *Cronache Ercolanesi* 28, 1998, 40; 55 Fig. 11.

196. Steffy 1994, 71.

197. Steffy 1985, 521.

198. Ibid.. put into perspective by Steffy 1994, 71.

199. Bockius 2000a, 119f.; 122 with Fig. 9.

200. See L. Casson, 'Harbour and river boats of ancient Rome', *Journal Roman Studies* 55, 1965, 31–9 pl. 1.1.

201. Marsden 1994, 109–29; 181f.

202. For earlier evidence from the continent, see Bockius 2002, 2 with Fig. 2; 2006, 198–9, map 2. Including the Mediterranean area: R. Bockius, Abdichten, Beschichten, Kalfatern. Schiffsversiegelung und ihre Bedeutung als Indikator für Technologietransfers zwischen den antiken Schiffbautraditionen, *Jahrbuch RGZM* 49, 2002, 189–96 Fig. 1 maps 1–2.

203. Thus Marsden 1994, 124.

204. Arnold 1992, 21–45 with appendix. Summary R. Bockius, Das Boot Yverdon 2, in: Mees and Pferdehirt 2002, 63ff.; idem, Yverdon, Hoops, *Reallex. Germ. Altkde.* 35, 2007, 797–800 s.v. Yverdon-les-Bains.

205. See, for example, the depictions in A. Maiuri, *La Casa del Menandro e il suo, Tesoro di Argenteria*, Rome, 1932, 266–7 Fig. 107, Plate XVI; Basch 1986, 471; 473 figs 1064; 1066; *Kunst der Antike. Gallerie Günter Puhze, Katalog 16*, Freiburg 2002, 13 No. 98 Fig. 98.

206. R. Bockius, in: Mees and Pferdehirt 2002, 65.

207. Providing that *Not. Dign., Occ.* 42.15 relates to Yverdon-les-Bains. See D. van Berchem, Ebrudunum-Yverdon, station d'une flotilla militaire au Bas-Empire, *Revue Hist. Suisse* 17, 1937, 83–95; Reddé 1986, 307–8.

END MATTER

Bibliography

A. Abbegg-Wigg and A. Rau (eds) 2008: *Aktuelle Forschungen zu Kriegsbeuteopfern und Fürstengräbern im Barbaricum* (Neumünster)

Ch. Albrecht 1938: *Das Römerlager in Oberaden und das Uferkastell Beckinghausen an der Lippe I.* Veröffentl. aus d. städt. Museum Dortmund (Dortmund)

Ch. Albrecht 1942: *Das Römerlager in Oberaden und das Uferkastell Beckinghausen an der Lippe II.* Veröffentl. aus d. städt. Museum Dortmund (Dortmund)

S. Albrecht 2010: Warum tragen wir einen Gürtel? Der Gürtel der Byzantiner – Symbolik und Funktion. In: Daim and Drauschke 2010, 79–95

C.-G. Alexandrescu 2007: VTERE FELIX – O Inchizatoare de BALTEUS din Colectiile Muzeului National de Antichitati din Bucuresti. In: S. Nemeti, F. Fodorean, E. Nemeth, S. Cocis, I. Nemeti, and M. Pislaru (eds), *DACIA FELIX. Studia Michaeli Barbulescu oblata* (Cluj-Napoca), 242–9

C.-G. Alexandrescu 2010: *Blasmusiker und Standartenträger im römischen Heer. Untersuchungen zur Benennung, Funktion und Ikonographie* (Cluj-Napoca)

C.-G. Alexandrescu 2011: Neue Erkenntnisse zum römischen Cornu. Die Aussagekraft eines Exemplars im Privatbesitz. *Jahrb. RGZM* 54, 2007 (2011), 497–516

M. R. Alföldi 2001: Das Jahr 8 v.Chr.: Augustus in Gallien. Zum Skyphos mit dem Bild der Germanen im Schatz von Boscoreale. In: *Rome et ses Provinces. Festschrift für J. Ch. Balty* (Brüssel) 15–27

G. Alföldy, B. Dobson, and W. Eck (eds) 2000: *Kaiser, Heer und Gesellschaft in der römischen Kaiserzeit* (Stuttgart)

L. Allason-Jones and M. C. Bishop 1988: *Excavations at Roman Corbridge: the Hoard.* HBMCE Archaeological Report 7 (London)

L. Allason-Jones and R. Miket 1984: *The Catalogue of Small Finds from South Shields Roman Fort.* Soc. Ant. of Newcastle upon Tyne Monogr. Ser. 2 (Newcastle upon Tyne)

R. Amy et al. 1962: *L'arc d'Orange*, Gallia Suppl. 15

E. Angelicoussis 1984: The panel reliefs of Marcus Aurelius, *Mitteilungen des Deutschen Archäologischen Instituts, Römische Abteilung* 91, 141–205

F. Annibali 1995: *Guida al museo civico di Assisi e agli scavi archeologici della città* (Assisi)

B. Armbruster 2001: s. v. Metallguss. *RGA* 19 (Berlin/New York), 622–42

B. Arnoldt 1992: *Batellerie gallo-romaine sur le lac de Neuchâtel, T. 2.* Arch. Neuchâteloise 13 (Saint-Blaise)

R. Aßkamp and Chr. Schäfer (eds) 2008: *Projekt Römerschiff. Nachbau und Erprobung für die Ausstellung 'Imperium Konflikt Mythos, 2000 Jahre Varusschlacht'* (Hamburg)

D. Atkinson and L. Morgan 1987: The Wellingborough and Nijmegen marches. In: Dawson 1987, 99–108

J. Aurrecoechea Fernández 2009: Evolución y chronología de las armaduras segmentadas Romanas (*loricae segmentatae*), basadas en los hallazgos Hispánicos. In: *Limeskongress 2006*, 433–44

D. Baatz 1966: Zur Geschützbewaffnung römischer Auxiliartruppen in der frühen und mittleren Kaiserzeit. *Bonner Jahrbücher* 166, 194–207. Reprinted in: Baatz 1994, 113–26

D. Baatz 1973: *Kastell Hesselbach und andere Forschungen am Odenwaldlimes.* Limesforschungen 12 (Berlin)

D. Baatz 1984: Quellen zur Bauplanung römischer Militärlager. In: *Bauplanung und Bautheorie der Antike* (Berlin), 315–25. Reprinted in: Baatz 1994, 91–101

D. Baatz 1989: *Die Wachttürme am Limes.* Ed. 2. Kl. Schr. z. Kenntnis d. röm. Besetzungsgesch. Südwestdeutschlands 15 (Stuttgart)

D. Baatz 1990: Schleudergeschosse aus Blei – eine waffentechnische Untersuchung. *Saalburg Jahrb.* 45, 59–67. Reprinted in: Baatz 1994, 294–302

D. Baatz 1994: *Bauten und Katapulte des römischen Heeres.* MAVORS 11 (Stuttgart)

D. Baatz 2000: *Der römische Limes. Archäologische Ausflüge zwischen Rhein und Donau* (4th ed. Berlin)

D. Baatz and F.-R. Herrmann (eds) 1982: *Die Römer in Hessen* (Stuttgart)

D. Baatz, A. Hauptmann, R. Maddin 1995: Die schweren Eisenträger von der Saalburg. Zur Form, Funktion und Metallurgie. *Saalburg-Jahrbuch* 46, 25–40

D. Baatz and R. Bockius 1997: *Vegetius und die römische Flotte.* RGZM Mon. 39 (Mainz)

K. Baika 2009: Greek harbours of the Aegean. In: X. Nieto and M. A. Cau (eds), *Arqueología náutica mediterránea.* Monografies des CASC 8 (Girona 2009) 429–51

L. Bakker 1993: Raetien unter Postumus – Das Siegesdenkmal einer Juthungenschlacht im Jahre 260 n. Chr. aus Augsburg. *Germania* 71, 369–86

J. C. Balty and W. van Rengen 1993: *Apamea in Syria. The Winter Quarters of Legio II Parthica. Roman Gravestones from the Military Cemetery* (Bruxelles)

F. Baratte 1986: *Le trésor d'orfèvrerie romaine de Boscoreale* (Paris)

H. Bernhard and R. Petrovszky et al. 2006: *Geraubt und im Rhein versunken. Der Barbarenschatz.* Ausstellung Hist. Museum der Pfalz Speyer (Speyer/Stuttgart)

D. Barbargli 2005: The Wreck C. In: Camilli and Setari 2005, 46–51

M. Barbulescu 1997: *Das Legionslager von Potaissa (Turda).* Führer zu den archäologischen Denkmälern aus Dacia Porolissensis No. 7 (Zalau)

P. S. Bartoli and A. P. Dzur 1941: *Die Traianssäule. Die Geschichte des ersten und zweiten dakischen Feldzuges. Kupferstiche aus dem Jahre 1667 von Pietro Santi Bartoli. Die Erklärungen der Reliefs Neubearbeitung und Ausstattung von E. A. P. Dzur* (Voorburg)

L. Basch 1987: *Le musée imaginaire de la marine antique* (Athens)

J. D. Bateson 1981: *Enamel-working in Iron Age, Roman and Sub-Roman Britain.* BAR 93 (Oxford)

G. Bauchhenß 1978: *Germania Inferior. Bonn und Umgebung, Militärische Grabdenkmäler. Corpus signorum imperii Romani. Deutschland III 1* (Frankfurt a.M.)

L. E. Baumer, T. Hölscher, and L. Winkler 1991: Narrative Systematik und politisches Konzept in den Reliefs der Traianssäule, *JdI* 106, 261–95

T. Bechert 1999: *Die Provinzen des römischen Reiches. Einführung und Überblick* (Mainz)

T. Bechert and W. Willems 1995: *Die römische Reichsgrenze zwischen Mosel und Nordseeküste* (Stuttgart)

F. Beck and H. Chew (eds) 1991: *Masques de fer. Un officier romain du temps de Caligula* (Paris)

W. Beck and D. Planck 1980: *Der Limes in Südwestdeutschland* (Stuttgart)

M. Becker 2010: *Das Fürstengrab von Gommern.* Veröffentl. des Landesamtes für Denkmalpflege und Archäologie Sachsen-Anhalt-Landesmuseum für Vorgeschichte 63 I und II

J. Beeser 1979: Pilum murale? In: *Fundber. Baden-Württemb.* 4, 133–42

G. Behrens 1927: Fundbericht (Depotfund aus dem Mainzer Legionslager). *Mainzer Zeitschr.* 22, 29–31

G. Behrens 1950: *Das Frühchristliche und Merowingische Mainz.* RGZM Kulturgeschichtliche Wegweiser 20 (Mainz)

G. und J. Bemmann 1998: *Der Opferplatz von Nydam. Die Funde aus den älteren Grabungen Nydam-I und Nydam-II* (Neumünster)

J. Bemmann, J. and G. Hahne 1994: Waffenführende Grabinventare der jüngeren römischen Kaiserzeit und der Völkerwanderungszeit in Skandinavien. Studie zur zeitlichen Ordnung anhand der norwegischen Funde. 75. *Ber. RGK* 1994, 283–640

H. Bender 2010: Die römische Armee und ihr Einfluss auf Produktion und Bevorratung im zivilen Bereich. Beispiele aus den nordwestlichen Provinzen des Imperium Romanum. In: Eich 2010, 165–76

D. Benea and R. Petrovszky 1987: Werkstätten zur Metallbearbeitung in Tibiscum im 2. und 3. Jahrhundert n. Chr. *Germania* 65, 226–39

J. Bennett 1989: A Roman helmet in the Dominican Republic. In: van Driel-Murray 1989, 235–45

J. Bennett 1991: Plumbatae from Pitsunda (Pythus), Georgia, and some observations in their probable use. *JRMES* 2, 59–63

D. van Berchem 1985: Le port de Séleucie de Piérie et l'infrastructure logistique des guerres parthiques. *BJ* 185, 47–87

D. Bérenger 1995: Ein möglicher Wachtposten augusteischer Zeit in Bielefeld auf der Sparrenberger Egge. In: Kühlborn 1995, 170–4

A. von Berg 2006: Thür, Kreis Mayern-Koblenz, Spätkeltisches Adelsgrab. In: J. Kunow and H.-H. Wegner, *Urgeschichte im Rheinland* (Cologne) 492f.

J. Bergemann 1990: *Römische Reiterstatuen. Ehrendenkmäler im öffentlichen Bereich.* DAI Beiträge zur Erschließung hellenistischer und römischer Skulptur und Architektur 11 (Mainz)

L. Berger and G. Helmig 1989: Die Erforschung der augusteischen Militärstation auf dem Baseler Münsterhügel. In: Trier 1989, 7–24

M. Bergmann 1981: Zu Fries B der flavischen Cancelleriareliefs, *Marburger Winckelmannsprogramm 1981*, 19–31

H. Bernhard, H.-J. Engels, R. Engels, and R. Petrovszky 1990: *Der römische Schatzfund von Hagenbach* (Mainz)

G. Bersu 1964: *Die spätrömische Befestigung 'Bürgle' bei Gundremmingen.* Münchner Beitr. Vor- und Frühgesch. 10 (München)

F. Berti 1990: *Fortuna Maris. La Nave Romana di Comacchio* (Bologna)

J. M. Beyer (ed.) 2010: *Archäologie. Von der Schatzsuche zur Wissenschaft* (Mainz)

M. Biborski and J. Ilkjaer 2006: *Illerup Ådal 11/12. Die Schwerter* (Aarhus)

P. Bidwell and S. Speak 1994: *Excavations at South Shields Roman Fort I.* Society of Antiquaries of Newcastle upon Tyne with Tyne and Wear Museums. Mon. Ser. 4 (Newcastle upon Tyne)

S. Biegert and B. Steidl 2011: Ein Keramikhändler im vicus des Limeskastells Ober-Florstadt. Terra sigillata und lokale Warengruppen des 3. Jahrhunderts n. Chr. In: B. Liesen (ed.) *Terra Sigillata in den Germanischen Provinzen.* Koll. Xanten 13.–14. Nov. 2008. Xantener Ber. 20 (Mainz) 221–332

E. Birley 1986: Limesforschung seit Ernst Fabricius, *Limeskongress 1983*, 7–19

R. Birley 1996: *The Weapons. Vindolanda Res. Rep. New Ser. IV1: The Small Finds* (Bardon Mill)

R. Birley 2009: *Vindolanda, A Roman Frontier Fort on Hadrian's Wall* (Stroud)

M. C. Bishop (ed.) 1983: *Roman Military Equipment. Proceedings of a Seminar Held in the Department of Ancient History and Classical Archaeology at the University of Sheffield, 21st March 1983* (Sheffield)

M. C. Bishop (ed.) 1985: *The Production and Distribution of Roman Military Equipment. Proceedings of the Second Roman Military Equipment Research Seminar.* BAR Int. Ser. 275 (Oxford)

M. C. Bishop 1985a: The military fabricae and the production of arms in the early principate. In: Bishop 1985, 1–42

M. C. Bishop 1988: Cavalry equipment of the Roman army in the first century A.D. In: Coulston 1988, 67–195

M. C. Bishop 1989 O Fortuna: a sideways look at the archaeological record and Roman military equipment. In: van Driel-Murray 1989, 1–11

M. C. Bishop 1990: Legio V Alaudae and the crested lark. *JRMES* 1, 161–4

M. C. Bishop 1991: Soldiers and military equipment in the towns of Roman Britain. In: V. A. Maxfield and M. J. Dobson (eds), *Roman Frontier Studies 1989. Proc. of the XVth Internat. Congress of Roman Frontier Studies.* (Exeter) 21–7

M. C. Bishop 1992: The early imperial 'apron'. *JRMES* 3, 81–104

M. C. Bishop 2002: *Lorica Segmentata vol. 1. JRMES* Mon. 1 (Chirnside)

M. C. Bishop and J. C. N. Coulston 2006: *Roman Military Equipment from the Punic Wars to the Fall of Rome* (ed. 2, Oxford)

D. J. Blackmann 1982: Ancient harbours in the Mediterranean. Parts 1 + 2, *Int. Journal Nautical Arch* 11/2, 79–104; 11/3, 185–211

D. Blackman 2008: Roman shipsheds. In: Hohlfelder 2008, 23–36

T. F. C. Blagg 2000: The architecture of the legionary principia. In: Brewer 2000, 139–147

R. Bockius 1997: Vegetius und die Klassifizierung römischer Kriegsschiffe in der kaiserzeitlichen Flotte. In: Baatz and Bockius 1997, 41–64

R. Bockius 2000a: Gleichmaß oder Vielfalt? Zum interscalmium bei Vitruv (De architectura I 2,21f.). In: *Studia Antiquaria. Festschrift für Niels Bantelmann zum sechzigsten Geburtstag.* Universitätsforsch. Prähist. Arch. 63 (Bonn) 111–25

R. Bockius 2000b: A Late Roman 'river cruiser' from Mainz? On the reconstruction of Mainz, Wreck No. 3. In: J. Litwin (ed.), *Down the River to the Sea. Proceedings of the Eighth International Symposium on Boat and Ship Archaeology, Gdańsk 1997.* ISBSA (Danzig) 121–6

R. Bockius 2002: *Die römerzeitlichen Schiffsfunde von Oberstimm in Bayern.* Monogr. RGZM 50 (Mainz)

R. Bockius 2006: *Die spätrömischen Schiffswracks aus Mainz. Schiffsarchäologisch-technikgeschichtliche Untersuchung spätantiker Schiffsfunde vom nördlichen Oberrhein.* Monogr. RGZM 67 (Mainz)

R. Bockius 2007: *Schifffahrt und Schiffbau in der Antike* (Stuttgart)

R. Bockius 2012: Uniformity or multiplicity? On Vitruvius' interscalmium. In: B. Rankov (ed.), *Trireme Olympias: The Final Report* (Oxford), 170–81

R. Bockius 2013: *Ruder-Sport im Altertum. Facetten von Wettkampf, Spiel und Spektakel.* Mosaiksteine. Forschungen am RGZM 10 (Mainz)

R. Bockius 2014: ein römischer Bleiankerstock aus Germersheim (Kreis Groß-Gerau). Zu Schiffausrüstung metiterraner Techniktradition aus dem Rhein. In: RGZM (Hrsg.), *Honesta missione. Festschr. f. Barbara Pferdehirt.* Monogr. RGZM 100 (Mainz)

S. Boedecker 2010: Waffen für Vagdavercustis. *Der Limes* 2, 16–19

M. Bofinger 2012: Scutum vs. Caelum – Über die Auswirkung von Feuchtigkeit auf römische Schilde. In: Koepfer u. a. 2012, 119–28

R. Bockius 2013: *Ruder-Sport im Altertum. Facetten von Wettkampf, Spiel und Spektakel.* Mosaiksteine. Forschungen am RGZM 10 (Mainz)

R. Bockius 2014: Ein römischer Bleiankerstock aus Germersheim (Kreis Groß-Gerau). Zu Schiffausrüstung metiterraner Techniktradition aus dem Rhein. In: RGZM (Hrsg.), *Honesta missione. Festschr. f. Barbara Pferdehirt.* Monogr. RGZM 100 (Mainz)

A. Böhme 1972: Die Fibeln der Kastelle Saalburg und Zugmantel. *Saalburg Jahrb.* 29, 5–122

H. W. Böhme 1974: *Germanische Grabfunde des 4. bis 5. Jahrhunderts zwischen unterer Elbe und Loire.* Münchner Beitr. Vor- und Frühgesch. 19 (Munich)

H. W. Böhme 1975: Archäologische Zeugnisse zur Geschichte der Markomannenkriege. *Jahrb. RGZM* 22, 153–217

H. W. Böhme 1986: Zum Ende der Römerherrschaft in Britannien und die angelsächsische Besiedlung Englands im 5. Jahrhundert. *Jahrb. RGZM* 33, 469–574

H. W. Böhme 1986a: Bemerkungen zum spätrömischen Militärstil. In: H. Roth (Hrsg.), *Zum Problem der Deutung frühmittelalterlicher Bildinhalte* (Sigmaringen) 25–49

A. Böhme-Schönberger 2009: *Hautnah. Römische Stoffe aus Mainz* (Mainz)

P. C. Bol 2007: *Die Geschichte der antiken Bildhauerkunst III. Hellenistische Plastik* (Mainz)

M. Bonino 2006: Il Gabbiano. Una barca a remi di età Augustea. In: A. Camilli, A. De Laurenzi, and E. Setari (eds), *Alkedo. Navi e commerci della Pisa romana.* Ausst.-Kat. Pisa 2006, 21–4

G. C. Boon 1972: *Isca. The Roman Legionáry Fortress at Caerleon, Monmouthshire* (Cardiff)

W. Boppert 1992: *Militärische Grabdenkmäler aus Mainz und Umgebung. Corpus signorum imperii Romani.* Deutschland II 5 (Frankfurt a.M.)

L. Borhy 1990: Zwei neue Parade-Brustplatten im Ungarischen Nationalmuseum. *Bayer. Vorgesch. Bl.* 55, 299–307

D. Boschung 1987: Römische Glasphalerae mit Porträtbüsten. In: *BJ* 187, 193–258

D. Boschung 1989: *Die Bildnisse des Caligula.* Herrscherbild I 4 (Berlin)

D. Boschung, H. von Hesberg, and A. Linfert 1997: *Die antiken Skulpturen in Chatsworth sowie in Dunham Massey und Withington Hall.* Monumenta Artis Romanae 26 (Mainz)

D. Boschung 1999: Militärische Aspekte im Bild des Kaisers. In: v. Hesberg 1999, 201–11

D. Boschung 2001: Überlegungen zum Denkmal des L. Aemilius Paullus in Delphi. In: *Rome et ses Provinces. Festschrift für J. Ch. Balty* (Brüssel) 59–72

D. Boschung 2004: Ordo senatorius: Gliederung und Rang des Senats als Thema der römischen Kunst. In: W. Eck and M. Heil (eds), *Senatores populi Romani. Realität und mediale Präsentation einer Führungsschicht* (Stuttgart) 97–110

D. Boschung 2005: Montfaucon, Spence, Winckelmann: Drei Versuche, die Antike zu ordnen. In: Fischer 2005, 105–44

D. Boschung 2006: Die Tetrarchie als Botschaft der Bildmedien. Zur Visualisierung eines Herrschaftssystems. In: Boschung and Eck 2006, 349–80

D. Boschung and W. Eck 2006: *Die Tetrarchie. Ein neues Regierungssystem und seine mediale Präsentation.* ZAKMIRA-Schriften 3 (Wiesbaden)

A. V. A. J. Bosman 1999: Battlefield Flevum Velsen 1, the latest excavations, results and interpretations from features and finds. In: W. Schlüter and R. Wiegels (eds), *Rom, Germanien und die Ausgrabungen von Kalkriese.* Osnabrücker Forschungen zu Altertum und Antike-Rezeption Band 1 (Osnabrück) 91–6

A. Bottini 1988: Apulisch-Korinthische Helme. In: Bottini *et al.* 1988, 107–36

A. Bottini, M. Egg, F.-W. von Hase, H. Pflug, U. Schaaff, P. Schauer, and G. Waurick 1988: *Antike Helme. Sammlung Lipperheide und andere Bestände des Antikenmuseums Berlin.* Monogr. RGZM 14 (Mainz)

Chr. Boube-Piccot1994: *Les bronzes antiques du Maroc IV. L'équipement militaire et l'armement* (Paris)

J. Bouzek, H. Friesinger, K. Pieta, and B. Komoróczy (eds) 2000: *Gentes, Reges und Rom. Auseinandersetzung – Anerkennung – Anpassung. Festschr. f. Jaroslav Tejral zum 65. Geburtstag* (Brno)

W. C. Braat 1967: Römische Schwerter und Dolche im Rijksmuseum von Oudheden. *Oudheidkde. Mededel.* 47, 56–61

J. W. Brailsford 1961: *Hod Hill I. Antiquities from Hod Hill in the Durden Collection* (London)

R. Braun 1992: Die Geschichte der Reichs-Limes-Kommission und ihre Forschungen. In: *Der römische Limes in Deutschland.* AiD Sonderheft (Stuttgart 1992) 9–32

D. J. Breeze 2011: *The Frontiers of Imperial Rome* (Barnsley)

D. J. Breeze and B. Dobson 2000: *Hadrian's Wall* (London, 4th ed.)

D. J. Breeze and M. C. Bishop (eds) 2013: *The Crosby Garrett Helmet* (Pewsey)

R. J. Brewer (ed.) 2000: *Roman Fortresses and their Legions. Papers in Honour of George C. Boon, FSA, FRHistS* (London)

C. Bridger 1994: Die römerzeitliche Besiedlung der Kempener Lehmplatte. *BJ* 194, 83

R. Brilliant 1967: *The Arch of Septimius Severus in the Roman Forum.* Memoirs of the American Academy in Rome 29 (Rome)

M. Brouwer 1982: Römische Phalerae und anderer Lederbeschlag aus dem Rhein. *Oudheidkundige Mededeelingen uit het Rijksmuseum von Oudheden te Leiden* 63, 145–87

M. Brüggler, M. Buess, M. Heinzelmann, and M. Nieberle 2010: Ein bislang unentdecktes Standlager am Niederrhein. *Der Limes* 4, Heft 1, 6–8

M. Brüggler, Ch. Dirsch, M. Drechsler, R. Schwab, and F. Willer 2012: Ein römischer Schienenarmschutz aus dem Auxiliarlager Till-Steincheshof und die Messingherstellung in der römischen Kaiserzeit. *BJ* 212, 121–52

P. A. Brunt 1975: Did Imperial Rome disarm her subjects? *Phoenix* 29, 260–70

O. Büchsenschütz 2008: Des champs de bataille nationaux aux 'oppida' européens. In: M. Reddé and S. von Schnurbein (eds) *Alésia et la bataille du Teutoburg. Un parallèle critique des sources.* Beiheft Francia 66 (Ostfildern) 181–3

T. Buijtendorp 2006: De voorganger van Forum Hadriani. Van inheemse nederzetting tot centrale plaats. In: *Forum Hadriani. Van Romeinse stad tot monument* (Utrecht) 66–76

H. Bullinger 1969: *Spätantike Gürtelbeschläge. Typen, Herstellung, Trageweise und Datierung* (Bügge)

A. Bursche 2013: The battle of Abritus, the Imperial treasury and aurei in Barbaricum. *Numismatic Chronicle* 173, 151–70; Taf. 1–37

A. Busch 2001: Von der Provinz zum Zentrum – Bilder auf den Grabdenkmälern einer Eliteeinheit. In: Noelke 2001, 679–94

A. W. Busch 2009b: Victoria auf der Wangenklappe – Ein klassisches Bildmotiv auf dem Helm eines Auxiliarsoldaten. *Xantener Ber.* 15 (Mainz) 329–46

A. W. Busch 2010: *Militär in Rom.* Palilia 20 (Wiesbaden)

A. W. Busch 2010a: Dalla villa imperiale ai Castra Albana: le nouve ricerche des DAI sull'acampamento della legio II Parthica e sui suoi dintorni. In: G. Ghini (ed.) *Lazio e Sabina 7* (Rome) 259–67

A. W. Busch 2011: Von der Kaiservilla zu den castra. Das Lager der legio II Parthica in Albano Laziale und seine Vorgängerbebauung – ein Vorbericht zu den Projektarbeiten in 2009. *KuBA* 1, 87–94

A. W. Busch and H.-J. Schalles 2009: *Waffen in Aktion. Akten der 16. Internationalen Roman Military Equipment Conference (ROMEC) Xanten, 13.–16. Juli 2007.* Xantener Ber. 19 (Mainz)

M. Buora (ed.) 2002: *Miles Romanus dal Po al Danubio nel Tardoantico* (Pordenone)

J. P. Bushe-Fox 1932: *Third Report on the Excavations of the Roman Fort at Richborough, Kent.* Reports Research Comm. Soc. Ant. London No. 10 (Oxford)

J. P. Bushe-Fox 1949: *Fourth Report on the Excavations of the Roman Fort at Richborough, Kent.* Reports Research Comm. Soc. Ant. London No. 14 (Oxford)

E. Cabré-Herreros and J. A. Morán Cabré 1991: Punales dobleglobulares con probale simbologia astral en el pomo de la empunadura. In: *XX Congreso Nacional de Arqueologia* (Zaragoza) 341–8

D. Calomino 2011: Sea rams from Sicily. *Minerva* 22, H. 6, 32–4

A. Camilli 2002: Pisa shipwrecks; the state of the art. In: H. Tzalas (ed.), *8th International Symposium on Ship Construction in Antiquity, Hydra 2002. Proceedings,* offprint (Athens)

A. Camilli and E. Setari (eds) 2005: *Ancient Shipwrecks of Pisa. A Guide* (Milano)

B. Cämmerer, Ph. Filtzinger, and D. Planck 1986: *Die Römer in Baden-Württemberg* (Stuttgart, 3rd ed.)

D. B. Campbell 2006: *Roman Fortresses 27 BC–AD 378.* Illustrated by B. Delf (Oxford)

D. B. Campbell 2009: *Roman Auxiliary Forts 27 BC–AD 378.* Illustrated by B. Delf (Oxford)

C. v. Carnap-Bornheim 1991: *Die Schwertriemenbügel aus dem Vimose (Fünen). Zur Typologie der Schwertriemenbügel der römischen Kaiserzeit im Barbarikum und in den römischen Provinzen.* Kleine Schr. Marburg 38 (Marburg)

C. v. Carnap-Bornheim (ed.) 1994a: *Beiträge zu römischer und barbarischer Bewaffnung in den ersten vier nachchristlichen Jahrhunderten.* Veröffentl. Vorgesch. Seminars Marburg Sonderband 8 (Lublin/Marburg)

C. v. Carnap-Bornheim 2003: Zu den Prachtgürteln aus Ejsbøl und Neudorf-Bornstein. In: *Sieg und Triumpf,* 240–5

M. Saliola and F. Casprini 2012: *Pugio - Gladius Brevis Est. History and Technology of the Roman Battle Dagger.* BAR Int. Ser. 2404 (Oxford)

L. Casson 1971: *Ships and Seamanship in the Ancient World* (Princeton/New Jersey)

L. Casson 1994: *Ships and Seafaring in Ancient Times* (London)

E. Chirila *et al.* 1972: *Das Römerlager von Buciumi* (Klausenburg)

K. Christ 1992: *Geschichte der römischen Kaiserzeit* (Munich ed.2)

R. Christlein and Th. Fischer 1979: Neues zum Lager Eining-Unterfeld. *Arch. Korr. Bl.* 9, 1979, 423–8

C. Cichorius 1896–1900: *Die Reliefs der Trajanssäule* (Berlin)

S. Ciglenecki 1987: *Höhenbefestigungen aus der Zeit vom 3. bis 6. Jh. im Ostalpenraum* (Ljubljana)

Ch.-O.-F.-J.-B. de Clarac 1841: *Musée de sculture antique et moderne II* (Paris) 747–50 Nr. 313 Taf. 221 Abb. 751

F. Coarelli 2008: *La Colonna di Marco Aurelio – The Column of Marcus Aurelius* (Rome)

J. Coates 2002: On working the Piraeus shipsheds. In: *Tropis VII. 7th International Symposium on Ship and Boat Construction in Antiquity* (Athen) 265–78

W. Coblenz 1960: Ein reiches kaiserzeitliches Grab aus Zauschwitz, Kreis Borna. *Arbeitsu. Forschungsber. Sachsen* 8, 29–38

P. Connolly 1976: *The Roman Army* (London)

P. Connolly 1987: The Roman saddle. In: Dawson 1987, 7–27

P. Connolly 1989: A note on the origin of the Imperial Gallic helmet. In: van Driel-Murray 1989, 227–34

P. Connolly 1990: *Tiberius Claudius Maximus: The Roman Legionary* (Oxford)

P. Connolly 1990a: *Tiberius Claudius Maximus: The Roman Cavalryman* (Oxford)

P. Connolly 1991: The Roman fighting technique deduced from armour and weaponry. In: *Roman Frontier Studies 1989* (Exeter) 358–63

P. Connolly 2002: The *pilum* from Marius to Nero – a reconsideration of its developement and function. *JRMES* 12/13, 1–8

P. Couissin 1926: *Les armes romaines* (Paris)

J. C. Coulston 1985: Roman archery equipment. In: Bishop 1985, 220–366

J. C. Coulston 1987: Roman military equipment in third century tombstones. In: Dawson 1987, 141–5

J. C. Coulston (ed.) 1988: *Military equipment and the identity of Roman Soldiers. Proceedings of the Fourth Roman Military Equipment Conference.* BAR Int. Ser. 394 (Oxford)

J. C. Coulston 1988a: Three legionaries from Croy Hill. In: Coulston 1988, 1–29

J. C. Coulston 1989: The value of Trajan's Column as a source for military equipment. In: van Driel-Murray 1989, 31–45

J. C. Coulston 2007: By the sword united: Roman fighting styles on the battlefield and in the arena. In: B. Molloy (ed.), *The Cutting Edge. Studies in Roman and Medieval Combat* (Stroud) 34–220

R. Cowan 2008: *Imperial Roman Legionary AD 161–284.* Illustrated by A. McBride (Oxford)

B. Cunliffe (ed.) 1988: *The Temple of Sulis Minerva at Bath, Vol. 2. The Finds from the Sacred Spring.* Oxford University Committee for Archaeology Mon. 16 (Oxford)

H. Cüppers (ed.) 1990: *Die Römer in Rheinland-Pfalz* (Stuttgart)

J. Curle 1911: *A Roman Frontier Post and Its People. The Roman Fort at Newstead* (Glasgow)

K. Czarnecka 1997: Germanic weaponry of the Przeworsk culture and its Celtic background. *JRMES* 8, 291–7

W. Czysz 1986: Ein spätrömisches Waffengrab aus Westendorf, Lkr. Augsburg. *Bayer. Vorgesch. Bl.* 51, 261–71

W. Czysz, Kh. Dietz, Th. Fischer, and H.-J., Kellner 1995: *Die Römer in Bayern* (Stuttgart)

B. van Daele 2005: Roman and Early Byzantine military equipment at Pisidian Sagalassos/Turkey. In: Jilek 2005, 233–40

F. Daim and J. Drauschke. 2010: *Byzanz – das Römerreich im Mittelalter. Teil 1. Welt der Ideen, Welt der Dinge.* Mon. RGZM 84, 1 (Mainz)

R. D'Amato 2009: *Imperial Roman Naval Forces 31 BC–AD 500.* Illustrated by G. Sumner (Oxford)

R. D'Amato and G. Sumner 2009: *Arms and Armour of the Imperial Roman Soldier. From Marius to Commodus, 112 BC–AD 192* (London)

K. Damianidis 2011: Roman ship graffiti in the Tower of the Winds in Athens. *Arch. Korr. Bl.* 41, H. 1, 85–99

D. P. Davison 1989: *The Barracks of the Roman Army from the 1st to 3rd Centuries A.D.* BAR Int. Ser. 427 (Oxford)

M. Dawson (ed.) 1987: *Roman Military Equipment: The Accoutrements of War. Proceedings of the Third Roman Military Equipment Research Seminar.* BAR Int. Ser. 336 (Oxford)

F. De Caprariis 2002: Druso, Giove Feretrio e le coppe 'imperiali' di Boscoreale, *MEFRA* 114, 717–37

S. De Maria 1988: *Gli archi onorari di Roma e dell' Italia romana* (Rome)

K. V. Decker 1993: Vier römische Reiterschwerter aus Mainz. *Mitt. Hist. Verein Pfalz* 91, 21–7

F. W. Deichmann 1969: *Ravenna: Hauptstadt des spätantiken Abendlandes. Bd. 1: Geschichte und Monumente* (Wiesbaden)

A. Demandt 2007: *Die Spätantike. Römische Geschichte von Diocletian bis Justinian 284–565 n.Chr.* Handb. d. Altertumswiss. III 6 (Munich²)

E. Deschler-Erb 1996: Die Kleinfunde aus Edelmetall, Bronze und Blei. In: *Beiträge zum römischen Oberwinterthur-Vitudurum 7. Ausgrabungen im Unteren Bühl.* Monogr. Kantonsarch. Zürich 27 (Zürich/Egg)

E. Deschler-Erb 1997: Vindonissa: Ein Gladius mit reliefverzierter Scheide und Gürtelteilen aus dem Legionslager. *Jber. GPV*, 13–30

E. Deschler-Erb 1999: *Ad Arma! Römisches Militär des 1. Jahrhunderts n. Chr. In Augusta Raurica.* Forsch. In August 28 (Augst)

E. Deschler-Erb 2000: Niellierung auf Buntmetall: Ein Phänomen der frühen römischen Kaiserzeit. *Kölner Jahrb.* 33, 383–96

E. Deschler-Erb 2004: Ein 'Fellhelm' aus Vindonissa. *Jber. GPV*, 3–12

E. Deschler-Erb, M. Peter, and S. Deschler-Erb 1991: *Das frühkaiserzeitliche Militärlager in der Kaiseraugster Unterstadt.* Forsch. Augst 12 (Augst)

E. Descher-Erb and P.-A. Schwarz 1993: Eine bronzene Speerspitze aus der Insula 22. *Jahresber. Augst u. Kaiseraugst* 14, 173–83

E. Deschler-Erb 1996: *Die Funde aus Metall. Ein Schrank mit Lararium des 3. Jahrhunderts. Ausgrabungen im Unteren Bühl. Beiträge zum römischen Oberwinterthur-Vitudurum 7.* Monogr. Kantonsarch. Zürich 27 (Zürich/Egg)

Kh. Dietz and Th. Fischer 1996: *Die Römer in Regensburg* (Regensburg)

B. Dobson 1978: *Die Primipilares. Entwicklung und Bedeutung, Laufbahnen und Persönlichkeiten eines römischen Offiziersranges*. Beih. BJ 37 (Köln, Bonn)

M. Dobson 2008: *The Army of the Roman Republic. The Second Century BC, Polybius and the Camps at Numantia, Spain* (Oxford)

H. Dolenz, Ch. Flügel, and Ch. Öllerer 1995: Militaria aus einer Fabrica auf dem Magdalensberg. In: *Festschr. G. Ulbert* (Espelkamp) 51–80

A. von Domaszewski 1967: *Die Rangordnung des römischen Heeres. Einführung, Berichtigungen und Nachträge von Brian Dobson*. Beih. BJ 14 (Köln, Graz²)

A. van Doorselaer 1963/64: Provinzialrömische Gräber mit Waffenbeigaben aus dem Rheinland und Nordfrankreich. *Saalburg Jahrb.* 21, 26–31

M. Döring 2003: Römische Häfen und Tunnelbauten der Phlegraeischen Felder. In: *Wasserhistorische Forschungen. Schwerpunkt Antike*. Schriften der Deutschen Wasserhistorischen Gesellschaft (DWhG) Vol. 2 (Siegburg) 35–53

W. von Dorow 1826/27: *Römische Alterthümer in und um Neuwied am Rhein; mit Grundrissen, Aufrissen und Durchschnitten des daselbst ausgegrabenen Kastells, und Darstellungen der darin gefundenen Gegenstände*. Die Denkmale germanischer und römischer Zeit in den Rheinisch-Westfälischen Provinzen 2 (Berlin)

A. Down and M. Rule 1971: *Chichester Excavations 1* (Oxford)

F. Dörschel 2012: Eine römische Pfeilspitze aus Augsburg-Oberhausen. In: Koepfer *et al.* 2012, 93–6

W. Drack 1990: Hufeisen in, auf und über römischen Straßen in Oberwinterthur. Ein Beitrag zur Geschichte des Hufeisens. *Bayer. Vorgesch. Bl.* 55, 191–239

H. Dragendorff, F. Koepp, and G. Krüger 1905: Das Uferkastell bei Haltern. Ausgrabungen in Haltern. Das Uferkastell 1903 und 1904. Mitt. Altertums-Komm. Westfalen 4 (Münster) 33–79

F. Drexel 1924: Römische Paraderüstung. In: M. Abranic and V. Hoffiller (eds), *Strena Bucolica* (Belgrad)

J. Driehaus (†) *et al.* 2010: Die Panzer von Augsburg und Vice. Eine Untersuchung zur Metalltechnologie im 1. Jahrhundert n. Chr. With contributions by Ch. Raub and L. Bakker, with a foreword by M. Radnoti-Alföldi. *91. Ber. RGK*, 239–408

C. van Driel-Murray 1985: The production and supply of military leatherwork in the first and second centuries AD, a review of the archaeological evidence. In: Bishop 1985, 43–81

C. van Driel-Murray (ed.) 1989: Roman military equipment: the sources of evidence. *Proceedings of the Fifth Roman Military Equipment Conference*. BAR Int. Ser. 476 (Oxford)

C. van Driel-Murray 1989a: The Vindolanda chamfrons and miscellaneous items of leather horsgear. In: van Driel-Murray 1989, 281–318

C. van Driel-Murray 1990: New light on old tents, *JRMES* 1, 109–37

C. van Driel-Murray 1994: Wapentiug voor Hercules. In: N. Roymans and T. Derks (eds), *De tempel van Empel. Een Hercules-heiligdom in het woongebied van de Bataven* ('s-Hertogenbosch 1994) 92–107

C. van Driel-Murray 1999: A rectangular shield cover of the Coh. XV. Voluntariorum. *JRMES* 10, 1999, 45–54

C. van Driel-Murray 2000: A late Roman assemblage from Deurne (Netherlands). *BJ* 200, 293–308

C. van Driel-Murray and M. Gechter 1983: Funde aus der Fabrika der legio I Minervia aus Bonner Berg. *Rhein. Ausgr.* 63, 1–83

C. Dulière 1964: Beschlagbleche aus Bronze mit dem Bild der römischen Wölfin. *Jahresber. GPV*, 5–14

W. Ebel-Zepezauer 2003: Die augusteischen Marschlager in Dorsten-Holsterhausen. *Germania* 81, 2, 539–55

W. Ebel-Zepezauer, Ch. Grünewald, P. Ilisch, J.-S. Kühlborn, and B. Tremmel 2009: *Augusteische Marschlager und Siedlungen des 1. bis 9. Jahrhunderts in Dorsten-Holsterhausen*. Bodenaltertümer Westfalens 47 (Mainz)

W. Eck 1990 Ein Armamentarium für die equites et pedites singulares in Köln. *Kölner Jahrb. Vor- und Frühgeschichte* 23, 127–30

W. Eck 1997: Lateinische Epigraphik. In: F. Graf (ed.) *Einleitung in die lateinische Philologie* (Stuttgart/Leipzig) 92–111

W. Eck 2004: *Köln in römischer Zeit. Geschichte einer Stadt im Rahmen des Imperium Romanum*. Geschichte der Stadt Köln Bd. 1 (Köln)

W. Eck 2010: Friedenssicherung und Krieg in der römischen Kaiserzeit. Wie ergänzt man das römische Heer? In: Eich 2010, 87–110

W. Eck 2010a: Epigraphik und Archäologie – zwei symbiotische Wissenschaften. In: Beyer 2010, 174–82

W. Eck and A. Pangerl 2006: Zur Herstellung der Diplomata Militaria: Tinte auf einem Diplom des Titus für Noricum. *ZPE* 157, 181–4

W. Eck and A. Pangerl 2008: Moesien und seine Truppen. Neue Diplome für Moesia und Moesia Superior. *Chiron* 38, 317–94

W. Eck and A. Pangerl 2009: Moesien und seine Truppen II. Neue Diplome für Moesia, Moesia Inferior und Moesia Superior. *Chiron* 39, 505–89

W. Eck and H. Wolff (eds) 1986: *Heer und Integrationspolitik. Die römischen Militärdiplome als historische Quelle*. Passauer Hist. Forsch. 2 (Cologne/Vienna)

H. J. Eggers 2004: *Einführung in die Vorgeschichte* (4th ed. Berlin)

M. K. H. Eggert 2001: *Prähistorische Archäologie. Konzepte und Methoden* (Tübingen/Basel)

A. Eich (ed.) 2010: *Die Verwaltung der kaiserzeitlichen römischen Armee. Studien für Hartmut Wolff*. Historia Einzelschr. 211 (Stuttgart)

K.-V.von Eickstedt 1991: *Beitrage zur Topographie des antikes Piraeus* (Athens)

M. El-Saghir, J.-C. Golvin, M. Reddé, E.-S. Hegazy, and G. Wagner 1986: *Le camp romain de Louqsor*. MIFAO 83 (Cairo)

R. Embleton and F. Graham 2003: *Hadrian's Wall in the Days of the Romans* (Newcastle upon Tyne)

C. Engelhardt 1863: *Thorsberg Mosefund*. Sønderjydske Mosefund 1 (Copenhagen)

P. Erdkamp (ed.) 2007: *A Companion to the Roman Army*. Blackwell Companions to the Ancient world (Oxford)

Ch. Ertel, V. Gassner, S. Jilek, and H. Stieglitz 1999: *Untersuchungen zu den Gräberfeldern in Carnuntum. Bd. 1 Der archäologische Befund*. RLÖ 40 (Vienna)

Ch. Ertel 1999a: *Das römische Hafenviertel von Brigantium/Bregenz*. Schriften des Vorarlberger Landesmuseums Reihe A: Landschaftsgeschichte und Archäologie 6 (Bregenz)

S. Estiot 2008: Sine arcu sagittae: La réprésentation numismatique de plumbatae/mattiobarbuli aux IIIe-IVe siècles (279–307 de n. è.). In: M. Alram and H. Winter (eds) *Festschr. f. Günther Dembski z. 65. Geburtstag Teil I*, Numismat. Zeitschr. 116/117 (Vienna) 177–201

R. Éttienne, I. Piso, and A. Diaconescu 2004: Les fouilles du Forum Vetus de Sarmizegetusa. Rapport général. *Acta Musei Napocensis* 39/40I, 202–23 (24) 59–154

E. Ettlinger and M. Hartmann 1984: Fragmente einer Schwertscheide aus Vindonissa und ihre Gegenstücke vom Grossen St. Bernhard. *Jber. GPV* 5–46

A. Faber 1994: *Das römische Auxiliarkastell und der Vicus von Regensburg-Kumpfmühl*. MBV 49 (Munich)

R. Fahr 2005: Frühkaiserzeitliche Militärausrüstung vom Gelände eines Feldlagers aus dem Bataveraufstand – Hinterlassenschaften eines Gefechtes? In: Jilek 2005, 109–36

R. Fahr and Ch. Miks 2001: Bewaffnung und Ausrüstung. In: Fischer 2001, 224–45

P. Fasold 1995: Ein keltisch-römischer Bronzehelm aus Frankfurt am Main. In: W. Czysz, C.-M. Hüssen, H.-P. Kuhnen, C. S. Sommer, and G. Weber (eds), *Festschrift für Günter Ulbert zum 65. Geburtstag* (Espelkamp), 81–8

R. Fellmann 1957: *Das Grab des Lucius Munatius Plancus bei Gaeta*. Schr. Inst. f. Ur- u. Frühgesch. d. Schweiz 11 (Basel)

R. Fellmann 1957/58: Die Principia des Legionslagers Vindonissa und das Zentralgebäude der römischen Lager und Kastelle. *Jber. GPV*, 1–174

R. Fellmann 1983: *Principia-Stabsgebäude*. Schr. Limesmus. Aalen 31 (Stuttgart)

R. Fellmann (with contributions by W. B. Stern, A. Burkhardt and Th. Rehren) 1999: Das Zink-Täfelchen vom Thormebodewald auf der Engehalbinsel bei Bern und seine keltische Inschrift. *Archaeologie im Kanton Bern* 4B, 133–75

M. Feugère 1985: Nouvelles observations sur les cabochons de bronze estampés du cingulum romain. In: Bishop 1985a, 117–41

M. Feugère 1993: L'évolution du mobiier non céramique dans les sépultures antique de Gaule méridionale (IIe sieécle av. J.-C.). In: M. Struck (ed.), *Römerzeitliche Gräber als Quellen zu Religion, Bevölkerungsstruktur und Sozialgeschichte*. Arch. Schr. Inst. Vor- u. Frühgesch. Johannes-Gutenberg-Univ. Mainz 3 (Mainz)

M. Feugère 1994: *Casques antiques. Les visages de la guerre de Mycènes à la fin de l'Empire Romaine* (Paris)

M. Feugère 2002: *Les armes des Romains de la République à Antiquité tardive* (ed. 2 Paris)

Ph. Filtzinger 1983: *Limesmuseum Aalen* (ed. 3 Stuttgart)

Ph. Filtzinger, D. Planck, and B. Cämmerer 1986: *Die Römer in Baden-Württemberg* (Stuttgart)

G. Fingerlin 1971/72: Dangstetten, ein augusteisches Lager am Hochrhein. Vorbericht über die Grabungen 1967–1969. *Ber. RGK* 51/52, 197–232

G. Fingerlin 1981: Eberzahnanhänger aus Dangstetten. *Fundber. Baden-Württemberg* 6, 417–432

G. Fingerlin 1986: *Dangstetten I. Katalog der Funde (Fundstellen 1 bis 603)*. Forsch. u. Ber. z. Vor- u. Frühgesch. Baden-Württemberg 22 (Stuttgart)

G. Fingerlin 1998: *Dangstetten II. Katalog der Funde (Fundstellen 604 bis 1358)*. Forsch. u. Ber. z. Vor- u. Frühgesch. Baden-Württemberg 69 (Stuttgart)

Th. Fischer 1984: Ein germanisches Gräberfeld der jüngeren Kaiserzeit aus Berching-Pollanten, Lkr. Neumarkt i. d. Oberpfalz, Oberpfalz. *AJB* 1983, 123–8

Th. Fischer 1985: Ein Halbfabrikat von der Wangenklappe eines römischen Reiterhelmes aus dem Lager von Eining-Unterfeld, Gde. Neustadt, Lkr. Kelheim. *Bayer. Vorgesch. Bl.* 50, 477–82

Th. Fischer 1988: Zur römischen Offiziersausrüstung im 3. Jahrhundert n. Chr. *Bayer. Vorgesch. Bl.* 53, 167–90

Th. Fischer 1990: *Das Umland des römischen Regensburg*. Münchner Beitr. Vor- u. Frühgesch. 42 (Munich)

Th. Fischer 1991: Zwei neue Metallsammelfunde aus Künzing/Quintana (Lkr. Deggendorf, Niederbayern). In: *Spurensuche. Festschr. f. H.-J. Kellner zum 70. Geburtstag* (Kallmünz) 125–75

Th. Fischer 1995: Ein römischer Hortfund aus Affecking, Stadt Kelheim. In: Festschr. G. Ulbert 1995, 339–47

Th. Fischer 1997: Gladius und caligae. Tracht und Bewaffnung des römischen Heeres in der frühen und mittleren Kaiserzeit. In: Schallmayer 1997, 126–133

Th. Fischer 1999: Materialhorte des 3. Jhs. in den römischen Grenzprovinzen zwischen Niedergermanien und Noricum. In: *Das mitteleuropäische Barbaricum und die Krise des römischen Weltreiches im 3. Jahrhundert*. Spisy Arch. Ústavu AV Brno (Brno) 19–50

Th. Fischer 1999a: Zum Einfluß des Militärs auf die zivile Besiedlung in den Nordwestprovinzen des römischen Reiches. In: von Hesberg 1999, 67–74

Th. Fischer 2000: Zur Herstellung militärischer Bronzen im spätrömischen Kastell Haus Bürgel. In: Friesinger, H., Pieta, K., Rajtár, J. (eds) *Metallgewinnung und -verarbeitung in der Antike (Schwerpunkt Eisen)* Arch. Inst. d. Slowakischen Ak. d. Wiss (Nitra) 113–16

Th. Fischer 2000a: Germanische Speer- und Lanzenspitzen aus dem Mündungsbereich der Naab in die Donau bei Regensburg-Großprüfening. In: Bouzek *et al.* 2000, 67–75

Th. Fischer 2000b: Die römische Armee als Wirtschaftsfaktor. In: Wamser 2000, 49–52

Th. Fischer 2000c: Neuere Forschungen zum römischen Flottenlager Köln-Alteburg. In: Grünewald and Schalles 2000, 547–64

Th. Fischer, (ed.) 2001: *Die römischen Provinzen. Eine Einführung in das Studium ihrer Archäologie* (Stuttgart)

Th. Fischer 2001a: Waffen und militärische Ausrüstung in zivilem Kontext – grundsätzliche Erklärungsmöglichkeiten. *Jber. GPV*, 13–18

Th. Fischer 2002: *Noricum* (Mainz)

Th. Fischer 2002a: Zu einer römischen Soldatendarstellung aus Lentia/Linz an der Donau. In: K. Kuzmová, K. Pieta, and J. Rajtár (eds), *Zwischen Rom und dem Barbarikum. Festschrift für Titus Kolnik zum 70. Geburtstag*. Archaeologica Slovaca Monographiae 5 (Nitra) 89–96

Fischer 2004: Th. Fischer, Ein römischer Legionärshelm des 1. Jahrhunderts n. Chr. aus dem Po bei Cremona im römisch-germanischen Museum zu Köln. *Kölner Jahrb.* 37, 61–76

Th. Fischer 2004a: Bemerkungen zu Grab 622 von Kemnitz, Kreis Potsdam in Brandenburg. In: Friesinger, H. and Stuppner, A. (eds) *Zentrum und Peripherie – Gesellschaftliche Phänomene in der Frühgeschichte. Mat. D. 13. Int. Symp. 'Grundprobleme der frühgeschichtlichen Entwicklung im mittleren Donauraum' Zwettl 4.–8. Dez. 2000* (Vienna) 131–41

Th. Fischer 2005: Militaria aus Zerstörungsschichten in dem römischen Flottenlager Köln-Alteburg. In: Jilek 2005, 153–64

Th. Fischer (ed.) 2005a: *Bilder von der Vergangenheit. Zur Geschichte der archäologischen Fächer.* ZAKMIRA-Schriften 2 (Wiesbaden)

Th. Fischer 2005b: Geschichte der Provinzialrömischen Archäologie in Deutschland. In: Fischer 2005b, 193–212

Th. Fischer 2006: Das römische Heer in der Zeit der Tetrarchie. Eine Armee zwischen Innovation und Kontinuität? In: Boschung and Eck 2006, 103–32

Th. Fischer 2008: Bemerkungen zum sogenannten Gesichtshelm aus Thorsberg. In: Abegg-Wigg and Rau 2008, 105–23

Th. Fischer 2008a: Der Helm des Bassus. *Antike Welt* 5, 28–9

Th. Fischer 2009: Zerstörungshorizonte. Germanische Übergriffe und ihr archäologischer Niederschlag. In: Konflikt 2009, 109–13

Th. Fischer 2009a: Römische Militärlager und zivile Siedlungen in Germanien zwischen Rhein und Elbe zur Zeit Marbods (von der Drusus-Offensive 12/9 v. Chr. bis zu der Aufgabe der römischen Eroberungspläne 17 n. Chr.). Ein aktueller Überblick. In: Salac and Bemmann 2009, 485–519

Th. Fischer 2009b: Römische Waffen in Aktion – Kampfspuren. In: Busch and Schalles 2009, 1–7

Th. Fischer 2009c: Von den Römern zu den Bayern. In: S. Bonk and P. Schmid (eds), *Bayern unter den Römern. Facetten einer folgenreichen Epoche* (Regensburg) 23–56

Th. Fischer 2010: Provinzialrömische Archäologie. In: Beyer 2010, 163–73

Th. Fischer 2011: Teile von römischen Waffen und militärischer Ausrüstung aus den Grabungen in Dülük Baba Tepesi in den Jahren 2004–2009. In: E. Winter (ed.) *Von Kummuh nach Telouch. Historische und archäologische Untersuchungen in Kommagene.* Asia Minor Studien 64. Dolichener und Kommagenische Forschungen IV (Bonn) 105–19

Th. Fischer 2012: Zur Dolchaufhängung im späten 2. und frühen 3. Jahrhundert n. Chr. In: *Festschr. für Jürgen Oldenstein* (Bonn)

Th. Fischer 2012a: Archaeological evidence of the Marcomannic Wars of Marcus Aurelius (AD 166–180). In: M. van Ackeren (ed.), *A Companion to Marcus Aurelius* (Oxford)

Fischer 2012b: Fischer, Th., Waffenweihungen und Tropaia im römischen Reich. In: W. Meighörner (ed.), *Waffen für die Götter. Krieger, Trophäen, Heiligtümer* (Innsbruck) 206–13

Th. Fischer 2013: Römische Militärgürtel aus Edelmetall. In: M. Hardt and O. Heinrich Tamáska (eds) *Macht des Goldes, Gold der Macht. Herrschafts- und Jenseitspräsentation zwischen Antike und Frühmittelalter im mittleren Donauraum.* Forsch. zu Spätantike und Mittelalter 2 (Weinstadt) 33–45

Th. Fischer 2013a: Zur Funktion des frühkaiserzeitlichen Glasmedaillons aus Rheingönheim (Stadt Ludwigshafen, Rheinland-Pfalz) und verwandter Stücke. In: *Palatinus Illustrandus. Festschrift für Helmut Bernhard zum 65. Geburtstag* (Mainz/Ruhpolding) 111–15

Th. Fischer 2013b: Die Soldaten des Maximinus Thrax. Die Einheiten und ihre Bewaffnung. In: Pöppelmann *et al.* 2013, 198–206

Th. Fischer 2013c: Ein bemerkenswerter Kavalleriehelm aus dem 3. Jh. n. Chr. – der Adlerhelm aus dem Museum in Mougins. In: Pöppelmann *et al.* 2013, 207

Th. Fischer 2013d: Zur Bewaffnung und Ausrüstung der Kavallerieformationen Roms in der Zeit des Maximinus Thrax. In: Pöppelmann *et al.* 2013, 228–34

Th. Fischer 2014: Bemerkungen zu römischem Pionierwerkzeug aus Künzing (Lkr. Deggendorf). In: *Festschr. für Karl Schmotz* (Rahden Westf.)

Th. Fischer and G. Moorbauer 2013: Schlachtfeldarchäologie. Römische Schlachten-archäologisch bezeugt. In: Pöppelmann *et al.* 2013, 51–6

Th. Fischer and E. Riedmeier-Fischer 2008b: *Der römische Limes in Bayern* (Regensburg)

K. Fittschen 1972: Das Bildprogramm des Trajansbogens zu Benevent, *AA* 1972, 742–88

F. Fless 1995: *Opferdiener und Kultmusiker auf stadtrömischen historischen Reliefs* (Mainz)

F. B. Florescu 1965: *Das Siegesdenkmal von Adamklissi-Tropaeum Traiani* (Bonn/Bucharest)

H. I. Flower 2001: A tale of two monuments: Domitian, Trajan and some Praetorians at Puteoli (*AE* 1973, 137). *American Journal of Archaeology* 105, 625–48

Ch. Flügel, E. Blumenau, E. Deschler-Erb, S. Hartmann, and E. Lehmann 2004:, Römische Cingulumbeschläge mit Millefiorieinlagen. *Arch. Korr. Bl.* 34, 531–46

Ch. Flügel 2004: Ein Brustschließblech der Legio I Adiutrix. *Bayer. Vorgesch. Bl.* 70, 153–8

Ch. Flügel 2010: Tribuli – römische Krähenfüße. *Bayer. Vorgesch. Bl.* 75, 143–6

R. Förtsch 1995: Villa und Praetorium. Zur Luxusarchitektur in frühkaiserzeitlichen Legionslagern. *Kölner Jahrb.* 28, 629–30

Ch. Flügel and J. Obmann 2008: Römische Architekturfibeln. Ein Beitrag zur römischen Militärarchitektur. *Quaderni Friulani di Archeologia* 18:1, 145–53

S. Fortner 1995: Ein Beschlagblech aus dem Kastell Gelduba, Krefeld Gellep. In: *Festschr. G. Ulbert*, 89–94

R. Franke 1998: Ein römischer Brandpfeil aus dem Südvicus von Sorviodurum-Straubing. *Jahresber. Hist. Verein Straubing* 100/I, 245–57

R. Franke 2003: *Arae Flaviae V. Die Kastelle I und II von Arae Flaviae/Rottweil und die römische Okkupation des oberen Neckargebietes.* Forsch. u. Ber. z. Vor- u. Frühgesch. in Baden-Württemberg 93 (Stuttgart)

R. Franke 2009: *Römische Kleinfunde aus Burghöfe 3.* Frühgeschichtliche und provinzial-römische Archäologie 9 (Rahden/Westfalen)

R. Franke 2013: The headquarters building in the tetrarchic fort at Nag´al-Hagar (Upper Egypt). *Journal of Roman Archaeology* 26, 456–63

G. Franzius 1999: Beschläge einer Gladiusscheide und Teile eines Cingulums aus Kalkriese, Lkr. Osnabrück. *Germania* 77, 567–608

U. von Freeden 1987: Das frühmittelalterliche Gräberfeld von Moos-Burgstall, Ldkr. Deggendorf, in Niederbayern. *Ber. RGK* 68, 493–637

U. von Freeden 2001: Awarische Funde in Süddeutschland? *Jahrb. RGZM* 38, 593–627

D. French and C. S. Lightfoot (eds) 1989: *The Eastern Frontier of the Roman Empire. Proc. Coll. Ankara 1988* (Oxford)

S. S. Frere and J. K. St. Joseph 1974: The Roman fort at Longthorpe. *Britannia* 5, 1–129

A. Frey (ed.) 2009: *Ludwig Lindenschmidt d. Ä. Mosaiksteine.* Forsch. Am RGZM 5 (Mainz)

S. Friedrich 2010: *Remagen. Das römische Auxiliarkastell Rigomagus.* Berichte zur Archäologie an Mittelrhein und Mosel 16 (Koblenz)

H. Friesinger and F. Krinzinger (eds) 1997: *Der römische Limes in Österreich. Führer zu den archäologischen Denkmälern* (Vienna)

H. Friesinger, J. Tejral, and A. Stupner (eds) 1994: *Markomannenkriege, Ursachen und Wirkung* (Brno/Vienna)

H. Froning 1981: *Marmor-Schmuckreliefs mit griechischen Mythen im 1. Jh. v. Chr.* (Mainz)

N. Fuentes 1987: The Roman military tunic. In: Dawson 1987, 41–75

N. Fuentes 1991: The mule of a soldier. *JRMES* 2, 65–99

G. Garbrecht 1991: Talsperre und Tunnel am Hafen Seleukeia. In: idem (ed.), *Historische Talsperren* (Stuttgart) 83–9

W. Gaitzsch 1980: *Eiserne römische Werkzeuge.* BAR, Int. Ser. 78 (Oxford)

W. Gaitzsch 1986: *Antike Korb und Seilerwaren.* Kleine Schriften des Limesmuseums Aalen 38 (Aalen)

M. Galinier 2007: *La Colonne Trajane et les forums impériaux* (Rome)

O. Gamber and Ch. Beaufort 1990: *Katalog der Leibrüstkammer II. Der Zeitraum von 1500–1560* (Busto Arsizio)

A. Gansser-Burckhardt 1942: *Das Leder und seine Verarbeitung im römischen Legionslager* Vindonissa (Basel)

J. Garbsch 1978: *Römische Paraderüstungen.* Münchner Beitr. Vor- und Frühgesch. 30 (Munich)

J. Garbsch 1984: Ein römisches Paradekettenhemd von Bertoldsheim, Lkr. Neuburg-Schrobenhausen. *Neuburger Kollektaneenblatt* 139, 239–53

J. Garbsch 1986: *Mann und Ross und Wagen. Transport und Verkehr im antiken Bayern.* Ausstellungskataloge der Prähistorischen Staatssammlung München 13 (Munich)

J. Garbsch 1986a: Donatus torquibus armillis phaleris. Römische Orden in Raetien. *Bayer. Vorgesch. Bl.* 51, 333–6

J. Garbsch 1988: Übersicht über den spätrömischen Donau-Iller-Rhein-Limes. In: J. Garbsch and P. Kos, *Das spätrömische Kastell Vemania bei Isny I. Zwei Schatzfunde des frühen 4. Jahrhunderts.* Münchner Beitr. Vor- u. Frühgesch. 44 (Munich) 105–27

J. Garbsch 1992: *Der römische Limes in Bayern. 100 Jahre Limesforschung* (Munich)

J. Garbsch 1994: *Römischer Alltag in Bayern. Das Leben vor 2000 Jahren. Festschr. Bayerische Handelsbank AG 1869–1994* (Munich)

R. Gardiner (ed.) 1995: *The Age of the Galley. Mediterranean Oared Vessels Since Pre-Classical Times. Conway's History of the Ship* (London)

R. Garland 1987: *The Piraeus, from the Fifth to the First Century B.C.* (Ithaca NY)

W. Gauer 1977: *Untersuchungen zur Trajanssäule* (Berlin)

Ch. Gazdac 2009: An unknown battle? Military artefacts and coin finds. In: Busch and Schalles 2009, 125–9

A. Gebhardt 2002: *Imperiale Politik und provinziale Entwicklung. Untersuchungen zum Verhältnis von Kaiser, Heer und Städten im Syrien der vorseverischen Zeit.* Klio Beih. N. F. 4 (Berlin)

M. Gechter 1984: Beobachtungen zur Sozialstruktur des römischen Militärs in den Nord-westprovinzen anhand des Fibelaufkommens. In: L. Pauli (ed.) *Archäologie und Kulturgeschichte 2. Beiträge zur Erforschung von Sozialstrukturen und Randkulturen. Symposion in Saerbeck 17.–19.2.1984,* (Munich) 5–9

M. Gechter and F. Willers 1996: Eine römische Helmmaske aus Dormagen. *Archäologie im Rheinland 1995* (Köln/Bonn) 88–90

K. Genser 1986: *Der österreichische Donaulimes in der Römerzeit. Ein Forschungsbericht RLÖ* (Vienna)

W. Geominy 1982: *Die Florentiner Niobiden* (Bonn)

M. Geschwinde, H. Haßmann, P. Lönne, M. Meyer, and G. Moosbauer 2009:, Roms vergessener Feldzug. Das neu entdeckte Schlachtfeld am Harzhorn in Niedersachsen. In: *Varusschlacht 2009,* 228–32

U. Giesler 1978: Jüngerkaiserzeitliche Nietknopfsporen mit Dreipunkthalterung vom Typ Leuna. *Saalburg Jahrb.* 35, 5–56, Taf. 1–11

F. Gilbert 2004: *Le Soldat Romain. À la fin de la République et sous le Haut-Empire* (Saint-Germain-du-Puy)

K.-J. Gilles 1985: *Spätrömische Höhensiedlungen in Eifel und Hunsrück.* Trierer Zeitschr. Beih. 7 (Trier)

J. F. Gilliam 1967: The deposita of an auxiliary soldier (P. Columbia inv. 325). *BJ* 167, 233–43

K. Gilliver 2007: *Auf dem Weg zum Imperium. Die Geschichte der römischen Armee* (Hamburg)

R. Girshmann 1962: *Iran. Parther und Sasaniden* (München)

L. Giuliani 2010: *Ein Geschenk für den Kaiser. Das Geheimnis des großen Kameos* (Munich)

A. Giuliano 1955: *Arco di Costantino* (Mailand)

D. Glad 2009: *Origine et diffusion de l'équipement défensif corporel en Méditerranée orientale (IVe–VIIIe s.). Contribution à l'étude historique et archéologique des armées antiques et médiévales.* Archaeological Studies on Late Antiquity and early medieval Europe (400–1000 A. D.) Mon. II. BAR Int. Ser. 1921 (Oxford)

P. Glüsing 2000: Ergänzende Anmerkungen zur Enddatierung der frührömischen Lippelager Anreppen und Haltern. Erweiterter Diskussionsbeitrag. In: Wiegels 2000, 119–20

F. Goddio and J. Yoyotte 2007: Der große Hafen in Alexandria. In: F. Goddio and M. Clauss (eds), *Ägyptens versunkene Schätze* (München, Berlin, New York) 324–34

K. P. Goethert 1996:, Neue römische Prunkschilde. In: Junkelmann 1996, 115–26

R. Gogräfe and J. Chehadé : Die Waffen führenden Gräber aus Chisphin im Golan. *JRMES* 10, 1999, 73–80

R. Goguey and M. Reddé 1995: *Le camp légionnaire de Mirebeau.* RGZM Mon. 36 (Mainz)

A. Goltz and U. Hartmann 2008: Valerianus und Gallienus. In: Johne *et al.* 2008, 223–95

J. Göpfrich 1986: Römische Lederfunde aus Mainz. *Saalburg Jahrb.* 42, 5–67

J. Gorecki 1997: 'Seid einig, bereichert die Soldaten, alles andere verachtet!'. Der römische Staatshaushalt und die Kosten der militärischen Besatzung der Saalburgkastelle. In: Schallmayer 1997, 147–57

M. Grab 2012: Das marianische Pilum. Der 'römische Mythos' im Test. In: Koepfer *et al.* 2012, 83–92

W. Grabert and H. Koch 1986: Militaria aus der villa rustica von Treuchtlingen-Weinbergshof. *Bayer. Vorgesch. Bl.* 51, 325–32

G. Grabherr 2001: *Michlhallberg. Die Ausgrabungen in der römischen Siedlung 1997–1999 und die Untersuchungen an der zugehörigen Straßentrasse.* Schriftenreihe des Kammerhofmuseums Bad Aussee 22 (Bad Aussee)

J. Gräf 2009: Die Schwertgurte aus dem Thorsberger Moor. In: Busch and Schalles 2009, 131–6

J. Graßler 2012: Versuch der Rekonstruktion augusteischer Klingen. In: Koepfer *et al.* 2012, 45–72

B. A. Greiner 2006: Zur Herstellungsweise römischer Kettenhemden (*lorica hamata*). In: Seitz 2006, 199–204

Grenzen 2006: various authors, *Grenzen des römischen Imperiums* (Mainz)

F. Grew and N. Griffiths 1991: The pre-Flavian military belt: the evidence from Britain. *Archaeologia* 109, 47–84

W. B. Griffiths 2000: Re-enactment as research: towards a set of guidelines for the re-enactors and academics. In: *JRMES* 11, 135–9

W. Groenmann-van Wateringe 1967: *Romeins lederwerk uit Valkenburg Z. H.* (Groningen)

E. Grönke and E. Weinlich 1991: *Die Nordfront des römischen Kastells Biriciana-Weissenburg. Die Ausgrabungen 1986/1987.* Kataloge der Prähist. Staatsslg. München 25 (Kallmünz)

J. Grohmayer and G. Veith 1963: *Heerwesen und Kriegsführung der Griechen und Römer.* Handb. d. Altertumswiss. 4.3.2 (München)

M. Groller v. Mildensee 1901: Römische Waffen. *RLÖ* 2, 85–132

K. Grote 2006: Das Römerlager im Werratal bei Hedemünden (Ldkr. Göttingen). Ein neuentdeckter Stützpunkt der augusteischen Okkupationsvorstöße im rechtsrheinischen Germanien. *Germania* 84:1, 27–59

K. Grote 2012: *Römerlager Hedemünden.* Veröffentl. d. arch. Sammlung d. Landesmus. Hannover 53 (Dresden)

M. Grünewald 1981: *Die Kleinfunde des Legionslagers von Carnuntum mit Ausnahme der Gefäßkeramik.* RLÖ 31 (Vienna)

Th. Grünewald and H.-J. Schalles (eds) 2000: *Germania Inferior.* RGA-E 28 (Berlin/New York)

Th. Grünewald and S. Seibel (eds) 2003: *Kontinuität und Diskontinuität. Germania inferior am Beginn und am Ende der römischen Herrschaft.* RGA-E 35 (Berlin/New York)

K. Gschwandler 1986: *Guß und Form* (Vienna)

M. Gschwind 1997: Bronzegießer am raetischen Limes, *Germania* 75, 607–38

M. Gschwind 1998: Pferdegeschirrbeschläge aus der zweiten Hälfte des 3. Jahrhunderts aus Abusina/Eining. *Saalburg Jahrb.* 49, 112–38

M. Gschwind 2004: *Abusina. Das römische Auxiliarkastell Eining an der Donau vom 1. bis 5. Jahrhundert n. Chr.* Münchner Beitr. Vor- und Frühgesch. BV 53 (Munich)

M. Gschwind 2009: Every square structure a Roman fort? Recent research in Qreye-Ayyash and its alleged bridgehead fort Tall ar-Rum on the Euphrates. In: *Limeskongress 2006,* 1593–1604

N. Gudea 1989: *Porolissum. Un complex arheologic daco-roman la marginea de nord a Imperiului-Roman* (Zalau)

N. Gudea 1994: Römische Waffen aus den Kastellen des westlichen Limes von Dacia Prolissensis. In: von Carnap-Bornheim 1994, 79–89

N. Gudea 1996: *Porolissum. Vama Romana (Das Zollgebäude. Beiträge zur Kenntnis des Zollsystems in den Dakischen Provnzen). Porolissum. Un complex arheologic daco-roman la marginea de nord a Imperiului-Roman II* (Cluj-Napoca)

N. Gudea 1997: Der Dakische Limes. Materialien zu seiner Geschichte. *Jahrb. RGZM* 44, 1–113

N. Gudea 2001: Die Nordgrenze der römischen Provinz Obermoesien. Materialien zu ihrer Geschichte (86–275 n. Chr.) *Jahrb. RGZM* 48, 3–118

N. Gudea 2005: Der untermoesische Donaulimes und die Verteidigung der moesischen Nord- und Westküste des Schwarzen Meeres. Limes et litus Moesiae inferioris (86–275 n. Chr.). *Jahrb. RGZM* 52, 319–566

N. Gudea and D. Baatz 1974: Teile spätrömischer Ballisten aus Gorea und Orsova (Rumänien) *Saalburg Jahrb.* 31, 50–72

Ch. Gugl 2007a: Die Anfänge des Carnuntiner Legionslagers. In: Humer 2007, 220–8

Ch. Gugl 2009: *Carnuntensis Scutaria* (*Not. Dign. Occ.* IX, 20) Archäologische Evidenz für spätantike Ledererzeugung im Legionslager Carnuntum? In: *Limeskongress 2006,* 1405–19

Ch. Gugl and R. Kastler (eds) 2007: *Legionslager Carnuntum. Ausgrabungen 1968–1977.* RLÖ 75 (Vienna)

J. K. Haalebos 1973: *Zwammerdam-Nigrum Pullum. Ein Auxiliarkastell am Niedergermanischen Limes* (Amsterdam)

T. Haines, G. Sumner, and J. Naylor 2000: Recreating the world of the Roman soldier: the work of the Ermine Street Guard. *JRMES* 11, 119–27

N. G. L. Hammond 1984: The Battle of Pydna, *JHS* 104, 31–47

N. Hanel 1995: *Vetera I. Die Funde aus den römischen Lagern auf dem Fürstenberg bei Xanten.* Rhein. Ausgr. 35 (Cologne)

N. Hanel 1995a: Ein römischer Kanal zwischen dem Rhein und Gross-Gerau? *Arch. Korr. Bl.* 25, 107–16

N. Hanel 2000: Militärische Thermen in Niedergermanien – Eine Bestandsaufnahme. In: C. Fernández Ochoa and V. García Entero (eds) *Rermas romanas en el Occidente del Imperio. Colloquio Internacional Gijón* (Gijón) 23–33

N. Hanel, U. Peltz, and F. Willer 2000: Untersuchungen zu römischen Reiterhelmmasken aus der Germania Inferior. *BJ* 200, 243–74

N. Hanel, S.-Wilbers-Rost, and F. Willer 2004: Die Helmmaske von Kalkriese. *BJ* 204, 71–91

N. Hanel 2007: Military camps, canabae and vici. The archaeological evidence. In: Erdkamp 2007, 395–416

N. Hanel and B. Song 2007: Neue Ergebnisse der Luftbildarchäologie zu den römischen Militäranlagen Vetera Castra I auf dem Fürstenberg bei Xanten. *Germania* 85, 349–57

W. S. Hanson 2007: *Elginhaugh. A Roman Frontier Fort in Scotland* (Chalford)

W. S. Hanson, K. Speller, P. A. Yeoman, and J. Teller 2007: *Elginhaugh: A Flavian Fort and its Annexe.* Britannia Mon. Ser. 23 (London)

D. B. Harden, H. Hellenkemper, K. Painter, and D. Whitehouse 1988: *Glas der Caesaren* (Mailand)

O. Harl 1996: Die Kataphraktarier im römischen Heer – Panegyrik und Realität. *Jahrb. RGZM* 43, 601–27; Taf. 90–3

J. Harnecker 1997: *Katalog der römischen Eisenfunde von Haltern.* Bodenaltertümer Westfalens 35 (Mainz)

J. Harnecker and G. Franzius 2008: *Kalkriese 4. Katalog der römischen Funde vom Oberesch. Die Schnitte 1 bis 22.* RGF 66 (Mainz)

J. Harnecker and E. Tolksdorf-Lienemann 2004: *Kalkriese 2. Sondierungen in der Kalkrieser Niewedder Senke. Archäologie und Bodenkunde.* RGF 62 (Mainz)

H. Harrauer and H. Seider 1979: Ein neuer lateinischer Schuldschein: P. Vindob. L 135. *ZPE* 36, 109–20

M. Hartmann 1982: Ein Helm vom Typ Weisenau aus Vindonissa. *Jber. GPV*, 5–9

M. Hartmann 1986: *Vindonissa* (Windisch)

U. Hartmann 2008: Claudius Gothicus und Aurelianus. In: Johne u. a. 2008, 297–323

F. J. Hassel 1985: *Die Münzen der Römischen Republik im Römisch-Germanischen Zentralmuseum.* Kat. Vor- u. Frühgesch. Altert. 24 (Mainz)

J. Heiligmann 1990: *Der 'Alb-Limes'.* Forschungen und Berichte zur Vor-und Frühgeschichte in Baden-Württemberg 35 (Stuttgart)

P. Henrich 2013: Neuzeitliche Schuppenketten von römischen Fundstellen. *Arch. Korr. Bl.* 43, 247–56

F. R. Hermann 1969: Der Eisenhortfund aus dem Kastell Künzing. *Saalburg Jahrb.* 26, 129–41

G. Herrmann 1983: *The Sasanian Rock Reliefs at Bishapur: 3.* Iranische Felsreliefs 6. Iranische Denkmäler, Lieferung 11 II (Berlin)

P. Herz 2010: Die Versorgung der römischen Armee mit Waffen und Ausrüstung. In: Eich 2010, 111–32

H. von Hesberg 1985: Coloniae maritimae. *Römische Mitt.* 92, 127–30

H. von Hesberg (ed.) 1999: *Das Militär als Kulturträger in römischer Zeit* (Cologne)

H. von Hesberg 1999a: Gestaltungsprinzipien römischer Militärarchitektur. In: v. Hesberg 1999, 87–116

C. Heucke 2001: s. v. Ravenna. *NP* 10, 795–288

J. Heurgon 1958: *Le Trésor de Ténès* (Paris)

F. Himmler 2005: Naves Lusoriae – Flusskriegsschiffe der Spätantike. *Revue Études Militaires Anciennes* 2, 153–79

F. Himmler 2010: Aus dem Alltag römischer Soldaten. Mit den Römern unterwegs – Ergebnisse eines im Jahre 2008 durchgeführten Erprobungsmarsches. *Der Limes* 2, 28–33

F. W. Himmler 2012: 'On the road again' – Ergebnisse zweier Erprobungsmärsche in den Jahren 2004 und 2008. In: Koepfer et al. 2012, 173–92

F. W. Himmler 2012a: 'These boots are made for walking – Rekonstruktion römischer Stiefel im Langstreckenexperiment.' In: Koepfer et al. 2012, 193–219

J. Hock 2001: Burgi. In: Fischer 2001, 143–51

N. Hodgson 1999: Wallsend-Segedunum. In: P. Bidwell (ed.), *Hadrian's Wall 1989–1999. A Summary of Recent Excavations and Research Prepared for The Twelfth Pilgrimage on Hadrian's Wall, 14–21 August 1999* (Carlisle), 83–94

O. Höckmann 1983: 'Keltisch' oder 'römisch'? Bemerkungen zur Typogenese der spätrömischen Ruderschiffe von Mainz. *Jahrb. RGZM* 30, 403–34

O. Höckmann 1984: Darstellungen von zwei römischen Ziegelstempeln aus Mainz. *Arch. Korrebl.* 14, 319–24

O. Höckmann 1985: *Antike Seefahrt* (München)

O. Höckmann 1986: Römische Schiffsverbände auf dem Ober- und Mittelrhein und die Verteidigung der Rheingrenze in der Spätantike. *Jahrb. RGZM* 33:1, 369–416

O. Höckmann 1996: Schiffsbilder auf antiken Münzen. In: R. Albert (ed.), *Rom und Rhein – Macht und Münzen.* Schr.-R. Numismat. Ges. Speyer e.V. 38 (Speyer) 61–72

O. Höckmann 1998: Das Lager Alteburg, die Germanische Flotte und die Römische Rheinschiffahrt. *Kölner Jahrb.* 31, 317–50

T. Hölscher 1979: Beobachtungen zu rômischen historischen Denkmäler. *AA*, 337–48

T. Hölscher 1980: Die Geschichtsauffassung in der römischen Repräsentationskunst, *JdI* 95, 265–321

T. Hölscher 1980a: Römische Siegesdenkmäler der späten Republik. In: Tainia. Festschrift für R. Hampe (Mainz) 351–71

T. Hölscher 1984: *Staatsdenkmal und Publikum vom Untergang der Republik bis zur Festigung des Kaisertums in Rom.* Xenia, Heft 9 (Konstanz)

T. Hölscher 1984a: Actium und Salamis, *JdI* 99, 187–214

T. Hölscher 1988: Die großen ideologischen Programme. Sockel vom Denkmal des Bocchus von Mauretanien für Sulla. In: M. R. Kaiser (ed.) *Augustus und die verlorene Republik* (Berlin) 384ff. Nr 214

T. Hölscher 1992: Monumenti politici di Domiziano. Stabilità e sviluppo dell' iconografia politica romana. In: Accademia Nazionale Virgiliana (eds), *La storia, la letteratura e l' arte a Roma da Tiberio a Domiziano. Atti del Convegno (Mantova, 4–7 ottobre 1990)*, (Mantua) 297–305

T. Hölscher 2000: Die Säule des Marcus Aurelius: Narrative Struktur und ideologische Botschaft. In: Scheid and Huet 2000, 89–105

T. Hölscher 2009: Rilievi provenienti da monumenti statali del tempo dei Flavi. In: F. Coarelli (ed.), *Divus Vespasianus. Il bimillenario dei Flavi* (Rome) 54–8

V. Hoffiller 1910/11: *Oprema rimskoga vojnika u prvo doba carstva.* Vjestnik Hrvatskoga Arheoloskoga Drustva n. s. 11 (Zagreb)

V. Hoffiler 1912: *Oprema rimskoga vojnika u prvo doba carstva II.* Vjestnik Hrvatskoga Arheoloskoga Drustva n. s. 11 (Zagreb)

D. Hoffmann 1970: *Das spätrömische Bewegungsheer und die Notitia Dignitatum II.* Epigr. Stud. 7/2 (Düsseldorf)

B. Hoffmann 2006: Melonenperlen und das Militär in Großbritannien, am Rhein und an der oberen Donau. In: Seitz 2006, 227–30

R. L. Hohlfelder (ed.) 2008: *The Maritime World of Ancient Rome. Proceedings of 'The Maritime World of Ancient Rome' Conference Held at the American Academy in Rome, 27–29 March 2003* (Ann Arbor)

Th. Homolle 1897: Le trophée de Paul-Émile vainqueur de Persée. *BCH* 21, 620–3

Th. Homolle 1903: Le trophée de Paul-Émile à Delphes. Une illustration antique pour le texte de Live. In: *Mélanges Boissier* (Paris) 297–302

E. Honigmann 1923: s. v. Seleukeia 2 *RE* II A,1, 1184–1200

H.-G. Horn (ed.) 1987: *Die Römer in Nordrhein-Westfalen* (Stuttgart)

J. Horvat 1997: Roman Republican weapons from Smihel in Slovenia. *JRMES* 8, 105–20

J. Horvat 2002: The hoard of Roman Republican weapons from Grad near Smihel. *Arheloski vestnik* 53, 117–92

J. Horvat and A. Bavdek 2009: *Ocra. The Gateway Between the Mediterranean and Central Europe* (Ljubljana)

S. Hoss 2006: VTERE FELIX und MNHMΛN – Zu den Gürteln mit Buchstabenbeschlägen. *Arch. Korr. Bl.* 36, 237–51

S. Hoss 2009: The military belts of the *equites*. In: Busch and Schalles 2009, 313–21

S. Hoss 2010: Der Gürtel als Standeszeichen der römischen Soldaten. *Mannheimer Gesch. Bl.* 19, 114–28

W. Hübener 1957: Ein römisches Gräberfeld in Neuburg an der Donau, *Bayer. Vorgesch. Bl.* 22, 1957, 71–96

W. Hübener 1963/64: Zu den provinzialrömischen Waffengräbern. *Saalburg Jahrb.* 21, 20–5

W. Hübener 1973: *Die römischen Metallfunde von Augsburg-Oberhausen. Ein Katalog.* Materialhefte Bayer. Vorgesch. 28 (Kallmünz)

F. Humer (ed.) 2007: *Legionsadler und Druidenstab. Vom Legionslager zur Donaumetropole. Katalog der Ausstellung '2000 Jahre Carnuntum' Bad Deutsch Altenburg* (Vienna)

F. Humer and G. Kremer (eds) 2011: *Götterbilder-Menschenbilder. Religion und Kulte in Carnuntum* (Bad Deutsch-Altenburg)

H. Hurst 1992: L'ilot de l'Amirauté, le port circulaire et l'avenue Bourguiba. In: A. Ennabil (ed.) *Pour sauver Carthage. Exploration et conservation de la cité punique, romaine et byzantine* (Paris), 79–94

H. R. Hurst and S. P. Roskams 1994: *Excavations at Carthage: The British Mission II 1. The Circular Harbour, North Side: the Site and Finds Other than Pottery.* British Academy Monographs in Archaeology 4 (Sheffield)

H. Hurst and L. E. Stager 1978: A metropolitan landscape: the Late Punic port of Carthage, *World Archaeology* 9:3, 334–46

J. Ilkjaer 1990: *Illerup Ådal 1/2. Die Lanzen und Speere* (Aarhus)

J. Ilkjaer 1993: *Illerup Ådal 3/4. Die Gürtel* (Aarhus)

Imperium Romanum 2005: *Imperium Romanum. Roms Provinzen an Neckar, Rhein und Donau. Ausstellungskatalog Archäolog.* Landesmuseum Baden-Württemberg (Stuttgart)

A. Iriarte, E. Gil, I. Filloy, and M. L. Garcia 1997: Votive deposit of Republican weapons at Gracurris. *JRMES* 8, 233–50

D. Isac and M. Bărbulescu 2008: Neue Paraderüstungen aus Dakien. *Acta Musei Napocensis* 43–44/I, 211–31

J. Istenic 2009: Roman military equipment and the beginning of the Roman use of brass in Europe. In: Busch/Schalles 2009, 237–42

J. Istenic 2000: A late-Republican gladius from the river Ljubljanica (Slovenia). *JMRES* 11, 1–9

J. Istenic 2005: Evidence for a very late Republican siege at Grad near Reka in Western Slowenia. In: Jilek 2005, 77–87

J. Istenic 2010: Late La Tène scabbards with non-ferrous openwork plates. *Arheologski Vestnik* 61, 121–64

L. Jacobi 1897: *Das Römerkastell Saalburg bei Homburg vor der Höhe* (Homburg)

O. Jahn 1860: *Die Lauersforter Phalerae. Fest-Programm zu Winckelmanns Geburtstag am 9. December 1860.* Herausgegeben vom Vorstande des Vereins von Altertumsfreunden in den Rheinlanden (Bonn)

S. James 1988: The *fabricae*: state arms factories of the Later Roman Empire. In: Coulston 1988a, 257–331

S. James 2004: *The Excavations at Dura-Europos Conducted by Yale University and the French Academy of Inscriptions and Letters 1928 to 1937. Final Report VII. The Arms and Armour and Other Military Equipment.* (London)

S. James 2005: The deposition of military equipment during the final siege at Dura Europos, with particular regard to the Tower 19 countermine. In: Jilek 2005, 189–206

A. Jacquemin 1999: *Offrandes monumentales à Delphes* (Paris)

A. Jacquemin and D. Laroche 1982: Notes sur trois piliers delphiques. *BCH* 106, 191–218

E. Jansma and J.-M. A. Morel (eds) 2007: *Een Romeinse Rijnaak, gevonden in Utrecht-De Meern. Resultaten van het onderzoek naar de platbodem 'De Meern 1'.* Rapportage Arch. Monumentenzorg 144 (Amersfoort)

I. Jenkins 1985: A group of silvered-bronze horse-trappings from Xanten (Castra Vetera). *Britannia* 16, 141–64

R. Jernej and Ch. Gugl (eds) 2004: *Virunum. Das römische Amphitheater. Die Grabungen 1998–2001.* Archäologie Alpen Adria 4 (Klagenfurt)

S. Jilek 1986: Kleinfunde. In: H. Stiglitz, *Auxiliarkastell Carnuntum.* Carnuntum Jahrb. 1986, 193–225

S. Jilek (ed.) 2005: *Archäologie der Schlachtfelder. Militaria aus Zerstörungshorizonten. Proceedings of the XIV Roman Military Equipment Conference (ROMEC).* Carnuntum Jahrb. 2005

S. Jilek 2005a: Militaria aus einem Zerstörungshorizont im Auxiliarkastell von Carnuntum. In: Jilek 2005, 165–80

K.-P. Johne, U. Hartmann, and Th. Gerhardt (ed.) 2008: *Die Zeit der Soldatenkaiser. Krise und Transformation des Römischen Reiches im 3. Jahrhundert n. Chr. (235–284)* (Berlin)

S. Johnson 1983: *Late Roman Fortifications* (London)

A. Johnson 1987: *Römische Kastelle des 1. und 2. Jahrhunderts n. Chr. in Britannien und in den germanischen Provinzen des Römerreiches* (Mainz)

B. Jones and D. Mattingly 1990: *An Atlas of Roman Britain* (London)

C. A. Jost 2006: *Der römische Limes in Rheinland-Pfalz* (Koblenz)

C. A. Jost 2007: Vorbericht zu den Ausgrabungen 2002–2004 im Limeskastell Niederberg bei Koblenz. In: Thiel 2007, 48–55

I. Jütting 1995: Die Kleinfunde aus dem römischen Lager Eining-Unterfeld. *Bayer. Vorgesch. Bl.* 60, 162–230

M. Junkelmann 1986: *Die Legionen des Augustus* (Mainz)

M. Junkelmann 1990: *Die Reiter Roms. Teil 1: Reise, Jagd, Triumph und Circusrennen* (Mainz)

M. Junkelmann 1991: *Die Reiter Roms. Teil 2: Reitweise und militärischer Einsatz* (Mainz)

M. Junkelmann 1992: *Die Reiter Roms. Teil 3: Zubehör, Reitweise, Bewaffnung* (Mainz)

M. Junkelmann 1996: *Reiter wie Statuen aus Erz* (Mainz)

M. Junkelmann 1997: Römische Kampf- und Turnierrüstungen. In: H. Born (ed.) *Sammlung Guttmann, Bd. VI* (Mainz)

M. Junkelmann 1999: Paradehelme? Zur funktionalen Einordnung frühkaiserzeitlicher Maskenhelme im Lichte von Neufunden und praktischen Versuchen. In Kemkes and Scheuerbrandt 1999, 39–43

M. Junkelmann 2000: *Römische Helme. Slg. Axel Guttmann Bd. 8* (Mainz)

M. Junkelmann 2000a: *Das Spiel mit dem Tod. So kämpften Roms Gladiatoren* (Mainz)

M. Junkelmann 2002: Das Phänomen der zeitgenössischen 'Römergruppen'. In: I. Jensen and A. Wieczorek (eds) *Dono, Asterix und Zeus. Zeitzeuge Archäologie in Werbung, Kunst und Alltag heute* (Mannheim/Weißbach) 73–90

M. Junkelmann 2006: *Panis militaris. Die Ernährung des römischen Soldaten oder der Grundstoff der Macht* (ed. 3 Mainz)

M. Junkelmann 2007: Bewaffnung und Ausrüstung der römischen Armee in der frühen römischen Kaiserzeit. In: Humer 2007, 296–305

M. Junkelmann 2009: *Hollywoods Traum von Rom* (ed. 2 Mainz)

M. Junkelmann 2011: Roman militaria. In: M. Merrony (ed.) *Mougins Museum of Classical Art* (Mougins), 235–66

I. Kader 1996: *Propylon und Bogentor. Untersuchungen zum Tetrapylon von Latakia und anderen frühkaiserzeitlichen Bogenmonumenten im Nahen Osten. Damaszener Forsch. 7* (Mainz)

H.-M. von Kaenel 1986: *Münzprägung und Münzbildnis des Claudius* (Berlin)

H. Kähler 1965: *Der Fries vom Reiterdenkmal des Aemilius Paullus in Delphi* (Berlin)

H. Kähler 1966: *Seethiasos und Census. Die Reliefs aus dem Palazzo Santa Croce in Rom* (Berlin)

H. Kähler 1968: *A. Rubeni dissertatio de gemma Augustea* (Berlin)

H. Kaiser and C. S. Sommer 1994: *LOPODVNVM I. Die römischen Befunde der Ausgrabungen an der Kellerei in Ladenburg 1981–1985 und 1990. Forsch. u. Ber. z. Vor- u. Frühgesch. in Baden-Württemberg 50* (Stuttgart)

C. A. Kalee 1989: Roman helmets and other militaria from Vechten. In: van Driel-Murray 1989, 193–226

M. Kandler 2007: Römische Reitereinheiten und ihr Lager in Carnuntum. In: Humer 2007, 261–9

Katalog Westfalen 1989: *2000 Jahre Römer in Westfalen* (Münster)

E. Kavanagh de Prado and F. Quesada Sanz 2009: Pugio Hispaniensis between Celtiberia and Rome. Current research and analysis of the construction of the sheaths. In: *Limeskongress 2006*, 339–50

S. Keay 2012: Portus. Trajan's shipsheds. *Current World Archaeology Magazine* 51, 35–40

P. Kehne 2004: Zur Logistik des römischen Heeres von der mittleren Republik bis zum Ende der hohen Kaiserzeit (241 v. Chr.–235 n. Chr.): Forschungen und Tendenzen. *Militärgeschichtl. Zeitschr.* 63, Heft 1, 207–32

J. Keim and H. Klumbach 1976: *Der römische Schatzfund von Straubing. Münchner Beitr. Vor- und Frühgesch. 3* (Munich)

E. Keller 1971: *Die spätrömischen Grabfunde in Südbayern. Münchner Beitr. Vor- und Frühgesch. 14* (Munich)

E. Keller 1979: *Das spätrömische Gräberfeld von Neuburg an der Donau. Materialhefte z. bayer. Vorgesch. 40* (Kallmünz)

H.-J. Kellner 1978: *Der römische Verwahrfund von Eining. Münchner Beitr. Vor- und Frühgesch. 29* (München)

H.-J. Kellner and G. Zahlhaas 1993: *Der römische Tempelschatz von Weißenburg i. B.* (Mainz)

M. Kemkes and J. Scheuerbrandt (eds) 1997: *Zwischen Patrouille und Parade. Die römische Reiterei am Limes. Schr. Limesmus. Aalen 51* (Aalen)

M. Kemkes and J. Scheuerbrandt 1999: *Fragen zur römischen Reiterei. Kolloquium zur Ausstellung 'Reiter wie Statuen aus Erz. Die römische Reiterei am Limes zwischen Parouille und Parade' im Limesmuseum Aalen am 25./26.2.1998* (Stuttgart)

D. L. Kennedy 2000: *The Roman Army in Jordan* (Amman)

D. L. Kennedy and M. C. Bishop 1998: Military equipment. In: D. L. Kennedy, *The Twin Towns of Zeugma on the Euphrates.* Journal of Roman archaeology. Suppl. Ser. 27 (Portsmouth) 135–7

J. P. C. Kent, B. Overbeck, and A. U. Stylow 1973: *Die römische Münze* (Munich)

J. P. C. Kent and K. S. Painter 1977: *Wealth of the Roman World. Gold and Silver A.D. 300–700* (London)

L. Keppie 1991: A centurion of legio Martia at Padova? *JRMES* 2, 115–21

D. Kienast 1966: *Untersuchungen zu den Kriegsflotten der Römischen Kaiserzeit. Antiquitas, R. 1. Abh. Alten Gesch. 13* (Bonn)

W. Kimmig 1940: Ein Keltenschild aus Ägypten. *Germania* 24, 106–11

M. Klee 2006: *Grenzen des Imperiums. Leben am römischen Limes* (Stuttgart)

M. Klee 2009: *Der römische Limes in Hessen. Geschichte und Schauplätze des UNESCO-Welterbes* (Regensburg)

M. Klein 1999: Votivwaffen aus einem Mars-Heligtum in Mainz. *JRMES* 10, 87–94

H. Klumbach 1961: Ein römischer Legionärshelm aus Mainz. *Jahrb. RGZM* 8, 96–105; Taf. 43–7

H. Klumbach (ed.) 1973: *Spätrömische Gardehelme. Münchner Beitr. Vor- und Frühgesch. 15* (München)

H. Klumbach 1974: *Römische Helme aus Niedergermanien. Kunst und Altertum am Rhein Nr. 51* (Cologne)

H. Klumbach and L. Wamser 1978: Ein Neufund zweier außergewöhnlicher Helme der römischen Kaiserzeit aus Theilenhofen (Lkr. Weißenburg-Gunzenhausen). In: *Jahresber. d. bayer. Bodendenkmalpflege 17/18* (Bonn) 41–61

L. Kocsis 1983: Ein neugefundener römischer Helm aus dem Legionslager von Aquincum. In: *Limeskongress 1983*, 350–4

L. Kocsis (ed.) 2008: *The Enemies of Rome. Proceedings of the 15th International Roman Military Equipment Conference, Budapest 2005. JRMES 16* (Budapest)

L. Kocsis 2008a: New data on the question of morphology an dating of the Intercisa III type helmets. In: Kocsis 2008, 249–72

Ch. Koepfer 2012: Rekonstruktion römischer Schilde. In: Koepfer et al. 2012, 113–18

Ch. Koepfer, F. W. Himmler, and J. Löffl (eds) 2012: *Die römische Armee im Experiment. Unter Mitarbeit von Ph. Egetenmeier* (Berlin)

G. M. Koeppel 1983: Die historischen Reliefs der römischen Kaiserzeit I. *BJ* 183, 61–144

G. M. Koeppel 1984: Die historischen Reliefs der römischen Kaiserzeit II. *BJ* 184, 1–65

G. M. Koeppel 1985: Die historischen Reliefs der römischen Kaiserzeit III. *BJ* 185, 143–213

G. M. Koeppel 1986: Die historischen Reliefs der römischen Kaiserzeit IV. *BJ* 186, 1–90

G. M. Koeppel 1987: Die historischen Reliefs der römischen Kaiserzeit V. *BJ* 1987, 101–58

G. M. Koeppel 1990: Die historischen Reliefs der römischen Kaiserzeit VII. *BJ* 190, 1–64

G. M. Koeppel 1991: Die historischen Reliefs der römischen Kaiserzeit VIII. *BJ* 191, 135–98

G. M. Koeppel 1992: Die historischen Reliefs der römischen Kaiserzeit IX. *BJ* 192, 61–121

F. Kolb 1973: Römische Mäntel: paenula, lacerna, μανδύη. *Röm. Mitt.* 80, 69–167; Taf. 22–46

F. Kolb 2001: *Herrscherideologie in der Spätantike* (Berlin)

T. G. Kolias 1988: *Byzantinische Waffen. Ein Beitrag zur byzantinischen Waffenkunde von den Anfängen bis zur Lateinischen Eroberung.* Byzantina Vindobonensia 17 (Vienna)

B. Komoróczy 2000: Panzerschuppentypen aus der römischen Befestigungsanlage am Burgstall bei Musov. In: Bouzek u. a. 2000, 79–86

B. Komoróczy 2009: Marcomannia. Der Militärschlag gegen die Markomannen und Quiaden - Ein archäologischer Survey. In: Konflikt 2009, 114–25

H. C. Konen 2000: *Classis Germanica: Die Römische Rheinflotte im 1–3. Jahrhundert n. Chr.* Pharos 15 (St. Katharinen)

Konflikt 2009: *2000 Jahre Varusschlacht. Konflikt. Ausstellungskatalog Kalkriese 2009* (Stuttgart)

M. Konrad 1997: *Das römische Gräberfeld von Bregenz-Brigantium I. Die Körpergräber des 3. bis 5. Jahrhunderts.* Münchner Beitr. Vor- und Frühgesch. 51 (Munich)

M. Konrad 2001: *Der spätrömische Limes in Syrien. Archäologische Untersuchungen an den Grenzkastellen von Sura, Tetrapyrgium, Cholle und in Resafa.* Resafa V (Mainz)

M. Korfmann 1972: *Schleuder und Bogen in Südwestasien von den frühesten Belegen bis zum Beginn der Historischen Stadtstaaten.* Antiquitas, Reihe 3, 13 (Bonn)

G. Kossack and G. Ulbert (eds) 1974: *Studien zur Vor- und Frühgeschichtlichen Archäologie. Festschrift für Joachim Werner zum 65. Geburtstag* (München)

H. Kotsidou 2000: *Time kai Doxa. Ehrungen für hellenistische Herrscher im griechischen Mutterland und in Kleinasien unter besonderer Berücksichtigung der archäologischen Denkmäler* (Frankfurt a. M.)

K. Kraft 1951: *Zur Rekrutierung der Alen und Kohorten an Rhein und Donau* (Bern)

O. Krause 2009: *Der Arzt und sein Instrumentarium in der römischen Legion* (Remshalden)

E. Krekovic and L. Snopko 1998: Der römische Prunkhelm von Gerulata. *Arch. Korr. Bl.* 28, 283–95

G. Kreucher 2008: Probus und Carus. In: Johne *et al.* 2008, 395–423

J. Krier and F. Reinert 1993: *Das Reitergrab von Hellingen. Die Treverer und das römische Militär in der frühen Kaiserzeit* (Luxemburg)

K. R. Krierer 1995: *Sieg und Niederlage. Untersuchungen physiognomischer und minischer Phänomene in Kampfdarstellungen der römischen Plastik* (Wien)

J. Krohmayer and G. Veith 1928: *Heerwesen und Kriegführung der Römer und Griechen. G. Otto (ed.) Handbuch der Altertumswissenschaft vierte Abteilung, dritter Teil, zweiter Band* (Munich reprinted 1963)

M. Kronberger 2007: Das frühe Vindobona/Wien. In: Humer 2007, 85–95

W. Kubitschek 1899: s.v. Census. In: *Paulys Real-Encyclopädie der Classischen Altertumswissenschaft III* (Stuttgart) 1914–24

J.-S. Kühlborn 1992: *Das Römerlager in Oberaden III.* Bodenaltertümer Westfalens 27 (Mainz)

J.-S. Kühlborn 1995: *Germaniam pacavi – Germanien habe ich befriedet: Archäologische Stätten augusteischer Okkupation* (Münster)

E. Künzl 1977: Cingula di Ercolano e Pompei. *Cronache Pompeiane* 3, 177–97

E. Künzl 1988: Schwert 'des Tiberus'. In: *Augustus und die verlorene Republik: eine Ausstellung im Martin-Gropius-Bau, Berlin, 7. Juni–14. August 1988* (Mainz) 558f. Nr. 383

E. Künzl 1991: Die medizinische Versorgung der römischen Armee zur Zeit des Kaisers Augustus und die Reaktion der Römer auf die Situation bei den Kelten und Germanen. In: Trier 1991, 185–202

E. Künzl 1993: *Die Alamannenbeute aus dem Rhein bei Neupotz.* Monogr. RGZM 34 (Mainz)

E. Künzl 1996: Gladiusdekorationen der frühen römischen Kaiserzeit, dynastische Legitimation, Victoria und Aurea Aetas. *Jahrb. RGZM* 43, 383–474

E. Künzl 1999: Fellhelme. Zu den mit organischem Material dekorierten römischen Helmen der frühen Kaiserzeit und der imitatio Alexandri des Germanicus. In: Schlüter and Wiegels 1999, 149–68

E. Künzl 2002: Der römische Schuppenpanzer (*lorica squamata*): Importwaffe und Prunkgrabelement. In: Pleska and Tejral 2002, 127–40

E. Künzl 2003: Waffendekor und Zoologie in Alexandrien. Der hellenistische Prunkschild im Württembergischen Landesmuseum Stuttgart. *Jahrb. RGZM* 50, 279–305; Taf. 7–2

E. Künzl 2004: Sol, Lupa, Zwillingsgottheiten und Hercules: Neue Funde und Bemerkungen zur Ikonographie römischer Paradewaffen. *Arch. Korr. Bl.* 34, 389–406

E. Künzl 2006: Römischer Waffendekor – Ein neuer Schildbuckel im RGZM. *Bayer. Vorgesch. Bl.* 71, 243–8

E. Künzl 2008: *Unter den goldenen Adlern. Der Waffenschmuck des römischen Imperiums* (Mainz/Regensburg)

E. Künzl 2009: Angsthorte und Plündererdepots. Die Reichskrise des 3. Jahrhunderts aus archäologischer Sicht. In: Varusschlacht 2009, 203–19

E. Künzl 2010: *Der Traum vom Imperium. Der Ludovisisarkophag – Grabmal eines Feldherrn Roms* (Regensburg/Mainz)

A. Kuttner 1995: *Dynasty and Empire in the Age of Augustus. The Case of the Boscoreale Cups* (Berkeley/Los Angeles/London)

P. La Baume 1983: *Römisches Kunstgewerbe zwischen Christi Geburt und 400* (Munich)

M. Langner 2001: *Antike Graffitizeichnungen. Motive, Gestaltung und Bedeutung.* Palilia 11 (Wiesbaden)

H. P. Laubscher 1975: *Der Reliefschmuck des Galeriusbogens in Thessaloniki,* Archäologische Forschung 1 (Berlin)

H. P. Laubscher 1993: Ein tetrarchisches Siegesdenkmal in Iznik (Nikaia), *JdI* 108, 375–97

A. K. Lawson 1978: Studien zum römischen Pferdegeschirr. *Jahrb. RGZM* 25, 131–72

A.-M. Leander Touati 1987: *The Great Trajanic Frieze* (Stockholm)

Y. Le Bohec 2010: *Das römische Heer in der Späten Kaiserzeit* (Stuttgart)

Y. Le Bohec and C. Wolff (eds) 2000: *Les légions de Rome sous le Haut-Empire* (Paris)

Y. Le Bohec and C. Wolff (eds) 2004: *L'armée Romaine de Dioclétien à Valentinien Ier* (Lyon)

K. Lehmann-Hartleben 1923: *Die antiken Hafenanlagen des Mittelmeeres: Beiträge zur Geschichte des Städtebaues im Altertum.* Klio Beih. 14 (Leipzig)

K. Lehmann-Hartleben 1926: *Die Trajanssäule* (Berlin/Leipzig)

G. A. Lehmann and R. Wiegels (eds) 2007: *Römische Präsenz und Herrschaft im Germanien der augusteischen Zeit. Der Fundplatz von Kalkriese im Kontext neuerer Forschungen und Ausgrabungsbefunde.* Abh. Akk. D. Wiss. zu Göttingen, Phil.–Hist. Klass. Dritte Folge, Bd. 279 (Göttingen)

O. Lendle 1983: *Texte und Untersuchungen zum technischen Bereich der antiken Poliorketik.* Palingenesia XIX (Wiesbaden)

K.-H. Lenz 2006: *Römische Waffen, militärische Ausrüstung und militärische Befunde aus dem Stadtgebiet der Colonia Ulpia Traiana (Xanten)* (Bonn)

L. Leoncini 1987: Frammenticon trofei navalie strumenti sacrificali dei Musei Capitolini. Nuova ipotesi ricostruttiva. *Xenia* 13, 13–24

L. Leoncini 1988: Storia e fortuna del cosiddetto 'Fregio di S. Lorenzo'. *Xenia* 14, 59–110

K. Liampi 1998: *Der makedonische Schild* (Bonn)

Limes 1992: *Der römische Limes in Deutschland. Archäologie in Deutschland. Sonderheft*

L. Lindenschmit 1858: *Die Alterthümer unserer heidnischen Vorzeit* (Mainz)

L. Lindenschmit 1870: *Die Alterthümer unserer heidnischen Vorzeit. Zweiter Band* (Mainz)

L. Lindenschmit 1881: *Die Alterthümer unserer heidnischen Vorzeit. Dritter Band* (Mainz)

L. Lindenschmit 1882: *Tracht und Bewaffnung des römischen Heeres während der Kaiserzeit mit besonderer Berücksichtigung der Rheinischen Denkmale und Fundstücke* (Braunschweig)

L. Lindenschmit 1892: *Die Alterthümer unserer heidnischen Vorzeit. Vierter Band* (Mainz)

L. Lindenschmit 1911: *Die Alterthümer unserer heidnischen Vorzeit. Fünfter Band* (Mainz)

J. Lipsius 1598: *De militia Romana libri quinque, commentarius ad Polybium* (Antwerpen)

J. Löffl 2012: Focale – Das Halstuch der römischen Armee im Experiment. In: Koepfer *et al.* 2012, 221–4

K. Löhberg 1969: Untersuchungen an Eisenfunden aus Limeskastellen. *Saalburg Jahrb.* 26, 1969, 142–6

H. Löhr 2009: Zur Botschaft und Datierung der Marcussäule. In: *Zurück zum Gegenstand. Festschrift für A. E. Furtwängler* (Langenweißbach) 123–35

H. Löhr and M. Trunk 2008: Ein neues Militärlager auf dem Petrisberg bei Trier. In: *Del imperium de Pompeyo a la auctoritas de Augusto. Homenaje a Michael Grant* (Madrid) 141–50

M. Lodewijckx *et al.* 1993: A third-century collection of decorativ objects from a Roman villa at Wange (Central Belgium). *JRMES* 4, 67–99

H. Lohmann 2009: *Die sogenannte Domitius-Ara. In: Zurück zum Gegenstand. Festschrift für A. E. Furtwängler* (Langenweißbach) 109–22

H. P. L'Orange and A. von Gerkan 1939: *Der spätantike Bildschmuck des Konstantinsbogens* (Berlin)

M. Luik 1997: Die römischen Militäranlagen der Iberischen Halbinsel von der Zeit der Republik bis zum Ausgang des Principats. Ein Forschungsüberblick. *Jahrb. RGZM* 44, 213–75

M. Luik 2000: Republikanische Pilumfunde vom 'Talamonaccio'/Italien. *Arch. Korr. Bl.* 30, 269–277

M. Luik 2001: Militaria in städtischen Siedlungen der Iberischen Halbinsel. *Jber. GPV* 2001, 97–104

M. Luik 2002: *Die Funde aus den römischen Lagern um Numantia im Römisch-Germanischen Zentralmuseum.* RGZM Kat. Vor- und frühgesch. Altertümer 31 (Mainz)

M. Luik 2009: 'Der feurige Krieg' – Archäologische Forschungen zu den römischen Lagern um Numantia/Spanien. Ein Überblick. In: Meller 2009, 49–57

M. Mackensen 1987: *Frühkaiserzeitliche Kleinkastelle bei Nersingen und Burlafingen an der oberen Donau.* Münchner Beitr. Vor- und Frühgesch. 41, (München)

M. Mackensen 1988: Frühkaiserzeitliche Kleinkastelle an der oberen Donau. In: *Zivile und militärische Strukturen im Nordwesten der römischen Provinz Raetien. 3. Heidenheimer Archäologie-Colloquium am 9. und 10. Oktober 1987* (Heidenheim) 13–32

M. Mackensen 1994: Das Kastell Caelius Mons (Kellmünz an der Iller) – eine tetrarchische Festungsbaumaßnahme in der Provinz Raetien. *Arch. Vestnik* 45, 145–63

M. Mackensen 1995: *Das spätrömische Genzkastell Caelius Mons in Kellmünz an der Iller.* Führer zu archäologischen Denkmälern in Bayern. Schwaben Bd. 3 (Stuttgart)

M. Mackensen 2001: Ein spätestrepublikanisch-augusteischer Dolch aus Tarent/Kalabrien. In: *Carinthia Romana und die römische Welt. Festschrift für Gernot Piccotini zum 60. Geburtstag* (Klagenfurt) 341–54

M. Mackensen 2002: Ein vergoldetes frühkaiserzeitliches Gladiusortband mit figürlich verziertem Scheidenblech aus Kleinasien oder Nordsyrien. *Bayer. Vorgesch. Bl.* 65, 125–42

M. Mackensen 2006: Die Grenze in Nordafrika am Beispiel der Provinzen Africa Proconsularis und Numidia. In: Grenzen 2006, 62–71

M. Mackensen 2007: Spätantike zweiteilige Gipsmatrize aus Nordafrika für Tonstatuetten eines behelmten östlichen Reiters. *Jahrb. RGZM* 54, 613–28

M. Mackensen 2008: Mannschaftsunterkünfte und Organisation einer severischen Legionsvexillation im tripolitanischen Kastell Gholaia/Bu Njem (Libyen). *Germania* 86, 271–306

M. Mackensen 2009: Silberner Zierstift aus Pons Aeni/Pfaffenhofen. Hinweis auf einen spätrömischen Kammhelm vom Typ Deurne-Berkasovo. *Bayer. Vorgesch. Bl.* 74, 2009, 289–94; Taf. 25

M. Mackensen 2010: Das commoduszeitliche Kleinkastell Tisavar/Ksar Rhilane am südtunesischen limes Tripolitanus. *Kölner Jahrb.* 43, 451–68

M. Mackensen 2010a: Das severische Vexillationskastell Myd (---/Gheriat el-Garbia am limes Tripolitanus/Libyen. Bericht über die Kampagne 2009. *Röm. Mitt.* 116, 2010, 363–458

M. Mackensen and R. Franke 2010: Eine Mannschaftsunterkunft im tetrarchischen Kastell Nag al-Hagar bei Kom Ombo (Oberägypten). In: *oleum non perdidit. Festschr. für Stephanie Martin-Kilcher zu ihrem 65. Geburtstag.* Antiqua 47 (Basel) 81–94

R. Madyda-Legutko 1986: *Die Gürtelschnallen der römischen Kaiserzeit und der frühen Völkerwanderungszeit im mitteleuropäischen Barbaricum.* BAR Int. Ser. 360 (Oxford)

F. Magi 1945: *I rilievi flavi del Palazzo della Cancelleria* (Rome)

A. Maiuri 1958: *Die Altertümer der phlegräischen Felder. Vom Grab des Vergil bis zur Höhle von Cumae* (Rome)

U. Mannering 2006: Questions and answers on textiles and their find spots: the Mons Claudianus Textile Project. In: S Schrenk (ed.), *Ikke angivet.* Riggisberger Berichte, no. 13, 149–59

W. H. Manning 2006: The Roman ironwork deposits from the fort at Newstead. *Bayer. Vorgesch. Bl.* 71, 15–32

D. Mano Zisi 1957: *Nalaz iz Tekije – Les Trouvailles de Tekija* (Belgrad)

D. Marchant 1990: Roman weapons in Great Britain, a case study: spearheads, problems in dating and typology. *JRMES* 1, 1–6

F. Marcu 2009: *The Internal Planning of Roman Forts of Dacia.* Bibliotheca Musei Napocensis 30 (Cluj-Napoca)

Ch. Marek 2003: *Pontus et Bithynia. Die römischen Provinzen im Norden Kleinasiens. Orbis Provinciarum* (Mainz)

E. W. Marsden 1969: *Greek and Roman Artillery. Vol. I: Historical Development* (Oxford)

E. W. Marsden 1972: *Greek and Roman Artillery. Vol. II: Technical Treatises* (Oxford)

P. Marsden 1994: *Ships of the Port of London, First to Eleventh Centuries AD.* English Heritage, Arch. Report 3 (London)

I. Martell 2001: Fibeln. In: Fischer 2001, 247–56

St. Martin-Kilcher 1985: Ein silbernes Schwertortband mit Niellodekor und weitere Militärfunde des 3. Jahrhunderts aus Augst. *Jahresber. Augst und Kaiseraugst* 5, 147–203

St. Martin-Kilcher 1993: A propos de la tombe d'un officier de Cologne (Severinstor) et de quelques tombes à armes vers 300. In: F. Vallet and M. Kazanski (eds), *L'Armée Romaine et les Barbares du III au VII siècle* (Paris) 299–312

St. Martin-Kilcher 2011: Römer und gentes Alpinae im Konflikt. In: Moosbauer and Wiegels 2011, 27–62

S. Martini 2010: Mittelalterliche und neuzeitliche Hufeisen im Rheinischen Landesmuseum Trier. *Funde und Ausgrabungen im Bezirk Trier* 42, 70–90

J. Marquart 1886: *Das Privatleben der Römer I und II* (ed. 2 Leipzig 1886; reprint Darmstadt 1980)

Ph. Mason 2003: Rimska vojaška utrdba. In: D. Preseren (ed.), *Zemlja pod vasimi nogami* (Ljubljana), 66–71

D. J. P. Mason 2003: *Roman Britain and the Roman Navy* (Stroud)

S. Matešič 2009: Some observations on scabbard slides from the Thorsberg bog. In: Busch and Schalles 2009, 152–63

D. Mauskopf Deliyannis 2010: *Ravenna in Late Antiquity* (Cambridge/New York)

V. A. Maxfield 1981: *The Military Decorations of the Roman Army* (London)

V. A. Maxfield (ed.) 1989: *The Saxon Shore. A Handbook.* Exeter Studies in History 25 (Exeter)

V. A. Maxfield and D. P. S. Peacock 2001: Survey and excavations Mons Claudianus (1987–1993) Bd. II: Excavations. Part I. Institut Francais d' archéologie Orientale 43 (Cairo)

E. Mayer 2002: *Rom ist dort, wo der Kaiser ist* (Mainz)

R. McMullen 1960: Inscriptions on armor and the supply of arms in the Roman Empire. *American Journal Arch.* 64, 23–40

R. McMullen 1965: The Celtic Renaissance. *Historia* 14, 93–104

A. Mees and B. Pferdehirt (ed.) 2002: *Römerzeitliche Schiffsfunde in der Datenbank 'Navis I'.* Kat. Vor- u. Frühgesch. Altert. 29 (Mainz)

W.-R. Megow 1987: *Kameen von Augustus bis Alexander Severus* (Berlin) 155f. A 10 Taf. 3–6

F. Meijer 1986: *A History of Seafaring in the Classical World* (London/Sidney)

R. Meijers and F. Willer (eds) 2007: *Hinter der silbernen Maske* (Nijmegen/Bonn)

H. Meyer 1991/92: Rom, Pergamon und Antiochus III: zu den Siegesreliefs von Sant'Omobono. *BullCom* 94, 17–32

H. Meyer 1993: Ein Denkmal des Consensus Civium, *BulCom* 95, 1993, 45–67

H. Meyer 2000: *Prunkkameen und Staatsdenkmäler römischer Kaiser. Neue Perspektiven zur Kunst der frühen Prinzipatszeit* (München) 124–39

A. Mees and B. Pferdehirt (eds) 2002: *Römerzeitliche Schiffsfunde in der Datenbank 'NAVIS I'.* Kat. Vor- u. Frühgesch. Altert. 29 (Mainz)

H. Meller (ed.) 2009: *Schlachtfeldarchäologie.* Tagungen des Landesmuseums für Vorgeschichte Halle Bd. 2 (Halle (Saale))

W. Menghin 1983: *Das Schwert im Frühen Mittelalter. Chronologisch-typologische Untersuchungen zu Langschwertern aus germanischen Gräbern des 5. bis 7. Jahrhunderts n. Chr.* Wissenschaftliche Beibände zum Anzeiger des Germanischen Nationalmuseums 1 (Stuttgart)

J. Metzler, R. Waringo, R. Bis, and N. Metzler-Zens 1991: *Clemency et les tombes de l'aristocratie en Gaule Belgique* (Luxemburg)

Ch. Miks 2001: Die Cheiroballistra des Heron. Überlegungen zu einer Geschützentwicklung der Kaiserzeit. *Saalburg Jahrb.* 51, 153–233

Ch. Miks 2007: *Studien zur römischen Schwertbewaffnung in der Kaiserzeit.* KSARP 8 (Rahden)

Ch. Miks 2008: *Vom Prunkstück zum Altmetall. Ein Depot spätrömischer Helme aus Koblenz.* Mosaiksteine. Forsch. am RGZM 4 (Mainz)

Ch. Miks 2008a: Ein römisches Schwert mit Ringknauf aus dem Rhein bei Mainz. *Mainzer Arch. Zeitschr.* 8, 129–65

Ch. Miks 2009: Das Schwert des Tiberius. In: Frey 2009, 25–8

Ch. Miks 2009a: Relikte eines frühmittelalterlichen Oberschichtgrabes? Überlegungen zu einem Konvolut bemerkenswerter Objekte aus dem Kunsthandel. *Jahrb. RGZM* 56, 395–538

Ch. Miks 2011: Römische Helme aus einem mittelkaiserzeitlichen Siedlungskontext in Poitiers/Lemonum (Dép. Vienne/F). *Jahrb. RGZM* 58, 591–660

Ch. Miks 2011a: Spätrömische Kammhelme mit hoher Kammscheibe. *Jahrb. RGZM* 22, 448–82

Ch. Miks and F. Ströbele (in preparation): Materialanalysen und Überlegungen zu den möglichen Fertigungsorten frühmittelalterlicher Spangenhelme des Typs Baldenheim. In: V. Ivanisevic (ed.) *Early Byzantine City and Society. Conference*

Dedicated to the Centenary of Archaeological Research in Caricin Grad; 3rd to 7th October 2012 – Ledscovac, Serbia. Caricin Grad

St. G. Miller 1993: *The Tomb of Lyson and Kallikles: A Painted Macedonian Tomb* (Mainz)

M. Mirkovic 2007: *Moesia superior. Eine Provinz an der mittleren Donau. Orbis Provinciarum* (Mainz)

A. Miron 1984: Das Gräberfeld von Olewig. In: H. Cüppers (ed.) *Trier. Augustusstadt der Treverer* (ed. 2 Mainz)

C. Mischka, J. Obmann, and P. Henrich 2010: Forum, Basilika und ein szenisches Theater am raetischen Limes ?. In: *Der Limes* 4:1, 10–13

S. Mitschke 2010: Was steckt dahinter? Fragen zur römischen Identität am Beispiel von Reiterhelmen. *Mannheimer Gesch. Bl.* 19, 99–113

C. Moneta 2010: *Der Vicus des römischen Kastells Saalburg* (Mainz)

D. W. von Moock 1998: *Die figürlichen Grabstelen Attikas in der Kaiserzeit. Studien zur Verbreitung, Chronologie und Ikonographie* (Mainz)

G. Moosbauer 2009: *Die Varusschlacht* (Munich)

G. Moosbauer and R. Wiegels (eds) 2011: *Fines imperii-imperium sine fine? Römische Okkupations- und Grenzpolitik im frühen Principat.* Ornabrücker Forsch. zu Altertum und Antike-Rezeption 14 (Rahden)

J.-M. A. W. Morel 1986: The early-Roman defended harbours at Velsen, North-Holland. In: *Limeskongress 1983*, 200–12

J.-M. A. W. Morel 1987: Frührömische Schiffshäuser in Haltern, Hofestatt. In: *Ausgrabungen und Funde in Westfalen-Lippe 5* (Mainz) 221–49

J.-M. A. W. Morel 1988: *De vroeg-romeinse versterking te Velsen 1. Fort en haven* (Diss. Amsterdam)

J.-M. A. W. Morel and A. V. A. J. Bosman 1989: An early Roman burial in Velsen I. In: van Driel-Murray 1989, 167–91

J.-M. A. W. Morel 1991: Die Entwicklung der frühen römischen Militärhäfen in Nordwesteuropa. In: *Die römische Okkupation nördlich der Alpen zur Zeit des Augustus. Kolloquium Bergkamen 1989. Vorträge* (Münster) 159–66

Á. Morillo Cerdán and F. García Diez 2000: Signum militaris del museo arqueologico nacional (Madrid). *Kölner Jahrb.* 33, 397–401

Á. Morillo Cerdán 2000: Neue Forschungen zu römischen Lagern der iulisch-claudischen Zeit in Nordspanien. *BJ* 200, 1–24

Á. Morillo Cerdán and J. Aurreecoecha, (eds) 2006: *The Roman Army in Hispania* (León)

J. S. Morrison 1996: *Greek and Roman Oared Warships*. Oxbow Monogr. 62 (Oxford)

J. S. Morrison and J. F. Coates 1990: *Die athenische Triere. Geschichte und Rekonstruktion eines Kriegsschiffs der griechischen Antike* (Mainz)

A. Müller 1873: *Das Cingulum militiae.* Programm des Gymnasiums zu Ploen (Ploen)

M. Müller 1999: *Faimingen-Phoebianae II. Die römischen Grabfunde.* Limesforsch. 26 (Mainz)

M. Müller 2002: *Die römischen Buntmetallfunde von Haltern.* Bodenaltertümer Westfalens 37 (Mainz)

M. Müller 2006: Ein römischer Helm vom Typ Weisenau aus Oberaden. In: G. Isenberg (ed.) *Varia Castrensia. Haltern,* Oberaden, Anreppen. Bodenaltertümer Westfalens 42 (Mainz), 287–303

M. Müller, H.-J. Schalles, and N. Zieling (eds) 2008: *Colonia Ulpia Traiana. Xanten und sein Umland in römischer Zeit* (Mainz)

W. Müller-Wiener 1994: *Die Häfen von Byzantion, Konstantinupolis, Istanbul* (Tübingen)

C. Munteanu 2013: Roman military pontoons sustained on inflated animal skins. *Arch. Korr. Bl.* 43, 545–52

A. Nabbefeld 2009: *Studien zur römischen Schildbewaffnung,* KSARP 9 (Rahden)

A. Nabbefeld 2010: Dionysos-Gott der Lüste auch Schutzgott im Krieg? *Antike Welt* 5, 78–82

J.-W. Neugebauer and M. Grünewald 1975: Weitere römische Grabfunde aus Klosterneuburg, P. G. Wien-Umgebung. *Röm. Österreich* 3, 143–65

R. Niblett 1985: *Sheepen: An Early Roman Industrial Site at Camulodunum* (London)

J. A. W. Nicolay 2003: The use and significance of military equipment and horse gear from non-military contexts in the Batavian area: continuity from the Late Iron Age into the early Roman period. In: Grünewald and Seibel 2003, 345–73

J. A. W. Nicolay 2007: *Armed Batavians: Use and Significance of Weaponry and Horse Gear from Non-military Contexts in the Rhine Delta (50 BC to AD 450).* AAS 11 (Amsterdam)

J. A. W. Nicolay 2009: Bürger Roms. Germanische Heimkehrer aus dem römischen Militärdienst. In: Konflikt 2009, 258–69

P. Noelke (ed.) 2001: *Romanisierung versus Resistenz und Wiederaufleben einheimischer Elemente. Koll. Köln 2001* (Mainz)

H. U. Nuber 1972: Zwei bronzene Besitzermarken aus Frankfurt/M.-Hedderheimein. Zur Kennzeichnung von Ausrüstungsgegenständen des römischen Heeres. *Chiron* 2, 484–507

H. U. Nuber 1985: Waffengräber aus Wehringen. In: *Die Römer in Schwaben. Jubiläumsaustellung 2000 Jahre Augsburg.* Arbeitshefte Bayer. Landesamt f. Denkmalpflege 27 (München) 209–10

H. U. Nuber 1986: Das Steinkastell Hofheim (Main-Taunus-Kreis). In: *Limeskongress 1972*, 226–34

J. Obmann 1999: Waffen – Statuszeichen oder alltäglicher Gebrauchsgegenstand?. In: v. Hesberg 1999, 189–200

J. Obmann 1999a: Aus alt mach neu. Vorbericht zu einer beidseitig verzierten Dolchscheidenplatte aus Xanten. In: *Xantener Ber. Grabung – Forschung – Präsentation*, Bd. 8 (Köln/Bonn) 331–9

J. Obmann 2000: *Römische Dolchscheiden im 1. Jahrhundert n. Chr.* KSARP 4 (Cologne)

J. Oldenstein 1979: Ein Numerum-Omnium-Beschlag aus Kreuzweingarten bei Euskirchen. *BJ* 179, 543–52

J. Oldenstein 1976: Zur Ausrüstung der römischen Auxiliareinheiten. Studien zu Beschlägen und Zierat an der Ausrüstung der römischen Auxiliareinheiten des obergermanisch-raetischen Limesgebietes aus dem zweiten und dritten Jahrhundert n. Chr. *Ber. RGK* 57, 49–284

J. Oldenstein 1985: Manufacture and supply of the Roman army with bronze fittings. In: Bishop 1985a, 82–94

J. Oldenstein 1990: Two Roman helmets from Eich, Alzey-Worms district. *JRMES* 1, 27–37

J. Oldenstein 1997: Mit *hasta* und *lorica* Wache schieben. Rekonstruktion der Ausrüstung eines Auxiliarsoldaten aus severischer Zeit. In: Schallmayer 1997, 134–46

J. Opladen-Kauder and S. Boedecker 2005: Vom Sondengänger zur Ausgrabung: Die Entdeckung eines römischen Heiligtums am Unteren Niederrhein. In: *Von Anfang an. Archäologie in Nordrhein-Westfalen* (Mainz) 442–5

E. M. Orlin 2002: *Temple, Religion and Politics in the Roman Republic* (Leiden/New York 2002)

S. Ortisi 2005: Pompeiji und Herculaneum – Soldaten in den Vesuvstädten. In: Jilek 2005, 143–51

S. Ortisi 2006: Gladii aus Pompeji, Herculaneum und Stabiae. *Germania* 84, 370–85

S. Ortisi 2009: *Römische Militärausrüstung und Pferdegeschirr aus Pompeji, Herculaneum und Stabiae*. Habil. Schr. Köln (Wiesbaden)

S. Ortisi 2009a: Vaginae catellis, baltea lamnis crepitent … Ein neues Zierelement am frühkaiserzeitlichen Schwertgehänge. *Arch. Korr. Bl.* 39:4, 539–45

B. Overbeck 1973: *Geschichte des Alpenrheintals in römischer Zeit aufgrund archäologischer Zeugnisse. Teil II: Die Fundmünzen der römischen Zeit im Alpenrheintal und Umgebung*. MBV 21 (München)

B. Overbeck 1974: Numismatische Zeugnisse zu den spätrömischen Gardehelmen. In: Kossack and Ulbert 1974, 217–25

B. Overbeck 1983: *Geschichte des Alpenrheintals in römischer Zeit aufgrund archäologischer Zeugnisse. Teil I: Topographie, Fundvorlage und Historische Auswertung. Unter Mitarbeit von L. Pauli*. MBV 20 (München)

A. Paetz gen. Schieck 2003: *Aus Gräbern geborgen. Koptische Textilien aus eigener Sammlung*. Ausstellungskatalog Deutsches Textilmuseum Krefeld (Krefeld)

A. Paetz gen Schieck 2010: Mumienportraits und ihre kulturellen Bezugssysteme – Formen der Selbstdarstellung und des Totengedenkens im römischen Ägypten. *Mannheimer Gesch. Bl.* 19, 81–98

A. Paetz gen. Schieck 2011: Über das Bildnis eines römischen Offiziers aus Ägypten und pfeilförmige Clavi als militärische Rangabzeichen im 3. Jahrhundert n. Chr. In: O. Heinrich-Tamaska, N. Krohn, and S. Ristow (eds) *Studien zu Spätantike und frühem Mittelalter 3* (Hamburg), 305–33

S. Palágyi 1989: Rekonstruktionsmöglichkeiten der Pferdegeschirrfunde aus Pannonien. In: van Driel-Murray 1989, 123–42

H. Pamir 2004: Eine Stadt stellt sich vor. Seleukeia Pieria und ihre Ruinen. *Antike Welt* 35/2, 17–21

S. T. Parker 1987: *The Roman Frontier in Central Jordan. Interim Report on the Limes Arabicus Project 1980–1985* (Oxford)

S. T. Parker 1990: The Limes Arabicus Projekt. The 1989 Campaign. *ADAJ* 34, 357–76

S. T. Parker 2000: Roman legionäry fortresses in the east. In: Brewer 2000, 121–38

K. Parlasca and H. Seemann (eds) 1999: *Augenblicke. Mumienporträts und ägyptische Grabkunst aus römischer Zeit* (Frankfurt)

P. Paulsen 1967: Einige Flügellanzen aus Schwaben. *Fundber. Schwaben* N. F. 18:1, 225–64; Taf. 49f.

L. Pauli 1987: Gewässerfunde aus Nersingen und Burlafingen. In: Mackensen 1987, 281–312

X. Pauli Jensen 2009: North Germanic archery. The practical approach – results and perspectives. In: Busch and Schalles 2009, 369–75

M. Pausch 2003: *Die römische Tunika. Ein Beitrag zur Peregrinisierung der antiken Kleidung* (Augsburg)

P. Pensabene and C. Panella (eds) 1999: *Arco di Costantino. Tra archeologia e archeometria* (Rome)

Th. Pekáry 1968: *Untersuchungen zu den römischen Reichsstraßen*. Antiquitas I 17 (Bonn)

I. Pekáry 1999: *Repertorium der hellenistischen und römischen Schiffsdarstellungen*. Boreas, Beih. 8 (Münster)

L. Pernet 2010: *Armement et auxiliaires gaulois (IIe et Ier siècles avant notre ère)*. Protohistoire Européenne 12 (Montagnac)

L. Petculescu 1990: Contributions to Roman decorated helmets and breastplates from Dacia. In: *Limeskongress 1986*, 843–54

L. Petculescu 1995: Military equipment graves in Roman Dacia. *JRMES* 6, 105–45

D. Petersen 1990: Significant Roman military finds from flea markets in Germany. *Arma. Newsletter of the Roman Military Equipment Conference* 2:1, 6–10

E. A. H. Petersen, A. Domaszewski, and G. Calderini 1896: *Die Marcus-Säule auf Piazza Colonna in Rom* (Munich)

H. von Petrikovits 1975: *Die Innenbauten römischer Legionslager während der Principatszeit*. Abhandlungen d. Rheinisch-Westfälischen Ak. d. Wiss. 56 (Opladen)

H. von Petrikovits, 1981: Die Canabae Legionis. In: *150 Jahre Deutsches Archäologisches Institut 1929–1979* (Mainz) 165–75

M. Pfaffenbichler 1996: Das Fortleben der antiken Schutzbewaffnung in der Florentiner Kunst der Frührenaissance. In: F. Blakolmer, K. R. Krierer, F. Krinzinger, A. Landskron-Dinstl, H. D. Szemethy, and K. Zhuber-Okrog (eds) *Fremde Zeiten. Festschr. f. J. Borchhardt zum sechzigsten Geburtstag* (Wien) 363–76

S. Pfahl 2013: Abschied von der Reiterei. Zu den Inschriften auf den Panzerverschlüssen der sogenannten Paraderüstungen. *SJ* 57, 127–38

S. Pfahl and M. Reuter 1996: Waffen aus römischen Einzelsiedlungen rechts des Rheins. Ein Beitrag zum Verhältnis von Militär- und Zivilbevölkerung im Limeshinterland. *Germania* 74:1, 119–67

B. Pferdehirt 1995: *Das Museum für antike Schiffahrt* (Mainz)

B. Pferdehirt 2004: *Römische Militärdiplome und Entlassungsurkunden in der Sammlung des Römisch-Germanischen Zentralmuseums I und II* (Mainz)

H. Pflug 1988: Korinthische Helme. In: Bottini *et al.* 1988, 65–106

H. Pflug 1989: *Römische Porträtstelen in Oberitalien. Untersuchungen zur Chronologie, Typologie und Ikonographie* (Mainz)

B. J. Philp 1981: *The Excavations of the Roman Forts of the Classis Britannica at Dover, 1970–1977*. Kent Monogr. Ser. 3 (Dover)

R. Pirling and R. Siepen 2006: *Die Funde aus den römischen Gräbern von Krefeld-Gellep*. GDVB Bd. 20 (Stuttgart)

M. Pietsch 1983: Die römischen Eisenwerkzeuge von Saalburg, Feldberg und Zugmantel. *SJ* 39, 5–132

M. Pietsch, D. Timpe, and L. Wamser 1991: Das augusteische Truppenlager Marktbreit. *Ber. RGK* 72, 263–324

F. Pirson 1996: Style and message on the Column of Marcus Aurelius, *Papers of the British School at Rome* 64, 139–79

L. F. Pitts and J. K. St. Joseph 1985: *Inchtuthil. The Roman Legionäry Fortress.* Britannia Monograph Series 6 (London)

D. Planck 1983: *Das Freilichtmuseum zum rätischen Limes im Ostalbkreis.* Führer zu arch. Denkmälern Baden-Württemberg 9 (Stuttgart)

R. Pleiner 1970: Zur Schmiedetechnik im römerzeitlichen Bayern. *Bayer. Vorgesch. Bl.* 35, 113–41

R. Pleiner 2000: *Iron in Archaeology. The European Bloomery Smelters* (Prague)

J. Pleska and J. Tejral 2002: *Das germanische Königsgrab von Musov in Mähren.* Mon. RGZM 55 (Mainz)

R. Ployer 2010: Ein Schwertgehänge der mittleren Kaiserzeit aus Palmyra. In: B. Bastl, V. Gassner, and U. Muss (eds) *Zeitreisen. Syrien-Palmyra-Rom. Festschr. f. Andreas Schmidt-Colinet zum 65. Geburtstag* (Wien) 185–96

R. Pogorzelski 2012: *Die Traianssäule in Rom. Dokumentation eines Krieges in Farbe* (Mainz)

R. Pogorzelski 2014: *Die Prätoriamner. Foterknechte oder Elitetruppe?* (Mainz)

H. Polenz (ed.) 1986: *Das römische Budapest. Neue Ausgrabungen und Funde in Aquincum* (Münster/Lengerich)

E. Polito 1998: *Fulgentibus armis. Introduzione allo studio dei fregi d' armi antichi* (Rome)

M. Pollak 2004: Funde entlang der Oberen Traun zwischen Hallstätter See und Traunsee. Kombinierter römischer Land-Wasser-Verkehr im Salzkammergut, Oberösterreich. *Fundber. Aus Österreich* 42, 331–85

J. Pollini 2002: *Gallo-Roman Bronzes and the Process of Ronmanization. The Cobannus Hoard.* Monumenta Graeca et Romana 9 (Leiden/Boston/Köln)

P. Pomey (ed.) 1997: *La Navigation dans l'Antiquité* (Aix-en-Provence)

H. Pöppelmann, K. Deppmeyer, and W.-D. Steinmetz (eds) 2013: *Roms vergessener Feldzug. Die Schlacht am Harzhorn* (Darmstadt)

M. Poux 2002: *Sur les traces de César. Militaria tardo-républicains en contexte gaulois.* Collection Bibracte 14 (Glux-en Glenne)

J. Prammer 1976: Die Ausgrabungen 1976 im Kastell Sorviodurum. In: R. Christlein (ed.), *Beiträge zur Topographie und Geschichte niederbayerischer Römerorte.* Beil. Z. Amtlichen Schul-Anzeiger f. d. Regierungsbezirk Niederbayern Nr. 5/6, 22–31

J. Prammer 2010: *Museumsführer Gäubodenmuseum Straubing* (Straubing)

D. Precht 2008: Das Forum. In: M. Müller, H.-J. Schalles, and N. Zieling (eds) *Colonia Ulpia Traiana. Xanten und sein Umland in römischer Zeit* (Mainz), 341–53

J. Prins 2000: The fortune of a late Roman officer. A hoard from the Meuse valley (Netherlands) with helmet and gold coins, *BJ* 200, 309–28

F. Pritchard 2004: *Clothing Culture. Dress in Egypt in the First Millennium AD. Clothing from Egypt in the Collection of The Whitworth Art Gallery, The University of Manchester* (Riggisberg)

H. H. von Prittwitz und Gaffron 1991: Der Reiterhelm des Tortikollis. *BJ* 191, 225–46

Ph. Pröttel 1988: Zur Chronologie der Zwiebelknopffibeln. *Jahrb. RGZM* 35, 347–72

H. Prückner 1997: Die Stellung des Tiberius. Vorschläge zur Ergänzung der gemma Augustea. In: *Komos. Festschrift T. Lorenz* (Vienna) 119–24

D. Quast 2009: *'Wanderer zwischen den Welten'. Die germanischen Prunkgräber von Stráze und Zakrów.* Mosaiksteine. Forsch. am RGZM 6 (Mainz)

D. Quast 2012: Einige alte und neue Waffenfunde aus dem frühbyzantinischen Reich. In: *Thesaurus Avarorum. Archaeological Studies in Honour of Èva Garam* (Budapest) 351–70

A. Raab 2012: Die Lederung einer Lorica Segmentata. In: Koepfer et al. 2012, 105–12

K. Raddatz 1987: *Der Thorsberger Moorfund: Teile von Waffen und Pferdegeschirr, sonstige Fundstücke aus Metall und Glas, Ton- und Holzgefäße, Steingeräte.* Offa-Bücher 65 (Neumünster)

I. Radman-Livaja 2004: *Militaria Sisciensia – Nalazi rimske vojne opreme iz Siska u fundusu Arheoloskoga muzeja u Zagrebu.* Musei Archaeologici Zagrabiensis Catalogi et monographiae 1, 1 (Zagreb)

I. Radman-Livaja (ed.) 2010: *Finds of the Roman Military Equipment in Croatia* (Zagreb)

G. Radoslavova, G. Dzanev, and N. Nikolov 2011: The Battle of Abritus in AD 251: written sources, archaeological and numismatic data. *Archäologica Bulgarica* 3, 23–50

J. Rageth 2010: Belege zum Alpenfeldzug aus dem Oberhalbstein GR. In: *Oleum non perdidit. Festschr. f. Stefanie Martin-Kilcher zu ihrem 65. Geburtstag.* Antiqua 47 (Basel) 59–69

J. Rageth and W. Zanier 2010: Crap Ses und Septimer: Archäologische Zeugnisse der römischen Alpeneroberung 16/15 v. Chr. aus Graubünden. Mit einem Beitrag von S. Klein. *Germania* 88, 241–311

J. Rajtar 1992: Das Holz-Erde-Lager aus der Zeit der Markomannenkriege in Iza. In: *Probleme der relativen und absoluten Chronologie ab Latènezeit bis zum Frühmittelalter* (Kraków), 149–70

J. Rajtar 1994: Waffen und Ausrüstungsteile aus dem Holz-Erde-Lager von Iza. In: *JRMES* 5, 83–95

J. Rajtar 2009: Im Handstreich genommen. Der Fall des Römerlagers von Iza. In: Konflikt 2009, 126–7

B. Rankov 2008: Roman shipsheds and Roman ships. In: Hohlfelder 2008, 51–67

M. Rathmann 2003: *Untersuchungen zu den Reichsstraßen in den westlichen Provinzen des Imperium Romanum.* Beih. BJ 55 (Mainz)

H. Ratsdorf 2009: Neue Gedanken zur Rekonstruktion römischer Schilde. In: Busch and Schalles 2009, 343–51

A. Rau 2010: *Jernalderen i Nordeuropa. Nydam Mose. Die personengebundenen Gegenstände. Grabungen 1989–1999* (Århus)

M. Reddé 1986: *Mare nostrum. Les infrastructures, le dispositif et l'histoire de la marine militaire sous l'empire romain.* Bibliothèque des Ecoles françaises d'Athènes et de Rome, 262 (Rome)

M. Reddé (ed.) 1996: *L'armée romaine en Gaule* (Paris) 212–19

M. Reddé and S. von Schnurbein 2001: *Alésia. Fouilles et recherches Franco-Allemandes sur les travaux militaires Romains autour du Mont-Auxois (1991–1997)* (Paris)

M. Reddé and J.-C. Golvin 2005: *Voyages sur la Méditerranée* (Arles)

M. Reddé, R. Brulet, R. Fellmann J. K. Haalebos, and S. von Schnurbein (eds) 2006: *Les fortifications militaires. L' architecture de la Gaule romaine.* Documents d'archéologie francaise 100 (Paris/Bordeaux)

M. Reddé 2006: *Alesia – Vom nationalen Mythos zur Archäologie* (Mainz)

M. Reddé 2014: *Les frontières de l'Empire romain (1er siècle avant J. C.–5e siècle après J. C.)* (Lacapelle-Marival)

Ch. Reichmann 1994: Römisch-germanische Schlachtfelder bei Krefeld. *Archäologie in Deutschland* 4, 11

C. Reichmann 1999: Archäologische Spuren der sogenannen Bataverschlacht vom November 69 n. Chr. und von Kämpfen des 3. Jahrhunderts n. Chr. im Umfeld des Kastells Gelduba (Krefeld-Gellep). In: Schlüter and Wiegels 1999, 97–115

P. Reinecke 1962: Römische und frühmittelalterliche Denkmäler vom Weinberg bei Eining a. d. Donau. In: *Kleine Schriften zur vor- und frühgeschichtlichen Topographie Bayerns* (München) 106–23

A. Reis 2001/2002: Roman military equipment of the 3rd century AD from the civitas capital of Nida-Hedernheim, Germania Superior. *JRMES* 12/13, 59–65

A. Reis 2010: *Nida-Heddernheim im 3. Jahrhundert n. Chr. Studien zum Ende einer Siedlung.* Schr. Arch. Mus. Frankfurt 34 (Regensburg)

Ch. Reusser 1993: *Der Fidestempel auf dem Kapitol und seine Ausstattung* (Rome)

M. Reuter 1999: Späte Militärdolche vom Typ Künzing. Anmerkungen zur Datierung und Verbreitung. In: *JRMES* 10, 121–4

M. Reuter 1999a: Studien zu den numeri des römischen Heeres in der mittleren Kaiserzeit. *Ber. RGK* 80, 357–569

M. Reuter 2001: Die 'keltische Renaissance' in den Nordwestprovinzen des römischen Reiches. In: P. Noelke, F. Naumann-Steckner, and B. Schneider (eds), *Romanisation und Resistenz in Plastik, Architektur und Inschriften der Provinzen des Imperium Romanum. Neue Funde und Forschungen. Akten des VII. Internationalen Colloquiums über Probleme des provinzialrömischen Kunstschaffens. Köln 2. Bis 6. Mai 2001* (Mainz), 21–6

M. Reuter 2007: Das Ende des raetischen Limes im Jahre 254 n. Chr. *Bayer. Vorgesch. Bl.* 72, 77–149

S. Reuter 2005: Ein Zerstörungshorizont der Jahre um 280 n. Chr. in der Retentura des Legionslagers Reginum/Regensburg. Die Ausgrabungen in der Grasgasse – Maximilianstraße 26 in den Jahren 1979/80. *Bayer. Vorgesch. Bl.* 70, 183–281

Sir I. Richmond 1968: *Hod Hill II. Excavations carried out between 1951 and 1958 for the Trustees of the British Museum* (London)

D. Richter 2010: *Das römische Heer auf der Trajanssäule.* MENTOR 3 (ed.2. Wiesbaden)

A. Riegl 1927: *Spätrömische Kunstindustrie* (ed. 2 Vienna)

S. E. Rigold 1969: The Roman haven of Dover. *Arch. Journal* 126, 78–100

E. Ritterling 1912: *Das frührömische Lager bei Hofheim im Taunus.* Nassauische Annalen 40 (Wiesbaden)

E. Ritterling 1924/25: Legio (Augustus bis Diocletian). In: *Realencylopädie der classischen Altertumswissenschaft* XII 1–2, 1211–1829

H. R. Robinson 1975: *The Armour of Imperial Rome* (London)

M. Roehmer 1997: *Der Bogen als Staatsmonument. Zur politischen Bedeutung der römischen Ehrenbögen des 1. Jhs. n. Chr.* Quellen und Forschungen zur antiken Welt 28 (München)

A. Rost and S. Wilbers-Rost 2012: *Kalkriese 6. Verteilung der Kleinfunde auf dem Oberesch in Kalkriese. Kartierung und Interpretation der römischen Militaria unter Einbeziehung der Befunde.* Römisch-Germanische Forschungen 70 (Mainz)

H. Roth 1986: *Kunst und Kunsthandwerk im frühen Mittelalter. Archäologische Zeugnisse von Childerich I. bis zu Karl dem Großen* (Stuttgart)

N. Roymans and T. Derks (eds) 1994: *De tempel van Empel. Een Hercules-heiligdom in het woongebied van de Bataven* (s'Hertogenbosch)

N. Roymans (ed.) 1996: *From the Sword to the Plough.* Amsterdam Arch. Studies 1 (Amsterdam)

E. M. Ruprechtsberger 1993: *Die römische Limeszone in Tripolitanien und der Kyrenaika, Tunesien – Libyen.* Schr. Limesmus. Aalen 47 (Stuttgart)

I. Scott Ryberg 1967: *Panel Reliefs of Marcus Aurelius* (New York)

M. El-Saghir, R. Migalla, and L. Gabolde 1986: *Le camp romain de Louqsor* (Cairo)

V. Salac and J. Bemmann (eds) 2009: *Mitteleuropa zur Zeit Marbods* (Prague/Bonn)

V. Saladino 2004: Lustrum. In: *Thesaurus Cultus Rituum Antiquorum (ThesCRA) II* (Los Angeles)

M. Sašel-Kos 2011: The Roman conquest of Dalmatia and Pannonia under Augustus – some of the latest results. In: Moosbauer and Wiegels 2011, 107–18

R. Saxer 1967: *Untersuchungen zu den Vexillationen des römischen Kaiserheeres von Augustus bis Diokletian.* Epigr. Stud. 1, Beihefte *BJ* 18, (Cologne/Graz)

U. Schaaff 1988: Keltische Helme. In: Bottini et al. 1988, 293–326

U. Schaaff 1990: *Keltische Waffen* (Mainz)

U. Schaaff 2003: *Münzen der römischen Kaiserzeit mit Schiffsdarstellungen.* Kat. Vor- u. Frühgesch. Altert. 35 (Mainz)

H. Schach-Dörges 1998: Zu süddeutschen Grabfunden alamannischer Zeit – Versuch einer Bestandsaufnahme. *Fundber. Baden Württemberg* 22:1, 627–54

Th. Schäfer 1979: Das Siegesdenkmal vom Kapitol. In: H. G. Horn and Ch. B. Rüger, *Die Numider* (Ausstellungskat. Bonn 1979) 243–50

Th. Schäfer 1989: *Imperii insignia. Sella curulis und Fasces. Zur Repräsentation römischer Magistrate.* Römische Abteilung, Erganzungsheft 29 (Mainz)

H.-J. Schalles and Ch. Schreiter 1993: *Geschichte aus dem Kies. Neue Funde aus dem Alten Rhein bei Xanten.* Xantener Ber. 3 (Köln)

H.-J. Schalles (ed.) 2010: *Die frühkaiserzeitliche Manuballista aus Xanten-Wardt.* Xantener Ber. 18 (Mainz)

E. Schallmayer (ed.) 1990: *Der römische Weihebezirk von Osterburken I. Corpus der griechischen und lateinischen Beneficiarier-Inschriften des Römischen Reiches.* Forsch. u. Ber. z. Vor- u. Frühgesch. in Baden Württemberg 40 (Stuttgart)

E. Schallmayer (ed.) 1992: *Der römische Weihebezirk von Osterburken II. Kolloquium 1990 und paläobotanische-osteologische Untersuchungen.* Forsch. u. Ber. z. Vor- u. Frühgesch. in Baden Württemberg 40 (Stuttgart)

E. Schallmayer (ed.) 1997: *Hundert Jahre Saalburg* (Mainz)

E. Schallmayer 2006: *Der Limes. Geschichte einer Grenze* (Munich)

E. Schallmayer 2010: *Der Odenwaldlimes* (Stuttgart)

J. Scheid and V. Huet (eds) 2000: *Autour de la Colonne Aurélienne. Geste et image sur la colonne de Marc Aurèle à Rome* (Turnhout)

M. Schleiermacher 1984: *Römische Reitergrabsteine. Die kaiserzeitlichen Reliefs des triumphierenden Reiters* (Bonn)

M. Schleiermacher 1995: Bemerkungen zum römischen Pferdegeschirr. In: Festschr. G. Ulbert 1995, 131–8

M. Schleiermacher 2000: Römisches Pferdegeschirr aus den Kastellen Saalburg, Zugmantel und Feldberg. *Saalburg Jahrb.* 50, 167–93

O. Schlippschuh 1974: *Die Händler im römischen Kaiserreich in Gallien, Germanien und den Donauprovinzen, Raetien, Noricum und Pannonien* (Amsterdam)

W. Schlüter with contributions by F. Berger, G. Franzius, J. Lienemann, A. Rost, E. Tolksdorf-Lienemann, R. Wiegels, and S. Wilbers-Rost 1992: Archäologische Zeugnisse der Varusschlacht? Die Untersuchungen in der Kalkrieser-Niewedder Senke bei Osnabrück. *Germania* 70, 307–402

W. Schlüter and R. Wiegels (eds) 1999: *Rom, Germanien und die Ausgrabungen von Kalkriese. Int. Kongress d. Univ. Osnabrück und des Landschaftsverbandes Osnabrücker Land e. V. vom 2. bis 5. September 1996* (Osnabrück)

J. Schmalhofer 2012: Der Einfluss von Regen auf römische scuta. In: Koepfer *et al.* 2012, 129–36

S. von Schnurbein 1974: Zum Ango. In: Kossack and Ulbert 1974, 411–33

S. von Schnurbein 1977: *Das römische Gräberfeld von Regensburg.* Materialhefte z. Bayer. Vorgesch. A31 (Kallmünz)

S. von Schnurbein 1981: Untersuchungen zur Geschichte der römischen Militärlager an der Lippe. *Ber. RGK* 62, 5–101

S. von Schnurbein 1986: Dakisch-thrakische Soldaten im Römerlager Oberaden. *Germania* 64, 409–31

S. von Schnurbein 1995: Merkur als Soldat? Zur Gürtelmode des 3. Jahrhunderts n. Chr. In: Festschr. G. Ulbert 1995, 139–48

H. Schönberger, 1975: *Kastell Künzing. Die Grabungen von 1958 bis 1966.* Limesforsch. 13 (Berlin)

H. Schönberger 1976: *Das augusteische Römerlager Rödgen.* Limesforsch. 15 (Berlin)

H. Schönberger 1978: *Kastell Oberstimm. Die Grabungen von 1968 bis 1971.* Limesforsch. 18 (Berlin)

H. Schönberger 1985: Die römischen Truppenlager der frühen und mittleren Kaiserzeit zwischen Nordsee und Inn. *Ber. RGK* 66, 321–497

M. Schönfelder 2009: Ludwig Lindenschmit und Frankreich. In: Frey 2009, 55–8

M. Schönfelder (ed.)2010: *Kelten! Kelten? Keltische Spuren in Italien.* Mosaiksteine. Forschungen am RGZM 7 (Mainz)

M. Scholz 2009: *Das Reiterkastell Aquileia/Heidenheim. Die Ergebnisse der Grabungen 2000–2004.* Forsch. u. Ber. Z. Vor- u. Frühgesch. Baden-Württemberg 110 (Stuttgart)

A. Schnapp 2009: *Die Entdeckung der Vergangenheit. Ursprünge und Abenteuer der Archäologie* (Stuttgart)

M. Schrader 2009: Rekonstruiertes römisches Militär. Zur Wirkung archäologischer Forschung in der gegenwärtigen Öffentlichkeit. In: Busch and Schalles 2009, 353–68

E. Schramm 1918: *Die antiken Geschütze der Saalburg* (Bad Homburg 1918; reprint with introduction by D. Baatz)

P.-E. Schramm 1955: *Herrschaftszeichen und Staatssymbolik.* Schr. d. Monumenta Germaniae Historica 13, 2 (Stuttgart)

W. Schüle 1969: *Die Meseta-Kulturen der Iberischen Halbinsel* (Berlin)

A. Schulten 1927: *Numantia: Die Ergebnisse der Ausgrabungen 1905–1919, Bd. 3* (Munich)

A. Schulten 1929: *Numantia: Die Ergebnisse der Ausgrabungen 1905–1919, Bd. 4* (Munich)

M. Schulze-Dörrlamm 1985: Germanische Kriegergräber mit Schwertbeigaben in Mitteleuropa aus dem späten 3. Jahrhundert und der ersten Hälfte des 4. Jahrhunderts n. Chr. *Jahrb. RGZM* 32, 509–69

M. Schulze-Dörrlamm 2009: *Byzantinische Gürtelschnallen und Gürtelbeschläge im Römisch-Germanischen Zentralmuseum. Teil 1 Die Schnallen ohne Beschläg, mit Laschenbeschläg und mit festem Beschläg des 5.–7. Jahrhunderts* Kat. Vorgesch. Altertümer 30, 1 (ed. 2 Mainz)

M. Schulze-Dörrlamm 2009a: *Byzantinische Gürtelschnallen und Gürtelbeschläge im Römisch-Germanischen Zentralmuseum. Teil 2 Die Schnallen mit Scharnierbeschläg und die Schnallen mit angegossenem Riemendurchzug des 7.–10. Jahrhunderts* Kat. Vorgesch. Altertümer 30, 2 (ed. Mainz)

I. R. Scott 1980: Spearheads of the British Limes. In: *Limeskongress 1989*, 333–43

Cl. Seillier 1977: Boulogne and coastal defences in the 4th and 5th centuries. In: D. E. Johnston (ed.), *The Saxon Shore.* Council for British Archaeology Report 18 (London) 35–8

Cl. Seillier 1994: Boulogne-sur-Mer. In: R. Delmarie et al. (eds), *Pas-de-Calais. Carte archéologique de Gaule* 62:1–2 (Paris) 214–301

Cl. Seillier 1996: Le camp de la Flotte de Bretagne à Boulogne-sur-Mer (Gesoriacum). In: M. Reddé (ed.), *L'armée romaine en Gaule* (Paris) 212–19

G. Seitz (ed.) 2006: *Im Dienste Roms. Festschrift für Hans Ulrich Nuber* (Remshalden)

W. Selzer, K.-V. Decker, and A. Do Paço 1988: *Römische Steindenkmäler. Mainz in römischer Zeit. Katalog der Steindenkmäler in der Steinhalle* (Mainz)

S. Settis, A. La Regina, G. Agosti, and V. Farinella 1988: *La Colonna Traiana* (Turin)

A. V. Siebert 1999: *Instrumenta sacra. Untersuchungen zu römischen Opfer-, Kult- und Priestergeräten* (Berlin/New York)

Sieg und Triumpf 2003: *Sieg und Triumpf. Der Norden im Schatten des römischen Reiches.* Ausstellungskatalog Nationalmuseum Kopenhagen (Kopenhagen)

S. Sievers 1995: Die Waffen. In: Reddé *et al.* 1995, 135–57

S. Sievers 1997: Alesia and Orsuna: Bemerkungen zur Normierung der spätrepublikanischen Bewaffnung und Ausrüstung. *JRMES* 8, 271–6

D. Sim 1997: Roman chain-mail: experiments to reproduce the techniques of manufacture. *Britannia* 28, 359–71

D. Sim and J. Kaminski 2012: *Imperial Roman Armour. The Production of Early Imperial Military Armour* (Oxford/Oakville)

M. Simkins and R. Embleton 2006: *Die römische Armee von Caesar bis Constantin 44 v. Chr.–333 n. Chr.* (Sankt Augustin)

E. Simon 1981: *Die Götter am Trajansbogen zu Benevent.* 1. Trierer Winckelmannsprogramm (Mainz)

E. Simon 1985: Virtus und Pietas. Zu den Friesen A und B von der Cancelleria. *JdI* 100, 543–56

M. Sommer 1984: *Die Gürtel und Gürtelbeschläge des 4. und 5. Jahrhunderts im römischen Reich*. Bonner Hefte zur Vorgesch. (Bonn)

C. S. Sommer 1984: *The Military Vici in Roman Britain. Aspects of Their Origins, Their Location and Layout, Administration, Function and End*. BAR British Series 129 (Oxford)

C. S. Sommer 1988: Kastellvicus und Kastell. Untersuchungen zum Zugmantel im Taunus und zu den Kastellvici in Obergermanien und Raetien. *Fundberichte aus Baden-Württemberg* 13, 457–707

C. S. Sommer 1995: Where did they put the horses? *Festschr. G. Ulbert* 149–68

C. S. Sommer 1999: Wohin mit den Pferden? – Stallbaracken sowie Aufmarsch- und Übungsplätze in römischer Zeit. In: Kemkes and Scheuerbrandt 1999, 84–90

C. S. Sommer 2002: Hoch und immer höher – Zur dritten Dimension römischer Gebäude in Obergermanien. In: R. Gogräfe and K. Kell (eds) *Haus und Siedlung in den römischen Nordwestprovinzen. Grabungsbefund, Architektur und Ausstattung*. Forsch. im röm. Schwarzenacker 4 (Homburg/Saar) 47–61

G. Sommer von Bülow 2006: Die Donaugrenze in Serbien. In: Genzen 2006, 157–62

A. Sorell 1981: *Reconstructing the Past*. Edited by M. Sorell (London)

J. E. H. Spaul 1994: *Ala². The Auxiliary Cavalry Units of the Pre-Diocletianic Imperial Roman Army* (Andover)

J. E. H. Spaul 2000: *Cohors². The Evidence for and a Short History of the Auxiliary Infantry Units of the Roman Imperial Army*. BAR Int. Ser. 841 (Oxford)

M. A. Speidel 1996: *Die römischen Schreibtafeln von Vindonissa*. Veröffentl. GPV 12 (Baden)

M. A. Speidel 2010: Auf kürzestem Weg und gut verpflegt an die Front. Zur Versorgung pannonischer Expeditionstruppen während der severischen Partherkriege. In: Eich 2010, 133–48

M. P. Speidel 1983: Legionsabteilungen aus Mainz beim Holzeinschlag im Odenwald. Der Odenwald 30, 111–14

M. P. Speidel 1992: The weapons keeper, the fisci curator and the ownership of weapons in the Roman army. In: M. P. Speidel, *Roman Army Studies II* (Stuttgart) 131–6

M. P. Speidel 1999: Bildnisse römischer Offiziere aus dem Fayum. In: Parlasca and Seemann 1999, 87–8

M. P. Speidel 2002: The framework of an imperial legion. In: R. J. Brewer (ed.): *Birthday of the Eagle: the Second Augustan Legion and the Roman Military Machine* (Cardiff) 125–43

M. P. Speidel 2008: Das Heer. In: Johne *et al.* 2008, 673–90

J. Spier 2010: *Treasures of the Ferrell Collection* (Wiesbaden)

J. Stäcker 2003: *Princeps und miles. Studien zum Bindungs- und Nahverhältnis von Soldat und Kaiser im 1. und 2. Jh. n.Chr.* (Zürich/New York)

P. F. Stary 1981: Ursprung und Ausbreitung der eisenzeitlichen Ovalschilde mit spindelförmigem Schildbuckel. *Germania* 59, 287–306

P. F. Stary 1981a: *Zur eisenzeitliche Bewaffnung und Kampfweise in Mittelitalien (ca. 9.–6. Jh. v. Chr.)*. Marburger Stud. Z. Vor- u. Frühgesch. 3 (Marburg)

P. F. Stary 1994: *Zur eisenzeitlichen Bewaffnung und Kampfweise auf der iberischen Halbinsel* (Berlin/New York)

K. Stauner, 2004: *Das offizielle Schriftwesen des römischen Heeres von Augustus bis Gallienus (27 v. Chr.–268 n. Chr.). Eine Untersuchung zu Struktur, Funktion und Bedeutung der offiziellen militärischen Verwaltungsdokumentation und zu deren Schreibern* (Bonn)

J. R. Steffy 1985: The Herculaneum boat: preliminary notes on hull details. *Am. Journal Arch.* 89, 519–21

J. R. Steffy 1994: *Wooden Ship Building and the Interpretation of Shipwrecks* (College Station)

B. Steidl 2000: Die Wetterau vom 3. bis 5. Jahrhundert n. Chr. Mat. z. Vor- u. Frühgesch. Von Hessen 22 (Wiesbaden)

B. Steidl 2008: *Welterbe Limes. Roms Grenze am Main* (Obernburg am Main)

E. M. Steinby (ed.) 1993: *Lexicon Topographicum Urbis Roma I* (Rome)

G. Steinhauer 1996: La découverte de l'arsenal de Philon. In: *Tropis IV. 4th International Symposium on Ship Construction in Antiquity* (Athens) 471–9

K. Stemmer 1978: *Untersuchungen zur Typologie, Chronologie und Ikonographie der Panzerstatuen*. Arch. Forsch. (Berlin)

H. Steuer 1990: Höhensiedlungen des 4. und 5. Jahrhunderts in Südwestdeutschland. Einordnung des Zähringer Burgberges, Gemeinde Gundelfingen, Kreis Breisgau-Hochschwarzwald. In: Nuber *et al.* 1990, 139–205

G. D. Stiebel 2003: The militaria from Herodium. In: G. C. Bottini, L. Di Segni, and L. D. Chrupcala (eds), *One Land – Many Cultures. Archaeological Studies in Honour of S. Loffreda*. Studium Biblicum Franciscanum, Coll. Maior 41 (Jerusalem)

G. D. Stiebel 2005: 'Dust to dust, ashes to ashes …' – military equipment from destruction layers in Roman Palestine. In: Jilek 2005, 99–108

G. D. Stiebel and J. Magness 2007: The Military Equipment From Masada. In: *Masada VII The Yigael Yadin Excavations 1963–1965, Final Reports* (Jerusalem)

O. Stoll 1992: *Die Skulpturenausstattung römischer Militäranlagen an Rhein und Donau. Der obergermanisch-raetische Limes*. Pharos 1.2 (St. Katharinen)

O. Stoll 2001: Die Adler im 'Käfig'. Zu einer Aquilifer-Grabstele aus Apamea in Syrien. *Arch Korr. Bl.* 21, 535–8

K. Strobel 2007: Strategy and army structure between Septimius Severus and Constantine the Great. In: Erdkamp 2007, 267–85

K. Strobel 2010: *Kaiser Traian. Eine Epoche der Weltgeschichte* (Regensburg)

G. Sumner 2002: *Roman Military Clothing (1) 100 BC–AD 200*, Osprey Men-at-Arms 374 (Oxford)

G. Sumner 2003: *Roman Military Clothing (2) AD 200–400*, Osprey Men-at-Arms 390 (Oxford)

G. Sumner 2007: *Die römische Armee. Bewaffnung und Ausrüstung zur Kaiserzeit* (Stuttgart)

G. Sumner 2009: *Roman Military Dress* (Stroud)

E. A. Sydenham: *The Coinage of the Roman Republic* (London)

K. Szabó 1986: Le casque romain de Intercisa – récente trouvaille du Danube. Avec une contribution de A. Mocsy. *Limeskongress 1983*, 421–5

A. K. Taylor 1975: Römische Hackamoren und Kappzäume aus Metall. *Jahrb. RGZM* 22, 106–33

J. Tejral 1992: Die Probleme der römisch-germanischen Beziehungen unter Berücksichtigung der neuen Forschungsergebnisse im niederösterreichisch-südmährischen Thayaflussgebiet. *Ber. RGK* 73, 377–468

J. Tejral 1994: Römische und germanische Militärausrüstung der antoninischen Periode im Licht norddanubischer Funde. In: Carnap-Bornheim 1994a, 28–60

J. Tejral 2002: Die Sporen. In: Pleska and Tejral 2002, 141–88

A. Thiel (ed.) 2007: *Forschungen zur Funktion des Limes*. Beitr. zum Welterbe Limes 2 (Bad Homburg)

M. D. Thomas 2003: *Lorica Segmentata Vol. 2. JRMES* Mon. 2 (Chirnside)

W. Torbrügge 1971/1972: Vor- und frühgeschichtliche Flußfunde. Zur Ordnung und Bestimmung einer Denkmälergruppe. *Ber. RGK* 51/52, 3–146

M. Torelli 1982: *Typology and Structure of Roman Historical Reliefs* (Ann Arbor)

M. Torelli 1993: Arcus Marci Aurelii, in Steinby 1993, 98–9

H. Travis and J. Travis 2011: *Roman Body Armour* (Chalford)

M. Treister 1994: Roman military equipment in the Kingdom of Bosporus. In: Carnap-Bornheim 1994a, 91–9

B. Trier (ed.) 1989: *2000 Jahre Römer in Westfalen*. Ausstellungskatalog des Westfälischen Museums für Archäologie in Münster (Mainz)

B. Trier (ed.) 1991: *Die römische Okkupation nördlich der Alpen zur Zeit des Augustus. Kolloquium Bergkamen 1989: Vorträge*. Bodenaltertümer Westfalens 26 (Münster)

J. Trumm 2001: Militaria, Ziegelstempel und eine gefälschte Inschrift: Veteranen im Umfeld von Schleitheim-Iuliomagus. *Jber. GPV* 2001, 109–17

S. Rinaldi Tufi 1988: *Militari romani sul Reno. L' iconografia degli 'stehende Soldaten' nelle stele funerarie del I secolo d. C.* (Rome)

S. Tusa and J. Royal 2012: The landscape of the naval battle at the Egadi Islans (241 B.C.). *Journal Roman Arch.* 25, 7–48

H. Ubl 1969: *Waffen und Uniformen des römischen Heeres der Principatsepoche nach den Grabreliefs Noricums und Pannoniens*. Ungedr. Diss. (Klosterneuburg)

H. Ubl 1975: Römische Helme vom Typus Weisenau in Wiener Sammlungen. *Röm. Österreich* 3, 195–235

H. Ubl 1976: Pilleus Pannonicus, die Feldmütze des spätrömischen Heeres. In: M. Mitscha-Märheim, H. Friesinger, and H. Kerchler (eds), *Festschr. f. Richard Pittioni*. Arch. Austriaca Beih. 14 (Vienna), 214–41

H. Ubl 1989: Was trug der römische Soldat unter dem Cingulum? In: van Driel-Murray 1989, 61–74

H. Ubl 1994: Wann verschwand der Dolch vom römischen Militärgürtel? In: Carnap-Bornheim 1994a, 137–44

H. Ubl (ed.) 1997: *Katalog zur Schausammlung 'Römerzeit' des Museums Lauriacum-Enns 2*. Forsch. in Lauriacum 12 (Enns)

H. Ubl 2001: Gedanken zu einem Benefiziarierabzeichen aus Lauriacum. In: *Carinthia Romana und die römische Welt. Festschrift für Gernot Piccotini zum 60. Geburtstag* (Klagenfurt) 379–90

H. Ubl 2006: Was trug der römische Soldat unter dem Panzer. *Bayer. Vorgesch. Bl.* 71, 261–76

H. Ubl 2013: *Waffen und Uniformen des römischen Heeres der Principatsepoche nach den Grabreliefs Noricums und Pannoniens*. Austria Antiqua 3 (Vienna)

G. Ulbert 1959: *Die römischen Donau-Kastelle Aislingen und Burghöfe*. Limesforsch. 1 (Berlin)

G. Ulbert 1962: Der Legionärsdolch von Oberammergau. In: J. Werner (ed.), *Aus Bayerns Frühzeit. Friedrich Wagner zum 75. Geburtstag* (Munich)

G. Ulbert 1968: *Römische Waffen des 1. Jahrhunderts n. Chr.* Kleine Schriften zur Kenntnis der römischen Besetzungsgeschichte Südwestdeutschlands 4 (Stuttgart)

G. Ulbert 1969: *Das frührömische Kastell Rheingönnheim. Die Funde aus den Jahren 1912 und 1913*. Limesforsch. 9 (Berlin)

G. Ulbert 1969a: Gladii aus Pompeji. Vorarbeiten zu einem Corpus römischer Gladii. *Germania* 47, 97–128

G. Ulbert 1970: *Das römische Donau-Kastell Rißtissen. Teil 1. Die Funde aus Metall, Horn und Knochen*. Urkunden zur Vor- und Frühgesch. aus Südwürttemberg-Hohenzollern Heft 4 (Stuttgart)

G. Ulbert 1971: Römische Bronzeknöpfe mit Reliefverzierung. *Fundber. Schwaben* N. F. 19, 278–97

G. Ulbert 1971a: GAIVS ANTONIVS, der Meister des silbertauschierten Dolches von Oberammergau. *Bayer. Vorgesch. Bl.* 36, 44–9

G. Ulbert, 1974: Straubing und Nydam. Zu römischen Langschwertern der späten Limeszeit. In: Kossack and Ulbert 1974, 197–216

G. Ulbert, J. Garbsch, and K. Raddatz 1976: s. v. Bewaffnung. In: J. Hoops *et al.* (eds) *Reallexikon der Germanischen Altertumskunde (RGA)* (Berlin/New York), 416–33

G. Ulbert 1984: *Cáceres el Viejo. Ein spätrepublikanisches Legionslager in Spanisch-Extremadura*. Madrider Beitr. 11 (Mainz)

Ch. Unz and E. Deschler-Erb 1997: *Katalog der Militaria aus Vindonissa*. Veröffentl. GPV 14 (Brugg)

O. von Vacano 1988: Regio instratu ornatus. Beobachtungen zur Deutung des Reliefs des L. Aemillius Paullus in Delphi. In: *Bathron, Festschrift für H. Drerup* (Saarbrücken), 375–86

D. Valbelle and J.-Y. Carrez-Maratray 2000: *Le camp romain du Bas-Empire à Tell el-Herr* (Paris)

V. Varsik 1996: Das römische Lager von Rusovce-Gerulata. Ein Beitrag zu Lokalisierung und Anfängen. *Jahrb. RGZM* 43, 531–600

Varusschlacht 2009: *2000 Jahre Varusschlacht. Konflikt* (Stuttgart)

Varusschlacht Katalog 2009: *Varusschlacht im Osnabrücker Land. Museum und Park Kalkriese (Katalog)* (Mainz)

C. C. Vermeule 1959/60: Hellenistic and Roman cuirassed statues. *Berytus* 13, 1–82

C. C. Vermeule 1960: A Roman silver helmet in the Toledo (Ohio) Museum of Art. *JRS* 50, 8–11

H. D. L. Viereck 1975: *Die römische Flotte. Classis Romana* (Herford)

B. Vierneisel-Schlörb 1979: *Glyptothek München, Katalog der Skulpturen II. Klassische Skulpturen des 5. und 4. Jhs. v. Chr.* (München)

Z. Visy 1985: *Der pannonische Limes in Ungarn* (Stuttgart)

Z. Visy (ed.) 2003: *The Roman Army in Pannonia. An Archaeological Guide of the Ripa Pannonica* (Pécs)

Z. Visy 2003a: *The Ripa Panonica in Hungary* (Budapest)

Th. Völling 1990: Funditores im römischen Heer. *Saalburg Jahrb.* 45, 24–58

Th. Völling 1991: Plumbata-mattiobarbulus-marzobarboulon. Bemerkungen zu einem Waffenfund aus Olympia. *Arch. Anz.* 287–98

Th. Völling 1997: Römische militaria in Griechenland. Ein Überblick. *JMRES* 8, 91–104

M. Vogt 2006: *Spangenhelme: Baldenheim und verwandte Typen*. Kat. Vor- und Frühgesch. Altertümer, Bd 39 (Mainz)

M.-L. Vollenweider and M. Avisseau-Bronstet 2003: *Camées et intailles II. Les portraits romains du Cabinet des médailles* (Paris)

N. Walke 1965: *Das römische Donaukastell Straubing-Sorviodurum*. Limesforschungen 3 (Berlin)

L. Wamser (ed.) 2000: *Die Römer zwischen Alpen und Nordmeer* (Mainz)

L. Wamser and B. Steidl (eds) 2002: *Neue Forschungen zur römischen Besiedlung zwischen Oberrhein und Enns*. Schriftenreihe d. Arch. Staatsslg. 3 (München)

G. Waurick 1983: Untersuchungen zur historisierenden Rüstung in der Römischen Kunst. *Jahrb. RGZM* 30, 265–301

G. Waurick 1988: Helme der hellenistischen Zeit und ihre Vorläufer. In: Bottini *et al.* 351–80

G. Waurick 1988a: Römische Helme. In: Bottini *et al.* 1988, 327–64

G. Waurick 1990: *Helme in Caesars Heer* (Mainz)

G. Waurick 1994: Zur Rüstung von frühkaiserzeitlichen Hilfstruppen und Verbündeten der Römer. In: v. Carnap-Bornheim 1994, 1–25

G. Weber (ed.) 2000: *Cambodunum-Kempten. Erste Hauptstadt der römischen Provinz Raetien?* (Mainz)

G. Webster 1969: *The Roman Imperial Army of the First and Second Centuries A.D.* (London)

G. Wegner 1976: *Die vorgeschichtlichen Flußfunde aus dem Main und dem Rhein bei Mainz*. Materialhefte z. Bayer. Vorgesch. A 30 (Kallmünz)

P. Weiß 2004: Zwei vollständige Konstitutionen für die Truppen von Noricum (8. Sept. 79) und Pannonia inferior (27. Sept. 154). *ZPE* 146, 239–46

K.-W. Welwei 1992: Die 'Löwen' Caracallas. *BJ* 192, 231–9

H. Welfare and V. Swan 1995: *Roman Camps in England. The Field Archeology* (London)

W. M. Werner 1983: Ein dakischer Trensenknebel aus Augsburg-Oberhausen. *Arch. Korr. Bl.* 13, 235–40

R. E. M. Wheeler 1929: The Roman lighthouse at Dover. *Arch. Journal* 86, 29–46

R. E. M. Wheeler 1943: *Maiden Castle, Dorset* (Oxford)

R. Wiegels (ed.) 2000: *Die Fundmünzen von Kalkriese und die frühkaiserzeitliche Münzprägung* (Möhnesee)

R. Wiegels (ed.) 2007: *Die Varusschlacht. Wendepunkt der Geschichte?* (Stuttgart)

L. Wierschowski 1984: *Heer und Wirtschaft. Das römische Heer der Prinzipatszeit als Wirtschaftsfaktor*. Habelts Dissertationsdrucke, Reihe Alte Geschichte, Heft 20 (Bonn)

M. Wijnhoven 2009: Lorica Hamata Squamataque: A Study of Roman Hybrid Feathered Armour. *Journal of the Mail Research Society*, 2:1, 3–29

J. P. Wild 1970: Button-and-loop fasteners in the Roman provinces. *Britannia* 1, 137–55

J. P. Wild 2010: Klassenunterschiede in einem römischen Kastell: Das Zeugnis der Textilreste und Dokumente aus Vindolanda. *Mannheimer Gesch. Bl.* 19, 129–31

W. J. H. Willems 1992: Roman face masks from the Kops Plateau, Nijmegen, the Netherlands, *JRMES* 3, 57–66

T. Wilmott 1997: *Birdoswald. Excavations of a Roman Fort on Hadrian's Wall and Its Successor Settlements: 1987–92*. English Heritage Archaeological Report 14 (London)

T. Wilmott 1997a: The Birdoswald basilica: a new type of building in an auxiliary fort. In: *Limeskongress 1995*, 581–6

S. Winterbottom 1989: Saddle covers, chamfrons and possible horse armour from Carlisle. In: van Driel-Murray 1989, 319–36

G. Wolf 1997: Prolegomena zur Erforschung der Heiligen Lanze. In: H.-J. Becker, *Die Reichskleinodien, Herrschaftszeichen des Heiligen römischen Reiches*. Schr. z. staufischen Kunst u. Gesch. 16, (Göppingen)

G. Wolf and F. Kirchweger 2005: *Die Heilige Lanze in Wien* (Mailand)

D. Woods 1993: The ownership and disposal of military equipment in the Late Roman army. *JRMES* 4, 55–65

P. Worm 2000: *Die Heilige Lanze. Bedeutungswandel und Verehrung eines Herrschaftszeichens*. Elementa diplomica 8. Arbeiten aus dem Marburger hilfswissenschaftl. Inst. (Marburg)

R. Wünsche 2005: *Glyptothek München. Meisterwerke griechischer und römischer Skulptur* (München)

M. P. Wuilleumier 1952: Lyon. La bataille de 197. *Gallia* 8, 146–50

M. Yacoub 1995: *Splendeurs des Mosaiques de Tunisie* (Tunis)

H. C. Youtie and J. G. Winter 1951: *Papyri and Ostraca from Karanis, Papyri in the University of Michigan Collection Vol. 8* (Ann Arbor)

S. Zabelicky-Scheffenegger 1979: *Burnum I. Erster Bericht über die Kleinfunde der Grabungen 1973 und 1974 auf dem Forum*. Schr. Balkankomm. Ant. Abt. 19 (Vienna)

W. Zanier 1993: *Das römische Kastell Ellingen*. Limesforschungen 23 (Berlin)

W. Zanier 1988: Römische dreiflügelige Pfeilspitzen. *Saalburg Jahrb.* 44, 5–27

W. Zanier 1994: Eine römische Katapultpfeilspitze der 19. Legion aus Oberammergau – Neues zum Alpenfeldzug des Drusus im Jahre 15 v. Chr. *Germania* 74, 587–96

W. Zanier 1995: Ein einheimischer Opferplatz mit römischen Waffen der frühesten Okkupation (15–10 v. Chr.) bei Oberammergau. In: *Limeskongress 1995*, 47–52

W. Zanier 2006: *Das Alpenrheintal in den Jahrzehnten um Christi Geburt. Forschungsstand zu den historischen und archäologischen Quellen der Spätlatène- und frühen römischen Kaiserzeit zwischen Bodensee und Bündner Pässen (Vorarlberg, Liechtenstein, Sankt Gallen, Graubünden)*. Münchner Beitr. Zur Vor- und Frühgesch. Veröffentl. D. Komm. z. Vergleichenden Archäologie Römischer Alpen- und Donauländer 59 (Munich)

P. Zanker 1970: Das Trajansforum in Rom. *AA* 85, 499–544

P. Zanker 1987: *Augustus und die Macht der Bilder* (Munich)

N. Zieling 1989: *Studien zu germanischen Schilden der Spätlatène- und der römischen Kaiserzeit im freien Germanien*. BAR Int. Ser. (Oxford)

G. Ziethen 1997: Ex Oriente ad Rhenum – Orientalen im römischen Mainz. *Mainzer Arch. Zeitschr.* 4, 111–86

E. Zweierlein-Diehl 2008: *Magie der Steine. Die antiken Prunkkameen im kunsthistorischen Museum* (Vienna)

Abbreviations

AA	Archäologischer Anzeiger	JdI	Jahrbuch des Deutschen Archäologischen Instituts
AAS	Les annales archéologiques arabes syriennes	JRMES	Journal of Roman Military Equipment Studies
Arch. Korr. Bl.	Archäologisches Korrespondenzblatt		
BAR	British Archaeological Reports (Oxford)	KSARP	Kölner Studien zur Archäologie der römischen Provinzen
Bayer. Vorgesch. Bl.	Bayerische Vorgeschichtsblätter		
BCH	Bulletin de correspondance hellénique	MBV	Münchner Beitr. Z. Vor- u. Frühgesch.
BJ	Bonner Jahrbücher	ORL	Der obergermanisch-raetische Limes des Römerreiches
BulCom	Bulletino della Commissione arceologica comunale di Roma	RIC	H. Mattingly and E. A. Sydenham (eds) Roman Imperial Coins (London 1923–1994)
CIL	Corpus Inscriptionum Latinarum		
Jber. GPV	Jahresberichte der Gesellschaft Pro Vindonissa	RLÖ	Der römische Limes in Österreich
JHS	The Journal of Hellenic Studies	ZPE	Zeitschr. f. Papyrologie und Epigraphik

Proceedings of the International Congresses of Roman Frontier Studies

Limeskongress 1949	E. Birley (ed.), The Congress of Roman Frontier Studies 1949 (Newcastle 1952)
Limeskongress 1955	E. Swoboda (ed.), Carnuntina. Ergebnisse der Forschung über die Grenzprovinzen des römischen Reiches. Vorträge beim internationalen Kongreß der Altertumsforscher Carnuntum 1955. Röm. Forsch. In Niederösterreich 3 (Carnuntum 1956)
Limeskongress 1957	R. Laur-Belart (ed.), Limes-Studien. Vorträge des 3. Internationalen Limes-Kongresses in Rheinfelden 1957 (Basel 1959)

Proceedings of the 4th Limeskongress in Durham in 1959 were not published

Limeskongress 1963	G. Novak (ed.), Quintus Congressus Internationalis Limitis Romani Studiosorum (Nitra 1964)
Limeskongress 1964	H. Schönberger (ed.), Studien zu den Militärgrenzen Roms. Vorträge des 6. Internationalen Limeskongresses in Süddeutschland 1964. BJ Beih. 19 (Bonn 1967)
Limeskongress 1967	Applebaum, S. (ed.), Roman Frontier Studies 1967. The Proceedings of the Seventh International Congress Held at Tel Aviv (Tel Aviv 1971)
Limeskongress 1969	E. Birley, B. Dobson, and M. Jarrett (eds), Roman Frontier Studies 1969. Eighth International Congress of Limesforschung (Cardiff) (Cardiff 1974)
Limeskongress 1972	M. Pippidi (ed.), D'Études sur les Frontières Romaines (Mamaia 1974)
Limeskongress 1974	D. Haupt and H. G. Horn (eds), Studien zu den Militärgrenzen Roms 1974 in der Germania Inferior (Bonn 1977)
Limeskongress 1976	J. Fitz (ed.), Akten des 11. Internationalen Limeskongresses, Székesfehévár 1976 (Budapest 1977)
Limeskongress 1979	W. S. Hanson and L. J. F. Keppie (eds), Roman Frontier Studies 1979. Proceedings of the XIIth International Congress of Roman Frontier Studies Stirling 1979. BAR Int. Ser. 71 (Oxford 1980)
Limeskongress 1983	Ch. Unz (ed.), Studien zu den Militärgrenzen Roms III. Akten des 13. Int. Limeskongresses Aalen 1983. Forsch. u. Ber. z. Vor- u. Frühgesch. in Baden-Württemberg 20 (Stuttgart 1986)
Limeskongress 1986	H. Vetters and M. Kandler (eds.) Akten des 14. Int. Limeskongresses in Carnuntum 1986. Österr. Ak. d. Wiss. Der Römische Limes in Österreich 36 (Vienna 1990)
Limeskongress 1989	V. A. Maxfield and M. J. Dobson (eds), Roman Frontier Studies 1989. Proceedings of the XVth International Congress of Roman Frontier Studies Canterbury (Exeter 1991)
Limeskongress 1995	W. Groenman-van Waateringe, B. L. van Beek, W. J. H. Willems, and S. L. Wynia (eds), Roman Frontier Studies 1995. Proceedings of the XVIth International Congress of Roman Frontier Studies Rolduc. Oxbow Monograph 91 (Oxford 1997)
Limeskongress 1997	N. Gudea (ed.), Roman Frontier Studies 1997. Proceedings of the XVIIth International Congress of Roman Frontier Studies 1997 Zalau (Zalau 1999)

Limeskongress 2000   P. Freeman, J. Bennett, Z. T. Fiema, and B. Hoffman (eds), *Limes XVIII. Proceedings of the XVIIIth International Congress of Roman Frontier Studies held in Amman, Jordan (September 2000)* (Oxford 2002)

Limeskongress 2003   Z. Visy (ed.), *Limes XIX. Proceedings of the XIXth International Congress of Roman Frontier Studies held in Pécs, Hungary, September 2003* (Pécs 2005)

Limeskongress 2006   A. Mortillo, N. Hanel, and E. Martin (eds), *Limes XX. Proceedings of the XXth International Congress of Roman Frontier Studies held in León, Spanien (September 2006)* (Madrid 2009)

Illustration credits

Deutsches Archäologisches Institut Athens: Fig. 49 (Thessaloniki-0222)

Deutsches Archäologisches Institut Roms: Figs 20 (99.1616), 23 (42.1351R), 30 (2007.0012), 32 (79.1052), 33 (91.148), 34 (91.101), 35 (89.750), 36 (37.329), 37 (37.328), 45 (dig2008.2375), 47 (33.51R), 52 (3135), 55 (3134)

http://arachne.uni-koeln.de/item/marbilder: Figs 12, 13, 14, 15, 16, 17, 18, 19, 21, 22, 24, 25, 26, 27, 29, 31, 38, 39, 40, 42, 44, 46, 48, 50, 51

http://commons.wikimedia.org: Fig. 56 (Gryffindor, CC BY-SA 3.0)

http://www.romancoins.info: Fig. 6

Hirmer, 561.3197: Fig. 53

after L'Orange – von Gerkan 1939 Taf. 4b: Fig. 54

after Ryberg 1967: Fig. 41 (Taf. 22), Fig. 43 (Taf. 24)

Private collection: Fig. 28 (photo: A. Pangerl)

Verlag Konrad Theiss, Stuttgart: Figs 456, 460, 461, 463, 464, 465, 466, 468, 472

Index

Persons and peoples

Places

Pfünz (Germany) 35, 43, 51, 322, *322*
Pisa (Italy) 347, 354, 363–4, *363–4*
Pisidia (Turkey) 39, 132
Plovdiv (Bulgaria) 195
Poetovio, *see* Pettau/Ptuj (Slovakia)
Poland 39, 107
Pomet/*Porolissum* (Romania) 65, 263, *264*, 267, *267*, 284
Pompeii (Italy) *33*, 48, *49*, *60*, 61, 66, 73 n163, *79*, *115*, 117,
    142, 148–9, *148–9*, 150, 152–3, *154*, 156, 162, *165*, 175,
    176, 177, *177*, 186, 187, 303, 308, 309, 329, 351, 369 n99,
    370 n117
Pontus (Turkey) 287
Porolissum, *see* Pomet
Port (Switzerland) 106–8, *107*, 109, 111, 215 n167
Porto Novo (Italy) 66, 148, *148*
Potaissa, *see* Turda
Praeneste (Italy) *349*, *352*, 369 n79
Ptuj, *see* Pettau/Ptuj
Puteoli (Italy) 61, *62*, 224, 269, 351
Pydna (Greece) 1, 3, 56, 200, 298, 299, 300

Raetia 35, 38, 42, 43, 44, 47, 52, 53, 54, 63, 64, 84, 88, 98, 119,
    132, 138, 165, 172, 173, 191, 192, 200, 205, 208, 223, 224,
    227, 234, 237, 239, 241, 252, 259, 264, 266, 267–8, 270,
    271, 272, 273, 275–6, 278, 279, *279*, 280–3, *281*, 292 n37,
    298, 306, 307, 311, 313–4, 319, 321, 322, *322, 323, 324*
Rainau-Buch (Germany) 119, *119*, 200, 201, 237, 239
Ratiaria (Belgium) 46, 284
Ravenna (Italy) 269, 332, 334, 335, *335*, 336, *336*, 337, 367 n30
Reculver (England) 277, *277*
Red Sea 287, 290
Regensburg/Reginum (Germany) 48, *48*, 51, 77, 213 n52, 214
    n78, 230, 231, 232, 251–3, *252*, 256, 259, 280, 322, 372 n
Regensburg-Großprüfening (Germany) 43, 48, 88–9, *89*, 207,
    213 n52, 313
Regensburg-Kumpfmühl (Germany) 43, 51, *198*, *205*, *316*, 317
    n172
Resca (Romania) 197–8, *197*
Rethel (France) 362, *362–3*
Rheingönnheim (Germany) 51, 53, 78, *78*, 142, *147*, *151*, 306
Rhilane (Tunisia) 256, *256*
Rhine, River/Rhineland, 8, 34, 37, 41, 42, 43, 45, 51, 52, 58, 93,
    98, 103, 105, *106*, 109, *110*, 111, 113, 114, 116, 126, 134,
    148, 149, 150, 174, 177, 187, 189, *190*, 201, 207, 223, 224,
    225, 227, 230, 231, *241, 243, 245, 246*, 247, 254–5, 268,
    270, 271, 272, 273, 277–9, *278*, 280, 281–2, *281*, 287, 291,
    301, 302, 306, 307, 309, *309–10*, 315, 317, 319, 322, 323–4,
    333, 337, 338, 339, 355, 362, 367 n11, 371–2 n158
Ribchester (England) 195–6, *196*
Richborough (England) 36, 277, *277*, 306
Rieti (Italy) 102, 103–4, *103*
Rißtissen (Germany) 38, 129
Rodez (France) 183, *183*
Rödgen (Germany) 257–8, *258*
Rohr (Germany) 32, *32*
Romania 39, 82, 85, 130, 195, 197, 198, 216 n188, 251, 262,
    263, 267, 309, 335
Rome (Italy) 3, 4, 5–6, *6–7*, 7, 8, 9, 12–13, 15–16, *15–16*, 18–21,
    18–19, 21, 23–6, *24*, 37, 41, 56, 61, 62, 97, 100, 116, *117*,

    136, 137, 171, 174, 176, *184*, 188, 210, 220 n516, 224, 230,
    235, 237, 242, 243, 245, 268–71, *269*, 272, 273, 277, 278,
    281, 283, 284, 286, 287, 291, 292, 297, 298, 301, 306, 307,
    311, 312, 313, 317, 319, 323, 324, 325, 327 n1, 332–3, *334*,
    342, 343, 348, *348*, 350, 352, 354, 355, 368 n61, 369 n77
Ruffenhofen (Germany) 280, 307, 313
Rusovce/Gerulata (Slovakia) 133, *133*, *182*, 186

Saalburg (Germany) 35, *36*, 37, 51, 228, 239, 322
Sagalassos (Turkey) 39, 132
Sahara 290, 291, 292
Samandag, *see* Seleukia Piereia
Sarmizegetusa (Romania) 309, *310–12*
Saxony 57, 84, *85, 92, 241, 277*
Scandinavia 58, 92, 93, 152, 322
Schaan (Liechtenstein) 106, *106*
Scotland 97, 170, 179, 228, 249, 263, 268, 309, 312, 313, 315
Sea of Marmara 333, 334
Segedunum, *see* Wallsend
Seleukia Piereia (Turkey) 336–7, *337*, *337*
Semendria (Serbia) 193, *193*
Serbia 39, 54, 78, 193, *193*, 335
Sicily 200, 224, 298, 343
Silistra (Belgium) *90*, 159, 195, *196*, 284
Singidunum, *see* Belgrade/Singidunum
Sirmium (Serbia) 46, 319
Sisak/Siscia (Croatia) 67, 124, *154*, *172*, 283
Slovakia 39, 133, 181, 186, 317
Slovenia 39, 54, *54*, 105, 107, 227
Smihel (Slovakia) 54, *54*, 170
Sorviodurum, *see* Straubing (Germany)
South Shields (England) 258, *258*
Spain 36, 39, 43, 45, 46, 51, 52, 78, 105, 110, 111, 130, 131, 137,
    141, 161, 162, 168, 170, 200, 225, 233, 241–3, *243–4*, 297,
    298, 299, 300, 301, 312, 317, 324
Steincheshof (Germany) 134, *135*
Strasbourg (France) 43, *147*, 249, 279, 323
Straubing/Sorviodurum (Germany) 32, 43, 51, 54, *55*, 65, *110*,
    153, *154*, 173, *173*, 197, *197*, 198, *206, 207*, 261, *262*, 321,
    322
Svistov (Bulgaria) 284, 367 n43
Switzerland 37, 39, 247, 365
Syria 37, 53, 64, 76, 89, 171, 174, 180, 192, *195*, 203, 243, 264,
    273, 287–8, *288*, 311, 314, 315, 317, 319, 320, 321, 324,
    337, 342, 357

Tapae (Romania) 14, 15
Taunus (Germany) 35, 36, 130, 266, 279, 306, 307
Tekije (Serbia) 54, 78, *79*
Telamon (Italy) 58, 300
Tell Oum Hauran (Syria) 101, 180–1, *180*, 195, *196*
Tell-el Herr (Egypt) 290, *290*
Ténès (Algeria) 94, *96–7*
Theilenhofen (Germany) 38, 48, 102, 114–5, *114*, 179, 181, *181*,
    184, 32, 321
Thessaloniki (Greece) 21–3, 46, 214 n106, 325
Thorsberg (Germany) 92, 159, 192
Thrace 53, 187, 193, 304, 319
Thür (Germany) 53,107, 215 n172

Subjects